# JUST WHAT THE DOCTOR ORDERED

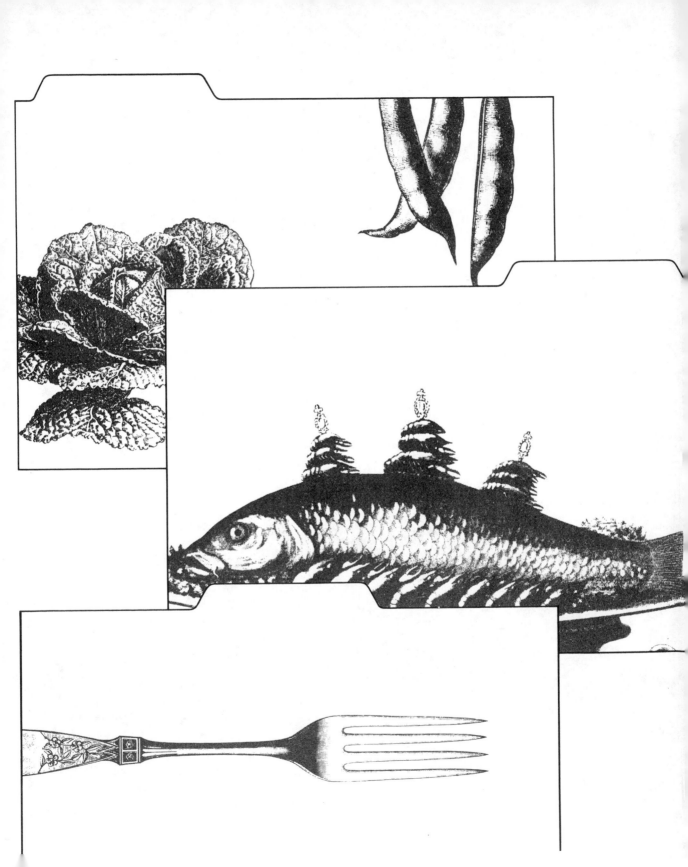

BOSTON'S BETH ISRAEL HOSPITAL

# JUST WHAT THE DOCTOR ORDERED

A Complete Medical Cookbook
with Over 250 Gourmet Recipes
for Low-Calorie, Diabetic, Low-Fat,
Low-Cholesterol, Low-Sodium,
Bland, High-Fiber, and Renal Diets

HARRIET WILINSKY GOODMAN
*and*
BARBARA MORSE

WINGS BOOKS
New York • Avenel, New Jersey

Portions of this book first appeared in *Woman's Day* magazine.

This 1995 edition is published by Wings Books,
distributed by Random House Value Publishing, Inc.,
40 Engelhard Avenue, Avenel, New Jersey 07001,
by arrangement with Henry Holt and Company, Inc.

Random House
New York • Toronto • London • Sydney • Auckland

Printed and bound in the United States of America

**Library of Congress Cataloging-in-Publication Data**
Goodman, Harriet Wilinsky.
    Just what the doctor ordered: gourmet recipes developed with Boston's Beth
Israel Hospital for low-calorie, diabetic, low-fat, low-cholesterol, low-sodium,
bland, high-fiber, and renal diets / Harriet Wilinsky Goodman and Barbara
Morse.
        p.    cm.
    Originally published: New York, Holt, Rinehart, and Winston, 1982.
    Includes bibliographical references and index.
    ISBN 0–517–14696–7
    1. Diet therapy. 2. Cookery for the sick. I. Morse, Barbara. II. Beth Israel
Hospital (Boston, Mass.) III. Title.
RM216.G67  1995
641.5'631—dc20                                                                95–15650
                                                                                        CIP

Designer: Joy Chu

8  7  6  5  4  3  2  1

DEDICATED TO
DR. CHARLES F. WILINSKY
DIRECTOR OF THE BETH ISRAEL HOSPITAL OF BOSTON
FROM 1928 TO 1953
WITHOUT WHOSE IMPERISHABLE INSPIRATION THIS BOOK
COULD NOT HAVE BEEN CONCEIVED OR WRITTEN

# Contents

# Acknowledgments

*T*hough the title page bears our names, this book could not have materialized without the efforts of dozens of committed people: physicians and dietitians from Boston's Beth Israel and other hospitals; educators and administrators from Harvard Medical School, Harvard School of Public Health, Framingham State College, and Simmons College; professional chefs, caterers, and dedicated volunteers.

First, our thanks to Dr. Mitchell T. Rabkin, Beth Israel's president, for recognizing the need for this book and for his support in accomplishing it.

It is impossible to name them all, but we take advantage of this opportunity to thank everyone in general, and the following participants in particular: Renée McHardy, R.D., who researched and coordinated all dietary and nutritional aspects of the book and who, in addition, piloted every recipe to completion; Lourdes Natividad, M.S., R.D., Clinical Chief of Dietetics, and Mary Lou Abruzzese, R.D., Clinical Dietitian and Renal Specialist, both at Beth Israel Hospital; Dr. Constance Jordan, R.D., Professor of Food and Nutrition, Department of Home Economics, Framingham State College, for arranging the testing and perfecting of more than half of the recipes, as well as for her thoughtful critique of the manuscript; Margaret Potter, Assistant Professor, Department of Home Economics, and Lisa Gould, Home Economist, who assisted her; Nancy Herbold, M.S., R.D., Assistant Professor of Nutrition, Simmons College, and Rena Mendellson, M.S., D.Sc., Assistant Professor, Faculty of Medicine, University of Toronto, formerly at Simmons, who supervised students in similar testing and evaluating procedures.

We are indebted to these physicians and nutritionists for their critique of the manuscript: Mark Altschule, M.D., Honorary Curator of Prints and Photographic Materials, Countway Library of Medicine; W. Gerald Austen, M.D., Surgeon-in-Chief, Massachusetts General Hospital; Eugene Braunwald, M.D., Physician-in-Chief, Joint Departments of Medicine, Beth Israel Hospital and Brigham & Women's Hospitals of Boston; the following Beth Israel Hospital physicians:

William Silen, M.D., Surgeon-in-Chief, Franklin H. Epstein, M.D., Director of the Renal Unit, James M. Rabb, M.D., Internist and Gastroenterologist, Mark Peppercorn, M.D., Internist and Gastroenterologist; Allan Sandler, M.D., Internist, Massachusetts General Hospital; Sigrid Hagg, M.D., Endocrinologist and Assistant Professor of Medicine, University of Pittsburgh School of Medicine, and Director, Diabetes Clinic, Pittsburgh Veterans Administration; Dr. Margaret Ross, R.D., Professor Emeritus and Head of Nutrition Department, Simmons College; Mary Ellen Collins, M.S., R.D., Director, Department of Dietetics and Nutrition, Brigham & Women's Hospital, Jelia C. Witchie, M.S., R.D., Professor, Harvard School of Public Health; Peggy Morrison, Ph.D., Assistant Director, Health Science and Computing Facilities, Harvard School of Public Health; Beth Israel's Gail M. Luca, R.D., Director of Nutrition Services, Terri Smith, M.S., R.D., Associate Director and Internship Director, and Adele Dronsick, R.D., Dietetic Internship Coordinator, Emeritus; Edith Syrgila, M.S., R.D., Executive Director, New England Dairy and Food Council.

For editing the chapter on Food Labeling, our thanks to Yolan Harsanyi, Consumer Affairs Office, U.S. Food and Drug Administration, Boston; to Rufus E. Lester, Vice-President, and Christine Filardo, M.S., R.D., Director of Consumer Affairs, both of Stop and Shop Companies, Inc., Boston.

We thank Catherine M. Breen, M.S., R.D., Director of Dietetics, Brookline Hospital; Barbara Ashburn, R.D., Sally Kotchin, M.S., R.D., and Joan Leon, M.S., R.D., for their help in developing both the content of the book and the guidelines for modifying recipes.

We congratulate the professional cooks who developed and tested our recipes: Odette Bery, Cordon Bleu trained restaurateur, chef, and culinary arts teacher; Sheryl Julian, food editor, *The Phoenix*, formerly Deputy Director, La Varenne, Paris; and Jean Kressy, M.S. in nutrition and foods, free-lance food writer; Nell Giles Ahern, cookbook editor; Gina Clegg, home economist; and Amy Cheng, M.S., home economist.

For her initial guidance, we thank Ruth Lockwood, television producer for "The French Chef, Julia Child," and Chinese food specialist and restaurateur Joyce Chen.

No thanks can adequately express our indebtedness to the hard working volunteers who did everything from testing recipes in their own kitchens to checking computer printouts, from researching supermarket shelves to typing manuscripts, from reading proof to supplying recipes: Janice Abrams, Doris Abramson, Sylvia Adelson, Lillian Adler, Helaine Allen, Idalia Banash, Marilyn Benson, Marion Bond, Laura Brody, Florence Bornstein, Beatrice Borteck, Jean Brenner, Rima Burroughs, Marcia Cable, Roseanne Cataldo, Joan Daniels,

Mae Dolby, Zelma Dorson, Eunice Duchin, Sybil Elkins, Charlotte Faneuil, Carol Feinberg, Shirley Feldman, Fan Freedman, Cecile Frost, Miriam Geller, Joan Genser, Gertrude Gilvar, Lillian Ginzberg, Ruth Glass, Barbara Ginns, Bernice Godine, Sheila Goldberg, Sophie Goldberg, Dorothy Goldman, Irene Goldman, Margaret Goldman, Ruth Goldstein, Blanch Gordon, Ellen Gordon, Tryna Gordon, Miriam Gould, Marjorie Burchard Greenough, Beatrice Gross, Evelyn Gross, Florence Gross, Helen Grossman, Emma Gutlon, Virginia Harris, Ellen Helman, Cecile Isenberg, Beatrice Kadetsky, Belle Kahn, Patricia Kannon, Nancy Katz, Maggie Katzenberg, Mirian Keesam, Gertrude Kleven, Diane Korelitz, Rona Kowal, Mildred Kuperman, Chris Kupferman, Bonnie Lane, Irene Lane, Rosalind Levine, Marian Levison, Dorothy Lider, Charlotte Litt, Dorothy Ludwig, Marjorie Marcus, Susan Markson, George Meister, Rita Mucera, Ruth Nathan, Sara Nelson, Thelma Newton, Nancy Nigrosh, Patricia Patricelli, Mae Podrin, Pauline Priede, Betty Rachlin, Mary Ravin, M.D., Mildred Remis, Ruth Roberts, Celia Robinson, Dorothy Rosen, Beatrice Rosenfield, Marilyn Rosenthal, Marilyn Ross, William Roth, Frances Rubinstein, Evelyn Rudman, Adele Saffron, Adele Schaye, Ruth Schaye, Gertrude Scheft, Kelly Schein, Edna Sears, Barbara Sherman, Selma Sherman, Evelyn Shohet, Beatrice Singer, Bertha Sobol, Ethel Sobol, Margaret Spear, Marilyn Stein, Blanche Taylor, Miriam Towvim, Elsie Weinberger, Florence Weiner, Sarah Weintraub, Lisa Weisman, Frances Werman, Ruth Werman, Mary Wilinsky, Thelma Wolbarsht, Sophie Wolk, and Marjorie Zinn.

A special thank you to Stanley Burnshaw, Publisher Emeritus and author, who identified a sketchy outline as a book and catalyzed us into action.

And finally, we are deeply grateful to our husbands, the late Sylvan A. Goodman and William B. Morse, who supported this endeavor from its inception with unflagging encouragement, patience, and generosity.

We believe that many people will live more happily because of this book. We ask them to join us in thanking everyone who participated in its development.

HARRIET WILINSKY GOODMAN
BARBARA MORSE

# Introduction

One answer to the problem of rising medical costs is to stay healthy or, in response to illness, to do everything possible to restore your own vitality. Of course, it's not easy to change habits and living patterns developed over a lifetime no matter how well-intentioned you are, and the challenge is even greater when you don't really know how to make those changes. Without the necessary information, such changes may appear hopelessly complex or impossibly disruptive to your day-to-day existence. But after all, it's your life or that of someone close to you that actually could be improved or even extended.

At Boston's Beth Israel Hospital, we are concerned not only with treating today's illness but also with protecting tomorrow's health. We know from experience that more patients are motivated to improve their diets and health than currently accomplish change. Almost everyone understands that it is the individual person who is ultimately responsible for his or her own health, but often information that might enable patients to take full responsibility is not made available to them. Although we all have been involved with our own diet and nutrition on a life-long basis, most of us are unfamiliar with special diet requirements. What was needed, we felt, was a clear-eyed, authoritative, scientifically sound book that could provide the lay person with the knowledge and skills to develop a healthful and appealing diet.

*Just What the Doctor Ordered* is designed to provide all the information you need once your doctor and dietitian have given you their nutritional prescription. Here is a step-by-step way to proceed, in order to work out the specific diet recommended for you. You will learn what is really meant by a "low-sodium," "low-cholesterol," "low-calorie," "high-fiber," "low-fat," "diabetic," or "bland" diet. You will be relieved to find that good food and happy dining can be consistent with all these variations, and that you can prepare any diet or combination of diets easily at home. Basic information is included to make you a knowledgeable shopper as you learn to read details on the labels that can make the difference between pleasurable dining and frustration. And where there may be stringent limitations, such as in kidney failure, the advice given on food preparation can indeed be crucial in keeping the patient functioning and out of the hospital.

But what if you are not ill? The basic recipes are all tried, true, and tasty, but—more important—this volume offers the opportunity to think about, and act on, the prevention of illness, too. Consider some of the common chronic conditions of mid- and later life—obesity, high blood pressure, heart disease, atherosclerosis, for example. Better nutrition can delay the onset of such illnesses or ameliorate their limitations should they arise. Knowledge of good nutrition and how to achieve it can give you an advantage you should not ignore.

*Just What the Doctor Ordered* covers everything from appetizers to desserts. And it does more, for there is a listing of the different types of foods, the assortments from which you should choose and why, calorie contents, and information about essential nutrients, vitamins, and minerals. Significantly, our emphasis is always on what you can enjoy rather than on what you must avoid.

One example of our positive approach is very special—a first-time solution to a common and growing dilemma. Many people are placed on *several* diets at once, and their problem is how to wend their way through a series of individually restricted recipes and still come up with something palatable. More and more people today are being advised by their physicians to cut down on calories, sugar, fat, and cholesterol, all at the same time. To meet their needs, we have modified, tested, and approved each recipe for that particular combination of all four restrictions. In addition, each recipe can be modified further to include the low-sodium limitation.

*Just What the Doctor Ordered* gives you the opportunity to help yourself to health. Harriet Wilinsky Goodman, Barbara Morse, and their colleagues have created a most useful volume that is straightforward and relevant. Whatever your diet, it is in excellent taste. Enjoy it!

MITCHELL T. RABKIN, M.D., PRESIDENT
BETH ISRAEL HOSPITAL, BOSTON;
ASSOCIATE PROFESSOR OF MEDICINE AT THE
BETH ISRAEL HOSPITAL, HARVARD MEDICAL SCHOOL

# JUST WHAT THE DOCTOR ORDERED

# The Purpose of This Book

*I*f you've been advised by your doctor to alter your diet for any one of a number of health-related reasons, this book is for you. Like most people, you probably experienced dismay and even a moment of panic when confronted with the need to change this basic and heretofore highly enjoyable aspect of your life. You may have realized that the only kind of special diet with which you are familiar is the slimming variety. Perhaps your doctor turned you over to the hospital dietitian for some explanation of your new eating regime. The diet may even have seemed clear enough when it was explained. Now that you are on your own, however, the guidelines seem sketchy indeed. But you feel hesitant about burdening your physician with dozens of questions about what to eat and what not to eat and the dietitian also struck you as a busy person. . . .

You could venture out to the supermarket for inspiration. Although you have been warned to read the labels on packages carefully (danger, you have been told, lurks in the fine print), you hope that you can pick and choose wisely from among all the products available. When you begin examining labels, you discover that there's a good chance that low-sodium, low-fat, sugar-free, and low-calorie products harbor several other forbidden ingredients. Your initial journey into the mysteries of proteins, fats, carbohydrates, riboflavin, niacin, thiamine, and a host of other equally baffling substances leads you nowhere.

If you've tried finding a book to enlighten you further, you probably have discovered hundreds on special diets of all kinds. There are cookbooks for many of these diets—for low-fat diets, low-sodium diets, low-calorie diets, diabetic diets, low-cholesterol diets, and for many others. But there is no one book that tells you how to cope with the restrictions of several of these diets simultaneously—which is why we've written this one.

For example, obesity is often the handmaiden of diabetes. To suggest a diet to an overweight diabetic without a low-calorie plan would be an exercise in futility. If you are both diabetic and obese, you may be running the risk of heart disease and hardening of the arteries, as well. If you can prepare meals that respect the combined requirements of diabetic, low-calorie, low-fat, and low-cholesterol diets, you may be setting yourself on the road to better health.

But the risk of heart disease is not confined to diabetics. If you have high blood pressure, you, too, may be vulnerable. Your doctor may prescribe a low-sodium diet for you. His or her advice could vary from "not another grain of salt" to "go easy with the salt shaker." The doctor may also want you to reduce the amount of fats and cholesterol you're ingesting with the foods you eat. You must now cope with not one but a combination of diets.

Similarly, if your problem is hyperlipidemia, a word your doctor is more apt to write in your record than use in conversation, you, also, stand a better than average chance of developing heart trouble. Hyperlipidemia means that the levels of fat and cholesterol in your bloodstream are higher than they should be. Your doctor may prescribe a low-cholesterol diet and suggest that you can do yourself a lot of good by watching the amount of fat you include in a meal. Of course, if you weigh more than you should, it would help to add a low-calorie diet to your growing list of considerations.

The challenge to change your eating habits is clear. It's the combination of recommended diets that complicates matters. Take away the salt, the butter, the sugar, the heavy cream, and the chocolate frosting and what's left, you may ask. In fact, there is plenty of good food and satisfying eating in your future, if you know how to provide for it. This book tells you how to do just that.

It includes hundreds of delicious basic recipes and tells you not only how to change them to meet the individual requirements of low-calorie, diabetic, low-fat, low-cholesterol, low-sodium, bland, high-fiber, and renal diets separately but, uniquely, it shows you how to modify these same recipes for the most useful diet combinations.

The most important of these are our "four-in-one" diet modifications with which, using a single set of ingredients and cooking instructions, we have altered basic recipes in the book to meet the combined restrictions of these four diets: Low-Calorie, Diabetic, Low-Fat, and Low-Cholesterol. You may use them for any one of the four diets, for any combination of two or more, or for all four, simultaneously.

In developing them, we used ingredients permitted for all of the four diets, and we eliminated (or used sparingly) those you should limit or avoid. We experimented with both the selection and the quantities of the ingredients we used, tried various cooking methods, tested, tasted, altered, and retested the recipes until we were satisfied with the results.

Finally, we calculated the calories, the nutrient values, and the food exchanges (see page 42 for an explanation of food exchanges) to be sure that they met the requirements of all four diets. Whether your diet problem is diabetes, or one that calls for less cholesterol or reduced fats or fewer calories, you'll find these "four-in-one" recipe modifications delectable. And, of course, if you must lose weight, these, used with your total calorie ration or your food exchange plan in mind, will make dieting a relatively agreeable experience. Our "four-in-one" recipes are as delicious as they are useful for the special diets they serve. What is more, they are so tasty that you can serve them to nondieters as well and know that your family or guests will enjoy them.

But *Just What the Doctor Ordered* is more than a cookbook. It is designed to answer the many questions you have about your newly imposed diet. What *can* you eat? What should you avoid? Why are you on this kind of diet? Must you buy special foods for it? Where do you find them? How will you know they're the right kinds of food for you? Is it a good idea to take vitamins? Will additives harm you? Will preservatives poison you? We hope that we have provided most of the answers.

*Just What the Doctor Ordered* includes an introduction to the basic facts of nutrition, gives you insight into the reasons why certain diets are proposed, tells you how to read a label on food packages, and provides a glossary to make the reading intelligible. It tells you about the key nutrients, explains what each does for the body, and directs you to the foods that supply them. It lists foods to enjoy for each diet and, in addition, presents basic information to make the relationship between diet and health easy to understand.

**Why Diets and Why These?**

All sound diets are based on known principles of good nutrition. They offer a variety of foods calculated to give you proteins, carbohydrates, fats, minerals, vitamins, and water, in the proportions and amounts your body needs. When your doctor believes that a change in these proportions, and sometimes in the variety, will be better for your health, he or she prescribes a special diet, temporarily or permanently; sometimes to prevent illness, sometimes to help ameliorate it. Often it is one or more of the eight included in this book: Low-Calorie, Diabetic, Low-Fat, Low-Cholesterol, Low-Sodium, Bland, High-Fiber, or Renal.

*Low-Calorie Diets* are usually suggested to help you lose weight. Like all sound diets, they offer a healthy assortment of foods but in controlled quantities so that the sum total of calories you consume will be fewer than your body uses up in the course of the day.

*Diabetic Diets* are designed to help keep your blood sugar within the range of normality. They are prescribed if you lack or suffer from inadequate amounts of insulin, the sugar-lowering hormone. All diabetic diets restrict carbohydrates. Since diabetics are prone to heart disease, diabetic diets also restrict saturated fats. Nevertheless, they include a great variety of foods and give clear guidelines for the quantities allowed to help you live comfortably and successfully with this disorder.

*Low-Fat Diets* offer a wide range of foods essential to good nutrition while reducing the amount of fat you eat daily. They pay careful attention to the fat content of all foods, not only obvious fats like butter, oil, or margarine but also the fats hidden in certain foods, like well-marbled meats, cheeses, nuts, and even some fruits like avocados. Though some doctors disagree, many favor low-fat diets if you have gall bladder problems.

*Low-Cholesterol Diets* are prescribed when there is danger that the cholesterol levels in your blood may be elevated beyond the point of good health. Foods high in saturated fats may also have adverse effects, so these diets often limit such foods as well. They are designed to prevent the potentially harmful effects that too much cholesterol may have on your arteries and your heart, and to minimize the amount of cholesterol you take in with your food. There is considerable controversy about whether healthy people need to limit their daily cholesterol consumption. Some doctors and nutritionists think such limitations are unnecessary. Others favor them. In any case, all of our recipes are modified to meet low-cholesterol diet restrictions should they be suggested.

*Low-Sodium Diets* are prescribed when your physician finds that you are consuming more sodium (salt) than your body can handle, and that you are retaining more water in your tissues than he or she believes is healthy. These diets are frequently suggested in the treatment of high blood pressure. In addition, doctors often prescribe sodium restrictions for patients with heart problems or with certain kinds of liver conditions. If you are on a low-sodium diet, you'll soon learn that although your salt shaker is one highly visible evil, there are dozens of others hiding in unexpected places, even in a package of frozen peas.

*Bland Diets* are primarily concerned with preventing or relieving irritations of the stomach and intestinal tract. These diets, most commonly associated with ulcers, favor a minimum amount of highly seasoned foods and sometimes emphasize small, frequent feedings. Recent research has cast doubt on their usefulness, so that some physicians have ceased to prescribe them. However, since many continue to recommend them, we have modified our recipes to meet bland diet requirements.

*High-Fiber Diets* encourage the use of foods that include substantial amounts of dietary fiber. Roughage, a synonym for dietary fiber found in foods like bran, whole-grain cereals, some raw vegetables, and many other foods, is the key word in the fiber diets. Dietary fiber works by absorbing moisture and adding bulk to other foods during passage through the intestinal tract; in a sense, it acts as a natural laxative. High-fiber diets are recommended by many doctors who believe that greater bulk in foods and frequent elimination of body wastes can help prevent certain diseases like cancer of the colon and diverticulosis.

*Renal Diets* are very special diets, as you know if you are on one. They are designed to help your body cope with kidney malfunctions and are almost always worked out on an individual basis. They retain a wide variety of foods that will deliver to you most of the nutrients you need, and they require close attention to your intake of certain proteins, potassium, and other minerals.

**About the Recipes**   If good eating has been one of life's pleasures, and you are suddenly bombarded with restrictions, your first reaction may be that you would rather die happily at the dinner table with a lovely taste on your tongue and a savory soufflé in your stomach than live without your favorite foods. Postpone that decision until you've glanced through this book and have tried some of the recipes we've developed with your needs in mind. The recipes have been tested and approved by dozens of people who know and appreciate good food, and they dispel the widely held belief that no food is good unless it is browned in butter, dipped in batter, topped with heavy cream, laced with liqueurs, or glazed with sugar.

Our basic recipes and their modifications have been developed especially for this cookbook by professional cooks and registered dietitians, working in tandem. In developing them, we accepted the current thinking of many distinguished doctors and nutritionists and consequently limited our use of animal fats, suggested polyunsaturated margarine and oil in most instances, resisted temptations to use the sugar scoop lavishly, and restrained our impulse to use more salt than is necessary to flavor foods. The result is that they are as healthful as they are delicious.

Our testing procedures have been extraordinarily thorough. The recipes have of course been tested by the professional chefs who developed them. In addition, they have been retested by nonprofessional cooks who prepared them in their own home kitchens. Most have been tested and evaluated a third time by students of dietetics at Framingham State College in Framingham, Massachusetts, and at Simmons College in Boston, working under the supervision of their professors, and by dietetic interns at Boston's Beth Israel Hospital. We worked with over a thousand recipes from which we made our final selection. We included in the book only those that met our pre-established standards of palatability, texture, and eye appeal for the basic recipe and all of its modifications for the special diets involved.

As you read through the list of ingredients in these recipes, you may be surprised by some of them. We permit limited amounts of sugar in our modifications for diabetics, though some doctors and dietitians may disagree. Occasionally we use ingredients that appear in the "Foods to Limit" lists for a special diet. In such cases, we have calculated the nutrient values carefully to be certain they are permissible for most people. If you are on a strict diet, you will want your doctor's approval to include these ingredients. We use no artificial sweeteners or salt substitutes in our recipes, but if your doctor prescribes them, by all means use them. We usually eliminate or use flour sparingly in our "four-in-one" modifications, but you may use it as long as you count it in calories or food exchanges.

We do not use fructose in our recipes, partly because, as of this writing, research is still being done to determine its applicability to diabetic diets in particular, and its effects on the metabolic processes in general. However, it is one of the natural sugars, and if your physician approves it, use it. But remember, our recipes have all been tested using the precise ingredients in the exact quantities we specify, so you will have to experiment if you decide to change ingredients or improvise.

Though most dietitians and doctors agree on the fundamentals of good nutrition and their contribution to good health, there is no inviolate, absolute rule about what is permitted in certain diets or even about whether specific diets must be prescribed for particular health problems. By all means, follow the advice of your doctor and dietitian. It is based on your needs as an individual.

We recommend you read the section called "How to Use the Recipes" (page 27). It tells you how to interpret our ingredients, how to cook for special diets in the easiest possible way, and how to stock your larder.

Finally, we offer advice on how to modify your own favorite recipes. Start with the few basic guidelines we outline, add a willingness to experiment, a little imagination, and you're on your way. Of course, if your special diet limits your calories or restricts any specific nutrient, consult your doctor or your dietitian before you add your new recipe to your menu.

You'll be able to adapt almost every good recipe you have, once you've learned what ingredients to eliminate, which to add, what to substitute, and how to change cooking methods. To help you do this, we include a list of spices and herbs with clear indications of what is allowed and what is discouraged for each of the special diets. We've also included lists of foods to enjoy and foods to limit or avoid. These are not absolute mandates, and we suggest that you ask your physician or dietitian to edit them for your specific needs.

We hope you will use and enjoy these recipes, and that you'll find great success in modifying your own favorites. Together they should make eating a happy experience for you and for everyone who shares your table.

# Nutrition—What Is It?

Nutrition is a synonym for nourishment. The science of nutrition explains how your body uses the food you eat for growth, energy, tissue repair, and replenishment, and for the day-to-day business of keeping your body alive and functioning. Good nutrition comes from a well-balanced diet, enjoyed in the quantities your body needs. Malnutrition can result not only from too little to eat but from a poor assortment of foods.

If you're healthy and want to stay that way, it is wise to learn the component parts of good nutrition and a well-balanced diet and to plan to eat accordingly for the rest of your life. Your chances of its being a longer one are better if you do.

Both the quantity and the quality of what you eat are important. It is equally important to eat a variety of foods. With a little judicious planning, you can continue to live as a gourmet chef and consumer, if this is part of your life-style. But remember, whether your meals are gourmet delights or the simplest fare, a well-balanced diet must include all the nutrients your body needs to keep you in good health: proteins, carbohydrates, fats, vitamins, and minerals. The surest way to get them is to eat a wide assortment of foods.

**What Are Nutrients?**

As of this writing there are about seventy known nutrients essential to your well-being. Probably more will be identified as the years go on. There are ten most important ones you should know about, and you should know, also, that if you choose the foods that provide these ten and eat them in the right amounts and proportions, the other sixty nutrients will most likely be included simultaneously in your diet. These ten, which nutritionists call the "Leader Nutrients," are proteins (amino acids), carbohydrates (starches and sugars), fats (fatty acids), vitamin A, vitamin C, thiamine ($B_1$), riboflavin ($B_2$), niacin, calcium, and iron.

Each of these ten nutrients, plus water, performs a different function.

Proteins build and repair your body tissues. They form an essential part of all body secretions, help retain the right balance of fluids, and help you resist infection. They are part of the cell structures that make up your muscles, blood, and bones. They are obviously vital to your health, and fortunately, they are easy to include with every meal, because so many everyday foods supply them: breads, cereals, nuts, cheese, fish, eggs, poultry, meat, peas, and beans, to name a few.

Carbohydrates are a major source of energy. You need them to supply fuel for your brain. They also help your body use fats efficiently. If you jog, run, dance, swim, walk, or just sit and swing your legs, it is the carbohydrates you eat that provide some of your physical mobility. In addition, they supply your body with important building materials and they keep you warm. Your body obtains them readily from starches—like cereal, pasta, rice, corn, potatoes; and from sugars—including fruits, jams, jellies, candies, and sweets.

Fats give you energy, but a little of them goes a long way. If you are like most of your friends and relatives, fats account for about 40 percent of the calories generated by the food you eat. Some fats are probably not as immediately recognizable as butter or cream would be, but they are there just the same, streaking the best prime beef, nestling under the chicken skin, hidden in the delectable flesh of olives. There are two kinds of fats: saturated fats, primarily from animal sources, and unsaturated fats, available usually from vegetable oil, nuts, or wheat germ.

An ounce of fat supplies more than twice the amount of calories as an ounce of protein or carbohydrate. But don't think for a moment that you can live without fats altogether. In addition to giving you energy in concentrated form, they help your body use vitamins A, D, E, and K, and they are essential to the health of all your body tissues. They make a noticeable contribution to the flavor of food, and they do a good job of satisfying your appetite. Nevertheless, most nutritionists agree it is wise to cut down fats from the usual 40 percent of your daily calorie intake to about 30 percent. (Note 1.)

Vitamins and minerals make vital contributions to your health, but if you are an average adult, you probably get enough of both to keep you in good shape if you eat a well-balanced diet every day. If, for any reason, your doctor prescribes a special diet for you, he will be the best judge of whether you need vitamin or mineral pills as supplements.

Each of the vitamins and minerals in the "Leader 10" (Note 2) makes its own special contribution, and each is readily available in

9

the food you eat. Our chart entitled "Nutrients: What They Do for You and Where to Find Them" (page 653) gives you a long list of foods that are sources of each essential vitamin and mineral.

If you work on the theory that if one vitamin is good, more is better, you are flirting with disaster. For example, vitamin A is alleged to be good for your eyes and there is some truth to this theory, but many experts believe that great excesses can be dangerous. It is almost impossible to get too much of a particular vitamin in the food you eat, but you can get too much from a bottle of pills.

Similarly, you need vitamin C daily. It helps heal wounds and broken bones, aids tooth formation, binds your body cells together, and assists your body in absorbing iron. It is plentiful in a long list of foods and rarely do you need more of it from the local drugstore.

Like the other vitamins, thiamine (vitamin $B_1$), riboflavin (vitamin $B_2$), and niacin are available in the foods you eat, but they are less apt to turn up routinely or in generous quantities. However, if your menu includes some meals planned with meat, poultry, fish, eggs, milk, yogurt, cereals, green beans, and peas, you will get your share. Thiamine encourages your appetite, improves your digestion, helps you maintain a healthy nervous system, and aids your body in converting carbohydrates to energy. Riboflavin also assists your body in turning food into energy. In addition, it helps keep your eyes healthy and the skin around your mouth and eyes smooth. Niacin, working with the other nutrients, reinforces their contributions.

Calcium helps build strong bones and teeth, helps your nerves, muscles, and heart to function, and enables your blood to clot normally.

Iron is the only mineral that everyday diets may deliver in skimpy quantities, particularly to infants, children under six, women of childbearing age, and the elderly. It combines with protein to form hemoglobin, the red substance of the blood. It helps the cells deliver oxygen, prevents anemia, and increases resistance to infection. Iron is readily available in iron pills and other dietary supplements. But if for any reason your doctor feels that you need extra vitamins, minerals, or other additions to your daily diet, he or she will prescribe them. Remember, it's dangerous to be your own doctor.

**How Much Do You Need?**

How much do you need of each nutrient? In what foods do you find them? Fortunately nutritionists have developed easy answers to these questions. They have divided foods into five food groups. Of these, four are basic and essential: the Meat Group, which includes meat, fish, poultry, eggs, dried beans, peas, and nuts; the Fruit and Vegetable Group; the Bread and Cereal Group; and the Milk Group, which includes milk, milk products, and cheeses. Together, the foods in these groups, eaten in adequate amounts, supply virtually all the nutrients you need in the course of a day. (Note 3.)

The foods in the Meat Group are good sources of protein, iron, and the B-complex vitamins: thiamine ($B_1$), riboflavin ($B_2$), niacin, pyridoxine ($B_6$), and cyanocobalamin ($B_{12}$).

The foods in the Fruit and Vegetable Group are major sources of vitamin C and vitamin A. In addition, they provide important minerals, fiber, and carbohydrates.

The foods in the Bread and Cereal Group are rich in carbohydrates. They also supply vitamins from the B complex and important amounts of iron.

The Milk Group is the major source of calcium. No other group can supply you with enough calcium to keep you fit. In addition, the foods in the Milk Group contribute protein as well as many of the B vitamins, especially riboflavin ($B_2$), vitamin A, and vitamin D, with which most milk is fortified.

No one group offers all the essential nutrients in adequate quantities, so your daily diet should include foods from each of these four basic groups.

There is a fifth group, for which nutritionists neither urge a daily ration nor suggest a serving size. This is the Fats, Sweets, and Alcohol Group. It may well include some of the goodies you like best: candy, jams, jellies, pastries, cakes, wines, beers and all kinds of alcoholic beverages, butter, margarine, oil, and salad dressings. It is wise to declare the foods in this group "extras." Consider them only if you can afford the calories after you have planned the day's menu to include the first four essential food groups. Except for a few items like vegetable oils, which supply vitamin E and essential fatty acids, the fifth group provides mainly calories.

If you're a normal, healthy adult, your chances of staying that way are improved if you eat two servings from the Meat Group, four from the Fruit and Vegetable Group, four from the Bread and Cereal Group, and two from the Milk Group daily. If you're on a special diet, your physician or dietitian may alter the number of servings you should have from each group, and may restrict your food choices within a group.

The size of the serving is a variable, of course. Obviously, an athletic teenager who jogs, plays tennis, and is trying out for the football team needs larger servings than a sedentary seventy-year-old. The correct serving size must be tailored to your age, sex, and way of life.

Here are a few typical foods from each of the basic groups. We've organized them in individual panels so that you can quickly see the wide assortment in each group as well as the daily allowances recommended for adults, the serving sizes, and the calories each item yields. (Note 4.)

THE MEAT, POULTRY, FISH, AND BEANS GROUP

Recommended adult minimum, 5 ounces per day. (All calories are approximate.)

*What Is a Serving?*
2 to 3 ounces fish or shellfish, not counting bones or shells
    ½ cup tuna, canned in water (127 calories)
    2 to 3 ounces fresh or frozen lean fish fillets, such as flounder or haddock (120 calories)
    4 fish sticks (160 calories)
    ½ cup cooked crabmeat or lobster (80 calories)
    4 large or 9 small clams (100 calories)
    ¾ cup oysters (120 calories)
    12 to 18 medium shrimp (200 calories)
2 to 3 ounces poultry, not counting skin, bone, or fat
    1 small chicken leg or thigh (90 calories)
    ½ small chicken breast (155 calories)
    2 slices (4 by 2¼ inches)
       chicken (160 calories)
       turkey (160 calories)
       game hen (180 calories)
       duck (200 calories)
2 to 3 ounces cooked lean meat, not counting bone or fat
    2 slices (4 by 2¼ inches)
       veal (120 calories)
       lamb (130 calories)
       liver (130 calories)
       beef (140 calories)
       ham (160 calories)
       pork (175 calories)
    1 thick or 2 thin lamb chops, trimmed (140 calories)
    2 to 3 slices Canadian bacon (160 calories)
    1 (3 by ½ inch) hamburger patty (245 calories)
    2 eggs (160 calories)
2 to 3 ounces cheese
    ½ cup cottage cheese (130 calories)
    2 slices or cubes Cheddar cheese (230 calories)

1 cup cooked dried peas, beans, lentils (200 calories, average)
4 tablespoons peanut butter (380 calories)
⅓ cup peanuts, salted and roasted in oil (280 calories)
½ cup almonds, cashews, salted and roasted in oil (480 calories, average)

THE BREAD AND
CEREAL GROUP

Recommended adult minimum, 4 servings per day. (All calories are approximate.)

*What Is a Serving?*
1 slice bread (65 calories)
½ to ¾ cup cooked cereal (60 to 100 calories)
1 roll, biscuit, or muffin (90 to 120 calories)
1 ounce (about 1 cup) ready-to-eat plain cereal (110 calories)
½ to ¾ cup cooked macaroni, spaghetti, noodles, or other pasta (100 to 150 calories)

THE FRUIT AND
VEGETABLE GROUP

Recommended adult minimum, 4 servings per day. (All calories are approximate.)

*What Is a Serving?*
1 cup raw salad (20 calories or less, dressing excluded)
½ cup raw vegetables (see below for calorie counts)
½ cup cooked or canned fruit or vegetables
raw fruit—varies with the fruit
  ½ medium cantaloupe (80 calories)
  ½ cup berries or fresh mixed fruit (40 calories)
  10 to 12 grapes or cherries (40 calories)
  ½ medium banana or grapefruit (40 calories)
  2 medium or 3 small plums or nectarines (65 calories)
  2 medium or 3 small figs (80 calories)
  1 medium or 2 small peaches, pears, oranges, apples (30 calories)
6 ounces unsweetened fruit juice (80 calories)
½ cup cooked or canned fruit
  without sugar (average 40 calories)
  with light syrup (average 60 calories)
  with medium syrup (average 80 calories)
  with heavy syrup (average 100 calories)
½ cup raw, cooked, or canned vegetables
  beets, carrots, onions, peas, pumpkin, squash (average 35 calories)
  leafy greens, asparagus, broccoli, Brussels sprouts, cabbage,

celery, eggplant, string beans, tomatoes (average 20 calories or less)

corn, lima beans, potatoes (average 70 calories)

THE MILK GROUP

Recommended adult minimum, 2 servings per day—a child should have at least 3 servings. (All calories are approximate.)

*What Is a Serving?*
1 cup skim milk, buttermilk, reconstituted nonfat dry milk (90 calories)
1 cup 2 percent low-fat milk (145 calories)
1 cup whole milk (160 calories)
1 cup reconstituted evaporated milk (170 calories)
1 cup cocoa or chocolate-flavored skim-milk drink (190 calories)
1 cup malted milk made with whole milk (245 calories)
1 slice (1 ounce) Swiss cheese (105 calories)
1 cup low-fat yogurt made with skim milk (125 calories)
1 cup whole-milk yogurt (150 calories)
1 cup yogurt with sweetened fruit added (250 calories)
1 cup baked custard (305 calories)

THE FATS, SWEETS, AND ALCOHOL GROUP

(All calories are approximate.)

1 tablespoon vegetable oil (120 calories)
1 tablespoon solid vegetable shortening (120 calories)
1 tablespoon mayonnaise (100 calories)
1 tablespoon margarine or butter (100 calories)
2 slices cooked bacon (90 calories)
2 tablespoons Roquefort cheese dressing (150 calories)
2 tablespoons tartar sauce (140 calories)
2 tablespoons French dressing (120 calories)

1 tablespoon granulated sugar (45 calories)
1 tablespoon honey (65 calories)
1 tablespoon maple syrup (50 calories)
1 tablespoon chocolate sauce (45 calories)
1 tablespoon jam or preserves (55 calories)
3 medium caramels (110 calories)
1-ounce chocolate bar with almonds (150 calories)
1 chocolate chip cookie (2½ by ½ inch) (50 calories)
1 fig bar (50 calories)

1 sandwich-type cookie (50 calories)
chocolate cake with chocolate icing, 1¾-inch piece of 9-inch round
   layer cake (235 calories)
pecan pie, ⅛ of 9-inch pie (430 calories)
½ cup chocolate pudding (70 calories)

12-ounce can cola-type beverage (145 calories)
1 cup quinine soda (75 calories)

12-ounce can beer (150 calories)
3½-ounce glass sweet sherry (140 calories)
3½-ounce glass dry vermouth (105 calories)
3½-ounce glass sweet vermouth (170 calories)
3½-ounce glass dry table wine (90 calories)
1-ounce glass brandy (75 calories)
1½-ounce jigger 86-proof gin, Scotch, whiskey (105 calories)
3½-ounce glass martini (140 calories)
8-ounce glass highball (165 calories)
⅔-ounce glass Curacao liqueur (55 calories)

Examine the suggested serving size in the meat group. You may be amazed by its modest size. True, it's the recommended adult minimum, but it's probably less than you imagined and possibly far less than you usually eat.

You may be equally surprised to learn that 4 slices of bread per day or the equivalent in the Bread and Cereal Group are considered adequate and that 3 ounces of Swiss cheese or 2 cups of milk are all you need from the Milk Group.

Notice how big a difference there can be between the calories in single servings of food within the same food group. A hamburger, 3 inches by ½ inch, adds up to 245 calories, and a small chicken leg only 90 calories. Each is a single serving in the meat group. You'll get your full complement of nutrients in either one, so the choice is yours. But remember before making it that this is only a part of your daily eating plan. If you are going to reap the rewards of a well-balanced diet, you should not only plan your daily menu to include each of the four essential food groups but you should also consider the total calorie count as well. If there is any room for extras, explore the fifth group and indulge yourself in the taste treat of your choice. But don't overindulge. There is considerable evidence that "thin is better," not just better to look at, by modern standards, but better for your general

# Desirable Weights—Ages 25 and Over

*Weights at ages 25-59 based on lowest mortality. Weight in pounds according to frame (in indoor clothing weighing 5 lbs. for men and 3 lbs. for women; shoes with 1" heels).\**

## Men

| HEIGHT | SMALL FRAME | MEDIUM FRAME | LARGE FRAME |
|---|---|---|---|
| 5' 2" | 128–134 | 131–141 | 138–150 |
| 5' 3" | 130–136 | 133–143 | 140–153 |
| 5' 4" | 132–138 | 135–145 | 142–156 |
| 5' 5" | 134–140 | 137–148 | 144–160 |
| 5' 6" | 136–142 | 139–151 | 146–164 |
| 5' 7" | 138–145 | 142–154 | 149–168 |
| 5' 8" | 140–148 | 145–157 | 152–172 |
| 5' 9" | 142–151 | 148–160 | 155–176 |
| 5' 10" | 144–154 | 151–163 | 158–180 |
| 5' 11" | 146–157 | 154–166 | 161–184 |
| 6' | 149–160 | 157–170 | 164–188 |
| 6' 1" | 152–164 | 160–174 | 168–192 |
| 6' 2" | 155–168 | 164–178 | 172–197 |
| 6' 3" | 158–172 | 167–182 | 176–202 |
| 6' 4" | 162–176 | 171–187 | 181–207 |

## Women

| HEIGHT | SMALL FRAME | MEDIUM FRAME | LARGE FRAME |
|---|---|---|---|
| 4' 10" | 102–111 | 109–121 | 181–131 |
| 4' 11" | 103–113 | 111–123 | 120–134 |
| 5' | 104–115 | 113–126 | 122–137 |
| 5' 1" | 106–118 | 115–129 | 125–140 |
| 5' 2" | 108–121 | 118–132 | 128–143 |
| 5' 3" | 111–124 | 121–135 | 131–147 |
| 5' 4" | 114–127 | 124–138 | 134–151 |
| 5' 5" | 117–130 | 127–141 | 137–155 |
| 5' 6" | 120–133 | 130–144 | 140–159 |
| 5' 7" | 123–136 | 133–147 | 143–163 |
| 5' 8" | 126–139 | 136–150 | 146–167 |
| 5' 9" | 129–142 | 139–153 | 149–170 |
| 5' 10" | 132–145 | 142–156 | 152–173 |
| 5' 11" | 135–148 | 145–159 | 155–176 |
| 6' | 138–151 | 148–162 | 158–179 |

\*Note 5.

well-being. Most physicians agree that you stand a better chance of maintaining good health if you know your desirable weight and stay at it.

The height and weight table on page 16 will give you an idea of what it should be.

Once you know what your weight should be, you can calculate your daily calorie needs by the following exercise in simple arithmetic. Using the middle of the range, multiply the weight the chart says is ideal for you by 16 if you're an adult woman, and by 18 if you're an adult man. For example, if you're female, 5 feet 4 inches (with 2-inch heels) and have a medium frame, you should weigh about 119 pounds wearing light clothes, and you should consume about 1900 calories per day. If you're a very active woman—a swimmer, bowler, tennis player, or a tireless dancer—you might add a few more calories in the course of a day, but if your life is extremely sedentary you'll need fewer calories. If you're an older adult you are probably less active, so you may need far fewer calories than this calculation method suggests. You might try using what you weighed in your mid-twenties as a weight goal. (Note 6.)

A calorie is a way of measuring the amount of energy you get from the food you eat. If you eat more calories than your body uses, you will gain weight. If you eat fewer, you will lose weight. Of course exercise plays a part in the final score.

If you're an average adult, it takes only about 3500 calories more than your body uses to gain a pound, and it takes only a little drinking and snacking to pile up a couple of thousand extra calories in a few hours. Two gin-and-tonics before dinner (about 360 calories) sipped to quench the thirst generated by eight small chunks of Cheddar cheese on crackers (about 550 calories), plus a handful or two of peanuts (about 400 calories) and a couple dozen potato chips used to scoop up a delicious sour cream dip (about 375 calories) will give you a good start toward that extra 3500. A generous helping of pecan pie à la mode for dessert (about 700 calories) and an after-dinner liqueur (about 55 calories) will take you to 2440 calories, or almost two-thirds of the way.

If you plan to lose weight by eating less but not exercising more, the rate at which you lose may disappoint you. (Note 7.)

*If you're sedentary you'll burn 80 to 100 calories an hour,* doing things like reading, watching television, eating, or sewing.
*If your activities are light you'll burn 110 to 160 calories an hour,* doing

things like ironing, dusting, cooking, or performing office work that requires some standing and some arm movement.

*If you're moderately active you'll burn 170 to 240 calories an hour,* doing light housework, gardening, or light carpentry.

*If you're vigorously active you'll burn 250 to 340 calories an hour,* walking fast, golfing, dancing, skating, or bowling.

*If you're strenuously active you'll burn 350 or more calories an hour,* playing singles tennis, jogging, skiing, or swimming fast.

Have you any idea of how much exercise it takes to compensate for the delights of a rich dessert? The chart below can take a lot of joy out

## Activity-Calorie Equivalents

*The more strenuously you exercise, the more quickly you burn up calories.*

Note that if you're sedentary, it will take you 209 minutes, about 3½ hours, to burn the calories in one slice of chocolate cake. The more active you are, the less time it will take. But even exercising strenuously, you will have to work for almost an hour.

MINUTES NEEDED TO BURN UP CALORIES DEPENDING ON THE FOLLOWING ACTIVITY LEVELS

| FOOD | CALORIES | SEDENTARY | LIGHT | MODERATE | VIGOROUS | STRENUOUS |
|---|---|---|---|---|---|---|
| *Breakfast Foods* | | | | | | |
| 1 egg, poached | 79 | 53 | 35 | 23 | 16 | 14 |
| 3 slices cooked bacon | 137 | 63 | 61 | 40 | 27 | 23 |
| 1 slice toast with margarine | 105 | 70 | 47 | 31 | 21 | 18 |
| 1 jelly doughnut | 226 | 151 | 100 | 66 | 45 | 39 |
| 3 pancakes with margarine and syrup | 628 | 419 | 279 | 184 | 126 | 108 |
| 1 cup cornflakes with skim milk and sugar | 168 | 112 | 75 | 49 | 34 | 29 |
| *Entrées* | | | | | | |
| ½ roasted chicken breast | 144 | 96 | 64 | 42 | 29 | 25 |
| 1 cup beef stew | 209 | 139 | 93 | 61 | 42 | 36 |
| 4 ounces porterhouse steak | 528 | 352 | 235 | 155 | 106 | 91 |
| ham and cheese sandwich with mayonnaise | 411 | 274 | 183 | 120 | 82 | 70 |
| 4 ounces baked haddock | 102 | 68 | 45 | 30 | 20 | 17 |
| 1 cheeseburger | 309 | 206 | 137 | 90 | 62 | 53 |
| 1 cup French fries | 301 | 201 | 134 | 88 | 60 | 52 |

of snacking. It may shock you to see how much activity it takes to use up the calories you eat in typical breakfast, lunch, and dinner foods. (Note 8.)

**How Can You Stay on Your Diet?**

Once your doctor proposes a special diet you have two choices: You can elect to follow every detail of the design for improving your health or you can decide to fight the whole idea. Your thinking may go something like this: "Doctors don't know everything," and "statistics can lie." You can read them almost any way you wish, especially if you're rationalizing about clinging to habits of long standing. You have

## Activity-Calorie Equivalents (*Cont'd*)

MINUTES NEEDED TO BURN UP CALORIES DEPENDING ON THE FOLLOWING ACTIVITY LEVELS

| FOOD | CALORIES | SEDENTARY | LIGHT | MODERATE | VIGOROUS | STRENUOUS |
|---|---|---|---|---|---|---|
| *Desserts* | | | | | | |
| 1 apple, medium | 80 | 53 | 36 | 23 | 16 | 14 |
| ½ nine-inch two-layer chocolate cake with frosting | 313 | 209 | 139 | 92 | 63 | 54 |
| ⅛ nine-inch apple pie | 302 | 201 | 139 | 88 | 60 | 52 |
| ½ cup vanilla ice cream | 134 | 89 | 60 | 39 | 27 | 23 |
| ½ cup Jell-O | 71 | 47 | 32 | 21 | 14 | 12 |
| *Beverages* | | | | | | |
| 1 cup whole milk | 160 | 102 | 70 | 47 | 32 | 27 |
| 1 cup beer | 101 | 67 | 45 | 30 | 20 | 17 |
| 1 cup cola-type beverage | 96 | 64 | 43 | 28 | 19 | 16 |
| 1 cup orange juice | 112 | 75 | 50 | 33 | 22 | 19 |
| *Snack Foods* | | | | | | |
| 10 potato chips | 114 | 76 | 51 | 33 | 23 | 20 |
| 1 cup popcorn, popped in oil | 64 | 43 | 28 | 19 | 13 | 11 |
| ½ cup peanuts, roasted in oil | 434 | 289 | 193 | 127 | 87 | 74 |
| 2 peanut butter cups | 206 | 137 | 92 | 60 | 41 | 35 |

heard all the warnings about smoking and lung cancer but you know an eighty-four-year-old man who has been chewing cigars since he was fifteen. You believe that exercise is good for you but what's the point of walking in an air-polluted city? You have read that sugar is bad for your teeth and that butter is a threat to your arteries. You're twenty pounds heavier than pleasingly plump, but you must have a sweet after dinner, and there is nothing so good for depression as a triple scoop of ice cream with fudge sauce and nuts. In any case, your life is your own and you can squander it as you please. But before you do, consider whether you owe it to yourself and to those who love you to safeguard your health.

Even if you do feel committed to the new diet, staying on it may be one of the greatest challenges you will ever face. Never underestimate the power of old habits. Write down everything you eat and drink for a solid week. You'll be amazed at how much you consume. Enlist all the help you can get from your friends, your family, the waitresses in restaurants, your colleagues at school or at work. Don't keep your diet a secret. You will soon find many others with the same problems, and in company there is strength.

Your doctor or dietitian may know of groups meeting regularly to help you and people like you over the early hurdles of changing your eating habits. Join one. Exchanging experiences, recipes, hints, and warnings with your fellow sufferers can be rewarding. There are no magic formulas with which to achieve instant behavior modification. Your will to succeed is your major weapon. Good luck.

# How to Read a Label

*L*abeling foods has been a time-honored custom ever since the earliest homemakers put up the first jars of pickles and preserves. Nowadays labels do much more than identify the contents of the wide variety of packages and containers that line our supermarket shelves. Most modern labels list the ingredients in the products, and many inform you of the nutritional values of the foods inside the packages as well.

If you've been buying food all these years, while ignoring the complicated information printed on the food packages, you're among the majority. You've quite reasonably put your faith in your government and your grocer.

Now that you must cope with a special diet, however, reading labels is no longer optional. You must examine every jar, can, tub, and package carefully to be certain that it is salt-free, sugar-free, low in fat, low in cholesterol, or well within whatever restrictions your doctor has ordered.

This very close look will open a whole new world to you, though not necessarily a likable one. You're entitled to a moment of dismay. The bewildering terminology and the strange arithmetic may well overwhelm you. They needn't and they won't, once you understand the current FDA regulations governing nutrition labeling.

Start with the letters FDA. They stand for the Food and Drug Administration, a division of the Department of Health and Human Services, formerly the Department of Health, Education, and Welfare (HEW).

The FDA's prime purpose is to safeguard you and the rest of the citizenry. One of its main challenges is to keep you from eating unsafe foods. The FDA has been exercising its role as guardian of your nutritional well-being for many years, constantly reviewing and updating its standards, as new data and new needs appear. Since Congress passed the Fair Packaging and Labeling Act in 1967, the FDA has worked with industry to develop as complete a labeling program as possible, standardizing the information that food labels disclose. As a result you can learn a lot about what you are eating and how nutritious it is, if you know what to look for and how to interpret what you find.

**What Must the Label Say?**

Labels in general conform to certain rules about the information they provide and the way in which they provide it. This is so that you can readily compare similar products. For example, the label must name the product; give the name and address of the manufacturer, packer, or distributor; state the quantity of the contents; list the ingredients; and say whether any artificial flavoring has been used. (Note 9.)

All ingredients must be listed in a rigidly specified order. The ingredient used in the largest quantity by weight must be named first, the second largest next, and so forth in descending order. If a canned beef stew lists water first, potatoes second, and meat third, it's apt to consist of a little meat drowning in a sea of gravy and jostled by too many potatoes. If, on the other hand, the label reads meat, potatoes, and water, in that order, you know that the most abundant ingredient is meat.

There are further labeling requirements if the food is for special dietary use, or if nutrients have been added, or if the package makes any nutritional claim for the product. When this is the case, the label must give the serving size, the number of servings in the container, the calories per serving, and the number of grams of protein, fat, and carbohydrate per serving. It must list eight nutrients, in addition, and show what percentage of the U.S. Recommended Daily Dietary Allowances (U.S. RDAs) one serving of this food yields for each of them. (Note 10.)

U.S. RDAs are the recommended amounts of protein, vitamins, and minerals you should eat every day to stay healthy. These recommendations are based on findings published by the Food and Nutrition Board, National Academy of Sciences–National Research Council. The FDA has based its nutrition labeling program on these findings, selecting protein, five vitamins, and two minerals that must be included on labels, and always in this order: protein, vitamin A, vitamin C, thiamine, riboflavin, niacin, calcium, and iron. In addition, the manufacturer has the option of stating amounts of other vitamins, minerals, sodium, and saturated and unsaturated fats the product contains.

The recommended amounts vary with people's weight, height, sex, age, and with the special demands of pregnancy. They are generous and offer a wide margin of safety to allow for the substantial varia-

## ENRICHED WHITE BREAD

NUTRITION INFORMATION, per serving
Serving Size = 2 Slices (Approx. 2 oz.)
Servings per Container = 8

|  | 2 Slices per serving | 6 Slices per day |
|---|---|---|
| CALORIES | 140 | 420 |
| PROTEIN, grams | 4 | 12 |
| CARBOHYDRATE, grams | 27 | 81 |
| FAT, grams | 2 | 6 |

PERCENTAGE OF U.S. RECOMMENDED DAILY ALLOWANCES (U.S. RDA)

|  |  |  |
|---|---|---|
| PROTEIN | 6 | 15 |
| VITAMIN A | 0 | 0 |
| VITAMIN C | 0 | 0 |
| THIAMINE | 15 | 45 |
| RIBOFLAVIN | 10 | 30 |
| NIACIN | 10 | 30 |
| CALCIUM | 6 | 20 |
| IRON | 8 | 25 |

INGREDIENTS: Flour, water, sugar, vegetable shortening,
yeast, salt, yeast nutrients, niacinamide,
iron, thiamine chloride, and riboflavin,
calcium propionate (a preservative).

### NET WT. 16 OZ. (1 LB.)

DISTRIBUTED BY D. C. CORPORATION, Chicago, Illinois 60605, U.S.A.

tions of the nutritional needs of individuals. The figures most commonly used on labels, however, are for adults and children over four. Most adults need only two-thirds to three-quarters of the amounts specified and children about half. Use the U.S. RDAs as guides, not gospel.

The label for enriched white bread pictured here is typical. (Note 11.) At the top of the panel, under the heading "Nutrition Information," are listed serving size, the number of servings for the entire container, the number of calories per serving, and the gram weights per serving for protein, carbohydrate, and fat. On the lower part of the panel you'll find the heading "Percentage of U.S. Recommended Daily Allowances (U.S. RDA)" and, under this, the required nutrients. The percentage figure beside the nutrient tells you what fraction of the total daily allowance one serving of this food will give you.

You may choose to ignore the U.S. RDAs as you handle your routine food shopping, but you may feel in better control of your market basket if you know what they're all about.

There are some foods that the FDA exempts from these labeling rules. These include catsup, mayonnaise, cheese and cheese products, milk and cream, eggs and egg products, margarine, and ice cream and other frozen desserts. The FDA has set standards of identity for them. The theory is that since these standards require that all such foods called by the same name include the same mandatory ingredients, they need not list them on their labels. (Note 12.)

**Required Reading**  Even if you must take a magnifying glass to market, read the list of ingredients with care. These are vital to you if you are on a diet that limits salt or sugar or cholesterol or any particular nutrient. The listing of cholesterol content, the kinds of fats, and the amounts of sodium in a product are optional. If your diet restricts the consumption of any of these, avoid packaged foods that give you no clues to their contents. Don't gamble with the unknown.

"No salt added" may still be too much. If you are on a low-sodium diet be wary of the packages that read "no salt added." All foods have some sodium in them. Therefore, even if no salt has been added, there may be more sodium in the food in its natural state than your diet permits.

"Sugar-free" may mean more calories—not fewer. Recognize that "sugar-free" does not mean sugar-substitute free, nor does it necessarily mean that this is a low-calorie product. Its carbohydrate content is even more important to you than calories if you are on a diabetic diet.

Low-calorie diet foods are worth a second look. Products advertised as low in calories, such as cake mixes, salad dressings, and margarine, imply miraculous help in losing weight. Because they make a nutritional claim, they require full nutrition labeling, whether or not nutrients have been added to them. It should be reassuring to know that by law, food-processing companies are not permitted to use the words "low-calorie" unless the product contains 40 calories or fewer per serving, nor may a food label say "reduced calories" unless its calorie content is at least one-third lower than a similar food for which it can serve as a low-calorie substitute. (Note 13.)

The words on the labels may be mysterious. Many of the ingredients listed on the labels will be familiar to you, but some may be baffling: lecithin, potassium caseinate, carotene, sodium benzoates, and dozens more. They may be emulsifiers, preservatives, vitamins, proteins, or any number of valuable nutrients listed by their chemical names. They have been approved by the FDA or they would not be in use. Nevertheless, it's wise to know what you are about to swallow, particularly if you're on a diet. Consult the glossary at the back of this book (page 657) for translations of these strange terms.

**What About Additives?**

Recently the word "additives" has taken on a sinister meaning when applied to food. Conversely, the word "natural" has come to imply virtue. Technically, an additive is any substance that, when added to food, becomes a part of that food. Additives are used to maintain or improve nutritional value, to help in processing or preparing food, to make food more appealing by means of color or flavor enhancers or both, or to maintain freshness and preserve food, in which case they are known as preservatives. Currently there are about 2,800 substances intentionally added to foods and almost 10,000 other compounds or combinations of compounds that may find their way into foods in the course of processing, packaging, or storage. (Note 14.)

The labeling act mandates that the presence of additives be revealed in the ingredient listing. All additives must be listed, but colors and flavors need not be given by name. The ingredient list may simply say "artificial color" or "artificial flavor" or "natural flavor." There are some exceptions: labels for butter, cheese, ice cream, and other foods for which the FDA has set standards of identity need not state that they include artificial color.

You may not recognize that certain ingredients whose validity you wouldn't dream of questioning are, indeed, widely used as additives. Vitamin D added to milk is an additive. In fact, virtually all the vitamins and minerals with which foods are enriched or fortified are additives, as are sugar, salt, corn syrup, baking soda, vegetable colors, mustard, and pepper. Together, these account for more than 98 percent, by weight, of all food additives used in the United States.

Additives are more strictly regulated now than at any time in history. The FDA has the power to authorize or reject them on the basis of their safety. Today the manufacturer must prove an additive is safe before it may be used. Every new additive must be subjected to an extensive battery of tests that may take years to complete. There are two major exceptions to this proving and approval process. The first is a group of 700 substances "Generally Recognized as Safe" (GRAS). (Note 15.) These are considered harmless because they have been used for a very long time and no harmful effects have been observed. The second is "prior sanctioned substances." These had been approved by

25

the FDA, and the U.S. Department of Agriculture (USDA) before the 1958 and 1960 amendments to the 1938 Food and Drug Cosmetic Act. The FDA is constantly reviewing all additives, however, and if there is any question about their safety, even though previously approved, the FDA may take them off the market and require the manufacturer to test and study them further.

It is almost impossible to eat a meal without additives. Your breakfast might include a fresh banana, sliced over a crunchy cereal and moistened with milk, followed by toast with margarine and a good cup of coffee. The cereal could be a high-protein variety, fortified with a host of vitamins and minerals, processed with some sugar and at least one preservative. The milk is fortified with vitamin D. The toast might be made from enriched white bread whose ingredients include niacin, thiamine, hydrochloride, riboflavin (all vitamins), and calcium propionate (a preservative). The margarine has had color added. You're almost certain to consume a number of additives with your breakfast, all of them designed to make you like the products better, to keep them in good condition on the shelf and in the refrigerator, and even to offer you extra nutrients.

If, as a matter of course, you cast a suspicious eye on additives, you have the option of rejecting them. Before you decide to grow your own crops and abandon your grocer, however, take comfort in the constant vigilance of the government consumer protection agencies. Decide for yourself whether you prefer to bake your own daily bread or buy enriched loaves at your supermarket. They include not only significant vitamins, but mold inhibitors as well.

Nutrition labeling is changing constantly as science, industry, and the government pool their knowledge on behalf of a healthier nation. Fresh fruits, vegetables, and some dairy products are not yet subject to nutritional labeling rules, but the FDA is developing programs for them. Meat, poultry, and fish products are under the jurisdiction of the USDA, which is currently working to develop clearer nutrition information for these foods.

As you will find with a little practice, label reading can be a good investment. It can help you count calories, choose foods that match your special diet needs, plan better meals for your whole family, compare prices of foods with identical nutrition values, and thus add power to your shopping dollar.

# How to Use This Book

**How to Use the
Recipes**

*I* n order to make the best use of the recipes in this book, first read the entire Basic Recipe through, and see that you have everything you need on hand. The Basic Recipes are designed for you if you need no special diet and like to eat well. If you must cook for a special diet, look for the diet or combination of diets that concerns you. You'll find all the diets listed by name after the Basic Recipe, and you'll see instructions beside each listing, telling you how to change the Basic Recipe to suit the diet you need. In dietitians' language this process of changing a recipe is called *modifying* it. Now, look back at the Basic Recipe. Plan to use all the ingredients listed for it and in the same amounts, unless these key words in the special diet modification signal a change: *decrease, increase, omit, substitute, add,* or *garnish.*

The word *increase* means we are using more of an ingredient than we did in the Basic Recipe. *Decrease* means we are using less. *Omit* means we have taken one or more of the Basic Recipe ingredients out of the modification entirely. *Substitute* means we are substituting a totally different ingredient in the modification for the one we used in the Basic Recipe. *Add* means that we have introduced an ingredient for the modification that was not present in the Basic Recipe. *Garnish* means that, after completing the cooking, we have added an ingredient with nutrient value for decoration, and we intend it to be eaten.

There may also be changes in cooking and preparation methods for some of the modifications. When these occur, we have spelled out the techniques. Once you have made the changes we propose in the ingredients and in the cooking methods, prepare the dish exactly as the Basic Recipe directs, unless we indicate otherwise.

When a "four-in-one" recipe modified for the combination of Low-Calorie, Diabetic, Low-Fat, and Low-Cholesterol diets needs several major changes, we have written a totally separate recipe for it. Similarly, when a modification for Renal Diets requires many changes, we have written a separate recipe for it also. Use these as you would any complete recipe, with no reference to the Basic Recipe from which they were derived. Read them through and follow them from start to finish.

So that you can make your own menu choices and know all that you want to know about what you are eating, we give the number of calories and the amounts of protein, fat, carbohydrate, cholesterol, sodium, and potassium per serving for the Basic Recipe and for its four-in-one modification—the combined Low-Calorie, Diabetic, Low-Fat, and Low-Cholesterol modification. For Low-Sodium and Renal modifications we give the amounts of the same nutrients and of phosphorus and calcium in addition. (Note 16.)

For Bland and High-Fiber Diets we give only the number of calories per serving. In most cases ingredient changes for these modifications are so minor that their nutrient values are very similar to those in the Basic Recipes. Certain Basic Recipes, though acceptable for High-Fiber Diets, are not in themselves high in fiber content. In these cases we either modify the Basic Recipe or suggest high-fiber foods to serve with them. When we modify the recipe, we add or substitute specific quantities of ingredients and include their nutrient values in our calorie counts per serving. When we suggest other foods to plan into the menu to provide extra fiber, we do not include their nutrient value in our calculations.

When recipes specify that vegetables, pasta, or other foods are to be boiled in salted water that is subsequently drained off, their nutrient values overstate the numbers of milligrams of sodium per serving.

We use the metric units gram (g) and milligram (mg) as the only practical way to express the weights of individual nutrients since they are so small. We have rounded off the nutrient value figures to the nearest digit. If knowing the precise gram or milligram content of a particular nutrient is important to your diet, skip the recipe until your doctor or dietitian gives you an okay to use it.

If you are comfortable with figuring food values in exchanges—the milk exchange, the vegetable exchange, the fruit exchange, the bread exchange, the meat exchange, and the fat exchange—you will find this information in both our Basic Recipes and their four-in-one variations.

Note that the serving size appears in the upper left-hand corner of each recipe. It represents the size of the portion for which we have calculated calories, nutrient values, and exchanges. Unless we indicate otherwise we use the same serving size for the Basic Recipe and all of its modifications. Often this serving size seems small. It is meant purely as a base for calculations, not as a guide to how much food you should eat. Your doctor and your dietitian have worked out quantities for you, possibly suggested a daily calorie allowance or quota of food exchanges, and you know how many servings of a particular recipe your diet permits.

Yields are approximate and are the same for the Basic Recipe and all of its modifications unless we suggest otherwise. Sometimes sauces and dressings that are integral parts of recipes yield larger amounts than the number of servings require. These extra amounts often may be refrigerated, frozen, used in other cooking, enjoyed in larger portions by nondieters or by you if your diet permits.

Some of our recipes require other recipes in the book to complete their preparation. They are always modified to suit your special diet, identified by name, and the page number on which to find them is always given. For a list of them see pages 32–33.

In developing our recipes we have used fresh foods wherever possible. We recognize that some of these are seasonal and are not always available. In some instances canned or frozen foods may be used. Before substituting canned or frozen foods, however, read the lists of ingredients. Then read the list of foods to enjoy and foods to limit, beginning on page 42, for your special diet and act accordingly.

Our recipes designed for Renal Diets are very specifically developed and state clearly whether fresh, canned, or frozen foods are to be used. Make no substitutions.

*Meat, Fish and Poultry:* Generally, frozen meat, fish, and poultry may be substituted for fresh, and in the same amounts.

Whenever we speak of ground beef, we mean ground round. This is a lean beef, the same as ground beef with 15 percent fat.

*Vegetables:* All vegetables are fresh unless we specify otherwise. Frozen and canned vegetables may sometimes be substituted if you're willing to compromise on flavor and texture and if you know how to adjust cooking time.

Fresh vegetables are decidedly preferable for salads. Frozen vegetables may be used, if you recognize that they will lack crispness.

Fresh mushrooms are always preferred, but in most cases canned may be substituted.

*Soups and Soup Stocks:* Soup stocks always refer to our own recipes. Commercial soup stock—canned, powdered, granulated, or in the form of bouillon cubes—may be substituted, assuming your special diet does not prohibit them. When using these products, reduce the amount of salt suggested in the recipe ingredient list, to compensate for the added salt in the commercial products.

*Dairy Products:* In accordance with the recommendations of many physicians and nutritionists, we have developed our recipes with poly-unsaturated vegetable oils and margarine rather than with butter, chicken fat, or lard. If, however, you prefer butter and your doctor authorizes you to use it, substitute butter for margarine. The calories are the same. In this case we prefer unsalted butter. Just use the same quantity that the recipe suggests.

Milk in our ingredient lists always means whole milk unless otherwise specified.

Plain yogurt in our ingredient lists always means whole-milk yogurt without flavoring or fruit added. Low-fat yogurt means partially skim-milk yogurt without flavoring or fruit added.

We use freshly grated Parmesan cheese in all recipes, but packaged grated Parmesan cheese may be substituted.

*Fruits and Fruit Juices:* We use fresh fruits unless the recipe notes some other kind. Canned or frozen fruits may be substituted, but, of course, textures and flavors will be altered. Read the package instructions carefully to be certain you are using equivalent quantities.

When our ingredient list calls for canned fruit, it means fruit packed in syrup. Light and heavy syrups are interchangeable unless the recipe specifies otherwise. For the Low-Calorie, Diabetic, Low-Fat, and Low-Cholesterol modifications only canned fruits packed in their own juices or in water may be used. If frozen fruit is substituted, be certain that no sugar has been added in the processing.

Citrus fruit juices are intended to be fresh, though bottled or frozen citrus juice may be substituted. Usually the package gives you clues to quantity equivalents.

Grated fruit peels always mean fresh peels. Dry versions may be substituted in accordance with the package instructions for refreshing them.

Our vegetable juices are canned or bottled. If you have a juice extractor or make your own fresh juices, they, of course, may be used, and in the same amounts.

*Bread, Flour, Rice, and Pasta:* Bread crumbs mean those you make at home. Unless we specify soft fresh bread crumbs, we mean dry bread crumbs. Commercial varieties may be substituted, but in this case read the ingredient list on the package carefully.

Flour is always white all-purpose flour, unsifted, unless otherwise stated. Stone-ground whole wheat flour is always to be used unsifted unless otherwise specified.

Rice refers to uncooked long-grain, regular white cooking rice, not the quick-cooking instant variety.

Unless otherwise indicated, pasta means commercially prepared varieties, but if you make your own, substitute it in the same amount that the recipe suggests.

*Herbs and Spices:* Unless we indicate otherwise, all the herbs we use are dried. Fresh herbs may be substituted, but quantities must be tripled—they are one-third as strong as dried herbs.

*Cooking Techniques and Tools:* When a recipe says "beat," we mean beat with an electric appliance. If you don't have an electric mixer or beater, use a rotary hand beater or a balloon whisk.

When a recipe says "mix," we mean mix ingredients thoroughly and blend by hand, with a fork or spoon.

We often refer to an electric blender to purée foods. This same process can be achieved by an electric food processor, a hand-operated food mill, or by pushing foods through a wire mesh strainer.

Nonstick pots and pans and utensils are useful for cooking with a minimum of fats and oils.

**How to Simplify Your Kitchen Work**

If you have only yourself to cook for, you have no problem. Design your menu, choose your recipe, and prepare it in the version your diet dictates. If, on the other hand, you must cook for yourself and other members of the family not on restricted diets at the same time, you have a different challenge. You may meet it by serving everyone the modified version of the recipe. Most of them are so palatable that you will not be imposing hardships on the healthy. Or, in most instances you can follow the Basic Recipe as far as the ingredients and the cooking techniques for your modification are identical with the Basic Recipe. Then, remove a portion to complete for yourself, separately.

There are several ways to minimize the work this double cooking can generate. Many of them are based on planning ahead and on stocking the kitchen, the pantry, the freezer, the refrigerator, the wine rack, and the spice shelf appropriately.

**Stocking the Kitchen**

Your supermarket shelves are full of frozen, bottled, jarred, packaged, dried, and canned foods, especially developed to suit your special diet needs. You'll have no trouble locating low-calorie, low-sodium, low-fat, low-cholesterol, and sugar-free items. If your diet permits, and if you read the labels carefully, you'll find them very useful.

However, we have developed a number of Basic Recipes that you will use so often you may prefer to prepare them yourself and be absolutely sure of their content. These include homemade soup stocks, mayonnaise, salad dressings, whipped topping, egg substitute, entrée sauces, and a number of others.

**Stocking the Refrigerator and Freezer**

Listed below are recipes that may be used as part of our Basic Recipes. Sometimes they are used as ingredients and are integral parts of the recipes themselves. Sometimes they serve as delicious accompaniments to other recipes in the book or to your own favorite recipe. We call them companion recipes, and have modified all of them for seven special diets, and modified several for Renal Diets as well.

Most of them can be frozen or refrigerated, and when this is the case you will find it helpful to prepare extra portions of these, modified for the diet you need, and have a reserve of them on hand. Store them in individual-portion containers and packages and have them ready to use. If you are apt to use very small portions, it is handy to freeze soups and gravies in ice cube trays and then store the individual cubes in the freezer in well-sealed bags.

COMPANION RECIPES

*Soup Stocks*

| | | |
|---|---|---|
| Beef Stock | Freezable | 113 |
| Chicken Stock | Freezable | 114 |
| Fish Stock | Freezable | 115 |
| Meat and Vegetable Stock | Freezable | 116 |

*Entrée Sauces and Gravies*

| | | |
|---|---|---|
| Béchamel Sauce | Refrigerate | 399 |
| Hollandaise Sauce | Make fresh | 390 |
| Brown Sauce | Freezable | 387 |
| Italian Tomato Sauce | Freezable | 392 |
| Mornay Sauce | Make fresh | 389 |
| Mushroom Sauce | Freezable | 395 |
| Velouté Sauce | Refrigerate | 403 |
| Velvet Dill Sauce | Refrigerate | 400 |

*Salad Dressings, Condiments, Miscellaneous*

| | | |
|---|---|---|
| Tarragon Mustard | Refrigerate | 520 |
| Homemade Mayonnaise | Refrigerate | 499 |
| Tomato Catsup | Refrigerate | 518 |
| Vinaigrette Dressing | Refrigerate | 500 |
| Low-Cholesterol Egg Substitute | Make fresh | 189 |

*Desserts, Fillings, Miscellaneous*

| | | |
|---|---|---|
| Vanilla Ice Cream | Freezable | 615 |
| Easy-Mix Flaky Pie Crust | Freezable | 555 |
| Pâte Brisée | Freezable | 557 |
| Custard Sauce | Make fresh | 632 |
| Apricot Sauce | Refrigerate | 622 |
| Whipped Topping | Make fresh | 636 |

In addition to having these basics on hand, consider further suggestions for stocking foods you will need often.

**Stocking the Pantry, Wine Rack, and Spice Shelf**

First, review your wine supplies and spice rack. Diet restrictions often minimize your use of fats and reduce or eliminate salt, sugar, and certain other common ingredients at the expense of your taste buds. How do you compensate? Wines, brandies, and many other alcoholic beverages used as ingredients can often save the recipe. Even if you are on a diabetic diet, you may use them in limited amounts and with your physician's approval, as long as you make certain that the alcohol burns off in the cooking. So, add brandy, both red and white wines, dry vermouth, and dry sherry to your larder.

Spices and herbs, too, can work miracles in converting a bland dish to a savory one. Two or three spices, used together in carefully measured amounts, can compensate deliciously for the "no salt" or "use salt sparingly" rule in low-sodium diets. Herbs add flavor and can replace certain spices that some diets prohibit. Many of our recipe modifications use interesting blends of both herbs and spices for this purpose, and with great success. See "Herbs and Spices to Enjoy" (page 643) for those approved for your diet, and stock up accordingly.

Now, check your pantry for the specific demands of your diet. Be certain it includes all the special ingredients your diet may require. Some of them will keep well on your pantry shelves, others need refrigeration, and many can be frozen. You will find it helpful to have a good supply of these on hand.

<table>
<tr><td>FOR LOW-CALORIE,<br>DIABETIC, LOW-FAT,<br>AND LOW-<br>CHOLESTEROL DIETS</td><td>

*For the Pantry Shelf:*
Vegetable cooking spray
Cornstarch
Arrowroot
Canned foods packed in water or in their own unsweetened juices
Evaporated skim milk
Powdered skim milk
Polyunsaturated oil
Bread crumbs, preferably homemade
Spices—see "Herbs and Spices to Enjoy"

*For the Refrigerator:*
Polyunsaturated margarine
Part-skim mozzarella cheese
</td></tr>
</table>

The following items are perishable and will keep only 4 to 7 days in the refrigerator:

Skim milk
Buttermilk
1 percent low-fat cottage cheese
Low-fat yogurt
Part-skim ricotta cheese

*For the Freezer:*
Multiple portions of freezable companion recipes appropriately modified (pages 32–33)
Individual servings of favorite dishes, cooked or uncooked, ready to defrost
Frozen vegetables
Frozen fruits with no sugar added
Soup stocks, homemade

<table>
<tr><td>FOR LOW-SODIUM<br>DIETS</td><td>

*For the Pantry Shelf:*
Low-sodium vegetable juices
Low-sodium or no-salt-added canned vegetables
Water-packed canned tuna and salmon
Low-sodium canned soups and bouillons
Jams and jellies without sodium benzoate preservative
Unsalted nuts
Red or white wine
</td></tr>
</table>

Spices—see "Herbs and Spices to Enjoy"
See our list of "Foods to Enjoy, Foods to Avoid" (page 57)

*For the Refrigerator:*
Low-sodium mayonnaise and salad dressings
Unsalted margarine
Unsalted peanut butter

*For the Freezer:*
Homemade soup stocks (pages 113–117)
Frozen vegetables—except peas, lima beans, and mixed vegetables

FOR HIGH-FIBER
DIETS

*For the Pantry Shelf:*
Stone-ground whole wheat flour
Wheat germ
All-bran cereal and flour
Coconut (dried flakes or grated)

*For the Refrigerator:*
Nuts
Sesame and other edible seeds

FOR BLAND DIETS

Bland diets are in the main very lenient. You will find that your pantry supplies can be very varied indeed. See "Foods to Enjoy for Bland Diets" (page 59).

FOR RENAL DIETS

Renal diets are the most individualized of all. Your grocery list must be tailored to the detailed instructions your physician or dietitian prescribes.

**Freezing, Storage, and Cooking Hints**

You can certainly freeze many of the foods prepared from recipes in this book. Here are some tips for doing that, plus other helpful suggestions about storing and cooking food. (Note 17.)

*Freezing Hints:* Add crumb and cheese toppings to frozen food just before reheating, not before freezing.
    Cool hot food quickly in the refrigerator to stop cooking, to retard bacterial growth, and to help retain the natural flavor, color, and texture.

Wrap foods well before freezing. Laminated freezer paper, plastic wraps, and heavy-duty aluminum foil are good materials to use.

Thaw frozen foods in the refrigerator, not at room temperature, to prevent bacterial growth.

Rigid containers that are flat on top and bottom stack well in the freezer and conserve space. Nonrigid containers will bulge and waste space.

Food expands as it freezes, so allow ample air space when filling containers.

Fresh berries, such as cranberries, blueberries, strawberries, raspberries, and blackberries, can be frozen in sealed containers without sugar or syrup if they are to be used for cooking later. Prepare all other fruits with sugar or syrup before freezing depending on their intended use.

Blanch all vegetables before freezing.

*Storage Hints:* Dried fruits will keep about six months in tightly covered containers. Store in a cool place. In humid weather, store in the refrigerator.

Store meats in the coldest part of the refrigerator.

Ground meats are more likely to spoil than roasts, chops, or steaks because more of the meat surface has been exposed to contamination from air and food handlers; use ground meat within one to two days and roasts, chops, or steaks within three to five days. Poultry and fish should be used within one to two days.

Keep dry milk in a tightly closed container. Nonfat dry milk will keep for several months on pantry shelf. Dry whole milk does not keep as well as nonfat, so store it in the refrigerator.

Hard cheeses such as Cheddar, Parmesan, and Swiss will keep for several months tightly covered in the refrigerator. If mold develops on the surface, cut it off before using.

Fresh vegetables are best kept in the refrigerator. Exceptions are potatoes, mature onions, garlic bulbs, shallots, winter squashes, and rutabagas—which should be stored in a cool, dry place. High temperatures hasten sprouting and shrinking in these vegetables.

Honey and syrups, after opening, are best protected against mold in the refrigerator. If crystals form, immerse container in a pan of hot water to dissolve them.

Shelled nuts are best stored in the refrigerator or freezer in airtight containers. Unshelled nuts may be stored at room temperature about six months. Unroasted nuts keep better than roasted nuts.

Canned foods, after opening, should be stored in the refrigerator in glass or plastic containers.

Bread stays fresh longer at room temperature than in the refrigerator except in hot, humid weather, when it is better protected against mold in the refrigerator.

Bread will keep frozen two to three months if stored in the original wrapper.

Store cereals, flours, pastas, spices, and sugar at room temperature, away from a stove or refrigerator. Store in tightly closed containers to keep out dust, moisture, and insects.

Buy flours and cereals in small quantities during the summer and inspect often for insects.

Eggs keep well in the refrigerator; for best quality use within a week. Cover leftover yolks with cold water and store covered in the refrigerator. Egg whites should also be refrigerated in a covered container. Both yolks and whites should be used within four days. You can freeze egg whites, however; put each in individual ice cube containers so you will be sure of the quantity.

Fats and oils in partially filled containers should be transferred to smaller containers with little or no air space to retain maximum freshness. For long storage, keep oils in the refrigerator. They may cloud and solidify, but this is not harmful; they will clear at room temperature.

Butter or margarine should be stored tightly wrapped in the refrigerator. Exposure to heat and light hastens rancidity.

Keep all homemade salad dressings refrigerated. Refrigerate commercial salad dressings after opening.

Store unripe fruit at room temperature until ready to eat, then refrigerate. Most fruits should be used within three to five days. Citrus fruits and apples will keep longer.

Bruised or decayed fruit will contaminate sound, firm fruit, so sort the fruit before storing.

Pineapples will not ripen further after purchasing. Select ripe fruit and use as soon as possible.

Cooked rice may be kept up to one week in the refrigerator or may be frozen for six to eight months. To reheat cooked rice, steam it in a colander over boiling water.

*Cooking Hints:* Use crushed cereals such as cornflakes in place of bread crumbs for coating or as a topping for casseroles.

Cook rice in soup stock instead of water for added flavor. Spices can be added also.

Shorten the cooking time slightly for pastas to be used in combination dishes that will need further cooking.

If cooked pasta is to be used cold in salads, drain well and add the salad dressing while the pasta is still hot to prevent sticking.

Turn your leftover bread into bread crumbs. For the crisp variety, leave the bread uncovered to dry out on the counter or dry in a low (225°F.) oven. Break one slice into pieces, place in the blender, and blend until crumbs are the size you wish, fine or coarse. For soft bread crumbs, remove crust from day-old bread. Pull bread apart in small bits and measure loosely into a measuring cup.

To peel tomatoes and peaches, slip into boiling water for 10 seconds. Remove and plunge into cold water, then peel.

If you are not sure of the volume of your baking dish, fill it with water. Then empty by pouring into a measuring cup to find out how many cups it holds.

To retain the maximum nutrient value of vegetables, steam them or cook them only until tender, in just enough water to prevent scorching. Use pan with a tight-fitting lid.

Bake or boil potatoes and other roots and tubers in their skins. Pare, trim, and cut them after they are cooked. This method retains vitamins and minerals.

To toast whole or slivered seeds and nuts, spread them on a pie plate and place in a 300°F. oven for about 15 minutes or until golden brown. Turn them frequently so they do not burn.

To toast coconut, spread it out on a pie plate and place in a 325°F. oven for about 10 minutes or until golden brown. Stir frequently to prevent scorching.

**How to Modify Your Own Favorite Recipes**

Of course, you must make changes in order to turn your favorite recipe into one you can still enjoy, in spite of your diet restrictions. Once the restrictions have been spelled out, you will know which foods to avoid and which to use freely.

As you modify your recipes, you will soon discover that you may have to change ingredients or cooking methods, or both. If you approach your experiments with daring and patience, the results will be rewarding. Here are a few tips on modifying a recipe for a special diet, though you should be aware that there are no pat answers. Many of these hints apply to most diets. Others apply specifically to a single diet or a combination of special diets, in which case we have arranged them under their relevant special diet headings.

TIPS ON HOW TO
MODIFY RECIPES FOR
LOW-CALORIE,
DIABETIC, LOW-FAT,
AND LOW-
CHOLESTEROL DIETS
After much experimentation with our Basic Recipes we have developed one modification to meet the restrictions of these four special diets simultaneously. If you must respect only one of them, modify your favorite recipe accordingly.

Substitute skim milk for whole milk.

Substitute evaporated skim milk or skim milk for cream.

Substitute 1 percent low-fat cottage cheese for regular cottage cheese.

Substitute a purée of 1 percent low-fat cottage cheese for cream cheese in dips and spreads.

Substitute buttermilk or low-fat yogurt for sour cream.

Substitute Low-Cholesterol Egg Substitute (page 189) for whole eggs, using the equivalent number of eggs suggested in the recipe.

Substitute part-skim mozzarella cheese for Cheddar or Swiss cheese. In sauces, substitute skim American cheese.

Substitute sapsago cheese for Parmesan cheese. It has a more pungent flavor, so try it first to see if you enjoy it.

Use pretoasted bread crumbs rather than buttered crumbs for toppings. If you are eager to save calories and fats, omit bread crumbs totally and garnish dish after baking with minced parsley, celery leaves, or scallions.

Substitute cornstarch or arrowroot for flour in thickening, for fewer calories. One tablespoon cornstarch equals 2 tablespoons flour.

Reduce the amount of sugar you use.

If you're using canned fruit, choose fruit packed in water or in its natural juices rather than in syrup.

When possible, substitute polyunsaturated oil for butter or for solid shortening. Since oil is 100 percent fat, and butter and other solid shortenings are about 85 percent fat, you will need less oil. For every cup of butter, reduce the amount of oil to ⅞ cup.

Use vegetable cooking spray for greasing pans in place of margarine, butter, or oil.

When sautéing fatty meats, drain all excess fat before continuing with the recipe.

When a recipe calls for ingredients to be sautéed in fat and then added to a liquid, omit the sautéing step and add ingredients directly to the liquid.

Use no-stick utensils and omit fat or reduce amounts.

Remove skin from chicken, preferably before cooking. Otherwise, remove skin before eating. Pat chicken with paper towel to reduce fat adhering to the meat.

Bake stuffing separately from meat or poultry to reduce fat and serve as a side dish.

Omit nuts. They add fat and calories.

Explore new products such as imitation cream cheese or imitation sour cream. Although they are lower in calories and cholesterol, they are not low in fat, so read the labels carefully to see whether your diet permits them.

Omit fat, and brown meat and vegetables in a small amount of soup stock that has been brought to the sizzle in a skillet, saucepan, or wok.

See Foods to Enjoy for Low-Calorie Diets (page 50), for Diabetic Diets (page 42), for Low-Fat Diets (page 54), and for Low-Cholesterol Diets (page 56).

See "Herbs and Spices to Enjoy" (page 643).

TIPS ON HOW TO MODIFY RECIPES FOR LOW-SODIUM DIETS

Omit all salt from cooking.

Use fresh vegetables whenever possible.

Add a little sugar to the cooking water in which you are preparing vegetables. This brings out the flavor.

If substituting canned vegetables, use low-sodium varieties.

Frozen vegetables may be used, except for frozen peas, lima beans, and mixed vegetables.

Substitute low-sodium vegetable juices for regular.

Substitute unsalted polyunsaturated margarine for regular margarine or butter.

If using butter, be sure it is unsalted.

Omit Parmesan, Cheddar, Swiss, and mozzarella cheeses and substitute low-sodium American, low-sodium Cheddar, or low-sodium Swiss cheese.

Substitute unsalted homemade soup stocks (pages 113–17) for canned stocks, bouillon powders, or cubes.

Substitute wines and vinegars for salt. They add excellent flavoring when judiciously used.

Substitute water-packed canned tuna and salmon for oil-packed.

Flavor beef with dry mustard, sage, marjoram, pepper, or thyme. A bay leaf or two adds a fresh, subtle taste.

Season chicken with paprika, parsley, tarragon, thyme, sage, or curry powder.

Rub lamb with a little curry powder or turmeric and sprinkle with chopped parsley, rosemary, mint, and turmeric.

Try sage and dry mustard with fresh pork.

Combine marjoram, crushed bay leaf, curry powder, powdered ginger, and oregano and pound gently into veal.

Add zest to fish with bay leaf, cayenne pepper, curry powder, paprika, fennel seed, dill, marjoram, and thyme.

For a mysterious but pleasant flavor, add brewed coffee to the roasting pan and baste lamb, mutton, or veal with it.

For salads and salad dressings, try coriander seed, dill, chervil, garlic, oregano, chives, mint, or tarragon.

For an unexpected but delicious flavor, add basil, marjoram, caraway seed, or savory to vegetables.

Add fresh tomatoes, garlic, and fresh mushrooms to chicken, beef, veal, fish, and egg dishes.

Marinate beef, chicken, veal, and lamb in salad dressings that include only the spices allowed, or sprinkle with lemon juice.

Apple slices, pineapple, dried apricots, and cranberries supply an appealing tang when roasted with pork, veal, and chicken.

Spark the taste of eggs with a little curry powder, parsley flakes, chives, pepper, oregano, or paprika.

See "Herbs and Spices to Enjoy" (page 643).

See Foods to Enjoy and Foods to Avoid for Low-Sodium Diets, page 57.

| TIPS ON HOW TO MODIFY RECIPES FOR BLAND DIETS | Bland diets permit a wide variety of food choices. For additional guidance in modifying favorite recipes, see Foods to Enjoy for Bland Diets (page 59) and "Herbs and Spices to Enjoy" (page 643). |
| --- | --- |
| TIPS ON HOW TO MODIFY RECIPES FOR HIGH-FIBER DIETS | If recipe calls for all-purpose flour in a bread, pancake, or shortcake, substitute stone-ground whole wheat flour for half the amount used. |

Sprinkle sesame seed in the skillet before pouring in pancake batter.

Use high-fiber foods such as nuts, coconut, wheat germ, all-bran, sesame seeds, or chopped fresh parsley in recipes, or add them as garnish, when feasible.

Add oatmeal to meatloaves.

See Foods to Enjoy for High-Fiber Diets (page 59).

# Food Exchanges and
# Foods to Enjoy

*N*ow that your doctor has prescribed a special diet for you, you will probably expect a list of everything you absolutely can or cannot eat. It is highly unlikely that you will get one. Every detail cannot be spelled out no matter how much you would like to have it that way, but the dietitian you consult at your doctor's suggestion will give you a great deal of dependable guidance.

As additional aids, we offer below lists of foods to enjoy and foods to limit or avoid for several diets. These lists are very general in nature and are subject to your doctor's and your dietitian's approval. Special diets are often so highly individualized that only someone who knows your special needs can tell you which foods are suitable for you.

Remember, too, dietary laws are neither sacred nor immutable. Medical and nutritional research goes on constantly. Almost daily, new evidence surfaces, challenging old beliefs. Our presentations here represent current thinking, but they are only broad guidelines.

**Foods to Enjoy for Diabetic Diets**

If you've been counting calories all your life and struggling to keep your potentially plump alter ego out of sight and under control, you may find food exchange lists one of the best friends you've ever had. Although they were developed primarily to guide diabetics in planning daily eating patterns, they offer such a wide variety of possibilities that they can add up to a much easier and healthier way to control weight than any of the dozens of diets you've tried so far.

Exchange lists, developed by the American Diabetic Association and the American Dietetic Association (Note 18) are a way of organizing foods of similar types and nutritional values into basic food groups, or exchanges. Each food within the group may be exchanged for any other in the same group as you plan your meals for the day. For example, strawberries and figs are members of the same group, the Fruit

Group. Each supplies approximately 10 grams of carbohydrate and 40 calories. Take your pick; you may have either.

**The Six Basic Food Exchange Lists**

There are six major exchange lists: the Milk Exchange, the Vegetable Exchange, the Fruit Exchange, the Bread Exchange, the Meat Exchange, the Fat Exchange. Every food in each exchange is similar to its colleagues in calories, carbohydrates, proteins, and fats. For the purpose of menu planning they are considered equal, although differences between them may be 20 to 30 calories per serving.

As you know, a balanced diet depends on eating a wide assortment of foods. Obviously, then, the foods from no one exchange list can supply you with all the nutrients you need, but if you select foods from all six lists you'll eat wisely and well.

Your physician and your dietitian will tell you how many exchanges you may have from each of the six lists, depending on your daily calorie quota and on other health considerations. Once these limits are prescribed, your menu for the day is entirely up to you.

Here are the six exchange lists, typical foods that compose them, and the approximate nutrient values each food unit provides. Certain foods listed in the milk and meat exchanges include fat exchanges, also—whole milk and high-fat meats, for example. The milk and meat exchange lists suggest that when you use these foods, you omit equivalent amounts of fat exchanges from your daily menu plan.

MILK EXCHANGES

Include nonfat, low-fat, and whole milk. One exchange of milk contains approximately 12 grams of carbohydrate, 8 grams of protein, a trace of fat, and 80 calories.

This list shows the kinds and amounts of milk and milk products to use for one milk exchange.

*Nonfat Fortified Milk*

| | |
|---|---|
| Skim or nonfat milk | 1 cup |
| Powdered (nonfat dry, before adding liquid) | ⅓ cup |
| Canned evaporated skim milk | ½ cup |
| Buttermilk made from skim milk | 1 cup |
| Yogurt made from skim milk (plain, unflavored) | 1 cup |

*Low-Fat Fortified Milk—Contains Saturated Fat*
1 percent fat, fortified milk
    (omit ½ fat exchange)     1 cup
2 percent fat, fortified milk,
    (omit 1 fat exchange)     1 cup
Yogurt, plain, unflavored,
    made from 2 percent
    fortified milk (omit 1 fat
    exchange)     1 cup

*Whole Milk (Omit 2 Fat Exchanges)—Contains Saturated Fat*
Whole milk     1 cup
Canned evaporated whole
    milk     ½ cup
Buttermilk made from
    whole milk     1 cup
Yogurt, plain, unflavored,
    made from whole milk     1 cup

VEGETABLE
EXCHANGES

One exchange of vegetables contains about 5 grams of carbohydrate, 2 grams of protein, and 25 calories.

This list shows the kinds of vegetables to use for one vegetable exchange. One exchange is ½ cup.

| | | |
|---|---|---|
| Asparagus | Brussels sprouts | Celery |
| Bean sprouts | Cabbage | Cucumbers |
| Beets | Carrots | Eggplant |
| Broccoli | Cauliflower | Green pepper |

*Greens:*

| | | |
|---|---|---|
| Beet | Mushrooms | Summer squash |
| Chard | Okra | Tomatoes |
| Collard | Onions | Tomato juice |
| Dandelion | Rhubarb | Turnips |
| Kale | Rutabaga | Vegetable juice cocktail |
| Mustard | Sauerkraut | Zucchini |
| Spinach | String beans— | |
| Turnip |    green or yellow | |

Eat as much of the following vegetables as you wish. (They need not be counted as an exchange.)

| | | |
|---|---|---|
| Chicory | Escarole | Radishes |
| Chinese cabbage | Lettuce | Watercress |
| Endive | Parsley | |

Starchy vegetables are found in the Bread Exchange list.

FRUIT EXCHANGES   One exchange of fruit contains approximately 10 grams of carbohydrate and 40 calories.

This list shows the kinds and amounts of fruits to use for one fruit exchange.

| | |
|---|---|
| Apple | 1 small |
| Apple juice | ⅓ cup |
| Applesauce (unsweetened) | ½ cup |
| Apricots, dried | 4 halves |
| Apricots, fresh | 2 medium |
| Banana | ½ small |
| Berries | |
|   Blackberries | ½ cup |
|   Blueberries | ½ cup |
|   Raspberries | ½ cup |
|   Strawberries | ¾ cup |
| Cherries | 10 large |
| Cider | ⅓ cup |
| Dates | 2 |
| Figs, dried | 1 |
| Figs, fresh | 1 |
| Grapefruit | ½ |
| Grapefruit juice | ½ cup |
| Grape juice | ¼ cup |
| Grapes | 12 |
| Mango | ½ small |
| Melon | |
|   Cantaloupe | ¼ small |
|   Honeydew | ⅛ medium |
|   Watermelon | 1 cup |
| Nectarine | 1 small |
| Orange | 1 small |
| Orange juice | ½ cup |
| Papaya | ¾ cup |
| Peach | 1 medium |

| Pear | 1 small |
| Persimmon, native | 1 medium |
| Pineapple | ½ cup |
| Pineapple juice | ⅓ cup |
| Plums | 2 medium |
| Prune juice | ¼ cup |
| Prunes | 2 medium |
| Raisins | 2 tablespoons |
| Tangerine | 1 medium |

No limits on cranberries as long as you don't use sugar.

Include bread, cereal, and starchy vegetables. One exchange of bread contains approximately 15 grams of carbohydrate, 2 grams of protein, and 70 calories.

This list shows the kinds and amounts of breads, cereals, starchy vegetables, and prepared foods to use for one bread exchange.

*Bread—All These Are Low-Fat*

| White (including French and Italian) | 1 slice |
| Whole wheat | 1 slice |
| Rye or pumpernickel | 1 slice |
| Raisin | 1 slice |
| Bagel, small | ½ |
| English muffin, small | ½ |
| Plain roll, bread | 1 |
| Frankfurter roll | ½ |
| Hamburger bun | ½ |
| Dried bread crumbs | 3 tablespoons |
| Tortilla, 6-inch | 1 |

*Cereal—All These Are Low-Fat*

| Bran flakes | ½ cup |
| Other ready-to-eat unsweetened cereal | ¾ cup |
| Puffed cereal (unfrosted) | 1 cup |
| Cereal (cooked) | ½ cup |
| Grits (cooked) | ½ cup |
| Rice or barley (cooked) | ½ cup |
| Pasta (cooked): spaghetti, noodles, macaroni | ½ cup |
| Popcorn (popped, no fat added) | 3 cups |

*Cereal (Cont'd)*

| | |
|---|---|
| Cornmeal (dry) | 2 tablespoons |
| Flour | 2½ tablespoons |
| Wheat germ | ¼ cup |

*Crackers—All These Are Low-Fat*

| | |
|---|---|
| Arrowroot | 3 |
| Graham, 2½ inches square | 3 |
| Matzo, 4 by 6 inches | ½ |
| Oyster | 20 |
| Pretzels, 3⅛ inches long by ⅛ inch wide | 25 |
| Rye wafers, 2 by 3½ inches | 3 |
| Saltines | 6 |
| Soda, 2½ inches square | 4 |

*Dried Beans, Peas, and Lentils—All These Are Low-Fat*

| | |
|---|---|
| Beans, peas, lentils (dried and cooked) | ½ cup |
| Baked beans, no pork (canned) | ¼ cup |

*Starchy Vegetables—All These Are Low-Fat*

| | |
|---|---|
| Corn | ⅓ cup |
| Corn on cob | 1 small |
| Lima beans | ½ cup |
| Parsnips | ⅔ cup |
| Peas, green (canned or frozen) | ½ cup |
| Potato, white | 1 small |
| Potato (mashed) | ½ cup |
| Pumpkin | ¾ cup |
| Winter squash, acorn or butternut | ½ cup |
| Yam or sweet potato | ¼ cup |

*Prepared Foods*

| | |
|---|---|
| Biscuit, 2 inches diameter (omit 1 fat exchange) | 1 |
| Cornbread, 2 by 2 by 1 inch (omit 1 fat exchange) | 1 |
| Corn muffin, 2 inches diameter (omit 1 fat exchange) | 1 |
| Crackers, round butter type (omit 1 fat exchange) | 5 |

*Prepared Foods (Cont'd)*

| | |
|---|---|
| Muffin, plain small (omit 1 fat exchange) | 1 |
| Potatoes, French fried, 2 to 3½ inches long (omit 1 fat exchange) | 8 |
| Potato or corn chips (omit 2 fat exchanges) | 15 |
| Pancake, 5 by ½ inch (omit 1 fat exchange) | 1 |
| Waffle, 5 by 5 by ½ inch (omit 1 fat exchange) | 1 |

MEAT EXCHANGES

*Lean Meat*

One exchange of lean meat (1 ounce) contains 7 grams of protein, 3 grams of fat, and 55 calories.

This list shows the kinds and amounts of lean meat and other protein-rich foods to use for one low-fat meat exchange.

| | |
|---|---|
| Beef: Baby beef (very lean), chipped beef, chuck, flank steak, tenderloin, plate ribs, plate skirt steak, round (bottom, top), all cuts rump, spare ribs, tripe | 1 ounce |
| Lamb: Leg, rib, sirloin, loin (roast and chops), shank, shoulder | 1 ounce |
| Pork: Leg (whole rump, center shank), ham, smoked (center slices) | 1 ounce |
| Veal: Leg, loin, rib, shank, shoulder, cutlets | 1 ounce |
| Poultry: Meat without skin of chicken, turkey, Cornish hen, guinea hen, pheasant | 1 ounce |
| Fish: Any fresh or frozen | 1 ounce |
| Canned salmon, tuna, crab, and lobster | ¼ cup or 1 ounce |
| Clams, oysters, scallops, shrimps | 5 or 1 ounce |
| Sardines, drained | 3 |
| Cheeses containing less than 5 percent butterfat | 1 ounce |
| Cottage cheese, dry and 2 percent butterfat | ¼ cup |
| Dried beans and peas (omit 1 bread exchange) | ½ cup |

*Medium-Fat Meat*

For each exchange of medium-fat meat omit one-half fat exchange.

48

This list shows the kinds and amounts of medium-fat meat and other protein-rich foods to use for one medium-fat meat exchange.

| | |
|---|---|
| Beef: Ground (15 percent fat), corned beef (canned), rib eye, round (ground commercial) | 1 ounce |
| Pork: Loin (all cuts tenderloin), shoulder arm (picnic), shoulder blade, Boston butt, Canadian bacon, boiled ham | 1 ounce |
| Liver, heart, kidney, and sweetbreads (these are high in cholesterol) | 1 ounce |
| Cottage cheese, creamed | ¼ cup |
| Cheese: Mozzarella, ricotta, farmer's cheese, Neufchâtel | 1 ounce |
| Parmesan | 3 tablespoons |
| Egg (high in cholesterol) | 1 |
| Peanut butter (omit 2 additional fat exchanges) | 2 tablespoons |

*High-Fat Meat*

For each exchange of high-fat meat omit one fat exchange.

This list shows the kinds and amounts of high-fat meat and other protein-rich foods to use for one high-fat meat exchange.

| | |
|---|---|
| Beef: Brisket, corned beef (brisket), ground beef (more than 20 percent fat), roasts (rib), steaks (club and rib) | 1 ounce |
| Lamb: Breast | 1 ounce |
| Pork: Spare ribs, loin (back ribs), pork (ground), country-style ham, deviled ham | 1 ounce |
| Veal: Breast | 1 ounce |
| Poultry: Capon, duck (domestic), goose | 1 ounce |
| Cheese: Cheddar types | 1 ounce |
| Cold cuts | 1 slice, 4½ by ⅛ inch |
| Frankfurter | 1 small |

FAT EXCHANGES   One exchange of fat contains about 5 grams of fat and 45 calories.

This list shows the kinds and amounts of fat-containing foods to use for one fat exchange.

| | |
|---|---|
| Margarine, soft—tub or stick* | 1 teaspoon |
| Avocado (4 inches in diameter)† | ⅛ avocado |
| Oil: corn, cottonseed, safflower, soy, sunflower | 1 teaspoon |
| Oil, olive† | 1 teaspoon |
| Oil, peanut† | 1 teaspoon |
| Olives† | 5 small |
| Almonds† | 10 whole |
| Pecans† | 2 large whole |
| Peanuts† | |
| Spanish | 20 whole |
| Virginia | 10 whole |
| Walnuts | 6 small |
| Nuts, other† | 6 small |

If your diet should be low in saturated fats, select your exchanges from the foods listed above. The fats in them are polyunsaturated or primarily monounsaturated.

| | |
|---|---|
| Margarine, regular stick | 1 teaspoon |
| Butter | 1 teaspoon |
| Bacon fat | 1 teaspoon |
| Bacon, crisp | 1 strip |
| Cream, light | 2 tablespoons |
| Cream, sour | 2 tablespoons |
| Cream, heavy | 1 tablespoon |
| Cream cheese | 1 tablespoon |
| French dressing‡ | 1 tablespoon |
| Italian dressing‡ | 1 tablespoon |
| Lard | 1 teaspoon |
| Mayonnaise‡ | 1 teaspoon |
| Salad dressing, mayonnaise type‡ | 2 teaspoons |
| Salt pork | ¾-inch cube |

**Foods to Enjoy for Low-Calorie Diets**    The challenge of living happily with a daily calorie allowance is a difficult one to meet. How each person meets it is a highly individual matter. Therefore, instead of organizing formal groups of foods to

*Made with corn, cottonseed, safflower, soy, or sunflower oil only.
†Fat content is primarily monounsaturated.
‡If made with corn, cottonseed, safflower, soy, or sunflower oil, it can be used in fat-modified diet.

enjoy and foods to limit, as we have for many other special diets, we give you an idea of the calories per serving in a long list of common foods. You will notice discrepancies between these and the approximate calorie values given in the food exchanges preceding. The figures below are more precise and are based on those developed by the Agricultural Research Service of the U.S. Department of Agriculture. (Note 19.) You can judge for yourself which foods to shun and which ones to enjoy.

Used with the food exchange lists, a must if you are diabetic, they can help you plan satisfying meals and still live within the calorie quota or number of food exchanges your doctor has prescribed.

CALORIE COUNTS FOR
BASIC FOODS

| Bread and Cereal Foods | Serving Size | Calories |
|---|---|---|
| Bread or toast | 1 slice | 65 |
| Hard roll | 1 roll | 80 |
| Cooked cereal | ½ cup | 70 |
| Dry cereal | 1 cup | 100 |
| Noodles, spaghetti, rice, barley, cooked | ½ cup | 100 |
| Matzo | 4 by 6 inches | 80 |
| Bagel | ½ | 80 |
| English muffin | ½ | 80 |
| Muffin (corn or bran) | 1 small | 90–120 |
| Biscuit | 1 | 90–120 |
| Pancake | 1 | 100–150 |
| Waffle | 1 (5 by 5 inches) | 100–150 |
| Crackers (graham) | 2 large | 110 |
| Crackers (saltines) | 4 small | 50 |

| Vegetables (Raw or Cooked) | Serving Size | Calories |
|---|---|---|
| Asparagus | ½ cup | 15 |
| Beans, dried or lima | ½ cup | 95 |
| Beans, wax or green | ½ cup | 15 |
| Beets | ½ cup | 25 |
| Broccoli | ½ cup | 25 |
| Brussels sprouts | ½ cup | 25 |
| Cabbage | ½ cup | 15 |
| Carrots | ½ cup | 25 |
| Cauliflower | ½ cup | 15 |
| Celery | ½ cup | 10 |
| Chicory | ½ cup | 5 |

51

| Vegetables (Cont'd) | Serving Size | Calories |
|---|---|---|
| Chinese cabbage | ½ cup | 5 |
| Corn | ½ cup | 90 |
| Cucumber | ½ cup | 10 |
| Eggplant | ½ cup | 20 |
| Endive | ½ cup | 5 |
| Escarole | ½ cup | 5 |
| Green peas | ½ cup | 75 |
| Green pepper | ½ cup | 10 |
| Lettuce | ½ cup | 5 |
| Mixed vegetables | ½ cup | 60 |
| Mushrooms | ½ cup | 10 |
| Okra | ½ cup | 25 |
| Onions | ½ cup | 30 |
| Parsley | ½ cup | 15 |
| Parsnip | ½ cup | 50 |
| Potato | ½ cup | 50 |
| Radishes | ½ cup | 10 |
| Sauerkraut | ½ cup | 20 |
| Scallions | ½ cup | 20 |
| Spinach, raw | ½ cup | 5 |
| Spinach, cooked | ½ cup | 20 |
| Squash, summer | ½ cup | 15 |
| Squash, winter | ½ cup | 65 |
| Sweet potato, mashed | ¼ cup | 150 |
| Tomatoes | ½ cup | 30 |
| Tomato juice | ½ cup | 25 |
| Tomato purée | ½ cup | 45 |
| Turnip, mashed | ½ cup | 25 |
| Watercress | ½ cup | 5 |
| Zucchini | ½ cup | 15 |

| Fruits and Juices | Serving Size | Calories |
|---|---|---|
| Berries | 1 cup | 50–100 |
| Cherries | 10 | 50 |
| Grapefruit | ½ | 40 |
| Apple juice | ⅓ cup | 60 |
| Grapefruit juice | ½ cup | 50 |
| Orange juice | ½ cup | 60 |
| Pineapple juice | ⅓ cup | 70 |
| Apple | 1 small | 60 |

| Fruits and Juices (Cont'd) | Serving Size | Calories |
|---|---|---|
| Orange | 1 small | 45 |
| Peach | 1 small | 40 |
| Plum | 2 small | 40 |
| Canned fruit without sugar | ½ cup | 40 |

| Milk and Dairy Products | Serving Size | Calories |
|---|---|---|
| Buttermilk | 1 cup | 100 |
| Milk, whole | 1 cup | 160 |
| Milk, low-fat, 99 percent | 1 cup | 100 |
| Milk, skim | 1 cup | 85 |
| Milk, flavored skim | 1 cup | 180 |
| Cottage cheese | 2 tablespoons (1 ounce) | 30 |
| Cheddar cheese | 1 ounce | 100 |
| Yogurt, fruited | 1 cup | 240 |
| Yogurt, plain | 1 cup | 140 |

| Meat and Other Protein Foods | Serving Size | Calories |
|---|---|---|
| Beef, lamb, pork | 4 ounces | 400 |
| Cold cuts | 4 ounces | 400 |
| Egg | 1 ounce | 80 |
| Fish, chicken, liver, veal | 4 ounces | 300 |
| Frankfurter | 1 | 140 |
| Peanut butter | 2 tablespoons | 190 |
| Shellfish, plain cooked | 4 ounces | 200 |

| Fats | Serving Size | Calories |
|---|---|---|
| Cream cheese | 1 tablespoon | 50 |
| Heavy cream | 1 tablespoon | 50 |
| Light cream | 1 tablespoon | 45 |
| Gravy | 1 tablespoon | 50 |
| Margarine, butter, or other solid fat | 1 teaspoon | 35 |
| Mayonnaise | 1 tablespoon | 100 |
| Oil | 1 teaspoon | 40 |

| Sweets | Serving Size | Calories |
|---|---|---|
| Candy bar | 1 ounce | 150 |
| Chocolates | 2 medium | 100 |
| Chocolate sauce | 2 tablespoons | 90 |

| Sweets (Cont'd) | Serving Size | Calories |
|---|---|---|
| Hard candy | 3 small | 75 |
| Jelly, pancake syrup | 1 tablespoon | 50 |
| Sugar | 1 teaspoon | 15 |

| Desserts | Serving Size | Calories |
|---|---|---|
| Angel food or sponge cake | 1 piece | 120 |
| Brownie | 1 small | 150 |
| Cookies, shortbread | 2 | 70 |
| Cupcake, with frosting | 1 | 150 |
| Custard | ½ cup | 150 |
| Danish pastry | 1 small | 150 |
| Doughnut | 1 | 150 |
| Eclair, custard filling | 1 medium | 320 |
| Flavored gelatin | ½ cup | 75 |
| Ice cream, plain | ½ cup | 130 |
| Pie | 1 slice | 400–500 |
| Sherbet | ½ cup | 130 |

| Snacks | Serving Size | Calories |
|---|---|---|
| Pizza | ⅛ of 14-inch pizza | 150 |
| Popcorn, without butter | 1 cup | 40 |
| Potato chips | 10 | 115 |
| Potatoes, French fried | 10 | 150 |
| Pretzels, thin twisted | 3 | 75 |

| Beverages | Serving Size | Calories |
|---|---|---|
| Beer, regular | 12 ounces | 150 |
| Beer, "light" | 12 ounces | 96 |
| Cocoa, whole milk | 8 ounces | 230 |
| Cola-type beverage | 8 ounces | 100 |
| Ice cream soda | 1 | 250–400 |
| Sweet wine | 4 ounces | 150 |
| Whiskey, 86 proof | 1½-ounce jigger | 105 |

**Foods to Enjoy for Low-Fat Diets**

If your gall bladder is misbehaving, or if your pancreas is functioning imperfectly, your doctor may suggest that you avoid all kinds of fats in your diet, both saturated and unsaturated. In addition he or she may caution you to avoid gaseous foods and any others that cause you discomfort. We list a few such possibilities under the heading "Foods to Limit." On the other hand, many physicians believe that, except for large quantities of fats, you should eat whatever appeals to you unless you find you cannot tolerate it. By all means follow your physician's counsel.

| *Foods to Enjoy* | *Foods to Limit* |
|---|---|
| Buttermilk made with skim milk, flavored skim-milk drinks, weak tea, coffee | Carbonated beverages, whole milk, chocolate milk |
| Any breads except those listed under Foods to Limit, saltines, soda crackers | Any bread made with eggs and a large amount of fat, e.g., breakfast rolls, quick breads |
| Angel food cake, arrowroot cookies, gelatin desserts, ices, puddings made without whole milk or fat, sherbets, vanilla wafers, desserts made from fruits listed in Foods to Enjoy for Low-Fat Diets | Desserts made with chocolate, cream, egg yolk, butter, margarine, other shortening, whole milk, nuts, coconut |
| Fruit juices, banana, cooked or canned apples, apricots, cherries, fruit cocktail, peaches, pears, pineapple, plums, dried fruit, stewed fruit, fresh fruit if tolerated, except melon | All fruits not listed under Foods to Enjoy |
| Three teaspoons of fat daily, if tolerated | More than amount of fat allowed under Foods to Enjoy |
| Lean beef, chicken, turkey, lamb, pork, ham, veal, fish, low-fat cottage cheese, egg white; nonfat cottage cheese | Liver, kidney, sweetbreads, heart, processed and spiced meats |
| Potatoes, hominy, macaroni, noodles, rice, spaghetti | Fried potatoes, potato chips |
|  | All creamed soups, chowders, and bisques |

*Foods to Enjoy*
Honey, jelly, jam, molasses, sugar, dry cocoa, and candies except those listed under Foods to Limit

*Foods to Limit*
Candies made with the following: cream, chocolate, butter, margarine and other shortenings, nuts, coconut, and fruits not listed under Foods to Enjoy for Low-Fat Diets

All vegetables except those listed under Foods to Limit
See "Herbs and Spices to Enjoy" (page 643)

Cucumber, Brussels sprouts, cabbage, cauliflower

**Foods to Enjoy for Low-Cholesterol Diets**

The food choices below may be recommended if you have tendencies toward vascular disorders or high blood pressure, or if for other reasons your doctor believes that eating this way is good for you.

Our list of foods to limit may represent more or fewer restrictions than your physician prescribes. Some have limited cholesterol content but are so high in saturated fats that your diet prohibits them. Remember, your doctor's advice is specifically addressed to you and to your state of health as an individual. By all means follow it.

*Foods to Enjoy*
Fresh skim milk, skim evaporated milk, nonfat dry milk solids, buttermilk, low-fat yogurt, dry cocoa, malt and fruit-flavored syrups, carbonated beverages, coffee, tea
Enriched or whole grain breads

*Foods to Limit*
Whole milk, whole milk drinks, cream or milk substitutes

Breads with high egg and/or butter content, pastries, doughnuts, coffee cakes, hot breads

All types of cereals
Gingersnaps, fig bars, sugar wafers, arrowroot cookies, gelatin desserts, angel food cake, sponge cake, fruit or water ices and nonmilk sherbets, pudding made with skim milk

Desserts made with butter, hydrogenated shortenings, chocolate, cream, egg yolks, whole milk, coconut, nuts

| *Foods to Enjoy* | *Foods to Limit* |
|---|---|
| Most vegetable oils (corn, soy, safflower, olive), soft margarine, salad dressings made with the above oils, walnuts, pecans | Sweet and sour creams, coconut oil, cocoa butter, lard, hydrogenated vegetable shortening, regular margarine, bacon, suet, chicken fat, gravies, coconut, cashew nuts, peanuts, peanut butter, most nondairy coffee lighteners and imitation cream products |
| Fruit juices and all fruits, including avocado | Coconut |
| Egg white | Whole eggs and dishes made with whole eggs |
| Salmon, sardines, tuna, mackerel, whitefish, herring | Shellfish |
| Pot and farmer's cheese, skim-milk cheeses such as dry cottage cheese and sapsago cheese, mozzarella cheese made from skim milk, creamed cottage cheese | Cream cheese, hard cheeses |
| Fresh veal, turkey, chicken, beef—round, rump, or sirloin steaks, lamb, pork, ham | Liver, kidney, tongue, luncheon meat, salami, pastrami, corned beef, frankfurters, spare ribs, bacon, sausage, poultry skins, duck, and goose |
| Sauces made from food allowed | Sauces made with butter, bacon, cream cheese, whole eggs, or shortening |
| All kinds of vegetables See "Herbs and Spices to Enjoy" (page 643) | |

**Foods to Enjoy for Low-Sodium Diets**

A low-sodium diet may be prescribed because you are retaining more fluid in your tissues than normal or because your blood pressure is elevated or because of other cardiovascular problems. These recommendations are for you if your sodium restriction is a moderate one—two grams of sodium per day. If yours is a more stringent restriction consult your doctor or dietitian before using this list.

| Foods to Enjoy | Foods to Avoid |
| --- | --- |
| Bread, plain matzo, melba toast, dry cereals, cooked cereals except instant cereals, rice, rolls, soda, graham and oyster crackers, muffins, and biscuits | Salted crackers, cheese crackers, cheese bread, quick-cooking or instant cereals; salted snacks such as pretzels, potato chips, corn chips, and salted popcorn |
| Whole or skim milk, milk-base beverages such as frappés, milkshakes, and cocoa | Instant beverage mixes, cultured buttermilk, cultured Dutch process cocoa, condensed milk |
| Coffee, tea, carbonated beverages | Chemically softened water |
| Fresh fruits, canned fruits, sun-dried fruits | Preserved and glazed fruits |
| Asparagus, all kinds of beans, broccoli, Brussels sprouts, cabbage, cauliflower, celery, chicory, corn, cucumbers, eggplant, endive, escarole, lettuce, mushrooms, okra, onions, parsley, parsnips, fresh peas, unsalted peas, peppers, sweet potatoes and white potatoes, pumpkin, radish, soybeans, summer and winter squash, tomatoes, low-sodium canned vegetables and vegetable juices | Frozen peas, frozen lima beans, frozen mixed vegetables, canned vegetables, sauerkraut, pickles or other vegetables prepared in brine, salted tomato and vegetable juices |
| Fresh and frozen beef, lamb, pork, rabbit, veal, fish (except shellfish), chicken, duck, turkey, tongue, tuna, salmon (without salt), peanut butter (without salt), cottage cheese, eggs, kidney, liver, sweetbreads, and heart | Salted, smoked meats, meats koshered by salting, low-cholesterol meat substitute, salted or smoked fish |
| Low-sodium American, low-sodium Swiss, and low-sodium Cheddar cheeses | All cheeses and cheese spreads except low-sodium cheeses listed in Foods to Enjoy. |
| Homemade soups, low-sodium canned soups | Bouillon cubes, regular canned soup, packaged soup mixes |

*Foods to Enjoy*
Unsalted butter, unsalted
  margarine, unsalted
  mayonnaise, heavy or light
  cream, cream substitute,
  cream cheese, unsalted
  cooking fat or oil, unsalted
  nuts, unsalted salad
  dressings

Chocolate, unflavored gelatin,
  low-sodium condiments,
  regular and low-sodium
  baking powder, white sugar,
  jams, jellies

See "Herbs and Spices to
  Enjoy" (page 643)

*Foods to Avoid*
Bacon and bacon fat, salt pork,
  olives, party spreads and
  dips, salted meat drippings,
  salted nuts, salted salad
  dressings

Salt in any form, commercially
  prepared catsup, mustard,
  steak sauces, meat sauces,
  soy sauce, seasoning salts,
  salted meat tenderizers,
  MSG, jams and jellies using
  sodium benzoate as
  preservative

**Foods to Enjoy for
Bland Diets**

Currently, there is considerable debate about the validity of bland
diets. Many doctors don't believe in them and think you should eat
everything that agrees with you. Others feel strongly that bland diets
can be useful and that certain foods should be avoided or eaten sparingly. If a bland diet is recommended, the lists below may be helpful.

*Foods to Enjoy*
All foods except those listed
  under Foods to Eat
  Sparingly

*Foods to Eat Sparingly*
Caffeine and caffeine-
  containing foods, such as
  coffee, decaffeinated coffee,
  tea, cocoa; alcoholic
  beverages, unless the alcohol
  is boiled off in cooking; any
  foods that cause you
  discomfort; some spices—see
  "Herbs and Spices to Enjoy"
  (page 643)

**Foods to Enjoy For
High-Fiber Diets**

You may think of dietary fiber as roughage. In a way it is, but, technically, dietary fiber is cellulose that comes from the fibrous part of

grains, fruits, and vegetables. These fibers are neither digested nor absorbed by the body, and therefore, they generate the bulk that accelerates the passage of foods through the intestinal tract.

High-fiber diets permit virtually all foods, but, of course, some foods are much higher in dietary fiber than others. We list here some that, if added to your diet, will increase its fiber content. Usually, high-fiber diets require a substantial amount of fluids, more than you would normally drink, so if you're eating a great many high-fiber foods, it is wise to drink seven to eight cups of liquid a day.

| *Foods to Enjoy* | *Foods to Limit* |
|---|---|
| Eat more whole wheat breads and flour. | None |
| Eat more coarse bran and bran cereal. | |
| Eat more raw fruits, vegetables, and legumes, including dried peas, dried beans, potato skins, and peelings on fruits and vegetables. | |
| Eat more nuts as snacks. Add them to cakes, cookies, and other foods whenever possible. | |
| See "Herbs and Spices to Enjoy" (page 643) | |

# A P P E T I Z E R S

Appetizers are literally foods that stimulate the appetite. This is essential for some special dieters. For others, it may be more important to curb the appetite. If you're on a low-calorie regime, for example, an appetizer may be the last thing in the world you need. If, however, you're on a low-fat diet, your taste buds may need cajoling. Interestingly enough, fats in food stimulate the appetite, and your zeal for your next meal may well be at low ebb if you've been cutting your fat intake down to new minimums.

In either case, the assortment of appetizers we offer is a varied one. It includes tasty tidbits built around fish, shellfish, eggs, meats, poultry, cheese, and vegetables. All may be presented as a first course or as an hors d'oeuvre. Some of them, like Cheese Knishes or Petite Meat Turnovers, can be luncheon dishes in themselves. Choose a recipe that appeals to you or skip this course and apply the calories and nutrients to the total eating plan you've made for today.

# Savory Cheese Spread

BASIC RECIPE

Serving size: 2 tablespoons
Calories per serving: 101
Approximate nutrient
    values per serving:
        Protein 2 g
        Fat 10 g
        Carbohydrate 1 g
        Sodium 94 mg
        Potassium 31 mg
        Cholesterol 21 mg
Exchanges:
    Fat 2

two 8-ounce packages cream cheese
½ cup polyunsaturated margarine
1½ teaspoons paprika
1 teaspoon dry mustard
1 teaspoon caraway seed
2 tablespoons thinly sliced scallions, white and green parts included
1 tablespoon capers

In large mixing bowl cream together cheese and margarine until light. Add remaining ingredients and stir until well blended. Serve at room temperature.

*Yield:* 3 cups

*Change Savory Cheese Spread as follows or use Basic Recipe, if indicated, for:*

LOW-CALORIE, DIABETIC, LOW-FAT, AND LOW-CHOLESTEROL DIETS

Calories per serving: 35
Approximate nutrient
    values per serving:
        Protein 3 g
        Fat 2 g
        Carbohydrate 1 g
        Sodium 105 mg
        Potassium 26 mg
        Cholesterol 1 mg
Exchanges:
    Fat 1

Substitute 16 ounces 1 percent low-fat cottage cheese, puréed in a blender, for cream cheese.
Reduce margarine to ¼ cup.
Proceed as in Basic Recipe.

*Yield:* 2¾ cups.

Calories per serving: 101
Approximate nutrient
  values same as Basic
  Recipe except for:
    Calcium 17 mg
    Phosphorus 22 mg
    Sodium 56 mg

Omit capers.
Substitute unsalted polyunsaturated margarine for margarine.
Proceed as in Basic Recipe.

BLAND DIETS

Calories per serving: 101

Omit capers and mustard.
Add 1 tablespoon fresh chopped chives.
Proceed as in Basic Recipe.

HIGH-FIBER DIETS

Use Basic Recipe. For extra fiber, use it to stuff celery or cherry
  tomatoes.

# Herbed Chicken Dip

BASIC RECIPE

Serving size: ¼ cup
Calories per serving: 59
Approximate nutrient
  values per serving:
    Protein 6 g
    Fat 2 g
    Carbohydrate 3 g
    Sodium 242 mg
    Potassium 166 mg
    Cholesterol 17 mg
Exchanges:
  Vegetable 1
  Meat ½

¾ cup finely chopped cooked chicken
2 cups plain yogurt
4 tablespoons chopped fresh parsley
4 tablespoons finely chopped onions
¾ teaspoon salt
½ teaspoon tarragon
½ teaspoon dillweed
⅛ teaspoon freshly ground pepper

Combine all ingredients in a large bowl. Mix to blend.
    Cover and refrigerate at least 1 hour before serving.

*Yield:* 2 cups

*Change Herbed Chicken Dip as follows or use Basic Recipe, if indicated, for:*

## LOW-CALORIE, DIABETIC, LOW-FAT, AND LOW-CHOLESTEROL DIETS

Substitute 2 cups plain low-fat yogurt for yogurt.
Proceed as in Basic Recipe.

Calories per serving: 59
Approximate nutrient
  values per serving:
    Protein 7 g
    Fat 1 g
    Carbohydrate 5 g
    Sodium 255 g
    Potassium 211 mg
    Cholesterol 13 mg
Exchanges:
  Vegetable 1
  Meat ½

## LOW-SODIUM AND RENAL DIETS

Omit salt.
Add 2 teaspoons chervil.
Proceed as in Basic Recipe.

Calories per serving: 59
Approximate nutrient
  values per serving:
    Protein 6 g
    Fat 2 g
    Carbohydrate 3 g
    Calcium 80 mg
    Phosphorus 91 mg
    Sodium 36 mg
    Potassium 174 mg
    Cholesterol 17 mg

## BLAND DIETS

Omit pepper.
Proceed as in Basic Recipe.

Calories per serving: 59

## HIGH-FIBER DIETS

Use Basic Recipe. For extra fiber, serve with sesame seed
  breadsticks or whole wheat toast points.

# Eggplant Caviar

BASIC RECIPE

Serving size: ¼ cup
Calories per serving: 67
Approximate nutrient
  values per serving:
    Protein 1 g
    Fat 5 g
    Carbohydrate 5 g
    Sodium 474 mg
    Potassium 198 mg
    Cholesterol 0 mg
Exchanges:
  Vegetable 1
  Fat 1

1 large eggplant
1 tablespoon salt
⅓ cup olive oil
1 teaspoon finely minced garlic
4 tomatoes, peeled and diced
2 tablespoons lemon juice
2 tablespoons tomato paste
¼ cup finely chopped fresh parsley
¼ cup finely chopped onions
½ teaspoon freshly ground pepper

Peel the eggplant, removing only half the skin. Slice in ¼-inch slices lengthwise, then dice into ¼-inch cubes.

Place a layer of eggplant in a colander and salt lightly. Continue to layer until all the eggplant and salt are used. Allow to stand 2 hours, then gently squeeze eggplant to remove liquid.

Heat the oil in a heavy saucepan, add the eggplant and garlic, cover, and cook over low heat 20 to 30 minutes, or until the eggplant is soft. Cool.

Mix the remaining ingredients thoroughly in a bowl. Stir in the cold eggplant.

Chill for at least 2 hours before serving.

*Yield:* 3½ cups

*Change Eggplant Caviar as follows or use Basic Recipe, if indicated, for:*

LOW-CALORIE, DIABETIC, LOW-FAT, AND LOW-CHOLESTEROL DIETS

Calories per serving: 30
Approximate nutrient
  values per serving:
    Protein 1 g
    Fat 1 g
    Carbohydrate 5 g
    Sodium 474 mg
    Potassium 198 mg
    Cholesterol 0 mg
Exchanges:
  Vegetable 1

Reduce oil to 1 tablespoon and cook eggplant in a covered pan over very low heat.
Proceed as in Basic Recipe.

LOW-SODIUM DIETS

Calories per serving: 67
Approximate nutrient
  values same as Basic
  Recipe except for:
    Sodium 3 mg

Omit salt.
Place eggplant in colander and cover with plate. Put heavy weight on plate and let eggplant drain for about 2 hours. Squeeze gently.
Proceed as in Basic Recipe.

BLAND DIETS

Calories per serving: 67

Omit pepper.
Proceed as in Basic Recipe.

HIGH-FIBER DIETS

Use Basic Recipe.

# Mushrooms and Herbs Vinaigrette

BASIC RECIPE

This recipe requires overnight refrigeration.

Serving size: ⅓ cup
Calories per serving: 101
Approximate nutrient
  values per serving:
    Protein 2 g
    Fat 9 g
    Carbohydrate 5 g
    Sodium 208 mg
    Potassium 244 mg
    Cholesterol 0 mg
Exchanges:
  Vegetable 1
  Fat 2

2 cups small fresh mushroom caps
9-ounce package frozen artichoke hearts, thawed
1 clove garlic, halved
8 peppercorns
1 tablespoon chopped fresh parsley
½ teaspoon salt
½ teaspoon coriander seed
½ teaspoon thyme
¼ teaspoon fennel seed
¼ cup red wine vinegar
½ cup olive oil
1½ cups water

In a medium saucepan combine all ingredients. Bring to a boil, reduce heat, and simmer, covered, for 10 minutes. Remove from heat and allow to cool.

Refrigerate, covered, overnight.

Remove garlic, drain off liquid, and serve at room temperature.

*Yield:* 6 servings

*Change Mushrooms and Herbs Vinaigrette as follows or use Basic Recipe, if indicated, for:*

## LOW-CALORIE, DIABETIC, LOW-FAT, AND LOW-CHOLESTEROL DIETS

Calories per serving: 57
Approximate nutrient
  values per serving:
    Protein 2 g
    Fat 5 g
    Carbohydrate 5 g
    Sodium 208 mg
    Potassium 244 mg
    Cholesterol 0 mg
Exchanges:
  Vegetable 1
  Fat 1

Reduce olive oil to ¼ cup.
Proceed as in Basic Recipe.

## LOW-SODIUM DIETS

Calories per serving: 101
Approximate nutrient
  values same as Basic
  Recipe except for:
    Sodium 25 mg

Omit salt.
Proceed as in Basic Recipe.

## BLAND DIETS

Calories per serving: 101

Omit peppercorns.
Proceed as in Basic Recipe.

## HIGH-FIBER DIETS

Use Basic Recipe.

## MUSHROOMS AND HERBS VINAIGRETTE FOR RENAL DIETS

This recipe requires overnight refrigeration.

1½ cups fresh small white onions
1 clove garlic, halved
8 peppercorns
1 tablespoon chopped fresh parsley
½ teaspoon coriander seed
½ teaspoon thyme
¼ teaspoon fennel seed
¼ cup red wine vinegar
½ cup olive oil
1½ cups water
two 4-ounce cans whole mushrooms, drained

In a medium saucepan combine all ingredients except the mushrooms. Bring to a boil, reduce heat, and simmer, covered, for 10 minutes. Add mushrooms and simmer 5 more minutes. Remove from heat and allow to cool. Refrigerate, covered, overnight. Remove garlic, drain off liquid, and serve at room temperature.

*Yield:* 6 servings

Serving size: ⅓ cup
Calories per serving: 117
Approximate nutrient
   values per serving:
      Protein 2 g
      Fat 8 g
      Carbohydrate 11 g
      Calcium 35 mg
      Phosphorus 66 mg
      Sodium 111 mg
      Potassium 219 mg
      Cholesterol 0 mg
Exchanges:
   Vegetable 2
   Fat 1½

# Salmon Brandade

BASIC RECIPE

1 pound salmon steak, approximately 1 inch thick
3 cups Fish Stock (page 115)
1¼ cups diced peeled potatoes
¼ cup olive oil
¼ cup heavy cream
1 teaspoon lemon juice
2 cloves garlic, put through garlic press

Serving size: 2 tablespoons
Calories per serving: 62
Approximate nutrient
   values per serving:
      Protein 4 g
      Fat 4 g
      Carbohydrate 1 g
      Sodium 42 mg

69

Potassium 95 mg
Cholesterol 11 mg
Exchanges:
Meat ½
Fat ½

¼ teaspoon salt
⅛ teaspoon cayenne pepper

In a skillet or casserole in which the salmon will fit comfortably, pour enough fish stock to cover fish. Bring to a boil, reduce heat so liquid simmers gently, and cook salmon approximately 7 to 10 minutes or until fish flakes when tested with a fork. Remove salmon to paper toweling and allow to drain thoroughly.

Cook potatoes in boiling water to cover, approximately 10 minutes or until tender. Drain thoroughly, return potatoes to saucepan, cover, and shake over low heat until potatoes are dry. Remove from heat.

Flake fish in a large mixing bowl. Add potatoes and mix well. Warm the olive oil and cream in a small saucepan and add it to the fish in a slow steady stream, stirring constantly.

Add remaining ingredients and stir until brandade is thoroughly blended and has the consistency of mashed potatoes.

Mound onto a serving dish and shape into a dome. Serve immediately.

*Yield:* 3 cups

*Change Salmon Brandade as follows for:*

LOW-CALORIE, DIABETIC, LOW-FAT, AND LOW-CHOLESTEROL DIETS

Calories per serving: 49
Approximate nutrient
  values per serving:
    Protein 5 g
    Fat 3 g
    Carbohydrate 1 g
    Sodium 42 mg
    Potassium 97 mg
    Cholesterol 7 mg
Exchanges:
  Meat ½
  Fat ½

Reduce oil to 3 tablespoons.
Substitute ¼ cup skim milk for cream.
Proceed as in Basic Recipe.

Calories per serving: 62
Approximate nutrient
  values same as Basic
  Recipe except for:
    Calcium 2 mg
    Phosphorus 69 mg
    Sodium 19 mg

Omit salt.
Proceed as in Basic Recipe.

### BLAND DIETS

Calories per serving: 62

Omit cayenne pepper.
Proceed as in Basic Recipe.

### HIGH-FIBER DIETS

Calories per serving: 62

Add 2 tablespoons chopped fresh parsley to seasonings. Proceed as in Basic Recipe. For extra fiber, serve with sesame crackers or rye bread rounds.

# Miniature Swordfish Kebabs

### BASIC RECIPE

Serving size: four 1-inch
  fish cubes, two cherry
  tomatoes
Calories per serving: 90
Approximate nutrient
  values per serving:
    Protein 11 g
    Fat 4 g
    Carbohydrate 3 g
    Sodium 56 mg
    Potassium 216 mg
    Cholesterol 17 mg
Exchanges:
  Meat 1½

1 pound swordfish, 1 inch thick
2 tablespoons chopped fresh dillweed
¼ cup dry vermouth
¼ cup orange juice
1 tablespoon polyunsaturated margarine, melted
juice of ½ lemon
1 crumbled bay leaf
¼ teaspoon freshly ground pepper
1 pint cherry tomatoes

Remove the skin from the swordfish and cut into 1-inch cubes.
  Combine the dillweed, vermouth, orange juice, margarine,

71

lemon juice, bay leaf, and pepper in a medium bowl. Add the fish and marinate for 1 hour in the refrigerator, turning occasionally.

Preheat broiler. Spread the fish cubes out on a shallow baking pan. Baste with marinade. Broil for 5 minutes or until fish is white and firm to the touch. Turn once during cooking.

Spear 4 swordfish cubes on small skewers and arrange the spears on a platter. Spoon the cooking juices over the fish until well moistened. Cover with foil and refrigerate several hours. Before serving, garnish the platter with cherry tomatoes. Serve at once.

*Yield:* 8 servings

*Change Miniature Swordfish Kebabs as follows or use Basic Recipe, if indicated, for:*

LOW-CALORIE, DIABETIC, LOW-FAT, LOW-CHOLESTEROL, AND HIGH-FIBER DIETS

Use Basic Recipe.

LOW-SODIUM DIETS

Calories per serving: 90
Approximate nutrient
values same as Basic
Recipe except for:
Sodium 42 mg

Substitute unsalted polyunsaturated margarine for margarine. Proceed as in Basic Recipe.

BLAND DIETS

Calories per serving: 90

Omit pepper.
Proceed as in Basic Recipe.

# Eggs Mayonnaise

BASIC RECIPE

4 eggs
⅛ teaspoon salt
⅛ teaspoon freshly ground pepper
½ cup Homemade Mayonnaise (page 499)
10-ounce package frozen green peas
2 tablespoons diced pimiento
1 cucumber, peeled in strips and thinly sliced
2 tablespoons chopped fresh parsley

Bring a large saucepan of water to a boil. Gently lower eggs into boiling water. When water returns to a boil, turn heat low and cook eggs for 12 minutes. Drain and plunge into cold water. Set aside.

Season mayonnaise with salt and pepper; if too thick, thin with 1 tablespoon cold water. Set aside.

Drop frozen peas into saucepan of boiling water and boil for 1 minute. Drain and rinse with cold water. Pile the peas into a bowl and stir in pimiento.

Peel eggs and halve lengthwise. Arrange them flat side down around edge of serving platter. Place peas in center. Cover eggs completely with mayonnaise. Place sliced cucumbers at each end of platter. Dust cucumbers and eggs with parsley. Refrigerate until ready to serve.

*Yield:* 4 servings

*Change Eggs Mayonnaise as follows or use Basic Recipe, if indicated, for:*

### LOW-CALORIE, DIABETIC, LOW-FAT, AND LOW-CHOLESTEROL DIETS

Calories per serving: 115
Approximate nutrient
   values per serving:
   Protein 9 g
   Fat 3 g
   Carbohydrate 14 g
   Sodium 289 mg
   Potassium 274 mg
   Cholesterol 35 mg
Exchanges:
   Vegetable 1
   Bread ½
   Meat ½
   Fat ½

Substitute low-calorie Homemade Mayonnaise (page 500) for basic Homemade Mayonnaise.
Split eggs in half, remove yolks and use only the whites.
Proceed as in Basic Recipe.

### LOW-SODIUM AND RENAL DIETS

Calories per serving: 329
Approximate nutrient
   values per serving:
   Protein 10 g
   Fat 28 g
   Carbohydrate 10 g
   Calcium 61 mg
   Phosphorus 152 mg
   Sodium 82 mg
   Potassium 224 mg
   Cholesterol 301 mg

Omit salt.
Substitute low-sodium Homemade Mayonnaise for basic Homemade Mayonnaise (page 499).
Omit frozen peas. Substitute 8-ounce can low-sodium peas, drained.
Omit pimiento. Substitute 2 tablespoons shredded red bell pepper.
Proceed as in Basic Recipe.

### BLAND DIETS

Calories per serving: 338

Substitute bland Homemade Mayonnaise (page 499) for basic Homemade Mayonnaise.
Omit pepper.
Proceed as in Basic Recipe.

### HIGH-FIBER DIETS

Use Basic Recipe.

# Baba Gânoosh

BASIC RECIPE

Serving size: ⅓ cup
Calories per serving: 53
Approximate nutrient
  values per serving:
    Protein 2 g
    Fat 2 g
    Carbohydrate 8 g
    Sodium 186 mg
    Potassium 272 mg
    Cholesterol 0 mg
Exchanges:
    Vegetable 1
    Fat ½

2 medium eggplants
¼ cup lemon juice
3 tablespoons tahini
2 cloves garlic, put through garlic press
½ teaspoon salt
¼ teaspoon freshly ground pepper
⅓ cup chopped fresh parsley

Preheat oven broiler.

Place eggplants on a cookie sheet approximately 8 inches below the broiler. Broil eggplant until skin starts to turn brown.

Gently pierce skin and turn, broiling on all sides until eggplant is soft, approximately 30 minutes.

Cool eggplants, halve them, and gently scoop out meat. Place meat in a blender with one-fourth of the charred skin from the eggplant.

Add all ingredients except parsley. Blend until the mixture is smooth. Scoop into a serving bowl, stir in parsley, and chill for at least 1 hour.

*Yield:* 6 servings

*Change Baba Gânoosh as follows or use Basic Recipe, if indicated, for:*

LOW-CALORIE, DIABETIC, LOW-FAT, AND LOW-CHOLESTEROL DIETS

Use Basic Recipe.

Calories per serving: 53
Approximate nutrient
   values same as Basic
   Recipe except for:
      Calcium 29 mg
      Phosphorus 37 mg
      Sodium 3 mg

## LOW-SODIUM AND RENAL DIETS

Omit salt.
Proceed as in Basic Recipe.

## BLAND DIETS

Calories per serving: 53

Omit pepper.
Proceed as in Basic Recipe.

## HIGH-FIBER DIETS

Use Basic Recipe.

# Chicken Pâté with Mushrooms

### BASIC RECIPE

Serving size: ¼ cup
Calories per serving: 139
Approximate nutrient
   values per serving:
      Protein 10 g
      Fat 9 g
      Carbohydrate 4 g
      Sodium 240 mg
      Potassium 394 mg
      Cholesterol 28 mg
Exchanges:
   Vegetable 1
   Meat 1
   Fat 1½

1 whole chicken breast (¾ pound)
1 cup Chicken Stock (page 114)
1 small onion, halved
¾ pound fresh mushrooms, sliced
1 tablespoon polyunsaturated oil
3 tablespoons Homemade Mayonnaise (page 499)
½ teaspoon salt
¼ teaspoon freshly ground pepper
⅛ teaspoon ground nutmeg
⅛ teaspoon allspice
1 sprig fresh parsley

Put chicken breast into a large saucepan with stock. Add enough water to almost cover it. Bring to a boil, skim the surface, add onion, and simmer gently, covered, for 20 minutes. Remove chicken and onion to a plate. Strain the stock and freeze it for future use.

Sauté mushrooms in oil over medium heat until all liquid evaporates. Remove mushrooms from pan and set aside.

Skin and bone the chicken, then dice the meat. Purée chicken, onion, and mushrooms in a blender.

Pour puréed mixture into a bowl. Add mayonnaise, salt, pepper, nutmeg, and allspice. Stir well. Spoon the pâté into small bowl or crock. Cover tightly and chill. Before serving, garnish with sprig of parsley.

*Yield:* 6 servings

*Change Chicken Pâté with Mushrooms as follows or use Basic Recipe, if indicated, for:*

LOW-CALORIE, DIABETIC, LOW-FAT, AND LOW-CHOLESTEROL DIETS

Calories per serving: 99
Approximate nutrient
  values per serving:
    Protein 11 g
    Fat 4 g
    Carbohydrate 4 g
    Sodium 247 mg
    Potassium 403 mg
    Cholesterol 30 mg
Exchanges:
  Vegetable 1
  Meat 1
  Fat ½

Substitute low-calorie Homemade Mayonnaise (page 500) for basic Homemade Mayonnaise.
Proceed as in Basic Recipe.

LOW-SODIUM DIETS

Calories per serving: 139
Approximate nutrient
  values same as Basic
  Recipe except for:
    Sodium 43 mg

Omit salt.
Substitute low-sodium Homemade Mayonnaise (page 499) for basic Homemade Mayonnaise.
Proceed as in Basic Recipe.

Calories per serving: 139

Omit pepper and nutmeg.
Substitute bland Homemade Mayonnaise (page 499) for basic
    Homemade Mayonnaise.
Proceed as in Basic Recipe.

## HIGH-FIBER DIETS

Use Basic Recipe. For extra fiber serve in a Bibb lettuce cup or
    add an edible garnish of celery sticks and radishes.

# Stuffed Artichokes

### BASIC RECIPE

Serving size: 1 artichoke, 2
    tablespoons mayonnaise,
    ⅛ cup chicken mixture
Calories per serving: 522
Approximate nutrient
    values per serving:
        Protein 21 g
        Fat 47 g
        Carbohydrate 14 g
        Sodium 329 mg
        Potassium 625 mg
        Cholesterol 94 mg
Exchanges:
    Vegetable 3
    Meat 2
    Fat 9

*The Artichokes*
4 medium-size artichokes
2 tablespoons lemon juice
½ teaspoon paprika

*The Stuffing*
1 cup Homemade Mayonnaise (page 499)
2 tablespoons lemon juice
¼ teaspoon salt
¼ teaspoon ground cumin
¼ teaspoon ground ginger
¼ teaspoon turmeric
⅛ teaspoon cayenne pepper
1½ cups finely minced cooked chicken

*To prepare the artichokes:* Cut off stem; discard small leaves
around base. Place the artichoke on its side; cut off the top one-
third. Snip off pointed tips of remaining leaves with scissors.
Dip cut parts in lemon juice to prevent discoloration. Turn
artichoke right side up and spread leaves; pull out cone of yel-
low-white young leaves that cover the fuzzy choke in the cen-

ter. Using a sturdy teaspoon, scrape out the choke and discard. The heart below is a great delicacy.

*To prepare the stuffing:* In a medium bowl, combine ½ cup of the mayonnaise, lemon juice, salt, cumin, ginger, turmeric, and cayenne pepper. Add chicken and blend in thoroughly. Cover and refrigerate.

Stand artichokes in a deep saucepan; cover with boiling water. Add lemon juice and simmer, covered, approximately 40 minutes, or until the outer leaves pull off easily.

Drain upside down in a colander. Cool to room temperature.

Immediately before serving, spoon ⅓ cup chicken mixture into center of each artichoke.

Top chicken mixture in each artichoke with 2 tablespoons mayonnaise sprinkled lightly with paprika.

To eat, tear off the leaves one at a time and dip in the mayonnaise. The chicken salad makes a delectable accompaniment to the remaining artichoke heart.

*Yield:* 4 servings

*Change Stuffed Artichokes as follows or use Basic Recipe, if indicated, for:*

LOW-CALORIE, DIABETIC, LOW-FAT, AND LOW-CHOLESTEROL DIETS

*The artichokes:* Use Basic Recipe.

*The stuffing:* Substitute low-calorie Homemade Mayonnaise (page 500) for basic Homemade Mayonnaise.

Proceed as in Basic Recipe.

Calories per serving: 201
Approximate nutrient
 values per serving:
  Protein 22 g
  Fat 7 g
  Carbohydrate 19 g
  Sodium 381 mg
  Potassium 701 mg
  Cholesterol 108 mg
Exchanges:
 Vegetable 2
 Bread ½
 Meat 2
 Fat 1

## LOW-SODIUM DIETS

*The artichokes:* Use Basic Recipe.

*The stuffing:* Omit salt.
   Substitute low-sodium Homemade Mayonnaise (page 499) for basic Homemade Mayonnaise.
   Proceed as in Basic Recipe.

## BLAND DIETS

*The artichokes:* Use Basic Recipe.

*The stuffing:* Omit cayenne pepper.
   Substitute bland Homemade Mayonnaise (page 499) for basic Homemade Mayonnaise. Proceed as in Basic Recipe.

## HIGH-FIBER DIETS

Use Basic Recipe.

# Miniature Meatballs

### BASIC RECIPE

*The Meatballs*
1½ pounds ground round beef
½ cup fresh bread crumbs (page 38)
1 egg
½ teaspoon salt
½ teaspoon freshly ground pepper
1 teaspoon ground cumin
1 teaspoon ground coriander
1 tablespoon polyunsaturated oil

*The Sauce*
2 tablespoons polyunsaturated oil
1 cup finely sliced onions

---

Calories per serving: 522
Approximate nutrient
   values same as Basic
   Recipe except for:
   Sodium 82 mg

Calories per serving 522

Serving size: 4 meatballs, 2
   tablespoons sauce
Calories per serving: 181
Approximate nutrient
   values per serving:
   Protein 16 g
   Fat 9 g
   Carbohydrate 9 g
   Sodium 311 mg
   Potassium 274 mg
   Cholesterol 70 mg
Exchanges:
   Bread ½
   Meat 2
   Fat 1

1½ tablespoons flour
1 teaspoon ground cumin
1 teaspoon ground coriander
½ teaspoon salt
2 cups plain yogurt

*To prepare the meatballs:* Combine the meat, bread crumbs, egg, salt, pepper, cumin, and coriander in a large mixing bowl.

Mix well and shape into 1-inch meatballs. Heat 1 tablespoon oil in a large skillet and sauté a layer of meatballs until brown on all sides; do not overcrowd. Remove meatballs and set aside. Sauté the rest in batches.

*To prepare the sauce:* Heat the remaining 2 tablespoons oil in a saucepan and sauté onions until soft. Stir in the flour, cumin, coriander, and salt and cook for 1 minute. Add the yogurt, bring to a boil, and continue stirring until well blended. Lower heat, add meatballs, and simmer gently for 10 minutes. Serve immediately.

*Yield:* **40** meatballs; 1¼ cups sauce

*Change Miniature Meatballs as follows or use Basic Recipe, if indicated, for:*

LOW-CALORIE, DIABETIC, LOW-FAT, AND LOW-CHOLESTEROL DIETS

*The meatballs:* Omit egg and use Low-Cholesterol Egg Substitute (page 189) equivalent to 1 large egg.

*The sauce:* Substitute plain low-fat yogurt for yogurt.
Proceed as in Basic Recipe.

Calories per serving: 179
Approximate nutrient
   values per serving:
      Protein 17 g
      Fat 8 g
      Carbohydrate 10 g
      Sodium 327 mg
      Potassium 319 mg
      Cholesterol 39 mg
Exchanges:
   Bread ½
   Meat 2
   Fat 1

*The meatballs:* Omit salt.

*The sauce:* Omit salt. Add 1 teaspoon curry powder with other spices.
    Proceed as in Basic Recipe.

Calories per serving: 181
Approximate nutrient
    values per serving:
        Protein 16 g
        Fat 9 g
        Carbohydrate 9 g
        Calcium 81 mg
        Phosphorus 178 mg
        Sodium 91 mg
        Potassium 277 mg
        Cholesterol 70 mg

## BLAND DIETS

*The meatballs:* Omit pepper. Proceed as in Basic Recipe.

*The sauce:* Use Basic Recipe.

Calories per serving: 181

## HIGH-FIBER DIETS

*The meatballs:* Omit bread crumbs. Substitute ½ cup wheat germ. Proceed as in Basic Recipe.

*The sauce:* Use Basic Recipe.

Calories per serving: 174

# Chicken Puffs

## BASIC RECIPE

½ cup Chicken Stock (page 114)
¼ cup polyunsaturated margarine for the puffs
3 tablespoons finely chopped onions
¾ teaspoon dry mustard
½ teaspoon salt
⅛ teaspoon freshly ground pepper

Serving size: 3 puffs
Calories per serving: 107
Approximate nutrient
    values per serving:
        Protein 5 g
        Fat 7 g
        Carbohydrate 5 g

Sodium 192 mg
Potassium 82 mg
Cholesterol 63 mg
Exchanges:
  Bread ½
  Meat ½
  Fat 1

1 tablespoon dry sherry
½ cup sifted flour
2 large eggs
¾ cup minced cooked chicken
¼ cup finely chopped green pepper
1 tablespoon polyunsaturated oil for greasing pan

In a medium saucepan bring to a boil chicken stock, margarine, onions, mustard, salt, pepper, and sherry.

Reduce heat and add flour, all at once, and stir vigorously, preferably with a wooden spoon, until mixture leaves the sides of the saucepan and forms a ball.

Remove from heat and add eggs, one at a time, beating after each addition until thoroughly blended.

Stir in chicken and green pepper. Drop by rounded teaspoons onto greased cookie sheet and refrigerate at least 1 hour.

Preheat oven to 425°F. Bake puffs 18 to 20 minutes or until golden brown.

*Yield:* 30 puffs

*Change Chicken Puffs as follows or use Basic Recipe, if indicated, for:*

LOW-CALORIE, DIABETIC, LOW-FAT, AND LOW-CHOLESTEROL DIETS

Omit oil for greasing pan. Spray pan with vegetable cooking spray.
Proceed as in Basic Recipe.

Calories per serving: 97
Approximate nutrient
  values per serving:
  Protein 5 g
  Fat 6 g
  Carbohydrate 5 g
  Sodium 181 mg
  Potassium 82 mg
  Cholesterol 63 mg
Exchanges:
  Bread ½
  Meat ½
  Fat 1

Omit salt.
Substitute unsalted polyunsaturated margarine for margarine.
Proceed as in Basic Recipe.

Calories per serving: 107
Approximate nutrient
  values same as Basic
  Recipe except for:
    Calcium 10 mg
    Phosphorus 56 mg
    Sodium 26 mg

### BLAND DIETS

Omit ground pepper and mustard.
Add ¼ teaspoon caraway seed.
Proceed as in Basic Recipe.

Calories per serving: 107

### HIGH-FIBER DIETS

Use Basic Recipe.

# Crabmeat Amandine

### BASIC RECIPE

Serving size: ½ cup
Calories per serving: 209
Approximate nutrient
  values per serving:
    Protein 15 g
    Fat 13 g
    Carbohydrate 7 g
    Sodium 807 mg
    Potassium 229 mg
    Cholesterol 75 mg
Exchanges:
  Bread ½
  Meat 2
  Fat 2

3 tablespoons polyunsaturated margarine
2 tablespoons flour
1⅓ cups plain yogurt
½ teaspoon grated lemon rind
2 tablespoons finely diced scallion greens
⅛ teaspoon salt
⅛ teaspoon freshly ground pepper
three 6½-ounce cans crabmeat
6 tablespoons slivered toasted almonds (page 38)

In a large skillet, melt the margarine over low heat and add the flour. Cook for 1 minute, stirring. Remove from heat and allow to cool briefly.

Stir in the yogurt. Return to heat and boil, stirring constantly. Then reduce heat and gently simmer for 3 minutes. Stir in the lemon rind, scallions, salt, pepper, and crabmeat. Heat about 5 minutes.

Serve in warmed ramekins or custard cups. Garnish each serving with 1 tablespoon toasted almonds.

*Yield:* 6 servings

*Change Crabmeat Amandine as follows or use Basic Recipe, if indicated, for:*

LOW-CALORIE, DIABETIC, LOW-FAT, AND LOW-CHOLESTEROL DIETS

Reduce margarine to 2 tablespoons.
Reduce flour to 1½ tablespoons.
Substitute 1 cup plain low-fat yogurt for yogurt.
Omit almonds.
Proceed as in Basic Recipe.

Calories per serving: 134
Approximate nutrient
  values per serving:
    Protein 14 g
    Fat 6 g
    Carbohydrate 5 g
    Sodium 791 mg
    Potassium 175 mg
    Cholesterol 70 mg
Exchanges:
  Bread ½
  Meat 2
  Fat 1

LOW-SODIUM DIETS

Omit salt.
Omit canned crabmeat and substitute 1 pound fresh crabmeat that has been run under cold water and moistened with 1 tablespoon lemon juice.
Proceed as in Basic Recipe.

Calories per serving: 214
Approximate nutrient
  values per serving:
    Protein 17 g
    Fat 13 g
    Carbohydrate 7 g
    Sodium 244 mg
    Potassium 298 mg
    Cholesterol 84 mg

Omit pepper.
Add 1 tablespoon lemon juice with crabmeat.
Proceed as in Basic Recipe.

HIGH-FIBER DIETS

Use Basic Recipe.

# Petite Meat Turnovers

BASIC RECIPE

Calories per serving: 210

Serving size: 2 turnovers
Calories per serving: 243
Approximate nutrient
  values per serving:
    Protein 7 g
    Fat 14 g
    Carbohydrate 21 g
    Sodium 252 mg
    Potassium 78 mg
    Cholesterol 36 mg
Exchanges:
  Bread 1½
  Meat ½
  Fat 2½

double the recipe for Easy-Mix Flaky Pie Crust (page 555)
½ pound ground round beef
2 tablespoons finely chopped onions
¼ teaspoon ground cumin
¼ teaspoon oregano
¼ teaspoon salt
⅛ teaspoon freshly ground pepper
1 clove garlic, put through garlic press
1 tablespoon sour cream
¼ cup grated Cheddar cheese
1 large egg yolk
1 teaspoon water

Prepare pastry and refrigerate while preparing meat filling.
    Preheat oven to 400°F.
    In a skillet sauté beef until meat starts to brown. Add onions and sauté mixture until onions are soft, stirring to break up large pieces of meat. Add cumin, oregano, salt, pepper, garlic, sour cream, and cheese. Mix thoroughly and remove from heat.
    Roll out pastry, half the dough at a time, to about ⅛ inch thick. Cut in circles, using a glass measuring 3 inches in diameter. As circles are cut remove them to an ungreased cookie sheet.

Place approximately 2 teaspoons meat filling on each pastry circle and fold dough over to make a turnover. Seal edges and prick top with a fork to allow steam to escape. Beat egg yolk with water and brush turnover with mixture. Bake 12 to 15 minutes or until golden brown. Serve hot.

*Yield:* 12 servings

*Change Petite Meat Turnovers as follows for:*

### LOW-CALORIE, DIABETIC, LOW-FAT, AND LOW-CHOLESTEROL DIETS

Calories per serving: 228
Approximate nutrient
  values per serving:
    Protein 7 g
    Fat 13 g
    Carbohydrate 21 g
    Sodium 241 mg
    Potassium 79 mg
    Cholesterol 10 mg
Exchanges:
    Bread 1½
    Meat ½
    Fat 2½

Substitute plain low-fat yogurt for sour cream.
Omit cheese.
Omit egg yolk and brush turnovers with 1 egg white, beaten.
Proceed as in Basic Recipe.

### LOW-SODIUM DIETS

Calories per serving: 243
Approximate nutrient
  values per serving:
    Protein 7 g
    Fat 14 g
    Carbohydrate 21 g
    Sodium 9 mg
    Potassium 75 mg
    Cholesterol 33 mg

Substitute double recipe low-sodium Easy-Mix Flaky Pie Crust
    (page 555) for basic Easy-Mix Flaky Pie Crust.
Omit salt.
Substitute low-sodium grated Cheddar cheese for Cheddar.
Proceed as in Basic Recipe.

### BLAND DIETS

Calories per serving: 243

Omit pepper.
Proceed as in Basic Recipe.

Calories per serving: 242

Substitute double recipe high-fiber Easy-Mix Flaky Pie Crust (page 556) for basic Easy-Mix Flaky Pie Crust.
Proceed as in Basic Recipe.

# Choux Puffs with Mushroom Filling

BASIC RECIPE

Crabmeat Amandine (page 84) and Chicken Paté with Mushrooms (page 76) also make tasty fillings.

*The Choux Puffs*
¼ cup polyunsaturated margarine
½ cup water
½ cup sifted all-purpose flour
¼ teaspoon salt
2 large eggs
1 tablespoon polyunsaturated oil

*The Filling*
⅓ cup polyunsaturated margarine
¾ cup finely chopped onions
3 cups finely chopped fresh mushrooms
¼ teaspoon salt
⅛ teaspoon freshly ground pepper

Serving size: 2 puffs
Calories per serving: 109
Approximate nutrient
  values per serving:
    Protein 2 g
    Fat 9 g
    Carbohydrate 5 g
    Sodium 167 mg
    Potassium 92 mg
    Cholesterol 39 mg
Exchanges:
  Vegetable 1
  Fat 2

The choux puffs should be prepared and refrigerated 1 hour before baking.

*To prepare the choux puffs:* In a medium saucepan, bring margarine and water to a boil. Reduce heat. Add flour and salt, all at once, and stir vigorously until mixture leaves the sides of the saucepan and forms a ball.

    Remove from heat. Add eggs one at a time, beating after each addition, until mixture is well blended.

    Cool choux puff mixture to room temperature.

    Preheat oven to 425°F.

Drop mixture by rounded teaspoons onto cookie sheets greased with oil. Bake puffs 18 to 20 minutes or until golden brown and crusty. Place on a rack to cool. When cool, cut in half for filling.

*To prepare the filling:* Turn oven down to 375°F.

In a medium skillet heat the margarine. Add onions and mushrooms and sauté until onions are soft. Remove from heat and season with salt and pepper. Mix gently to blend.

Fill choux puff halves with rounded teaspoons of mushroom mixture.

Place on ungreased cookie sheets and bake 10 minutes or until hot.

*Yield:* 14 servings

*Change Choux Puffs with Mushroom Filling as follows or use Basic Recipe, if indicated, for:*

### LOW-CALORIE, DIABETIC, LOW-FAT, AND LOW-CHOLESTEROL DIETS

*The puffs:* Use Basic Recipe.

*The filling:* Omit margarine. Simmer onions and mushrooms in 2 cups Chicken Stock (page 114) until soft. Drain and season with salt and pepper.

Proceed as in Basic Recipe.

### LOW-SODIUM DIETS

*The puffs:* Omit salt. Substitute unsalted polyunsaturated margarine for margarine.

Calories per serving: 71
Approximate nutrient
  values per serving:
    Protein 2 g
    Fat 5 g
    Carbohydrate 5 g
    Sodium 124 mg
    Potassium 91 mg
    Cholesterol 39 mg
Exchanges:
  Vegetable 1
  Fat 1

Calories per serving: 109
Approximate nutrient

values same as Basic
Recipe except for:
    Sodium 13 mg

*The filling:* Omit salt. Substitute unsalted polyunsaturated margarine for margarine.
    Proceed as in Basic Recipe.

### RENAL DIETS

*The puffs:* Omit salt. Substitute unsalted polyunsaturated margarine for margarine.

*The filling:* Omit salt. Substitute unsalted polyunsaturated margarine for margarine.
    Substitute three 8-ounce cans drained, chopped mushrooms for fresh mushrooms.
    Proceed as in Basic Recipe.

Calories per serving: 115
Approximate nutrient
    values per serving:
        Protein 2 g
        Fat 9 g
        Carbohydrate 6 g
        Calcium 11 mg
        Phosphorus 67 mg
        Sodium 182 mg
        Potassium 114 mg
        Cholesterol 39 mg

### BLAND DIETS

*The puffs:* Use Basic Recipe.

Calories per serving: 109

*The filling:* Omit pepper.
    Proceed as in Basic Recipe.

### HIGH-FIBER DIETS

Use Basic Recipe.

# Baked Stuffed Mushrooms

### BASIC RECIPE

Serving size: 2 mushrooms
Calories per serving: 92
Approximate nutrient
    values per serving:
        Protein 2 g

12 large mushrooms
2 tablespoons polyunsaturated margarine
¼ cup finely chopped pecans
3 tablespoons finely chopped onions

Fat 8 g
Carbohydrate 5 g
Sodium 157 mg
Potassium 195 mg
Cholesterol 0 mg
Exchanges:
Vegetable 1
Fat 1½

1 clove garlic, put through garlic press
1 tablespoon dry sherry
¼ teaspoon marjoram
¼ teaspoon salt
⅛ teaspoon freshly ground pepper
½ cup fresh bread crumbs (page 38)
½ teaspoon paprika

Preheat oven to 375°F.

Remove stems from mushrooms and chop fine. Reserve caps.

Melt margarine in a medium skillet. Add chopped mushroom stems, pecans, onions, and garlic and sauté until onion is tender. Add sherry and simmer uncovered for about 1 minute longer or until almost all liquid has evaporated. Remove from heat and add remaining ingredients except paprika.

Fill mushroom caps with mixture. Arrange in shallow baking dish. Bake in preheated oven for about 15 minutes.

Sprinkle tops with paprika before serving.

*Yield:* 6 servings

*Change Baked Stuffed Mushrooms as follows or use Basic Recipe, if indicated, for:*

LOW-CALORIE, DIABETIC, LOW-FAT, AND LOW-CHOLESTEROL DIETS

Omit margarine. Omit pecans and substitute ¼ cup minced celery.

Instead of sautéing chopped mushroom stems, celery, onions, and garlic, simmer them in ½ cup Chicken Stock (page 114), covered, for 5 minutes.

Proceed as in Basic Recipe.

Calories per serving: 26
Approximate nutrient
values per serving:
Protein 2 g
Fat 0 g
Carbohydrate 5 g
Sodium 132 mg
Potassium 194 mg
Cholesterol 0 mg
Exchanges:
Vegetable 1

Omit salt.
Substitute unsalted polyunsaturated margarine for margarine.
Proceed as in Basic Recipe.

Calories per serving: 92
Approximate nutrient
   values same as Basic
   Recipe except for:
      Sodium 27 mg

BLAND DIETS

Omit pepper.
Proceed as in Basic Recipe.

Calories per serving: 92

HIGH-FIBER DIETS

Use Basic Recipe.

# Cheese Knishes

BASIC RECIPE

Serving size: 1 knish
Calories per serving: 134
Approximate nutrient
   values per serving:
      Protein 4 g
      Fat 7 g
      Carbohydrate 13 g
      Sodium 170 mg
      Potassium 55 mg
      Cholesterol 39 mg
Exchanges:
   Bread 1
   Meat ½
   Fat 1

*The Dough*
4 cups sifted flour
2 teaspoons baking powder
1 teaspoon salt
⅔ cup polyunsaturated margarine
1 large egg
⅔ cup cold water
4 tablespoons flour for board
1 teaspoon polyunsaturated margarine for greasing cookie
   sheets

*The Cheese Filling*
3 tablespoons polyunsaturated margarine
1½ cups chopped onions
1 large egg
1 egg white
2 cups firmly packed farmer's cheese

*The Glaze*
2 egg yolks
2 tablespoons water

*To prepare dough:* In a large bowl sift together the flour, baking powder, and salt. Cut in the margarine. Add egg and enough water to make a soft dough. Refrigerate dough while preparing filling.

*To prepare filling:* Melt margarine in skillet, add onions, and sauté until tender.

In a medium bowl beat the egg plus egg white lightly. Add sautéed onion and the cheese to eggs and mix thoroughly.

Preheat oven to 350°F.

Divide dough in half. On floured board roll one half into a 14-inch square. Cut into 3½-inch squares.

Place 1 tablespoon filling on each square and fold dough over to form rectangular pillows. Seal edges with a fork. Repeat with remaining dough. Place knishes on lightly greased cookie sheets.

*To prepare glaze:* Beat the 2 egg yolks and water together. Brush on tops of knishes.

Bake about 25 minutes or until golden brown.

*Yield:* 32 knishes

*Change Cheese Knishes as follows or use Basic Recipe, if indicated, for:*

LOW-SODIUM AND RENAL DIETS

*The dough:* Omit salt.

Substitute unsalted polyunsaturated margarine for margarine.

Proceed as in Basic Recipe.

*The filling:* Substitute unsalted polyunsaturated margarine for margarine. Proceed as in Basic Recipe.

*The glaze:* Use Basic Recipe.

Calories per serving: 134
Approximate nutrient
values same as Basic
Recipe except for:
Calcium 54 mg
Phosphorus 62 mg
Sodium 51 mg

## BLAND DIETS

Use Basic Recipe.

## HIGH-FIBER DIETS

Calories per serving: 136

*The dough:* Use Basic Recipe.

*The filling:* Add 1 tablespoon poppy seeds to cheese filling. Proceed as in Basic Recipe.

## CHEESE KNISHES FOR LOW-CALORIE, DIABETIC, LOW-FAT, AND LOW-CHOLESTEROL DIETS

Serving size: 1 knish
Calories per serving: 118
Approximate nutrient
  values per serving:
    Protein 4 g
    Fat 5 g
    Carbohydrate 13 g
    Sodium 166 mg
    Potassium 63 mg
    Cholesterol 5 mg
Exchanges:
  Bread 1
  Meat ½
  Fat ½

*The Dough*
4 cups sifted flour
2 teaspoons baking powder
1 teaspoon salt
⅔ cup polyunsaturated margarine
1 cup cold water
4 tablespoons flour for board
vegetable cooking spray for cookie sheets

*The Cheese Filling*
1½ cups chopped onions
1 cup Chicken Stock (page 114)
2 cups firmly packed farmer's cheese

*The Glaze*
1 egg white
4 drops yellow food color

*To prepare the dough:* In a large bowl sift together the flour, baking powder, and salt. Cut in the margarine. Add enough water to make a soft dough. Refrigerate dough while preparing filling.

*To prepare the filling:* Simmer onions in stock until tender. Drain thoroughly. Combine the onions and farmer's cheese.
    Preheat oven to 350°F.

Divide dough in half. On a floured board, roll one half into a 14-inch square. Cut dough into 3½-inch squares.

Place 1 tablespoon filling on each square and fold dough over to form rectangular pillows. Seal edges with a fork. Repeat with remaining dough.

Place knishes on cookie sheets well sprayed with vegetable cooking spray.

*To prepare the glaze:* Beat egg white with food color.

Brush tops of knishes. Bake about 25 minutes or until golden brown.

*Yield:* 32 knishes

# SOUPS

Soup can be the heart of a meal or an introduction to it. Soup stocks can be an essential ingredient in a casserole or a stew, or can be used as the cooking liquid for vegetables. Our soups run the entire gamut from chowders, bisques, and thick soups like hearty Turkey Venezia to classic stocks. Except in the case of renal diets, where it was not possible to modify every recipe, all recipes have been modified for low-calorie, diabetic, low-fat, low-cholesterol, low-sodium, bland, and high-fiber diets.

Note that our soup stocks have been developed to be useful for all diets. However, they contain no fiber, and if a high-fiber diet is proposed for you, your daily menu plan should include entrées, salads, vegetables, or desserts that offer the complement of roughage your diet requires.

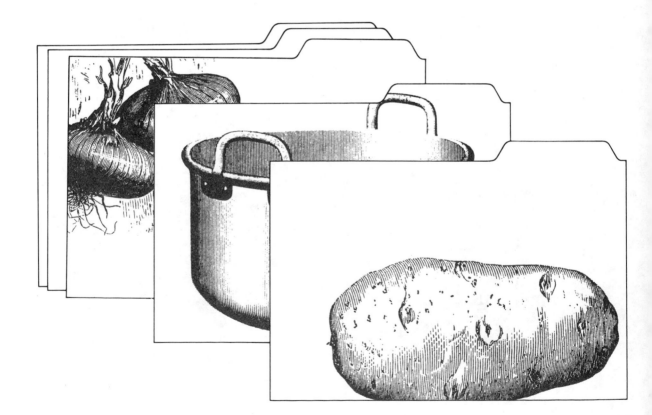

# Cream of Carrot Soup

BASIC RECIPE

Serving size: 1 cup
Calories per serving: 204
Approximate nutrient
  values per serving:
    Protein 2 g
    Fat 17 g
    Carbohydrate 12 g
    Sodium 352 mg
    Potassium 402 mg
    Cholesterol 41 mg
Exchanges:
  Bread 1
  Fat 3

3 cups thinly sliced carrots
¾ cup coarsely chopped onions
4 tablespoons polyunsaturated margarine
2 cups diced peeled raw potatoes
5 cups Chicken Stock (page 114)
¾ teaspoon salt
¾ teaspoon dillweed
⅛ teaspoon freshly ground pepper
1 cup heavy cream
⅓ cup minced fresh parsley

In a large saucepan, sauté carrots and onions in margarine until onions are soft.

Add potatoes, chicken stock, salt, dillweed, and pepper. Simmer, covered, approximately 15 minutes or until vegetables are tender. Remove from heat, uncover, and let cool to room temperature.

Purée mixture in an electric blender. Return soup to saucepan and bring to a simmer. Stir in cream and heat thoroughly. Serve garnished with parsley.

*Yield:* 8 servings

*Change Cream of Carrot Soup as follows or use Basic Recipe, if indicated, for:*

## LOW-CALORIE, DIABETIC, LOW-FAT, AND LOW-CHOLESTEROL DIETS

Omit margarine.
Simmer carrots, onions, potatoes, salt, dillweed, and pepper in chicken stock, covered, 15 minutes or until vegetables are tender.
Substitute skim milk for cream.
Proceed as in Basic Recipe.

Calories per serving: 61
Approximate nutrient
 values per serving:
  Protein 3 g
  Fat 0 g
  Carbohydrate 13 g
  Sodium 299 mg
  Potassium 429 mg
  Cholesterol 1 mg
Exchanges:
 Bread 1

## LOW-SODIUM DIETS

Omit salt.
Substitute unsalted polyunsaturated margarine for margarine.
Proceed as in Basic Recipe.

Calories per serving: 204
Approximate nutrient
 values same as Basic
 Recipe except for:
  Sodium 89 mg

## BLAND DIETS

Omit pepper.
Proceed as in Basic Recipe.

Calories per serving: 204

## HIGH-FIBER DIETS

Use Basic Recipe.

# Cucumber Vichyssoise

BASIC RECIPE

4 tablespoons polyunsaturated margarine
3 cups diced unpeeled cucumber
1½ cups thinly sliced leeks, white part only
1 cup diced peeled potato
4 cups Chicken Stock (page 114)
½ cup chopped fresh parsley
1 cup heavy cream
1 teaspoon salt
⅛ teaspoon white pepper
2 tablespoons snipped chives

In a large saucepan heat margarine. Add cucumbers and leeks; sauté until leeks are tender. Do not brown.

Add potato, stock, and parsley. Simmer, covered, 20 minutes or until vegetables are tender.

When soup is cool, purée in two batches in blender or processor. Stir in cream, salt, and white pepper; refrigerate until thoroughly chilled. Garnish with chives before serving.

*Yield:* 8 servings

*Change Cucumber Vichyssoise as follows or use Basic Recipe, if indicated, for:*

LOW-SODIUM DIETS

Omit salt.
Substitute unsalted polyunsaturated margarine for margarine.
Add 1 teaspoon curry powder with pepper.
Proceed as in Basic Recipe.

BLAND DIETS

Omit pepper.
Proceed as in Basic Recipe.

Use Basic Recipe.

## CUCUMBER VICHYSSOISE FOR LOW-CALORIE, DIABETIC, LOW-FAT, AND LOW-CHOLESTEROL DIETS

Serving size: 1 cup
Calories per serving: 45
Approximate nutrient
   values per serving:
      Protein 2 g
      Fat 0 g
      Carbohydrate 9 g
      Sodium 342 mg
      Potassium 343 mg
      Cholesterol 1 mg
Exchanges:
   Vegetable 2

3 cups diced unpeeled cucumber
1½ cups thinly sliced leeks, white part only
1 cup diced peeled potato
4 cups Chicken Stock (page 114)
½ cup chopped fresh parsley
1 cup skim milk
1 teaspoon salt
⅛ teaspoon white pepper
2 tablespoons snipped chives

In a large saucepan, combine cucumber, leeks, potato, chicken stock, and parsley. Simmer, covered, about 40 minutes or until vegetables are tender.

When soup is cool, purée in two batches in an electric blender or processor. Stir in milk, salt, and white pepper. Refrigerate until thoroughly chilled. Garnish with chives before serving.

*Yield:* 8 servings

# Eggdrop Soup

## BASIC RECIPE

Serving size: 1 cup
Calories per serving: 49
Approximate nutrient
   values per serving:
      Protein 3 g
      Fat 3 g
      Carbohydrate 2 g

2 large eggs
1 tablespoon dry sherry
¼ teaspoon ground ginger
4 cups Chicken Stock (page 114)
1 teaspoon salt
½ cup thinly sliced scallions, both green and white parts

Sodium 672 mg
Potassium 231 mg
Cholesterol 137 mg
Exchanges:
Meat 1

Beat eggs, sherry, and ginger together.

In a large saucepan, bring chicken stock and salt to a boil. Turn off heat and pour beaten egg mixture into soup in a slow, steady stream, stirring constantly.

Serve garnished with scallions.

*Yield:* 4 servings

*Change Eggdrop Soup as follows or use Basic Recipe, if indicated, for:*

LOW-CALORIE, DIABETIC, LOW-FAT, AND LOW-CHOLESTEROL DIETS

Calories per serving: 25
Approximate nutrient
 values per serving:
  Protein 4 g
  Fat 0 g
  Carbohydrate 3 g
  Sodium 687 mg
  Potassium 244 mg
  Cholesterol 0 mg
Exchanges:
 Meat ½

Omit whole eggs. Substitute 4 large egg whites beaten lightly with 8 drops yellow food color.

Proceed as in Basic Recipe.

LOW-SODIUM DIETS

Calories per serving: 49
Approximate nutrient
 values same as Basic
 Recipe except for:
  Sodium 123 mg

Omit salt.

Proceed as in Basic Recipe.

BLAND AND HIGH-FIBER DIETS

Use Basic Recipe.

# Gazpacho

BASIC RECIPE

Serving size: 1 cup
Calories per serving: 95
Approximate nutrient
  values per serving:
    Protein 2 g
    Fat 5 g
    Carbohydrate 11 g
    Sodium 505 mg
    Potassium 515 mg
    Cholesterol 0 mg
Exchanges:
  Vegetable 2
  Fat 1

2½ cups tomato juice
3 cups coarsely chopped peeled tomatoes
1½ cups diced green pepper
⅔ cup chopped onions
⅛ cup minced fresh parsley
1 clove garlic, minced
3 tablespoons olive oil
3 tablespoons wine vinegar
1¼ teaspoons salt
⅛ teaspoon cayenne pepper
½ cup diced peeled cucumber

In a large bowl, combine all ingredients except diced cucumber. Purée one-third of the mixture at a time in electric blender. Refrigerate until very cold. Mix well before serving. Garnish with reserved cucumber.

*Yield:* 8 servings

*Change Gazpacho as follows or use Basic Recipe, if indicated, for:*

LOW-CALORIE, DIABETIC, LOW-FAT, LOW-CHOLESTEROL, AND HIGH-FIBER DIETS

Use Basic Recipe.

LOW-SODIUM DIETS

Calories per serving: 95
Approximate nutrient
  values same as Basic
  Recipe except for:
    Sodium 12 mg
    Potassium 514 mg

Omit salt.
Substitute low-sodium tomato juice for tomato juice.
Proceed as in Basic Recipe.

102

Calories per serving: 95

Omit cayenne pepper.
Proceed as in Basic Recipe.

# German Potato Soup

### BASIC RECIPE

Serving size: 1 cup
Calories per serving: 108
Approximate nutrient
  values per serving:
    Protein 2 g
    Fat 5 g
    Carbohydrate 15 g
    Sodium 565 mg
    Potassium 444 mg
    Cholesterol 0 mg
Exchanges:
  Bread 1
  Fat 1

3 cups thinly sliced leeks, white part only
1 cup thinly sliced carrots
1 cup thinly sliced celery
4 tablespoons polyunsaturated margarine
4 cups diced peeled potatoes
6 cups Chicken Stock (page 114)
2 teaspoons salt
¼ teaspoon freshly ground pepper
½ cup chopped fresh parsley

In a large saucepan, sauté leeks, carrots, and celery in margarine until leeks are soft. Do not brown. Add potatoes, stock, salt, and pepper. Simmer, covered, about 15 to 20 minutes or until vegetables are tender. When the soup is cool enough to handle, purée in batches in a blender. Return to saucepan and heat. Garnish with parsley before serving.

*Yield:* 10 servings

*Change German Potato Soup as follows or use Basic Recipe, if indicated, for:*

## LOW-CALORIE, DIABETIC, LOW-FAT, AND LOW-CHOLESTEROL DIETS

Omit margarine. Do not sauté leeks, carrots, and celery. Place them and the potatoes in a large saucepan and simmer in stock about 15 to 20 minutes or until tender.
Proceed as in Basic Recipe.

Calories per serving: 68
Approximate nutrient
  values per serving:
    Protein 2 g
    Fat 0 g
    Carbohydrate 15 g
    Sodium 519 mg
    Potassium 443 mg
    Cholesterol 0 mg
Exchange:
  Bread 1

## LOW-SODIUM DIETS

Omit salt.
Substitute unsalted polyunsaturated margarine for margarine. Add 1 teaspoon thyme to stock with seasonings.
Proceed as in Basic Recipe.

Calories per serving: 108
Approximate nutrient
  values same as Basic
  Recipe except for:
    Sodium 80 mg
    Potassium 446 mg

## BLAND DIETS

Omit pepper.
Proceed as in Basic Recipe.

Calories per serving: 108

## HIGH-FIBER DIETS

Use Basic Recipe.

# Scallop Chowder

BASIC RECIPE

Serving size: 1½ cups
Calories per serving: 254
Approximate nutrient
  values per serving:
    Protein 22 g
    Fat 9 g
    Carbohydrate 21 g
    Sodium 720 mg
    Potassium 863 mg
    Cholesterol 43 mg
Exchanges:
  Vegetable 1
  Bread 1
  Meat 3
  Fat 1½

4 tablespoons polyunsaturated margarine
1½ cups chopped onions
1½ cups diced carrots
½ cup diced green pepper
3 tablespoons flour
3 cups Chicken Stock (page 114)
3 cups diced peeled potatoes
1 teaspoon thyme
1 teaspoon salt
¼ teaspoon freshly ground pepper
1½ pounds sea scallops, cut into bite-size pieces

Melt the margarine in a large saucepan. Add onions, carrots, and green pepper; sauté until onions are soft. Stir in flour, then gradually add chicken stock, stirring until smooth. Add potatoes, thyme, salt, and pepper.

Cover and simmer slowly about 15 to 20 minutes or until vegetables are tender.

Rinse scallops under cool running water and pat dry with paper towels. Add scallops to chowder and simmer, covered, for 5 minutes.

*Yield:* 6 servings

*Change Scallop Chowder as follows or use Basic Recipe, if indicated, for:*

LOW-CALORIE, DIABETIC, LOW-FAT, AND LOW-CHOLESTEROL DIETS

Use Basic Recipe.

Omit salt.
Substitute unsalted polyunsaturated margarine for margarine.
Proceed as in Basic Recipe.

Calories per serving: 254
Approximate nutrient
values same as Basic
Recipe except for:
Sodium 278 mg

## BLAND DIETS

Omit ground pepper.
Proceed as in Basic Recipe.

Calories per serving: 254

## HIGH-FIBER DIETS

Use Basic Recipe.

# Sicilian Fish Soup

BASIC RECIPE

⅓ cup olive oil
1 cup coarsely chopped onions
½ cup chopped green pepper
3 cloves garlic, put through garlic press
28-ounce can Italian plum tomatoes
1 cup water
½ cup white wine
2 cups diced peeled potatoes
1 teaspoon fennel seed
2 teaspoons salt
¼ teaspoon freshly ground pepper
½ teaspoon oregano
½ teaspoon basil
½ teaspoon thyme
2 pounds haddock fillets, fresh or frozen, cut in 2-inch-wide
    pieces
7 tablespoons grated Parmesan cheese

Serving size: 1¼ cups soup,
    1 tablespoon cheese
Calories per serving: 300
Approximate nutrient
    values per serving:
    Protein 27 g
    Fat 14 g
    Carbohydrate 16 g
    Sodium 1152 mg
    Potassium 823 mg
    Cholesterol 70 mg
Exchanges:
    Bread 1
    Meat 3½
    Fat 2

Heat the oil in a large saucepan. Add onions, green pepper, and garlic and sauté until onions are soft. Add tomatoes, water, wine, potatoes, fennel, salt, and pepper. Simmer, covered, for 30 minutes. Add oregano, basil, thyme, and haddock and cook approximately 10 minutes longer, or until fish flakes when tested. Ladle into warm soup plates, sprinkle each serving with 1 tablespoon Parmesan cheese, and serve immediately.

*Yield:* 7 servings

*Change Sicilian Fish Soup as follows or use Basic Recipe, if indicated, for:*

LOW-CALORIE, DIABETIC, LOW-FAT, AND LOW-CHOLESTEROL DIETS

Calories per serving: 199
Approximate nutrient
  values per serving:
    Protein 23 g
    Fat 5 g
    Carbohydrate 15 g
    Sodium 964 mg
    Potassium 821 mg
    Cholesterol 62 mg
Exchanges:
  Bread 1
  Meat 3
  Fat 1

Reduce oil to 2 tablespoons.
Proceed as in Basic Recipe.
Omit Parmesan cheese.
Substitute 1 teaspoon chopped fresh parsley per serving for garnish.

LOW-SODIUM DIETS

Calories per serving: 255
Approximate nutrient
  values per serving:
    Protein 23 g
    Fat 11 g
    Carbohydrate 15 g
    Sodium 193 mg
    Potassium 821 mg
    Cholesterol 62 mg

Omit salt.
Substitute 3½ cups canned tomatoes packed in tomato juice without added salt for Italian plum tomatoes.
Proceed as in Basic Recipe.
Omit Parmesan cheese.
Substitute 1 teaspoon chopped fresh parsley per serving for garnish.

## BLAND DIETS

Omit ground pepper.
Proceed as in Basic Recipe.

## HIGH-FIBER DIETS

Use Basic Recipe.

# Fresh Spinach Soup

BASIC RECIPE

Serving size: 1 cup
Calories per serving: 274
Approximate nutrient
  values per serving:
    Protein 5 g
    Fat 23 g
    Carbohydrate 14 g
    Sodium 571 mg
    Potassium 617 mg
    Cholesterol 60 mg
Exchanges:
  Bread 1
  Fat 5

4 tablespoons polyunsaturated margarine
¾ cup chopped onions
1 cup thinly sliced celery
1 cup thinly sliced carrots for soup
1¼ cups diced peeled potatoes
1 teaspoon salt
⅛ teaspoon freshly ground pepper
2 cups Chicken Stock (page 114)
10 ounces fresh spinach
⅛ teaspoon nutmeg
½ cup milk
1 cup heavy cream
½ cup grated raw carrots for garnish

Melt the margarine in a large saucepan. Add onions and sauté until soft. Add celery, sliced carrots, potatoes, salt, pepper, and chicken stock. Cover and simmer 30 minutes.

Meanwhile wash spinach, remove stems, and tear leaves into bite-size pieces. Drain leaves thoroughly. Add spinach to saucepan, cover, and simmer 5 minutes longer.

Pour into an electric blender or food processor and purée. Return purée to saucepan and stir in nutmeg, milk, and cream.

Cook, stirring, until soup is hot. Do not allow to boil. Garnish with grated carrots and serve.

*Yield:* 6 servings

*Change Fresh Spinach Soup as follows or use Basic Recipe, if indicated, for:*

## LOW-CALORIE, DIABETIC, LOW-FAT, AND LOW-CHOLESTEROL DIETS

Calories per serving: 112
Approximate nutrient
  values per serving:
    Protein 5 g
    Fat 4 g
    Carbohydrate 15 g
    Sodium 539 mg
    Potassium 657 mg
    Cholesterol 4 mg
Exchanges:
  Bread 1
  Fat 1

Reduce margarine to 2 tablespoons.
Substitute 1½ cups skim milk for milk and cream.
Proceed as in Basic Recipe.

## LOW-SODIUM DIETS

Calories per serving: 274
Approximate nutrient
  values same as Basic
  Recipe except for:
    Sodium 129 mg

Omit salt.
Substitute unsalted polyunsaturated margarine for margarine.
Proceed as in Basic Recipe.

## BLAND DIETS

Calories per serving: 274

Omit pepper and nutmeg.
Proceed as in Basic Recipe.

## HIGH-FIBER DIETS

Use Basic Recipe.

# Squash Bisque with Pecans

BASIC RECIPE

Serving size: 1 cup
Calories per serving: 293
Approximate nutrient
    values per serving:
        Protein 4 g
        Fat 23 g
        Carbohydrate 24 g
        Sodium 666 mg
        Potassium 650 mg
        Cholesterol 41 mg
Exchanges:
    Fruit 1
    Bread 1
    Fat 4½

4 tablespoons polyunsaturated margarine
1 cup coarsely chopped onions
2 cups chopped peeled apples
4 cups butternut squash, peeled and cut into cubes (about 3
    pounds)
4 cups Chicken Stock (page 114)
2 teaspoons salt
¼ teaspoon freshly ground pepper
1 teaspoon chervil
¼ teaspoon nutmeg
1 cup heavy cream
½ cup coarsely chopped pecans

In a large, heavy saucepan heat the margarine until foamy.
Add onions and sauté until soft. Add apples, squash, stock, salt,
pepper, chervil, and nutmeg. Cover and simmer 15 to 20 minutes or until squash is tender.

   Allow soup to cool. Pour into an electric blender or food processor and purée until smooth. Return purée to saucepan and
bring to a simmer. Stir in ½ cup of the cream and continue
cooking until heated through.

   Whip remaining ½ cup cream. Spoon 2 tablespoons whipped
cream on each serving, and garnish with 1 tablespoon pecans.

*Yield:* 8 servings

*Change Squash Bisque with Pecans as follows or use Basic Recipe, if indicated, for:*

## LOW-CALORIE, DIABETIC, LOW-FAT, AND LOW-CHOLESTEROL DIETS

Reduce margarine to 2 tablespoons.
Omit the heavy cream. Substitute ½ cup buttermilk for stirring into the purée. Omit cream for spooning on top of soup. Omit pecans and substitute ½ cup chopped unpeeled apples for garnish.
Proceed as in Basic Recipe.

Calories per serving: 125
Approximate nutrient
 values per serving:
  Protein 3 g
  Fat 4 g
  Carbohydrate 23 g
  Sodium 641 mg
  Potassium 613 mg
  Cholesterol 1 mg
Exchanges:
  Fruit 1
  Bread 1
  Fat 1

## LOW-SODIUM DIETS

Omit salt.
Substitute unsalted polyunsaturated margarine for margarine.
Proceed as in Basic Recipe.

Calories per serving: 293
Approximate nutrient
 values same as Basic
 Recipe except for:
  Sodium 60 mg

## BLAND DIETS

Omit pepper and nutmeg.
Proceed as in Basic Recipe.

Calories per serving: 293

## HIGH-FIBER DIETS

Use Basic Recipe.

# Bahamian Fish Chowder

BASIC RECIPE

Serving size: 1 cup
Calories per serving: 137
Approximate nutrient
  values per serving:
    Protein 17 g
    Fat 5 g
    Carbohydrate 6 g
    Sodium 431 mg
    Potassium 460 mg
    Cholesterol 27 mg
Exchanges:
  Vegetable 1
  Meat 2
  Fat 1

2 tablespoons polyunsaturated oil
½ cup finely chopped onions
2 cloves garlic, finely chopped
2 teaspoons curry powder
2 cups sliced peeled tomatoes
1 teaspoon salt
¼ teaspoon Tabasco
2½ cups water
1 pound skinless cod, cut into 1-inch cubes

Heat oil in a large, deep skillet. Add onions and garlic; cook until onions are soft. Stir in the curry powder; cook for 1 minute. Add tomatoes, salt, Tabasco, and water. Simmer for 15 minutes. Add cod to the soup; simmer for 4 minutes. Serve immediately.

*Yield:* 6 servings

*Change Bahamian Fish Chowder as follows or use Basic Recipe, if indicated, for:*

LOW-CALORIE, DIABETIC, LOW-FAT, AND LOW-CHOLESTEROL DIETS

Use Basic Recipe.

LOW-SODIUM DIETS

Calories per serving: 137
Approximate nutrient
  values same as Basic
  Recipe except for:
    Sodium 66 mg

Omit salt.
Increase Tabasco to ½ teaspoon.
Proceed as in Basic Recipe.

Calories per serving: 137

Omit Tabasco.
Proceed as in Basic Recipe.


HIGH-FIBER DIETS

Calories per serving: 139

Use Basic Recipe. Just before serving stir in ⅛ cup chopped
fresh parsley and cook for 1 more minute.


# Beef Stock

SUITABLE FOR LOW-CALORIE, DIABETIC, LOW-FAT,
LOW-CHOLESTEROL, LOW-SODIUM, BLAND, AND
HIGH-FIBER DIETS, AND FOR RENAL DIETS IN
LIMITED QUANTITIES

This recipe requires overnight refrigeration.

Serving size: 1 cup
Calories per serving: 0
Approximate nutrient
  values per serving:
    Protein 0 g
    Fat 0 g
    Carbohydrate 0 g
    Calcium 1 mg
    Phosphorus 20 mg
    Sodium 131 mg
    Potassium 313 mg
    Cholesterol 0 mg
Exchanges: 0

2 pounds soup bones, with meat
3 pounds beef shin bones
2 marrow bones
3 quarts cold water
2 carrots, sliced
2 stalks celery, sliced
2 medium onions
2 sprigs fresh parsley
1 bay leaf
½ teaspoon thyme
4 large egg whites
2 tablespoons cold water
4 eggshells

Cut meat off soup bones. Trim off excess fat and discard. Place
meat in a large, heavy saucepan with soup bones, shin bones,
and marrow bones. Add cold water, enough to cover bones and

meat. Bring to a boil and skim foam from surface as it rises. Reduce heat and simmer, continuing to skim if necessary.

Add carrots, celery, onions, parsley, bay leaf, and thyme. Partially cover and simmer very slowly for 5 hours. Skim as foam rises.

Strain the stock through a colander lined with a double thickness of cheesecloth. Allow to cool. Cover and refrigerate overnight. The next day, remove fat hardened on surface.

*To clarify stock:* Bring stock to a boil. Beat egg whites with the 2 tablespoons cold water until foamy. Break the eggshells into small pieces and stir into egg whites.

Slowly add this mixture to the boiling stock, stirring constantly. Reduce heat, cover, and simmer for 15 minutes without stirring.

Strain through a fine-mesh sieve lined with several thicknesses of cheesecloth. Allow to cool thoroughly, uncovered.

Stock may be stored, covered, in the refrigerator for a few days or frozen for long-term use.

*Yield:* 2 quarts

# Chicken Stock

SUITABLE FOR LOW-CALORIE, DIABETIC, LOW-FAT, LOW-CHOLESTEROL, LOW-SODIUM, BLAND, AND HIGH-FIBER DIETS, AND FOR RENAL DIETS IN LIMITED QUANTITIES

This recipe requires overnight refrigeration.

Serving size: 1 cup
Calories per serving: 0
Approximate nutrient
  values per serving:
    Protein 0 g
    Fat 0 g
    Carbohydrate 0 g
    Calcium 1 mg

2 pounds chicken necks
1 pound chicken wings
2 quarts cold water
2 medium onions, sliced
½ cup diced celery
½ cup diced carrots
1 bay leaf

Phosphorus 28 mg
Sodium 98 mg
Potassium 317 mg
Cholesterol 0 mg
Exchanges: 0

2 tablespoons chopped fresh parsley
½ teaspoon thyme

Wash chicken parts under cool running water and place them in a large, heavy saucepan. Add cold water and cover. Bring to a simmer and skim off the foam as it rises to the surface.

Add remaining ingredients, cover, and simmer slowly for 3 hours. Strain the stock through a colander lined with a double thickness of cheesecloth. Refrigerate overnight.

The next day, remove the hardened fat. Stock may be stored in the refrigerator for a few days or frozen for long-term use.

*Yield:* 1½ quarts

# Fish Stock

SUITABLE FOR LOW-CALORIE, DIABETIC, LOW-FAT, LOW-CHOLESTEROL, LOW-SODIUM, BLAND, AND HIGH-FIBER DIETS, AND FOR RENAL DIETS IN LIMITED QUANTITIES

Serving size: 1 cup
Calories per serving: 0
Approximate nutrient
  values per serving:
  Protein 0 g
  Fat 0 g
  Carbohydrate 0 g
  Calcium 1 mg
  Phosphorus 56 mg
  Sodium 318 mg
  Potassium 411 mg
  Cholesterol 0 mg
Exchanges: 0

3 pounds bones and heads from halibut, haddock, or any other white fish
3 quarts water
3 stalks celery, sliced
3 carrots, thinly sliced
1 medium onion
3 sprigs fresh parsley
2 bay leaves
1 teaspoon thyme

Wash fish trimmings under cool running water and place in a large, heavy saucepan. Add remaining ingredients. Bring to a boil and skim foam from surface as it rises. Reduce heat and simmer, uncovered, for 30 minutes. Continue to skim surface to remove foam.

Strain fish stock through a colander lined with a double

thickness of cheesecloth. Allow to cool before using to poach fish. Refrigerate if stock is to be used within a few days. Freeze for long-term use.

*Yield:* 9 cups

# Meat and Vegetable Stock

BASIC RECIPE

This recipe requires overnight refrigeration.

3 pounds chicken backs, necks, and wings
1 marrow bone
2 pounds veal bones, with meat, trimmed of excess fat
3 quarts cold water
1 cup chopped tomatoes
1 cup chopped onions
1 cup sliced celery
1 cup sliced carrots
¼ cup chopped green pepper
1 bay leaf
2 tablespoons chopped fresh parsley
1 teaspoon thyme
1 teaspoon basil
¼ teaspoon peppercorns

Wash the chicken parts under cool running water and place in large, heavy saucepan. Add marrow bone, veal bones with meat, and water. Bring to a boil and skim foam from surface as it rises. Reduce heat and simmer. Continue to skim surface to remove foam.

Add remaining ingredients and simmer slowly, partially covered, for 3 hours. Skim as necessary. Strain stock through a colander lined with a double thickness of cheesecloth. Allow to

Serving size: 1 cup
Calories per serving: 0
Approximate nutrient
  values per serving:
    Protein 0 g
    Fat 0 g
    Carbohydrate 0 g
    Calcium 1 mg
    Phosphorus 34 mg
    Sodium 147 mg
    Potassium 444 mg
    Cholesterol 0 mg
Exchanges: 0

cool, uncovered. Refrigerate overnight. The next day, remove fat hardened on the surface. Refrigerate if stock is to be used within a few days. Freeze for long-term use.

*Yield:* 2 quarts

*Change Meat and Vegetable Stock as follows or use Basic Recipe, if indicated, for:*

LOW-CALORIE, DIABETIC, LOW-FAT, LOW-CHOLESTEROL, LOW-SODIUM, HIGH-FIBER DIETS, AND FOR RENAL DIETS IN LIMITED QUANTITIES

Use Basic Recipe.

BLAND DIETS

Calories per serving: 0

Omit peppercorns.
Proceed as in Basic Recipe.

# Mushroom Bouillon

BASIC RECIPE

Serving size: ¾ cup
Calories per serving: 0
Approximate nutrient
  values per serving:
    Protein 0 g
    Fat 0 g
    Carbohydrate 0 g
    Sodium 138 mg
    Potassium 466 mg
    Cholesterol 0 mg
Exchanges: 0

¾ pound fresh mushrooms
2 tablespoons lemon juice
6 cups Beef Stock (page 113)
¼ teaspoon salt
⅛ teaspoon freshly ground pepper
¼ cup dry sherry

Gently wipe mushrooms with paper towels. Reserve a few unblemished mushrooms for garnish. Slice, sprinkle with lemon juice, and set aside. Mince remaining mushrooms.

In a medium saucepan add minced mushrooms to beef stock. Simmer very slowly, partially covered, for 20 minutes. Add salt, pepper, and sherry. Simmer, uncovered, for 2 minutes longer.

Strain bouillon through a fine-mesh sieve, pressing down to extract as much juice as possible from the mushrooms. Serve bouillon in cups, garnished with reserved mushroom slices.

*Yield:* 6 servings

*Change Mushroom Bouillon or use Basic Recipe, if indicated, for:*

LOW-CALORIE, DIABETIC, LOW-FAT, LOW-CHOLESTEROL, AND HIGH-FIBER DIETS

Use Basic Recipe.

LOW-SODIUM DIETS

Calories per serving: 0
Approximate nutrient values same as Basic Recipe except for:
Sodium 49 mg

Omit salt.
Proceed as in Basic Recipe.

BLAND DIETS

Calories per serving: 0

Omit pepper.
Proceed as in Basic Recipe.

# Turkey Venezia Soup

BASIC RECIPE

Serving size: 1 cup
Calories per serving: 314
Approximate nutrient
  values per serving:
    Protein 12 g
    Fat 21 g
    Carbohydrate 20 g
    Sodium 712 mg
    Potassium 386 mg
    Cholesterol 64 mg
Exchanges:
  Vegetable 1
  Bread 1
  Meat 1
  Fat 4

⅓ cup polyunsaturated margarine
1½ cups chopped onions
1½ cups chopped celery
1½ cups chopped carrots
4 tablespoons flour
1 quart cold water
½ cup raw rice
2 teaspoons salt
¼ teaspoon freshly ground pepper
½ teaspoon thyme
½ teaspoon marjoram
1 bay leaf
1 cup heavy cream
1 cup milk
1½ cups minced cooked turkey

Melt the margarine in a large casserole. Add onions, celery, and carrots and sauté until onions are soft. Sprinkle with flour and stir gently until thoroughly blended.

Add water, turn heat up, and bring to a boil. Gradually stir in rice. Season with salt, pepper, thyme, marjoram, and bay leaf.

Reduce heat, cover, and simmer slowly 30 minutes or until rice and vegetables are tender. Stir occasionally.

Add cream, milk, and turkey and simmer 10 minutes longer. Remove bay leaf before serving.

*Yield:* 8 servings

*Change Turkey Venezia Soup as follows or use Basic Recipe, if indicated, for:*

## LOW-CALORIE, DIABETIC, LOW-FAT, AND LOW-CHOLESTEROL DIETS

Calories per serving: 132
Approximate nutrient
  values per serving:
    Protein 12 g
    Fat 1 g
    Carbohydrate 18 g
    Sodium 642 mg
    Potassium 414 mg
    Cholesterol 20 mg
Exchanges:
  Milk ¼
  Vegetable 1
  Bread ½
  Meat 1

Omit margarine and flour. Place vegetables in a large casserole. Add the cold water, bring to a boil, add rice and seasonings, and cook as in the Basic Recipe.

Finally, omit cream and milk, substitute 2 cups of skim milk, and add with the turkey. Simmer and serve as in the Basic Recipe.

## LOW-SODIUM DIETS

Calories per serving: 314
Approximate nutrient
  values same as Basic
  Recipe except for:
    Sodium 88 mg

Omit salt.
Substitute unsalted polyunsaturated margarine for margarine.
Proceed as in Basic Recipe.

## BLAND DIETS

Calories per serving: 314

Omit pepper.
Proceed as in Basic Recipe.

## HIGH-FIBER DIETS

Use Basic Recipe.

# BREADS

Breads, biscuits, rolls, and muffins of all types are readily available in your local supermarket; but we present several here for your own production and pleasurable consumption. The satisfying aroma of baking bread will perk up the most jaded appetite. What's more, you will have the advantage of knowing every ingredient that goes into the ultimate product, as well as the nutrient values of the glorious sum total. This way, you can precisely figure one or more servings of the bread of your choice into your daily calorie or food exchange plan.

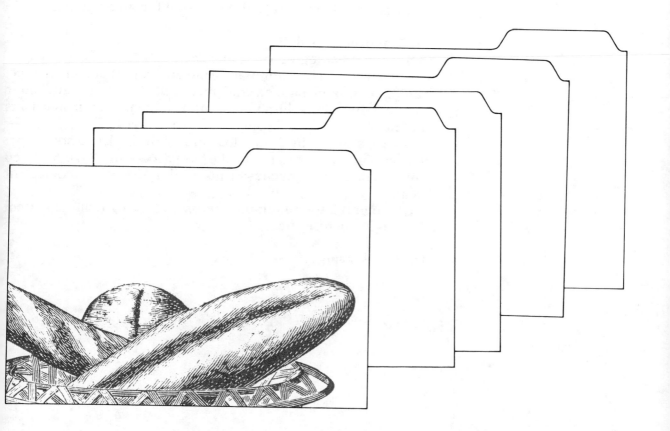

# Banana Nut Bread

BASIC RECIPE

Serving size: ½-inch slice
Calories per serving: 173
Approximate nutrient
  values per serving:
    Protein 3 g
    Fat 8 g
    Carbohydrate 24 g
    Sodium 134 mg
    Potassium 122 mg
    Cholesterol 16 mg
Exchanges:
  Fruit ½
  Bread 1½
  Fat 1½

2 cups sifted all-purpose flour
2 teaspoons baking powder
¼ teaspoon salt
½ cup polyunsaturated margarine
⅔ cup sugar
½ teaspoon allspice
1 teaspoon vanilla extract
1 large egg
1 cup mashed bananas
⅓ cup milk
½ cup raisins
½ cup chopped walnuts
1 teaspoon polyunsaturated margarine for greasing pan

Preheat oven to 350°F.
  Sift flour, baking powder, and salt.
  In a large bowl cream margarine and sugar; stir in allspice, vanilla, egg, and banana and mix well. Gradually add flour mixture alternately with milk, until just blended. Stir in raisins and nuts.
  Grease a 9-by-5-by-3-inch loaf pan with the 1 teaspoon margarine. Turn the batter into the prepared pan. Bake 55 to 60 minutes or until a cake tester inserted in the center comes out clean.
  Cool on rack for 10 minutes before removing from pan. Cool thoroughly before slicing.

*Yield:* 18 servings

*Change Banana Nut Bread as follows or use Basic Recipe, if indicated, for:*

## LOW-SODIUM DIETS

Omit salt.
Substitute unsalted polyunsaturated margarine for margarine wherever used.
Proceed as in Basic Recipe.

Calories per serving: 173
Approximate nutrient
    values same as Basic
    Recipe except for:
      Sodium 51 mg

## BLAND AND HIGH-FIBER DIETS

Use Basic Recipe.

## BANANA NUT BREAD FOR LOW-CALORIE, DIABETIC, LOW-FAT, AND LOW-CHOLESTEROL DIETS

Serving size: ½-inch slice
Calories per serving: 106
Approximate nutrient
    values per serving:
      Protein 2 g
      Fat 3 g
      Carbohydrate 19 g
      Sodium 109 mg
      Potassium 83 mg
      Cholesterol 0 mg
Exchanges:
    Fruit ½
    Bread 1
    Fat ½

2 cups sifted all-purpose flour
2 teaspoons baking powder
¼ teaspoon salt
¼ cup polyunsaturated margarine
½ cup sugar
½ teaspoon allspice
1 teaspoon vanilla extract
Low-Cholesterol Egg Substitute (page 189) equivalent to 1
    large egg
1 cup mashed bananas
⅓ cup skim milk
vegetable cooking spray

Preheat oven to 350°F.
    Sift flour, baking powder, and salt.
    In a large bowl cream margarine and sugar; stir in the allspice, vanilla, egg substitute, and banana and mix well. Gradually add flour mixture alternately with milk until just blended.
    Spray a 9-by-5-by-3-inch loaf pan with vegetable cooking spray. Turn batter into the prepared pan. Bake 55 to 60 minutes or until a cake tester inserted in the center comes out clean.

Cool on rack for 10 minutes before removing from pan. Cool thoroughly before slicing.

*Yield:* 18 servings

# Oatmeal Molasses Bread

BASIC RECIPE

Serving size: ½-inch slice
Calories per serving: 140
Approximate nutrient
  values per serving:
    Protein 4 g
    Fat 3 g
    Carbohydrate 24 g
    Sodium 232 mg
    Potassium 93 mg
    Cholesterol 1 mg
Exchanges:
  Bread 1½
  Fat 1

6½ cups all-purpose flour
1 cup rolled oats
2 packages active dry yeast
1 tablespoon salt
⅓ cup molasses
⅓ cup polyunsaturated margarine
1 cup water
1 cup milk
2 tablespoons flour for bread board
2 teaspoons polyunsaturated oil for oiling bowl and greasing
  pans
1 large egg white
1 tablespoon sesame seeds

In a large bowl mix 2 cups of the flour, the oats, undissolved yeast, and salt.

In a saucepan heat molasses, margarine, water, and milk until warm. Margarine does not have to melt. Add liquids to flour mixture and beat until blended. Gradually beat in remaining 4½ cups flour to form a soft dough. Turn out onto board dusted with 2 tablespoons flour. Knead until smooth and elastic.

Oil medium-size bowl, using 1 teaspoon of oil. Place dough in it, and rotate to oil it on all sides. Let rise in a warm place, free from draft, approximately 45 minutes or until dough doubles in size.

Punch down dough, divide in half, and shape into two loaves. Place in 9-by-5-by-3-inch loaf pans greased with remaining teaspoon of oil. Let rise in warm place about 45 minutes or until dough doubles in size.

Preheat oven to 375°F.

Beat egg white lightly and brush tops of loaves. Sprinkle with sesame seeds. Bake 35 minutes. Remove from pans and allow to cool on racks.

*Yield:* 2 loaves (32 slices)

*Change Oatmeal Molasses Bread as follows or use Basic Recipe, if indicated, for:*

LOW-CALORIE, DIABETIC, LOW-FAT, AND LOW-CHOLESTEROL DIETS

Calories per serving: 132
Approximate nutrient
  values per serving:
    Protein 4 g
    Fat 2 g
    Carbohydrate 24 g
    Sodium 228 mg
    Potassium 86 mg
    Cholesterol 0 mg
Exchanges:
  Bread 1½
  Fat ½

Reduce molasses to ¼ cup.
Reduce margarine to ¼ cup.
Substitute skim milk for milk.
Proceed as in Basic Recipe.

LOW-SODIUM DIETS

Calories per serving: 141
Approximate nutrient
  values same as Basic
  Recipe except for:
    Sodium 145 mg
    Potassium 96 mg

Reduce salt to 2 teaspoons.
Substitute unsalted polyunsaturated margarine for margarine
  wherever used.
Add 1 tablespoon fennel seed to flour, oats, and yeast mixture.
Proceed as in Basic Recipe.

BLAND DIETS

Use Basic Recipe.

Calories per serving: 138

Reduce all-purpose flour to 4½ cups. Add 2 cups stone-ground whole wheat flour and ⅓ cup all-bran cereal to the flour, oats, and yeast mixture.
Proceed as in Basic Recipe.

# Challah

BASIC RECIPE

This bread is good toasted and freezes well.

Serving size: 1 slice
Calories per serving: 100
Approximate nutrient
  values per serving:
    Protein 3 g
    Fat 2 g
    Carbohydrate 16 g
    Sodium 187 mg
    Potassium 34 mg
    Cholesterol 27 mg
Exchanges:
    Bread 1
    Fat ½

6 cups flour for dough
¼ cup sugar
1 tablespoon salt
2 packages active dry yeast
⅓ cup polyunsaturated margarine, at room temperature
1¼ cups hot tap water
4 large eggs, separated
3 tablespoons flour for bread board
2 teaspoons polyunsaturated oil for greasing bowl and baking sheet
1 teaspoon cold water
¾ teaspoon poppy seeds

Combine 2 cups of the flour with the sugar, salt, and yeast in a large bowl. Beat in margarine and hot water. Gradually beat in 4 egg whites and 3 egg yolks. (Reserve 1 egg yolk for glazing.) Add remaining 4 cups flour to form a soft dough. Turn out onto board dusted with 3 tablespoons flour. Knead until smooth and elastic.

Lightly grease a large bowl with 1 teaspoon oil, place dough in bowl, and rotate dough to oil it on all sides. Let rise in a warm place, free from draft, about 50 minutes or until dough doubles in size.

Punch dough down and divide in half. Divide each half into two pieces, one piece about one-third of the dough and the other piece two-thirds of the dough. Divide larger piece into three equal pieces and roll each piece into a 12-inch rope. Braid ropes, pinch ends to seal, and place on a baking sheet lightly greased with remaining teaspoon of oil, leaving room for a second loaf.

Divide smaller piece into three equal pieces and roll each piece into a 10-inch rope. Braid ropes, pinch ends to seal, and place on top of large braid. Repeat the process with the remaining dough to form a second loaf. Place on the baking sheet, allowing room between loaves for bread to rise.

Beat remaining egg yolk with 1 teaspoon cold water and brush braids with mixture. Sprinkle with poppy seeds and let loaves rise in warm place about 50 minutes or until loaves double in size.

Preheat oven to 375°F.

Bake loaves about 30 to 35 minutes or until nicely browned. Remove to racks to cool.

*Yield:* 2 loaves, 20 slices per loaf

*Change Challah as follows or use Basic Recipe, if indicated, for:*

## LOW-SODIUM AND RENAL DIETS

Reduce salt to 2 teaspoons.
Substitute unsalted polyunsaturated margarine for margarine.
Proceed as in Basic Recipe.

Calories per serving: 100
Approximate nutrient
   values same as Basic
   Recipe except for:
      Calcium 8 mg
      Phosphorus 32 mg
      Sodium 117 mg

## BLAND DIETS

Use Basic Recipe.

## HIGH-FIBER DIETS

Use Basic Recipe. For extra fiber, spread with strawberry preserves or marmalade.

## CHALLAH FOR LOW-CALORIE, DIABETIC, LOW-FAT, AND LOW-CHOLESTEROL DIETS

This bread is good toasted and freezes well.

Serving size: 1 slice
Calories per serving: 90
Approximate nutrient
  values per serving:
    Protein 3 g
    Fat 2 g
    Carbohydrate 16 g
    Sodium 180 mg
    Potassium 31 mg
    Cholesterol 14 mg
Exchanges:
  Bread 1
  Fat ½

6 cups flour for dough
2 tablespoons sugar
1 tablespoon salt
2 packages active dry yeast
¼ cup polyunsaturated margarine, at room temperature
1⅔ cups hot tap water
2 large eggs, separated
3 tablespoons flour for bread board
1 teaspoon polyunsaturated oil
vegetable cooking spray
1 teaspoon cold water
¾ teaspoon poppy seeds

In a large bowl combine 2 cups of the flour with the sugar, salt, and undissolved yeast. Beat in margarine and hot water. Gradually beat in 2 egg whites and 1 egg yolk. (Reserve 1 egg yolk for glazing.) Add remaining 4 cups flour to form a soft dough. Turn out onto board dusted with 3 tablespoons flour. Knead until smooth and elastic.

Lightly grease a large bowl with 1 teaspoon of oil, place dough in bowl, and rotate the dough to oil it on all sides. Let rise in a warm place, free from draft, about 50 minutes or until double in size.

Punch dough down and divide in half. Divide each half into two pieces, one piece about one-third of the dough and the other piece two-thirds of the dough. Divide larger piece into three equal pieces and roll each piece into a 12-inch rope. Braid ropes, pinch ends to seal, and place on a baking sheet sprayed with vegetable cooking spray, leaving room for a second loaf.

Divide smaller piece into three equal pieces and roll each piece into a 10-inch rope. Braid ropes, pinch ends to seal, and place on top of larger braid.

Repeat the process with the remaining dough to form a second loaf. Place on the baking sheet, allowing room between loaves for bread to rise.

Beat remaining egg yolk with 1 teaspoon cold water and

brush braids with mixture. Sprinkle with poppy seeds and let loaves rise in warm place about 50 minutes or until loaves double in size.

Preheat oven to 375°F.

Bake loaves about 30 to 35 minutes or until nicely browned. Remove to racks to cool.

*Yield:* 2 loaves, 20 slices per loaf

# Zucchini Bread

BASIC RECIPE

Serving size: ½-inch slice
Calories per serving: 215
Approximate nutrient
  values per serving:
    Protein 3 g
    Fat 12 g
    Carbohydrate 24 g
    Sodium 130 mg
    Potassium 58 mg
    Cholesterol 34 mg
Exchanges:
    Bread 1½
    Fat 2½

2 cups sifted all-purpose flour
2 teaspoons baking powder
½ teaspoon salt
2 large eggs
⅔ cup polyunsaturated oil
1 cup sugar
1 teaspoon ground cinnamon
½ teaspoon allspice
⅛ teaspoon ground cloves
1½ cups finely grated zucchini
½ cup chopped walnuts
1 teaspoon polyunsaturated margarine for greasing bread pan

Preheat oven to 350°F.

Sift flour, baking powder, and salt. Set aside.

In a large bowl beat eggs, oil, sugar, cinnamon, allspice, and cloves. Stir in zucchini, flour mixture, and nuts until well blended.

Grease a 9-by-5-by-3-inch loaf pan with the margarine. Turn batter into pan and bake 1 hour or until cake tester inserted in center comes out clean. Cool on rack for 10 minutes. Remove bread from pan and cool thoroughly before slicing.

*Yield:* 16 slices

*Change Zucchini Bread as follows or use Basic Recipe, if indicated, for:*

## LOW-SODIUM DIETS

Omit salt.
Substitute unsalted polyunsaturated margarine for margarine for greasing bread pan.
Proceed as in Basic Recipe.

Calories per serving: 215
Approximate nutrient
  values same as Basic
  Recipe except for:
    Sodium 59 mg

## BLAND DIETS

Omit cloves.
Proceed as in Basic Recipe.

Calories per serving: 215

## HIGH-FIBER DIETS

Use Basic Recipe.

## ZUCCHINI BREAD FOR LOW-CALORIE, DIABETIC, LOW-FAT, AND LOW-CHOLESTEROL DIETS

2 cups sifted all-purpose flour
2 teaspoons baking powder
½ teaspoon salt
Low-Cholesterol Egg Substitute (page 189) equivalent to 2 large eggs
⅓ cup polyunsaturated oil
½ cup sugar
1 teaspoon ground cinnamon
½ teaspoon allspice
⅛ teaspoon ground cloves
1 teaspoon grated orange rind
1½ cups finely grated zucchini
vegetable cooking spray

Preheat oven to 350°F.
  Sift flour, baking powder, and salt. Set aside.
  In a large bowl beat egg substitute, oil, sugar, cinnamon,

Serving size: ½-inch slice
Calories per serving: 124
Approximate nutrient
  values per serving:
    Protein 3 g
    Fat 5 g
    Carbohydrate 18 g
    Sodium 134 mg
    Potassium 57 mg
    Cholesterol 0 mg
Exchanges:
  Bread 1
  Fat 1

allspice, cloves, and orange rind. Stir in zucchini and flour mixture until well blended.

Spray a 9-by-5-by-3-inch loaf pan generously with cooking spray. Turn batter into pan and bake 1 hour or until cake tester inserted in center comes out clean. Allow to cool on rack for 10 minutes. Remove bread from pan and cool thoroughly before slicing.

*Yield:* 16 slices

# Apple Muffins

BASIC RECIPE

Serving size: 1 muffin
Calories per serving: 166
Approximate nutrient
  values per serving:
    Protein 3 g
    Fat 8 g
    Carbohydrate 21 g
    Sodium 273 mg
    Potassium 59 mg
    Cholesterol 25 mg
Exchanges:
    Bread 1½
    Fat 1½

2 tablespoons polyunsaturated margarine for greasing muffin
  cups
1¾ cups sifted all-purpose flour
⅓ cup sugar
1 tablespoon baking powder
½ teaspoon salt
⅓ cup polyunsaturated margarine
½ teaspoon ground cinnamon
¼ teaspoon ground ginger
1 large egg, lightly beaten
¾ cup milk
1 cup diced peeled apples

Preheat oven to 425°F.

Grease twelve 2-inch muffin cups with 2 tablespoons margarine.

Sift flour, sugar, baking powder, and salt into a large bowl.

Melt the ⅓ cup margarine in a small saucepan. Remove from heat and stir in cinnamon and ginger. Stir in egg and milk. Add this mixture to dry ingredients and stir just until flour is moistened. Stir in apples. Spoon batter into muffin cups. Bake 15 to 20 minutes or until cake tester inserted in the middle comes out clean. Serve warm.

*Yield:* 12 muffins

*Change Apple Muffins as follows or use Basic Recipe, if indicated, for:*

### LOW-SODIUM AND RENAL DIETS

Omit salt.
Substitute unsalted polyunsaturated margarine for margarine wherever used.
Proceed as in Basic Recipe.

Calories per serving: 166
Approximate nutrient values same as Basic Recipe except for:
Calcium 42 mg
Phosphorus 63 mg
Sodium 112 mg

### BLAND DIETS

Use Basic Recipe.

### HIGH-FIBER DIETS

Add 2 teaspoons grated orange rind and ⅓ cup chopped walnuts to the batter.
Proceed as in Basic Recipe.

Calories per serving: 184

### APPLE MUFFINS FOR LOW-CALORIE, DIABETIC, LOW-FAT, AND LOW-CHOLESTEROL DIETS

1¾ cups sifted all-purpose flour
3 tablespoons sugar
1 tablespoon baking powder
½ teaspoon salt
3 tablespoons polyunsaturated margarine
½ teaspoon ground cinnamon
¼ teaspoon ground ginger
Low-Cholesterol Egg Substitute (page 189) equivalent to 1 large egg
¾ cup skim milk
1 cup diced peeled apples
vegetable cooking spray

Serving size: 1 muffin
Calories per serving: 114
Approximate nutrient values per serving:
Protein 3 g
Fat 3 g
Carbohydrate 19 g
Sodium 237 mg
Potassium 68 mg
Cholesterol 0 mg
Exchanges:
Bread 1½
Fat ½

Preheat oven to 425°F.

Sift flour, sugar, baking powder, and salt into a large bowl.

Melt the margarine in a small saucepan. Remove from heat and stir in cinnamon and ginger. Stir in egg substitute and milk. Add this mixture to dry ingredients and stir just until flour is moistened. Stir in apples.

Spray twelve 2-inch muffin cups well with vegetable cooking spray. Spoon batter into muffin cups. Bake 15 to 20 minutes or until cake tester inserted in the middle comes out clean. Serve warm.

*Yield:* 12 muffins

# Yogurt Corn Muffins

BASIC RECIPE

2 tablespoons polyunsaturated margarine for greasing muffin
  cups
1⅛ cups all-purpose flour
¼ cup sugar
2 teaspoons baking powder
1 teaspoon baking soda
¼ teaspoon salt
⅔ cup cornmeal
⅓ cup chopped dates
1 large egg
¼ cup polyunsaturated oil for batter
1 cup plain yogurt

Preheat oven to 400°F.

Grease twelve 2-inch muffin cups with 2 tablespoons margarine.

Sift flour, sugar, baking powder, soda, and salt into a large mixing bowl. Mix in cornmeal. Add dates and stir to coat them with flour mixture.

In a separate bowl beat egg lightly. Stir in oil and yogurt.

Pour this mixture into flour and stir only until flour is moistened. Spoon batter into muffin cups.

Bake 20 minutes or until golden brown. Serve warm.

*Yield:* 12 muffins

*Change Yogurt Corn Muffins as follows or use Basic Recipe, if indicated, for:*

## LOW-SODIUM DIETS

Omit salt.
Substitute unsalted polyunsaturated margarine for margarine.
Proceed as in Basic Recipe.

Calories per serving: 183
Approximate nutrient
values same as Basic
Recipe except for:
Sodium 174 mg

## BLAND AND HIGH-FIBER DIETS

Use Basic Recipe.

## YOGURT CORN MUFFINS FOR LOW-CALORIE, DIABETIC, LOW-FAT, AND LOW-CHOLESTEROL DIETS

Serving size: 1 muffin
Calories per serving: 123
Approximate nutrient
values per serving:
Protein 4 g
Fat 3 g
Carbohydrate 20 g
Sodium 229 mg
Potassium 87 mg
Cholesterol 1 mg
Exchanges:
Bread 1½
Fat ½

vegetable cooking spray
1⅓ cups all-purpose flour
2 tablespoons sugar
2 teaspoons baking powder
1 teaspoon baking soda
¼ teaspoon salt
⅔ cup cornmeal
Low-Cholesterol Egg Substitute (page 189) equivalent to
1 large egg
2 tablespoons polyunsaturated oil
1 cup plain low-fat yogurt

Preheat oven to 400°F.

Spray twelve 2-inch muffin cups with vegetable cooking spray.

Sift flour, sugar, baking powder, soda, and salt into a large mixing bowl. Mix in cornmeal.

In a separate bowl beat egg substitute lightly. Stir in oil and yogurt. Pour this mixture into flour mixture and stir only until flour is moistened.

Spoon batter into muffin cups. Bake 20 minutes or until golden brown. Serve warm.

*Yield:* 12 muffins

# Homemade English Muffins

BASIC RECIPE

Serving size: 1 muffin
Calories per serving: 206
Approximate nutrient
   values per serving:
      Protein 6 g
      Fat 5 g
      Carbohydrate 37 g
      Sodium 381 mg
      Potassium 158 mg
      Cholesterol 2 mg
Exchanges:
   Bread 2½
   Fat 1

4 cups all-purpose flour
1 cup all-bran cereal
2 tablespoons sugar
1½ teaspoons salt
1 package active dry yeast
1 cup milk
½ cup water
¼ cup polyunsaturated margarine
2 tablespoons all-purpose flour for dusting board
1 teaspoon polyunsaturated oil
3 tablespoons cornmeal

In a large bowl combine 2 cups of the flour, the bran cereal, sugar, salt, and undissolved yeast.

In a saucepan heat milk, water, and margarine until warm. Add milk mixture to flour mixture and beat until well blended. Stir in additional 2 cups flour to make a stiff dough. Turn out onto board dusted with 2 tablespoons flour. Knead until smooth and elastic.

Place dough in bowl oiled with the 1 teaspoon polyunsaturated oil. Rotate dough to grease all surfaces. Let rise in a warm place free from draft approximately 45 minutes or until dough doubles in size.

Punch down dough and roll out to ½-inch thickness. Cut into rounds using a glass measuring 3 inches in diameter. Press a dusting of cornmeal lightly on each side. Place muffins on ungreased cookie sheet. Let rise in warm place approximately 35 minutes or until muffins double in size.

Preheat oven to 375°F.

Bake muffins 8 minutes. Turn on other side and bake 8 minutes. Cool on racks. To serve, split with a fork and toast.

*Yield:* 14 muffins

*Change Homemade English Muffins as follows or use Basic Recipe, if indicated, for:*

LOW-CALORIE, DIABETIC, LOW-FAT, AND LOW-CHOLESTEROL DIETS

Calories per serving: 194
Approximate nutrient
 values per serving:
  Protein 6 g
  Fat 3 g
  Carbohydrate 37 g
  Sodium 374 mg
  Potassium 160 mg
  Cholesterol 0 mg
Exchanges:
  Bread 2½
  Fat ½

Substitute skim milk for milk.
Reduce margarine to 3 tablespoons.
Proceed as in Basic Recipe.

LOW-SODIUM DIETS

Calories per serving: 206
Approximate nutrient
 values same as Basic
 Recipe except for:
  Sodium 270 mg

Reduce salt to 1 teaspoon.
Substitute unsalted polyunsaturated margarine for margarine.
Proceed as in Basic Recipe.

BLAND AND HIGH-FIBER DIETS

Use Basic Recipe.

# Popovers

BASIC RECIPE

Serving size: 1 popover
Calories per serving: 156
Approximate nutrient
  values per serving:
    Protein 5 g
    Fat 7 g
    Carbohydrate 17 g
    Sodium 135 mg
    Potassium 101 mg
    Cholesterol 97 mg
Exchanges:
  Milk ¼
  Bread 1
  Meat ½
  Fat 1

2 large eggs
1 cup milk
1 cup sifted all-purpose flour
¼ teaspoon salt
1 tablespoon polyunsaturated oil for batter
2 teaspoons polyunsaturated oil for greasing cups

Preheat oven to 375°F.

Arrange six 6-ounce glass custard cups on a cookie sheet or shallow pan and place in oven to heat.

Beat eggs lightly in a medium mixing bowl. Add milk, flour, salt, and the 1 tablespoon oil. Beat until blended. Do not overbeat.

Remove cups from oven and brush with remaining 2 teaspoons oil. Divide batter among cups; they should be approximately half full. Bake 1 hour or until tops are dark brown. Remove popovers from cups and serve at once. (If necessary, use the point of a sharp knife to loosen popovers from baking cups.)

*Yield:* 6 popovers

*Change Popovers as follows or use Basic Recipe, if indicated, for:*

LOW-CALORIE, DIABETIC, LOW-FAT, AND LOW-CHOLESTEROL DIETS

Calories per serving: 133
Approximate nutrient
  values per serving:
    Protein 6 g
    Fat 4 g
    Carbohydrate 18 g
    Sodium 154 mg
    Potassium 140 mg
    Cholesterol 1 mg
Exchanges:
  Milk ¼
  Bread 1
  Fat 1

Omit eggs. Use Low-Cholesterol Egg Substitute (page 189) equivalent to 2 large eggs.
Substitute skim milk for milk.
Proceed as in Basic Recipe.

LOW-SODIUM AND RENAL DIETS

Calories per serving: 156
Approximate nutrient
  values same as Basic
  Recipe except for:
    Calcium 61 mg
    Phosphorus 85 mg
    Sodium 43 mg

Omit salt.
Proceed as in Basic Recipe.

BLAND DIETS

Use Basic Recipe.

HIGH-FIBER DIETS

Calories per serving: 154

Reduce all-purpose flour to ½ cup. Add to it ½ cup stone-ground whole wheat flour.
Proceed as in Basic Recipe.

# Baking Powder Biscuits

BASIC RECIPE

Serving size: 1 biscuit
Calories per serving: 113
Approximate nutrient
  values per serving:
    Protein 2 g
    Fat 6 g
    Carbohydrate 14 g
    Sodium 168 mg
    Potassium 30 mg
    Cholesterol 1 mg
Exchanges:
  Bread 1
  Fat 1

2 cups sifted all-purpose flour
1 tablespoon baking powder
½ teaspoon salt
⅓ cup solid vegetable shortening
½ cup milk
1 tablespoon flour for board
1 teaspoon polyunsaturated oil

Preheat oven to 450°F.

Sift flour, baking powder, and salt into a large bowl. Cut in shortening until mixture is crumbly. Stir in milk. The mixture will be quite moist.

Turn dough onto a floured board and knead gently for 2 minutes. Roll the dough out to ½-inch thickness. Cut into 2-inch rounds. Grease cookie sheet with the oil, place biscuits on it, and bake 10 to 15 minutes or until lightly browned.

*Yield:* 14 biscuits

*Change Baking Powder Biscuits as follows or use Basic Recipe, if indicated, for:*

LOW-SODIUM AND RENAL DIETS

Calories per serving: 113
Approximate nutrient
  values same as Basic
  Recipe except for:
    Calcium 23 mg
    Phosphorus 38 mg
    Sodium 61 mg

Omit salt.
Reduce baking powder to 2 teaspoons.
Proceed as in Basic Recipe.

BLAND DIETS

Use Basic Recipe.

Calories per serving: 112

Reduce all-purpose flour to 1 cup. Add to it 1 cup stone-ground whole wheat flour.
Proceed as in Basic Recipe.


BAKING POWDER BISCUITS FOR LOW-CALORIE, DIABETIC, LOW-FAT, AND LOW-CHOLESTEROL DIETS

Serving size: 1 biscuit
Calories per serving: 99
Approximate nutrient
 values per serving:
  Protein 2 g
  Fat 4 g
  Carbohydrate 14 g
  Sodium 166 mg
  Potassium 27 mg
  Cholesterol 0 mg
Exchanges:
  Bread 1
  Fat 1

2 cups sifted all-purpose flour
1 tablespoon baking powder
½ teaspoon salt
¼ cup polyunsaturated oil
⅓ cup skim milk
1 tablespoon flour for board
vegetable cooking spray

Preheat oven to 450°F.

Sift flour, baking powder, and salt into a large bowl. Add oil and milk and stir with a fork until a soft dough is formed.

Turn dough onto a floured board and knead gently for 2 minutes. Roll the dough out to ½-inch thickness. Cut into 2-inch rounds. Spray cookie sheet with vegetable cooking spray. Place biscuits on cookie sheet and bake 10 to 15 minutes or until lightly browned.

*Yield:* 14 biscuits

# RICE AND CEREALS

Rice and cereals come in a dazzling array of sizes, shapes, and even colors; rice can be white or brown, long-grain, short-grain, instant, converted, or even wild, although the latter is actually a grain, not a rice. Cereals, too, come in a wide assortment: bran, corn, wheat, farina, hominy, oatmeal, Grape-Nuts; and some come in a choice of forms: flakes, buds, meals, flour, crumbs, and grits. Commercial varieties may be fortified with vitamins, mixed with fruits or sugar, toasted, puffed, and processed in many different ways.

Rice and cereals can be adjuncts for cooking: for coating or stuffing poultry, for topping or including in casseroles, for thickening stews. They can be companions to the entrée or the pivotal point around which breakfast, lunch, or dinner is planned. Many of our rice and cereal recipes are designed to serve as the main course in the meal, though a few may also serve as side dishes.

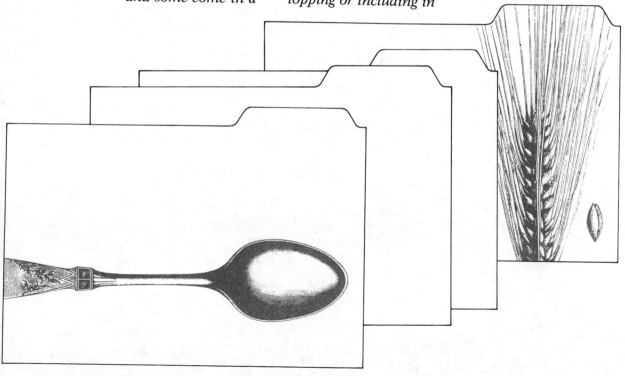

# Baked Rice with Herbs

BASIC RECIPE

3 tablespoons polyunsaturated margarine
¼ cup finely chopped onions
1 clove garlic, put through garlic press
1 cup raw long-grain rice
1¾ cups Chicken Stock (page 114)
½ teaspoon basil
½ teaspoon rosemary
1 teaspoon salt
⅛ teaspoon freshly ground pepper
1 bay leaf

Preheat oven to 375°F.

Melt margarine in a medium-size ovenproof casserole. Add onions and garlic and sauté until soft. Add rice and stir until well coated with margarine. Stir in remaining ingredients and bring to a boil.

Remove from heat, cover tightly, and bake 18 minutes or until all the liquid is absorbed.

Remove bay leaf and stir gently before serving.

*Yield:* 6 servings

*Change Baked Rice with Herbs as follows or use Basic Recipe, if indicated, for:*

LOW-SODIUM AND RENAL DIETS

Omit salt.
Substitute unsalted polyunsaturated margarine for margarine.
Proceed as in Basic Recipe.

## BLAND DIETS

Omit pepper.
Proceed as in Basic Recipe.

Calories per serving: 166

## HIGH-FIBER DIETS

Use Basic Recipe. Add 3 tablespoons chopped fresh parsley
before serving.

Calories per serving: 167

## BAKED RICE WITH HERBS FOR LOW-CALORIE, DIABETIC, LOW-FAT, AND LOW-CHOLESTEROL DIETS

Serving size: ½ cup
Calories per serving: 133
Approximate nutrient
values per serving:
Protein 2 g
Fat 2 g
Carbohydrate 26 g
Sodium 412 mg
Potassium 92 mg
Cholesterol 0 mg
Exchanges:
Bread 2

1 cup raw long-grain rice
¼ cup finely chopped onions
1 clove garlic, put through garlic press
1¾ cups Chicken Stock (page 114)
½ teaspoon basil
½ teaspoon rosemary
1 teaspoon salt
⅛ teaspoon freshly ground pepper
1 bay leaf
1 tablespoon polyunsaturated margarine

Preheat oven to 375°F.
Combine all ingredients except margarine in medium-size
ovenproof casserole. Bring to a boil over high heat. Remove
from heat, cover tightly, and bake 18 minutes or until all the
liquid is absorbed. Remove bay leaf and stir in margarine
before serving.

*Yield:* 6 servings

# Rice with Green Peppers and Mushrooms

BASIC RECIPE

Serving size: ½ cup
Calories per serving: 173
Approximate nutrient
  values per serving:
    Protein 3 g
    Fat 6 g
    Carbohydrate 27 g
    Sodium 451 mg
    Potassium 186 mg
    Cholesterol 0 mg
Exchanges:
  Bread 2
  Fat 1

3 tablespoons polyunsaturated margarine
1 cup chopped fresh mushrooms
1 cup chopped green pepper
1 clove garlic, put through garlic press
1 cup raw long-grain rice
1½ cups Chicken Stock (page 114)
1 teaspoon salt
¼ teaspoon freshly ground pepper
3 tablespoons chopped fresh parsley

Preheat oven to 375°F.

Melt margarine in a medium-size ovenproof casserole. Add mushrooms, green pepper, and garlic. Sauté until mushrooms are tender. Add rice. Mix gently. Stir in chicken stock, salt, and pepper. Bring to a boil.

Remove from heat, cover tightly, place in oven, and bake 20 minutes or until the liquid is absorbed.

Add parsley. Stir gently to blend.

*Yield:* 6 servings

*Change Rice with Green Peppers and Mushrooms as follows or use Basic Recipe, if indicated, for:*

LOW-SODIUM DIETS

Omit salt.
Substitute unsalted polyunsaturated margarine for margarine.
Add ½ teaspoon rosemary with stock and seasonings.
Proceed as in Basic Recipe.

Calories per serving: 173
Approximate nutrient
  values same as Basic
  Recipe except for:
    Sodium 28 mg
    Potassium 187 mg

Calories per serving: 173

## BLAND DIETS

Omit ground pepper.
Add ½ teaspoon rosemary with stock and seasonings.
Proceed as in Basic Recipe.

## HIGH-FIBER DIETS

Use Basic Recipe. For extra fiber, garnish with additional chopped fresh parsley.

## RICE WITH GREEN PEPPERS AND MUSHROOMS FOR LOW-CALORIE, DIABETIC, LOW-FAT, AND LOW-CHOLESTEROL DIETS

Serving size: ½ cup
Calories per serving: 139
Approximate nutrient
 values per serving:
  Protein 3 g
  Fat 2 g
  Carbohydrate 27 g
  Sodium 413 mg
  Potassium 185 mg
  Cholesterol 0 mg
Exchanges:
  Bread 2

1 cup raw long-grain rice
1 cup chopped fresh mushrooms
1 cup chopped green pepper
1 clove garlic, put through garlic press
1½ cups Chicken Stock (page 114)
1 teaspoon salt
¼ teaspoon freshly ground pepper
3 tablespoons chopped fresh parsley
1 tablespoon polyunsaturated margarine

Preheat oven to 375°F.
  Combine rice, mushrooms, green pepper, garlic, stock, salt, and pepper in a medium-size ovenproof casserole. Bring to a boil. Remove from heat and cover tightly. Place in preheated oven and bake 20 minutes or until the liquid is absorbed.
  Just before serving, stir in parsley and margarine.

*Yield:* 6 servings

## RICE WITH GREEN PEPPERS AND MUSHROOMS FOR RENAL DIETS

Serving size: ½ cup
Calories per serving: 172
Approximate nutrient
  values per serving:
    Protein 3 g
    Fat 6 g
    Carbohydrate 27 g
    Calcium 21 mg
    Phosphorus 52 mg
    Sodium 55 mg
    Potassium 129 mg
    Cholesterol 0 mg
Exchanges:
  Bread 2
  Fat 1

3 tablespoons unsalted polyunsaturated margarine
4-ounce can mushroom pieces, drained
1 cup chopped green pepper
1 clove garlic, put through garlic press
1 cup raw long-grain rice
1½ cups water
½ teaspoon ground cumin
¼ teaspoon freshly ground pepper
3 tablespoons chopped fresh parsley

Preheat oven to 375°F.

Melt margarine in a medium-size ovenproof casserole. Add mushrooms, green peppers, and garlic.

Add rice and mix gently. Stir in water, cumin, and pepper. Bring to boil, remove from heat, cover tightly, and place in oven. Bake for 20 minutes or until liquid is absorbed.

Gently stir in fresh parsley just before serving.

*Yield:* 6 servings

# Rice Pilaf

BASIC RECIPE

Serving size: ½ cup
Calories per serving: 177
Approximate nutrient
  values per serving:
    Protein 3 g
    Fat 7 g
    Carbohydrate 26 g
    Sodium 337 mg
    Potassium 102 mg
    Cholesterol 9 mg
Exchanges:
  Bread 2
  Fat 1

2 tablespoons polyunsaturated oil
2 tablespoons polyunsaturated margarine
1 cup raw long-grain rice
1 cup broken fine noodles
⅓ cup chopped onions
3 cups Chicken Stock (page 114)
1 teaspoon salt
¼ teaspoon freshly ground pepper
1 bay leaf

Heat oil and margarine in a medium saucepan. Add rice, noodles, and onions. Sauté until rice is golden brown. Add remaining ingredients.

Cover tightly; simmer slowly 20 minutes or until all the liquid is absorbed.

Remove bay leaf; stir gently. Serve immediately.

*Yield:* 8 servings

*Change Rice Pilaf as follows for:*

### LOW-CALORIE, DIABETIC, LOW-FAT, AND LOW-CHOLESTEROL DIETS

Omit polyunsaturated oil and margarine. Do not sauté rice, noodles, and onions. Place them in a medium saucepan with chicken stock and remaining ingredients.
Proceed as in Basic Recipe.
Garnish with ½ cup chopped fresh parsley before serving.

Calories per serving: 123
Approximate nutrient
  values per serving:
    Protein 3 g
    Fat 1 g
    Carbohydrate 26 g
    Sodium 310 mg
    Potassium 129 mg
    Cholesterol 9 mg
Exchanges:
  Bread 2

### LOW-SODIUM DIETS

Omit salt.
Substitute unsalted polyunsaturated margarine for margarine.
Add 1 clove garlic, put through garlic press. Sauté with rice, noodles, and onions.
Proceed as in Basic Recipe.

Calories per serving: 177
Approximate nutrient
  values same as Basic
  Recipe except for:
    Sodium 34 mg
    Potassium 104 mg

### BLAND DIETS

Omit pepper.
Proceed as in Basic Recipe.

Calories per serving: 177

Calories per serving: 179

Add ½ cup chopped green pepper to the saucepan with the rice, noodles, and onions, and sauté.

Proceed as in Basic Recipe.

# Barley Casserole

BASIC RECIPE

Serving size: ½ cup
Calories per serving: 168
Approximate nutrient
  values per serving:
    Protein 3 g
    Fat 7 g
    Carbohydrate 25 g
    Sodium 95 mg
    Potassium 192 mg
    Cholesterol 0 mg
Exchanges:
  Bread 1½
  Fat 1½

1 cup pearl barley
½ cup chopped onions
2 cups sliced fresh mushrooms
4 tablespoons polyunsaturated margarine
2 cups Chicken Stock (page 114).

In a 3-quart saucepan, sauté barley, onions, and mushrooms in margarine until onions are soft and barley is lightly browned.

Add chicken stock. Cover and simmer slowly, 40 minutes. Remove cover; cook 5 minutes longer, stirring gently, until barley is tender and all the liquid is absorbed.

*Yield:* 7 servings

*Change Barley Casserole as follows or use Basic Recipe, if indicated, for:*

### LOW-CALORIE, DIABETIC, LOW-FAT, AND LOW-CHOLESTEROL DIETS

Omit margarine. Do not sauté barley, onions, and mushrooms. Place them in saucepan with the chicken stock and simmer 45 minutes or until barley is tender and all the liquid is absorbed.
Proceed as in Basic Recipe.

Calories per serving: 110
Approximate nutrient
  values per serving:
    Protein 3 g
    Fat 0 g
    Carbohydrate 25 g
    Sodium 30 mg
    Potassium 190 mg
    Cholesterol 0 mg
Exchanges:
    Bread 1½

### LOW-SODIUM DIETS

Substitute unsalted polyunsaturated margarine for margarine. Proceed as in Basic Recipe.

Calories per serving: 168
Approximate nutrient
  values same as Basic
  Recipe except for:
    Sodium 30 mg

### BLAND DIETS

Use Basic Recipe.

### HIGH-FIBER DIETS

Use Basic Recipe up to point where all liquid is absorbed; remove from heat. Add 3 tablespoons finely chopped scallions, both white and green parts, and stir into casserole. Immediately before serving, add 3 tablespoons minced fresh parsley for edible garnish.

Calories per serving: 170

149

# Cheddar Rice Mold

BASIC RECIPE

Serving size: ½ cup
Calories per serving: 226
Approximate nutrient
  values per serving:
    Protein 6 g
    Fat 12 g
    Carbohydrate 23 g
    Sodium 514 mg
    Potassium 184 mg
    Cholesterol 17 mg
Exchanges:
  Bread 1½
  Meat 1
  Fat 1½

2½ cups Chicken Stock (page 114)
1 cup raw long-grain rice
1 teaspoon salt
⅛ teaspoon freshly ground pepper
½ teaspoon ground cumin
¼ teaspoon ground ginger
3 tablespoons polyunsaturated margarine for sautéing
1½ cups coarsely chopped fresh mushrooms
½ cup chopped sweet red pepper
1 cup grated sharp Cheddar cheese
1 tablespoon polyunsaturated margarine for greasing mold

In a medium saucepan bring stock to a boil. Stir in rice, salt, pepper, cumin, and ginger. Cover, reduce heat, and simmer slowly 20 to 25 minutes or until rice is tender and all the liquid has been absorbed. Spoon rice into a large bowl.

Preheat oven to 350°F.

In a medium skillet heat the margarine. Add mushrooms and red pepper and sauté until mushrooms are tender. Add mushroom mixture and cheese to rice and mix gently to blend.

Grease a 3½-cup ring mold with remaining margarine. Spoon rice mixture into mold.

Set in a pan filled with 1 inch hot water and bake 30 minutes.

Place mold on rack and allow to cool for 5 minutes.

Invert on serving dish before serving.

*Yield:* 7 servings

*Change Cheddar Rice Mold as follows or use Basic Recipe, if indicated, for:*

## LOW-CALORIE, DIABETIC, LOW-FAT, AND LOW-CHOLESTEROL DIETS

Reduce margarine for sautéing to 2 tablespoons.
Substitute 1 cup grated part-skim mozzarella cheese for Cheddar.
Omit margarine for greasing mold. Before filling the mold with rice mixture, spray it thoroughly with vegetable cooking spray.
Proceed as in Basic Recipe.

Calories per serving: 173
Approximate nutrient
   values per serving:
      Protein 6 g
      Fat 6 g
      Carbohydrate 23 g
      Sodium 457 mg
      Potassium 181 mg
      Cholesterol 9 mg
Exchanges:
   Bread 1½
   Meat 1
   Fat ½

## LOW-SODIUM DIETS

Omit salt.
Substitute unsalted polyunsaturated margarine for margarine wherever used.
Substitute grated low-sodium Cheddar for Cheddar.
Proceed as in Basic Recipe.

Calories per serving: 223
Approximate nutrient
   values per serving:
      Protein 6 g
      Fat 12 g
      Carbohydrate 23 g
      Sodium 38 mg
      Potassium 191 mg
      Cholesterol 6 mg

## BLAND DIETS

Omit pepper.
Proceed as in Basic Recipe.

Calories per serving: 226

## HIGH-FIBER DIETS

Use Basic Recipe.

# Fried Rice

BASIC RECIPE

Serving size: ½ cup
Calories per serving: 160
Approximate nutrient
   values per serving:
      Protein 6 g
      Fat 8 g
      Carbohydrate 15 g
      Sodium 477 mg
      Potassium 179 mg
      Cholesterol 54 mg
Exchanges:
   Bread 1
   Meat ½
   Fat 1½

2 large eggs
1 teaspoon cold water
2 tablespoons polyunsaturated oil for the eggs
¼ cup polyunsaturated oil for sautéing rice and celery
3 cups cold cooked rice
1½ cups thinly sliced celery
1 cup diced cooked chicken
1 cup fresh bean sprouts
½ cup thinly sliced scallions
¼ cup soy sauce
¾ teaspoon ground ginger
1 clove garlic, put through garlic press

Beat eggs lightly with water.

Heat 2 tablespoons oil in a medium skillet. Add eggs. Cook over medium heat, without stirring, to make a pancake. Turn once, cooking until eggs are set. Remove to a plate and cut into thin strips.

Heat the remaining oil in a large skillet over medium heat. Add rice and celery; sauté until coated with oil. Add remaining ingredients and cook, stirring gently, until thoroughly heated. Garnish with egg strips before serving.

*Yield:* 12 servings

*Change Fried Rice as follows or use Basic Recipe, if indicated, for:*

### LOW-CALORIE, DIABETIC, LOW-FAT, AND LOW-CHOLESTEROL DIETS

Omit eggs. Substitute Low-Cholesterol Egg Substitute (page 189) equivalent to 2 large eggs.
Omit 2 tablespoons oil to cook pancake. Spray pan well with vegetable cooking spray instead.
Reduce oil for sautéing rice and celery to 1 tablespoon.
Proceed as in Basic Recipe.

Calories per serving: 105
Approximate nutrient
   values per serving:
      Protein 7 g
      Fat 2 g
      Carbohydrate 15 g
      Sodium 487 mg
      Potassium 195 mg
      Cholesterol 9 mg
Exchanges:
   Bread 1
   Meat ½

### LOW-SODIUM AND RENAL DIETS

Omit soy sauce. Substitute ¼ cup dry sherry.
Add ¼ teaspoon freshly ground pepper.
Proceed as in Basic Recipe.

Calories per serving: 158
Approximate nutrient
   values per serving:
      Protein 6 g
      Fat 8 g
      Carbohydrate 15 g
      Calcium 23 mg
      Phosphorus 71 mg
      Sodium 38 mg
      Potassium 158 mg
      Cholesterol 54 mg

### BLAND AND HIGH-FIBER DIETS

Use Basic Recipe.

# Hominy Grits with Cheese

BASIC RECIPE

Serving size: ½ cup
Calories per serving: 160
Approximate nutrient
  values per serving:
    Protein 4 g
    Fat 9 g
    Carbohydrate 16 g
    Sodium 390 mg
    Potassium 33 mg
    Cholesterol 10 mg
Exchanges:
  Bread 1
  Meat ½
  Fat 1½

3 cups water
¾ teaspoon salt
¾ cup quick-cooking hominy grits
⅛ teaspoon freshly ground pepper
3 tablespoons polyunsaturated margarine
½ cup grated sharp Cheddar cheese

In a medium saucepan bring water to a boil. Add salt. Slowly stir in hominy grits. Return water to boil; then reduce heat. Simmer 5 to 7 minutes or until all the liquid is absorbed and mixture is thick. Stir frequently.

Stir in remaining ingredients. Cook, stirring, until cheese melts. Serve immediately.

*Yield:* 6 servings

*Change Hominy Grits with Cheese as follows or use Basic Recipe, if indicated, for:*

LOW-CALORIE, DIABETIC, LOW-FAT, AND LOW-CHOLESTEROL DIETS

Reduce polyunsaturated margarine to 2 tablespoons. Substitute grated part-skim mozzarella cheese for Cheddar. Proceed as in Basic Recipe.

Calories per serving: 129
Approximate nutrient
  values per serving:
    Protein 4 g
    Fat 5 g
    Carbohydrate 16 g
    Sodium 357 mg
    Potassium 31 mg
    Cholesterol 5 mg
Exchanges:
  Bread 1
  Meat ½
  Fat 1

## LOW-SODIUM DIETS

Calories per serving: 158
Approximate nutrient
  values per serving:
    Protein 4 g
    Fat 9 g
    Carbohydrate 16 g
    Sodium 2 mg
    Potassium 37 mg
    Cholesterol 3 mg

Omit salt.
Substitute unsalted polyunsaturated margarine for margarine.
Substitute low-sodium Cheddar cheese for Cheddar.
Proceed as in Basic Recipe.

## BLAND DIETS

Calories per serving: 160

Omit pepper.
Proceed as in Basic Recipe.

## HIGH-FIBER DIETS

Use Basic Recipe. For extra fiber, Grape-Nuts make a nice addition.

# PASTAS AND PANCAKES

Pastas and pancakes have a lot in common. They are endlessly versatile and can be baked, fried, stuffed, toasted, enriched with butter, or blanketed with sauces. They can be served as main courses, as side dishes, as appetizers, or—in the case of pancakes—as desserts. Both pastas and pancakes are nutritious and economical, and starting with two essential ingredients—eggs and flour—have been developed into thousands of delectable recipes by inspired cooks all over the world.

Here we present an interesting variety of recipes, including crêpes, waffles, blintzes, casseroles, and dessert pancakes, with an assortment of suggested sauces and fillings.

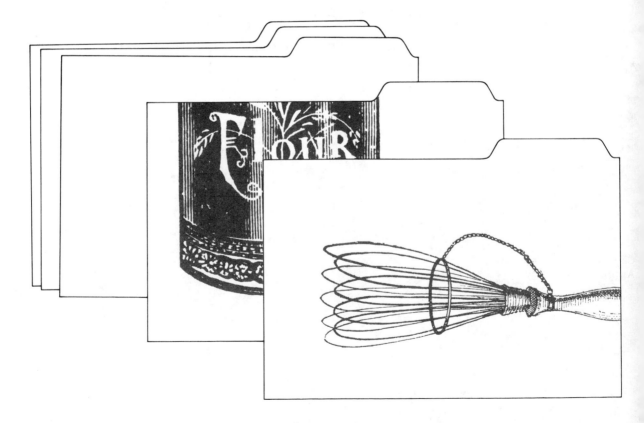

# Cheese Noodle Pudding

BASIC RECIPE

Serving size: ½ cup
Calories per serving: 220
Approximate nutrient
   values per serving:
      Protein 6 g
      Fat 15 g
      Carbohydrate 16 g
      Sodium 262 mg
      Potassium 103 mg
      Cholesterol 95 mg
Exchanges:
   Bread 1
   Meat ½
   Fat 3

1 teaspoon salt
2 quarts water
8 ounces cream cheese, at room temperature
2 large eggs, beaten
¼ teaspoon freshly ground pepper
1 cup sour cream
½ cup milk
2 tablespoons polyunsaturated oil
8 ounces medium-width noodles

Preheat oven to 350°F.

Add salt to water and bring to a boil.

Meanwhile, in a large bowl, mash cream cheese. Add eggs and pepper; mix thoroughly. Stir in sour cream, milk, and oil. Set aside.

Add noodles to boiling water and cook 8 to 10 minutes or until tender. Drain well. Then stir gently into cream cheese mixture until blended. Turn into an ungreased 8-by-8-by-2-inch baking dish. Bake 45 minutes or until lightly browned.

*Yield:* 12 servings

*Change Cheese Noodle Pudding as follows for:*

LOW-SODIUM AND RENAL DIETS

Calories per serving: 220
Approximate nutrient
   values same as Basic
   Recipe except for:
      Calcium 60 mg
      Phosphorus 95 mg
      Sodium 84 mg

Omit salt.
Proceed as in Basic Recipe.

Calories per serving: 220

Omit pepper.
Proceed as in Basic Recipe.


HIGH-FIBER DIETS

Calories per serving: 241
Serving size ½ cup

Add ½ cup raisins with noodles.
Proceed as in Basic Recipe.


CHEESE NOODLE PUDDING FOR LOW-CALORIE, DIABETIC, LOW-FAT, AND LOW-CHOLESTEROL DIETS

Serving size: ½ cup
Calories per serving: 130
Approximate nutrient
  values per serving:
    Protein 7 g
    Fat 4 g
    Carbohydrate 17 g
    Sodium 295 mg
    Potassium 131 mg
    Cholesterol 20 mg
Exchanges:
  Bread 1
  Meat ½
  Fat ½

1 teaspoon salt
2 quarts water
1 cup 1 percent low-fat cottage cheese
Low-Cholesterol Egg Substitute (page 189) equivalent to
    2 large eggs
¼ teaspoon freshly ground pepper
1 cup plain low-fat yogurt
½ cup skim milk
2 tablespoons polyunsaturated oil
8 ounces medium-width noodles

Preheat oven to 350°F.
    Add salt to water and bring to a boil.
    Meanwhile, in a large mixing bowl, beat cottage cheese, egg substitute, and pepper until well blended. Stir in yogurt, skim milk, and oil. Set aside.
    Add noodles to boiling water and cook 8 to 10 minutes or until tender. Drain well. Then stir gently into cottage cheese mixture until blended. Turn into an ungreased 8-by-8-by-2-inch baking dish. Bake 45 minutes or until lightly browned.

*Yield:* 12 servings

# Eggplant Manicotti

BASIC RECIPE

Serving size: 2 manicotti
Calories per serving: 483
Approximate nutrient
  values per serving:
    Protein 23 g
    Fat 31 g
    Carbohydrate 32 g
    Sodium 456 mg
    Potassium 1177 mg
    Cholesterol 56 mg
Exchanges:
  Vegetable 5
  Bread ½
  Meat 2
  Fat 5

⅓ cup olive oil
3 cups diced peeled eggplant
1 cup ricotta cheese for filling
1 cup grated mozzarella cheese for filling
⅓ cup grated Parmesan cheese for filling
¼ cup chopped fresh parsley
¾ teaspoon marjoram
⅛ teaspoon freshly ground pepper
12 manicotti (5½ ounces)
4 quarts boiling water
3½ cups Italian Tomato Sauce (page 392)
½ cup grated mozzarella cheese for topping
⅓ cup grated Parmesan cheese for topping

In a large skillet heat the olive oil. Add eggplant and sauté over medium heat until tender, about 7 minutes.

In a large bowl combine sautéed eggplant, the 1 cup ricotta, 1 cup mozzarella, and ⅓ cup Parmesan cheeses planned for filling. Mix in parsley, marjoram, and pepper.

Preheat oven to 350°F.

In a large saucepan, cook manicotti in 4 quarts boiling water 7 minutes or until almost tender. Drain thoroughly. Cool to room temperature, then fill with eggplant mixture.

Spoon 1½ cups of the tomato sauce into a large, shallow baking dish. Arrange manicotti on it and top with remaining 2 cups sauce. Sprinkle with the ½ cup mozzarella and ⅓ cup Parmesan cheeses planned for topping.

Bake, uncovered, for 20 minutes, or until very hot. Then place under broiler until top is nicely browned.

*Yield:* 6 servings

*Change Eggplant Manicotti as follows or use Basic Recipe, if indicated, for:*

### LOW-SODIUM DIETS

Calories per serving: 461
Approximate nutrient
values per serving:
Protein 18 g
Fat 30 g
Carbohydrate 31 g
Sodium 117 mg
Potassium 1181 mg
Cholesterol 31 mg

Omit all mozzarella and Parmesan cheese. Substitute 1 cup grated low-sodium Swiss cheese for the filling and ½ cup grated low-sodium Swiss cheese for the topping.
Proceed as in Basic Recipe.

### BLAND DIETS

Calories per serving: 483

Omit pepper.
Proceed as in Basic Recipe.

### HIGH-FIBER DIETS

Use Basic Recipe.

### EGGPLANT MANICOTTI FOR LOW-CALORIE, DIABETIC, LOW-FAT, AND LOW-CHOLESTEROL DIETS

Serving size: 2 manicotti
Calories per serving: 262
Approximate nutrient
values per serving:
Protein 19 g
Fat 8 g
Carbohydrate 32 g
Sodium 877 mg
Potassium 1182 mg
Cholesterol 18 mg
Exchanges:
Vegetable 5
Bread ½
Meat 1½
Fat ½

2 cups water
½ teaspoon salt for cooking eggplant
3 cups diced peeled eggplant
1 cup 1 percent low-fat cottage cheese
1 cup grated part-skim mozzarella cheese for filling
1 teaspoon salt
Low-Cholesterol Egg Substitute (page 189) equivalent to 1 large egg
¼ cup chopped fresh parsley
¾ teaspoon marjoram
⅛ teaspoon freshly ground pepper
12 manicotti (5½ ounces)
4 quarts boiling water

3½ cups Italian Tomato Sauce (page 392)
½ cup grated part-skim mozzarella cheese for topping

In a saucepan bring 2 cups water and ½ teaspoon salt to a simmer; add eggplant and cook 5 minutes or until tender. Drain thoroughly on paper toweling.

In a large bowl, combine eggplant, cottage cheese, 1 cup mozzarella planned for filling, 1 teaspoon salt, egg substitute, parsley, marjoram, and pepper.

Preheat oven to 350°F.

In a large saucepan, cook manicotti in 4 quarts boiling water 7 minutes or until almost tender. Drain thoroughly. Cool to room temperature.

Fill with eggplant mixture.

Spoon 1½ cups tomato sauce into large shallow baking dish. Arrange manicotti on it and top with remaining 2 cups sauce. Sprinkle with the ½ cup mozzarella cheese planned for topping and bake, uncovered, 20 minutes or until very hot. Place under broiler until top is nicely browned.

*Yield:* 6 servings

EGGPLANT MANICOTTI FOR RENAL DIETS

*The Manicotti and Filling*
⅓ cup olive oil
3 cups diced peeled eggplant
1 cup ricotta cheese
1 cup grated mozzarella cheese
¼ cup chopped fresh parsley
½ teaspoon oregano
¾ teaspoon marjoram
⅛ teaspoon freshly ground pepper
12 manicotti (5½ ounces)
4 quarts boiling water

*The Sauce*
6 tablespoons unsalted polyunsaturated margarine
6 tablespoons flour
3 cups milk
⅛ teaspoon freshly ground pepper

Serving size: 2 manicotti
Calories per serving: 512
Approximate nutrient
  values per serving:
    Protein 17 g
    Fat 40 g
    Carbohydrate 24 g
    Calcium 400 mg
    Phosphorus 327 mg
    Sodium 203 mg
    Potassium 445 mg
    Cholesterol 60 mg
Exchanges:
  Milk ½
  Vegetable 1
  Bread 1
  Meat 1½
  Fat 7

*161*

⅛ teaspoon nutmeg
½ cup grated mozzarella cheese for topping

*To prepare the manicotti and filling:* Heat the olive oil in a large skillet. Add eggplant and sauté until tender, about 7 minutes.
In a large bowl, combine eggplant, 1 cup ricotta, 1 cup mozzarella, parsley, oregano, marjoram, and pepper.
Preheat oven to 350°F.
Cook manicotti in boiling water 7 minutes or until almost tender. Drain thoroughly. Cool to room temperature.

*To prepare the sauce:* Melt margarine in a medium saucepan over low heat. Stir in flour; then gradually stir in milk. Raise heat to moderate and cook, stirring constantly, until sauce is thick and smooth. Boil and stir 1 minute. Remove from heat and stir in pepper and nutmeg.
Fill manicotti with eggplant mixture. Spoon 1½ cups of the sauce into a large shallow baking dish. Arrange manicotti in dish and top with remaining sauce. Sprinkle the remaining ½ cup mozzarella on top and bake, uncovered, for 20 minutes or until hot. Place under broiler and cook until top is nicely browned.

*Yield:* 6 servings

# Vermicelli with Tomato and Red Pepper Sauce

BASIC RECIPE

Serving size: ½ cup pasta, ⅓ cup sauce
Calories per serving: 185
Approximate nutrient values per serving:
    Protein 5 g
    Fat 7 g
    Carbohydrate 27 g

¼ cup olive oil
1 cup chopped onions
1 cup sliced carrots
1 cup sliced celery
3 cloves garlic, finely chopped
4 cups coarsely chopped peeled tomatoes
1 teaspoon oregano

Sodium 239 mg
Potassium 502 mg
Cholesterol 0 mg
Exchanges:
  Vegetable 2
  Bread 1
  Fat 1½

1 teaspoon red pepper flakes
¾ teaspoon salt
2 quarts water
8 ounces vermicelli
⅓ cup chopped fresh parsley

Heat oil in large saucepan over medium heat. Add onions, carrots, celery, and garlic. Sauté until onions are soft. Add tomatoes; lower heat and simmer, uncovered, 45 minutes or until sauce is thickened.

Purée sauce in a blender, a third at a time. Return to saucepan. Add oregano, red pepper flakes, and salt; simmer 15 minutes. The sauce can be made ahead of time and reheated.

While sauce is simmering or being reheated, prepare vermicelli. Bring 2 quarts water to a boil, add vermicelli, and cook 8 to 10 minutes or until tender. Drain well.

Pour sauce over vermicelli. Garnish with parsley and serve immediately.

*Yield:* 8 servings

*Change Vermicelli with Tomato and Red Pepper Sauce as follows or use Basic Recipe, if indicated, for:*

LOW-SODIUM DIETS

Calories per serving: 185
Approximate nutrient
  values same as Basic
  Recipe except for:
    Sodium 33 mg

Omit salt.
Proceed as in Basic Recipe.

BLAND DIETS

Calories per serving: 185

Omit red pepper flakes.
Proceed as in Basic Recipe.

## HIGH-FIBER DIETS

Use Basic Recipe.

### VERMICELLI WITH TOMATO AND RED PEPPER SAUCE FOR LOW-CALORIE, DIABETIC, LOW-FAT, AND LOW-CHOLESTEROL DIETS

Serving size: ½ cup pasta, ⅓ cup sauce
Calories per serving: 125
Approximate nutrient values per serving:
Protein 5 g
Fat 1 g
Carbohydrate 27 g
Sodium 239 mg
Potassium 502 mg
Cholesterol 0 mg
Exchanges:
Vegetable 2
Bread 1

4 cups coarsely chopped peeled tomatoes
1 cup chopped onions
1 cup sliced carrots
1 cup sliced celery
3 cloves garlic, finely chopped
1 teaspoon oregano
1 teaspoon red pepper flakes
¾ teaspoon salt
2 quarts water
8 ounces vermicelli
⅓ cup chopped fresh parsley

Simmer tomatoes in saucepan, covered, over low heat for 20 minutes.

Add onions, carrots, celery, and garlic. Cook, uncovered, 45 minutes or until sauce is thickened.

Purée sauce in a blender, a third at a time. Return to saucepan; add oregano, red pepper, and salt; simmer 15 minutes.

While sauce is simmering, prepare vermicelli. Bring 2 quarts water to a boil, add vermicelli, and cook 8 to 10 minutes or until tender. Drain well.

Pour sauce over vermicelli. Garnish with parsley and serve immediately.

*Yield:* 8 servings

# Fettucine with Cheese

BASIC RECIPE

3 quarts water
1 teaspoon salt
8 ounces fettucine
⅛ cup polyunsaturated margarine, melted
1 cup grated Parmesan cheese
½ cup chopped fresh parsley
2 teaspoons basil
1 clove garlic, put through garlic press
⅛ teaspoon freshly ground pepper

Boil the water and salt in a large saucepan. Add fettucine; cook 5 to 8 minutes or until tender. Place in colander and drain quickly, but not too thoroughly. Transfer moist fettucine to dry, clean saucepan. Place on low heat and add remaining ingredients. Toss gently to mix thoroughly.
Serve immediately on warmed plates.

*Yield:* 8 servings

*Change Fettucine with Cheese as follows or use Basic Recipe, if indicated, for:*

LOW-CALORIE, DIABETIC, LOW-FAT, AND LOW-CHOLESTEROL DIETS

Omit margarine and Parmesan cheese; substitute 1 cup 1 percent low-fat cottage cheese mixed with ¼ cup plain low-fat yogurt.
Proceed as in Basic Recipe.

Calories per serving: 196
Approximate nutrient
  values per serving:
    Protein 5 g
    Fat 11 g
    Carbohydrate 17 g
    Sodium 26 mg
    Potassium 104 mg
    Cholesterol 4 mg

## LOW-SODIUM DIETS

Omit salt.
Substitute unsalted polyunsaturated margarine for margarine.
Omit Parmesan cheese. Substitute ¾ cup grated low-sodium Swiss cheese.
Proceed as in Basic Recipe.

Calories per serving: 229

## BLAND DIETS

Omit pepper.
Proceed as in Basic Recipe.

## HIGH-FIBER DIETS

Use Basic Recipe. For extra fiber, garnish with caraway or poppy seeds.

# Gnocchi Verdi

### BASIC RECIPE

Serving size: 6 gnocchi
Calories per serving: 222
Approximate nutrient
  values per serving:
    Protein 13 g
    Fat 12 g
    Carbohydrate 16 g
    Sodium 1347 mg
    Potassium 292 mg
    Cholesterol 72 mg
Exchanges:
  Bread 1
  Meat 1½
  Fat 1½

*The Dough*
¾ pound fresh spinach
⅔ cup ricotta cheese
¾ cup flour
⅓ cup grated Parmesan cheese
1 large egg
¼ teaspoon salt
⅛ teaspoon freshly ground pepper
3½ quarts water for boiling gnocchi
2½ teaspoons salt for boiling gnocchi

*The Topping*
2 tablespoons polyunsaturated margarine, melted
⅓ cup grated Parmesan cheese

*To prepare the dough:* Wash spinach thoroughly and trim off any tough stems. Put in a large pot with only the water clinging to the leaves. Cook over medium heat, covered, for 5 to 10 minutes or until tender. Drain thoroughly and chop coarsely.

In a large bowl, thoroughly mix spinach, ricotta cheese, flour, ⅓ cup Parmesan cheese, egg, ¼ teaspoon salt, and pepper. Refrigerate gnocchi 1 hour or until dough is easy to handle.

Preheat oven to 375°F.

Pour the water into a large saucepan and add the 2½ teaspoons salt. Bring to a boil.

Shape gnocchi by using rounded teaspoons to form the dough into balls. Reduce heat to a simmer. Add gnocchi, a few at a time. As gnocchi rise to the surface, remove with a slotted spoon to a shallow baking dish.

*To prepare the topping:* Drizzle melted margarine over gnocchi and sprinkle with remaining ⅓ cup Parmesan cheese.

Bake 25 minutes or until golden brown.

*Yield:* 6 servings

*Change Gnocchi Verdi as follows or use Basic Recipe, if indicated, for:*

LOW-SODIUM DIETS

Calories per serving: 208
Approximate nutrient
  values per serving:
    Protein 10 g
    Fat 12 g
    Carbohydrate 15 g
    Sodium 89 mg
    Potassium 292 mg
    Cholesterol 66 mg

*The dough:* Omit salt from dough and cooking water. Omit Parmesan cheese. Add ¼ teaspoon nutmeg and proceed as in Basic Recipe.

*The topping:* Substitute unsalted polyunsaturated margarine for margarine.

Omit Parmesan cheese. Substitute ½ cup grated low-sodium Swiss cheese.

Proceed as in Basic Recipe.

## BLAND DIETS

Omit pepper.
Proceed as in Basic Recipe.


## HIGH-FIBER DIETS

Use Basic Recipe.


## GNOCCHI VERDI FOR LOW-CALORIE, DIABETIC, LOW-FAT, AND LOW-CHOLESTEROL DIETS

Serving size: 6 gnocchi
Calories per serving: 174
Approximate nutrient
  values per serving:
    Protein 10 g
    Fat 8 g
    Carbohydrate 16 g
    Sodium 1269 mg
    Potassium 308 mg
    Cholesterol 16 mg
Exchanges:
  Bread 1
  Meat 1
  Fat 1

*The Dough*
¾ pound fresh spinach
⅔ cup part-skim ricotta cheese
¾ cup flour
Low-Cholesterol Egg Substitute (page 189) equivalent to
    1 large egg
½ teaspoon salt
⅛ teaspoon freshly ground pepper
3½ quarts water for boiling gnocchi
2½ teaspoons salt for boiling gnocchi


*The Topping*
2 tablespoons polyunsaturated margarine, melted
½ cup grated part-skim mozzarella cheese


*To prepare the dough:* Wash spinach thoroughly and trim off any tough stems. Put in a large pot with only the water clinging to the leaves. Cook over medium heat, covered, 5 to 10 minutes or until tender. Drain thoroughly and chop coarsely.

In a large bowl, thoroughly mix spinach, ricotta cheese, flour, egg substitute, ½ teaspoon salt, and pepper. Refrigerate 1 hour or until dough is easy to handle.

Preheat oven to 375°F.

Pour the water into a large saucepan and add the 2½ teaspoons salt. Bring to a boil.

Shape gnocchi by using rounded teaspoons to form the dough into balls. Reduce heat to a simmer. Add gnocchi, a few at a time. As gnocchi rise to the surface, remove with slotted spoon to a shallow baking dish.

*To prepare the topping:* Drizzle melted margarine over gnocchi. Sprinkle with mozzarella cheese. Bake 25 minutes or until golden brown.

*Yield:* 6 servings

# Rotini with Cauliflower

BASIC RECIPE

Serving size: 1 cup, 1½ tablespoons grated cheese
Calories per serving: 293
Approximate nutrient values per serving:
  Protein 10 g
  Fat 10 g
  Carbohydrate 43 g
  Sodium 1102 mg
  Potassium 499 mg
  Cholesterol 6 mg
Exchanges:
  Vegetable 1
  Fruit 1
  Bread 2
  Meat ½
  Fat 1½

½ cup raisins
4 tablespoons olive oil
½ cup chopped onions
2 cloves garlic, put through garlic press
28-ounce can Italian plum tomatoes
½ teaspoon nutmeg
1 tablespoon salt
⅛ teaspoon freshly ground pepper
3 cups raw cauliflower flowerets in bite-size pieces
3 quarts water
4 cups rotini macaroni
¾ cup grated Parmesan cheese

The preparation of the vegetables and pasta should be timed so that both are hot and ready to be mixed at the same time.

Place raisins in a small cup, cover with boiling water, and let stand.

Heat the oil in a medium saucepan. Add onions and garlic and sauté over medium heat until onions are soft. Add undrained tomatoes, nutmeg, ½ teaspoon of the salt, and pepper, and simmer, uncovered, about 40 minutes or until sauce has thickened and reduced to about 2½ cups. The sauce can be made ahead of time.

Meanwhile, place the cauliflower in another saucepan. Add just enough water to cover and ½ teaspoon salt. Cover and bring to boil. Reduce heat and boil gently about 5 to 8 minutes or until tender. Drain, then cover to keep warm.

Bring 3 quarts water to a boil in a large pot and add remaining 2 teaspoons salt. Add rotini and boil, uncovered, about 9 to 12 minutes or until tender but still firm, stirring occasionally.

Drain pasta, put in a warm serving bowl, and add tomato sauce and cauliflower. Drain raisins and add to pasta; mix gently to blend. Garnish each serving with 1½ tablespoons grated Parmesan cheese.

*Yield:* 8 servings

*Change Rotini with Cauliflower as follows or use Basic Recipe, if indicated, for:*

LOW-CALORIE, DIABETIC, LOW-FAT, AND LOW-CHOLESTEROL DIETS

Omit raisins.
Reduce oil to 2 tablespoons.
Substitute grated sapsago cheese for Parmesan.
Proceed as in Basic Recipe.

Calories per serving: 232
Approximate nutrient
   values per serving:
     Protein 10 g
     Fat 6 g
     Carbohydrate 35 g
     Sodium 1022 mg
     Potassium 431 mg
     Cholesterol 8 mg
Exchanges:
   Vegetable 1
   Bread 2
   Meat ½
   Fat 1

LOW-SODIUM DIETS

Omit salt.
Substitute 3½ cups canned tomatoes, without added salt, for tomatoes.
Omit Parmesan cheese. Garnish with ⅛ cup chopped fresh Italian parsley.
Proceed as in Basic Recipe.

Calories per serving: 260
Approximate nutrient
   values per serving:
     Protein 7 g
     Fat 8 g
     Carbohydrate 43 g
     Sodium 13 mg
     Potassium 509 mg
     Cholesterol 0 mg

Omit pepper and nutmeg.
Proceed as in Basic Recipe.

HIGH-FIBER DIETS

Use Basic Recipe.

# Macaroni and Cheese au Gratin

BASIC RECIPE

Serving size: ½ cup
Calories per serving: 329
Approximate nutrient
  values per serving:
    Protein 9 g
    Fat 24 g
    Carbohydrate 20 g
    Sodium 495 mg
    Potassium 152 mg
    Cholesterol 63 mg
Exchanges:
  Vegetable 1
  Bread 1
  Meat 1
  Fat 4

4 tablespoons polyunsaturated margarine
½ cup fresh bread crumbs (page 38)
2 cups chopped onions
1½ cups elbow macaroni
1½ quarts boiling water
1 teaspoon salt
¼ teaspoon freshly ground pepper
⅛ teaspoon nutmeg
1½ cups grated Cheddar cheese
1 cup heavy cream

Preheat oven to 375°F.

Melt 1 tablespoon of the margarine in a medium skillet. Add bread crumbs and toss gently to coat. Remove crumbs and set aside.

Melt remaining 3 tablespoons margarine in the same skillet. Add onions and sauté until soft. Remove from heat.

Cook macaroni in 1½ quarts boiling water for 7 to 9 minutes or until tender. Drain in a colander and rinse under cold water.

Transfer macaroni to 2½-quart baking dish. Add sautéed onions, salt, pepper, nutmeg, cheese, and cream. Mix gently to blend. Top with buttered crumbs and bake, uncovered, 15 to 20 minutes or until crumbs are golden brown.

*Yield:* 8 servings

*Change Macaroni and Cheese au Gratin as follows or use Basic Recipe, if indicated, for:*

### LOW-SODIUM DIETS

Omit salt.
Substitute unsalted polyunsaturated margarine for margarine.
Substitute low-sodium Cheddar cheese for Cheddar.
Proceed as in Basic Recipe.
Garnish with ⅓ cup chopped fresh parsley just before serving.

Calories per serving: 326
Approximate nutrient
  values per serving:
    Protein 9 g
    Fat 24 g
    Carbohydrate 20 g
    Sodium 37 mg
    Potassium 179 mg
    Cholesterol 49 mg

### BLAND DIETS

Omit pepper and nutmeg.
Proceed as in Basic Recipe.

Calories per serving: 329

### HIGH-FIBER DIETS

Use Basic Recipe.
Garnish with ⅓ cup chopped fresh parsley just before serving.
For extra fiber, serve with stewed tomatoes or crisp green
    salad.

Calories per serving: 330

### MACARONI AND CHEESE AU GRATIN FOR LOW-CALORIE, DIABETIC, LOW-FAT, AND LOW-CHOLESTEROL DIETS

2 cups chopped onions
1½ cups Beef Stock (page 113)
1½ cups elbow macaroni
1½ quarts boiling water
1 teaspoon salt
¼ teaspoon freshly ground pepper
⅛ teaspoon nutmeg
1½ cups grated part-skim mozzarella cheese
1 cup skim milk
½ cup fresh bread crumbs (page 38)

Serving size: ½ cup
Calories per serving: 155
Approximate nutrient
  values per serving:
    Protein 9 g
    Fat 4 g
    Carbohydrate 21 g
    Sodium 427 mg
    Potassium 203 mg
    Cholesterol 13 mg
Exchanges:
  Vegetable 1
  Bread 1
  Meat 1

Preheat oven to 375°F.

In a small saucepan, simmer onions in beef stock for 10 minutes or until tender. Drain.

Cook macaroni in 1½ quarts boiling water for 7 to 9 minutes or until tender. Drain in a colander and rinse under cold water.

Transfer macaroni to a 2½-quart baking dish. Add onions, salt, pepper, nutmeg, cheese, and milk. Mix gently to blend.

Top with bread crumbs and bake, uncovered, 15 to 20 minutes or until golden.

*Yield:* 8 servings

# Noodles à la Russe

BASIC RECIPE

Serving size: ½ cup
Calories per serving: 290
Approximate nutrient
  values per serving:
    Protein 11 g
    Fat 16 g
    Carbohydrate 25 g
    Sodium 260 mg
    Potassium 172 mg
    Cholesterol 61 mg
Exchanges:
  Vegetable ½
  Bread 1½
  Meat 1
  Fat 2½

2 quarts water
8 ounces wide noodles
2 cups sour cream
1 cup cottage cheese
¼ cup chopped fresh parsley
3 tablespoons finely chopped onions
1 teaspoon Worcestershire sauce
⅛ teaspoon cayenne pepper
⅓ cup grated Parmesan cheese

Preheat oven to 350°F.

In a large saucepan bring 2 quarts water to a boil.

Meanwhile, in a medium-size casserole, combine sour cream, cottage cheese, parsley, onions, Worcestershire sauce, and cayenne pepper.

Cook noodles in boiling water for 5 minutes, drain, and add to the sour cream mixture. Toss gently until well blended. Sprinkle with Parmesan cheese and bake, uncovered, for 30 minutes.

*Yield:* 8 servings

*Change Noodles à la Russe as follows or use Basic Recipe, if indicated, for:*

### LOW-SODIUM AND RENAL DIETS

Calories per serving: 263
Approximate nutrient
   values per serving:
      Protein 9 g
      Fat 15 g
      Carbohydrate 24 g
      Calcium 96 mg
      Phosphorus 138 mg
      Sodium 140 mg
      Potassium 164 mg
      Cholesterol 57 mg

Omit Worcestershire sauce and Parmesan cheese.
Proceed as in Basic Recipe.

### BLAND DIETS

Calories per serving: 290

Omit cayenne pepper.
Proceed as in Basic Recipe.

### HIGH-FIBER DIETS

Calories per serving: 322

Use Basic Recipe. Add ⅓ cup chopped, toasted almonds (page 38) to the Parmesan cheese as garnish.

### NOODLES À LA RUSSE FOR LOW-CALORIE, DIABETIC, LOW-FAT, AND LOW-CHOLESTEROL DIETS

Serving size: ½ cup
Calories per serving: 151
Approximate nutrient
   values per serving:
      Protein 10 g
      Fat 2 g
      Carbohydrate 24 g
      Sodium 169 mg
      Potassium 127 mg
      Cholesterol 29 mg
Exchanges:
  Vegetable ½
  Bread 1½
  Meat ½

8 ounces wide noodles
2 quarts boiling water
1 cup 1 percent low-fat cottage cheese
Low-Cholesterol Egg Substitute (page 189) equivalent to
   2 large eggs
¼ cup chopped fresh parsley
3 tablespoons finely chopped onions
1 teaspoon Worcestershire sauce
⅛ teaspoon cayenne pepper
⅓ cup fresh bread crumbs (page 38)

Preheat oven to 350°F.

Cook noodles in boiling water for 5 minutes. Meanwhile, in a medium-size ovenproof casserole combine cottage cheese, egg substitute, parsley, onions, Worcestershire sauce, and cayenne pepper. Drain noodles, add to the cottage cheese mixture, and toss gently. Sprinkle with bread crumbs. Bake uncovered for 30 minutes.

*Yield:* 8 servings

# Meat and Macaroni

BASIC RECIPE

Serving size: 1 cup
Calories per serving: 304
Approximate nutrient
  values per serving:
    Protein 25 g
    Fat 11 g
    Carbohydrate 25 g
    Sodium 411 mg
    Potassium 486 mg
    Cholesterol 61 mg
Exchanges:
  Vegetable ½
  Bread 1½
  Meat 3
  Fat 1½

2 quarts water
8 ounces elbow macaroni
3 tablespoons polyunsaturated oil
1½ pounds ground round beef
½ cup finely sliced onions
3 cloves garlic, put through garlic press
2 teaspoons thyme
1½ cups sliced peeled tomatoes
1 teaspoon salt
½ teaspoon freshly ground pepper

In a large saucepan bring 2 quarts water to a boil. Add the macaroni and cook about 15 minutes or until tender. Drain in a colander, rinse under cold water, and drain again thoroughly. Set aside.

Heat 2 tablespoons of the oil in a large skillet. Add the meat and stir over high heat until browned. Remove the meat and drain off fat. Add remaining 1 tablespoon oil to skillet and sauté onions, garlic, and thyme until onions are soft. Add the tomatoes, salt, and pepper and simmer for 10 minutes.

Add the macaroni and meat to the onion mixture. Stir until thoroughly mixed and heated through. Serve immediately.

*Yield:* 6 servings

175

*Change Meat and Macaroni as follows for:*

## LOW-CALORIE, DIABETIC, LOW-FAT, AND LOW-CHOLESTEROL DIETS

Reduce oil to 3 teaspoons, using 2 teaspoons to sauté the ground beef, and 1 teaspoon to sauté the onions.
Proceed as in Basic Recipe.

Calories per serving: 264
Approximate nutrient
  values per serving:
    Protein 25 g
    Fat 7 g
    Carbohydrate 25 g
    Sodium 411 mg
    Potassium 486 mg
    Cholesterol 61 mg
Exchanges:
  Vegetable ½
  Bread 1½
  Meat 3
  Fat ½

## LOW-SODIUM DIETS

Omit salt.
Proceed as in Basic Recipe.

Calories per serving: 304
Approximate nutrient
  values same as Basic
  Recipe except for:
    Sodium 45 mg

## BLAND DIETS

Omit pepper.
Proceed as in Basic Recipe.

Calories per serving: 304

## HIGH-FIBER DIETS

After onion and tomato mixture has simmered for 10 minutes, add 1 cup shredded fresh spinach with the macaroni and meat. Stir thoroughly and proceed as in Basic Recipe.

Calories per serving: 306

# Cannelloni col Vitello

BASIC RECIPE

*The Manicotti*
8 manicotti (3½ ounces)
2 quarts boiling water

*The Filling*
1 tablespoon polyunsaturated oil
1 tablespoon basil
½ cup finely chopped celery
½ cup finely chopped onions
½ cup finely chopped carrots
½ cup finely chopped fresh parsley
¼ cup dry white wine
½ pound ground veal
½ teaspoon salt
¼ teaspoon freshly ground pepper
¼ cup dry bread crumbs (page 38)

*The Sauce*
2 tablespoons polyunsaturated margarine
1½ tablespoons flour
½ teaspoon salt
¼ teaspoon white pepper
1¾ cups milk
½ cup grated mozzarella cheese

Preheat oven to 300°F.

*To prepare the manicotti:* In a large saucepan, cook the manicotti in 2 quarts boiling water for 15 minutes or until just tender. Drain in a colander, rinse under cold water, and drain again thoroughly.

*To prepare the filling:* Heat oil in a large skillet. Add basil, celery, onions, and carrots, and sauté until cooked. Add parsley, wine, and veal and cook over high heat 3 to 5 minutes.

Remove from heat and blend in ½ teaspoon salt, ¼ teaspoon pepper, and bread crumbs.

Serving size: 2 manicotti
Calories per serving: 368
Approximate nutrient
   values per serving:
      Protein 20 g
      Fat 21 g
      Carbohydrate 25 g
      Sodium 821 mg
      Potassium 631 mg
      Cholesterol 66 mg
Exchanges:
  Milk ½
  Vegetable 1
  Bread 1
  Meat 2
  Fat 3

177

Fill each manicotti shell with 4 tablespoons of the filling. Place in an ovenproof dish and set aside.

*To prepare the sauce:* In a medium saucepan melt the margarine, blend in the flour, and cook for 1 minute. Add ½ teaspoon salt, ¼ teaspoon pepper, then the milk all at once. Bring to a boil, stirring constantly, then lower heat and continue to cook for 3 minutes.

Pour sauce over manicotti and sprinkle with cheese. Cover with foil. Bake for 20 minutes, then remove foil and continue baking for 10 minutes or until heated through.

*Yield:* 4 servings

*Change Cannelloni col Vitello as follows or use Basic Recipe, if indicated, for:*

LOW-CALORIE, DIABETIC, LOW-FAT, AND LOW-CHOLESTEROL DIETS

*The manicotti and the filling:* Use Basic Recipe.

*The sauce:* Substitute skim milk for milk.

Substitute grated part-skim mozzarella cheese for mozzarella.

Proceed as in Basic Recipe.

Calories per serving: 333
Approximate nutrient
 values per serving:
  Protein 21 g
  Fat 17 g
  Carbohydrate 25 g
  Sodium 838 mg
  Potassium 650 mg
  Cholesterol 50 mg
Exchanges:
 Milk ½
 Vegetable 1
 Bread 1
 Meat 2
 Fat 2

LOW-SODIUM DIETS

*The manicotti:* Use Basic Recipe.

Calories per serving: 392

Approximate nutrient
values per serving:
    Protein 21 g
    Fat 23 g
    Carbohydrate 25 g
    Sodium 192 mg
    Potassium 641 mg
    Cholesterol 60 mg

*The filling:* Omit salt.

*The sauce:* Omit salt.
    Substitute unsalted polyunsaturated margarine for margarine.
    Substitute low-sodium grated Swiss cheese for mozzarella.
    Proceed as in Basic Recipe.

### BLAND DIETS

*The manicotti:* Use Basic Recipe.

*The filling and the sauce:* Omit pepper.
    Proceed as in Basic Recipe.

### HIGH-FIBER DIETS

Use Basic Recipe.

Calories per serving: 368

# Blintzes

### BASIC RECIPE

*The Blintz Batter*
2 large eggs
1⅛ cups milk
2 tablespoons polyunsaturated oil for batter
¼ teaspoon salt
1 cup sifted all-purpose flour
1 teaspoon polyunsaturated oil for greasing crêpe pan
4 teaspoons polyunsaturated margarine for sautéing blintzes

*The Filling*
½ cup raisins
2 cups small-curd cottage cheese
½ teaspoon ground cinnamon

Serving size: 2 blintzes
Calories per serving: 237
Approximate nutrient
    values per serving:
    Protein 11 g
    Fat 11 g
    Carbohydrate 23 g
    Sodium 408 mg
    Potassium 208 mg
    Cholesterol 82 mg
Exchanges:
    Bread 1½
    Meat 1
    Fat 1½

¼ teaspoon salt
1 teaspoon vanilla extract

*To prepare the blintz batter:* Combine eggs, milk, 2 tablespoons oil, salt, and flour in a mixing bowl and beat until smooth. Cover and refrigerate at least 2 hours.

Heat a 6-inch crêpe pan or skillet over medium heat. Brush with 1 teaspoon oil. Then pour 2 tablespoons batter into pan and tip pan to distribute batter evenly over the bottom. Cook blintz until lightly browned on the bottom. Turn and cook until spotted brown on the other side.

Place blintzes on a plate as they are cooked and continue to make blintzes with remaining batter. Do not grease pan again.

*To prepare the filling:* Place raisins in a small cup, cover with boiling water, and let stand for 10 minutes. Drain. Meanwhile, mix all remaining ingredients until thoroughly blended. Add raisins and mix thoroughly.

*To assemble blintzes:* Spread 2 tablespoons of the cottage cheese filling across the center of each blintz. Fold up bottom over filling. Fold over sides and bring top down to form a cylinder-shaped blintz.

Preheat oven to 250°F.

Melt 2 teaspoons margarine reserved for sautéing in a large, heavy skillet. Sauté as many blintzes as will fit, seam side down, until golden brown. Turn carefully with a wide spatula and brown the other side. Transfer to a platter and keep warm in the oven while you repeat the process with the rest of the blintzes, adding the 2 remaining teaspoons of margarine as needed. Serve immediately.

*Yield:* 8 servings

*Change Blintzes as follows or use Basic Recipe, if indicated, for:*

## LOW-CALORIE, DIABETIC, LOW-FAT, AND LOW-CHOLESTEROL DIETS

*The batter:* Substitute skim milk for milk.
   Proceed as in Basic Recipe.

*The filling:* Substitute 1 percent low-fat cottage cheese for cottage cheese.
   Proceed as in Basic Recipe.

*To cook the blintzes:* Preheat oven to 425°F. Omit margarine planned for frying and the frying process. Instead, spray shallow glass baking dish with vegetable cooking spray. Arrange filled blintzes, seam side down, in dish. Bake for 15 minutes or until lightly browned.

## LOW-SODIUM DIETS

*The batter and the filling:* Omit salt.
   Substitute unsalted polyunsaturated margarine for margarine.
   Proceed as in Basic Recipe.

## BLAND DIETS

Use Basic Recipe.

## HIGH-FIBER DIETS

*The batter:* Reduce all-purpose flour to ½ cup. Add ½ cup stone-ground whole wheat flour.
   Proceed as in Basic Recipe.

*The filling:* Use Basic Recipe.

Calories per serving: 190
Approximate nutrient
   values per serving:
      Protein 12 g
      Fat 6 g
      Carbohydrate 23 g
      Sodium 407 mg
      Potassium 219 mg
      Cholesterol 72 mg
Exchanges:
   Bread 1½
   Meat 1
   Fat ½

Calories per serving: 237
Approximate nutrient
   values same as Basic
   Recipe except for:
      Sodium 271 mg

Calories per serving: 236

# Apple Cider Pancakes

BASIC RECIPE

Apple Purée with Rum (Page 633) makes a delicious topping for these pancakes.

Serving size: 2 pancakes
Calories per serving: 268
Approximate nutrient
  values per serving:
    Protein 6 g
    Fat 8 g
    Carbohydrate 44 g
    Sodium 363 mg
    Potassium 140 mg
    Cholesterol 69 mg
Exchanges:
    Fruit 1½
    Bread 2
    Meat ½
    Fat 1

1½ cups sifted all-purpose flour
1½ teaspoons baking powder
¼ teaspoon salt
2 tablespoons polyunsaturated margarine
¼ teaspoon ground cinnamon
1 teaspoon grated orange rind
1¼ cups unsweetened apple cider
1 large egg, slightly beaten

Sift flour, baking powder, and salt together into large mixing bowl.

Melt margarine in a small saucepan and blend in cinnamon and orange rind. Add to flour mixture with cider and beaten egg and stir just until blended. Let batter stand 30 minutes before making pancakes.

Cook pancakes on a preheated nonstick griddle, allowing ¼ cup batter per pancake. Unused batter may be stored, tightly covered, in the refrigerator.

*Yield:* 4 servings

*Change Apple Cider Pancakes as follows or use Basic Recipe, if indicated, for:*

### LOW-CALORIE, DIABETIC, LOW-FAT, AND LOW-CHOLESTEROL DIETS

Calories per serving: 235
Approximate nutrient
   values per serving:
     Protein 7 g
     Fat 3 g
     Carbohydrate 45 g
     Sodium 349 mg
     Potassium 163 mg
     Cholesterol 0 mg
Exchanges:
   Fruit 1½
   Bread 2
   Meat ½
   Fat ½

Reduce margarine to 1 tablespoon.
Omit egg and use Low-Cholesterol Egg Substitute (page 189) equivalent to 1 large egg.
Proceed as in Basic Recipe.

### LOW-SODIUM AND RENAL DIETS

Calories per serving: 268
Approximate nutrient
   values same as Basic
   Recipe except for:
     Calcium 47 mg
     Phosphorus 108 mg
     Sodium 169 mg

Omit salt.
Substitute unsalted polyunsaturated margarine for margarine.
Proceed as in Basic Recipe.

### BLAND DIETS

Use Basic Recipe.

### HIGH-FIBER DIETS

Calories per serving: 265

Reduce 1½ cups all-purpose flour to 1 cup. Add to it ½ cup stone-ground whole wheat flour.
Proceed as in Basic Recipe.

# Crêpes

For entrée fillings, you could use Crabmeat Amandine (Page 84) or Turkey Curry (Page 381). As a dessert, they would go well with Orange Cream Filling (Page 635) or Strawberry Pineapple Conserve (Page 639).

Serving size: 2 crêpes
Calories per serving: 133
Approximate nutrient
   values per serving:
     Protein 4 g
     Fat 7 g
     Carbohydrate 13 g
     Sodium 106 mg
     Potassium 91 mg
     Cholesterol 74 mg
Exchanges:
   Bread 1
   Meat ½
   Fat 1

2 large eggs
1⅛ cups milk
2 tablespoons polyunsaturated oil for batter
¼ teaspoon salt
1 cup sifted all-purpose flour
1 teaspoon polyunsaturated oil for greasing pan

Place eggs, milk, the 2 tablespoons oil, salt, and flour in the container of an electric blender. Blend until smooth. Cover batter and refrigerate at least 2 hours.

Heat a 6-inch crêpe pan and brush with 1 teaspoon oil. Pour 2 tablespoons batter into pan and tip to distribute evenly over the bottom of pan.

Cook until lightly browned on bottom. Turn and cook another minute. Place on wax paper to cool. Do not brush pan with any more oil. Repeat process until all the crêpes are cooked.

*Yield:* 16 crêpes

*Change Crêpes as follows or use Basic Recipe, if indicated, for:*

## LOW-CALORIE, DIABETIC, LOW-FAT, AND LOW-CHOLESTEROL DIETS

Substitute skim milk for milk.
Proceed as in Basic Recipe.

Calories per serving: 121
Approximate nutrient
  values per serving:
    Protein 4 g
    Fat 6 g
    Carbohydrate 13 g
    Sodium 107 mg
    Potassium 98 mg
    Cholesterol 69 mg
Exchanges:
  Bread 1
  Meat ½
  Fat ½

## LOW-SODIUM AND RENAL DIETS

Omit salt.
Proceed as in Basic Recipe.

Calories per serving: 133
Approximate nutrient
  values same as Basic
  Recipe except for:
    Calcium 58 mg
    Phosphorus 73 mg
    Sodium 37 mg

## BLAND AND HIGH-FIBER DIETS

Use Basic Recipe.

# Scandinavian Waffles

BASIC RECIPE

Serving size: 1 waffle
Calories per serving: 379
Approximate nutrient
    values per serving:
        Protein 5 g
        Fat 29 g
        Carbohydrate 24 g
        Sodium 373 mg
        Potassium 85 mg
        Cholesterol 148 mg
Exchanges:
    Bread 1½
    Meat ½
    Fat 5½

1½ cups sifted all-purpose flour
2 tablespoons sugar
1 tablespoon baking powder
¼ teaspoon salt
1½ cups heavy cream
⅓ cup polyunsaturated margarine, melted
2 large eggs, separated
vegetable cooking spray

Sift flour, sugar, baking powder, and salt into a large mixing bowl.

In a medium bowl, mix together cream, margarine, and egg yolks. Add to flour mixture and stir only until flour is moist.

In a separate bowl, beat egg whites until stiff and fold into batter. Let batter stand for 1 hour. Spray waffle iron with vegetable cooking spray and preheat. Use ½ cup batter for each waffle.

*Yield:* 7 servings

*Change Scandinavian Waffles as follows or use Basic Recipe, if indicated, for:*

LOW-SODIUM AND RENAL DIETS

Calories per serving: 379
Approximate nutrient
    values same as Basic
    Recipe except for:
        Calcium 75 mg
        Phosphorus 124 mg
        Sodium 209 mg

Omit salt.
Substitute unsalted polyunsaturated margarine for margarine.
Proceed as in Basic Recipe.

BLAND DIETS

Use Basic Recipe.

Calories per serving: 378

Serving size: 1 waffle
Calories per serving: 195
Approximate nutrient
  values per serving:
    Protein 7 g
    Fat 8 g
    Carbohydrate 25 g
    Sodium 362 mg
    Potassium 181 mg
    Cholesterol 3 mg
Exchanges:
  Bread 2
  Meat ½
  Fat 1

## HIGH-FIBER DIETS

Reduce all-purpose flour to 1 cup; add to it ½ cup stone-ground whole wheat flour.
Proceed as in Basic Recipe.

## SCANDINAVIAN WAFFLES FOR LOW-CALORIE, DIABETIC, LOW-FAT, AND LOW-CHOLESTEROL DIETS

1½ cups sifted all-purpose flour
1 tablespoon sugar
1 teaspoon baking soda
¼ teaspoon salt
1½ cups plain low-fat yogurt
½ cup skim milk
¼ cup polyunsaturated margarine, melted
2 large egg whites
vegetable cooking spray

Sift flour, sugar, baking soda, and salt into a large mixing bowl.

In a medium bowl, mix together yogurt, milk, and margarine. Add to flour mixture and stir only until flour is moist.

In a separate bowl, beat egg whites until stiff and fold into batter. Let batter stand 1 hour. Spray waffle iron with vegetable cooking spray and preheat. Use ½ cup batter for each waffle.

*Yield:* 7 servings

# E G G S

*Eggs are high in protein and relatively low in price. They combine readily with cheeses, vegetables, and sauces and, as an entrée, are a substitute for a meat, fish, or poultry course. Your doctor may have limited you to no more than three eggs a week, suggested an even smaller quota, or given you no limitations whatsoever. Although research has suggested that whole eggs may elevate cholesterol in the bloodstream of some people, the nutritive merits of eggs are undisputed. Our egg dishes run the gamut from Asparagus Soufflé to Tomato Custard, from Eggs Benedict to Omelet Mexicana. All are delicious and have been modified to preserve their appeal, even when egg yolks have been eliminated in behalf of special diet needs and our own egg substitute used instead.*

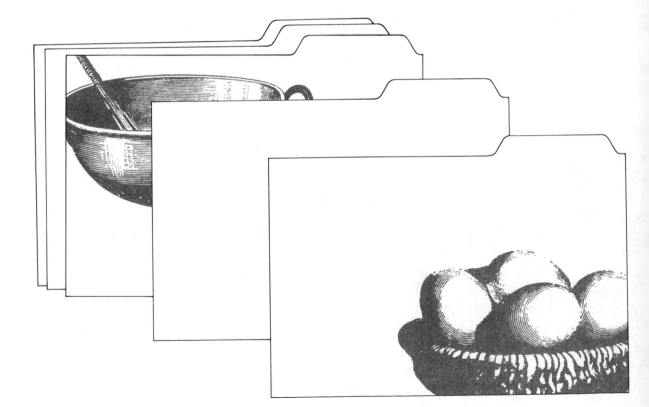

# Low-Cholesterol Egg Substitute

SUITABLE FOR LOW-CALORIE, DIABETIC, LOW-FAT, LOW-CHOLESTEROL, LOW-SODIUM, RENAL, BLAND, AND HIGH-FIBER DIETS

Serving size: equivalent of
   1 large egg
Calories per serving: 48
Approximate nutrient
   values per serving:
      Protein 8 g
      Fat 0 g
      Carbohydrate 3 g
      Calcium 60 mg
      Phosphorus 49 mg
      Sodium 124 mg
      Potassium 163 mg
      Cholesterol 1 mg
Exchanges:
   Milk ¼
   Meat ½

1 tablespoon nonfat dry milk powder
2 large egg whites
4 drops yellow food color

Sprinkle dry milk powder over egg whites and beat with fork until smooth. Add food color and beat until well blended.

*Yield:* Equivalent of 1 large egg

# Eggs Benedict

BASIC RECIPE

Serving size: 1 egg, ½
   muffin, 2 ounces ham, 2
   tablespoons sauce
Calories per serving: 512
Approximate nutrient
   values per serving:
      Protein 20 g
      Fat 39 g
      Carbohydrate 22 g
      Sodium 1324 mg
      Potassium 367 mg
      Cholesterol 440 mg
Exchanges:
   Bread 1½
   Meat 2½
   Fat 6

3 Homemade English Muffins (page 135)
¾ cup Hollandaise Sauce (page 390)

*The Eggs and Ham*
6 large eggs
6 thin slices cooked ham (12 ounces)
2 tablespoons polyunsaturated margarine
6 watercress sprigs

For this recipe, make the English muffins first. When ready to assemble, first make the hollandaise sauce and keep it warm. You can sauté the ham and toast the muffins while you are poaching the eggs. Though you can prepare the eggs ahead of time and then reheat them briefly in hot, not boiling, water, it is best to coordinate the dish with close timing.

*To poach eggs:* Fill a large skillet with 1 inch of water and bring to a slow simmer. Working quickly, break eggs, one at a time, into a cup, then slip each egg into the water. Cover and simmer 3 to 5 minutes. When eggs are poached, carefully remove with a slotted spoon and drain on paper towels. If eggs are prepared ahead of time, they may be reheated briefly in hot, not boiling, water.

*To assemble Eggs Benedict:* Sauté ham in margarine until warm. Split and toast English muffins.

Place one-half English muffin on a warm serving plate; top with a slice of ham. Carefully place a poached egg on ham and spoon hollandaise sauce over all. Garnish with sprig of watercress and serve at once.

*Yield:* 6 servings

*Change Eggs Benedict as follows or use Basic Recipe, if indicated, for:*

LOW-CALORIE, DIABETIC, LOW-FAT, AND LOW-CHOLESTEROL DIETS

*The English muffins:* Substitute low-calorie English Muffins (page 136) for basic English Muffins.

*The hollandaise sauce:* Substitute low-calorie Hollandaise Sauce (page 391) for basic Hollandaise Sauce.

*The eggs and ham:* Use 1 tablespoon polyunsaturated margarine for sautéing ham.

Proceed as in Basic Recipe.

Serving size: 1 egg, ½ muffin, 2 ounces ham, 2 tablespoons sauce
Calories per serving: 345
Approximate nutrient values per serving:
Protein 19 g
Fat 20 g
Carbohydrate 23 g
Sodium 1160 mg
Potassium 389 mg
Cholesterol 303 mg
Exchanges:
Bread 1½
Meat 2½
Fat 2

Calories per serving: 482
Approximate nutrient
 values per serving:
  Protein 29 g
  Fat 32 g
  Carbohydrate 20 g
  Sodium 256 mg
  Potassium 419 mg
  Cholesterol 455 mg

Calories per serving: 512

## LOW-SODIUM DIETS

*The English muffins:* Substitute low-sodium English Muffins (page 136) for basic English Muffins.

*The hollandaise sauce:* Substitute low-sodium Hollandaise Sauce (page 391) for basic Hollandaise Sauce.

*The eggs and ham:* Substitute sliced cooked turkey for the ham. Substitute unsalted polyunsaturated margarine for margarine.

## BLAND DIETS

*The English muffins:* Use Basic Recipe.

*The hollandaise sauce:* Use bland Hollandaise Sauce (page 391).

*The eggs and ham:* Use Basic Recipe.

## HIGH-FIBER DIETS

Use Basic Recipe.

# Gratin of Eggs and Mushrooms

BASIC RECIPE

Serving size: ⅔ cup
Calories per serving: 306
Approximate nutrient
 values per serving:
  Protein 15 g
  Fat 22 g
  Carbohydrate 12 g
  Sodium 625 mg
  Potassium 301 mg
  Cholesterol 297 mg
Exchanges:
 Vegetable 1
 Bread ½
 Meat 2
 Fat 3

1 cup sliced leeks, white part only
1½ cups sliced fresh mushrooms
⅓ cup polyunsaturated margarine
⅓ cup flour
1 cup Chicken Stock (page 114)
1 cup milk
1 teaspoon salt
½ teaspoon marjoram
¼ teaspoon oregano
¼ teaspoon freshly ground pepper
6 hard-cooked large eggs
1 cup grated Swiss cheese

Sauté leeks and mushrooms in margarine until tender. Stir in flour. Gradually add stock and milk, then cook over moderate heat, stirring constantly, until sauce comes to a boil and thickens.

Remove from heat; season with salt, marjoram, oregano, and pepper.

Preheat broiler.

Slice eggs ½ inch thick. Mix gently into sauce.

Spoon into a shallow 1½-quart baking dish. Sprinkle with cheese and broil until golden brown.

*Yield:* 6 servings

*Change Gratin of Eggs and Mushrooms as follows or use Basic Recipe, if indicated, for:*

### LOW-CALORIE, DIABETIC, LOW-FAT, AND LOW-CHOLESTEROL DIETS

Calories per serving: 216
Approximate nutrient
  values per serving:
    Protein 14 g
    Fat 13 g
    Carbohydrate 12 g
    Sodium 603 mg
    Potassium 301 mg
    Cholesterol 286 mg
Exchanges:
  Vegetable 1
  Bread ½
  Meat 2

Reduce margarine to 2 tablespoons.
Substitute skim milk for milk.
Substitute grated part-skim mozzarella cheese for Swiss.
Proceed as in Basic Recipe.

### LOW-SODIUM DIETS

Calories per serving: 321
Approximate nutrient
  values per serving:
    Protein 14 g
    Fat 23 g
    Carbohydrate 11 g
    Sodium 149 mg
    Potassium 307 mg
    Cholesterol 287 mg

Omit salt.
Substitute unsalted polyunsaturated margarine for margarine.
Substitute grated low-sodium Swiss cheese for Swiss.
Proceed as in Basic Recipe.

### BLAND DIETS

Calories per serving: 306

Omit pepper.
Proceed as in Basic Recipe.

### HIGH-FIBER DIETS

Use Basic Recipe.

# Omelet Mexicana

BASIC RECIPE

Serving size: ½ omelet
Calories per serving: 330
Approximate nutrient
  values per serving:
    Protein 9 g
    Fat 30 g
    Carbohydrate 11 g
    Sodium 409 mg
    Potassium 847 mg
    Cholesterol 274 mg
Exchanges:
  Vegetable 2
  Meat 1
  Fat 5½

1 tablespoon polyunsaturated margarine
2 tablespoons minced shallots
2 tablespoons minced sweet red pepper
1 large avocado
1½ tablespoons lemon juice
2 large eggs
2 tablespoons water
¼ teaspoon salt
⅛ teaspoon freshly ground pepper
4 sprigs watercress

Heat margarine in a 6-inch skillet. Add shallots and sweet pepper; sauté until shallots are soft but not brown. Remove from heat.

Dice half the avocado and slice the other half in 4 crescents. Sprinkle thoroughly with the lemon juice to keep from darkening. Set aside.

Beat eggs, water, salt, and ground pepper until yolks and whites are well blended. Return skillet with shallots and sweet pepper to burner, turn heat to medium, and add egg mixture. As omelet sets at edges, move eggs toward center with a spatula to allow uncooked egg to flow underneath. When omelet is browned on bottom and the top is barely set, transfer to a heated serving dish.

Spoon diced avocado over half of omelet. Fold omelet and garnish with avocado slices and watercress sprigs.

*Yield:* 2 servings

*Change Omelet Mexicana as follows or use Basic Recipe, if indicated, for:*

## LOW-SODIUM DIETS

Calories per serving: 330
Approximate nutrient
   values same as Basic
   Recipe except for:
     Sodium 77 mg

Omit salt.
Substitute unsalted polyunsaturated margarine for margarine.
Proceed as in Basic Recipe.

## BLAND DIETS

Calories per serving: 330

Omit ground pepper.
Proceed as in Basic Recipe.

## HIGH-FIBER DIETS

Use Basic Recipe.

## OMELET MEXICANA FOR LOW-CALORIE, DIABETIC, LOW-FAT, AND LOW-CHOLESTEROL DIETS

Serving size: ½ omelet
Calories per serving: 94
Approximate nutrient
   values per serving:
     Protein 9 g
     Fat 4 g
     Carbohydrate 6 g
     Sodium 442 mg
     Potassium 284 mg
     Cholesterol 1 mg
Exchanges:
   Vegetable 1
   Meat 1
   Fat ½

2 teaspoons polyunsaturated margarine
2 tablespoons minced shallots
2 tablespoons minced sweet red pepper
¼ cup diced green pepper
Low-Cholesterol Egg Substitute (page 189) equivalent to
   2 large eggs
¼ teaspoon salt
⅛ teaspoon freshly ground pepper
4 sprigs watercress

Heat margarine in a 6-inch skillet. Add shallots, sweet red pepper, and green pepper and sauté until shallots are soft. Remove from heat.

    Beat egg substitute, salt, and pepper with a fork. Return skillet with shallots and peppers to heat and add egg mixture. As omelet sets at edges, move eggs toward center with a spatula to allow uncooked egg to flow underneath. When omelet is browned on bottom and top is set, transfer to a heated serving dish.

Fold omelet in half and garnish with watercress.

*Yield:* 2 servings

OMELET MEXICANA FOR RENAL DIETS

1 tablespoon unsalted polyunsaturated margarine
2 tablespoons minced shallots
2 tablespoons minced sweet red pepper
2 large eggs
2 tablespoons water
⅛ teaspoon freshly ground pepper
¼ cup diced cooked fresh asparagus
4 cooked fresh asparagus tips for garnish

Heat the margarine in a small skillet. Add shallots and sweet pepper; sauté until shallots are soft but not brown. Remove from heat.

Beat eggs, water, and ground pepper until yolks and whites are well blended. Return skillet with shallots and sweet pepper to heat and add egg mixture.

As omelet sets at edges, move eggs toward center to allow uncooked egg to flow to bottom. When omelet is browned on bottom and the top is set, transfer to a heated serving dish. Spoon diced asparagus over half of omelet. Fold omelet and garnish with asparagus tips.

*Yield:* 2 servings

Serving size: ½ omelet
Calories per serving: 149
Approximate nutrient
  values per serving:
    Protein 8 g
    Fat 11 g
    Carbohydrate 5 g
    Calcium 46 mg
    Phosphorus 130 mg
    Sodium 72 mg
    Potassium 228 mg
    Cholesterol 274 mg
Exchanges:
    Vegetable 1
    Meat 1
    Fat 1½

# Omelet Supreme

BASIC RECIPE

Serving size: ⅙ omelet
Calories per serving: 274
Approximate nutrient
    values per serving:
        Protein 12 g
        Fat 22 g
        Carbohydrate 6 g
        Sodium 541 mg
        Potassium 173 mg
        Cholesterol 294 mg
Exchanges:
    Bread ½
    Meat 1½
    Fat 3½

*The Sauce*
4 tablespoons polyunsaturated margarine
3 tablespoons flour
1 cup milk
½ teaspoon basil
¼ teaspoon oregano
⅓ cup prosciutto ham, thinly sliced and cut in bite-size strips
⅓ cup grated mozzarella cheese

*The Omelet*
6 large eggs
½ teaspoon salt
⅛ teaspoon freshly ground pepper
2 tablespoons polyunsaturated margarine
⅓ cup grated mozzarella cheese

*To prepare the sauce:* In a small saucepan, heat 4 tablespoons margarine. Blend in flour. Gradually add milk; cook and stir over moderate heat until sauce comes to a boil. Boil and stir 1 minute. Remove from heat; season with basil and oregano. Mix in prosciutto ham and ⅓ cup mozzarella. Set aside.

Preheat broiler.

*To prepare the omelet:* In a mixing bowl beat together eggs, salt, and pepper.

In an omelet pan or skillet with an ovenproof handle, heat 2 tablespoons margarine until foamy. When foam has almost subsided, pour in egg mixture.

Cook over low heat, gently lifting cooked portion at edge with a spatula to allow uncooked egg to flow underneath. When bottom of omelet is browned and top is soft but not runny, remove from heat.

Cover omelet with sauce and sprinkle with remaining cheese. Broil until golden brown. Cut into 6 wedges and serve.

*Yield:* 6 servings

*Change Omelet Supreme as follows or use Basic Recipe, if indicated, for:*

LOW-CALORIE, DIABETIC, LOW-FAT, AND LOW-CHOLESTEROL DIETS

*The sauce:* Reduce polyunsaturated margarine to 2 tablespoons. Substitute skim milk for milk.

*The omelet:* Omit eggs. Use Low-Cholesterol Egg Substitute (page 189) equivalent to 6 large eggs.
   Proceed as in Basic Recipe.

Calories per serving: 197
Approximate nutrient
   values per serving:
      Protein 14 g
      Fat 12 g
      Carbohydrate 9 g
      Sodium 559 mg
      Potassium 276 mg
      Cholesterol 15 mg
Exchanges:
   Bread ½
   Meat 2
   Fat 1½

LOW-SODIUM DIETS

*The sauce:* Substitute unsalted polyunsaturated margarine for margarine.
   Substitute diced cooked shrimp for the prosciutto ham.
   Substitute ⅓ cup grated low-sodium Swiss cheese for mozzarella. Proceed as in Basic Recipe.

*The omelet:* Omit salt.
   Substitute unsalted polyunsaturated margarine for margarine.
   Substitute ⅓ cup grated low-sodium Swiss cheese for mozzarella. Proceed as in Basic Recipe.

Calories per serving: 288
Approximate nutrient
   values per serving:
      Protein 13 g
      Fat 22 g
      Carbohydrate 6 g
      Sodium 133 mg
      Potassium 169 mg
      Cholesterol 296 mg

BLAND DIETS

*The sauce:* Use Basic Recipe.

*The omelet:* Omit pepper. Proceed as in Basic Recipe.

Calories per serving: 274

Calories per serving: 275

*The sauce:* Add ¼ cup chopped green pepper to sauce with the seasonings.

Proceed as in Basic Recipe.

*The omelet:* Use Basic Recipe.

# Farmer's Omelet

## BASIC RECIPE

Serving size: ⅙ omelet
Calories per serving: 187
Approximate nutrient
  values per serving:
    Protein 8 g
    Fat 13 g
    Carbohydrate 10 g
    Sodium 424 mg
    Potassium 267 mg
    Cholesterol 274 mg
Exchanges:
  Vegetable 2
  Meat 1
  Fat 2

4 tablespoons polyunsaturated margarine
1½ cups diced cooked potatoes
½ cup chopped onions
⅓ cup chopped green pepper
6 large eggs
¼ cup water
¾ teaspoon salt
⅛ teaspoon freshly ground pepper
1½ cups fresh bean sprouts

Preheat broiler.

Heat the margarine in a medium-size ovenproof skillet. Add potatoes, onions, and green pepper and sauté until onions are soft.

In a large bowl beat eggs, water, salt, and pepper. Pour over vegetables in skillet and cook over low heat, gently pushing the edge of the omelet toward the center to allow the uncooked egg to flow to the bottom. When bottom of omelet is nicely browned and top is set, place skillet under preheated broiler and cook until golden brown, about 1 minute.

Cut in wedges and garnish with bean sprouts before serving.

*Yield:* 6 servings

*Change Farmer's Omelet as follows or use Basic Recipe, if indicated, for:*

## LOW-SODIUM AND RENAL DIETS

Calories per serving: 187
Approximate nutrient
  values same as Basic
  Recipe except for:
    Calcium 40 mg
    Phosphorus 128 mg
    Sodium 74 mg

Omit salt.
Substitute unsalted polyunsaturated margarine for margarine.
Proceed as in Basic Recipe.

## BLAND DIETS

Calories per serving: 187

Omit ground pepper.
Proceed as in Basic Recipe.

## HIGH-FIBER DIETS

Use Basic Recipe.

## FARMER'S OMELET FOR LOW-CALORIE, DIABETIC, LOW-FAT, AND LOW-CHOLESTEROL DIETS

Serving size: ⅙ omelet
Calories per serving: 122
Approximate nutrient
  values per serving:
    Protein 10 g
    Fat 4 g
    Carbohydrate 12 g
    Sodium 441 mg
    Potassium 363 mg
    Cholesterol 1 mg
Exchanges:
  Bread 1
  Meat 1

2 tablespoons polyunsaturated margarine
½ cup chopped onions
⅓ cup chopped green pepper
Low-Calorie Egg Substitute (page 189) equivalent to 6 large
  eggs
¾ teaspoon salt
⅛ teaspoon freshly ground pepper
1½ cups diced cooked potatoes
1½ cups fresh bean sprouts

Preheat broiler.
  Heat the margarine in a medium-size ovenproof skillet. Add onions and green pepper and sauté until onions are soft.
  In a large bowl combine the egg substitute, salt, and pepper. Pour over vegetables in skillet and cook over low heat, gently

pushing the edge of the omelet toward the center to allow the uncooked egg to flow to the bottom. When bottom of omelet is nicely browned and the top is set, arrange cooked potatoes over omelet, place skillet under broiler, and cook until golden brown, about 1 minute.

Cut into wedges and garnish with bean sprouts before serving.

*Yield:* 6 servings

# Tomato and Basil Omelet

BASIC RECIPE

*The Sauce*
1½ tablespoons olive oil
⅓ cup finely chopped onions
2 cloves garlic, finely chopped
1½ teaspoons basil
2 cups diced peeled tomatoes

*The Omelet*
6 large eggs
6 tablespoons water
½ teaspoon salt
¼ teaspoon freshly ground pepper
½ tablespoon olive oil

*To prepare the sauce:* Heat 1½ tablespoons olive oil in a large skillet over medium heat. Add onions, garlic, and basil. Sauté until onions are soft. Add tomatoes and cook over high heat for 10 to 15 minutes, stirring occasionally, until the tomato mixture thickens. Set aside.

*To prepare the omelet:* Preheat a second large skillet. Whisk eggs with water, salt, and pepper in a large bowl until well blended.

Pour remaining ½ tablespoon oil into the preheated skillet. Reduce heat and add the omelet mixture. Cook over low heat,

Serving size: ⅙ omelet, 2½ tablespoons sauce
Calories per serving: 143
Approximate nutrient values per serving:
Protein 7 g
Fat 10 g
Carbohydrate 6 g
Sodium 256 mg
Potassium 299 mg
Cholesterol 274 mg
Exchanges:
Vegetable 1
Meat 1
Fat 1½

gently pushing the edge of the omelet toward the center, allowing the uncooked egg to flow to the bottom. When the bottom of the omelet is nicely browned and the top is set, remove to a warm serving dish.

Spoon tomato sauce over omelet; fold in half. Serve immediately.

*Yield:* 6 servings omelet, 1 cup sauce

*Change Tomato and Basil Omelet as follows or use Basic Recipe, if indicated, for:*

LOW-CALORIE, DIABETIC, LOW-FAT, AND LOW-CHOLESTEROL DIETS

*The sauce:* Reduce oil to 1 tablespoon.
Proceed as in Basic Recipe.

*The omelet:* Omit whole eggs. Use Low-Cholesterol Egg Substitute (page 189) equivalent to 6 large eggs.
Omit oil reserved for cooking omelet. Spray skillet with vegetable cooking spray.
Proceed as in Basic Recipe.

LOW-SODIUM DIETS

*The sauce:* Use Basic Recipe.

*The omelet:* Omit salt. Substitute 1 teaspoon dillweed and whisk into egg mixture.
Proceed as in Basic Recipe.

Calories per serving: 92
Approximate nutrient
  values per serving:
    Protein 9 g
    Fat 3 g
    Carbohydrate 8 g
    Sodium 310 mg
    Potassium 397 mg
    Cholesterol 1 mg
Exchanges:
  Vegetable 1
  Meat 1
  Fat ½

Calories per serving: 143
Approximate nutrient
  values same as Basic
  Recipe except for:
    Sodium 73 mg
    Potassium 305 mg

Calories per serving: 143

*The sauce:* Use Basic Recipe.

*The omelet:* Omit pepper.
    Proceed as in Basic Recipe.

HIGH-FIBER DIETS

Calories per serving: 146

*The sauce:* Add ½ cup diced green peppers and sauté with onions, garlic, and basil in preparing the sauce.
    Proceed as in Basic Recipe.

*The omelet:* Use Basic Recipe.

# Spanish Omelets

BASIC RECIPE

Serving size: ½ omelet, ¼
    cup sauce
Calories per serving: 171
Approximate nutrient
    values per serving:
    Protein 7 g
    Fat 14 g
    Carbohydrate 5 g
    Sodium 520 mg
    Potassium 273 mg
    Cholesterol 274 mg
Exchanges:
    Vegetable 1
    Meat 1
    Fat 2

*The Sauce*
3 tablespoons olive oil
½ cup thinly sliced leeks, white part only
⅓ cup chopped green pepper
⅓ cup chopped celery
2 cloves garlic, put through garlic press
2 cups coarsely chopped peeled tomatoes
½ teaspoon salt
⅛ teaspoon freshly ground pepper
½ teaspoon oregano
½ teaspoon basil
1 bay leaf

*The Omelets*
8 large eggs
8 tablespoons water
1 teaspoon salt
¼ teaspoon freshly ground pepper
2 tablespoons polyunsaturated margarine

*To prepare the sauce:* Heat the olive oil in a medium saucepan. Add leeks, green pepper, celery, and garlic. Sauté until leeks are soft. Add tomatoes, salt, pepper, oregano, basil, and bay leaf. Simmer, uncovered, 30 minutes or until sauce is thickened and reduced to 2 cups. Stir occasionally. Remove bay leaf.

*To prepare the omelets:* Divide remaining ingredients into 4 equal parts. For each omelet, beat 2 eggs with 2 tablespoons water, ¼ teaspoon salt, and 1 twist of the pepper mill.

Heat 1½ teaspoons of the margarine in a 6-inch omelet pan until foam subsides. Pour in 2 beaten eggs. As edges set, lift with a spatula so the uncooked eggs run under the omelet. When eggs are almost done, spoon ¼ cup sauce in center of omelet and fold in half.

Transfer to a heated serving dish and spoon another ¼ cup sauce over top of omelet.

Repeat until 4 omelets are completed.

*Yield:* 8 servings (4 omelets, 2 cups sauce)

*Change Spanish Omelets as follows or use Basic Recipe, if indicated, for:*

LOW-CALORIE, DIABETIC, LOW-FAT, AND LOW-CHOLESTEROL DIETS

*The sauce:* Omit olive oil and sautéing. Combine all vegetables and spices in saucepan and simmer, uncovered, as in Basic Recipe.

*The omelets:* Omit eggs. Use Low-Cholesterol Egg Substitute (page 189) equivalent to 8 large eggs. When bottom of omelet is browned, turn and cook on other side. Fill and top with sauce and fold as in Basic Recipe.

Calories per serving: 94
Approximate nutrient
  values per serving:
    Protein 9 g
    Fat 3 g
    Carbohydrate 8 g
    Sodium 574 mg
    Potassium 371 mg
    Cholesterol 1 mg
Exchanges:
  Vegetable 1½
  Meat 1

## LOW-SODIUM DIETS

*The sauce:* Omit salt.

*The omelet:* Substitute unsalted polyunsaturated margarine for margarine. Omit salt.
    Proceed as in Basic Recipe.

Calories per serving: 171
Approximate nutrient
    values same as Basic
    Recipe except for:
        Sodium 79 mg

## BLAND DIETS

*The sauce and the omelet:* Omit ground pepper.
    Proceed as in Basic Recipe.

Calories per serving: 171

## HIGH-FIBER DIETS

Use Basic Recipe.

# Spinach Frittata

BASIC RECIPE

10 ounces fresh spinach
6 large eggs
⅓ cup grated Parmesan cheese
¼ cup chopped fresh parsley
½ teaspoon salt
⅛ teaspoon freshly ground pepper
2 cloves garlic, put through garlic press
2 tablespoons polyunsaturated margarine

Wash spinach thoroughly and trim off tough stems. Place spinach in a large pot with only the water that clings to the leaves. Cook, covered, about 5 minutes or until just tender. Drain thoroughly and chop coarsely.

Serving size: ⅙ frittata
Calories per serving: 163
Approximate nutrient
    values per serving:
        Protein 11 g
        Fat 12 g
        Carbohydrate 4 g
        Sodium 472 mg
        Potassium 321 mg
        Cholesterol 283 mg
Exchanges:
    Vegetable 1
    Meat 1½
    Fat 1½

In a large bowl beat eggs with cheese, parsley, salt, pepper, and garlic. Stir the spinach into this mixture. Set aside.

Preheat broiler.

Heat margarine in heavy ovenproof 8-inch skillet. Add egg and spinach mixture and cook over low heat 10 to 15 minutes or until bottom of frittata is nicely browned; the top need not be set.

Place skillet under broiler and broil until top has set and egg is golden brown. Serve in wedges.

*Yield:* 6 servings

*Change Spinach Frittata as follows or use Basic Recipe, if indicated, for:*

LOW-CALORIE, DIABETIC, LOW-FAT, AND LOW-CHOLESTEROL DIETS

Omit eggs. Use Low-Cholesterol Egg Substitute (page 189) equivalent to 6 large eggs.

Increase salt to ¾ teaspoon.

Omit Parmesan cheese. Sprinkle ½ cup grated part-skim mozzarella cheese over frittata before broiling; then broil until cheese melts and becomes golden brown.

LOW-SODIUM DIETS

Omit salt and Parmesan cheese.

Combine ¼ teaspoon oregano and ¼ teaspoon basil and add to egg mixture.

Substitute unsalted polyunsaturated margarine for margarine.

Sprinkle ½ cup grated low-sodium Swiss cheese over frittata before broiling. Then broil until cheese melts and becomes golden brown.

Calories per serving: 112
Approximate nutrient
  values per serving:
    Protein 11 g
    Fat 5 g
    Carbohydrate 6 g
    Sodium 500 mg
    Potassium 415 mg
    Cholesterol 7 mg
Exchanges:
  Vegetable 1
  Meat 1½
  Fat 1

Calories per serving: 170
Approximate nutrient
  values per serving:
    Protein 10 g
    Fat 13 g
    Carbohydrate 3 g
    Sodium 124 mg
    Potassium 327 mg
    Cholesterol 280 mg

Omit pepper.
Proceed as in Basic Recipe.

HIGH-FIBER DIETS

Use Basic Recipe.

Calories per serving: 163

# Asparagus Soufflé

BASIC RECIPE

*The Soufflé*
3 tablespoons polyunsaturated margarine
3 tablespoons flour
1 cup milk
½ teaspoon salt
⅛ teaspoon cayenne pepper
4 large eggs, at room temperature, separated
1 cup finely chopped cooked asparagus
¼ teaspoon cream of tartar

*The Sauce*
1 cup Chicken Stock (page 114)
½ cup dry white wine
1 small carrot, sliced
2 mushrooms, sliced
¼ cup chopped onions
1 sprig fresh parsley
1 small bay leaf
4 tablespoons polyunsaturated margarine
1½ tablespoons flour
¼ teaspoon salt
⅛ teaspoon freshly ground pepper
½ teaspoon dillweed

Serving size: ¼ soufflé, 2
   tablespoons sauce
Calories per serving: 279
Approximate nutrient
   values per serving:
      Protein 10 g
      Fat 22 g
      Carbohydrate 11 g
      Sodium 599 mg
      Potassium 250 mg
      Cholesterol 283 mg
Exchanges:
   Milk ¼
   Bread ½
   Meat 1
   Fat 4

Preheat oven to **400°F**.

*To prepare the soufflé:* In a medium saucepan melt 3 tablespoons margarine. Using a wire whisk, blend in 3 tablespoons flour. Gradually add the milk and cook over moderate heat, stirring constantly, until the sauce is thickened and smooth.

Remove from heat and season with salt and cayenne pepper. Add the egg yolks, one at a time, beating well after each addition. Stir in asparagus.

In a separate bowl, beat egg whites until foamy. Add cream of tartar and continue to beat until stiff peaks form. Stir about one-fourth of whites into the asparagus sauce, then fold in remaining whites.

Turn into ungreased 1½-quart soufflé dish and place in preheated oven. Immediately reduce temperature to 375°F. and bake about 35 minutes or until soufflé is nicely browned and firm on top.

*To prepare the sauce:* Do this while soufflé is cooking. You will want it to be ready when the soufflé is. In a medium saucepan place stock, wine, carrot, mushrooms, onions, parsley, and bay leaf. Simmer, tightly covered, for 20 minutes. Strain and reserve 1 cup.

In same saucepan melt 2 tablespoons margarine over moderate heat without letting it brown. Add flour and stir with a wire whisk until it is well blended.

Gradually add 1 cup strained liquid and cook over moderate heat, stirring constantly, until sauce is thickened and smooth. Boil and stir 1 minute.

Remove from heat, stir in salt, pepper, and dillweed, then the remaining 2 tablespoons margarine. If soufflé is not ready, put sauce in double boiler over hot water and cover.

Spoon warm sauce over individual portions of soufflé and serve at once.

*Yield:* 4 servings soufflé, 1 cup sauce

*Change Asparagus Soufflé as follows or use Basic Recipe, if indicated, for:*

LOW-SODIUM DIETS

*The soufflé:* Omit salt. Substitute unsalted polyunsaturated margarine for margarine.

*The sauce:* Omit salt. Substitute unsalted polyunsaturated margarine for margarine.
   Proceed as in Basic Recipe.

Calories per serving: 279
Approximate nutrient
   values same as Basic
   Recipe except for:
   Sodium 113 mg

BLAND DIETS

*The soufflé:* Omit cayenne pepper.
   Proceed as in Basic Recipe.

*The sauce:* Omit pepper.
   Proceed as in Basic Recipe.

Calories per serving: 279

HIGH-FIBER DIETS

Use Basic Recipe.

ASPARAGUS SOUFFLÉ FOR LOW-CALORIE, DIABETIC, LOW-FAT, AND LOW-CHOLESTEROL DIETS

*The Soufflé*
2 tablespoons polyunsaturated margarine
3 tablespoons flour
1 cup skim milk
½ teaspoon salt
⅛ teaspoon cayenne pepper
1 cup finely chopped cooked asparagus
6 large egg whites
¼ teaspoon cream of tartar

Serving size: ¼ soufflé, 2
   tablespoons sauce
Calories per serving: 144
Approximate nutrient
   values per serving:
   Protein 8 g
   Fat 7 g
   Carbohydrate 11 g
   Sodium 536 mg
   Potassium 260 mg
   Cholesterol 1 mg

*The Sauce*
1 cup Chicken Stock (page 114)
½ cup dry white wine
1 small carrot, sliced
2 mushrooms, sliced
¼ cup chopped onions
1 sprig fresh parsley
1 small bay leaf
1 tablespoon polyunsaturated margarine for sauce
1½ tablespoons flour
¼ teaspoon salt
⅛ teaspoon freshly ground pepper
½ teaspoon dillweed

Preheat oven to 400°F.

*To prepare the soufflé:* In a small saucepan melt the 2 table-spoons margarine. Using a wire whisk, blend in flour. Gradually add the milk and cook over moderate heat, stirring constantly, until the mixture is thickened and smooth. Boil and stir 1 minute. Remove from heat and season with salt and cayenne pepper. Stir in asparagus.

In a separate bowl, beat the egg whites until foamy. Add the cream of tartar and continue to beat until stiff peaks form. Stir about one-fourth of whites into the asparagus mixture, then fold in remaining whites.

Turn into ungreased 1½-quart soufflé dish and place in oven. Immediately reduce the temperature to 375°F and bake about 35 minutes or until nicely browned and firm on top.

*To prepare the sauce:* Do this while soufflé is baking. Place stock, wine, carrot, mushrooms, onions, parsley, and bay leaf in a medium saucepan. Simmer, tightly covered, for 20 minutes. Strain and reserve 1 cup.

In same saucepan melt 1 tablespoon margarine over moderate heat without letting it brown. Add flour and stir with a wire whisk until it is well blended.

Gradually add the 1 cup strained liquid and cook over moderate heat, stirring constantly, until sauce is thickened and smooth. Boil and stir 1 minute.

Remove from heat and blend in seasonings. If soufflé is not

ready, keep sauce warm: place in double boiler over hot water and cover.

Spoon warm sauce over individual portions of soufflé and serve at once.

*Yield:* 4 servings soufflé, 1 cup sauce

ASPARAGUS SOUFFLÉ FOR RENAL DIETS

*The Soufflé*
3 tablespoons unsalted polyunsaturated margarine
3 tablespoons flour
1 cup light cream
⅛ teaspoon cayenne pepper
4 large eggs, at room temperature, separated
1 cup finely chopped cooked fresh asparagus
¼ teaspoon cream of tartar

*The Sauce*
¼ cup dry white wine
4 tablespoons unsalted polyunsaturated margarine
1½ tablespoons flour
⅔ cup milk
¼ cup water
⅛ teaspoon freshly ground pepper
½ teaspoon dillweed

Preheat oven to 400°F.

*To prepare the soufflé:* Melt the 3 tablespoons margarine in a small saucepan. Blend in flour. Gradually add cream and cook over moderate heat, stirring constantly, until sauce is thickened and smooth. Remove from heat and season with cayenne pepper. Add egg yolks, one at a time, beating well after each addition. Stir in asparagus.

In a separate bowl, beat egg whites until foamy. Add cream of tartar and continue beating until stiff peaks form. Fold one-fourth of the whites into the asparagus sauce, then fold in remaining whites.

Turn into ungreased 1½-quart soufflé dish and place in oven. Reduce oven temperature immediately to 375°F. Bake for 35

Serving size: ¼ soufflé, ¼ cup sauce
Calories per serving: 492
Approximate nutrient values per serving:
  Protein 10 g
  Fat 45 g
  Carbohydrate 12 g
  Calcium 125 mg
  Phosphorus 181 mg
  Sodium 110 mg
  Potassium 232 mg
  Cholesterol 346 mg
Exchanges:
  Bread 1
  Meat 1
  Fat 8½

minutes or until nicely browned and firm to the touch. Meanwhile, toward end of cooking time, make the sauce.

*To prepare the sauce:* Place wine in a small saucepan. Boil for 2 minutes. Set aside.

Melt 2 tablespoons of the margarine in a saucepan. Blend in flour. Gradually add milk, wine, and water, stirring constantly. Cook and stir over moderate heat until sauce is thickened and smooth. Remove from heat. Blend in pepper and dillweed, then the remaining 2 tablespoons margarine. If soufflé is not ready, keep sauce warm in a covered double boiler over hot water.

When soufflé is browned, serve at once, with dill sauce.

*Yield:* 4 servings soufflé, 1 cup sauce

# Chicken Soufflé with Wine Sauce

BASIC RECIPE

*The Soufflé*
3 tablespoons polyunsaturated margarine
3 tablespoons flour
1 cup milk
¾ teaspoon salt
¼ teaspoon tarragon
⅛ teaspoon freshly ground pepper
4 large eggs, at room temperature, separated
1 cup minced cooked chicken
¼ teaspoon cream of tartar

*The Sauce*
2 cups Chicken Stock (page 114)
1 cup dry white wine
1 medium carrot, sliced
3 fresh mushrooms, sliced
¼ cup chopped onions
1 sprig fresh parsley

Serving size: ¾ cup soufflé,
2 tablespoons sauce
Calories per serving: 217
Approximate nutrient
  values per serving:
    Protein 13 g
    Fat 15 g
    Carbohydrate 8 g
    Sodium 523 mg
    Potassium 256 mg
    Cholesterol 206 mg
Exchanges:
  Bread ½
  Meat 2
  Fat 2

1 small bay leaf
4 tablespoons polyunsaturated margarine
3 tablespoons flour
½ teaspoon salt
⅛ teaspoon freshly ground pepper

Preheat oven to 400°F.

*To prepare the soufflé:* Melt the 3 tablespoons margarine in a medium saucepan. Blend in flour with a whisk. Gradually stir in milk and then cook over moderate heat, stirring constantly, until sauce is thickened and smooth. Boil and stir 1 minute.

Remove from heat; blend in salt, tarragon, and pepper. Add egg yolks, one at a time, beating well after each addition. Stir in chicken.

In a large bowl, beat egg whites until foamy. Beat in cream of tartar and continue beating until stiff peaks form. Fold about one-fourth of the whites into chicken mixture. Then fold in remaining whites.

Turn into 1½-quart soufflé dish. Place in oven and immediately lower temperature to 375°F. Bake about 35 minutes or until top is browned and soufflé is firm in the center. Meanwhile, make the sauce.

*To prepare the sauce:* In a medium saucepan place stock, wine, carrot, mushrooms, onions, parsley, and bay leaf. Simmer, tightly covered, for 20 minutes. Strain and reserve liquid.

In the same saucepan melt the margarine over moderate heat without letting it brown. Add the flour and stir until it is well blended. Gradually add 2 cups strained liquid and cook over moderate heat, stirring constantly, until thickened and smooth. Boil and stir 1 minute.

Remove from heat and blend in seasonings.

When soufflé is done, remove from oven and serve at once with wine sauce.

*Yield:* 6 servings soufflé, 2 cups sauce

*Change Chicken Soufflé with Wine Sauce as follows or use Basic Recipe, if indicated, for:*

LOW-CALORIE, DIABETIC, LOW-FAT, AND LOW-CHOLESTEROL DIETS

*The soufflé:* Reduce margarine to 2 tablespoons. Substitute skim milk for milk. Proceed as in Basic Recipe.

*The sauce:* Reduce margarine to 2 tablespoons. Proceed as in Basic Recipe.

Calories per serving: 176
Approximate nutrient
　values per serving:
　　Protein 13 g
　　Fat 10 g
　　Carbohydrate 8 g
　　Sodium 491 mg
　　Potassium 261 mg
　　Cholesterol 201 mg
Exchanges:
　Bread ½
　Meat 2
　Fat 1

LOW-SODIUM DIETS

*The soufflé:* Omit salt.
　Substitute unsalted polyunsaturated margarine for margarine.
　Add 2 tablespoons minced green pepper with chicken. Proceed as in Basic Recipe.

*The sauce:* Omit salt.
　Substitute unsalted polyunsaturated margarine for margarine.
　Proceed as in Basic Recipe.

Calories per serving: 217
Approximate nutrient
　values same as Basic
　Recipe except for:
　　Sodium 95 mg
　　Potassium 263 mg

BLAND DIETS

*The soufflé and the sauce:* Omit ground pepper. Proceed as in Basic Recipe.

Calories per serving: 217

Calories per serving: 218

*The soufflé:* Add 2 tablespoons minced green pepper with chicken. Proceed as in Basic Recipe.

*The sauce:* Use Basic Recipe.

## CHICKEN SOUFFLÉ WITH WINE SAUCE FOR RENAL DIETS

Serving size: ¾ cup soufflé, ¼ cup sauce
Calories per serving: 267
Approximate nutrient
   values per serving:
     Protein 14 g
     Fat 19 g
     Carbohydrate 10 g
     Calcium 117 mg
     Phosphorus 198 mg
     Sodium 99 mg
     Potassium 265 mg
     Cholesterol 211 mg
Exchanges:
   Bread 1
   Meat 1½
   Fat 3

*The Soufflé*
3 tablespoons unsalted polyunsaturated margarine
3 tablespoons flour
1 cup milk
¼ teaspoon tarragon
⅛ teaspoon freshly ground pepper
4 large eggs, at room temperature, separated
1 cup cooked minced chicken
¼ teaspoon cream of tartar

*The Sauce*
½ cup dry white wine
4 tablespoons unsalted polyunsaturated margarine
3 tablespoons flour
1¼ cups milk
½ cup water
⅛ teaspoon freshly ground pepper

*To prepare the soufflé:* In a medium saucepan, melt the margarine. Blend in flour and gradually stir in milk. Cook over moderate heat, stirring constantly, until sauce is thickened and smooth. Boil and stir 1 minute.

Remove from heat and stir in tarragon and pepper. Add egg yolks, one at a time, beating well after each addition. Stir in chicken.

In a separate bowl, beat egg whites until foamy. Beat in cream of tartar and continue beating until stiff peaks form. Fold one-fourth of the whites into chicken mixture; then fold in remaining whites.

Pour into 1½-quart soufflé dish. Place in oven and lower temperature immediately to 375°F. Bake for about 35 minutes or until soufflé is firm to the touch.

*To prepare the sauce:* Put wine in small saucepan. Simmer for 5 minutes. Set aside. Melt margarine in saucepan. Blend in flour, then gradually add milk, wine, and water. Cook and stir until sauce is thickened and smooth. Season with pepper.

*Yield:* 6 servings soufflé, 2 cups sauce

# Tomato Custard

BASIC RECIPE

Serving size: 1 custard cup
Calories per serving: 141
Approximate nutrient
  values per serving:
    Protein 5 g
    Fat 10 g
    Carbohydrate 11 g
    Sodium 221 mg
    Potassium 515 mg
    Cholesterol 119 mg
Exchanges:
  Vegetable 2
  Meat ½
  Fat 1½

4½ cups coarsely chopped peeled tomatoes
½ cup chopped onions
½ teaspoon basil
¼ teaspoon oregano
2 large eggs
½ cup heavy cream
½ teaspoon salt
⅛ teaspoon freshly ground pepper

In a medium saucepan cook tomatoes, onions, basil, and oregano, covered, over low heat 15 minutes. Uncover and simmer 45 minutes longer or until mixture is thick, stirring occasionally. Purée the sauce in a blender.
    Preheat oven to 350°F.
    In a large bowl beat eggs lightly. Stir in cream, salt, pepper, and the tomato purée. Pour into six 6-ounce custard cups. Set cups in a shallow baking dish and fill dish with hot water to approximately ¾ inch from top of cups. Bake 30 minutes or until a knife inserted in the center comes out clean. Cool cups on rack for 5 minutes before serving.

*Yield:* 6 servings

*Change Tomato Custard as follows for:*

## LOW-CALORIE, DIABETIC, LOW-FAT, AND LOW-CHOLESTEROL DIETS

Calories per serving: 70
Approximate nutrient
  values per serving:
    Protein 6 g
    Fat 0 g
    Carbohydrate 12 g
    Sodium 242 mg
    Potassium 566 mg
    Cholesterol 1 mg
Exchanges:
  Milk ¼
  Vegetable 2

Omit eggs. Use Low-Cholesterol Egg Substitute (page 189) equivalent to 2 large eggs.
Substitute skim milk for cream.
Proceed as in Basic Recipe.

## LOW-SODIUM DIETS

Calories per serving: 141
Approximate nutrient
  values same as Basic
  Recipe except for:
    Sodium 38 mg

Omit salt.
Proceed as in Basic Recipe.

## BLAND DIETS

Calories per serving: 141

Omit pepper.
Proceed as in Basic Recipe.

## HIGH-FIBER DIETS

Calories per serving: 142

Add ½ teaspoon celery seed to custard mixture.
Proceed as in Basic Recipe.

217

# C H E E S E S

Rejoice that you are living at a time when there are almost as many fine cheeses as there are good wines. Rejoice, too, that you may continue to enjoy many of them in spite of your diet restrictions. There is an excellent assortment of savory cheeses carefully developed for special diets, including low-fat cottage cheese, skim American cheeses, low-sodium Swiss cheese, low-sodium Cheddar cheese, part-skim ricotta cheese, and part-skim mozzarella cheese. You will find them not only in stores specializing in cheeses but in many supermarkets. We offer plenty of recipes to satisfy your taste for cheese—successfully modified to meet your needs. They include a wide range of luncheon and dinner dishes—tarts, quiches, soufflés, rarebits, and even cheese custard pie.

# Primavera Rarebit

BASIC RECIPE

2 cups water
1 pound fresh broccoli spears, trimmed and split
1½ cups milk
1 cup cooked rice
1½ cups grated sharp Cheddar cheese
4 large eggs
1 teaspoon dry mustard
½ teaspoon salt
¼ teaspoon cayenne pepper
2 teaspoons Worcestershire sauce

Bring water to a boil in a deep saucepan. Add broccoli in steamer, lower heat, and steam for 5 minutes. Turn off heat and keep broccoli covered.

Heat milk and rice together in a medium saucepan. Gradually add cheese and cook, stirring, until cheese melts. Turn off heat.

In a medium bowl beat eggs lightly. Stir in mustard, salt, cayenne pepper, and Worcestershire sauce. Then stir eggs gently into rice mixture. Over low heat, cook, stirring, until thickened. Serve over warm broccoli.

*Yield:* 4 servings

*Change Primavera Rarebit as follows or use Basic Recipe, if indicated, for:*

## LOW-CALORIE, DIABETIC, LOW-FAT, AND LOW-CHOLESTEROL DIETS

Calories per serving: 285
Approximate nutrient
    values per serving:
        Protein 27 g
        Fat 8 g
        Carbohydrate 28 g
        Sodium 703 mg
        Potassium 808 mg
        Cholesterol 27 mg
Exchanges:
    Milk ½
    Vegetable 1
    Bread 1
    Meat 2½

Substitute skim milk for milk.
Substitute grated part-skim mozzarella cheese for Cheddar.
Omit eggs. Use Low-Cholesterol Egg Substitute (page 189) equivalent to 4 large eggs.
Proceed as in Basic Recipe.

## LOW-SODIUM DIETS

Calories per serving: 397
Approximate nutrient
    values per serving:
        Protein 25 g
        Fat 23 g
        Carbohydrate 24 g
        Sodium 138 mg
        Potassium 716 mg
        Cholesterol 302 mg

Omit salt and Worcestershire sauce.
Substitute low-sodium grated Cheddar cheese for Cheddar.
Proceed as in Basic Recipe.

## BLAND DIETS

Calories per serving: 406

Omit mustard and cayenne pepper. Add ½ teaspoon basil and ¼ teaspoon oregano to seasonings.
Proceed as in Basic Recipe.

## HIGH-FIBER DIETS

Use Basic Recipe.

# Cheese Fondue

BASIC RECIPE

Serving size: ½ cup fondue,
    ¾ cup bread cubes
Calories per serving: 474
Approximate nutrient
    values per serving:
    Protein 29 g
    Fat 30 g
    Carbohydrate 21 g
    Sodium 445 mg
    Potassium 99 mg
    Cholesterol 100 mg
Exchanges:
    Bread 1½
    Meat 3
    Fat 4

3 tablespoons Kirsch
1 tablespoon cornstarch
1 clove garlic, cut in half
1½ cups dry white wine
1 pound Gruyère cheese, grated
⅛ teaspoon nutmeg
4 cups French bread, cut into 1-inch cubes

Mix the Kirsch and cornstarch together until smooth. Set aside.

Rub the inside of a fondue dish with the cut garlic. Pour wine into dish and heat, uncovered, until it starts to simmer. Do not boil. Add cheese gradually, stirring constantly. Gradually stir the Kirsch mixture into the melted cheese. Cook and stir until the fondue is creamy. Season with nutmeg. Keep fondue hot over low heat; do not allow it to boil. Serve with French bread cubes.

*Yield:* 5 servings

*Change Cheese Fondue as follows or use Basic Recipe, if indicated, for:*

## LOW-CALORIE, DIABETIC, LOW-FAT, AND LOW-CHOLESTEROL DIETS

Increase cornstarch to 2 tablespoons.
Substitute part-skim grated mozzarella cheese for Gruyère.
Proceed as in Basic Recipe.

Calories per serving: 335
Approximate nutrient
  values per serving:
    Protein 24 g
    Fat 15 g
    Carbohydrate 24 g
    Sodium 563 mg
    Potassium 101 mg
    Cholesterol 53 mg
Exchanges:
  Bread 1½
  Meat 3
  Fat 1

## LOW-SODIUM DIETS

Substitute grated low-sodium Swiss cheese for Gruyère.
Proceed as in Basic Recipe.

Calories per serving: 526
Approximate nutrient
  values per serving:
    Protein 25 g
    Fat 31 g
    Carbohydrate 25 g
    Sodium 331 mg
    Potassium 153 mg
    Cholesterol 32 mg

## BLAND DIETS

Omit nutmeg.
Proceed as in Basic Recipe.

Calories per serving: 474

## HIGH-FIBER DIETS

Use Basic Recipe. For extra fiber, serve with celery sticks.

# Onion Cheese Tart

BASIC RECIPE

9-inch Easy-Mix Flaky Pie Crust, unbaked (page 555)
1½ cups thinly sliced onions
2 tablespoons polyunsaturated margarine
1½ cups grated Swiss cheese
3 large eggs
1½ cups milk
½ teaspoon salt
⅛ teaspoon freshly ground pepper
⅛ teaspoon ground nutmeg

Make the pie crust.

Preheat oven to 375°F.

In a medium-size skillet, sauté onions in margarine until soft.

Sprinkle grated cheese in pie crust. Top with onions.

In a large mixing bowl, beat eggs lightly. Add milk, salt, pepper, and nutmeg. Beat until well blended. Pour over onions and cheese.

Place tart in the lower third of the oven. Bake 45 minutes or until top is lightly browned and a knife inserted in center comes out clean.

Remove to rack; let stand 5 minutes before serving.

*Yield:* 6 servings

*Change Onion Cheese Tart as follows for:*

LOW-SODIUM DIETS

Omit salt.
Substitute 2 tablespoons unsalted polyunsaturated margarine for margarine.
Substitute 9-inch low-sodium Easy-Mix Flaky Pie Crust (page 555) for basic Easy-Mix Flaky Pie Crust.
Substitute grated low-sodium Swiss cheese for Swiss.
Proceed as in Basic Recipe.

Calories per serving: 439

Omit pepper and nutmeg.
Proceed as in Basic Recipe.

## HIGH-FIBER DIETS

Calories per serving: 440

Sauté ¾ cup chopped celery with onions.
Substitute 9-inch high-fiber Easy-Mix Flaky Pie Crust (page 556) for basic Easy-Mix Flaky Pie Crust.
Proceed as in Basic Recipe.

## ONION CHEESE TART FOR LOW-CALORIE, DIABETIC, LOW-FAT, AND LOW-CHOLESTEROL DIETS

Serving size: ⅙ tart
Calories per serving: 304
Approximate nutrient
  values per serving:
    Protein 16 g
    Fat 13 g
    Carbohydrate 31 g
    Sodium 778 mg
    Potassium 271 mg
    Cholesterol 3 mg
Exchanges:
  Vegetable 1
  Bread 1½
  Meat 1½
  Fat 2½

9-inch Easy-Mix Flaky Pie Crust, unbaked (page 555)
1½ cups thinly sliced onions
1 cup Beef Stock (page 113)
Low-Cholesterol Egg Substitute (page 189) equivalent to
    3 large eggs
⅔ cup skim milk
1½ cups 1 percent low-fat cottage cheese
2 tablespoons flour
¾ teaspoon salt
¾ teaspoon Dijon mustard
⅛ teaspoon freshly ground pepper

Make the pie crust.
    Preheat oven to 425°F.
    Simmer onions in beef stock 7 to 10 minutes or until tender. Drain thoroughly; pat dry with paper towels. Arrange onions in the bottom of unbaked pie crust.
    In a large bowl, beat the remaining ingredients. Pour over onions.
    Bake tart for 15 minutes. Reduce oven temperature to 325°F. Bake 35 minutes longer or until top is browned and knife inserted in center comes out clean. Remove to rack; let stand 5 minutes before serving.

*Yield:* 6 servings

# Zucchini Quiche

BASIC RECIPE

Serving size: ⅙ quiche
Calories per serving: 558
Approximate nutrient
  values per serving:
    Protein 16 g
    Fat 43 g
    Carbohydrate 29 g
    Sodium 568 mg
    Potassium 337 mg
    Cholesterol 207 mg
Exchanges:
  Vegetable 1
  Bread 1½
  Meat 1½
  Fat 7½

9-inch Easy-Mix Flaky Pie Crust, unbaked (page 555)
4 tablespoons polyunsaturated margarine
4 cups diced zucchini
½ cup chopped onions
3 tablespoons chopped fresh parsley
½ teaspoon thyme
½ teaspoon salt
⅛ teaspoon freshly ground pepper
2 tablespoons dry sherry
1½ cups grated Swiss cheese
3 large eggs
1 cup light cream

Make the pie crust.

Preheat oven to 425°F.

Heat the margarine in a large skillet. Add zucchini and onions and sauté until they are soft. Add parsley, thyme, salt, pepper, and sherry. Increase heat and cook, stirring gently, until liquid has evaporated.

Sprinkle cheese over bottom of unbaked pie shell. Spoon vegetable mixture on top of cheese.

In a large bowl, beat eggs and cream. Pour this mixture over vegetables and cheese.

Bake quiche 15 minutes; then reduce oven temperature to 325°F. and bake approximately 25 minutes longer or until a skewer or sharp knife inserted in center comes out clean.

Allow to cool 5 minutes before serving.

*Yield:* 6 servings

*Change Zucchini Quiche as follows for:*

LOW-SODIUM DIETS

Calories per serving: 580
Approximate nutrient
   values per serving:
     Protein 15 g
     Fat 45 g
     Carbohydrate 28 g
     Sodium 112 mg
     Potassium 345 mg
     Cholesterol 191 mg

Substitute 9-inch low-sodium Easy-Mix Flaky Pie Crust (page 555) for basic Easy-Mix Flaky Pie Crust.
Omit salt.
Substitute unsalted polyunsaturated margarine for margarine.
Substitute grated low-sodium Swiss cheese for Swiss.
Proceed as in Basic Recipe.

BLAND DIETS

Calories per serving: 558

Omit pepper.
Proceed as in Basic Recipe.

HIGH-FIBER DIETS

Calories per serving: 557

Substitute 9-inch high-fiber Easy-Mix Flaky Pie Crust (page 556) for basic Easy-Mix Flaky Pie Crust.
Proceed as in Basic Recipe.

ZUCCHINI QUICHE FOR LOW-CALORIE, DIABETIC, LOW-FAT, AND LOW-CHOLESTEROL DIETS

Serving size: ⅙ quiche
Calories per serving: 122
Approximate nutrient
   values per serving:
     Protein 11 g
     Fat 5 g
     Carbohydrate 10 g
     Sodium 391 mg
     Potassium 334 mg
     Cholesterol 11 mg
Exchanges:
   Vegetable 1
   Bread ½
   Meat 1

4 cups diced zucchini
½ cup chopped onions
1 cup Beef Stock (page 113)
3 tablespoons chopped fresh parsley
½ teaspoon thyme
½ teaspoon salt
⅛ teaspoon freshly ground pepper
2 tablespoons dry sherry
2 teaspoons polyunsaturated margarine for greasing pie plate
⅔ cup fresh bread crumbs for lining pie plate (page 38)
1 cup grated part-skim mozzarella cheese
Low-Cholesterol Egg Substitute (page 189) equivalent to 3 large eggs

Preheat oven to 425°F.

In a large saucepan simmer zucchini and onions in beef stock, covered, approximately 15 minutes or until vegetables are tender. Add parsley, thyme, salt, pepper, and sherry. Increase heat and cook, uncovered, until liquid evaporates.

Prepare 9-inch pie plate by greasing bottom and sides with margarine, then spread with bread crumbs. Sprinkle cheese over crumbs; top with vegetables. Pour egg substitute over all.

Bake 15 minutes; then reduce oven temperature to 325°F. and bake 25 minutes more or until custard is set. Allow to cool 5 minutes before serving.

*Yield:* 6 servings

# Fresh Tomato Quiche

BASIC RECIPE

Serving size: ⅙ quiche
Calories per serving: 392
Approximate nutrient
  values per serving:
    Protein 13 g
    Fat 34 g
    Carbohydrate 11 g
    Sodium 511 mg
    Potassium 298 mg
    Cholesterol 211 mg
Exchanges:
  Vegetable 1
  Bread ½
  Meat 1½
  Fat 6

Pâte Brisée 9-inch pastry shell, unbaked (page 557)
3 firm, ripe, medium tomatoes (¾ pound)
2½ tablespoons flour
4 tablespoons polyunsaturated margarine
⅓ cup chopped onions
⅓ cup chopped green pepper
1½ cups grated sharp Cheddar cheese
3 large eggs
1 cup light cream
½ teaspoon basil
½ teaspoon chervil
¼ teaspoon oregano
½ teaspoon salt
⅛ teaspoon freshly ground pepper

Prepare Pâte Brisée and roll to fit a 9-inch pie plate. Flute edge.
  Preheat oven to 425°F.
  Cut tomatoes vertically in ½-inch slices. Dredge in flour.

In a medium skillet heat 2 tablespoons of the margarine until foamy. Add tomatoes and sauté until golden brown on both sides. Remove to paper towels to drain.

Melt remaining 2 tablespoons margarine in skillet, add onions and green pepper, and sauté until onions are soft.

Arrange tomato slices in pastry shell. Spoon onion mixture over them and sprinkle cheese on top.

In a large bowl beat eggs lightly. Beat in cream and remaining ingredients. Pour egg mixture over cheese and bake 15 minutes.

Reduce oven temperature to 325°F. and bake 35 minutes longer or until a skewer or sharp knife inserted in center comes out clean. Place quiche on rack and let stand 10 minutes before serving.

*Yield:* 6 servings

*Change Fresh Tomato Quiche as follows or use Basic Recipe, if indicated, for:*

LOW-SODIUM DIETS

Calories per serving: 386
Approximate nutrient
values per serving:
Protein 13 g
Fat 33 g
Carbohydrate 11 g
Sodium 57 mg
Potassium 310 mg
Cholesterol 191 mg

Substitute 9-inch low-sodium Pâte Brisée (page 557) for basic Pâte Brisée.
Omit salt.
Substitute unsalted polyunsaturated margarine for margarine.
Substitute grated low-sodium Cheddar cheese for Cheddar.
Proceed as in Basic Recipe.

BLAND DIETS

Calories per serving: 392

Omit ground pepper.
Proceed as in Basic Recipe.

HIGH-FIBER DIETS

Use Basic Recipe.

## FRESH TOMATO QUICHE FOR LOW-CALORIE, DIABETIC, LOW-FAT, AND LOW-CHOLESTEROL DIETS

Serving size: ⅙ quiche
Calories per serving: 188
Approximate nutrient
   values per serving:
      Protein 13 g
      Fat 10 g
      Carbohydrate 12 g
      Sodium 450 mg
      Potassium 326 mg
      Cholesterol 17 mg
Exchanges:
   Vegetable 1
   Bread ½
   Meat 1½
   Fat 1

Pâte Brisée 9-inch pastry shell, unbaked (page 557)
3 firm, ripe, medium tomatoes (¾ pound)
2½ tablespoons flour
2 tablespoons polyunsaturated margarine
⅓ cup chopped onions
⅓ cup chopped green pepper
1½ cups grated part-skim mozzarella cheese
Low-Cholesterol Egg Substitute (page 189) equivalent to
   3 large eggs
⅓ cup skim milk
½ teaspoon basil
½ teaspoon chervil
¼ teaspoon oregano
½ teaspoon salt
⅛ teaspoon freshly ground pepper

Prepare Pâte Brisée and roll to fit a 9-inch pie plate. Flute edge.
   Preheat oven to 425°F.
   Cut tomatoes vertically in ½-inch slices. Dredge in flour. In a medium skillet heat 1 tablespoon margarine until foamy. Sauté tomatoes until golden brown on both sides. Remove to paper towels to drain.
   Melt remaining 1 tablespoon margarine in skillet, add onions and green pepper and sauté until onions are soft.
   Arrange tomato slices in pastry shell. Spoon onion mixture over them and sprinkle cheese on top.
   In a bowl beat egg substitute lightly. Beat in milk with remaining ingredients and pour over cheese. Bake 15 minutes. Reduce oven temperature to 325°F. and bake 35 minutes longer or until knife inserted in center comes out clean. Place quiche on rack and let stand 10 minutes before serving.

*Yield:* 6 servings

# Vegetable Cheese Custard Pie

BASIC RECIPE

Serving size: ⅙ pie
Calories per serving: 175
Approximate nutrient
 values per serving:
    Protein 9 g
    Fat 11 g
    Carbohydrate 11 g
    Sodium 402 mg
    Potassium 383 mg
    Cholesterol 166 mg
Exchanges:
  Vegetable 2
  Meat 1
  Fat 1½

1 cup coarsely chopped peeled tomatoes
2 cups peeled zucchini cubes
2 cups unpeeled eggplant cubes
½ cup chopped onions
2 tablespoons chopped fresh parsley
½ teaspoon basil
¼ teaspoon oregano
¾ teaspoon salt
¼ teaspoon freshly ground pepper
⅓ cup fresh bread crumbs (page 38)
3 large eggs
⅓ cup light cream
¼ pound mozzarella cheese, thinly sliced

In a large saucepan combine tomatoes, zucchini, eggplant, and onions. Cover and simmer slowly 15 minutes or until vegetables are soft. Stir occasionally. Add parsley, basil, oregano, ½ teaspoon of the salt, and ⅛ teaspoon of the pepper. Continue cooking, uncovered, until all of the liquid has evaporated. Stir occasionally. Cool to room temperature.

Preheat oven to 375°F.

Sprinkle bread crumbs in a 9-inch pie plate.

Spoon vegetable mixture on top of crumbs.

Prepare a custard as follows: beat eggs, cream, and remaining salt and pepper together and pour over vegetables.

Arrange cheese on top. Bake 35 minutes or until custard is set.

Place pie plate on rack and allow to cool 10 minutes before serving.

*Yield:* 6 servings

*Change Vegetable Cheese Custard Pie as follows for:*

## LOW-SODIUM DIETS

Calories per serving: 209
Approximate nutrient
 values per serving:
  Protein 10 g
  Fat 14 g
  Carbohydrate 10 g
  Sodium 97 mg
  Potassium 397 mg
  Cholesterol 159 mg

Omit salt.
Substitute low-sodium Swiss cheese for mozzarella.
Proceed as in Basic Recipe.

## BLAND DIETS

Calories per serving: 175

Omit pepper.
Proceed as in Basic Recipe.

## HIGH-FIBER DIETS

Calories per serving: 175

Substitute fresh stone-ground whole wheat bread crumbs for
  bread crumbs.
Proceed as in Basic Recipe.

## VEGETABLE CHEESE CUSTARD PIE FOR LOW-CALORIE, DIABETIC, LOW-FAT, AND LOW-CHOLESTEROL DIETS

Serving size: ⅙ pie
Calories per serving: 120
Approximate nutrient
 values per serving:
  Protein 11 g
  Fat 3 g
  Carbohydrate 12 g
  Sodium 450 mg
  Potassium 445 mg
  Cholesterol 12 mg
Exchanges:
 Vegetable 2
 Meat 1

1 cup coarsely chopped peeled tomatoes
2 cups peeled zucchini cubes
2 cups unpeeled eggplant cubes
½ cup chopped onions
2 tablespoons chopped fresh parsley
½ teaspoon basil
¼ teaspoon oregano
½ teaspoon salt for vegetable mixture
⅛ teaspoon freshly ground pepper for vegetable mixture
⅓ cup fresh bread crumbs (page 38)
Low-Cholesterol Egg Substitute (page 189) equivalent to
  3 large eggs

⅓ cup skim milk
¼ teaspoon salt for custard mixture
⅛ teaspoon pepper for custard mixture
¼ pound part-skim mozzarella cheese, thinly sliced

In a large saucepan combine tomatoes, zucchini, eggplant, and onions. Cover and simmer slowly 15 minutes or until vegetables are soft. Stir occasionally. Add parsley, basil, oregano, ½ teaspoon of the salt and ⅛ teaspoon of the pepper. Continue cooking, uncovered, until all of the liquid has evaporated. Stir occasionally. Cool to room temperature.

Preheat oven to 375°F. Sprinkle crumbs in 9-inch pie plate. Spoon vegetable mixture on top of crumbs. Beat together egg substitute, milk, ¼ teaspoon salt, and ⅛ teaspoon pepper, and pour over vegetables. Arrange cheese on top. Bake 35 minutes or until custard is set. Place pie plate on rack and allow custard to cool 10 minutes before serving.

*Yield:* 6 servings

# Tomato Rarebit

BASIC RECIPE

Serving size: ½ cup tomato rarebit, 1 slice toast
Calories per serving: 444
Approximate nutrient values per serving:
    Protein 18 g
    Fat 32 g
    Carbohydrate 22 g
    Sodium 882 mg
    Potassium 370 mg
    Cholesterol 60 mg
Exchanges:
    Vegetable 1
    Bread 1
    Meat 2
    Fat 5

3 tablespoons polyunsaturated margarine for the rarebit
⅓ cup chopped onions
1 tablespoon cornstarch
1 teaspoon dry mustard
½ teaspoon salt
⅛ teaspoon freshly ground pepper
1½ cups peeled, seeded, cored, and chopped fresh tomatoes, cooked
2 cups grated sharp Cheddar cheese
4 slices white bread, toasted
4 teaspoons polyunsaturated margarine for the toast

Melt 3 tablespoons margarine in medium saucepan. Add onions and sauté until soft. Blend in cornstarch, mustard, salt, and pepper.

Add tomatoes and cook over moderate heat, stirring constantly, until mixture comes to a simmer.

Gradually add cheese and cook, stirring, until cheese melts.

Spread toast with remaining margarine and serve rarebit over toast.

*Yield:* 4 servings

*Change Tomato Rarebit as follows for:*

LOW-CALORIE, DIABETIC, LOW-FAT, AND LOW-CHOLESTEROL DIETS

Reduce margarine for the rarebit to 1½ tablespoons.
Substitute 1½ cups grated part-skim mozzarella cheese for Cheddar.
Proceed as in Basic Recipe.
Serve rarebit on dry toast.

Calories per serving: 286
Approximate nutrient
  values per serving:
    Protein 14 g
    Fat 16 g
    Carbohydrate 22 g
    Sodium 686 mg
    Potassium 349 mg
    Cholesterol 25 mg
Exchanges:
  Vegetable 1
  Bread 1
  Meat 1½
  Fat 2

LOW-SODIUM DIETS

Omit salt. Substitute unsalted polyunsaturated margarine for margarine wherever used.
Substitute 2 cups grated low-sodium Cheddar cheese for Cheddar.
Proceed as in Basic Recipe.

Calories per serving: 434
Approximate nutrient
  values per serving:
    Protein 18 g
    Fat 31 g
    Carbohydrate 21 g
    Sodium 142 mg
    Potassium 395 mg
    Cholesterol 20 mg

Calories per serving: 443

Omit mustard and pepper.
Proceed as in Basic Recipe.

HIGH-FIBER DIETS

Calories per serving: 432

Substitute 4 slices stone-ground whole wheat toast for toasted
  white bread.
Proceed as in Basic Recipe.

# Rarebit with Corn

BASIC RECIPE

Serving size: ⅔ cup rarebit,
  1 slice toast, 1 tomato
Calories per serving: 576
Approximate nutrient
  values per serving:
    Protein 24 g
    Fat 38 g
    Carbohydrate 38 g
    Sodium 1097 mg
    Potassium 603 mg
    Cholesterol 205 mg
Exchanges:
  Milk ½
  Vegetable 1
  Bread 2
  Meat 2
  Fat 6

3 tablespoons polyunsaturated margarine
1 tablespoon cornstarch
1 cup milk
1 teaspoon dry mustard
1 teaspoon paprika
½ teaspoon salt
⅛ teaspoon cayenne pepper
2 cups grated sharp Cheddar cheese
2 large eggs
1 cup cream-style corn
4 slices white toast
4 teaspoons polyunsaturated margarine for toast
4 small tomatoes, sliced
2 tablespoons minced fresh parsley

In a medium saucepan melt 3 tablespoons margarine. Blend in
cornstarch. Gradually add milk and cook over moderate heat,
stirring, until sauce thickens. Mix in mustard, paprika, salt,
and cayenne. Add cheese and cook, stirring, until cheese melts.
Remove from heat.

In a medium bowl beat eggs lightly. Stir in corn. Add to sauce and cook over low heat, stirring, until well blended.

Spread toast with margarine reserved for toast.

Arrange sliced tomatoes on toast, spoon rarebit over tomatoes, and garnish with parsley.

*Yield:* 4 servings

*Change Rarebit with Corn as follows or use Basic Recipe, if indicated, for:*

LOW-SODIUM DIETS

Omit salt.

Substitute unsalted polyunsaturated margarine for margarine wherever used.

Substitute grated low-sodium Cheddar cheese for Cheddar.

Substitute cream-style corn packed without salt for cream-style corn.

Proceed as in Basic Recipe.

Calories per serving: 565
Approximate nutrient
 values per serving:
  Protein 25 g
  Fat 37 g
  Carbohydrate 36 g
  Sodium 207 mg
  Potassium 627 mg
  Cholesterol 166 mg

BLAND DIETS

Omit cayenne pepper and mustard.

Proceed as in Basic Recipe.

Calories per serving: 575

HIGH-FIBER DIETS

Use Basic Recipe.

RAREBIT WITH CORN FOR LOW-CALORIE, DIABETIC, LOW-FAT, AND LOW-CHOLESTEROL DIETS

2 tablespoons polyunsaturated margarine
2 tablespoons cornstarch
1 cup skim milk

Serving size: ⅔ cup rarebit,
 1 slice toast, 1 tomato
Calories per serving: 382

235

1 teaspoon dry mustard
1 teaspoon paprika
½ teaspoon salt
⅛ teaspoon cayenne pepper
2 cups grated part-skim mozzarella cheese
1 cup cream-style corn
4 slices white toast
4 small tomatoes, sliced
2 tablespoons minced fresh parsley

In a medium saucepan melt the margarine. Blend in cornstarch. Gradually add milk and cook over moderate heat, stirring, until sauce thickens. Mix in mustard, paprika, salt, and cayenne pepper. Add cheese and cook, stirring, until cheese melts. Add cream corn and stir until blended.

Arrange tomato slices on toast, spoon rarebit over tomatoes, and garnish with parsley.

*Yield:* 4 servings

# Cheese Soufflé

BASIC RECIPE

4 tablespoons polyunsaturated margarine
3 tablespoons flour
1 cup milk, heated
¼ teaspoon salt
⅛ teaspoon freshly ground pepper
⅛ teaspoon ground nutmeg
4 large eggs, at room temperature, separated
¼ teaspoon cream of tartar
1½ cups grated sharp Cheddar cheese

Preheat oven to 400°F.

Melt the margarine in a large, heavy saucepan. Blend in flour. Add milk, salt, pepper, and nutmeg and cook over moderate heat, stirring constantly, until it forms a thickened, smooth sauce. Stir and continue cooking for 2 minutes. Remove from heat.

Beat egg yolks in a medium-size bowl. Add about 3 tablespoons of sauce to egg yolks and mix in well. Then add the egg mixture to remaining sauce and stir until thoroughly blended.

In a large mixing bowl beat egg whites until foamy. Beat in cream of tartar and continue beating until stiff peaks form.

Stir one-third of the beaten whites and the grated cheese into the sauce.

Fold in remaining whites quickly but gently.

Turn into a 1½-quart soufflé dish and place in oven. Immediately reduce heat to 375°F. and bake 35 minutes or until puffed and nicely browned.

Serve at once.

*Yield:* 6 servings

*Change Cheese Soufflé as follows or use Basic Recipe, if indicated, for:*

LOW-SODIUM DIETS

Calories per serving: 270
Approximate nutrient
values per serving:
    Protein 13 g
    Fat 22 g
    Carbohydrate 5 g
    Sodium 71 mg
    Potassium 151 mg
    Cholesterol 198 mg

Omit salt.
Substitute unsalted polyunsaturated margarine for margarine.
Substitute grated low-sodium Cheddar cheese for Cheddar.
Proceed as in Basic Recipe.

BLAND DIETS

Calories per serving: 275

Omit pepper and nutmeg.
Proceed as in Basic Recipe.

Calories per serving: 276

Use Basic Recipe. Garnish each serving with 1 tablespoon sliced scallions, both white and green parts. For extra fiber, serve with broiled tomato halves.

## CHEESE SOUFFLE FOR LOW-CALORIE, DIABETIC, LOW-FAT, AND LOW-CHOLESTEROL DIETS

Serving size: 1 cup
Calories per serving: 139
Approximate nutrient
  values per serving:
    Protein 12 g
    Fat 6 g
    Carbohydrate 8 g
    Sodium 624 mg
    Potassium 177 mg
    Cholesterol 3 mg
  Exchanges:
    Bread ½
    Meat 1½
    Fat 1

2 tablespoons polyunsaturated margarine
3 tablespoons flour
⅓ cup skim milk
½ teaspoon salt
⅛ teaspoon freshly ground pepper
1 cup 1 percent low-fat cottage cheese
3 tablespoons snipped chives
⅓ cup chopped fresh parsley
4 large egg whites
¼ teaspoon cream of tartar

Preheat oven to 350°F.

In a large, heavy saucepan melt margarine. Blend in flour. Add milk, salt, and pepper. Cook over moderate heat, stirring constantly, until thick and smooth. Remove from heat and blend in cottage cheese, chives, and parsley.

In a large mixing bowl, beat egg whites until foamy. Beat in cream of tartar and continue beating until stiff peaks form.

Fold one-fourth of the whites into cheese mixture, then fold in remaining whites quickly but gently. Turn into 1½-quart soufflé dish. Set soufflé dish in a shallow pan and fill pan halfway with hot water. Bake for 1 hour or until puffed and nicely browned. Serve immediately.

*Yield:* 4 servings

# FISH AND SHELLFISH

Although we no longer think of fish as "brain food," there is wisdom in trying to include fish in your menus. Lean fish, particularly, rates high in nutrients and low in calories, and is generally a food beneficial to your well-being.

Haddock, halibut, fillet of sole, and scrod fall into the lean fish category, so we use them often in our recipes.

Our selection includes fish to be enjoyed as entrées prepared in many ways—poached, boiled, skewered, sautéed, baked, and prepared in casseroles. There are additional recipes throughout the book using fish in appetizers, soups, and salads. You'll find them all listed in the index.

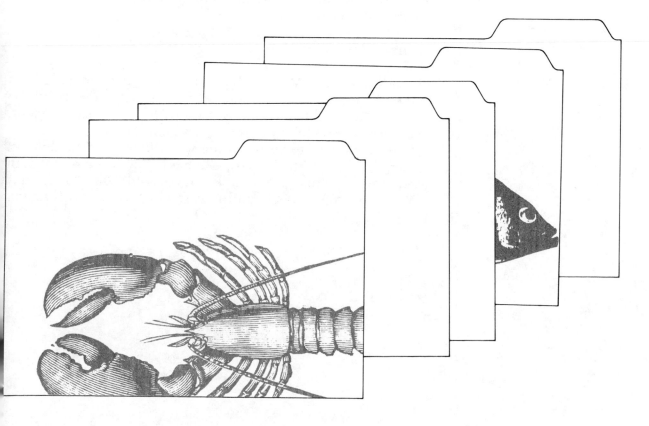

# Stuffed Trout

BASIC RECIPE

Serving size: 1 trout, ⅛ cup
  stuffing
Calories per serving: 472
Approximate nutrient
  values per serving:
    Protein 38 g
    Fat 32 g
    Carbohydrate 7 g
    Sodium 475 mg
    Potassium 654 mg
    Cholesterol 82 mg
Exchanges:
    Bread ½
    Meat 5
    Fat 3

4 tablespoons polyunsaturated margarine for stuffing
1 cup finely chopped fresh mushrooms
½ cup chopped onions
½ cup minced celery
1 teaspoon thyme
½ teaspoon salt
⅛ teaspoon freshly ground pepper
2 tablespoons chopped fresh parsley
¾ cup fresh bread crumbs (page 38)
six 6-ounce rainbow trout, cleaned, with head and tail intact
1 teaspoon polyunsaturated margarine for greasing baking
  dish
2 tablespoons melted polyunsaturated margarine for basting
6 lemon wedges

Preheat oven to 350°F.

*To prepare stuffing:* Melt 4 tablespoons margarine in a medium skillet. Add mushrooms, onions, and celery . Sauté until onions are soft. Remove from heat. Season with thyme, salt, pepper, and parsley. Add bread crumbs; mix gently to blend.

Stuff trout with mixture; fasten with skewers or toothpicks. Arrange trout in a shallow greased baking dish and baste them with remaining margarine. Bake, uncovered, 20 to 25 minutes or until fish flakes easily and is still moist. Serve with lemon wedges.

*Yield:* 6 servings trout, 2 cups stuffing

*Change Stuffed Trout as follows for:*

LOW-CALORIE, DIABETIC, LOW-FAT, AND LOW-CHOLESTEROL DIETS

Reduce margarine to 3 tablespoons for sautéing vegetables for stuffing.
Omit all remaining margarine. Spray baking dish with vegetable cooking spray.
Proceed as in Basic Recipe.

Calories per serving: 415
Approximate nutrient
    values per serving:
    Protein 38 g
    Fat 26 g
    Carbohydrate 7 g
    Sodium 411 mg
    Potassium 653 mg
    Cholesterol 82 mg
Exchanges:
    Bread ½
    Meat 5
    Fat 2

LOW-SODIUM DIETS

Calories per serving: 472
Approximate nutrient
    values same as Basic
    Recipe except for:
    Sodium 172 mg
    Potassium 658 mg

Omit salt.
Substitute unsalted polyunsaturated margarine for margarine wherever used.
Add ½ teaspoon tarragon to stuffing.
Proceed as in Basic Recipe.

BLAND DIETS

Calories per serving: 472

Omit pepper.
Proceed as in Basic Recipe.

HIGH-FIBER DIETS

Calories per serving: 496

Add 3 tablespoons toasted slivered almonds (page 38) to stuffing.
Proceed as in Basic Recipe.

# Rainbow Trout

BASIC RECIPE

Serving size: 1 trout
Calories per serving: 584
Approximate nutrient
values per serving:
Protein 40 g
Fat 39 g
Carbohydrate 11 g
Sodium 505 mg
Potassium 610 mg
Cholesterol 88 mg
Exchanges:
Bread 1
Meat 5
Fat 4½

six 6-ounce rainbow trout, cleaned, with head and tail intact
1 cup milk
½ cup flour
¾ teaspoon salt
⅛ teaspoon freshly ground pepper
⅓ cup polyunsaturated oil
4½ tablespoons polyunsaturated margarine
6 lemon wedges
6 fresh parsley sprigs

Rinse trout thoroughly under cool running water and pat dry with paper towels.

Arrange trout in a single layer in a shallow pan, cover with milk, and let stand about 30 minutes.

Combine flour, salt, and pepper. Drain fish and dredge with flour mixture.

In a large skillet heat the oil. Add trout and fry about 5 minutes on each side or until fish is browned. Remove with a wide spatula to a warm serving platter.

Pour off excess oil from skillet. Add margarine to skillet and cook until lightly browned. Pour over trout and garnish with lemon wedges and parsley before serving.

*Yield:* 6 servings

*Change Rainbow Trout as follows or use Basic Recipe, if indicated, for:*

LOW-SODIUM AND RENAL DIETS

Calories per serving: 584
Approximate nutrient
values same as Basic
Recipe except for:
Calcium 94 mg
Phosphorus 458 mg
Sodium 145 mg

Omit salt.
Substitute unsalted polyunsaturated margarine for margarine.
Proceed as in Basic Recipe.

## BLAND DIETS

Omit pepper.
Proceed as in Basic Recipe.

## HIGH-FIBER DIETS

Use Basic Recipe.
For extra fiber, garnish with toasted slivered almonds (page 38) or grated lemon rind.

## RAINBOW TROUT FOR LOW-CALORIE, DIABETIC, LOW-FAT, AND LOW-CHOLESTEROL DIETS

Serving size: 1 trout
Calories per serving: 355
Approximate nutrient
  values per serving:
    Protein 38 g
    Fat 20 g
    Carbohydrate 5 g
    Sodium 494 mg
    Potassium 580 mg
    Cholesterol 82 mg
Exchanges:
  Vegetable 1
  Meat 5
  Fat 1

six 6-ounce rainbow trout, cleaned, with head and tail intact
1 cup chopped onions
1 teaspoon salt
⅛ teaspoon freshly ground pepper
1 cup white wine
6 lemon wedges
6 sprigs fresh parsley

Preheat oven to 350°F.

Rinse trout under cold running water. Pat dry with paper towels. Arrange trout in a shallow baking dish. Sprinkle with onions, salt, and pepper. Pour wine over all.

Bake about 20 minutes or until fish flakes when tested with a fork; baste occasionally. Garnish with lemon wedges and parsley before serving.

*Yield:* 6 servings

# Fillets of Sole Poached in Vermouth

BASIC RECIPE

Serving size: 4 ounces fish,
  2½ tablespoons sauce
Calories per serving: 339
Approximate nutrient
  values per serving:
    Protein 36 g
    Fat 18 g
    Carbohydrate 7 g
    Sodium 361 mg
    Potassium 705 mg
    Cholesterol 69 mg
Exchanges:
  Bread ½
  Meat 4½
  Fat 1

2 pounds fillets of sole
1 cup dry vermouth
1 cup water
2 tablespoons polyunsaturated margarine
2 tablespoons flour
½ cup grated sharp Cheddar cheese
¼ cup sour cream
⅛ teaspoon freshly ground pepper
6 lemon wedges
6 watercress sprigs

In a large skillet, simmer half the fillets in vermouth and water until fish barely flakes with a fork—about 5 minutes. Repeat until all fillets are poached. If necessary, add more water to barely cover fish. Drain well. Strain poaching liquid and reserve ¾ cup. Arrange fillets in a shallow baking dish about 11 by 7 inches.

Preheat broiler.

Melt margarine in a small saucepan. Blend in flour. Gradually stir in reserved poaching liquid and cook, stirring constantly, until sauce comes to a boil. Boil and stir 1 minute. Remove from heat and allow to cool 1 minute. Stir in cheese, sour cream, and pepper. Pour sauce over fish, place under broiler, and broil until lightly browned—about 5 minutes. Garnish with lemon wedges and watercress.

*Yield:* 6 servings

*Change Fillets of Sole Poached in Vermouth as follows or use Basic Recipe, if indicated, for:*

## LOW-CALORIE, DIABETIC, LOW-FAT, AND LOW-CHOLESTEROL DIETS

Calories per serving: 280
Approximate nutrient
    values per serving:
        Protein 36 g
        Fat 12 g
        Carbohydrate 7 g
        Sodium 413 mg
        Potassium 696 mg
        Cholesterol 57 mg
Exchanges:
    Bread ½
    Meat 4½

Poach fish as in Basic Recipe. Reduce margarine to 1 tablespoon for the sauce.
Increase reserved poaching liquid to 1 cup by adding ¼ cup water.
Substitute 2 ounces grated skim American cheese for Cheddar.
Omit sour cream.
Proceed as in Basic Recipe.

## LOW-SODIUM DIETS

Calories per serving: 337
Approximate nutrient
    values per serving:
        Protein 36 g
        Fat 18 g
        Carbohydrate 7 g
        Sodium 266 mg
        Potassium 709 mg
        Cholesterol 62 mg

Omit salt.
Substitute unsalted polyunsaturated margarine for margarine.
Substitute low-sodium Cheddar for Cheddar.
Proceed as in Basic Recipe.

## BLAND DIETS

Calories per serving: 339

Omit pepper.
Proceed as in Basic Recipe.

## HIGH-FIBER DIETS

Calories per serving: 340

Use Basic Recipe. Add ⅛ cup celery leaves to lemon wedges and watercress for garnish.

# Sole Florentine

BASIC RECIPE

Serving size: 4 ounces fish,
   ⅓ cup spinach
Calories per serving: 739
Approximate nutrient
   values per serving:
      Protein 45 g
      Fat 56 g
      Carbohydrate 15 g
      Sodium 745 mg
      Potassium 1110 mg
      Cholesterol 185 mg
Exchanges:
   Vegetable 2
   Bread ½
   Meat 5
   Fat 8

*The Fish*
2 pounds sole fillets
1½ cups Fish Stock (page 115)

*The Creamed Spinach*
two 10-ounce packages frozen chopped spinach
2 tablespoons polyunsaturated margarine
2 tablespoons flour
1 cup heavy cream
½ teaspoon salt
⅛ teaspoon freshly ground pepper
⅛ teaspoon nutmeg
1 tablespoon lemon juice

*The Mornay Sauce*
4 tablespoons polyunsaturated margarine
4 tablespoons flour
1 cup milk
1 cup heavy cream
¾ cup grated Swiss cheese
⅛ teaspoon salt
⅛ teaspoon cayenne pepper
3 tablespoons grated Swiss cheese for topping

You may do the recipe in the following order or make the creamed spinach a little ahead of time. The fish should not stand a long time, and do not overcook it.

Preheat oven to 350°F.

*To prepare the fish:* Arrange sole in shallow baking dish. Pour fish stock over fish. Cover and bake approximately 15 minutes or until fish barely flakes. Remove fillets with slotted spoon and set aside. Pour off liquid and wipe out baking dish.

*To prepare the creamed spinach:* Place spinach in saucepan and cook according to directions on package. Drain thoroughly and put in top of double boiler, over simmering water, to keep warm.

In a second saucepan, melt the margarine. Blend in flour. Add cream and cook over low heat, stirring constantly, until thickened and smooth. Cook and stir for 1 minute.

Remove from heat and blend in salt, pepper, nutmeg, and lemon juice. Add to the cooked, drained spinach and mix thoroughly. Then spread spinach over bottom of shallow baking dish and set aside.

*To prepare the Mornay sauce:* Melt the margarine in a medium-size saucepan over low heat. Blend in flour. Gradually add milk and cream, and cook, stirring constantly, until sauce comes to a boil and thickens. Boil and stir 1 minute.

Remove from heat and blend in all remaining ingredients except the cheese topping.

*To assemble the fish, spinach, and sauce:* Preheat broiler. Carefully place fish on spinach that has been previously arranged in baking dish. Cover with Mornay sauce. Sprinkle with 3 tablespoons Swiss cheese and broil until golden brown, 2 or 3 minutes.

*Yield:* 6 servings

*Change Sole Florentine as follows or use Basic Recipe, if indicated, for:*

LOW-SODIUM DIETS

Calories per serving: 752
Approximate nutrient
values per serving:
Protein 44 g
Fat 57 g
Carbohydrate 14 g
Sodium 396 mg
Potassium 1116 mg
Cholesterol 175 mg

*The fish:* Use Basic Recipe.

*The creamed spinach:* Omit salt wherever used. Substitute unsalted polyunsaturated margarine for margarine. Proceed as in Basic Recipe.

*The Mornay sauce:* Substitute unsalted polyunsaturated margarine for margarine.

Substitute ¾ cup low-sodium grated Swiss cheese for Swiss. Omit salt. Proceed as in Basic Recipe.

*The fish:* Use Basic Recipe.

*The creamed spinach:* Omit pepper and nutmeg. Proceed as in Basic Recipe.

*The Mornay sauce:* Omit cayenne pepper. Proceed as in Basic Recipe.

Calories per serving: 739

HIGH-FIBER DIETS

Use Basic Recipe and add 2 tablespoons chopped fresh parsley for edible garnish.

Calories per serving: 739

SOLE FLORENTINE FOR LOW-CALORIE, DIABETIC, LOW-FAT, AND LOW-CHOLESTEROL DIETS

*The Fish*
2 pounds sole fillets
1½ cups Fish Stock (page 115)

*The Creamed Spinach*
two 10-ounce packages frozen chopped spinach
2 tablespoons polyunsaturated margarine
2 tablespoons flour
1 cup skim milk
½ teaspoon salt
⅛ teaspoon freshly ground pepper
1 tablespoon lemon juice

*The Mornay Sauce*
3 tablespoons polyunsaturated margarine
4 tablespoons flour
2 cups skim milk
¾ cup grated skim American cheese
⅛ teaspoon salt
⅛ teaspoon cayenne pepper
3 tablespoons chopped fresh parsley

Serving size: 4 ounces fish,
⅓ cup spinach
Calories per serving: 434
Approximate nutrient
values per serving:
Protein 44 g
Fat 22 g
Carbohydrate 17 g
Sodium 897 mg
Potassium 1209 mg
Cholesterol 62 mg
Exchanges:
Milk ½
Vegetable 1
Bread ½
Meat 5
Fat 2

*To prepare the fish:* Preheat oven to 350°F.

Arrange sole in shallow baking dish. Pour fish stock over fish. Cover and bake about 15 minutes or until fish barely flakes. Remove fillets with slotted spoon and set aside. Pour off liquid. Wipe out baking dish.

*To prepare the creamed spinach:* Place spinach in saucepan and cook according to directions. Drain thoroughly. Return to saucepan, cover, and reserve.

In a second saucepan, melt the margarine. Blend in flour. Add milk and cook over low heat, stirring constantly, until thickened and smooth. Cook and stir for 1 minute. Remove from heat and blend in salt, pepper, and lemon juice. Add sauce to the cooked, drained spinach and mix thoroughly. Spread spinach over bottom of baking dish and set aside.

*To prepare the Mornay sauce:* In a medium saucepan, melt the margarine over low heat. Using wire whisk, blend in the flour. Gradually add milk and cook, stirring constantly, until sauce comes to a boil and thickens. Boil and stir 1 minute. Remove from heat and blend in cheese, salt, and cayenne pepper.

*To assemble fish, spinach, and Mornay sauce:* Preheat broiler. Carefully place fish on creamed spinach previously arranged in baking dish. Cover with Mornay sauce. Broil until golden brown, 2 or 3 minutes.

Garnish with parsley before serving.

*Yield:* 6 servings

# Baked Halibut with Cucumber Sauce ·

BASIC RECIPE

Serving size: 4 ounces fish,
    ⅓ cup sauce
Calories per serving: 416
Approximate nutrient
    values per serving:
        Protein 33 g
        Fat 28 g
        Carbohydrate 7 g
        Sodium 740 mg
        Potassium 768 mg
        Cholesterol 224 mg
Exchanges:
    Bread ½
    Meat 4
    Fat 5

*The Fish*
6 halibut steaks (2 pounds)
½ cup thinly sliced celery
½ cup chopped onions
¼ cup chopped fresh parsley
1 teaspoon salt
⅛ teaspoon freshly ground pepper
½ teaspoon thyme
1 cup dry vermouth

*The Sauce*
3 large egg yolks
¼ teaspoon salt
⅛ teaspoon dry mustard
2 tablespoons lemon juice
½ cup polyunsaturated margarine
½ cup diced peeled cucumber
½ cup heavy cream, whipped

Preheat oven to 350°F.

*To prepare the fish:* Arrange halibut steaks in a shallow baking dish in which they will fit comfortably. Top with celery, onions, parsley, salt, pepper, and thyme. Pour vermouth over fish and bake, uncovered, about 20 to 25 minutes or until fish flakes when tested with a fork. Baste once or twice with vermouth.

Remove fish and vegetables with a slotted spoon to warm serving dish. Cover and set aside.

*To prepare the sauce:* Place egg yolks, salt, mustard, and lemon juice in an electric blender. Cover and blend briefly.

In a small saucepan heat margarine until it foams. Add melted margarine to the egg mixture in the blender in a slow, steady stream while continuing to blend for about 30 seconds.

Transfer sauce to the top of a double boiler over simmering

water. Add cucumber and stir gently until it is warmed through. Fold in the whipped cream.

Spoon over fish and serve immediately.

*Yield:* 6 servings fish, 2 cups sauce

*Change Baked Halibut with Cucumber Sauce as follows or use Basic Recipe, if indicated, for:*

LOW-SODIUM DIETS

Calories per serving: 416
Approximate nutrient
values same as Basic
Recipe except for:
Sodium 130 mg

*The fish:* Omit salt.
Proceed as in Basic Recipe.

*The sauce:* Omit salt. Substitute unsalted polyunsaturated margarine for margarine.
Proceed as in Basic Recipe.

BLAND DIETS

Calories per serving: 416

*The fish:* Omit pepper.
Proceed as in Basic Recipe.

*The sauce:* Omit mustard.
Proceed as in Basic Recipe.

HIGH-FIBER DIETS

Use Basic Recipe.

## BAKED HALIBUT WITH CUCUMBER SAUCE FOR LOW-CALORIE, DIABETIC, LOW-FAT, AND LOW-CHOLESTEROL DIETS

Serving size: 4 ounces fish,
  ¼ cup sauce
Calories per serving: 202
Approximate nutrient
  values per serving:
    Protein 33 g
    Fat 4 g
    Carbohydrate 6 g
    Sodium 597 mg
    Potassium 775 mg
    Cholesterol 61 mg
Exchanges:
  Bread ½
  Meat 4

*The Fish*
6 halibut steaks (2 pounds)
½ cup thinly sliced celery
½ cup chopped onions
¼ cup chopped fresh parsley
1 teaspoon salt
⅛ teaspoon freshly ground pepper
½ teaspoon thyme
1 cup dry vermouth

*The Sauce*
1 tablespoon polyunsaturated margarine
1 tablespoon cornstarch
¾ cup Chicken Stock (page 114)
¼ teaspoon salt
⅛ teaspoon dry mustard
2 tablespoons lemon juice
Low-Cholesterol Egg Substitute (page 189) equivalent to 1
  large egg
1 large egg white, beaten to hold stiff peaks
½ cup minced peeled cucumber

Preheat oven to 350°F.

*To prepare the fish:* Arrange halibut steaks in a shallow baking dish in which they will fit comfortably. Top with celery, onions, parsley, salt, pepper, and thyme. Pour vermouth over fish and bake, uncovered, about 20 to 25 minutes or until fish flakes when tested with a fork. Baste once or twice with vermouth.

Remove fish and vegetables with a slotted spoon to warm serving dish. Cover and set aside.

*To prepare the sauce:* In a small saucepan, melt margarine. Blend in cornstarch. Gradually add stock and continue cooking over low heat, stirring until sauce thickens. Bring to a boil for 1 minute. Remove from heat and blend in salt, mustard, and lemon juice.

In a medium bowl, beat egg substitute. Pour sauce into egg substitute in a slow, steady stream, stirring constantly. Fold in beaten egg white and cucumber. Place in saucepan and stir gently over low heat for 2 or 3 minutes or until sauce is warmed through.

Spoon on fish and serve immediately.

*Yield:* 6 servings fish, 1½ cups sauce

# Haddock St. Moritz

BASIC RECIPE

Serving size: 4 ounces fish
Calories per serving: 219
Approximate nutrient
  values per serving:
    Protein 25 g
    Fat 9 g
    Carbohydrate 9 g
    Sodium 701 mg
    Potassium 554 mg
    Cholesterol 72 mg
Exchanges:
  Bread ½
  Meat 4
  Fat 1½

1 cup chopped fresh mushrooms
1 cup fresh bread crumbs (page 38)
½ cup chopped onions
1 teaspoon salt
1 teaspoon rosemary
¾ teaspoon tarragon
¼ teaspoon freshly ground pepper
1 clove garlic, put through garlic press
2 pounds haddock fillets
½ cup dry vermouth
4 tablespoons polyunsaturated margarine, melted
⅓ cup chopped fresh parsley
6 lemon wedges

Preheat oven to 350°F.

In a large bowl combine mushrooms, bread crumbs, onions, salt, rosemary, tarragon, pepper, and garlic. Mix gently.

Arrange haddock in a shallow baking dish. Pour vermouth over fish and top with mushroom mixture. Drizzle margarine over all.

Bake uncovered 20 to 25 minutes or until fish flakes when tested with a fork. Garnish with parsley and lemon wedges before serving.

*Yield:* 6 servings fish, 1½ cups sauce

*Change Haddock St. Moritz as follows or use Basic Recipe, if indicated, for:*

LOW-CALORIE, DIABETIC, LOW-FAT, AND LOW-CHOLESTEROL DIETS

Reduce margarine to 2 tablespoons.
Proceed as in Basic Recipe.

Calories per serving: 185
Approximate nutrient
  values per serving:
    Protein 25 g
    Fat 5 g
    Carbohydrate 9 g
    Sodium 663 mg
    Potassium 552 mg
    Cholesterol 72 mg
Exchanges:
  Bread ½
  Meat 4
  Fat 1

LOW-SODIUM DIETS

Omit salt. Substitute unsalted polyunsaturated margarine for margarine.
Proceed as in Basic Recipe.

Calories per serving: 219
Approximate nutrient
  values same as Basic
  Recipe except for:
    Sodium 259 mg

RENAL DIETS

Omit salt. Substitute unsalted polyunsaturated margarine for margarine.
Substitute 4-ounce can drained sliced mushrooms for fresh mushrooms.
Proceed as in Basic Recipe.

Calories per serving: 217
Approximate nutrient
  values per serving:
    Protein 25 g
    Fat 9 g
    Carbohydrate 9 g
    Calcium 71 mg
    Phosphorus 329 mg
    Sodium 307 mg
    Potassium 515 mg
    Cholesterol 72 mg

Calories per serving: 219

HIGH-FIBER DIETS

Use Basic Recipe.

# Haddock Mousse with Carrot Sauce

BASIC RECIPE

Serving size: ⅔ cup
  mousse, 2 tablespoons
  sauce
Calories per serving: 286
Approximate nutrient
  values per serving:
    Protein 15 g
    Fat 23 g
    Carbohydrate 6 g
    Sodium 586 mg
    Potassium 368 mg
    Cholesterol 91 mg
Exchanges:
  Vegetable 1
  Meat 2
  Fat 4½

*The Mousse*
1 pound haddock fillets
½ cup chopped onions
½ cup cooked diced carrots
¾ teaspoon salt
⅛ teaspoon freshly ground pepper
3 large egg whites
1 cup heavy cream
1 tablespoon polyunsaturated margarine for greasing mold

*The Sauce*
1 cup Chicken Stock (page 114)
½ cup dry white wine
½ medium carrot, sliced
2 fresh mushrooms, sliced
¼ cup chopped onions
1 sprig fresh parsley
1 small bay leaf
2 tablespoons polyunsaturated margarine for making the sauce
1½ tablespoons flour
¼ teaspoon salt
⅛ teaspoon freshly ground pepper

255

½ teaspoon dillweed

2 tablespoons polyunsaturated margarine for enriching the sauce

*To prepare the mousse:* Put fish, onions, and carrots through a food grinder or processor, using the fine blade. Place mixture in a medium bowl. Add salt and pepper. Beat egg whites until foamy. Whip heavy cream until stiff. Gradually fold whites into the fish mixture, then fold in whipped cream. Fill a large bowl with cracked ice and place the medium bowl with fish mixture in ice. Let stand over ice for 1 hour. Stir occasionally.

Preheat oven to 350°F.

Grease a 5-cup fish mold with margarine. Spoon haddock mixture into mold and cover with waxed paper. Place mold in shallow pan and pour 1 inch hot water around the mold. Bake 40 to 50 minutes or until mousse is set. Remove waxed paper and place mold on a rack. Allow to cool 10 minutes before unmolding.

*To prepare the sauce:* In a medium saucepan simmer stock, wine, carrot, mushrooms, onions, parsley, and bay leaf, tightly covered, for 20 minutes. Strain and reserve 1 cup.

In the same saucepan, melt the 2 tablespoons margarine, blend in flour, and gradually add the 1 cup strained liquid. Cook over moderate heat, stirring constantly, until sauce is thickened and smooth. Boil and stir 1 minute. Mix in seasonings and remaining margarine. Unmold mousse and serve with sauce.

*Yield:* 6 servings mousse, 1 cup sauce

*Change Haddock Mousse with Carrot Sauce or use Basic Recipe, if indicated, for:*

LOW-CALORIE, DIABETIC, LOW-FAT, AND LOW-CHOLESTEROL DIETS

*The mousse:* Substitute skim milk for cream. Set aside.

Place 1 packet unflavored gelatin in a large bowl and soften in ¼ cup cold water. Then add ½ cup boiling water and stir until gelatin dissolves. Cool.

Prepare fish, vegetables, and seasonings as in Basic Recipe. Beat egg whites and add to fish mixture.

Next, stir skim milk into fish mixture and turn into the dissolved gelatin. Blend thoroughly. Set in bowl of cracked ice and let stand for 1 hour.

Omit margarine.

Prepare mold by spraying with vegetable cooking spray.

Proceed as in Basic Recipe.

*The sauce:* Reduce margarine for making the sauce to 1 tablespoon. Omit margarine for enriching the sauce.

Proceed as in Basic Recipe.

LOW-SODIUM DIETS

*The mousse and the sauce:* Omit salt.

Substitute unsalted polyunsaturated margarine for margarine wherever used.

Proceed as in Basic Recipe.

BLAND DIETS

*The mousse and the sauce:* Omit pepper.

Proceed as in Basic Recipe.

HIGH-FIBER DIETS:

Use Basic Recipe.

For extra fiber, add edible garnish of carrot curls and fresh parsley.

Calories per serving: 109
Approximate nutrient
  values per serving:
    Protein 16 g
    Fat 2 g
    Carbohydrate 7 g
    Sodium 530 mg
    Potassium 405 mg
    Cholesterol 37 mg
Exchanges:
  Vegetable 1
  Meat 2

Calories per serving: 286
Approximate nutrient
  values same as Basic
  Recipe except for:
    Sodium 167 mg

Calories per serving: 286

257

# Baked Scrod with Herbs

BASIC RECIPE

Serving size: 3 ounces fish,
   ¼ cup sauce
Calories per serving: 188
Approximate nutrient
   values per serving:
      Protein 25 g
      Fat 7 g
      Carbohydrate 7 g
      Sodium 428 mg
      Potassium 633 mg
      Cholesterol 41 mg
Exchanges:
   Vegetable 1
   Meat 3
   Fat 1

½ cup chopped onions
1 clove garlic, put through garlic press
2 tablespoons polyunsaturated margarine
1½ cups coarsely chopped peeled tomatoes
½ teaspoon thyme
½ teaspoon basil
½ teaspoon salt
⅛ teaspoon freshly ground pepper
1 pound scrod fillets
¼ cup chopped fresh parsley

Preheat oven to 350°F.

In a medium skillet sauté onions and garlic in margarine until onions are soft.

Add tomatoes, thyme, basil, salt, and pepper. Simmer, uncovered, until sauce thickens and is reduced to approximately 1¼ cups.

Place scrod in a shallow baking dish large enough to hold fish comfortably. Spoon sauce over fish. Bake, uncovered, about 15 to 20 minutes or until fish flakes when tested with a fork.

Garnish with parsley before serving.

*Yield:* 4 servings

*Change Baked Scrod with Herbs as follows or use Basic Recipe, if indicated, for:*

## LOW-CALORIE, DIABETIC, LOW-FAT, AND LOW-CHOLESTEROL DIETS

Omit margarine. Instead of sautéing, place onions, garlic, tomatoes, thyme, basil, salt, and pepper in a heavy skillet and simmer, uncovered, until onions are soft and sauce thickens and is reduced to approximately 1¼ cups.
Proceed as in Basic Recipe.

Calories per serving: 138
Approximate nutrient
  values per serving:
    Protein 25 g
    Fat 1 g
    Carbohydrate 7 g
    Sodium 371 mg
    Potassium 631 mg
    Cholesterol 41 mg
Exchanges:
  Vegetable 1
  Meat 3

## LOW-SODIUM DIETS

Omit Salt.
Substitute unsalted polyunsaturated margarine for margarine.
Proceed as in Basic Recipe.

Calories per serving: 188
Approximate nutrient
  values same as Basic
  Recipe except for:
    Sodium 97 mg

## BLAND DIETS

Omit pepper.
Proceed as in Basic Recipe.

Calories per serving: 188

## HIGH-FIBER DIETS

Use Basic Recipe.

## BAKED SCROD WITH HERBS FOR RENAL DIETS

½ cup chopped onions
1 clove garlic, put through garlic press
1 pound scrod fillets
2 tablespoons unsalted polyunsaturated margarine
½ teaspoon thyme

Serving size: 3 ounces fish
Calories per serving: 172
Approximate nutrient
  values per serving:
    Protein 24 g
    Fat 6 g

Carbohydrate 4 g
Calcium 47 mg
Phosphorus 237 mg
Sodium 94 mg
Potassium 407 mg
Cholesterol 41 mg
Exchanges:
  Vegetable 1
  Meat 3
  Fat 1

½ teaspoon basil
⅛ teaspoon freshly ground pepper
¼ cup dry vermouth
2 tablespoons water
¼ cup chopped fresh parsley

Preheat oven to 350°F.

In a medium skillet sauté onions and garlic in margarine until onions are soft.

Place fish in a shallow baking dish. Spoon sautéed vegetables over fish. Sprinkle thyme, basil, and pepper over the fish. Dribble vermouth and water over all. Bake, uncovered, approximately 15 to 20 minutes or until fish flakes easily when tested with a fork. Garnish with parsley before serving.

*Yield:* 4 servings

# Baked Salmon Steaks

BASIC RECIPE

Serving size: 4-ounce steak
Calories per serving: 280
Approximate nutrient
  values per serving:
    Protein 32 g
    Fat 13 g
    Carbohydrate 7 g
    Sodium 597 mg
    Potassium 685 mg
    Cholesterol 53 mg
Exchanges:
  Bread ½
  Meat 4
  Fat 1

2 cups chopped celery with leaves
5 salmon steaks (2 pounds)
2 tablespoons polyunsaturated margarine
¾ cups fresh bread crumbs (page 38)
¾ teaspoon tarragon
¾ teaspoon rosemary
¾ teaspoon salt
⅛ teaspoon freshly ground pepper
6 lemon wedges

Preheat oven to 350°F.

Arrange celery in bottom of a shallow baking dish; place salmon steaks on top. Set aside.

Melt the margarine in a medium skillet. Add bread crumbs, tarragon, rosemary, salt, and pepper; mix gently to blend.

Spread bread crumb mixture evenly over fish. Bake, uncovered, 25 minutes or until fish flakes when tested with a fork. Garnish with lemon wedges before serving.

*Yield:* 5 servings

*Change Baked Salmon Steaks as follows or use Basic Recipe, if indicated, for:*

LOW-CALORIE, DIABETIC, LOW-FAT, AND LOW-CHOLESTEROL DIETS

Use Basic Recipe.

LOW-SODIUM DIETS

Calories per serving: 289
Approximate nutrient
  values per serving:
    Protein 32 g
    Fat 14 g
    Carbohydrate 7 g
    Sodium 223 mg
    Potassium 691 mg
    Cholesterol 53 mg

Omit salt.
Substitute unsalted polyunsaturated margarine for margarine.
Add 1 tablespoon toasted sesame seeds (page 38) to crumb mixture.
Proceed as in Basic Recipe.

BLAND DIETS

Calories per serving: 280

Omit pepper.
Proceed as in Basic Recipe.

HIGH-FIBER DIETS

Calories per serving: 290

Add 1 tablespoon toasted sesame seeds (page 38) to crumb mixture.
Proceed as in Basic Recipe.

# Salmon Jambalaya

BASIC RECIPE

Serving size: 1 cup
Calories per serving: 360
Approximate nutrient
  values per serving:
    Protein 23 g
    Fat 14 g
    Carbohydrate 35 g
    Sodium 689 mg
    Potassium 775 mg
    Cholesterol 39 mg
Exchanges:
  Vegetable 2
  Bread 1½
  Meat 2½
  Fat 1

3 tablespoons polyunsaturated margarine
1 cup chopped onions
1 cup sliced celery
1 cup coarsely chopped green pepper
2 cloves garlic, put through garlic press
1 cup diced cooked ham
2 cups coarsely chopped peeled tomatoes
1½ cups Chicken Stock (page 114)
½ teaspoon thyme
½ teaspoon chili powder
½ teaspoon salt
¼ teaspoon freshly ground pepper
1 cup raw long-grain rice
1½ cups flaked cooked fresh salmon

In a large skillet, melt the margarine. Add onions, celery, green pepper, and garlic. Sauté until onions are soft. Add ham, tomatoes, stock, thyme, chili powder, salt, and pepper. Bring to a boil and stir in rice. Reduce heat, cover, and simmer slowly 20 minutes or until rice is tender, stirring occasionally. Add salmon and cook approximately 5 minutes or until heated through.

*Yield:* 6 servings

*Change Salmon Jambalaya as follows or use Basic Recipe, if indicated, for:*

LOW-CALORIE, DIABETIC, LOW-FAT, LOW-CHOLESTEROL, AND HIGH-FIBER DIETS

Use Basic Recipe.

Omit salt.
Substitute unsalted polyunsaturated margarine for margarine.
Substitute cooked chicken for ham.
Proceed as in Basic Recipe.

Calories per serving: 343
Approximate nutrient
   values per serving:
     Protein 26 g
     Fat 11 g
     Carbohydrate 34 g
     Sodium 139 mg
     Potassium 790 mg
     Cholesterol 44 mg

BLAND DIETS

Omit chili powder.
Omit freshly ground pepper.
Add ¼ teaspoon oregano and ¼ teaspoon ground cumin.
Proceed as in Basic Recipe.

Calories per serving: 360

# Salmon Patties with Wine Sauce

BASIC RECIPE

This recipe needs at least 1 hour of refrigeration.

*The Salmon*
15½-ounce can salmon
3 tablespoons polyunsaturated margarine
4 tablespoons flour
¾ cup milk
¼ teaspoon basil
¼ teaspoon oregano
½ teaspoon salt
⅛ teaspoon freshly ground pepper
2 tablespoons lemon juice
½ cup fresh bread crumbs (page 38)
⅓ cup polyunsaturated margarine for sautéing

Serving size: 1 patty, 2
   tablespoons sauce
Calories per serving: 331
Approximate nutrient
   values per serving:
     Protein 17 g
     Fat 24 g
     Carbohydrate 11 g
     Sodium 771 mg
     Potassium 387 mg
     Cholesterol 32 mg
Exchanges:
   Milk ¼
   Bread ½
   Meat 2
   Fat 4

*The Wine Sauce*
1 cup Chicken Stock (page 114)
½ cup dry white wine
1 small carrot, sliced
2 fresh mushrooms, sliced
2 tablespoons chopped onions
1 sprig fresh parsley
1 small bay leaf
2 tablespoons polyunsaturated margarine
1½ tablespoons flour
¼ teaspoon salt
⅛ teaspoon freshly ground pepper

*To prepare the salmon:* Drain salmon well. Place in medium-size bowl, remove bones, and flake with a fork.

Melt margarine in a small saucepan. Blend in flour and gradually stir in milk. Cook over moderate heat, stirring constantly, until mixture comes to a boil. It will be very thick. Remove from heat and add to salmon. Add basil, oregano, salt, pepper, and lemon juice and mix until thoroughly blended. Refrigerate 1 hour.

Shape salmon mixture into 6 patties, approximately ½ inch thick. Coat with bread crumbs and refrigerate again for at least 1 hour.

*To prepare the sauce:* In a medium saucepan place stock, wine, carrot, mushrooms, onions, parsley, and bay leaf. Simmer, tightly covered, for 20 minutes. Strain and reserve 1 cup liquid.

In the same saucepan melt the margarine over moderate heat without letting it brown. Add flour and stir until well blended. Gradually add the 1 cup reserved liquid and cook over moderate heat, stirring constantly, until sauce is thickened and smooth. Boil and stir 1 minute. Remove from heat and stir in salt and pepper. Set aside and keep warm.

*To complete recipe:* Remove salmon patties from refrigerator. Melt ⅓ cup margarine in medium-size skillet. Add patties and sauté until brown on both sides.

Serve with wine sauce.

*Yield:* 6 servings salmon, 1 cup sauce

Change Salmon Patties with Wine Sauce as follows or use Basic Recipe, if indicated, for:

LOW-CALORIE, DIABETIC, LOW-FAT, AND LOW-CHOLESTEROL DIETS

*The salmon:* Preheat oven to 400°F. Reduce margarine to 2 tablespoons to blend with flour.

Substitute skim milk for milk.

Omit margarine for sautéing. Instead, spray cookie sheet with vegetable cooking spray. Bake patties for 10 minutes, turn with spatula, and bake 10 minutes more, or until brown on both sides.

*The wine sauce:* Reduce margarine to 1 tablespoon.

Proceed as in Basic Recipe.

Calories per serving: 204
Approximate nutrient
  values per serving:
    Protein 17 g
    Fat 10 g
    Carbohydrate 11 g
    Sodium 639 mg
    Potassium 388 mg
    Cholesterol 29 mg
Exchanges:
  Milk ¼
  Bread ½
  Meat 2
  Fat 1

LOW-SODIUM DIETS

*The salmon:* Omit salt.

Substitute unsalted polyunsaturated margarine for margarine wherever used.

Substitute two 7¾-ounce cans salmon with no salt added for salmon.

Proceed as in Basic Recipe.

*The wine sauce:* Omit salt.

Substitute unsalted polyunsaturated margarine for margarine.

Proceed as in Basic Recipe.

Calories per serving: 327
Approximate nutrient
  values per serving:
    Protein 18 g
    Fat 24 g
    Carbohydrate 11 g
    Sodium 89 mg
    Potassium 369 mg
    Cholesterol 30 mg

BLAND DIETS

*The salmon and the wine sauce:* Omit pepper.

Proceed as in Basic Recipe.

Calories per serving: 331

Calories per serving: 332

*The salmon:* Add ¼ cup chopped fresh parsley to salmon mixture.
    Proceed as in Basic Recipe.

*The wine sauce:* Use Basic Recipe.
    For extra fiber, serve with broccoli spears or lima beans.

# Marinated Swordfish Steaks

BASIC RECIPE

The swordfish should be marinated for 2 hours.

Serving size: 4 ounces fish
Calories per serving: 339
Approximate nutrient
   values per serving:
     Protein 36 g
     Fat 20 g
     Carbohydrate 3 g
     Sodium 912 mg
     Potassium 569 mg
     Cholesterol 55 mg
Exchanges:
   Meat 4
   Fat 2½

6 swordfish steaks (2½ pounds)
3 bay leaves, crumbled into large pieces
⅓ cup lemon juice
⅓ cup soy sauce
½ cup polyunsaturated oil
2 cloves garlic, put through garlic press
¼ teaspoon freshly ground pepper

Place swordfish in a shallow baking dish in which it fits comfortably. Sprinkle bay leaves on top.
    Make a marinade with the remaining ingredients. Beat thoroughly and pour over fish. Cover and refrigerate 2 hours, turning once.
    Preheat broiler. Remove swordfish from marinade. Broil about 10 minutes per side, brushing each side once or twice with remaining marinade. The fish is done when a thin knife gently inserted shows flesh is white.

*Yield:* 6 servings

*Change Marinated Swordfish Steaks as follows for:*

## LOW-CALORIE, DIABETIC, LOW-FAT, AND LOW-CHOLESTEROL DIETS

Reduce oil to 2 tablespoons.
Proceed as in Basic Recipe.

Calories per serving: 274
Approximate nutrient
  values per serving:
    Protein 36 g
    Fat 12 g
    Carbohydrate 3 g
    Sodium 912 mg
    Potassium 569 mg
    Cholesterol 55 mg
Exchanges:
  Meat 4
  Fat 1

## LOW-SODIUM AND RENAL DIETS

Omit soy sauce and substitute ⅓ cup dry vermouth.
Proceed as in Basic Recipe.

Calories per serving: 335
Approximate nutrient
  values per serving:
    Protein 36 g
    Fat 20 g
    Carbohydrate 2 g
    Calcium 37 mg
    Phosphorus 353 mg
    Sodium 138 mg
    Potassium 530 mg
    Cholesterol 55 mg

## BLAND DIETS

Omit pepper.
Proceed as in Basic Recipe.

Calories per serving: 339

## HIGH-FIBER DIETS

Add 1 teaspoon grated lemon rind to marinade.
Proceed as in Basic Recipe.
For extra fiber, serve with julienned sweet red or green
  peppers.

Calories per serving: 339

# Turkish Swordfish on Skewers

BASIC RECIPE

The swordfish should be marinated for about 4 hours.

2½ pounds swordfish cut in 1-inch cubes
12 bay leaves
⅔ cup olive oil
⅔ cup lemon juice
1½ teaspoons marjoram
1 teaspoon oregano
1 teaspoon salt
¼ teaspoon freshly ground pepper
2 cloves garlic, put through garlic press
⅔ cup chopped onions
1 large eggplant, cut into 24 one-inch cubes
12 large mushrooms
2 green peppers, cut into 12 one-inch squares

Arrange fish in a single layer in a large, shallow glass baking dish. Place bay leaves over fish.

Combine oil, lemon juice, marjoram, oregano, salt, pepper, garlic, and onions and pour over fish. Let fish stand in marinade at room temperature 4 hours, turning occasionally. Discard bay leaves before making kabobs.

Thread fish, eggplant, mushrooms, and green peppers alternately on skewers and grill over charcoal or under broiler, about 7 to 10 minutes, turning and basting with marinade. Fish is done when it flakes easily with a fork.

*Yield:* 6 servings

Serving size: 4 ounces fish, 4 cubes eggplant, 2 mushrooms, 2 squares green pepper
Calories per serving: 496
Approximate nutrient values per serving:
    Protein 39 g
    Fat 32 g
    Carbohydrate 14 g
    Sodium 520 mg
    Potassium 1018 mg
    Cholesterol 55 mg
Exchanges:
    Vegetable 3
    Meat 4
    Fat 5

*Change Turkish Swordfish on Skewers as follows or use Basic Recipe, if indicated, for:*

## LOW-CALORIE, DIABETIC, LOW-FAT, AND LOW-CHOLESTEROL DIETS

Calories per serving: 363
Approximate nutrient
  values per serving:
    Protein 39 g
    Fat 17 g
    Carbohydrate 14 g
    Sodium 520 mg
    Potassium 1018 mg
    Cholesterol 55 mg
Exchanges:
  Vegetable 3
  Meat 4
  Fat 2

Omit olive oil. Substitute ¼ cup polyunsaturated oil.
Proceed as in Basic Recipe.

## LOW-SODIUM DIETS

Calories per serving: 496
Approximate nutrient
  values same as Basic
  Recipe except for:
    Sodium 154 mg

Omit salt.
Proceed as in Basic Recipe.

## BLAND DIETS

Calories per serving: 496

Omit ground pepper.
Proceed as in Basic Recipe.

## HIGH-FIBER DIETS

Use Basic Recipe.

# Tuna Catch

BASIC RECIPE

Serving size: 1½ cups
Calories per serving: 577
Approximate nutrient
  values per serving:
    Protein 25 g
    Fat 43 g
    Carbohydrate 26 g
    Sodium 1140 mg
    Potassium 670 mg
    Cholesterol 196 mg
Exchanges:
  Milk ¼
  Vegetable 2
  Bread 1
  Meat 2
  Fat 8

*The Casserole*
4 cups cooked fresh broccoli in bite-size pieces
6 tablespoons polyunsaturated margarine
½ cup chopped onions
½ cup diced green pepper
6 tablespoons flour
1½ cups milk
1½ cups light cream
½ teaspoon basil
½ teaspoon marjoram
1 teaspoon salt
¼ teaspoon freshly ground pepper
2 tablespoons lemon juice
two 6½-ounce cans chunk tuna packed in water, drained
2 hard-cooked large eggs, coarsely chopped

*The Topping*
4 tablespoons polyunsaturated margarine
2 cups fresh bread crumbs (page 38)

Preheat oven to 375°F.

*To prepare the casserole:* Arrange cooked broccoli in bottom of a shallow baking dish.

Heat 6 tablespoons margarine in a medium saucepan, add onions and green pepper, and sauté until onions are soft.

Blend in flour. Gradually stir in milk and cream and cook over moderate heat, stirring constantly, until sauce thickens and comes to a boil.

Remove from heat. Add basil, marjoram, salt, pepper, and lemon juice. Add drained tuna and chopped eggs and mix gently. Spoon sauce over broccoli.

*To prepare the topping:* In a medium skillet melt remaining 4 tablespoons margarine. Add bread crumbs and toss gently. Sprinkle crumbs over casserole and bake, uncovered, about 20 minutes or until topping has browned.

*Yield:* 6 servings

*Change Tuna Catch as follows or use Basic Recipe, if indicated, for:*

## LOW-CALORIE, DIABETIC, LOW-FAT, AND LOW-CHOLESTEROL DIETS

Calories per serving: 279
Approximate nutrient
  values per serving:
    Protein 23 g
    Fat 9 g
    Carbohydrate 27 g
    Sodium 1016 mg
    Potassium 698 mg
    Cholesterol 32 mg
Exchanges:
  Milk ½
  Vegetable 2
  Bread 1
  Meat 2
  Fat 1½

*The casserole:* Reduce margarine to 4 tablespoons.
  Substitute 3 cups skim milk for milk and cream.
  Omit eggs.
  Proceed as in Basic Recipe.

*The topping:* Omit margarine. Sprinkle bread crumbs over casserole and bake until browned.

## LOW-SODIUM DIETS

Calories per serving: 575
Approximate nutrient
  values same as Basic
  Recipe except for:
    Sodium 188 mg
    Potassium 672 mg

*The casserole:* Omit salt.
  Substitute unsalted polyunsaturated margarine for the margarine.
  Substitute tuna with no salt added for tuna.
  Proceed as in Basic Recipe.

*The topping:* Substitute unsalted polyunsaturated margarine for margarine.
  Proceed as in Basic Recipe.

## BLAND DIETS

Calories per serving: 577

*The casserole:* Omit ground pepper. Proceed as in Basic Recipe.

*The topping:* Use Basic Recipe.

## HIGH-FIBER DIETS

Use Basic Recipe.

271

# Scallops in Lemon Sauce

BASIC RECIPE

Serving size: 3 ounces
    scallops
Calories per serving: 174
Approximate nutrient
    values per serving:
        Protein 23 g
        Fat 8 g
        Carbohydrate 2 g
        Sodium 327 mg
        Potassium 504 mg
        Cholesterol 52 mg
Exchanges:
    Meat 3
    Fat 1

1½ pounds sea or bay scallops
3 tablespoons polyunsaturated margarine
¼ cup lemon juice
¼ teaspoon dillweed
1 clove garlic, put through garlic press
⅛ teaspoon freshly ground pepper
3 tablespoons chopped fresh parsley

Wash scallops and dry thoroughly. If using large sea scallops, cut them into bite-size pieces.

Heat 2 tablespoons of the margarine in a large heavy skillet. Add half the scallops and sauté over moderately high heat, turning them, until lightly browned—about 4 or 5 minutes.

As scallops are cooked, transfer with a slotted spoon to a warm serving dish. Add the remaining scallops and 1 tablespoon margarine to skillet and sauté until lightly browned. Transfer to serving dish.

Reduce heat and add lemon juice, dillweed, garlic, and pepper to skillet. Cook briefly, stirring to remove brown particles on bottom of skillet. Then pour sauce over scallops, garnish with chopped parsley, and serve immediately.

*Yield:* 5 servings

*Change Scallops in Lemon Sauce as follows or use Basic Recipe, if indicated, for:*

LOW-CALORIE, DIABETIC, LOW-FAT, AND LOW-CHOLESTEROL DIETS

Use Basic Recipe.

Substitute unsalted polyunsaturated margarine for margarine.
Proceed as in Basic Recipe.

Calories per serving: 174
Approximate nutrient
   values same as Basic
   Recipe except for:
      Calcium 119 mg
      Phosphorus 333 mg
      Sodium 259 mg

### BLAND DIETS

Omit pepper.
Proceed as in Basic Recipe.

Calories per serving: 174

### HIGH-FIBER DIETS

Use Basic Recipe.
Mix ¼ cup toasted slivered almonds (page 38) with parsley for
   garnish.

Calories per serving: 213

# Scallops and Asparagus

### BASIC RECIPE

Serving size: ¾ cup
Calories per serving: 192
Approximate nutrient
   values per serving:
      Protein 17 g
      Fat 8 g
      Carbohydrate 14 g
      Sodium 840 mg
      Potassium 683 mg
      Cholesterol 32 mg
Exchanges:
   Vegetable 3
   Meat 2
   Fat 1

½ cup Chicken Stock (page 114)
2 tablespoons soy sauce
3 tablespoons dry sherry
1 clove garlic, put through garlic press
1 tablespoon cornstarch
1 pound thin asparagus, stalks peeled
2 tablespoons polyunsaturated oil
¾ pound bay or sea scallops
½ cup sliced water chestnuts

Mix chicken stock, soy sauce, sherry, and garlic. Stir in cornstarch and set aside.

Cut each asparagus spear diagonally into 1½-inch pieces.

Heat the oil in a large, heavy skillet until hot. Add asparagus and stir-fry about 3 minutes or until asparagus is coated with oil.

Add scallops, water chestnuts, and reserved chicken broth mixture. Blend carefully and simmer, covered, stirring occasionally, 3 to 5 minutes or until scallops are tender.

*Yield:* 4 servings

*Change Scallops and Asparagus as follows or use Basic Recipe, if indicated, for:*

LOW-SODIUM DIETS

Omit soy sauce.
Proceed as in Basic Recipe.

Calories per serving: 186
Approximate nutrient
  values per serving:
    Protein 17 g
    Fat 8 g
    Carbohydrate 13 g
    Sodium 180 mg
    Potassium 650 mg
    Cholesterol 32 mg

BLAND AND HIGH-FIBER DIETS

Use Basic Recipe.

SCALLOPS AND ASPARAGUS FOR LOW-CALORIE, DIABETIC, LOW-FAT, AND LOW-CHOLESTEROL DIETS

Serving size: ¾ cup
Calories per serving: 132
Approximate nutrient
  values per serving:
    Protein 17 g
    Fat 1 g
    Carbohydrate 14 g
    Sodium 845 mg
    Potassium 692 mg
    Cholesterol 32 mg

1 pound thin asparagus, stalks peeled
¾ cup Chicken Stock (page 114)
2 tablespoons soy sauce
3 tablespoons dry sherry
1 clove garlic, put through garlic press
1 tablespoon cornstarch
¾ pound bay or sea scallops
½ cup sliced water chestnuts

Cut each asparagus spear diagonally into 1½-inch pieces. Simmer asparagus, covered, in chicken stock for 3 minutes.

Mix soy sauce, sherry, and garlic; stir in cornstarch. Pour mixture into asparagus and mix gently. Add scallops and water chestnuts. Simmer, covered, stirring occasionally, 5 minutes or until scallops are tender.

*Yield:* 4 servings

# Creamed Oysters

BASIC RECIPE

1 teaspoon polyunsaturated margarine for greasing dish
2 cups coarsely crumbled soda crackers
½ cup polyunsaturated margarine, melted
1½ pints shucked oysters with liquor
½ teaspoon salt
⅛ teaspoon freshly ground pepper
3 tablespoons chopped fresh parsley
¼ cup heavy cream
2 tablespoons dry sherry

Preheat oven to 400°F.

Grease bottom of a shallow 1½-quart baking dish with 1 teaspoon margarine. Add cracker crumbs to the melted margarine and mix gently to blend. Cover bottom of baking dish with half the cracker mixture.

Drain the liquor from oysters and reserve ¼ cup. Arrange drained oysters on top of crackers and sprinkle with salt, pepper, and parsley.

Combine reserved liquor with cream and sherry and pour over oysters. Top with remaining crumbs and bake, uncovered, about 15 to 20 minutes or until golden brown and bubbling.

*Yield:* 4 servings

*Change Creamed Oysters as follows or use Basic Recipe, if indicated, for:*

## LOW-CALORIE, DIABETIC, LOW-FAT, AND LOW-CHOLESTEROL DIETS

Calories per serving: 391
Approximate nutrient
  values per serving:
    Protein 19 g
    Fat 20 g
    Carbohydrate 32 g
    Sodium 927 mg
    Potassium 310 mg
    Cholesterol 90 mg
Exchanges:
  Bread 2
  Meat 2
  Fat 3

Reduce margarine to ¼ cup for mixing with crackers.
Substitute skim milk for cream.
Proceed as in Basic Recipe.

## LOW-SODIUM AND RENAL DIETS

Calories per serving: 535
Approximate nutrient
  values per serving:
    Protein 19 g
    Fat 37 g
    Carbohydrate 35 g
    Calcium 192 mg
    Phosphorus 300 mg
    Sodium 178 mg
    Potassium 299 mg
    Cholesterol 110 mg

Omit salt.
Substitute same amounts unsalted polyunsaturated margarine
  for margarine wherever used.
Substitute unsalted soda crackers for crackers.
Proceed as in Basic Recipe.

## BLAND DIETS

Calories per serving: 538

Omit pepper.
Proceed as in Basic Recipe.

## HIGH-FIBER DIETS

Use Basic Recipe.
For extra fiber serve with fresh peas or minted carrots.

# MEATS

Meats are currently the newest entries on the maligned foods list. There is some evidence that too much meat of the fatty variety may be less than ideal for your daily diet, but, of course, you should avoid eating excess quantities of any one food.

Meats are a superb source of protein, and most supply important amounts of many other nutrients: fat, calcium, phosphorus, sodium, potassium, and cholesterol.

Lean meats, round steak, and choice rather than prime cuts of beef (always with the fat trimmed off) should be acceptable for most special diets. Veal, of course, is lean but expensive. Chicken or white meat of turkey can be substituted for veal in most of our recipes, although the flavors and the nutrient values will change.

Most gourmet recipes using lamb and pork lose so much flavor in the translation from basic to special diets that although we tried dozens of them we retained only a very few for the book, all of them delicious.

The serving sizes we suggest may be smaller than those to which you are accustomed. Let your doctor or nutritionist guide you in choosing the number of servings you should include in your daily meal plan.

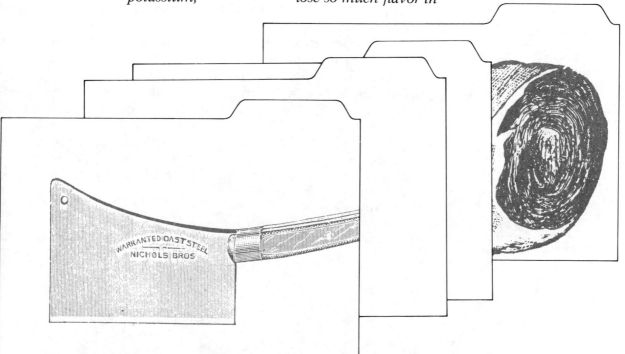

# Pot Roast with Madeira and Onions

BASIC RECIPE

Serving size: 3 ounces
beef, ⅓ cup gravy and
vegetables
Calories per serving: 227
Approximate nutrient
values per serving:
Protein 25 g
Fat 11 g
Carbohydrate 7 g
Sodium 549 mg
Potassium 434 mg
Cholesterol 70 mg
Exchanges:
Bread ½
Meat 3
Fat 1

4-pound boneless beef chuck roast, trimmed of excess fat
3 tablespoons flour
2 tablespoons polyunsaturated oil
2 tablespoons polyunsaturated margarine
2 cups sliced onions
1 cup sliced carrots
1 cup sliced celery
1 teaspoon ground cumin
1 teaspoon dry mustard
½ teaspoon ground cloves
2 teaspoons salt
¼ teaspoon freshly ground pepper
2 teaspoons freshly grated peeled ginger root
1 cup Madeira or sherry
2 cups Beef Stock (page 113)

Preheat oven to 325°F.

Dredge beef in flour. Heat together the oil and margarine in a large casserole. Add meat and brown on all sides. Remove beef to a platter.

Add onions to casserole and sauté until soft, stirring to remove any meat particles on bottom.

Return beef to casserole and arrange carrots and celery around it. Season with cumin, mustard, cloves, salt, and pepper. Stir ginger into Madeira or sherry and pour over meat. Cover with beef stock and bring to a simmer.

Cover and transfer to oven. Bake about 2 hours or until beef is tender, turning meat every hour. Carve beef into thin slices and spoon pan gravy and vegetables over meat before serving.

*Yield:* 10 servings

*Change Pot Roast with Madeira and Onions as follows or use Basic Recipe, if indicated, for:*

### LOW-CALORIE, DIABETIC, LOW-FAT, AND LOW-CHOLESTEROL DIETS

Omit margarine. Instead, spray casserole with vegetable cooking spray. Heat 2 tablespoons polyunsaturated oil in the casserole, add beef, and brown on all sides.
Proceed as in Basic Recipe.

Calories per serving: 206
Approximate nutrient
  values per serving:
    Protein 25 g
    Fat 8 g
    Carbohydrate 7 g
    Sodium 526 mg
    Potassium 433 mg
    Cholesterol 70 mg
Exchanges:
  Bread ½
  Meat 3
  Fat ½

### LOW-SODIUM DIETS

Omit salt.
Substitute unsalted polyunsaturated margarine for margarine.
Proceed as in Basic Recipe.

Calories per serving: 227
Approximate nutrient
  values same as Basic
  Recipe except for:
    Sodium 87 mg

### BLAND DIETS

Omit pepper, mustard, and ground cloves.
Proceed as in Basic Recipe.

Calories per serving: 226

### HIGH-FIBER DIETS

Use Basic Recipe.

# Boeuf Bourguignon

BASIC RECIPE

Serving size: 3 ounces
  beef, ⅛ cup sauce
Calories per serving: 353
Approximate nutrient
  values per serving:
    Protein 28 g
    Fat 21 g
    Carbohydrate 13 g
    Sodium 358 mg
    Potassium 647 mg
    Cholesterol 77 mg
Exchanges:
  Vegetable 3
  Meat 3
  Fat 2½

3 pounds boneless beef chuck, trimmed of excess fat and cut
  into 2-inch cubes
¼ cup flour
3 tablespoons polyunsaturated margarine for browning beef
3 tablespoons polyunsaturated oil for browning beef
2 cups diced carrots
3 cups coarsely chopped onions
1 teaspoon finely minced garlic
1 teaspoon thyme
1 teaspoon salt
¼ teaspoon freshly ground pepper
2 bay leaves
2 cups Burgundy wine
1 cup Beef Stock (page 113)
2 tablespoons polyunsaturated margarine for sautéing
mushrooms
2 tablespoons polyunsaturated oil for sautéing mushrooms
¾ pound medium whole mushrooms
½ cup chopped fresh parsley

Dredge beef with flour.

Heat 3 tablespoons each of the margarine and oil in a large, heavy casserole. Add beef, a few pieces at a time, and sauté until browned on all sides. As beef browns remove to a platter.

Add carrots, onions, and garlic to casserole and sauté until onions are soft. Return beef to casserole and add thyme, salt, pepper, bay leaves, wine, and stock.

Bring to a simmer; then cover and cook slowly 2 hours or until beef is tender. Remove cover and continue cooking until sauce thickens, stirring occasionally.

In a medium saucepan heat 2 tablespoons each of margarine and oil. Sauté mushrooms until lightly browned.

Serve beef garnished with mushrooms and parsley.

*Yield:* 10 servings

*Change Boeuf Bourguignon as follows or use Basic Recipe, if indicated, for:*

## LOW-SODIUM DIETS

Calories per serving: 353
Approximate nutrient
  values same as Basic
  Recipe except for:
    Sodium 81 mg

Omit salt.
Substitute unsalted polyunsaturated margarine for margarine
  wherever used.
Proceed as in Basic Recipe.

## BLAND DIETS

Calories per serving: 353

Omit pepper.
Proceed as in Basic Recipe.

## HIGH-FIBER DIETS

Use Basic Recipe.

## BOEUF BOURGUIGNON FOR LOW-CALORIE, DIABETIC, LOW-FAT, AND LOW-CHOLESTEROL DIETS

Serving size: 3 ounces
  beef, ⅛ cup sauce
Calories per serving: 230
Approximate nutrient
  values per serving:
    Protein 28 g
    Fat 8 g
    Carbohydrate 11 g
    Sodium 301 mg
    Potassium 642 mg
    Cholesterol 77 mg
Exchanges:
  Vegetable 2
  Meat 3

vegetable cooking spray
3 pounds boneless chuck beef, trimmed of excess fat and cut
  into 2-inch cubes
2 cups diced carrots
3 cups coarsely chopped onions
1 teaspoon finely minced garlic
1 teaspoon thyme
1 teaspoon salt
¼ teaspoon freshly ground pepper
2 bay leaves
2 cups Burgundy wine
1 cup Beef Stock (page 113)
¾ pound medium whole mushrooms
½ cup chopped fresh parsley

Spray a large, heavy casserole well with vegetable cooking spray. Add beef, a few pieces at a time, and sauté until brown on all sides. As beef browns, remove to a platter. Drain excess fat from pan.

Add carrots, onions, and garlic to casserole and sauté over low heat until onions are soft. Return beef to casserole and add thyme, salt, pepper, bay leaves, wine, and stock.

Bring to a simmer; then cover and cook slowly for 2 hours or until beef is tender. Remove cover, add mushrooms, and continue cooking until sauce thickens. Stir occasionally.

Serve beef garnished with parsley.

*Yield:* 10 servings

# Belgian Beef Casserole

BASIC RECIPE

This recipe requires overnight refrigeration.

Serving size: 3 ounces meat, ¼ cup gravy
Calories per serving: 209
Approximate nutrient values per serving:
    Protein 24 g
    Fat 10 g
    Carbohydrate 4 g
    Sodium 305 mg
    Potassium 368 mg
    Cholesterol 70 mg
Exchanges:
    Vegetable 1
    Meat 3
    Fat 1

3 tablespoons polyunsaturated oil
3 pounds boneless beef chuck, trimmed of excess fat and cut into 2-inch cubes
2 cups sliced onions
1 clove garlic, finely chopped
6-ounce can V-8 vegetable juice
12-ounce bottle beer
2 bay leaves
1 teaspoon thyme
1 teaspoon salt
⅛ teaspoon freshly ground pepper

Heat the oil in a heavy casserole large enough to hold the meat comfortably. Brown the beef on all sides, a few pieces at a time. As the pieces are browned, remove them to a platter and set aside. Add onions and garlic to remaining oil in casserole and sauté over low heat until lightly browned. Return meat to casserole.

Add remaining ingredients and bring to a simmer. Cover tightly and simmer slowly 2 to 2½ hours or until meat is tender. Allow to cool; refrigerate overnight.

Before reheating remove the hardened fat on the surface. Simmer 30 minutes or until stew is very hot. Remove meat to a heated platter. Spoon gravy over meat before serving.

*Yield:* 10 servings

*Change Belgian Beef Casserole as follows or use Basic Recipe, if indicated, for:*

LOW-CALORIE, DIABETIC, LOW-FAT, AND LOW-CHOLESTEROL DIETS

Calories per serving: 171
Approximate nutrient
  values per serving:
    Protein 24 g
    Fat 6 g
    Carbohydrate 3 g
    Sodium 305 mg
    Potassium 368 mg
    Cholesterol 70 mg
Exchanges:
  Vegetable 1
  Meat 3

Omit oil. Instead, spray casserole well with vegetable cooking spray. Trim excess fat from meat and brown beef in casserole. Drain off excess fat.
Substitute 12 ounces "light" beer for beer.
Add onions and garlic to casserole with remaining ingredients.
Proceed as in Basic Recipe.

LOW-SODIUM DIETS

Calories per serving: 209
Approximate nutrient
  values same as Basic
  Recipe except for:
    Sodium 57 mg

Omit salt.
Substitute low-sodium V-8 juice for V-8 juice.
Proceed as in Basic Recipe.

BLAND DIETS

Calories per serving: 209

Omit pepper.
Proceed as in Basic Recipe.

Use Basic Recipe.
For extra fiber, serve with barley or brown rice.

# Stuffed Cabbage Leaves

### BASIC RECIPE

Serving size: 2 rolls, ⅓ cup
    sauce
Calories per serving: 230
Approximate nutrient
    values per serving:
        Protein 25 g
        Fat 6 g
        Carbohydrate 21 g
        Sodium 796 mg
        Potassium 685 mg
        Cholesterol 107 mg
Exchanges:
    Vegetable 1
    Bread 1
    Meat 3

12 large cabbage leaves (use outer leaves)
1½ pounds lean ground round beef
1 cup cooked long-grain rice
1 large egg
¼ cup chopped fresh parsley
2 teaspoons salt
¾ teaspoon thyme
¼ teaspoon freshly ground pepper
3 cups coarsely chopped peeled tomatoes
½ cup sliced onions
1 tablespoon honey
1 tablespoon lemon juice
½ teaspoon allspice

In a large pot simmer cabbage leaves, in enough hot water to cover, for 5 minutes or until tender. Drain thoroughly.

In a large bowl combine beef, rice, egg, parsley, 1 teaspoon of the salt, thyme, and pepper. Mix thoroughly.

Place approximately ⅓ cup of meat mixture in center of each cabbage leaf. Fold sides over stuffing and roll up to form a cylinder.

In a large, heavy casserole combine tomatoes, onions, honey, lemon juice, allspice, and the remaining 1 teaspoon salt. Place cabbage rolls in pot seam side down. Spoon the mixture over cabbage rolls, cover, and simmer 1 hour. Remove cabbage rolls to warm serving plate.

Boil the sauce until reduced to about 2 cups. Spoon over cabbage rolls. Serve immediately.

*Yield:* 6 servings

*Change Stuffed Cabbage Leaves as follows for:*

### LOW-CALORIE, DIABETIC, LOW-FAT, AND LOW-CHOLESTEROL DIETS

Calories per serving: 225
Approximate nutrient
  values per serving:
    Protein 25 g
    Fat 5 g
    Carbohydrate 21 g
    Sodium 805 mg
    Potassium 701 mg
    Cholesterol 61 mg
Exchanges:
  Vegetable 1
  Bread 1
  Meat 3

Omit egg. Use Low-Cholesterol Egg Substitute (page 189) equivalent to 1 large egg.
Proceed as in Basic Recipe.

### LOW-SODIUM DIETS

Calories per serving: 230
Approximate nutrient
  values same as Basic
  Recipe except for:
    Sodium 64 mg

Omit salt.
Proceed as in Basic Recipe.

### BLAND DIETS

Calories per serving: 230

Omit pepper.
Proceed as in Basic Recipe.

### HIGH-FIBER DIETS

Calories per serving: 231

Substitute cooked brown rice for long-grain rice.
Proceed as in Basic Recipe.

# Tzimmes

BASIC RECIPE

Serving size: 3 ounces
  beef, ½ cup vegetables
  and prunes
Calories per serving: 370
Approximate nutrient
  values per serving:
    Protein 24 g
    Fat 8 g
    Carbohydrate 52 g
    Sodium 726 mg
    Potassium 728 mg
    Cholesterol 64 mg
Exchanges:
  Fruit 2
  Bread 2
  Meat 3

3 pounds brisket of beef
1 quart water
2 cups carrots, sliced 1 inch thick
1 large onion, quartered
½ cup dark-brown sugar, firmly packed
1 tablespoon salt
¼ teaspoon freshly ground pepper
4 cups cubed peeled sweet potatoes
1 cup pitted prunes
4 tablespoons flour
4 tablespoons cold water

Place brisket in heavy casserole in which it will fit comfortably. Add the water. Bring to a boil and skim off foam as it rises. Reduce heat. Add carrots, onion, sugar, salt, and pepper. Cover and simmer slowly for 2 hours.

Add sweet potatoes and prunes. Simmer about 20 minutes longer or until beef is tender.

Preheat oven to 400°F.

Transfer beef to a shallow roasting pan. Using a slotted spoon, arrange prunes and vegetables around meat. In a small bowl, blend flour and 4 tablespoons cold water until smooth.

Bring cooking liquid in casserole to a boil. Gradually stir in flour mixture and cook, stirring constantly, until liquid returns to a boil. Boil and stir for 2 minutes.

Pour sauce over meat and vegetables and bake, uncovered, 15 minutes or until meat is nicely browned.

*Yield:* 10 servings

*Change Tzimmes as follows for:*

## LOW-CALORIE, DIABETIC, LOW-FAT, AND LOW-CHOLESTEROL DIETS

Omit sugar.
Reduce sweet potatoes to 3 cups.
Reduce prunes to ¼ cup.
Proceed as in Basic Recipe.

Calories per serving: 270
Approximate nutrient
  values per serving:
    Protein 23 g
    Fat 8 g
    Carbohydrate 27 g
    Sodium 720 mg
    Potassium 547 mg
    Cholesterol 64 mg
Exchanges:
    Fruit 1
    Bread 1
    Meat 3

## LOW-SODIUM DIETS

Omit salt.
Add 2 teaspoons caraway seed to the seasonings.
Proceed as in Basic Recipe.

Calories per serving: 371
Approximate nutrient
  values same as Basic
  Recipe except for:
    Sodium 67 mg
    Potassium 734 mg

## BLAND DIETS

Omit pepper.
Proceed as in Basic Recipe.

Calories per serving: 370

## HIGH-FIBER DIETS

Add 2 teaspoons caraway seed to the seasonings.
Proceed as in Basic Recipe.

Calories per serving: 371

# Eggplant and Beef Casserole

BASIC RECIPE

The tomato sauce may be made the day before and refrigerated.

Serving size: ⅙ casserole
Calories per serving: 447
Approximate nutrient
  values per serving:
    Protein 27 g
    Fat 28 g
    Carbohydrate 24 g
    Sodium 548 mg
    Potassium 1098 mg
    Cholesterol 112 mg
Exchanges:
  Vegetable 2
  Bread 1
  Meat 3
  Fat 4

1 large eggplant (approximately 1¼ pounds)
1 large egg
2 tablespoons water
⅔ cup fresh bread crumbs (page 38)
½ teaspoon salt
⅓ cup polyunsaturated oil
¾ pound lean ground round beef
3 cups Italian Tomato Sauce (page 392)
8 ounces mozzarella cheese, sliced
⅓ cup grated Parmesan cheese

*To prepare the casserole:* Wash eggplant and remove a thin slice from both stem and blossom ends. Do not peel. Cut eggplant in slices about ½ inch thick. Beat egg with water. Dip eggplant slices in beaten egg and coat with bread crumbs mixed with salt.

In a large, heavy skillet heat the oil and sauté eggplant, a few slices at a time, until lightly browned on both sides. Remove eggplant and set aside.

Preheat oven to 350°F.

Wipe skillet with paper towel and sauté beef until it starts to brown, stirring to break up large pieces. Drain off any fat that may have accumulated. Add tomato sauce to the beef and stir to blend.

*To assemble the casserole:* Spoon a thin layer of the beef and tomato sauce mixture into a large, shallow baking dish. Next arrange layers of eggplant, the remaining beef and tomato sauce mixture, and mozzarella cheese, ending with cheese. Sprinkle with Parmesan cheese. Bake, uncovered, for 1 hour.

*Yield:* 6 servings

*Change Eggplant and Beef Casserole as follows or use Basic Recipe, if indicated, for:*

### LOW-SODIUM DIETS

Omit salt.
Substitute low-sodium Cheddar cheese for mozzarella.
Omit Parmesan cheese.
Proceed as in Basic Recipe.

Calories per serving: 451
Approximate nutrient
   values per serving:
     Protein 26 g
     Fat 30 g
     Carbohydrate 23 g
     Sodium 83 mg
     Potassium 1117 mg
     Cholesterol 89 mg

### BLAND AND HIGH-FIBER DIETS

Use Basic Recipe.

### EGGPLANT AND BEEF CASSEROLE FOR LOW-CALORIE, DIABETIC, LOW-FAT, AND LOW-CHOLESTEROL DIETS

The tomato sauce may be made the day before and refrigerated.

Serving size: ⅙ casserole
Calories per serving: 268
Approximate nutrient
   values per serving:
     Protein 24 g
     Fat 11 g
     Carbohydrate 21 g
     Sodium 397 mg
     Potassium 1080 mg
     Cholesterol 52 mg
Exchanges:
  Vegetable 1
  Bread 1
  Meat 3
  Fat ½

1 large eggplant (1¼ pounds)
½ teaspoon salt
1½ cups water
¾ pound lean ground round beef
3 cups Italian Tomato Sauce (page 392)
8 ounces part-skim mozzarella cheese, sliced

*To prepare the casserole:* Wash eggplant and remove a thin slice from stem and blossom ends. Do not peel. Cut eggplant into slices about ½ inch thick.

In a large saucepan add salt to 1½ cups water and cook eggplant slices until tender but still firm, about 5 to 10 minutes. Drain thoroughly on paper towels.

Preheat oven to 350°F.

In a large, heavy skillet sauté ground beef until it loses its red color, stirring to break up large pieces. Drain off any fat that may have accumulated. Add tomato sauce and stir to blend.

Spoon a thin layer of beef and tomato sauce into a large shallow baking dish. Arrange alternating layers of eggplant, sauce, and mozzarella cheese, ending with cheese. Bake, uncovered, for 1 hour.

*Yield:* 6 servings

# Hamburgers Aux Fines Herbes

BASIC RECIPE

*The Mushroom Sauce*
2½ tablespoons polyunsaturated margarine
1 tablespoon cornstarch
¾ cup Meat and Vegetable Stock (page 116)
2 cups coarsely chopped fresh mushrooms
¼ teaspoon salt
⅛ teaspoon freshly ground pepper
1 tablespoon dry sherry

*The Hamburgers*
2¼ pounds lean ground round beef
¼ cup chopped fresh parsley
2 tablespoons snipped fresh chives
1 teaspoon salt
¾ teaspoon tarragon
¾ teaspoon chervil
⅛ teaspoon freshly ground pepper

*To prepare the mushroom sauce:* In a large skillet heat the margarine. Blend in cornstarch. Gradually add stock, stirring constantly.

Add mushrooms, salt, pepper, and sherry. Simmer 10 minutes until sauce is thickened and smooth. Keep warm in a double boiler.

Serving size: 3 ounces beef, 2 tablespoons sauce
Calories per serving: 185
Approximate nutrient values per serving:
    Protein 24 g
    Fat 8 g
    Carbohydrate 2 g
    Sodium 436 mg
    Potassium 390 mg
    Cholesterol 69 mg
Exchanges:
    Meat 3
    Fat 1

*To prepare the hamburgers:* Preheat broiler. Mix beef lightly with all seasonings. Shape into 8 patties, each about ¾ inch thick. Broil hamburgers about 8 to 12 minutes, turning once, or until they reach the desired doneness.

Spoon mushroom sauce over hamburgers and serve.

*Yield:* 8 hamburgers, 1 cup sauce

*Change Hamburgers aux Fines Herbes as follows or use Basic Recipe, if indicated, for:*

### LOW-CALORIE, DIABETIC, LOW-FAT, AND LOW-CHOLESTEROL DIETS

*The mushroom sauce:* Omit margarine and cornstarch. Simmer all other ingredients together, in covered saucepan, about 10 minutes.

Proceed as in Basic Recipe.

*The hamburgers:* Use Basic Recipe.

### LOW-SODIUM DIETS

*The mushroom sauce:* Omit salt.
Substitute ½ teaspoon tarragon.
Substitute unsalted polyunsaturated margarine for margarine.

Proceed as in Basic Recipe.

*The hamburgers:* Omit salt.
Proceed as in Basic Recipe.

### BLAND DIETS

*The mushroom sauce and the hamburgers:* Omit pepper. Proceed as in Basic Recipe.

Calories per serving: 150
Approximate nutrient
values per serving:
Protein 24 g
Fat 5 g
Carbohydrate 1 g
Sodium 400 mg
Potassium 389 mg
Cholesterol 69 mg
Exchanges:
Meat 3

Calories per serving: 185
Approximate nutrient
values same as Basic
Recipe except for:
Sodium 57 mg
Potassium 393 mg

Calories per serving: 185

Calories per serving: 192

*The mushroom sauce:* Use Basic Recipe.

*The hamburgers:* Add ⅛ cup bran to beef mixture with herbs. Proceed as in Basic Recipe.

# Steak with Brandied Sauce

BASIC RECIPE

Serving size: 3 ounces
Calories per serving: 260
Approximate nutrient
 values per serving:
  Protein 28 g
  Fat 16 g
  Carbohydrate 1 g
  Sodium 110 mg
  Potassium 347 mg
  Cholesterol 77 mg
Exchanges:
 Meat 3
 Fat 2

1½ pounds sirloin steak, 1 inch thick, trimmed of excess fat
2 teaspoons whole peppercorns
1 tablespoon polyunsaturated margarine for sautéing steak
1 tablespoon olive oil
1 tablespoon polyunsaturated margarine for sauce
¼ cup brandy
2 tablespoons chopped fresh parsley
2 tablespoons snipped fresh chives

Wipe steak dry with a paper towel.

Crush peppercorns coarsely between 2 pieces of wax paper with a rolling pin; press the pepper into both sides of the steak. Cover with wax paper and refrigerate for about 2 hours.

Heat 1 tablespoon of the margarine with the olive oil in a large, heavy skillet. Sauté steak 4 minutes on each side, or until it has reached the desired degree of doneness. Remove to a warm platter.

Pour off any accumulated fat in skillet. Add the remaining 1 tablespoon margarine and the brandy. Bring sauce to a boil and cook for 1 minute.

Spoon sauce over steak; sprinkle with parsley and chives. Serve immediately.

*Yield:* 4 servings

*Change Steak with Brandied Sauce as follows or use Basic Recipe, if indicated, for:*

### LOW-CALORIE, DIABETIC, LOW-FAT, AND LOW-CHOLESTEROL DIETS

Prepare steak as in Basic Recipe and refrigerate it. Just before cooking, preheat broiler.

Omit margarine and olive oil for sautéing. Broil steak instead. Place steak under broiler and cook for 4 to 8 minutes on each side depending on desired degree of doneness. Remove to warm platter.

Omit margarine for sauce. Place ½ cup Beef Stock (page 113) and brandy in small saucepan. Bring to a boil and cook 2 minutes. Spoon over steak. Sprinkle with parsley and chives.

### LOW-SODIUM AND RENAL DIETS

Substitute unsalted polyunsaturated margarine for margarine wherever used.
Proceed as in Basic Recipe.

### BLAND DIETS

Omit peppercorns.
Proceed as in Basic Recipe.

### HIGH-FIBER DIETS

Use Basic Recipe.

Calories per serving: 180
Approximate nutrient
  values per serving:
    Protein 28 g
    Fat 7 g
    Carbohydrate 1 g
    Sodium 63 mg
    Potassium 364 mg
    Cholesterol 77 mg
Exchanges:
  Meat 3

Calories per serving: 260
Approximate nutrient
  values same as Basic
  Recipe except for:
    Calcium 21 mg
    Phosphorus 226 mg
    Sodium 53 mg

Calories per serving: 258

# Stir-Fried Beef with Green Peppers

BASIC RECIPE

Serving size: 1 cup
Calories per serving: 355
Approximate nutrient
  values per serving:
    Protein 33 g
    Fat 20 g
    Carbohydrate 10 g
    Sodium 785 mg
    Potassium 719 mg
    Cholesterol 91 mg
Exchanges:
    Vegetable 2
    Meat 4
    Fat 3

1½ tablespoons cornstarch
2 tablespoons soy sauce
¼ cup cold water
4 tablespoons polyunsaturated oil
1½ pounds round steak, ¼ inch thick, cut in 2-inch lengths
  across the grain and trimmed of excess fat
2 cups green pepper strips (cut lengthwise)
1 cup thinly sliced celery
½ cup sliced onions
1 clove garlic, finely chopped
¾ cup Beef Stock (page 113)

Mix cornstarch, soy sauce, and water; set aside.

Heat the oil in a large skillet over high heat. Add beef strips and stir-fry for about 2 minutes. Remove beef to a platter.

Turn heat to medium and add green pepper, celery, onions, and garlic to skillet. Sauté until onions are soft—about 3 minutes.

Return beef to skillet. Add stock, reduce heat, and simmer, covered, about 8 to 10 minutes or until beef and vegetables are tender.

Uncover, raise heat, and add cornstarch mixture. Cook, stirring gently, until sauce comes to a boil and thickens. Serve immediately.

*Yield:* 4 servings

*Change Stir-Fried Beef with Green Peppers as follows or use Basic Recipe, if indicated, for:*

LOW-CALORIE, DIABETIC, LOW-FAT, AND LOW-CHOLESTEROL DIETS

Reduce oil to 1 tablespoon. Spray skillet with vegetable cooking spray and add the oil.

Heat skillet; add beef, stir-fry for 2 minutes, and remove to plate. Then sauté vegetables; return beef to skillet, and proceed as in Basic Recipe.

Calories per serving: 264
Approximate nutrient
 values per serving:
  Protein 33 g
  Fat 10 g
  Carbohydrate 10 g
  Sodium 785 mg
  Potassium 719 mg
  Cholesterol 91 mg
Exchanges:
 Vegetable 2
 Meat 4
 Fat ½

LOW-SODIUM DIETS

Omit soy sauce. Substitute 2 tablespoons dry sherry.
Proceed as in Basic Recipe.

Calories per serving: 349
Approximate nutrient
 values per serving:
  Protein 33 g
  Fat 20 g
  Carbohydrate 9 g
  Sodium 126 mg
  Potassium 686 mg
  Cholesterol 91 mg

BLAND AND HIGH-FIBER DIETS

Use Basic Recipe.

# Beef Stroganoff

BASIC RECIPE

Serving size: 3 ounces beef, ⅓ cup sauce
Calories per serving: 435
Approximate nutrient values per serving:
Protein 31 g
Fat 31 g
Carbohydrate 9 g
Sodium 801 mg
Potassium 701 mg
Cholesterol 96 mg
Exchanges:
Vegetable 2
Meat 3
Fat 5

1½ pounds lean beef sirloin, cut into strips 2 inches long, ½ inch wide
⅓ cup polyunsaturated margarine
1 cup sliced onions
3 cups sliced fresh mushrooms
⅔ cup Beef Stock (page 113)
⅓ cup dry sherry
1 bay leaf
¾ cup sour cream
1 teaspoon salt
⅛ teaspoon freshly ground pepper
⅓ cup chopped fresh parsley

Trim off any excess fat from the steak.

In a large, heavy skillet, melt 3 tablespoons of the margarine. Sauté beef quickly, a few pieces at a time. As beef is cooked, remove with a slotted spoon to a large dish.

Melt the remaining margarine in the skillet. Add onions and mushrooms; sauté until onions are soft. Remove with spoon and set aside with beef.

Add beef stock, sherry, and bay leaf to skillet. Simmer, uncovered, until liquid is reduced by half, stirring to lift any particles from the bottom of the pan.

Return beef, vegetables, and any juices to skillet. Stir in sour cream, salt, and pepper. Cook over low heat, mixing gently, until heated through. Garnish with parsley before serving.

*Yield:* 4 servings

*Change Beef Stroganoff as follows or use Basic Recipe, if indicated, for:*

## LOW-SODIUM DIETS

Calories per serving: 435
Approximate nutrient
  values same as Basic
  Recipe except for:
    Sodium 101 mg

Omit salt.
Substitute unsalted polyunsaturated margarine for margarine.
Proceed as in Basic Recipe.

## RENAL DIETS

Calories per serving: 423
Approximate nutrient
  values per serving:
    Protein 30 g
    Fat 31 g
    Carbohydrate 7 g
    Calcium 82 mg
    Phosphorus 318 mg
    Sodium 242 mg
    Potassium 537 mg
    Cholesterol 96 mg

Omit salt.
Substitute unsalted polyunsaturated margarine for margarine.
Reduce onions to ½ cup.
Substitute two 4-ounce cans sliced mushrooms, drained, for fresh mushrooms.
Proceed as in Basic Recipe.

## BLAND DIETS

Calories per serving: 435

Omit pepper.
Proceed as in Basic Recipe.

## HIGH-FIBER DIETS

Use Basic Recipe.
For extra fiber, serve with groats or chickpeas.

## BEEF STROGANOFF FOR LOW-CALORIE, DIABETIC, LOW-FAT, AND LOW-CHOLESTEROL DIETS

Serving size: 3 ounces
  beef, ⅓ cup sauce
Calories per serving: 228

1½ pounds lean beef sirloin, cut into strips 2 inches long, ½ inch wide
vegetable cooking spray

297

1 cup sliced onions
3 cups sliced mushrooms
⅔ cup Beef Stock (page 113)
⅓ cup dry sherry
1 bay leaf
¾ cup buttermilk
1 teaspoon salt
⅛ teaspoon freshly ground pepper
⅓ cup chopped fresh parsley

Trim off any excess fat from the steak.

Spray a large, heavy skillet with vegetable cooking spray.

Rapidly sauté beef strips, a few at a time, about 2 minutes. Remove beef to a large platter and set aside.

Add onions, mushrooms, beef stock, sherry, and bay leaf to skillet. Simmer, covered, 5 minutes or until onions are soft. Stir occasionally.

Return beef to skillet. Add buttermilk, salt, and pepper, stirring to lift particles from the bottom of the pan. Heat through without boiling. Garnish with parsley before serving.

*Yield:* 4 servings

# Chili, Beef, and Noodle Casserole

BASIC RECIPE

2 tablespoons polyunsaturated margarine
1 cup chopped onions
⅔ cup thinly sliced celery
½ cup chopped green pepper
1 clove garlic, put through garlic press
1 pound lean ground round beef
3 cups coarsely chopped peeled tomatoes
1 cup fresh corn cut from the cob
1 tablespoon chili powder

¾ teaspoon oregano
¾ teaspoon salt
4 ounces wide noodles
1½ cups grated sharp Cheddar cheese

In a large skillet melt margarine and sauté onion, celery, green pepper, and garlic until tender. Add meat and sauté until brown. Add tomatoes, corn, chili powder, oregano, and salt and mix gently.

Preheat oven to 350°F.

Cook noodles in 1 quart of boiling water for 5 minutes. Drain quickly so the noodles are still moist; add to tomato-meat mixture and toss gently.

Transfer to a 2½-quart casserole. Sprinkle with cheese and bake, covered, 30 minutes or until cheese melts and casserole is hot.

*Yield:* 6 servings

*Change Chili, Beef, and Noodle Casserole as follows or use Basic Recipe, if indicated, for:*

LOW-CALORIE, DIABETIC, LOW-FAT, AND LOW-CHOLESTEROL DIETS

Omit margarine. Brown vegetables and beef in skillet that has been sprayed with vegetable cooking spray.
Substitute grated part-skim mozzarella cheese for Cheddar.
Proceed as in Basic Recipe.

Calories per serving: 372
Approximate nutrient
   values per serving:
      Protein 27 g
      Fat 17 g
      Carbohydrate 29 g
      Sodium 71 mg
      Potassium 723 mg
      Cholesterol 69 mg

Omit salt.
Substitute grated low-sodium Cheddar cheese for Cheddar.
Proceed as in Basic Recipe.

BLAND DIETS

Calories per serving: 373

Omit chili powder. Substitute ½ teaspoon ground cumin.
Proceed as in Basic Recipe.

HIGH-FIBER DIETS

Use Basic Recipe.

# Short Ribs with Raisins

BASIC RECIPE

This recipe requires overnight refrigeration.

Serving size: 3 ounces
   meat, 1 potato, ½ cup
   sauce
Calories per serving: 342
Approximate nutrient
   values per serving:
      Protein 28 g
      Fat 9 g
      Carbohydrate 38 g
      Sodium 989 mg

3 pounds short ribs of beef, cut into 3-inch pieces
2 tablespoons polyunsaturated oil
3 cups sliced carrots
2 teaspoons salt
¼ teaspoon freshly ground pepper
1 teaspoon rosemary
1 teaspoon thyme
1 teaspoon marjoram

Potassium 825 mg
Cholesterol 70 mg
Exchanges:
  Vegetable 1
  Fruit 1
  Bread 1½
  Meat 3
  Fat ½

½ cup raisins
¾ cup red wine
½ cup water
6 medium potatoes
½ teaspoon salt for boiling potatoes
2 tablespoons flour
4 tablespoons water

Trim excess fat from short ribs.

Heat the oil in a casserole large enough to hold the ribs comfortably in a single layer. Place the ribs in the casserole and brown on all sides. Arrange carrots over them. Season with 2 teaspoons salt, pepper, rosemary, thyme, and marjoram; sprinkle with raisins. Add wine and ½ cup water. Bring to a boil; then cover and simmer slowly for 1½ hours or until beef is tender. Refrigerate overnight.

The next day, remove all the hardened fat on the surface. Bring to a simmer and cook 30 minutes.

Meanwhile, peel potatoes and cut in quarters; add remaining ½ teaspoon salt and cook in boiling water 15 minutes or until tender. Drain thoroughly.

Remove beef to a warm platter. Arrange potatoes around beef.

In a small cup, mix flour with the 4 tablespoons water until smooth. Add to carrot and raisin sauce in casserole, increase heat, and boil, stirring constantly, until sauce is thickened and reduced to approximately 3 cups. Pour over ribs and potatoes. Serve immediately.

*Yield:* 6 servings

*Change Short Ribs with Raisins as follows or use Basic Recipe, if indicated, for:*

## LOW-CALORIE, DIABETIC, LOW-FAT, AND LOW-CHOLESTEROL DIETS

Omit oil. Spray casserole with vegetable cooking spray. Omit raisins.
Reduce potatoes to 3.
Proceed as in Basic Recipe.

Calories per serving: 240
Approximate nutrient
  values per serving:
    Protein 26 g
    Fat 7 g
    Carbohydrate 18 g
    Sodium 985 mg
    Potassium 553 mg
    Cholesterol 70 mg
Exchanges:
  Vegetable 1
  Bread 1
  Meat 3

## LOW-SODIUM DIETS

Omit salt.
Proceed as in Basic Recipe.

Calories per serving: 342
Approximate nutrient
  values same as Basic
  Recipe except for:
    Sodium 74 mg

## BLAND DIETS

Omit pepper.
Proceed as in Basic Recipe.

Calories per serving: 342

## HIGH-FIBER DIETS

Use Basic Recipe.

# Yankee Beef Stew

BASIC RECIPE

This recipe requires overnight refrigeration.

2½ pounds short ribs of beef, cut into 3-inch pieces
1 cup sliced carrots
1 cup sliced onions
½ cup sliced celery
1 bay leaf
2 teaspoons salt
¼ teaspoon freshly ground pepper
2 cups cold water
2 tablespoons lemon juice
1 cup coarsely chopped peeled fresh tomatoes
2 cups peeled quartered fresh beets
2 cups shredded raw cabbage

Trim excess fat from short ribs.

In a large casserole place beef, carrots, onions, and celery. Add bay leaf, salt, pepper, and water. Bring to a boil; then reduce heat and simmer slowly, covered, about 2½ hours or until beef is tender.

Transfer stew to a large bowl. Remove meat, separate meat from the bones, and return the meat to the bowl. Refrigerate overnight.

The next day, remove all the hardened fat on the surface. Bring stew to a simmer. Add lemon juice, tomatoes, and beets; simmer, covered, approximately 20 minutes or until beets are tender—add cabbage during last 5 minutes.

*Yield:* 8 servings

Serving size: 1 cup
Calories per serving: 138
Approximate nutrient
  values per serving:
    Protein 17 g
    Fat 4 g
    Carbohydrate 9 g
    Sodium 616 mg
    Potassium 424 mg
    Cholesterol 47 mg
Exchanges:
  Vegetable 2
  Meat 2

*Change Yankee Beef Stew as follows or use Basic Recipe, if indicated, for:*

LOW-CALORIE, DIABETIC, LOW-FAT, LOW-CHOLESTEROL, AND HIGH-FIBER DIETS

Use Basic Recipe.

LOW-SODIUM DIETS

Calories per serving: 138
Approximate nutrient
   values same as Basic
   Recipe except for:
      Sodium 67 mg

Omit salt.
Proceed as in Basic Recipe.

BLAND DIETS

Calories per serving: 138

Omit pepper.
Proceed as in Basic Recipe.

# Breast of Veal with Fruit Stuffing

BASIC RECIPE

Serving size: 4 ounces veal,
   ⅓ cup stuffing, ⅓ cup
   gravy
Calories per serving: 481
Approximate nutrient
   values per serving:
      Protein 33 g
      Fat 32 g
      Carbohydrate 15 g
      Sodium 620 mg
      Potassium 450 mg
      Cholesterol 119 mg

*The Stuffing*
¼ cup raisins
4 tablespoons polyunsaturated margarine
½ cup chopped onions
2 cups fresh bread crumbs (page 38)
1½ cups diced peeled apple
¼ cup chopped walnuts
1 teaspoon salt
⅛ teaspoon freshly ground pepper
¾ teaspoon ground cinnamon
½ teaspoon allspice

Exchanges:
  Fruit 1
  Bread ½
  Meat 4
  Fat 4

*The Roast*
5-pound veal breast, cut with a pocket
1 teaspoon salt
⅛ teaspoon freshly ground pepper
1 cup thinly sliced carrots
1 cup thinly sliced celery
1 cup thinly sliced onions
1 cup Chicken Stock (page 114)

*To prepare the stuffing:* Cover raisins with boiling water and set aside.

Heat the margarine in a medium skillet. Add chopped onions and sauté until soft. Remove to a large bowl. Add bread crumbs, apple, walnuts, salt, pepper, cinnamon, and allspice. Drain raisins and add. Stir gently until well mixed.

*To prepare the roast:* Preheat oven to 375°F. Combine 1 teaspoon salt and ⅛ teaspoon pepper, and rub inside of veal pocket with the mixture.

Fill pocket with stuffing. Close with skewers.

Arrange carrots, celery, and sliced onions in roasting pan. Place veal on vegetables and bake, uncovered, 30 minutes or until top begins to brown.

Lower heat to 350°F. Pour stock over veal, cover, and bake 2 hours more, or until tender.

Remove veal breast to heated platter and cover to keep warm. Purée pan juices and vegetables in blender and serve over veal.

*Yield:* 10 servings

*Change Breast of Veal with Fruit Stuffing as follows or use Basic Recipe, if indicated, for:*

## LOW-CALORIE, DIABETIC, LOW-FAT, AND LOW-CHOLESTEROL DIETS

Calories per serving: 444
Approximate nutrient
  values per serving:
    Protein 33 g
    Fat 28 g
    Carbohydrate 15 g
    Sodium 597 mg
    Potassium 438 mg
    Cholesterol 119 mg
Exchanges:
  Fruit 1
  Bread ½
  Meat 4
  Fat 3

Omit walnuts.
Reduce margarine to 2 tablespoons.
Proceed as in Basic Recipe.

## LOW-SODIUM DIETS

Calories per serving: 481
Approximate nutrient
  values same as Basic
  Recipe except for:
    Sodium 135 mg

Omit salt.
Substitute unsalted polyunsaturated margarine for margarine.
Proceed as in Basic Recipe.

## BLAND DIETS

Calories per serving: 481

Omit pepper.
Proceed as in Basic Recipe.

## HIGH-FIBER DIETS

Use Basic Recipe.

# Osso Buco

BASIC RECIPE

Serving size: 4 ounces veal,
  ½ cup sauce with
  vegetables
Calories per serving: 500
Approximate nutrient
  values per serving:
    Protein 34 g
    Fat 33 g
    Carbohydrate 16 g
    Sodium 748 mg
    Potassium 570 mg
    Cholesterol 119 mg
Exchanges:
  Vegetable 2
  Bread ½
  Meat 4
  Fat 4

3 pounds veal shanks, cut in 2-inch pieces
3 tablespoons flour
3 tablespoons olive oil
3 tablespoons polyunsaturated margarine
1 cup chopped onions
1 cup chopped celery
1 cup thinly sliced carrots
1 teaspoon salt
¼ teaspoon freshly ground pepper
1 teaspoon basil
2 bay leaves
1 cup white wine
1 tablespoon grated lemon rind
⅓ cup chopped fresh parsley

Dredge veal in flour.

Heat oil and margarine together in a heavy casserole. Add veal, a few pieces at a time, and sauté until brown on all sides. Remove to platter and reserve. Repeat process until all veal is browned.

Add onions, celery, and carrots to casserole. Return veal to casserole and spoon vegetables on it. Season with salt, pepper, basil, and bay leaves. Pour wine over all. Bring wine to a boil, then cover and simmer over low heat 1 hour or until meat is tender.

Transfer veal to a heated platter. Add lemon rind and parsley to casserole. Boil, stirring to lift any particles from bottom, until sauce is reduced to about 2 cups. Spoon sauce over veal and serve immediately.

*Yield:* 4 servings

*Change Osso Buco as follows or use Basic Recipe, if indicated, for:*

## LOW-CALORIE, DIABETIC, LOW-FAT, AND LOW-CHOLESTEROL DIETS

Calories per serving: 369
Approximate nutrient
values per serving:
Protein 34 g
Fat 19 g
Carbohydrate 16 g
Sodium 701 mg
Potassium 568 mg
Cholesterol 119 mg
Exchanges:
Vegetable 2
Bread ½
Meat 4
Fat 1

Omit oil.
Reduce margarine to 4 teaspoons.
Sauté veal in casserole that has been well sprayed with vegetable cooking spray and add the margarine.
Proceed as in Basic Recipe.

## LOW-SODIUM DIETS

Calories per serving: 500
Approximate nutrient
values same as Basic
Recipe except for:
Sodium 114 mg

Omit salt.
Substitute unsalted polyunsaturated margarine for margarine.
Proceed as in Basic Recipe.

## BLAND DIETS

Calories per serving: 500

Omit pepper.
Proceed as in Basic Recipe

## HIGH-FIBER DIETS

Use Basic Recipe.

# Veal Stew with Sage

BASIC RECIPE

Serving size: 4 ounces veal,
½ cup vegetables and
sauce
Calories per serving: 463
Approximate nutrient
values per serving:
Protein 38 g
Fat 26 g
Carbohydrate 19 g
Sodium 778 mg
Potassium 1092 mg
Cholesterol 119 mg
Exchanges:
Vegetable 1
Bread 1
Meat 4
Fat 3

4 tablespoons polyunsaturated margarine
4 tablespoons polyunsaturated oil
3 pounds boneless stewing veal, cut in 1-inch cubes
1 cup sliced onions
2 teaspoons sage
2 teaspoons salt
¼ teaspoon freshly ground pepper
2 cups coarsely chopped peeled tomatoes
two 10-ounce packages frozen Fordhook lima beans, thawed

Heat margarine and oil in a large casserole. Add veal, a few pieces at a time, and sauté until lightly browned on all sides. As veal browns, remove to a plate.

Add onions to casserole; sauté until soft. Return veal to casserole; add sage, salt, pepper, and tomatoes; mix gently.

Cover tightly; simmer slowly 1¼ hours or until veal is tender. Add lima beans; cook 10 minutes longer. Serve immediately.

*Yield:* 8 servings

*Change Veal Stew with Sage as follows or use Basic Recipe, if indicated, for:*

## LOW-CALORIE, DIABETIC, LOW-FAT, AND LOW-CHOLESTEROL DIETS

Calories per serving: 368
Approximate nutrient
  values per serving:
    Protein 38 g
    Fat 15 g
    Carbohydrate 18 g
    Sodium 721 mg
    Potassium 1090 mg
    Cholesterol 119 mg
Exchanges:
  Vegetable 1
  Bread 1
  Meat 4
  Fat ½

Omit margarine.
Reduce oil to 1 tablespoon.
Spray casserole with vegetable cooking spray.
Proceed as in Basic Recipe.

## LOW-SODIUM DIETS

Calories per serving: 412
Approximate nutrient
  values per serving:
    Protein 34 g
    Fat 26 g
    Carbohydrate 9 g
    Sodium 121 mg
    Potassium 930 mg
    Cholesterol 119 mg

Omit salt.
Substitute unsalted polyunsaturated margarine for margarine
    wherever used.
Substitute 3½ cups diced carrots for lima beans.
Proceed as in Basic Recipe.

## BLAND DIETS

Calories per serving: 463

Omit pepper.
Proceed as in Basic Recipe.

## HIGH-FIBER DIETS

Use Basic Recipe.

# Fricassee of Veal

BASIC RECIPE

Serving size: 1 cup
Calories per serving: 475
Approximate nutrient
  values per serving:
    Protein 37 g
    Fat 25 g
    Carbohydrate 26 g
    Sodium 546 mg
    Potassium 1212 mg
    Cholesterol 119 mg
Exchanges:
  Vegetable 5
  Meat 4
  Fat 2½

4 tablespoons polyunsaturated margarine for sautéing veal
3 pounds boneless stewing veal, cut in 1½-inch cubes
1 large onion studded with 4 whole cloves
2 cups carrots, sliced ¼ inch thick
1 teaspoon salt
¼ teaspoon freshly ground pepper
1 teaspoon thyme
1 bay leaf
2 cups Chicken Stock (page 114)
½ cup white wine
24 small whole white onions
2 tablespoons cornstarch
4 tablespoons cold water
3 cups small whole fresh mushrooms
4 tablespoons polyunsaturated margarine for sautéing mushrooms

Melt 4 tablespoons margarine in a large casserole. Add veal, a few pieces at a time, and sauté until lightly browned on all sides. As veal browns, remove to a plate.

When all meat is browned, return to casserole. Add large onion with cloves and carrots. Season with salt, pepper, thyme, and bay leaf. Add stock and wine. Bring to a boil; then cover and simmer slowly 1 hour or until veal is tender.

While veal is cooking, blanch small onions in boiling water for 1 minute. Scoop them out with a slotted spoon and peel them. Then return onions to the boiling water and cook, covered, 15 to 20 minutes or until tender. If you cook them ahead of time, drain off water and cover them.

When veal is done, remove the pieces to a warm plate. Discard the large clove-studded onion.

In a small bowl blend cornstarch with cold water until smooth. Stir into casserole and cook, stirring constantly, until sauce is lightly thickened. Return veal and small onions to pot. Simmer 5 minutes longer.

Meanwhile, sauté mushrooms in remaining margarine until lightly browned. Spoon over veal and serve.

*Yield:* 8 servings

*Change Fricassee of Veal as follows or use Basic Recipe, if indicated, for:*

LOW-SODIUM DIETS

Omit salt.
Substitute unsalted polyunsaturated margarine for margarine wherever used.
Proceed as in Basic Recipe.

Calories per serving: 475
Approximate nutrient values same as Basic Recipe except for:
Sodium 158 mg

BLAND DIETS

Omit pepper and cloves.
Proceed as in Basic Recipe.

Calories per serving: 475

HIGH-FIBER DIETS

Use Basic Recipe.

FRICASSEE OF VEAL FOR LOW-CALORIE, DIABETIC, LOW-FAT, AND LOW-CHOLESTEROL DIETS

Serving size: 1 cup (includes onions and mushrooms)
Calories per serving: 399
Approximate nutrient values per serving:
Protein 37 g
Fat 17 g
Carbohydrate 26 g

vegetable cooking spray
2 tablespoons polyunsaturated margarine
3 pounds boneless stewing veal, cut in 1½-inch cubes
1 large onion studded with 4 whole cloves
2 cups carrots, sliced ¼ inch thick
1 teaspoon salt
¼ teaspoon freshly ground pepper
1 teaspoon thyme

1 bay leaf
2 cups Chicken Stock (page 114)
½ cup white wine
24 small whole white onions, blanched and peeled
3 cups small whole fresh mushrooms
2 tablespoons cornstarch
4 tablespoons cold water

Prepare large casserole by spraying well with vegetable cooking spray.

Melt margarine in casserole. Add veal a few pieces at a time and sauté until lightly browned on all sides. As veal browns, remove to plate. When all meat is browned, return to casserole and add large clove-studded onion and carrots. Season with salt, pepper, thyme, and bay leaf. Add stock and wine. Bring to a boil; then cover and simmer gently 45 minutes. Add small onions and mushrooms and simmer 15 minutes longer or until meat and vegetables are tender. Remove veal to a warm plate. Remove large clove-studded onion and discard.

Blend cornstarch with cold water until smooth. Stir into casserole and cook, stirring constantly, until slightly thickened. Return veal to casserole, heat it through, and serve immediately.

*Yield:* 8 servings

# Veal Scallopini with Marsala

BASIC RECIPE

1 pound veal scallopini (4 cutlets)
2 tablespoons flour for coating
1½ tablespoons polyunsaturated oil
1½ tablespoons polyunsaturated margarine
¼ cup Marsala wine
2 tablespoons lemon juice
½ teaspoon salt

Potassium 445 mg
Cholesterol 79 mg
Exchanges:
  Bread ½
  Meat 3
  Fat 2

⅛ teaspoon freshly ground pepper
¼ cup chopped fresh parsley

Pound scallopini between waxed paper with flat side of a cleaver until thin. Dust both sides with flour.

Heat oil and margarine in a large, heavy skillet. On medium heat, sauté veal until brown on both sides. This browning should take no more than 5 minutes—do not overcook. Remove to a warm platter.

Reduce heat. Add Marsala, lemon juice, salt, and pepper to skillet. Bring to a boil, stirring to lift brown particles from bottom.

Return scallopini and juices to pan. Cook, turning and basting with sauce, until heated through. Spoon sauce over veal and garnish with parsley. Serve immediately.

*Yield:* 4 servings

*Change Veal Scallopini with Marsala as follows or use Basic Recipe, if indicated, for:*

LOW-CALORIE, DIABETIC, LOW-FAT, AND LOW-CHOLESTEROL DIETS

Calories per serving: 237
Approximate nutrient
  values per serving:
  Protein 22 g
  Fat 15 g
  Carbohydrate 2 g
  Sodium 369 mg
  Potassium 441 mg
  Cholesterol 79 mg
Exchanges:
  Meat 3
  Fat 1½

Omit flour.
Reduce oil and margarine to 1 tablespoon each.
Spray a skillet with vegetable cooking spray and add oil and margarine. Heat skillet; sauté veal.
Proceed as in Basic Recipe.

Calories per serving: 279
Approximate nutrient
  values per serving:
    Protein 22 g
    Fat 18 g
    Carbohydrate 5 g
    Calcium 19 mg
    Phosphorus 192 mg
    Sodium 66 mg
    Potassium 447 mg
    Cholesterol 79 mg

Omit salt.
Substitute unsalted polyunsaturated margarine for margarine.
Add ⅛ teaspoon each basil and oregano to skillet with the wine.
Proceed as in Basic Recipe.

## BLAND DIETS

Calories per serving: 279

Omit pepper.
Proceed as in Basic Recipe.

## HIGH-FIBER DIETS

Use Basic Recipe.
For extra fiber, serve with a spinach and mushroom salad.

# Patio Veal with Oregano

## BASIC RECIPE

Serving size: 3 ounces veal,
  ¼ cup vegetables
Calories per serving: 262
Approximate nutrient
  values per serving:
    Protein 23 g
    Fat 15 g
    Carbohydrate 7 g
    Sodium 373 mg

4 veal cutlets (1 pound)
2 tablespoons flour
1 tablespoon polyunsaturated margarine
1 tablespoon polyunsaturated oil
1 cup sliced fresh mushrooms
½ cup chopped onions
¼ cup vermouth
1 tablespoon chopped fresh parsley for sauce

Potassium 530 mg
Cholesterol 79 mg
Exchanges:
 Bread ½
 Meat 3
 Fat 1½

½ teaspoon salt
¼ teaspoon freshly ground pepper
½ teaspoon oregano
1 tablespoon chopped fresh parsley for garnish

Pound cutlets between wax paper with flat side of cleaver until thin. Place flour in paper bag, add one cutlet, and shake until dusted with flour. Remove, and repeat until all cutlets are lightly floured.

Heat margarine and oil together in large heavy skillet. Add 2 veal cutlets (do not crowd) and sauté until browned on both sides—2 to 3 minutes per side. Remove to a warm platter and sauté the other 2 cutlets.

Place mushrooms and onions in the same skillet and sauté until onions are soft. Reduce heat and add vermouth, parsley, salt, pepper, and oregano. Cook and stir until sauce bubbles.

Return all veal cutlets to skillet and cook, turning and basting with sauce, until heated through.

Arrange cutlets on heated platter, and spoon vegetables and sauce over them. Garnish with parsley before serving.

*Yield:* 4 servings

*Change Patio Veal with Oregano as follows or use Basic Recipe, if indicated, for:*

LOW-SODIUM DIETS

Calories per serving: 263
Approximate nutrient
 values same as Basic
 Recipe except for:
 Sodium 70 mg
 Potassium 534 mg

Omit salt.
Substitute unsalted polyunsaturated margarine for margarine.
Add 1 clove garlic, put through garlic press, to skillet with
 onions and mushrooms.
Proceed as in Basic Recipe.

RENAL DIETS

Calories per serving: 263
Approximate nutrient
 values per serving:

Omit salt.
Substitute unsalted polyunsaturated margarine for margarine.
Substitute 4-ounce can sliced mushrooms, drained, for fresh

Protein 23 g
Fat 15 g
Carbohydrate 8 g
Calcium 25 mg
Phosphorus 220 mg
Sodium 143 mg
Potassium 500 mg
Cholesterol 79 mg

mushrooms. Add 1 clove garlic, put through a garlic press, and sauté it in a heavy skillet with the ½ cup chopped onions and the mushrooms.
Proceed as in Basic Recipe.

## BLAND DIETS

Calories per serving: 262

Omit pepper.
Proceed as in Basic Recipe.

## HIGH-FIBER DIETS

Use Basic Recipe.

## PATIO VEAL WITH OREGANO FOR LOW-CALORIE, DIABETIC, LOW-FAT, AND LOW-CHOLESTEROL DIETS

Serving size: 3 ounces veal,
 ¼ cup vegetables
Calories per serving: 211
Approximate nutrient
 values per serving:
  Protein 23 g
  Fat 11 g
  Carbohydrate 4 g
  Sodium 376 mg
  Potassium 563 mg
  Cholesterol 79 mg
Exchanges:
 Vegetable 1
 Meat 3
 Fat ½

4 veal cutlets (1 pound)
vegetable cooking spray
1 teaspoon polyunsaturated margarine
1 teaspoon polyunsaturated oil
1 cup Beef Stock (page 113)
1 cup sliced fresh mushrooms
½ cup chopped onions
¼ cup dry vermouth
1 tablespoon chopped fresh parsley for sauce
½ teaspoon salt
¼ teaspoon freshly ground pepper
½ teaspoon oregano
1 tablespoon chopped fresh parsley for garnish

Pound cutlets between sheets of wax paper with flat side of cleaver until veal is thin.
 Heat margarine and oil in a large, heavy skillet that has been

sprayed with vegetable cooking spray. Sauté 2 veal cutlets until browned on both sides—about 2 to 3 minutes per side. Remove to warm platter and sauté the other 2 cutlets.

Put beef stock, mushrooms, onions, and vermouth in the skillet and bring to a boil. Reduce heat and simmer about 10 minutes or until vegetables are tender.

Add 1 tablespoon parsley, salt, pepper, and oregano; cook a little longer, stirring, until sauce thickens.

Return veal to skillet, turning and basting with sauce until heated through.

Arrange veal cutlets on heated platter. Spoon vegetables and sauce over them, and garnish with remaining parsley.

*Yield:* 4 servings

# Scandinavian Veal Chops

BASIC RECIPE

Serving size: 4 ounces veal, ½ cup vegetables and sauce
Calories per serving: 509
Approximate nutrient values per serving:
    Protein 37 g
    Fat 36 g
    Carbohydrate 9 g
    Sodium 875 mg
    Potassium 637 mg
    Cholesterol 149 mg
Exchanges:
  Vegetable 2
  Meat 4½
  Fat 4½

3 tablespoons polyunsaturated margarine
4 veal chops (1¾ pounds)
½ cup chopped onions
1 cup diced carrots
1 cup diced peeled turnips
1 teaspoon salt
¼ teaspoon freshly ground pepper for meat
⅓ cup Chicken Stock (page 114)
½ cup sour cream
½ teaspoon cornstarch
¾ teaspoon dillweed
¼ teaspoon freshly ground pepper for sauce
½ cup diced Muenster cheese

Heat the margarine in a large skillet. Add veal chops and sauté them until golden brown on both sides, about 3 to 4 minutes on each side. Remove from skillet and set aside.

Add onions to skillet; sauté until soft.

Return meat to pan. Arrange carrots and turnips on top. Sea-

318

son with salt and ¼ teaspoon pepper; pour stock over all. Cover tightly and simmer 40 minutes or until veal is tender.

Meanwhile, blend sour cream, cornstarch, dill, and remaining ¼ teaspoon pepper in a small bowl.

When veal is done, remove chops to a warm platter. Lower heat under skillet; stir sour cream mixture into pan juices. Keep stirring gently until sauce thickens. Do not let it boil.

Add cheese and cook, stirring, until cheese melts.

Return veal to skillet. Cook briefly, basting with sauce, until hot. Serve immediately.

*Yield:* 4 servings

*Change Scandinavian Veal Chops as follows or use Basic Recipe, if indicated, for:*

LOW-CALORIE, DIABETIC, LOW-FAT, AND LOW-CHOLESTEROL DIETS

Spray skillet with vegetable cooking spray. Reduce margarine to 1½ tablespoons. Add to skillet and cook chops as in Basic Recipe.
Omit sour cream. Substitute plain low-fat yogurt.
Omit Muenster cheese. Substitute diced part-skim mozzarella.
Proceed as in Basic Recipe.

Calories per serving: 407
Approximate nutrient
  values per serving:
    Protein 38 g
    Fat 23 g
    Carbohydrate 10 g
    Sodium 808 mg
    Potassium 652 mg
    Cholesterol 127 mg
Exchanges:
  Vegetable 2
  Meat 4½
  Fat 2

LOW-SODIUM DIETS

Omit salt. Substitute unsalted polyunsaturated margarine for margarine.
Omit Muenster cheese. Substitute diced low-sodium Swiss.
Proceed as in Basic Recipe.

Calories per serving: 523
Approximate nutrient
  values per serving:
    Protein 37 g
    Fat 36 g
    Carbohydrate 9 g
    Sodium 167 mg
    Potassium 638 mg
    Cholesterol 138 mg

Calories per serving: 509

Omit pepper.
Proceed as in Basic Recipe.

HIGH-FIBER DIETS

Calories per serving: 510

Use Basic Recipe and garnish with 3 tablespoons chopped fresh parsley.

# Swedish Roast Lamb

BASIC RECIPE

Serving size: 3 ounces
  lamb, 2 tablespoons
  gravy
Calories per serving: 190
Approximate nutrient
  values per serving:
    Protein 26 g
    Fat 7 g
    Carbohydrate 6 g
    Sodium 159 mg
    Potassium 291 mg
    Cholesterol 88 mg
Exchanges:
  Bread ½
  Meat 3

4-pound leg of lamb, boned, excess fat trimmed, rolled, and
  tied
½ cup water
2 tablespoons dark-brown sugar
1 tablespoon instant decaffeinated coffee granules
½ cup milk
2 tablespoons flour
2 tablespoons currant jelly
½ teaspoon salt
⅛ teaspoon freshly ground pepper

Preheat oven to 325°F.
  Place lamb skin side up on a rack in a roasting pan and begin roasting, 15 minutes per pound for medium rare.

*To prepare the basting sauce:* In a small saucepan, bring water, brown sugar, and coffee granules to a boil. Remove from heat and stir to dissolve sugar and coffee.
  Baste lamb frequently with coffee mixture until it is roasted through but not overcooked. Then remove lamb to warm serving platter and cover with aluminum foil.

*To make the gravy:* Pour off excess fat from pan juices; then scrape up and pour remaining juices into a measuring cup, adding enough water to make 1 cup. Pour juices into a saucepan. Mix milk and flour in a small bowl until smooth. Heat juices to boiling, then add milk and flour mixture and cook over moderate heat, stirring until thickened. Blend in currant jelly, salt, and pepper and simmer 5 minutes. Serve in a gravy boat with the roast lamb.

*Yield:* 12 servings

*Change Swedish Roast Lamb as follows for:*

LOW-CALORIE, DIABETIC, LOW-FAT, AND LOW-CHOLESTEROL DIETS

Reduce brown sugar to 1 tablespoon.
Substitute skim milk for milk.
Reduce currant jelly to 1 tablespoon.
Proceed as in Basic Recipe.

Calories per serving: 179
Approximate nutrient
  values per serving:
    Protein 26 g
    Fat 6 g
    Carbohydrate 4 g
    Sodium 159 mg
    Potassium 287 mg
    Cholesterol 87 mg
Exchanges:
  Bread ½
  Meat 3

LOW-SODIUM AND RENAL DIETS

Omit salt.
Proceed as in Basic Recipe.

Calories per serving: 190
Approximate nutrient
  values same as Basic
  Recipe except for:
    Calcium 27 mg
    Phosphorus 220 mg
    Sodium 67 mg

Calories per serving: 190

Omit water and coffee for basting sauce. Instead, rub lamb with the 2 tablespoons brown sugar and place directly in the roasting pan.
Omit currant jelly and substitute mint jelly in the gravy.
Omit pepper.
Proceed as in Basic Recipe.

HIGH-FIBER DIETS

Calories per serving: 190

Substitute stone-ground whole wheat flour for flour.
Proceed as in Basic Recipe.

# African Lamb

BASIC RECIPE

Serving size: 4 ounces lamb, 1 cup vegetables and gravy, ⅓ cup barley
Calories per serving: 459
Approximate nutrient values per serving:
    Protein 40 g
    Fat 15 g
    Carbohydrate 41 g
    Sodium 831 mg
    Potassium 1019 mg
    Cholesterol 109 mg
Exchanges:
    Vegetable 2
    Bread 2
    Meat 4
    Fat 1½

3 tablespoons polyunsaturated oil
2½ pounds boneless leg of lamb, trimmed of excess fat and cut in 1½-inch cubes
1 cup coarsely chopped onions
1 clove garlic, finely chopped
2 teaspoons salt
2 teaspoons ground cinnamon
¾ teaspoon ground cumin
¼ teaspoon cayenne pepper
2 cups coarsely chopped peeled tomatoes
½ cup pearl barley
1½ cups water
2 cups sliced zucchini
1½ cups sliced carrots
20-ounce can chickpeas, drained

Heat the oil in a large casserole. Add lamb, a few pieces at a time. Sauté until brown on all sides. As lamb browns, remove to a platter.

Add onions and garlic to casserole; sauté until soft, stirring to lift particles on bottom of pot.

Return lamb to casserole; season with salt, cinnamon, cumin, and cayenne. Stir meat gently to coat with spices. Add tomatoes; cover and simmer for 1 hour.

While lamb is simmering, prepare barley. Rinse the pearl barley and put it in saucepan with the water. Bring to a boil; then cover tightly and simmer for 1 hour or until barley is tender. Stir occasionally. Set aside. If finished before stew is done, transfer to a large sieve and place over pot of simmering water.

When lamb has cooked 1 hour, add zucchini and carrots; simmer 15 minutes longer. Add chickpeas and cook for an additional 10 minutes or until meat is tender.

Serve the barley with the stew.

*Yield:* 6 servings; 2 cups cooked barley

*Change African Lamb as follows or use Basic Recipe, if indicated, for:*

LOW-CALORIE, DIABETIC, LOW-FAT, AND LOW-CHOLESTEROL DIETS

Omit oil. Brown lamb in casserole that has been well sprayed with vegetable cooking spray.
Proceed as in Basic Recipe.

Calories per serving: 399
Approximate nutrient
  values per serving:
    Protein 40 g
    Fat 9 g
    Carbohydrate 41 g
    Sodium 831 mg
    Potassium 1019 mg
    Cholesterol 109 mg
Exchanges:
  Vegetable 2
  Bread 2
  Meat 4

Calories per serving: 459
Approximate nutrient
  value same as Basic
  Recipe except for:
    Sodium 99 mg

## LOW-SODIUM DIETS

Omit salt.
Proceed as in Basic Recipe.

## BLAND DIETS

Calories per serving: 459

Omit cayenne pepper.
Proceed as in Basic Recipe.

## HIGH-FIBER DIETS

Use Basic Recipe.

# Lamb and Lentil Ragout

### BASIC RECIPE

Serving size: 1½ cups
Calories per serving: 251
Approximate nutrient
  values per serving:
    Protein 20 g
    Fat 5 g
    Carbohydrate 33 g
    Sodium 452 mg
    Potassium 592 mg
    Cholesterol 30 mg
Exchanges:
  Vegetable 1
  Bread 2
  Meat 1
  Fat ½

1 tablespoon polyunsaturated oil
1 pound boned lamb shoulder, trimmed of excess fat and cut
  in 1-inch cubes
1 large onion, finely diced
1 large carrot, finely diced
2 cups lentils
½ teaspoon ground cinnamon
4 whole cloves
1 small bay leaf
½ teaspoon red chili powder
1½ teaspoons salt
6 cups water
½ cup chopped fresh parsley
1 cup shredded fresh spinach
8 slices lemon

Heat the oil in a large saucepan. Add half the lamb and sauté until lightly browned on all sides. Remove from pan, add remaining lamb, and repeat until all meat is browned. Remove lamb and set aside.

Pour off all but 1 tablespoon fat, add the onions and carrot, and sauté lightly for 3 minutes. Add the lamb, lentils, seasonings, and water. Cover and gently simmer for 1 hour or until the lentils and lamb are tender.

Just before serving, stir in parsley and spinach and cook for 1 minute.

Garnish each serving with a slice of lemon.

*Yield:* 8 servings

*Change Lamb and Lentil Ragout as follows or use Basic Recipe, if indicated, for:*

LOW-CALORIE, DIABETIC, LOW-FAT, AND LOW-CHOLESTEROL DIETS

Reduce lentils to 1 cup.
Reduce water to 5 cups.
Proceed as in Basic Recipe.

*Yield:* 7 servings

Calories per serving: 196
Approximate nutrient
    values per serving:
        Protein 17 g
        Fat 6 g
        Carbohydrate 21 g
        Sodium 514 mg
        Potassium 463 mg
        Cholesterol 34 mg
Exchanges:
    Vegetable 1
    Bread 1
    Meat 1
    Fat ½

LOW-SODIUM DIETS

Omit salt.
Add 2 teaspoons curry powder with seasonings.
Proceed as in Basic Recipe.

Calories per serving: 252
Approximate nutrient
    values same as Basic
    Recipe except for:
        Sodium 40 mg
        Potassium 600 mg

Calories per serving: 251

Omit chili powder and cloves.
Proceed as in Basic Recipe.

HIGH·FIBER DIETS

Use Basic Recipe.

# Holiday Ham

BASIC RECIPE

Serving size: 3 ounces ham
Calories per serving: 209
Approximate nutrient
    values per serving:
        Protein 22 g
        Fat 8 g
        Carbohydrate 12 g
        Sodium 822 mg
        Potassium 299 mg
        Cholesterol 78 mg
Exchanges:
    Bread 1
    Meat 3

*The Ham*
7-pound bone-in fully cooked smoked ham
2 tablespoons whole cloves

*The Honey Glaze*
1½ tablespoons orange juice
1½ teaspoons grated orange rind
1½ teaspoons dry mustard
¾ cup honey

Preheat oven to 325°F.
    Place ham, fat side up, on a rack in a shallow roasting pan. Bake ham, uncovered, about 18 minutes per pound—a little over 2 hours.
    While ham is baking prepare glaze. In a small bowl blend orange juice, orange rind, and mustard. Stir in honey.
    Approximately 30 minutes before ham is done, remove from oven. Using a sharp knife, score surface of ham in a diamond pattern, the lines ¾ inch apart. Insert cloves in diamond pattern and brush the top with glaze. Return ham to oven and continue baking, occasionally brushing with the glaze.

*Yield:* 18 servings

*Change Holiday Ham as follows or use Basic Recipe, if indicated, for:*

LOW-CALORIE, DIABETIC, LOW-FAT, AND LOW-CHOLESTEROL DIETS

*The ham:* Use Basic Recipe.

*Omit glaze:* Substitute 1 cup orange juice and baste with this every 15 minutes.
Proceed as in Basic Recipe.

Calories per serving: 171
Approximate nutrient
   values per serving:
   Protein 22 g
   Fat 8 g
   Carbohydrate 1 g
   Sodium 821 mg
   Potassium 315 mg
   Cholesterol 78 mg
Exchanges:
   Meat 3

LOW-SODIUM AND RENAL DIETS

*The ham:* Omit cloves.
Substitute 7-pound bone-in fresh ham for smoked ham.
Bake 25 to 30 minutes per pound or until meat thermometer registers 170°F.
Proceed as in Basic Recipe.

*The glaze:* Approximately 30 minutes before ham is done, brush with honey glaze. Do not score.
Proceed as in Basic Recipe.

*Yield:* 13 servings

Calories per serving: 255
Approximate nutrient
   values per serving:
   Protein 27 g
   Fat 9 g
   Carbohydrate 16 g
   Calcium 14 mg
   Phosphorus 279 mg
   Sodium 59 mg
   Potassium 364 mg
   Cholesterol 79 mg

BLAND DIETS

*The ham:* Omit cloves.
Proceed as in Basic Recipe.

*The glaze:* Omit mustard.
Proceed as in Basic Recipe.

Calories per serving: 208

Use Basic Recipe.
For extra fiber, serve with pineapple or raisin sauce.

# Roast Pork Hawaiian

BASIC RECIPE

This recipe needs 8 hours of refrigeration.

Serving size: 3 ounces
   pork, 1 tablespoon sauce
Calories per serving: 262
Approximate nutrient
   values per serving:
      Protein 25 g
      Fat 12 g
      Carbohydrate 12 g
      Sodium 177 mg
      Potassium 393 mg
      Cholesterol 75 mg
Exchanges:
   Fruit 1
   Meat 3
   Fat 1

3½-pound boneless pork loin, trimmed of excess fat
two 8-ounce cans crushed pineapple in heavy syrup
½ cup cider vinegar
¼ cup dry sherry
½ cup chopped onions
½ cup firmly packed dark-brown sugar
1 teaspoon salt
¼ teaspoon freshly ground pepper
2 teaspoons grated peeled fresh ginger root
2 cloves garlic, put through garlic press

Place pork in shallow glass pan large enough to hold the roast comfortably.

*To prepare the pineapple sauce:* Combine remaining ingredients in a medium saucepan. Simmer, uncovered, for 10 minutes. Pour sauce over pork and refrigerate at least 8 hours, or overnight, brushing occasionally with sauce.
   The next day preheat oven to 325°F.
   Place pork on a rack in a roasting pan and insert meat thermometer.
   Drain pineapple sauce from pan and reserve 1 cup. Use remaining sauce to baste meat as it roasts.
   Roast pork 30 to 35 minutes per pound or until a meat thermometer registers 170°F.

Remove to a heated serving platter, cover with aluminum foil, and let stand 20 minutes before serving.

Heat reserved pineapple sauce and serve with pork.

*Yield:* 10 servings pork, 1 cup sauce

*Change Roast Pork Hawaiian as follows or use Basic Recipe, if indicated, for:*

LOW-CALORIE, DIABETIC, LOW-FAT, AND LOW-CHOLESTEROL DIETS

Calories per serving: 246
Approximate nutrient
  values per serving:
    Protein 25 g
    Fat 12 g
    Carbohydrate 8 g
    Sodium 176 mg
    Potassium 396 mg
    Cholesterol 75 mg
Exchanges:
    Fruit 1
    Meat 3
    Fat 1

Substitute two 8-ounce cans crushed pineapple packed in unsweetened juice for the pineapple in heavy syrup.
Reduce brown sugar to ¼ cup.
Proceed as in Basic Recipe.

LOW-SODIUM AND RENAL DIETS

Calories per serving: 262
Approximate nutrient
  values same as Basic
  Recipe except for:
    Calcium 21 mg
    Phosphorus 269 mg
    Sodium 58 mg

Omit salt.
Proceed as in Basic Recipe.

BLAND DIETS

Calories per serving: 262

Omit pepper.
Proceed as in Basic Recipe.

Use Basic Recipe.

# Pork Chops and Apples

BASIC RECIPE

Serving size: 6-ounce pork
   chop, ½ cup sauce
Calories per serving: 294
Approximate nutrient
   values per serving:
      Protein 20 g
      Fat 19 g
      Carbohydrate 9 g
      Sodium 337 mg
      Potassium 350 mg
      Cholesterol 77 mg
Exchanges:
   Vegetable 1
   Fruit ½
   Meat 3
   Fat 2

four 6-ounce loin pork chops
1 tablespoon polyunsaturated oil
⅓ cup finely chopped onions
⅓ cup finely chopped celery
1 tablespoon flour
1 cup dry white wine
¾ cup chopped peeled tart apples
1 teaspoon thyme
½ teaspoon salt
¼ teaspoon freshly ground pepper
⅓ cup light cream

Preheat oven to 325°F.
   Trim excess fat from the pork chops.
   Heat the oil in an ovenproof casserole. Add the chops and brown on both sides. Remove from the casserole and pour off all but 2 tablespoons fat.
   Add the onions and celery to casserole and sauté until the onions are soft. Stir in flour and cook for 1 minute. Remove from heat and stir in wine. Return to heat and bring to boil, stirring constantly.
   Lower heat and add the pork chops, apples, thyme, salt, and pepper.
   Cover and place in oven for 1 hour or until pork is tender.
   Stir in cream just before serving.

*Yield:* 4 servings, 2 cups sauce

*Change Pork Chops and Apples as follows for:*

### LOW-CALORIE, DIABETIC, LOW-FAT, AND LOW-CHOLESTEROL DIETS

Calories per serving: 237
Approximate nutrient
  values per serving:
    Protein 20 g
    Fat 13 g
    Carbohydrate 9 g
    Sodium 337 mg
    Potassium 343 mg
    Cholesterol 55 mg
Exchanges:
    Vegetable 1
    Fruit ½
    Meat 3
    Fat 1

Omit cream. Add ⅓ cup Chicken Stock (page 114) and stir in with the wine.
Proceed as in Basic Recipe.

### LOW-SODIUM AND RENAL DIETS

Calories per serving: 294
Approximate nutrient
  values same as Basic
  Recipe except for:
    Calcium 38 mg
    Phosphorus 228 mg
    Sodium 62 mg

Omit salt.
Proceed as in Basic Recipe.

### BLAND DIETS

Calories per serving: 294

Omit pepper.
Proceed as in Basic Recipe.

### HIGH-FIBER DIETS

Calories per serving: 294

Use unpeeled apples.
Proceed as in Basic Recipe.

# POULTRY

Chicken and turkey are highly adaptable to the restrictions that special diets impose. For example, if you're on a low-sodium diet, you'll welcome the fact that poultry can be prepared without salt and still taste superb. A blend of thyme, sage, and marjoram makes an excellent salt substitute, and many of our recipes incorporate these seasonings.

Or if you're on a low-fat diet, you'll find a number of chicken and turkey recipes that use very little or no margarine or cooking oil, and still taste like sophisticated gourmet dishes.

For best results, be certain to use the kind of poultry specified in the recipe—broiler, fryer, roaster, and so on—because the age of the bird as well as its fat content affects both the recipe and the nutrient values.

# Herb Baked Chicken

BASIC RECIPE

1 cup thinly sliced carrots
1 cup thinly sliced onions
3½-pound broiler chicken, cut into serving pieces
1 cup Chicken Stock (page 114)
2 tablespoons lemon juice
½ teaspoon rosemary
½ teaspoon thyme
½ teaspoon marjoram
1 teaspoon salt
¼ teaspoon freshly ground pepper
⅓ cup chopped fresh parsley

Preheat oven to 325°F.

Arrange carrots and onions in a shallow baking dish. Place chicken, skin side up, over vegetables. Pour ½ cup of the stock over chicken. Cover tightly and bake 45 minutes.

Meanwhile, in a small saucepan bring to a boil remaining stock, lemon juice, rosemary, thyme, marjoram, salt, and pepper. Remove from heat.

Increase oven temperature to 400°F. Uncover chicken and bake, basting liberally with the herb mixture, for approximately 20 minutes or until chicken is tender and skin is lightly browned. Spoon vegetables and pan juices over chicken, garnish with parsley, and serve immediately.

*Yield:* 4 servings

*Change Herb Baked Chicken as follows or use Basic Recipe, if indicated, for:*

LOW-CALORIE, DIABETIC, LOW-FAT, AND LOW-CHOLESTEROL DIETS

Remove skin from chicken.
Proceed as in Basic Recipe.

Calories per serving: 163
Approximate nutrient
  values per serving:
    Protein 25 g
    Fat 3 g
    Carbohydrate 8 g
    Sodium 656 mg
    Potassium 564 mg
    Cholesterol 47 mg
Exchanges:
  Vegetable 1½
  Meat 3

LOW-SODIUM AND RENAL DIETS

Omit salt.
Proceed as in Basic Recipe.

Calories per serving: 252
Approximate nutrient
  values same as Basic
  Recipe except for:
    Calcium 52 mg
    Phosphorus 259 mg
    Sodium 107 mg

BLAND DIETS

Omit pepper.
Proceed as in Basic Recipe.

Calories per serving: 252

HIGH-FIBER DIETS

Use Basic Recipe.

# Poulet en Cocotte

BASIC RECIPE

4-pound roasting chicken
½ teaspoon salt
¼ teaspoon freshly ground pepper
½ teaspoon tarragon
3 tablespoons polyunsaturated margarine for browning
chicken
2 tablespoons polyunsaturated oil
12 small white onions, blanched
12 small new potatoes
¾ cup tomato juice
1 bay leaf
2 tablespoons chopped fresh parsley
¼ teaspoon thyme
½ pound medium-size sliced fresh mushrooms
2 tablespoons polyunsaturated margarine for sautéing
mushrooms
9-ounce package frozen artichoke hearts, thawed

Preheat oven to 325°F.

Wash chicken and dry thoroughly with paper towels. Rub inside of chicken with salt, pepper, and tarragon. Heat 3 tablespoons margarine and 2 tablespoons oil in an ovenproof casserole large enough to hold the chicken comfortably. Brown chicken on all sides, turning carefully to avoid breaking the skin.

While chicken is browning, parboil onions in a covered saucepan for 5 minutes. Drain and set onions aside.

In the same saucepan, cover potatoes with cold water, bring to a boil. Boil 2 minutes and drain.

Remove chicken from casserole. Add onions and potatoes to casserole and sauté until lightly browned. Stir gently to lift any drippings on bottom of pot. Return chicken to casserole.

Combine tomato juice, bay leaf, parsley, and thyme and pour over the chicken. Cover tightly and bake for 45 minutes.

Meanwhile, in a small skillet, sauté mushrooms in the 2 tablespoons margarine until lightly browned. Add to casserole with artichoke hearts and bake, tightly covered, about 45 minutes longer, or until chicken is tender.

*Yield:* 6 servings

*Change Poulet en Cocotte as follows or use Basic Recipe, if indicated, for:*

### LOW-CALORIE, DIABETIC, LOW-FAT, AND LOW-CHOLESTEROL DIETS

Skin chicken, dry thoroughly with paper towels, and season as in Basic Recipe.
Omit margarine and oil for browning. Spray casserole with vegetable cooking spray and brown chicken on all sides. Remove chicken and set aside.
Add boiled onions and potatoes to casserole and toss gently until coated with pan juices. Then add raw mushrooms and artichoke hearts and toss to coat with pan juices. Add tomato juice mixture. Return chicken to casserole and bake for 90 minutes or until tender.

Calories per serving: 281
Approximate nutrient
  values per serving:
    Protein 28 g
    Fat 4 g
    Carbohydrate 36 g
    Sodium 345 mg
    Potassium 1195 mg
    Cholesterol 47 mg
Exchanges:
  Vegetable 3
  Bread 1½
  Meat 3

### LOW-SODIUM DIETS

Omit salt.
Substitute unsalted polyunsaturated margarine for margarine wherever used.
Substitute low-sodium tomato juice for tomato juice.

Calories per serving: 478
Approximate nutrient
  values same as Basic
  Recipe except for:
    Sodium 102 mg
    Potassium 1197 mg

### BLAND DIETS

Omit pepper.
Proceed as in Basic Recipe.

Calories per serving: 478

### HIGH-FIBER DIETS

Use Basic Recipe.

# Stewed Chicken

BASIC RECIPE

Serving size: 4 ounces
   chicken, ¼ cup gravy
Calories per serving: 222
Approximate nutrient
   values per serving:
      Protein 28 g
      Fat 11 g
      Carbohydrate 3 g
      Sodium 789 mg
      Potassium 408 mg
      Cholesterol 87 mg
Exchanges:
   Bread ½
   Meat 4
   Fat 1

5-pound stewing chicken
1 cup sliced carrots
1 cup sliced celery
1 cup sliced leeks, white part only
1 bay leaf
2 teaspoons salt
¼ teaspoon peppercorns
3½ cups water
4 tablespoons polyunsaturated margarine
3 tablespoons flour

Rinse chicken and place in a casserole in which it will fit comfortably.

Add carrots, celery, leeks, bay leaf, salt, peppercorns, and water. Cover casserole and bring to a boil; then reduce heat and simmer gently 2 to 2½ hours or until chicken is tender. Skim foam as it rises to the surface.

Take chicken from stock and remove skin. Set aside on a warm platter.

Strain stock and boil, uncovered, until it is reduced to approximately 1¾ cups.

In a saucepan melt the margarine. Blend in flour. Then gradually add stock and cook over moderate heat, stirring constantly, until gravy is thickened and smooth.

Serve over chicken.

*Yield:* 7 servings

*Change Stewed Chicken as follows or use Basic Recipe, if indicated, for:*

### LOW-CALORIE, DIABETIC, LOW-FAT, AND LOW-CHOLESTEROL DIETS

Reduce stock to 1⅛ cups.
Reduce margarine to 2 tablespoons.
Reduce flour to 2½ tablespoons.
Proceed as in Basic Recipe.

Serving size: 4 ounces chicken, 3 tablespoons gravy
Calories per serving: 191
Approximate nutrient values per serving:
    Protein 28 g
    Fat 7 g
    Carbohydrate 2 g
    Sodium 752 mg
    Potassium 400 mg
    Cholesterol 87 mg
Exchanges:
    Meat 4
    Fat ½

### LOW-SODIUM AND RENAL DIETS

Omit salt.
Substitute unsalted polyunsaturated margarine for margarine.
Proceed as in Basic Recipe.

Calories per serving: 222
Approximate nutrient values same as Basic Recipe except for:
    Calcium 12 mg
    Phosphorus 243 mg
    Sodium 96 mg

### BLAND DIETS

Omit peppercorns.
Proceed as in Basic Recipe.

Calories per serving: 222

### HIGH-FIBER DIETS

Use Basic Recipe.

338

# Chicken Cacciatore

BASIC RECIPE

Serving size: 3 ounces chicken, ½ cup gravy
Calories per serving: 323
Approximate nutrient values per serving:
- Protein 26 g
- Fat 20 g
- Carbohydrate 10 g
- Sodium 625 mg
- Potassium 725 mg
- Cholesterol 77 mg

Exchanges:
- Vegetable 2
- Meat 3
- Fat 2

2 tablespoons polyunsaturated oil
3½-pound broiler-fryer chicken, cut into serving pieces
½ cup chopped onions
½ cup diced green pepper
1 clove garlic, put through garlic press
2 cups coarsely chopped peeled and seeded tomatoes
¼ cup dry white wine
3 tablespoons chopped fresh parsley
1 teaspoon salt
¼ teaspoon freshly ground pepper
½ teaspoon oregano

Heat oil in a large, heavy skillet. Add chicken, and brown on all sides. Remove chicken and set aside.

Add onions, green pepper, and garlic to skillet; sauté until onions are soft. Stir to lift any brown particles from the bottom of the pan. Drain off excess fat.

Return chicken to skillet. Add tomatoes and remaining ingredients. Cover tightly and simmer slowly for approximately 40 minutes or until chicken is tender.

Remove chicken to warm platter. Stir vegetable sauce briefly and spoon over chicken before serving.

*Yield:* 4 servings

*Change Chicken Cacciatore as follows or use Basic Recipe, if indicated, for:*

LOW-SODIUM DIETS

Calories per serving: 323
Approximate nutrient values same as Basic Recipe except for:
- Sodium 76 mg

Omit salt.
Proceed as in Basic Recipe.

Calories per serving: 323

Omit ground pepper.
Proceed as in Basic Recipe.


HIGH-FIBER DIETS

Use Basic Recipe.


CHICKEN CACCIATORE FOR LOW-CALORIE, DIABETIC, LOW-FAT, AND LOW-CHOLESTEROL DIETS

Serving size: 3 ounces
  chicken, ½ cup gravy
Calories per serving: 174
Approximate nutrient
  values per serving:
    Protein 26 g
    Fat 3 g
    Carbohydrate 10 g
    Sodium 625 mg
    Potassium 725 mg
    Cholesterol 47 mg
Exchanges:
  Vegetable 2
  Meat 3

3½-pound broiler-fryer chicken, cut into serving pieces
vegetable cooking spray
½ cup chopped onions
½ cup diced green pepper
1 clove garlic, put through garlic press
2 cups coarsely chopped peeled and seeded tomatoes
¼ cup dry white wine
3 tablespoons chopped fresh parsley
1 teaspoon salt
½ teaspoon oregano
¼ teaspoon freshly ground pepper

Remove skin from chicken. Spray a large, heavy skillet with vegetable cooking spray. Brown chicken on all sides. Add all remaining ingredients to skillet.

Cover tightly and simmer slowly for approximately 40 minutes or until chicken is tender.

Remove chicken to warm platter. Stir vegetable sauce briefly and spoon over chicken before serving.

*Yield:* 4 servings

# Chicken in Plum Sauce

BASIC RECIPE

Serving size: 3 ounces
    chicken, ½ cup sauce
Calories per serving: 431
Approximate nutrient
    values per serving:
    Protein 25 g
    Fat 24 g
    Carbohydrate 29 g
    Sodium 769 mg
    Potassium 628 mg
    Cholesterol 77 mg
Exchanges:
    Fruit 2
    Bread ½
    Meat 3
    Fat 3

1-pound 14-ounce can whole purple plums
¼ cup brandy
2 tablespoons cornstarch
4 tablespoons polyunsaturated margarine
3-pound broiler-fryer chicken, cut into serving pieces
1 cup chopped celery
1 teaspoon salt
¼ teaspoon marjoram
¼ teaspoon thyme
¼ teaspoon sage
⅛ teaspoon freshly ground pepper
1 clove garlic, put through garlic press
½ cup thinly sliced scallions, both white and green parts

Preheat oven to 350°F.

Drain plums and reserve 1 cup of the juice. Set plums aside.

In a small bowl stir brandy and cornstarch until smooth. Stir in reserved plum juice and set aside. Heat the margarine in a medium-size ovenproof casserole. Add the chicken pieces and sauté until brown on all sides.

Turn chicken skin side up in casserole. Add celery, salt, marjoram, thyme, sage, pepper, and garlic. Add brandy mixture. Cover and bake 30 minutes.

Add reserved plums and bake 10 minutes more or until chicken is done.

Garnish with sliced scallions before serving.

*Yield:* 4 servings

*Change Chicken in Plum Sauce as follows or use Basic Recipe, if indicated, for:*

### LOW-CALORIE, DIABETIC, LOW-FAT, AND LOW-CHOLESTEROL DIETS

Calories per serving: 262
Approximate nutrient
  values per serving:
    Protein 25 g
    Fat 9 g
    Carbohydrate 21 g
    Sodium 714 mg
    Potassium 654 mg
    Cholesterol 47 mg
Exchanges:
  Fruit 1½
  Bread ½
  Meat 3
  Fat 1

Remove skin from chicken.
Spray skillet well with vegetable cooking spray. Reduce margarine to 2 tablespoons.
Substitute 16-ounce can whole plums packed in water.
Proceed as in Basic Recipe.

### LOW-SODIUM DIETS

Calories per serving: 431
Approximate nutrient
  values same as Basic
  Recipe except for:
    Sodium 106 mg

Omit salt.
Substitute unsalted polyunsaturated margarine for margarine.
Proceed as in Basic Recipe.

### BLAND DIETS

Calories per serving: 431

Omit pepper.
Proceed as in Basic Recipe.

### HIGH-FIBER DIETS

Use Basic Recipe.

# Baked Chicken and Rice

BASIC RECIPE

Serving size: 3 ounces
chicken, 1 cup rice and
vegetables
Calories per serving: 427
Approximate nutrient
values per serving:
Protein 26 g
Fat 20 g
Carbohydrate 37 g
Sodium 955 mg
Potassium 851 mg
Cholesterol 68 mg
Exchanges:
Vegetable 2
Bread 2
Meat 3
Fat 2

4-pound broiler-fryer chicken, cut into serving pieces
¼ cup polyunsaturated margarine
¾ cup chopped red onions
1 cup thinly sliced carrots
1 cup thinly sliced celery
2 cloves garlic, put through garlic press
1 cup raw long-grain rice
2 cups coarsely chopped peeled tomatoes
2 cups Chicken Stock (page 114)
2 teaspoons salt
¼ teaspoon freshly ground pepper
1 teaspoon rosemary
1 teaspoon chervil
½ teaspoon oregano
9-ounce package frozen artichoke hearts
¼ cup pimiento pieces

Preheat oven to 350°F.

In an ovenproof casserole, sauté chicken pieces in margarine until brown on all sides. As pieces brown, remove them to a warm platter.

Add onions, carrots, celery, and garlic to casserole and sauté until onions are soft. Stir in rice, tomatoes, stock, salt, pepper, rosemary, chervil, and oregano. Add chicken and mix gently. Cover and bake 35 minutes or until chicken and rice are tender.

Shortly before chicken is done, cook artichoke hearts according to package directions, drain thoroughly, and cut in bite-size pieces. Garnish chicken with artichokes and pimiento before serving.

*Yield:* 6 servings

*Change Baked Chicken and Rice as follows or use Basic Recipe, if indicated, for:*

## LOW-CALORIE, DIABETIC, LOW-FAT, AND LOW-CHOLESTEROL DIETS

Calories per serving: 318
Approximate nutrient
  values per serving:
    Protein 26 g
    Fat 7 g
    Carbohydrate 37 g
    Sodium 917 mg
    Potassium 850 mg
    Cholesterol 47 mg
Exchanges:
  Vegetable 2
  Bread 2
  Meat 3
  Fat ½

Remove skin from chicken.
Reduce margarine to 2 tablespoons.
Spray casserole with vegetable cooking spray.
Proceed as in Basic Recipe.

## LOW-SODIUM DIETS

Calories per serving: 427
Approximate nutrient
  values same as Basic
  Recipe except for:
    Sodium 147 mg

Omit salt.
Substitute unsalted polyunsaturated margarine for margarine.
Proceed as in Basic Recipe.

## BLAND DIETS

Calories per serving: 427

Omit pepper.
Proceed as in Basic Recipe.

## HIGH-FIBER DIETS

Use Basic Recipe.

# Chicken Baked in Yogurt

BASIC RECIPE

This recipe requires at least 8 hours of refrigeration.

Serving size: 3 ounces of
  chicken
Calories per serving: 265
Approximate nutrient
  values per serving:
    Protein 26 g
    Fat 15 g
    Carbohydrate 5 g
    Sodium 918 mg
    Potassium 477 mg
    Cholesterol 84 mg
Exchanges:
  Milk ¼
  Meat 3
  Fat 1

3½-pound broiler-fryer chicken, cut into serving pieces
1 cup plain yogurt
1½ teaspoons salt
½ teaspoon ground cumin
½ teaspoon dry mustard
¼ teaspoon red pepper flakes
¼ teaspoon ground ginger
1 clove garlic, put through garlic press
½ cup scallions sliced diagonally in 1-inch pieces, including
  green part

Rinse chicken under cool running water; dry with paper towels.

In a large bowl, stir together yogurt, salt, cumin, mustard, pepper flakes, ginger, and garlic until blended.

Add chicken and turn to coat pieces with yogurt mixture. Cover and refrigerate at least 8 hours.

The next day, preheat oven to 325°F.

Arrange chicken, skin side up, in a shallow baking dish. Spoon any sauce remaining in bowl over chicken. Bake, uncovered, 1 hour or until chicken is tender and skin is nicely browned. Garnish with scallions before serving.

*Yield:* 4 servings

*Change Chicken Baked in Yogurt as follows or use Basic Recipe, if indicated, for:*

LOW-CALORIE, DIABETIC, LOW-FAT, AND LOW-CHOLESTEROL DIETS

Calories per serving: 177
Approximate nutrient
  values per serving:
    Protein 27 g
    Fat 4 g
    Carbohydrate 7 g
    Sodium 931 mg
    Potassium 522 mg
    Cholesterol 47 mg
Exchanges:
  Milk ¼
  Meat 3

Remove skin from chicken.
Substitute plain low-fat yogurt for yogurt.
Proceed as in Basic Recipe.

LOW-SODIUM AND RENAL DIETS

Calories per serving: 265
Approximate nutrient
  values same as Basic
  Recipe except for:
    Calcium 93 mg
    Phosphorus 279 mg
    Sodium 94 mg

Omit salt.
Proceed as in Basic Recipe.

BLAND DIETS

Calories per serving: 264

Omit pepper and mustard.
Proceed as in Basic Recipe.

HIGH-FIBER DIETS

Use Basic Recipe.
For extra fiber, serve with peas or broccoli and a green salad.

# California Chicken

BASIC RECIPE

Serving size: 3 ounces
  chicken, ⅔ cup sauce
Calories per serving: 461
Approximate nutrient
  values per serving:
    Protein 26 g
    Fat 31 g
    Carbohydrate 22 g
    Sodium 595 mg
    Potassium 819 mg
    Cholesterol 77 mg
Exchanges:
  Fruit 2
  Meat 3
  Fat 4

*The Chicken*
4 tablespoons polyunsaturated margarine
3½-pound broiler-fryer chicken, cut into serving pieces
¾ teaspoon salt
⅛ teaspoon cayenne pepper
1 cup orange juice

*The Sauce*
1 tablespoon cornstarch
2 tablespoons cold water
2 tablespoons orange liqueur
¼ teaspoon ground cloves
1½ teaspoons grated orange rind
1 clove garlic, put through garlic press
1½ cups orange sections in bite-size pieces
1 cup avocado cubes

*To prepare the chicken:* Heat the margarine in a large skillet. Add chicken and sauté until brown on both sides. Turn chicken skin side up; season with salt and cayenne pepper and add orange juice. Cover and simmer 30 minutes or until chicken is tender. Remove chicken to a heated platter.

*To prepare the sauce:* Blend cornstarch, water, and orange liqueur. Add to skillet and bring to a boil. Reduce heat, add cloves, orange rind, and garlic. Cook, stirring, until sauce thickens. Remove sauce from heat; stir in orange sections and avocado cubes.

Return chicken to skillet, place over low heat, and baste with sauce until chicken is heated through. Serve immediately.

*Yield:* 4 servings

Change California Chicken as follows or use Basic Recipe, if indicated, for:

LOW-CALORIE, DIABETIC, LOW-FAT, AND LOW-CHOLESTEROL DIETS

*The chicken:* Remove skin from chicken.
Reduce margarine to 2 tablespoons and heat in skillet that has been well sprayed with vegetable cooking spray. Proceed as in Basic Recipe.

*The sauce:* Proceed as in Basic Recipe. Omit avocado.
Add ½ cup minced scallions, both white and green parts, for garnish.

Serving size: 3 ounces chicken, ½ cup sauce
Calories per serving: 266
Approximate nutrient values per serving:
  Protein 25 g
  Fat 9 g
  Carbohydrate 21 g
  Sodium 538 mg
  Potassium 640 mg
  Cholesterol 47 mg
Exchanges:
  Fruit 2
  Meat 3
  Fat 1

LOW-SODIUM DIETS

*The chicken:* Omit salt.
Substitute unsalted polyunsaturated margarine for margarine.
Proceed as in Basic Recipe.

*The sauce:* Use Basic Recipe.

Calories per serving: 461
Approximate nutrient values same as Basic Recipe except for:
  Sodium 69 mg

BLAND DIETS

*The chicken:* Omit cayenne pepper.
Proceed as in Basic Recipe.

*The sauce:* Omit cloves.
Proceed as in Basic Recipe.

Calories per serving: 461

HIGH-FIBER DIETS

Use Basic Recipe.

# Marinated Broiled Chicken

BASIC RECIPE

4-pound roasting chicken, cut into serving pieces
½ cup lemon juice
3 cloves garlic, put through garlic press
2 tablespoons polyunsaturated oil
2 teaspoons crushed peppercorns
1 teaspoon thyme
¾ teaspoon salt

Place chicken pieces in large mixing bowl. Combine remaining ingredients and pour over the chicken; turn pieces so all are coated with seasonings. Refrigerate at least 4 hours, turning chicken occasionally.

   Preheat oven broiler. Arrange chicken skin side down in an ovenproof dish. Place dish 3 to 4 inches below the broiler. Broil 15 to 18 minutes on each side.

*Yield:* 6 servings

*Change Marinated Broiled Chicken as follows for:*

LOW-CALORIE, DIABETIC, LOW-FAT, AND LOW-CHOLESTEROL DIETS

Reduce oil to 2 teaspoons.
Proceed as in Basic Recipe.
Remove skin before serving.

Calories per serving: 243
Approximate nutrient
  values per serving:
    Protein 21 g
    Fat 16 g
    Carbohydrate 3 g
    Calcium 20 mg
    Phosphorus 193 mg
    Sodium 59 mg
    Potassium 328 mg
    Cholesterol 68 mg

Omit salt. Add 2 teaspoons rosemary.
Proceed as in Basic Recipe.

## BLAND DIETS

Calories per serving: 242

Omit peppercorns.
Proceed as in Basic Recipe.

## HIGH-FIBER DIETS

Calories per serving: 244

Add ½ cup coarsely chopped fresh parsley with seasoning.
Proceed as in Basic Recipe.
For extra fiber, serve with cauliflower or acorn squash.

# Chicken Breasts with Tarragon

### BASIC RECIPE

Serving size: 4 ounces
  chicken, ¼ cup sauce
Calories per serving: 413
Approximate nutrient
  values per serving:
    Protein 28 g
    Fat 28 g
    Carbohydrate 11 g

6 skinned, boned chicken breast halves (2 pounds)
⅔ cup dry bread crumbs (page 38)
4 tablespoons polyunsaturated oil
⅓ cup chopped onions
1 teaspoon salt
¼ teaspoon freshly ground pepper
¾ teaspoon tarragon

Sodium 518 mg
Potassium 426 mg
Cholesterol 118 mg
Exchanges:
  Bread 1
  Meat 4
  Fat 5

½ cup dry white wine
1 cup heavy cream
⅓ cup chopped fresh parsley

Coat chicken breasts with bread crumbs. Heat the oil in a large skillet. Add chicken and sauté until brown on both sides—about 2 minutes per side. Remove chicken and set aside.

Add onions to skillet and sauté until soft. Then return chicken to pan and season with salt, pepper, and tarragon. Pour wine over all.

Cover and simmer slowly for 15 to 20 minutes or until chicken is tender. Remove chicken to a warm platter.

Add cream to skillet. Increase heat and boil, stirring to lift brown particles from bottom of pan, until sauce is thickened and reduced to 1½ cups.

Spoon sauce over chicken and garnish with parsley.

*Yield:* 6 servings

*Change Chicken Breasts with Tarragon as follows for:*

LOW-SODIUM AND RENAL DIETS

Calories per serving: 413
Approximate nutrient
  values same as Basic
  Recipe except for:
    Calcium 60 mg
    Phosphorus 261 mg
    Sodium 152 mg

Omit salt.
Proceed as in Basic Recipe.

BLAND DIETS

Calories per serving: 413

Omit pepper.
Proceed as in Basic Recipe.

HIGH-FIBER DIETS

Calories per serving: 413

Substitute ⅔ cup stone-ground whole wheat dry bread crumbs for bread crumbs.
Proceed as in Basic Recipe.

## CHICKEN BREASTS WITH TARRAGON FOR LOW-CALORIE, DIABETIC, LOW-FAT, AND LOW-CHOLESTEROL DIETS

Serving size: 4 ounces chicken, 2 tablespoons sauce
Calories per serving: 162
Approximate nutrient values per serving:
    Protein 26 g
    Fat 4 g
    Carbohydrate 4 g
    Sodium 422 mg
    Potassium 479 mg
    Cholesterol 63 mg
Exchanges:
    Vegetable 1
    Meat 4

vegetable cooking spray
6 skinned, boned chicken breast halves (2 pounds)
⅓ cup chopped onions
1 teaspoon salt
¼ teaspoon freshly ground pepper
¾ teaspoon tarragon
½ cup dry white wine
1 cup coarsely chopped peeled tomatoes
⅓ cup chopped fresh parsley

Spray a large skillet with vegetable spray. Add chicken and sauté until brown on both sides—about 2 minutes per side. Remove chicken and set aside.

Add onions to skillet and sauté until soft. Then return chicken to pan and season with salt, pepper, and tarragon. Pour wine and tomatoes over all. Cover and simmer slowly for 15 to 20 minutes or until chicken is tender. Remove chicken to warm platter.

Increase heat and boil, stirring to lift brown particles from bottom of pan, until sauce is thickened and reduced to ¾ cup.

Spoon sauce over chicken and garnish with parsley.

*Yield:* 6 servings

# Chicken Romano

BASIC RECIPE

The tomato sauce may be prepared the day before.

Serving size: 4 ounces chicken, ¼ cup sauce, 3 tablespoons mushrooms and ham

¼ cup polyunsaturated margarine for sautéing chicken
8 skinned, boned chicken breast halves (2⅔ pounds)
2 cups Italian Tomato Sauce (page 392)
⅓ cup red wine

Calories per serving: 338
Approximate nutrient
  values per serving:
    Protein 31 g
    Fat 19 g
    Carbohydrate 11 g
    Sodium 558 mg
    Potassium 858 mg
    Cholesterol 72 mg
Exchanges:
  Vegetable 2
  Meat 4
  Fat 2½

½ teaspoon salt
⅛ teaspoon freshly ground pepper
¼ teaspoon allspice
¼ cup polyunsaturated margarine for sautéing mushrooms and ham
2 cups sliced fresh mushrooms
1 cup diced cooked ham

Heat the ¼ cup margarine in a large skillet. Add chicken breasts (a few at a time if necessary) and sauté until brown on both sides—about 2 minutes per side.

Combine 2 cups tomato sauce, wine, salt, pepper, and allspice, and pour over all the chicken breasts. Cover and simmer about 20 minutes or until chicken is tender. Baste occasionally.

While chicken is simmering, melt ¼ cup margarine in a medium skillet. Add mushrooms and ham and sauté until mushrooms are tender.

To serve, spoon sauce over chicken and top with mushrooms and ham.

*Yield:* 8 servings chicken

*Change Chicken Romano as follows or use Basic Recipe, if indicated, for:*

LOW-CALORIE, DIABETIC, LOW-FAT, AND LOW-CHOLESTEROL DIETS

Spray large skillet well with vegetable cooking spray. Reduce margarine to 1 tablespoon to sauté chicken. Add tomato sauce, wine, and seasonings, and proceed as in Basic Recipe.
Spray medium skillet well with vegetable cooking spray. Reduce margarine to 1½ tablespoons to sauté mushrooms and ham.
Proceed as in Basic Recipe.

Calories per serving: 269
Approximate nutrient
  values per serving:
    Protein 31 g
    Fat 11 g
    Carbohydrate 11 g
    Sodium 479 mg
    Potassium 856 mg
    Cholesterol 72 mg
Exchanges:
  Vegetable 2
  Meat 4
  Fat 1

Calories per serving: 344
Approximate nutrient
  values per serving:
    Protein 34 g
    Fat 19 g
    Carbohydrate 10 g
    Sodium 76 mg
    Potassium 874 mg
    Cholesterol 80 mg

Omit salt.
Substitute unsalted polyunsaturated margarine for margarine wherever used.
Substitute 1 cup diced cooked pork tenderloin for ham.
Proceed as in Basic Recipe.

## BLAND DIETS

Calories per serving: 338

Omit pepper.
Proceed as in Basic Recipe.

## HIGH-FIBER DIETS

Use Basic Recipe. For extra fiber, add minced scallions or chopped green pepper to garnish.

# Chicken Breasts with Ginger

BASIC RECIPE

Serving size: 4 ounces
  chicken, ⅛ cup carrots
  and sauce
Calories per serving: 358
Approximate nutrient
  values per serving:
    Protein 29 g
    Fat 22 g
    Carbohydrate 11 g
    Sodium 547 mg
    Potassium 556 mg
    Cholesterol 104 mg

8 skinned, boned chicken breast halves (2⅔ pounds)
½ cup dry bread crumbs (page 38)
¼ cup polyunsaturated oil
3 cups thinly sliced carrots
1½ teaspoons salt
¼ teaspoon freshly ground pepper
½ cup Chicken Stock (page 114)
1½ teaspoons grated peeled fresh ginger root
1 cup heavy cream
2 cups alfalfa sprouts

Dredge chicken in bread crumbs.

Heat the oil in a large skillet. Add the chicken and sauté until browned on both sides—about 2 minutes per side. Arrange the carrots on top of chicken, season with salt and pepper, and add chicken stock. Cover and simmer slowly approximately 20 minutes or until chicken and carrots are tender.

Remove chicken to a heated platter.

Add ginger and cream to the skillet, increase the heat, and boil gently. Stir, lifting the brown particles from the bottom of the skillet, until the sauce is thickened.

Spoon carrots and cream sauce over chicken and garnish with alfalfa sprouts.

*Yield:* 8 servings

*Change Chicken Breasts with Ginger as follows or use Basic Recipe, if indicated, for:*

LOW-SODIUM AND RENAL DIETS

Calories per serving: 358
Approximate nutrient
  values same as Basic
  Recipe except for:
    Calcium 61 mg
    Phosphorus 280 mg
    Sodium 135 mg

Omit salt.
Proceed as in Basic Recipe.

BLAND DIETS

Omit pepper.
Proceed as in Basic Recipe.

HIGH-FIBER DIETS

Use Basic Recipe.

## CHICKEN BREASTS WITH GINGER FOR LOW-CALORIE, DIABETIC, LOW-FAT, AND LOW-CHOLESTEROL DIETS

Serving size: 4 ounces
   chicken, ⅓ cup carrots
   and sauce
Calories per serving: 217
Approximate nutrient
   values per serving:
      Protein 28 g
      Fat 8 g
      Carbohydrate 8 g
      Sodium 522 mg
      Potassium 570 mg
      Cholesterol 64 mg
Exchanges:
   Vegetable 1
   Meat 4
   Fat 1

vegetable cooking spray
2 tablespoons polyunsaturated oil
8 skinned, boned chicken breast halves (2⅔ pounds)
3 cups thinly sliced carrots
1½ teaspoons salt
¼ teaspoon freshly ground pepper
½ cup Chicken Stock (page 114)
1 tablespoon cornstarch
1 cup buttermilk
1½ teaspoons grated peeled fresh ginger root
2 cups alfalfa sprouts

Spray a large skillet well with vegetable cooking spray, add the oil, and heat.

Sauté the chicken until browned on both sides—about 2 minutes per side. Arrange carrots on top of chicken, season with salt and pepper, and add chicken stock. Cover and simmer slowly about 20 minutes or until chicken and carrots are tender.

Remove chicken to a heated platter.

Blend cornstarch and buttermilk.

Add buttermilk mixture and ginger to skillet, increase the heat, and bring to boil. Stir, lifting particles from bottom of pan, until sauce is thickened.

Spoon carrots and sauce over chicken and garnish with alfalfa sprouts. Any extra sauce may be frozen.

*Yield:* 8 servings

# Chicken Breasts with Cucumber

BASIC RECIPE

Serving size: 4 ounces
chicken, ⅓ cup sauce
Calories per serving: 371
Approximate nutrient
values per serving:
Protein 27 g
Fat 26 g
Carbohydrate 7 g
Sodium 526 mg
Potassium 458 mg
Cholesterol 118 mg
Exchanges:
Bread ½
Meat 4
Fat 4½

6 skinned, boned chicken breast halves (2 pounds)
⅛ cup fresh bread crumbs (page 38)
¼ cup polyunsaturated margarine
1 teaspoon salt
¼ teaspoon freshly ground pepper
3 tablespoons Cognac
½ cup dry vermouth
1 cup heavy cream
1½ cups diced peeled cucumber
½ cup sliced scallions, white and green parts

Coat chicken breasts with bread crumbs.

Heat the margarine in a large skillet and sauté chicken until brown on both sides—about 2 minutes per side. Season with salt and pepper and add Cognac and vermouth. Cover and simmer slowly approximately 20 minutes or until chicken is tender. Remove chicken to a warm platter.

Add cream to skillet and boil, stirring to lift particles from bottom of skillet, until sauce is slightly thickened. Reduce heat, and stir in cucumber and scallions. Return chicken to pan and cook, basting with sauce, until hot.

*Yield:* 6 servings

*Change Chicken Breasts with Cucumber as follows or use Basic Recipe, if indicated, for:*

LOW-SODIUM AND RENAL DIETS

Calories per serving: 371
Approximate nutrient
values same as Basic
Recipe except for:
Calcium 50 mg
Phosphorus 254 mg
Sodium 84 mg

Omit salt.
Substitute unsalted polyunsaturated margarine for margarine.
Proceed as in Basic Recipe.

Calories per serving: 371

Omit pepper.
Proceed as in Basic Recipe.

HIGH-FIBER DIETS

Calories per serving: 372

Use Basic Recipe.
Just before serving add 3 tablespoons chopped fresh parsley
for garnish.

CHICKEN BREASTS WITH CUCUMBER FOR LOW-
CALORIE, DIABETIC, LOW-FAT, AND LOW-
CHOLESTEROL DIETS

Serving size: 4 ounces
chicken, ⅓ cup sauce
Calories per serving: 211
Approximate nutrient
values per serving:
Protein 27 g
Fat 8 g
Carbohydrate 7 g
Sodium 491 mg
Potassium 471 mg
Cholesterol 64 mg
Exchanges:
Bread ½
Meat 4
Fat 1

vegetable cooking spray
2 tablespoons polyunsaturated margarine
6 skinned, boned chicken breast halves (2 pounds)
1 teaspoon salt
¼ teaspoon freshly ground pepper
3 tablespoons Cognac
½ cup dry vermouth
1 tablespoon cornstarch
¾ cup buttermilk
1½ cups diced peeled cucumber
½ cup sliced scallions, white and green parts

Spray a large skillet well with vegetable cooking spray. Heat
the margarine and sauté the chicken until brown on both
sides—about 2 minutes per side. Season with salt and pepper,
add Cognac and vermouth, cover, and simmer slowly approximately 20 minutes or until chicken is tender. Remove chicken
to a warm platter.

Blend cornstarch and buttermilk until smooth. Gradually
stir into pan juices and simmer gently over low heat until sauce
thickens. Remove from heat and stir in cucumber and scallions. Return chicken to skillet, turn heat low, and baste with
sauce until chicken is heated through. Serve immediately.

*Yield:* 6 servings

# Chicken Sautéed with Vegetables

BASIC RECIPE

Serving size: ¾ cup
Calories per serving: 316
Approximate nutrient
  values per serving:
    Protein 27 g
    Fat 18 g
    Carbohydrate 12 g
    Sodium 751 mg
    Potassium 662 mg
    Cholesterol 63 mg
Exchanges:
  Vegetable 2
  Meat 4
  Fat 3

1 tablespoon cornstarch
2 tablespoons dry sherry
2 tablespoons soy sauce
4 tablespoons polyunsaturated oil
2 cups uncooked chicken, without skin, in bite-size pieces
½ cup diced green pepper
½ cup thinly sliced celery
½ cup sliced water chestnuts
1 clove garlic, finely chopped
½ cup Chicken Stock (page 114)

Stir cornstarch, sherry, and soy sauce until smooth. Set aside.

Heat oil in a large skillet. Add chicken and sauté for 2 minutes, stirring constantly. Add green pepper, celery, water chestnuts, and garlic and mix gently. Add chicken stock, reduce heat, cover, and simmer slowly for 5 minutes or until chicken is tender.

Uncover skillet, add reserved sherry mixture and cook, mixing gently, until sauce comes to a boil and thickens.

*Yield:* 4 servings

*Change Chicken Sautéed with Vegetables as follows or use Basic Recipe, if indicated, for:*

## LOW-CALORIE, DIABETIC, LOW-FAT, AND LOW-CHOLESTEROL DIETS

Spray skillet with vegetable cooking spray. Reduce oil for sautéing chicken to 2 tablespoons and add to skillet. Proceed as in Basic Recipe.

Calories per serving: 256
Approximate nutrient
  values per serving:
    Protein 27 g
    Fat 11 g
    Carbohydrate 12 g
    Sodium 751 mg
    Potassium 662 mg
    Cholesterol 63 mg
Exchanges:
  Vegetable 2
  Meat 4
  Fat 1½

## LOW-SODIUM DIETS

Omit soy sauce.
Increase sherry to 3 tablespoons.
Proceed as in Basic Recipe.

Calories per serving: 311
Approximate nutrient
  values per serving:
    Protein 26 g
    Fat 18 g
    Carbohydrate 11 g
    Sodium 92 mg
    Potassium 629 mg
    Cholesterol 63 mg

## BLAND AND HIGH-FIBER DIETS

Use Basic Recipe.

# Chicken Tetrazzini

BASIC RECIPE

Serving size: 1 cup
Calories per serving: 277
Approximate nutrient
 values per serving:
  Protein 23 g
  Fat 12 g
  Carbohydrate 18 g
  Sodium 623 mg
  Potassium 423 mg
  Cholesterol 57 mg
Exchanges:
 Bread 1
 Meat 3
 Fat 1½

5-pound roasting chicken
1 onion, sliced
4 whole cloves
1 bay leaf
2 celery stalks, sliced
1 carrot, sliced
2 teaspoons salt
1 teaspoon white pepper
½ cup dry sherry
8 ounces thin spaghetti
2 tablespoons polyunsaturated margarine for sautéing mushrooms
¼ pound fresh mushrooms, sliced
3 tablespoons polyunsaturated margarine for sauce
1½ tablespoons flour
¼ cup heavy cream
½ teaspoon polyunsaturated margarine for greasing baking dish
¼ cup grated Parmesan cheese

Place the chicken, onion, cloves, bay leaf, celery, carrot, salt, and pepper in a large pot. Add enough water to cover two-thirds of the chicken—you will need 2 quarts cooking liquid later. Cover and simmer gently approximately 45 minutes or until chicken is tender. Be careful not to overcook. Cool in the stock about 20 minutes. Remove the chicken, take the meat off the bones, and cut meat into 1-inch cubes. You may do this in advance; cover and refrigerate the chicken and stock separately.

Remove chicken from refrigerator and bring to room temperature. Skim the fat off chicken stock, strain, measure 2 quarts into a large saucepan, and add sherry. Bring to a boil, add spaghetti, and cook until just tender, 6 or 7 minutes. Remove from heat and drain in a colander, reserving 2 cups of the stock. Run cold water over spaghetti so it won't stick. Set aside.

Preheat oven to 300°F.

In a small skillet heat 2 tablespoons margarine, add mushrooms, and sauté over medium heat until light brown. Set aside.

Melt 3 tablespoons margarine reserved for sauce in a small saucepan over moderate heat and add flour, stirring until it is well mixed. Gradually add cream and the 2 cups reserved stock, stirring for 2 to 3 minutes or until mixture thickens into a smooth cream sauce. Remove from heat.

To assemble, grease an ovenproof casserole with the remaining ½ teaspoon margarine.

Transfer spaghetti to a large bowl. Add mushrooms and mix gently. Then add chicken and cream sauce and mix until well blended.

Pour the mixture into the casserole, sprinkle with Parmesan cheese, and bake covered for 40 minutes. Remove cover and bake 10 minutes longer, until lightly browned.

*Yield:* 10 servings

*Change Chicken Tetrazzini as follows or use Basic Recipe, if indicated, for:*

LOW-CALORIE, DIABETIC, LOW-FAT, AND LOW-CHOLESTEROL DIETS

Substitute skim milk for cream in the sauce.
Omit margarine for greasing casserole. Instead, spray with vegetable cooking spray.
Omit Parmesan cheese on top of casserole.
Proceed as in Basic Recipe.

Calories per serving: 244
Approximate nutrient
  values per serving:
    Protein 22 g
    Fat 9 g
    Carbohydrate 18 g
    Sodium 570 mg
    Potassium 425 mg
    Cholesterol 47 mg
Exchanges:
  Bread 1
  Meat 3
  Fat 1

## LOW-SODIUM DIETS

Calories per serving: 276
Approximate nutrient
  values per serving:
    Protein 23 g
    Fat 13 g
    Carbohydrate 18 g
    Sodium 73 mg
    Potassium 428 mg
    Cholesterol 56 mg

Omit salt.

Substitute unsalted polyunsaturated margarine for margarine
  wherever used.

Add 2 tablespoons lemon juice to sherry when cooking the
  spaghetti.

Omit Parmesan cheese. Substitute grated low-sodium Cheddar
  cheese sprinkled on top of casserole.

Proceed as in Basic Recipe.

## BLAND DIETS

Calories per serving: 277

Omit pepper and cloves.

Proceed as in Basic Recipe.

## HIGH-FIBER DIETS

Calories per serving: 302

Use Basic Recipe.

Garnish with ⅓ cup toasted slivered almonds (page 38).

## CHICKEN TETRAZZINI FOR RENAL DIETS

Serving size: 1 cup
Calories per serving: 340
Approximate nutrient
  values per serving:
    Protein 23 g
    Fat 19 g
    Carbohydrate 19 g
    Calcium 68 mg
    Phosphorus 260 mg
    Sodium 149 mg
    Potassium 456 mg
    Cholesterol 83 mg
Exchanges:
  Bread 1
  Meat 3
  Fat 3

5-pound roasting chicken
1 onion, sliced
4 whole cloves
2 celery stalks, sliced
1 carrot, sliced
½ teaspoon freshly ground pepper
2 tablespoons unsalted polyunsaturated margarine for sautéing mushrooms
two 4-ounce cans sliced mushrooms, drained
3 tablespoons unsalted polyunsaturated margarine for sauce
1½ tablespoons flour
1 cup heavy cream
1 cup milk
¼ cup dry sherry
2 tablespoons lemon juice
2 quarts water

8 ounces thin spaghetti
½ teaspoon unsalted polyunsaturated margarine for greasing
    baking dish

Place the chicken, onion, cloves, celery, carrot, and pepper in a large pot. Add enough water to cover two-thirds of the chicken. Cover and simmer gently approximately 45 minutes or until chicken is tender. Be careful not to overcook. Cool in the stock about 20 minutes. Remove the chicken, take the meat off the bones, and cut into 1-inch cubes. Set aside. You may prepare the chicken in advance; cover and refrigerate.

Preheat oven to 300°F.

In a separate saucepan heat the margarine and sauté the mushrooms on medium heat. Set aside.

Melt 3 tablespoons margarine for sauce in a small saucepan over moderate heat. Add flour and stir until it is well mixed. Gradually add cream, milk, sherry, and lemon juice, stirring constantly until mixture is thickened and smooth. Remove from heat.

Measure 2 quarts water into a large saucepan. Bring to a boil, add spaghetti, and cook 6 to 7 minutes, or until just tender. Drain well in a colander and run cold water over the spaghetti so it won't stick.

To assemble, grease an ovenproof dish with remaining ½ teaspoon unsalted polyunsaturated margarine. Transfer spaghetti to a large bowl and add mushrooms, mixing gently. Then mix in the chicken and cream sauce. Pour mixture into casserole and bake, covered, for 30 minutes. Remove cover and bake 10 minutes longer, to brown the top lightly.

*Yield:* 10 servings

# Kentucky Cassoulet

BASIC RECIPE

Serving size: ¾ cup
Calories per serving: 307
Approximate nutrient
  values per serving:
    Protein 32 g
    Fat 13 g
    Carbohydrate 16 g
    Sodium 634 mg
    Potassium 847 mg
    Cholesterol 83 mg
Exchanges:
  Vegetable 2
  Bread ½
  Meat 4
  Fat ½

1 cup navy beans
½ bay leaf
1½ teaspoons salt
1¾ cups water
1 tablespoon red wine vinegar
½ teaspoon Tabasco
1 teaspoon fennel seeds
4 teaspoons polyunsaturated oil
1 pound lean cubed pork
6 chicken thighs, skinned and boned
1 cup finely chopped onions
4 cloves garlic, finely chopped
6 tomatoes, peeled and sliced
⅓ cup chopped fresh parsley

Soak beans for 2 hours in cold water to cover. Drain.

Put beans, bay leaf, salt, water, vinegar, Tabasco, and fennel seeds in a 3-quart saucepan. Cover and gently simmer for 1 hour.

Heat 2 teaspoons of the oil in a large skillet. Add the pork and brown on all sides, tossing and turning constantly—about 5 minutes.

Add browned pork to the beans and continue to cook for 30 minutes longer.

Heat the other 2 teaspoons oil in the same skillet. Add chicken, and brown on both sides—about 3 to 4 minutes per side. Remove and add to the beans.

Sauté the onions and garlic in the same skillet until onions are soft. Add to beans. Finally, add tomatoes to the bean mixture, cover, and gently simmer 40 minutes. Just before serving, stir in parsley.

*Yield:* 6 servings

*Change Kentucky Cassoulet as follows or use Basic Recipe, if indicated, for:*

LOW-CALORIE, DIABETIC, LOW-FAT, AND LOW-CHOLESTEROL DIETS

Use Basic Recipe.

LOW-SODIUM DIETS

Calories per serving: 308
Approximate nutrient
  values per serving:
    Protein 32 g
    Fat 13 g
    Carbohydrate 17 g
    Sodium 85 mg
    Potassium 853 mg
    Cholesterol 83 mg

Omit salt.
Increase vinegar to 2 tablespoons.
Increase fennel seeds to 2 teaspoons.
Proceed as in Basic Recipe.

BLAND DIETS

Calories per serving: 307

Omit Tabasco.
Proceed as in Basic Recipe.

HIGH-FIBER DIETS

Calories per serving: 309

Use Basic Recipe. Just before serving, add 1 cup shredded raw spinach to the chopped parsley and stir into the cassoulet. Cook 2 additional minutes.

# Cornish Game Hens with Wild Rice

BASIC RECIPE

Serving size: ½ hen, ⅓ cup
  stuffing, 2 tablespoons
  sauce
Calories per serving: 338
Approximate nutrient
  values per serving:
    Protein 30 g
    Fat 16 g
    Carbohydrate 17 g
    Sodium 430 mg
    Potassium 614 mg
    Cholesterol 63 mg
Exchanges:
  Bread 1
  Meat 4
  Fat 2

*The Poultry Sauce*
3 tablespoons polyunsaturated margarine for sautéing
⅓ cup chopped onions
2 cloves garlic, finely chopped
3 ripe tomatoes, peeled, seeded, and diced
6 fresh mushroom caps, thinly sliced
2 cups Chicken Stock (page 114)
¼ cup Cognac
¼ teaspoon salt
1 tablespoon polyunsaturated margarine
1 tablespoon flour

*The Hens and Stuffing*
½ cup wild rice
3 cups cold water
3 tablespoons polyunsaturated margarine for sautéing
⅓ cup chopped onions
⅓ cup chopped fresh mushrooms
⅓ cup diced water chestnuts, drained
1 teaspoon thyme
¾ teaspoon tarragon
½ teaspoon salt
⅛ teaspoon freshly ground pepper
4 Cornish game hens
2 tablespoons plus 1 teaspoon polyunsaturated margarine

In this recipe, start the poultry sauce before putting Cornish hens in the oven, since it takes a little longer to cook than they do.

*To prepare the sauce:* Melt 3 tablespoons of the margarine in a medium saucepan and sauté onions and garlic until onions are soft. Add tomatoes, mushrooms, stock, Cognac, and salt. Simmer over low heat, uncovered, 1½ hours, stirring occasionally.

*To prepare the hens and stuffing:* Rinse rice in cold water; place in medium saucepan. Add cold water; simmer, uncovered, 25

367

minutes or until most of the grains have opened. Add more water if necessary. Remove from heat, cover, and let stand 20 minutes. Drain and spoon into a large bowl.

In a medium skillet, heat 3 tablespoons margarine. Add onions and mushrooms; sauté until onions are soft.

Combine mushroom mixture with rice. Add water chestnuts, thyme, tarragon, salt, and pepper; mix gently.

Preheat oven to 400°F.

Stuff hens with rice mixture; close with skewers or toothpicks. Arrange birds, breast side up, in a shallow baking dish that has been greased with 1 teaspoon margarine. Melt remaining margarine for basting.

Roast the Cornish hens, uncovered, 1 hour or until tender. Baste occasionally.

About 10 minutes before hens are ready, finish the sauce. In a separate saucepan, melt remaining tablespoon of margarine. Blend in flour. Just before serving add this to poultry sauce mixture to thicken, stirring until smooth and heated through.

Remove hens to warm platter and serve. Pass the sauce separately.

*Yield:* 8 servings, 1 cup sauce

*Change Cornish Game Hens with Wild Rice as follows, or use Basic Recipe, if indicated, for:*

LOW-CALORIE, DIABETIC, LOW-FAT, AND LOW-CHOLESTEROL DIETS

*The poultry sauce:* Omit margarine for sautéing. Instead, sauté onions in pan sprayed with vegetable cooking spray.

Proceed as in Basic Recipe.

*The Cornish hens:* Omit margarine for greasing baking dish. Spray dish well with vegetable cooking spray instead.

Reduce margarine for sautéing vegetables to 2 tablespoons.

Reduce margarine for basting birds to 2 teaspoons.

Proceed as in Basic Recipe.

Calories per serving: 279
Approximate nutrient
  values per serving:
    Protein 30 g
    Fat 10 g
    Carbohydrate 17 g
    Sodium 363 mg
    Potassium 613 mg
    Cholesterol 63 mg
Exchanges:
  Bread 1
  Meat 4
  Fat 1

Calories per serving: 338
Approximate nutrient
values same as Basic
Recipe except for:
Sodium 105 mg

*The poultry sauce:* Omit salt.
   Substitute unsalted polyunsaturated margarine for margarine wherever used.
   Proceed as in Basic Recipe.

*The Cornish hens:* Omit salt.
   Substitute unsalted polyunsaturated margarine for margarine wherever used.
   Proceed as in Basic Recipe.

BLAND DIETS

Calories per serving: 338

*The poultry sauce:* Use Basic Recipe.

*The Cornish hens:* Omit pepper.
   Proceed as in Basic Recipe.

HIGH-FIBER DIETS

Calories per serving: 355

*The poultry sauce:* Use Basic Recipe.

*The Cornish hens:* Substitute ⅓ cup chopped walnuts for the water chestnuts.
   Proceed as in Basic Recipe.

# Roast Turkey with Prune and Apple Stuffing

BASIC RECIPE

Serving size: 4 ounces
turkey, ½ cup stuffing
Calories per serving: 456

2 cups dried prunes
3 cups water
½ cup polyunsaturated margarine

Approximate nutrient
values per serving:
Protein 35 g
Fat 25 g
Carbohydrate 23 g
Sodium 418 mg
Potassium 596 mg
Cholesterol 88 mg
Exchanges:
Fruit 1½
Bread ½
Meat 4
Fat 2½

2 cups chopped onions
2 cups chopped celery
1 teaspoon sage
1 teaspoon marjoram
1 teaspoon thyme
1 tablespoon salt
½ teaspoon freshly ground pepper
4½ cups chopped peeled apples
8 cups cubed stale bread
12-pound turkey

*To prepare the stuffing:* Simmer prunes in 3 cups water in a small covered saucepan for 10 minutes or until tender. Remove prunes to a bowl. Pit and chop them. Reserve 1½ cups of the cooking liquid.

Heat margarine in a large skillet. Add onions and celery; sauté until onions are soft. Season with sage, marjoram, thyme, salt, and pepper. Remove from heat and set aside.

Combine apples and bread cubes in a large bowl. Add celery mixture, prunes, and reserved prune liquid. Mix gently to blend.

Preheat oven to 325°F.

*To prepare the turkey:* Rinse turkey under cool running water. Drain thoroughly and pat dry with paper towels. Fill neck pocket and body cavity loosely with stuffing—secure neck flap with a skewer and do the same with body cavity. Tie wings and legs close to body.

Place turkey breast side up on a rack in a shallow roasting pan; cover lightly with aluminum foil. Roast approximately 18 minutes per pound. Remove foil during the last hour of roasting to allow bird to brown.

The turkey is done when a meat thermometer inserted in the center of the inside thigh muscle, not touching bone, registers 185°F.

Remove roast turkey from oven to a heated platter; cover lightly with foil. Let stand in a warm place 30 minutes before serving.

*Yield:* 24 servings

*Change Roast Turkey with Prune and Apple Stuffing or use Basic Recipe, if indicated, for:*

### LOW-SODIUM DIETS

Calories per serving: 456
Approximate nutrient
 values same as Basic
 Recipe except for:
 Sodium 106 mg

Omit salt.
Substitute unsalted polyunsaturated margarine for margarine.
Proceed as in Basic Recipe.

### BLAND DIETS

Calories per serving: 456

Omit pepper.
Proceed as in Basic Recipe.

### HIGH-FIBER DIETS

Calories per serving: 456

Use Basic Recipe. For additional fiber, use unpeeled apples.

### ROAST TURKEY WITH APPLE STUFFING FOR LOW-CALORIE, DIABETIC, LOW-FAT, AND LOW-CHOLESTEROL DIETS

Serving size: 4 ounces
 turkey, ½ cup stuffing
Calories per serving: 280
Approximate nutrient
 values per serving:
 Protein 35 g
 Fat 10 g
 Carbohydrate 14 g
 Sodium 381 mg
 Potassium 518 mg
 Cholesterol 63 mg
Exchanges:
 Fruit ½
 Bread ½
 Meat 4

2 cups chopped onions
2 cups chopped celery
2 cups Chicken Stock (page 114)
1 teaspoon sage
1 teaspoon marjoram
1 teaspoon thyme
1 tablespoon salt
½ teaspoon ground black pepper
6 cups diced peeled apples
8 cups cubed stale bread
12-pound turkey

Preheat oven to 325°F.

*To prepare the stuffing:* Simmer onions and celery in the chicken stock until tender. Add sage, marjoram, thyme, salt, and pepper to the mixture.

Blend apples and bread cubes in a large bowl. Add stock mixture and mix gently until thoroughly combined.

*To prepare the turkey:* Rinse turkey under cool water. Drain thoroughly and pat dry with paper towels. Fill the neck pocket and body cavity loosely with stuffing. Secure neck flap with a skewer and do the same with the body cavity. Tie wings and legs close to body. Place turkey breast side up on a rack in a shallow roasting pan; cover lightly with aluminum foil. Roast approximately 18 minutes per pound. Remove foil in the last hour to allow bird to brown.

The turkey is done when a meat thermometer inserted in the center of the inside thigh muscle, not touching bone, registers 185°F.

Put roast turkey on a heated platter; cover with foil. Let stand in a warm place 30 minutes before serving. Do not eat turkey skin.

*Yield:* 24 servings

# Old-Fashioned Turkey Pie

BASIC RECIPE

Serving size: 1 biscuit, ¾ cup turkey mixture
Calories per serving: 408
Approximate nutrient values per serving:
Protein 21 g
Fat 21 g
Carbohydrate 34 g
Sodium 743 mg
Potassium 489 mg
Cholesterol 47 mg

*The Turkey Mixture*
⅓ cup polyunsaturated margarine
½ cup sliced celery
½ cup chopped green pepper
⅓ cup flour
2¾ cups Chicken Stock (page 114)
1 teaspoon salt
½ teaspoon thyme
½ teaspoon rosemary
½ teaspoon tarragon

Exchanges:
Vegetable 1
Bread 2
Meat 2
Fat 3½

¼ teaspoon freshly ground pepper
¼ cup dry sherry
1 cup cooked small white onions
1 cup cooked sliced carrots
3 cups cubed cooked turkey

*The Topping*
2 cups sifted flour
1 tablespoon baking powder
½ teaspoon salt
¼ cup chopped fresh parsley
⅓ cup polyunsaturated oil
⅔ cup milk

*To prepare the turkey mixture:* Heat the margarine in a medium skillet. Sauté the celery and green pepper until celery is soft. Blend in flour. Gradually add stock and cook over moderate heat, stirring constantly, until sauce comes to a boil. Remove from heat and add salt, thyme, rosemary, tarragon, pepper, and sherry.

Combine the celery mixture with onions, carrots, and turkey. Spoon into a shallow 2½-quart baking dish.

Preheat oven to 425°F.

*To prepare the topping:* Make a biscuit crust by sifting flour, baking powder, and salt into a large bowl. Stir in parsley. Add oil and milk and blend with a fork to make a soft dough.

Turn onto a piece of waxed paper and knead lightly.

Roll between pieces of waxed paper to approximately the size of the casserole, then cut into eight 2-inch biscuits.

Arrange dough circles on top of turkey-vegetable mixture in casserole, leaving space between biscuits for steam to escape. Bake about 25 minutes or until biscuits are golden brown.

*Yield:* 8 servings

*Change Old-Fashioned Turkey Pie as follows or use Basic Recipe, if indicated, for:*

### LOW-CALORIE, DIABETIC, LOW-FAT, AND LOW-CHOLESTEROL DIETS

Serving size: ¾ cup turkey mixture
Calories per serving: 204
Approximate nutrient values per serving:
Protein 19 g
Fat 8 g
Carbohydrate 14 g
Sodium 415 mg
Potassium 495 mg
Cholesterol 44 mg
Exchanges:
Vegetable 1
Bread ½
Meat 2
Fat 1

*The turkey mixture:* Reduce margarine to 3 tablespoons.
Add ¼ cup chopped fresh parsley with herbs.
Proceed as in Basic Recipe.

*The topping:* Omit biscuit dough. Instead, top with ¾ cup wheat germ sprinkled on turkey mixture. Bake 15 minutes or until wheat germ is lightly browned.

*Yield:* 8 servings

### LOW-SODIUM DIETS

Calories per serving: 408
Approximate nutrient values same as Basic Recipe except for:
Sodium 256 mg

*The turkey mixture:* Omit salt. Substitute unsalted polyunsaturated margarine for margarine.
Proceed as in Basic Recipe.

*The topping:* Omit salt.
Proceed as in Basic Recipe.

### BLAND DIETS

Calories per serving: 408

*The turkey mixture:* Omit ground pepper.
Proceed as in Basic Recipe.

*The topping:* Use Basic Recipe.

### HIGH-FIBER DIETS

Use Basic Recipe.

374

# Turkey in Bangkok Sauce

BASIC RECIPE

Serving size: 4 asparagus spears, 3 ounces turkey, ⅓ cup sauce
Calories per serving: 393
Approximate nutrient values per serving:
Protein 32 g
Fat 23 g
Carbohydrate 15 g
Sodium 667 mg
Potassium 675 mg
Cholesterol 66 mg
Exchanges:
Bread 1
Meat 4
Fat 4

*The Casserole*
½ teaspoon salt
24 medium-size fresh asparagus spears, trimmed
6 slices cooked turkey (18 ounces)

*The Bangkok Sauce*
2 cups Chicken Stock (page 114)
1 cup dry white wine
1 medium carrot, sliced
3 fresh mushrooms, sliced
¼ cup chopped onions
1 sprig fresh parsley
1 small bay leaf
4 tablespoons polyunsaturated margarine
3 tablespoons flour
½ teaspoon salt
⅛ teaspoon freshly ground pepper
1½ teaspoons curry powder

*The Topping*
4 tablespoons polyunsaturated margarine
1 cup fresh bread crumbs (page 38)
⅓ cup toasted slivered almonds (page 38)

*To prepare the casserole:* Fill a large skillet with water to 1-inch depth. Add salt, bring to a boil, and slip in the asparagus. Boil, uncovered, for 5 minutes. Cover tightly and reduce heat. Boil gently 5 minutes longer or until asparagus spears are tender. Drain thoroughly.

In a shallow baking dish arrange asparagus spears with tips pointing in the same direction. Place turkey slices over asparagus.

Preheat oven to 375°F.

*To prepare the sauce:* In a medium saucepan place stock, wine, carrot, mushrooms, onions, parsley, and bay leaf. Simmer, tightly covered, for 20 minutes. Strain and reserve liquid.

In the same saucepan melt the margarine. Using a wire whisk, blend in the flour. Gradually add 2 cups strained liquid and cook over moderate heat, stirring constantly, until sauce is thickened and smooth. Boil and stir 1 minute. Remove from heat and stir in the salt, pepper, and curry powder.

*To prepare the topping:* Melt margarine in a medium skillet. Add crumbs and almonds and mix gently to blend.

*To assemble the casserole:* Pour curry sauce over turkey. Spoon topping over sauce.
   Bake casserole, uncovered, for 25 minutes or until browned.

*Yield:* 6 servings


*Change Turkey in Bangkok Sauce as follows or use Basic Recipe, if indicated, for:*

LOW-CALORIE, DIABETIC, LOW-FAT, AND LOW-CHOLESTEROL DIETS

Calories per serving: 250
Approximate nutrient
   values per serving:
      Protein 31 g
      Fat 8 g
      Carbohydrate 13 g
      Sodium 552 mg
      Potassium 616 mg
      Cholesterol 66 mg
Exchanges:
   Bread 1
   Meat 4
   Fat 1

*The casserole:* Use Basic Recipe.

*The sauce:* Reduce margarine to 2 tablespoons.
   Proceed as in Basic Recipe.

*The topping:* Omit margarine, fresh bread crumbs, and almonds. Substitute 1 cup dry bread crumbs (page 38). Sprinkle on top of sauce in casserole. Bake as in Basic Recipe.


LOW-SODIUM DIETS

Calories per serving: 393
Approximate nutrient
   values same as Basic
   Recipe except for:
      Sodium 149 mg

*The casserole:* Omit salt.
   Proceed as in Basic Recipe.

*The sauce:* Omit salt.

Substitute unsalted polyunsaturated margarine for margarine.
Proceed as in Basic Recipe.

*The topping:* Substitute unsalted polyunsaturated margarine for margarine.
Proceed as in Basic Recipe.

### BLAND DIETS

Calories per serving: 393

*The casserole and the topping:* Use Basic Recipe.

*The sauce:* Omit pepper.
Proceed as in Basic Recipe.

### HIGH-FIBER DIETS

Use Basic Recipe.

# Scalloped Turkey

### BASIC RECIPE

Serving size: ½ cup noodles, 1 cup turkey mixture
Calories per serving: 676
Approximate nutrient values per serving:
Protein 29 g
Fat 44 g
Carbohydrate 42 g
Sodium 1178 mg
Potassium 618 mg
Cholesterol 150 mg
Exchanges:
Bread 3
Meat 3
Fat 7½

6 tablespoons polyunsaturated margarine for sautéing vegetables
1½ cups sliced fresh mushrooms
1 cup sliced celery
½ cup chopped onions
6 tablespoons flour
1½ cups Chicken Stock (page 114)
1½ cups light cream
¼ cup chopped fresh parsley
¼ teaspoon sage
¼ teaspoon marjoram
¼ teaspoon thyme
1 teaspoon salt for turkey mixture

¼ teaspoon freshly ground pepper
3 cups cubed cooked turkey
3 quarts water
1 teaspoon salt for cooking noodles
4½ cups uncooked broad noodles
¼ cup polyunsaturated margarine for sautéing bread crumbs
3 cups fresh bread crumbs (page 38)

Preheat oven to 350°F.

Melt margarine in a large skillet. Add mushrooms, celery, and onions and sauté until onions are soft. Sprinkle with flour and stir gently. Gradually add stock and cream and cook over moderate heat, stirring constantly, until sauce is smooth and thickened. Remove from heat and add parsley, sage, marjoram, thyme, 1 teaspoon salt, and pepper. Gently stir in cooked turkey. Set aside.

In a large pot bring water and 1 teaspoon salt to a boil. Add noodles and cook 5 to 7 minutes or until almost tender. Drain, but while still moist transfer the noodles to a 2½-quart casserole. Spoon turkey mixture over noodles and mix lightly.

Melt remaining ¼ cup margarine in a small skillet. Add crumbs and mix thoroughly. Spread crumb mixture evenly over turkey and bake, uncovered, 25 to 30 minutes or until crumbs are golden brown.

*Yield:* 6 servings

*Change Scalloped Turkey as follows or use Basic Recipe, if indicated, for:*

### LOW-CALORIE, DIABETIC, LOW-FAT, AND LOW-CHOLESTEROL DIETS

Reduce margarine to 4 tablespoons for sautéing vegetables.
Substitute skim milk for cream.
Omit margarine for sautéing bread crumbs. Reduce bread crumbs to 1 cup, sprinkle on top of casserole, and bake uncovered as in Basic Recipe.

Calories per serving: 379
Approximate nutrient
values per serving:
   Protein 29 g
   Fat 13 g
   Carbohydrate 35 g
   Sodium 994 mg
   Potassium 642 mg
   Cholesterol 85 mg
Exchanges:
   Milk ⅛
   Bread 2
   Meat 3
   Fat 1½

### LOW-SODIUM DIETS

Omit salt.
Substitute unsalted polyunsaturated margarine for margarine wherever used.
Proceed as in Basic Recipe.

Calories per serving: 676
Approximate nutrient
values same as Basic
Recipe except for:
   Sodium 256 mg

### BLAND DIETS

Omit pepper.
Proceed as in Basic Recipe.

Calories per serving: 676

### HIGH-FIBER DIETS

Use Basic Recipe.

# Turkey Hash

BASIC RECIPE

Serving size: 1½ cups
Calories per serving: 325
Approximate nutrient
  values per serving:
    Protein 34 g
    Fat 12 g
    Carbohydrate 19 g
    Sodium 429 mg
    Potassium 961 mg
    Cholesterol 88 mg
Exchanges:
  Vegetable 1
  Bread 1
  Meat 4
  Fat 1

4 fresh tomatoes, peeled and chopped
¼ cup water
2 tablespoons polyunsaturated margarine
½ cup chopped onions
1 teaspoon thyme
2 cups diced cooked potatoes
½ teaspoon salt
¼ teaspoon freshly ground pepper
3 cups diced cooked turkey

Put tomatoes in a saucepan with water and simmer for 3 minutes. Set aside.

Heat margarine. Add onions and thyme; sauté until soft. Add potatoes and continue to sauté until the potatoes turn golden brown. Add the tomatoes, salt, and pepper; mix thoroughly and cook for 3 minutes. Add turkey. Toss over high heat until the turkey is hot.

*Yield:* 4 servings

*Change Turkey Hash as follows for:*

LOW-CALORIE, DIABETIC, LOW-FAT, AND LOW-CHOLESTEROL DIETS

Reduce margarine to 1 tablespoon.
Proceed as in Basic Recipe.

Calories per serving: 300
Approximate nutrient
  values per serving:
    Protein 34 g
    Fat 9 g
    Carbohydrate 19 g
    Sodium 400 mg
    Potassium 960 mg
    Cholesterol 88 mg
Exchanges:
  Vegetable 1
  Bread 1
  Meat 4
  Fat ½

## LOW-SODIUM DIETS

Substitute unsalted polyunsaturated margarine for margarine.
Omit salt; increase pepper to ½ teaspoon.
Add 2 tablespoons cider vinegar when adding the tomatoes.
Proceed as in Basic Recipe.

Calories per serving: 326
Approximate nutrient
  values per serving:
    Protein 34 g
    Fat 12 g
    Carbohydrate 20 g
    Sodium 97 mg
    Potassium 970 mg
    Cholesterol 88 mg

## BLAND DIETS

Omit pepper.
Proceed as in Basic Recipe.

Calories per serving: 325

## HIGH-FIBER DIETS

Add ½ cup finely sliced celery with the onions.
Proceed as in Basic Recipe.

Calories per serving: 327

# Turkey Curry

BASIC RECIPE

⅓ cup currants
1 cup boiling water
⅓ cup polyunsaturated margarine
½ cup chopped onions
½ cup sliced celery
¼ cup flour
1¼ cups Chicken Stock (page 114)
1¼ cups milk
2½ teaspoons curry powder
1 teaspoon salt
2 cups cubed cooked turkey
1⅓ cups cubed unpeeled apples

Serving size: ¾ cup
Calories per serving: 276
Approximate nutrient
  values per serving:
    Protein 17 g
    Fat 15 g
    Carbohydrate 19 g
    Sodium 566 mg
    Potassium 453 mg
    Cholesterol 46 mg
Exchanges:
  Fruit 1
  Bread ½
  Meat 2
  Fat 2½

Put currants in a small bowl; cover with boiling water and let stand 10 minutes or until plump.

Melt margarine in a medium saucepan. Add onions and celery; sauté until onions are soft.

Using a wire whisk, blend in flour. Gradually add chicken stock and milk. Cook over moderate heat, stirring constantly, until sauce comes to a boil and thickens. Blend in curry powder and salt.

Drain currants. Add to curry sauce with turkey and apples. Simmer 5 minutes or until very hot. Mix gently.

*Yield:* 6 servings

*Change Turkey Curry as follows or use Basic Recipe, if indicated, for:*

LOW-CALORIE, DIABETIC, LOW-FAT, AND LOW-CHOLESTEROL DIETS

Reduce margarine to 2 tablespoons.
Substitute skim milk for milk.
Proceed as in Basic Recipe.

Calories per serving: 206
Approximate nutrient
  values per serving:
    Protein 17 g
    Fat 7 g
    Carbohydrate 20 g
    Sodium 505 mg
    Potassium 460 mg
    Cholesterol 40 mg
Exchanges:
  Fruit 1
  Bread ½
  Meat 2
  Fat 1

LOW-SODIUM DIETS

Omit salt.
Substitute unsalted polyunsaturated margarine for margarine.
Proceed as in Basic Recipe.

Calories per serving: 276
Approximate nutrient
  values same as Basic
  Recipe except for:
    Sodium 99 mg

BLAND DIETS

Use Basic Recipe.


HIGH-FIBER DIETS

Use Basic Recipe. Add ¼ cup coarsely chopped peanuts and
sprinkle on top of casserole.


TURKEY CURRY FOR RENAL DIETS

⅓ cup unsalted polyunsaturated margarine
½ cup chopped onions
½ cup sliced celery
¼ cup flour
1¼ cups water
1¼ cups light cream
2½ teaspoons curry powder
2 cups cooked cubed turkey
1⅛ cups cubed unpeeled apples

Melt margarine in a medium saucepan. Add onions and celery
and sauté until onions are soft.

Blend in flour. Gradually add water and light cream, and
cook over moderate heat, stirring constantly, until sauce comes
to a boil and thickens. Blend in curry powder.

Add turkey and apples to curry sauce and simmer 5 minutes
or until heated through.

*Yield:* 6 servings

Calories per serving: 311

Serving size: ¾ cup
Calories per serving: 360
Approximate nutrient
  values per serving:
    Protein 16 g
    Fat 28 g
    Carbohydrate 11 g
    Calcium 61 mg
    Phosphorus 223 mg
    Sodium 72 mg
    Potassium 331 mg
    Cholesterol 94 mg
Exchanges:
  Fruit ½
  Bread ½
  Meat 2
  Fat 5

# Broiled Deviled Turkey

BASIC RECIPE

Serving size: 1 cup
Calories per serving: 285
Approximate nutrient
   values per serving:
     Protein 35 g
     Fat 12 g
     Carbohydrate 8 g
     Sodium 377 mg
     Potassium 526 mg
     Cholesterol 94 mg
Exchanges:
   Bread ½
   Meat 4
   Fat 1

2 tablespoons polyunsaturated margarine
1½ tablespoons flour
1½ cups Chicken Stock (page 114)
1 tablespoon dry mustard
2 tablespoons cold water
1 tablespoon Worcestershire sauce
1 tablespoon tomato paste
¼ teaspoon salt
4 cups coarsely diced cooked turkey
⅓ cup dry bread crumbs (page 38)

Preheat broiler.

Melt the margarine in a medium saucepan. Add the flour and stir for 1 minute. Gradually stir in the chicken stock. Bring to a boil, stirring constantly. Then lower the heat and simmer gently for 3 minutes.

Stir the mustard and water together until smooth and whisk mustard into the chicken stock mixture. Add Worcestershire sauce, tomato paste, and salt. Remove from heat and stir in the turkey.

Pour deviled turkey into an ovenproof dish, sprinkle with bread crumbs, and place under broiler until light golden brown.

*Yield:* 5 servings

*Change Broiled Deviled Turkey as follows for:*

## LOW-CALORIE, DIABETIC, LOW-FAT, AND LOW-CHOLESTEROL DIETS

Omit margarine.
Pour ⅛ cup of the chicken stock into a medium saucepan and stir in the flour until smooth. Then slowly add the remaining stock. Bring mixture to a boil, stirring constantly.
Proceed as in Basic Recipe.

Calories per serving: 245
Approximate nutrient
  values per serving:
    Protein 35 g
    Fat 7 g
    Carbohydrate 8 g
    Sodium 332 mg
    Potassium 525 mg
    Cholesterol 94 mg
Exchanges:
  Bread ½
  Meat 4

## LOW-SODIUM DIETS

Omit salt and Worcestershire sauce.
Add 2 tablespoons lemon juice.
Substitute unsalted polyunsaturated margarine for margarine.
Proceed as in Basic Recipe.

Calories per serving: 284
Approximate nutrient
  values same as Basic
  Recipe except for:
    Sodium 172 mg
    Potassium 529 mg

## BLAND DIETS

Omit mustard; substitute 1 teaspoon curry powder. Stir it into the 2 tablespoons cold water and whisk into the chicken stock mixture. Proceed as in Basic Recipe.

Calories per serving: 281

## HIGH-FIBER DIETS

Omit bread crumbs. Substitute wheat germ.
Proceed as in Basic Recipe.

Calories per serving: 276

# ENTRÉE SAUCES

We include two kinds of entrée sauces here. Some are essential ingredients in the preparation of particular recipes. Others are accompaniments that change a good dish into a superb one. A tender, melt-in-your-mouth soufflé can be memorable in itself, but a Béchamel sauce, spooned over it in champagne-colored ribbons, can turn a basic entrée into a rare delicacy.

We present both kinds in their basic forms, and in carefully modified versions. In all instances we have preserved the essence of the original sauce so well that the flavors they generate justify the extra calories they add. Many of our sauces, although designed primarily to enhance meat, fish, and poultry, make delicious additions to egg, cheese, and vegetable dishes as well.

If a high-fiber diet has been suggested for you, please recognize that certain sauces like Brown Sauce, Mornay, and Béchamel, though suitable for high-fiber diets, do not themselves provide substantial amounts of roughage. When you use them, it will be wise to include high-fiber foods in your entrées, salads, vegetables, or other courses.

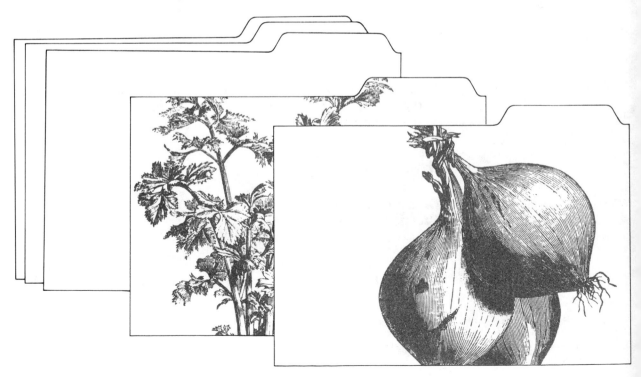

# Brown Sauce

BASIC RECIPE

Serving size: 2 tablespoons
Calories per serving: 55
Approximate nutrient
  values per serving:
    Protein 1 g
    Fat 5 g
    Carbohydrate 3 g
    Sodium 74 mg
    Potassium 113 mg
    Cholesterol 0 mg
Exchanges:
  Vegetable ½
  Fat 1

½ cup polyunsaturated margarine
1 cup diced carrots
1 cup chopped onions
1 cup chopped celery
¼ cup flour
4 cups Beef Stock (page 113)
1 cup chopped peeled tomatoes
2 sprigs fresh parsley
1 bay leaf
¼ teaspoon peppercorns

Heat the margarine in a large saucepan. Add carrots, onions, and celery; sauté until onions are soft.

Add flour; cook over moderate heat, stirring constantly, until mixture is golden brown. Gradually add the beef stock, stirring constantly. Add remaining ingredients and simmer slowly, uncovered, 1½ to 2 hours or until thickened. Skim as necessary. Strain and cool, uncovered, stirring occasionally.

Cover and refrigerate or freeze.

*Yield:* 2½ cups

*Change Brown Sauce as follows or use Basic Recipe, if indicated, for:*

LOW-CALORIE, DIABETIC, LOW-FAT, AND LOW-CHOLESTEROL DIETS

Reduce margarine to ¼ cup.
Proceed as in Basic Recipe.

Calories per serving: 35
Approximate nutrient
   values per serving:
      Protein 1 g
      Fat 2 g
      Carbohydrate 3 g
      Sodium 51 mg
      Potassium 112 mg
      Cholesterol 0 mg
Exchanges:
   Vegetable ½
   Fat ½

LOW-SODIUM DIETS

Substitute unsalted polyunsaturated margarine for margarine.
Proceed as in Basic Recipe.

Calories per serving: 55
Approximate nutrient
   values same as Basic
   Recipe except for:
      Sodium 29 mg

BLAND DIETS

Omit peppercorns.
Proceed as in Basic Recipe.

Calories per serving: 55

HIGH-FIBER DIETS

Use Basic Recipe.

# Mornay Sauce

BASIC RECIPE

This is delicious with egg and vegetable dishes.

4 tablespoons polyunsaturated margarine
4 tablespoons flour
1 cup milk
1 cup heavy cream
¾ cup grated Swiss cheese
⅛ teaspoon salt
⅛ teaspoon cayenne pepper

In a medium saucepan, melt margarine over low heat. Blend in flour. Gradually stir in milk and cream. Cook, stirring constantly, until sauce comes to a boil and thickens.

Boil, stirring constantly, 1 minute longer. Remove from heat; mix in remaining ingredients. Serve warm.

*Yield:* 2 cups

*Change Mornay Sauce as follows or use Basic Recipe, if indicated, for:*

LOW-CALORIE, DIABETIC, LOW-FAT, AND LOW-CHOLESTEROL DIETS

Reduce margarine to 3 tablespoons.
Substitute 2 cups skim milk for milk and cream.
Substitute grated skim American cheese for Swiss.
Proceed as in Basic Recipe.

Calories per serving: 117
Approximate nutrient
  values per serving:
    Protein 2 g
    Fat 11 g
    Carbohydrate 3 g
    Calcium 79 mg
    Phosphorus 57 mg
    Sodium 24 mg
    Potassium 45 mg
    Cholesterol 25 mg

Omit salt.
Substitute unsalted polyunsaturated margarine for margarine.
Substitute low-sodium Swiss cheese for Swiss.
Proceed as in Basic Recipe.

BLAND DIETS

Calories per serving: 114

Omit cayenne pepper.
Proceed as in Basic Recipe.

HIGH-FIBER DIETS

Use Basic Recipe.

# Hollandaise Sauce

BASIC RECIPE

This sauce is good spooned over asparagus, broccoli, or cauliflower.

Serving size: 2 tablespoons
Calories per serving: 167
Approximate nutrient
  values per serving:
    Protein 2 g
    Fat 18 g
    Carbohydrate 1 g
    Sodium 248 mg

3 large egg yolks
¼ teaspoon salt
⅛ teaspoon dry mustard
2 tablespoons lemon juice
½ cup polyunsaturated margarine

Place egg yolks, salt, mustard, and lemon juice in the container

Potassium 19 mg
Cholesterol 136 mg
Exchanges:
Fat 4

of an electric blender. Cover and blend until well mixed. Turn off motor.

Heat the margarine in a small saucepan until it foams. Turn on blender and add the melted margarine in a slow, steady stream. Turn off motor.

Keep sauce warm in the top of a double boiler over barely simmering water until ready to use.

*Yield:* ¾ cup

*Change Hollandaise Sauce as follows or use Basic Recipe, if indicated, for:*

### LOW-SODIUM AND RENAL DIETS

Calories per serving: 167
Approximate nutrient values same as Basic Recipe except for:
Calcium 13 mg
Phosphorus 44 mg
Sodium 4 mg

Omit salt.
Substitute unsalted polyunsaturated margarine for margarine.
Proceed as in Basic Recipe.

### BLAND DIETS

Calories per serving: 167

Omit mustard.
Proceed as in Basic Recipe.

### HIGH-FIBER DIETS

Use Basic Recipe.

### HOLLANDAISE SAUCE FOR LOW-CALORIE, DIABETIC, LOW-FAT, AND LOW-CHOLESTEROL DIETS

Serving size: 2 tablespoons
Calories per serving: 23

1 tablespoon polyunsaturated margarine
1 tablespoon cornstarch

¾ cup Chicken Stock (page 114)
¼ teaspoon salt
⅛ teaspoon dry mustard
2 tablespoons lemon juice
Low-Cholesterol Egg Substitute (page 189) equivalent to
    1 large egg

In a small saucepan, melt margarine. Whisk in cornstarch. Gradually stir in chicken stock, and continue cooking over moderate heat, stirring constantly, until sauce thickens. Bring to a boil for 1 minute. Remove from heat and blend in salt, mustard, and lemon juice.

In a small bowl, whisk egg substitute until foamy. Pour sauce into egg substitute in a slow, steady stream, stirring constantly.

*Yield:* 1 cup

# Italian Tomato Sauce

SUITABLE FOR LOW-CALORIE, DIABETIC, LOW-FAT, LOW-CHOLESTEROL, LOW-SODIUM, BLAND, AND HIGH-FIBER DIETS

¾ cup chopped onions
1 clove garlic, minced
1 tablespoon olive oil
4 pounds peeled, quartered tomatoes
6-ounce can tomato paste
½ cup water
1 bay leaf
1 teaspoon basil
½ teaspoon oregano

In a large saucepan, sauté onions and garlic in olive oil until onions are soft. Add tomatoes, tomato paste, water, and bay leaf. Simmer very slowly, uncovered, for 1½ hours or until sauce is thick. Stir occasionally. Add basil and oregano and simmer 20 minutes longer.

*Yield:* 4 cups

# Pasta Sauce Trieste

BASIC RECIPE

In addition to using this over pasta, try it as a sauce for meatloaf.

Serving size: ½ cup
Calories per serving: 165
Approximate nutrient
  values per serving:
    Protein 2 g
    Fat 14 g
    Carbohydrate 8 g
    Sodium 377 mg
    Potassium 369 mg
    Cholesterol 27 mg
Exchanges:
  Vegetable 1½
  Fat 3

3 tablespoons olive oil
½ cup chopped celery
½ cup chopped onions
½ teaspoon minced garlic
28-ounce can Italian plum tomatoes
½ teaspoon salt
⅛ teaspoon freshly ground pepper
½ teaspoon basil
¼ teaspoon oregano
½ cup heavy cream

In a large saucepan heat the oil and sauté celery, onions, and garlic until celery is soft. Add undrained tomatoes, salt, and pepper. Simmer, uncovered, approximately 40 minutes or until sauce is thickened and reduced by half. Stir occasionally.

Add basil and oregano. Simmer 10 minutes longer. Remove sauce from heat. Allow to cool. Transfer to an electric blender and purée until smooth. Return to saucepan. Bring to a simmer, add cream, and cook until heated through.

*Yield:* 3 cups

*Change Pasta Sauce Trieste as follows for:*

LOW-CALORIE, DIABETIC, LOW-FAT, AND LOW-CHOLESTEROL DIETS

Calories per serving: 85
Approximate nutrient
  values per serving:
    Protein 2 g
    Fat 5 g
    Carbohydrate 9 g
    Sodium 391 mg
    Potassium 385 mg
    Cholesterol 1 mg
Exchanges:
  Vegetable 1½
  Fat 1

Reduce oil to 2 tablespoons.
Substitute buttermilk for heavy cream.
Proceed as in Basic Recipe.

LOW-SODIUM DIETS

Calories per serving: 165
Approximate nutrient
  values same as Basic
  Recipe except for:
    Sodium 26 mg

Omit salt.
Substitute 3½ cups canned tomatoes, packed without added salt, for tomatoes.
Proceed as in Basic Recipe.

BLAND DIETS

Calories per serving: 165

Omit pepper.
Proceed as in Basic Recipe.

HIGH-FIBER DIETS

Calories per serving: 166

Add ½ teaspoon fennel seed with the basil and oregano.
Proceed as in Basic Recipe.

# Mushroom Sauce

BASIC RECIPE

This is excellent with beef.

⅓ cup polyunsaturated margarine
2 tablespoons cornstarch
1½ cups Meat and Vegetable Stock (page 116)
4 cups coarsely chopped fresh mushrooms
½ teaspoon salt
⅛ teaspoon freshly ground pepper
2 tablespoons dry sherry

In a large skillet heat the margarine. Blend in cornstarch. Gradually add stock, stirring constantly.

Add mushrooms, salt, pepper, and sherry. Simmer 10 minutes, stirring occasionally, until sauce has thickened.

*Yield:* 2 cups

*Change Mushroom Sauce as follows or use Basic Recipe, if indicated, for:*

LOW-CALORIE, DIABETIC, LOW-FAT, AND LOW-CHOLESTEROL DIETS

Omit margarine and cornstarch. Instead, simmer all ingredients, covered, about 10 minutes or until mushrooms are tender.
Proceed as in Basic Recipe.

Serving size: 2 tablespoons
Calories per serving: 42
Approximate nutrient
 values per serving:
    Protein 1 g
    Fat 4 g
    Carbohydrate 2 g
    Sodium 117 mg
    Potassium 88 mg
    Cholesterol 0 mg
Exchanges:
    Fat 1

Calories per serving: 6
Approximate nutrient
 values per serving:
    Protein 1 g
    Fat 0 g
    Carbohydrate 1 g
    Sodium 79 mg
    Potassium 87 mg
    Cholesterol 0 mg
Exchanges: 0

Omit salt.
Substitute unsalted polyunsaturated margarine for margarine.
Add ½ teaspoon tarragon with seasonings.
Proceed as in Basic Recipe.

Calories per serving: 42
Approximate nutrient
   values same as Basic
   Recipe except for:
      Sodium 11 mg
      Potassium 89 mg

BLAND DIETS

Omit pepper. Substitute 1½ cups bland Meat and Vegetable Stock (page 117) for basic Meat and Vegetable Stock.
Proceed as in Basic Recipe.

Calories per serving: 42

HIGH-FIBER DIETS

Use Basic Recipe. For extra fiber, mix 1 tablespoon All-Bran cereal or wheat germ into the sauce.

# Cucumber Mousseline Sauce

BASIC RECIPE

This is particularly good with poached salmon or any white fish fillets.

Serving size: 2 tablespoons
Calories per serving: 89
Approximate nutrient
   values per serving:
      Protein 1 g
      Fat 10 g
      Carbohydrate 1 g
      Sodium 96 mg
      Potassium 20 mg
      Cholesterol 61 mg
Exchanges:
   Fat 2

3 large egg yolks
¼ teaspoon salt
⅛ teaspoon dry mustard
2 tablespoons lemon juice
½ cup polyunsaturated margarine
½ cup heavy cream, whipped
½ cup minced peeled cucumber

Place egg yolks, salt, mustard, and lemon juice in the container of an electric blender. Cover and blend.

Heat the margarine in a small saucepan until it foams. Remove the cover from the blender and add the melted margarine in a slow, steady stream. When all the margarine has been added, turn off blender.

If not using sauce immediately, put it in the top of a double boiler over barely simmering water to keep warm.

Immediately before serving, fold in the whipped cream and cucumber.

*Yield:* 2 cups

*Change Cucumber Mousseline Sauce as follows or use Basic Recipe, if indicated, for:*

### LOW-SODIUM AND RENAL DIETS

Omit salt.
Substitute unsalted polyunsaturated margarine for margarine.
Proceed as in Basic Recipe.

Calories per serving: 89
Approximate nutrient
  values same as Basic
  Recipe except for:
    Calcium 11 mg
    Phosphorus 22 mg
    Sodium 5 mg

### BLAND DIETS

Omit mustard.
Proceed as in Basic Recipe.

Calories per serving: 89

### HIGH-FIBER DIETS

Use Basic Recipe. For extra fiber, do not peel cucumber.

## CUCUMBER MOUSSELINE SAUCE FOR LOW-CALORIE, DIABETIC, LOW-FAT, AND LOW-CHOLESTEROL DIETS

Serving size: 2 tablespoons
Calories per serving: 13
Approximate nutrient
  values per serving:
    Protein 1 g
    Fat 1 g
    Carbohydrate 1 g
    Sodium 57 mg
    Potassium 30 mg
    Cholesterol 0 mg
Exchanges:
  Fat ½

1 tablespoon polyunsaturated margarine
1 tablespoon cornstarch
¾ cup Chicken Stock (page 114)
¼ teaspoon salt
⅛ teaspoon dry mustard
2 tablespoons lemon juice
Low-Cholesterol Egg Substitute (page 189) equivalent to
  1 large egg
½ cup minced peeled cucumber
1 large egg white

Melt margarine in a small saucepan. Whisk cornstarch into margarine; then gradually add chicken stock and continue cooking over moderate heat, stirring constantly, until sauce thickens. Bring to a boil for 1 minute.

Remove from heat and stir in salt, mustard, and lemon juice.

In a small bowl, whisk egg substitute until foamy. Pour sauce into egg substitute in a slow, steady stream, stirring constantly.

If not using sauce immediately, put it in the top of a double boiler over barely simmering water to keep warm.

Just before serving, mix cucumber into the sauce. Beat egg white until stiff and fold into the sauce.

*Yield:* 2 cups

# Béchamel Sauce

BASIC RECIPE

Lovely with vegetables, and as a base for other cream sauces.

4 tablespoons polyunsaturated margarine
4 tablespoons flour
2 cups milk
½ teaspoon salt
⅛ teaspoon freshly ground pepper
⅛ teaspoon nutmeg

Melt margarine in a medium saucepan. Blend in flour. Gradually stir in milk. Cook over moderate heat, stirring constantly, until sauce is thickened and smooth. Boil and stir 1 minute. Remove from heat; blend in salt, pepper, and nutmeg.

*Yield:* 2 cups

*Change Béchamel Sauce as follows or use Basic Recipe, if indicated, for:*

LOW-CALORIE, DIABETIC, LOW-FAT, AND LOW-CHOLESTEROL DIETS

Reduce margarine to 3 tablespoons.
Substitute skim milk for milk.
Proceed as in Basic Recipe.

Serving size: 2 tablespoons
Calories per serving: 52
Approximate nutrient
  values per serving:
    Protein 1 g
    Fat 4 g
    Carbohydrate 3 g
    Sodium 112 mg
    Potassium 49 mg
    Cholesterol 4 mg
Exchanges:
  Milk ¼
  Fat 1

Calories per serving: 37
Approximate nutrient
  values per serving:
    Protein 1 g
    Fat 2 g
    Carbohydrate 3 g
    Sodium 106 mg
    Potassium 54 mg
    Cholesterol 1 mg
Exchanges:
  Milk ¼
  Fat ½

## LOW-SODIUM AND RENAL DIETS

Omit salt.
Substitute unsalted polyunsaturated margarine for margarine.
Proceed as in Basic Recipe.

Calories per serving: 52
Approximate nutrient
values same as Basic
Recipe except for:
Calcium 37 mg
Phosphorus 30 mg
Sodium 15 mg

## BLAND DIETS

Omit pepper and nutmeg.
Proceed as in Basic Recipe.

Calories per serving: 52

## HIGH-FIBER DIETS

Use Basic Recipe.

# Velvet Dill Sauce

### BASIC RECIPE

This sauce goes well with chicken or fish.

Serving size: 2 tablespoons
Calories per serving: 61
Approximate nutrient
values per serving:
Protein 0 g
Fat 6 g
Carbohydrate 2 g
Sodium 140 mg
Potassium 56 mg
Cholesterol 0 mg
Exchanges:
Fat 1

2 cups Chicken Stock (page 114)
1 cup dry white wine
1 medium carrot, sliced
3 fresh mushrooms, sliced
¼ cup chopped onions
1 sprig fresh parsley
1 small bay leaf
8 tablespoons polyunsaturated margarine
3 tablespoons flour
½ teaspoon salt
⅛ teaspoon freshly ground pepper
1 teaspoon dillweed

In a medium saucepan place stock, wine, carrot, mushrooms, onions, parsley, and bay leaf. Simmer, tightly covered, for 20 minutes. Strain and reserve 2 cups.

In the same saucepan melt 4 tablespoons of the margarine over moderate heat without letting it brown. Add the flour and stir with a wire whisk until it is well blended. Gradually add the 2 cups strained liquid and cook over moderate heat, stirring constantly, until sauce is thickened and smooth. Boil and stir 1 minute. Remove from heat and blend in salt, pepper, dill-weed, and remaining 4 tablespoons margarine.

*Yield:* 2 cups

*Change Velvet Dill Sauce as follows or use Basic Recipe, if indicated, for:*

LOW-CALORIE, DIABETIC, LOW-FAT, AND LOW-CHOLESTEROL DIETS

Reduce margarine to 2 tablespoons for the sauce and omit the margarine added with the seasonings.
Proceed as in Basic Recipe.

LOW-SODIUM DIETS

Omit salt.
Substitute unsalted polyunsaturated margarine for margarine.
Proceed as in Basic Recipe.

Calories per serving: 23
Approximate nutrient values per serving:
Protein 0 g
Fat 2 g
Carbohydrate 2 g
Sodium 97 mg
Potassium 55 mg
Cholesterol 0 mg
Exchanges:
Fat ½

Calories per serving: 61
Approximate nutrient values same as Basic Recipe except for:
Sodium 14 mg

Calories per serving: 61

Omit pepper.
Proceed as in Basic Recipe.


## HIGH-FIBER DIETS

Use Basic Recipe. For extra fiber, plan to serve raw vegetable salad and stone-ground whole wheat toast with your meal.


## VELVET DILL SAUCE FOR RENAL DIETS

Serving size: ¼ cup
Calories per serving: 136
Approximate nutrient
   values per serving:
     Protein 2 g
     Fat 13 g
     Carbohydrate 5 g
     Calcium 51 mg
     Phosphorus 41 mg
     Sodium 19 mg
     Potassium 68 mg
     Cholesterol 5 mg
Exchanges:
   Bread ½
   Fat 2½

½ cup dry white wine
8 tablespoons unsalted polyunsaturated margarine
3 tablespoons flour
1¼ cups milk
½ cup water
⅛ teaspoon freshly ground pepper
1 teaspoon dillweed

Put wine in a small saucepan and simmer for 5 minutes. Set aside.

Melt 4 tablespoons of the margarine in a saucepan. Blend in flour. Gradually stir in milk, wine, and water. Cook and stir until thickened and smooth. Remove from heat and blend in pepper, dillweed, and remaining 4 tablespoons margarine.

*Yield:* 2 cups

# Velouté Sauce

BASIC RECIPE

This sauce complements chicken dishes very well.

Serving size: 2 tablespoons
Calories per serving: 37
Approximate nutrient
  values per serving:
    Protein 0 g
    Fat 3 g
    Carbohydrate 3 g
    Sodium 111 mg
    Potassium 53 mg
    Cholesterol 0 mg
Exchanges:
    Fat 1

2 cups Chicken Stock (page 114)
1 cup dry white wine
1 medium carrot, sliced
3 fresh mushrooms, sliced
¼ cup chopped onions
1 sprig fresh parsley
1 small bay leaf
4 tablespoons polyunsaturated margarine
3 tablespoons flour
½ teaspoon salt
⅛ teaspoon freshly ground pepper

Combine stock, wine, carrot, mushrooms, onions, parsley, and bay leaf in a medium saucepan. Simmer, tightly covered, for 20 minutes. Strain and reserve 2 cups liquid.

In the same saucepan melt the margarine over moderate heat. Add flour and stir until it is well blended. Gradually add the reserved liquid and cook over moderate heat, stirring constantly, until thickened and smooth. Boil and stir 1 minute. Remove from heat and blend in salt and pepper.

*Yield:* 2 cups

*Change Velouté Sauce as follows or use Basic Recipe, if indicated, for:*

## LOW-CALORIE, DIABETIC, LOW-FAT, AND LOW-CHOLESTEROL DIETS

Reduce the margarine to 2 tablespoons.
Proceed as in Basic Recipe.

Calories per serving: 24
Approximate nutrient
values per serving:
Protein 0 g
Fat 2 g
Carbohydrate 3 g
Sodium 97 mg
Potassium 53 mg
Cholesterol 0 mg
Exchanges:
Fat ½

## LOW-SODIUM DIETS

Omit salt.

Calories per serving: 37
Approximate nutrient
values same as Basic
Recipe except for:
Sodium 14 mg

## BLAND DIETS

Omit pepper.
Proceed as in Basic Recipe.

Calories per serving: 37

## HIGH-FIBER DIETS

Use Basic Recipe.

½ cup dry white wine
4 tablespoons unsalted polyunsaturated margarine
3 tablespoons flour
1¼ cups milk
½ cup water
⅛ teaspoon freshly ground pepper

Pour wine in a small saucepan and simmer for 5 minutes. Set aside.

Melt the margarine in a medium saucepan. Stir in flour and cook until it is well blended. Gradually add milk, wine, and water and cook over moderate heat, stirring constantly, until thickened and smooth. Boil and stir 1 minute. Remove from heat and blend in pepper.

*Yield:* 2 cups

Serving size: ¼ cup
Calories per serving: 87
Approximate nutrient
  values per serving:
    Protein 2 g
    Fat 7 g
    Carbohydrate 5 g
    Calcium 46 mg
    Phosphorus 38 mg
    Sodium 19 mg
    Potassium 62 mg
    Cholesterol 5 mg
Exchanges:
  Milk ¼
  Fat 1½

# Poultry or Lamb Marinade

BASIC RECIPE

1 cup white wine
½ cup polyunsaturated oil
1 small onion, sliced
1 bay leaf
1½ teaspoons minced fresh mint
1½ teaspoons chervil
1½ teaspoons rosemary
1 teaspoon salt
¼ teaspoon freshly ground pepper
1 clove garlic, put through garlic press

Combine all ingredients in a small saucepan. Bring to a boil. Remove from heat.

Chill thoroughly before using.

*Yield:* 1½ cups

Serving size: 2 tablespoons
Calories per serving: 87
Approximate nutrient
  values per serving:
    Protein 0 g
    Fat 9 g
    Carbohydrate 2 g
    Sodium 184 mg
    Potassium 18 mg
    Cholesterol 0 mg
Exchanges:
  Fat 2

*Change Poultry or Lamb Marinade as follows or use Basic Recipe, if indicated, for:*

LOW-CALORIE, DIABETIC, LOW-FAT, AND LOW-CHOLESTEROL DIETS

Reduce oil to ⅛ cup.
Proceed as in Basic Recipe.

*Yield:* 1⅛ cups

Calories per serving: 65
Approximate nutrient
  values per serving:
    Protein 0 g
    Fat 7 g
    Carbohydrate 2 g
    Sodium 201 mg
    Potassium 20 mg
    Cholesterol 0 mg
Exchanges:
  Fat 1½

LOW-SODIUM AND RENAL DIETS

Omit salt.
Proceed as in Basic Recipe.

Calories per serving: 87
Approximate nutrient
  values same as Basic
  Recipe except for:
    Calcium 5 mg
    Phosphorus 4 mg
    Sodium 1 mg

BLAND DIETS

Omit pepper.
Proceed as in Basic Recipe

Calories per serving: 87

HIGH-FIBER DIETS

Use Basic Recipe.

# Tarragon Sauce

BASIC RECIPE

This goes beautifully with meats, particularly pork or veal.

¼ cup polyunsaturated margarine
⅓ cup chopped onions
1 clove garlic, finely chopped
1 cup white wine
¼ cup Cognac
1½ cups Brown Sauce (page 387)
1 teaspoon tarragon
2 tablespoons chopped fresh parsley

In a medium saucepan melt the margarine and sauté onions and garlic until onions are soft. Add wine and Cognac; simmer, uncovered, until reduced by half. Add brown sauce, tarragon, and parsley; simmer, uncovered, for 10 minutes.

*Yield:* 2 cups

*Change Tarragon Sauce as follows or use Basic Recipe, if indicated, for:*

LOW-CALORIE, DIABETIC, LOW-FAT, AND LOW-CHOLESTEROL DIETS

Reduce margarine to 2 tablespoons.
Substitute 1½ cups low-calorie Brown Sauce (page 388) for Brown Sauce.
Proceed as in Basic Recipe.

Substitute unsalted polyunsaturated margarine for margarine.
Substitute low-sodium Brown Sauce (page 388) for basic Brown Sauce.
Proceed as in Basic Recipe.

Calories per serving: 70
Approximate nutrient
  values same as Basic
  Recipe except for:
    Sodium 22 mg

BLAND DIETS

Substitute bland Brown Sauce (page 388) for basic Brown Sauce.
Proceed as in Basic Recipe.

Calories per serving: 71

HIGH-FIBER DIETS

Use Basic Recipe.

# Marchand de Vin Sauce

BASIC RECIPE

This is excellent with beef—hamburgers as well as steaks.

Serving size: 2 tablespoons
Calories per serving: 84
Approximate nutrient
  values per serving:
    Protein 1 g
    Fat 8 g
    Carbohydrate 4 g
    Sodium 192 mg
    Potassium 116 mg
    Cholesterol 0 mg
Exchanges:
  Vegetable ½
  Fat 1½

½ cup polyunsaturated margarine
¾ cup chopped fresh mushrooms
2 tablespoons minced shallots
⅔ cup red wine
½ teaspoon salt
½ cup diced carrots
½ cup chopped onions
½ cup chopped celery
2 tablespoons flour
2 cups Beef Stock (page 113)
½ cup chopped peeled tomatoes
1 sprig fresh parsley
1 bay leaf
⅛ teaspoon peppercorns

In a medium saucepan melt ¼ cup of the margarine. Sauté mushrooms and shallots until tender. Add wine and salt; simmer, uncovered, until liquid is reduced to ½ cup. Remove from heat and set aside.

In a large saucepan melt remaining ¼ cup margarine. Add the carrots, onions, and celery and sauté until onions are soft. Add flour and cook over moderate heat, stirring constantly, about 10 minutes or until flour is browned.

Add remaining ingredients and simmer slowly, uncovered, 1½ to 2 hours or until thick. Skim as necessary. Strain and allow to cool. Then stir in the mushroom mixture and reheat. Sauce may be stored in the freezer.

*Yield:* 1½ cups

*Change Marchand de Vin Sauce as follows or use Basic Recipe, if indicated, for:*

LOW-CALORIE, DIABETIC, LOW-FAT, AND LOW-CHOLESTEROL DIETS

Calories per serving: 50
Approximate nutrient
  values per serving:
    Protein 1 g
    Fat 4 g
    Carbohydrate 4 g
    Sodium 154 mg
    Potassium 115 mg
    Cholesterol 0 mg
Exchanges:
  Vegetable ½
  Fat 1

Reduce margarine to 4 tablespoons.
Proceed as in Basic Recipe.

LOW-SODIUM DIETS

Calories per serving: 84
Approximate nutrient
  values same as Basic
  Recipe except for:
    Sodium 25 mg

Omit salt.
Substitute unsalted polyunsaturated margarine for margarine.
Proceed as in Basic Recipe.

Calories per serving: 84

BLAND DIETS

Omit peppercorns.
Proceed as in Basic Recipe.


HIGH-FIBER DIETS

Use Basic Recipe.


# Pineapple Sweet-and-Sour Sauce

BASIC RECIPE

This is delicious with pork, ham, or tongue.


Serving size: 2 tablespoons
Calories per serving: 35
Approximate nutrient
  values per serving:
    Protein 0 g
    Fat 0 g
    Carbohydrate 9 g
    Sodium 94 mg
    Potassium 47 mg
    Cholesterol 0 mg
Exchanges:
  Fruit 1

two 8-ounce cans crushed pineapple in heavy syrup
½ cup cider vinegar
¼ cup dry sherry
½ cup chopped onions
½ cup firmly packed dark-brown sugar
1 teaspoon salt
¼ teaspoon freshly ground pepper
2 teaspoons grated peeled fresh ginger root
2 cloves garlic, put through garlic press

In a small saucepan combine pineapple and syrup with remaining ingredients. Simmer, uncovered, for 10 minutes, stirring occasionally.
    Serve warm.

*Yield:* 3 cups

*Change Pineapple Sweet-and-Sour Sauce as follows or use Basic Recipe, if indicated, for:*

## LOW-CALORIE, DIABETIC, LOW-FAT, AND LOW-CHOLESTEROL DIETS

Calories per serving: 23
Approximate nutrient
values per serving:
   Protein 0 g
   Fat 0 g
   Carbohydrate 6 g
   Sodium 93 mg
   Potassium 49 mg
   Cholesterol 0 mg
Exchanges:
   Fruit ½

Substitute two 8-ounce cans crushed pineapple packed in unsweetened juice for pineapple.
Reduce sugar to ¼ cup.
Proceed as in Basic Recipe.

## LOW-SODIUM AND RENAL DIETS

Calories per serving: 35
Approximate nutrient
values same as Basic
Recipe except for:
   Calcium 8 mg
   Phosphorus 4 mg
   Sodium 2 mg

Omit salt.
Proceed as in Basic Recipe.

## BLAND DIETS

Calories per serving: 35

Omit pepper.
Proceed as in Basic Recipe.

## HIGH-FIBER DIETS

Use Basic Recipe.

# Fresh Cranberry Sauce

BASIC RECIPE SUITABLE FOR LOW-SODIUM,
BLAND, AND HIGH-FIBER DIETS

Use this with roast turkey or chicken.

Serving size: ⅓ cup
Calories per serving: 170
Approximate nutrient
    values per serving:
        Protein 1 g
        Fat 7 g
        Carbohydrate 29 g
        Sodium 2 mg
        Potassium 103 mg
        Cholesterol 0 mg
Exchanges:
    Fruit 3
    Fat 1

4 cups fresh cranberries
1 cup sugar
1 cup chopped unpeeled apples
⅔ cup chopped pecans
1 tablespoon grated orange rind

Rinse cranberries and remove any stems. Using a medium blade, put cranberries through a food grinder or chop coarsely by hand. Add sugar and mix gently to blend. Cover and refrigerate overnight.

Before serving stir in remaining ingredients.

*Yield:* 3 cups

FRESH CRANBERRY SAUCE FOR LOW-CALORIE,
DIABETIC, LOW-FAT, AND LOW-CHOLESTEROL
DIETS

*The Purée*
½ cup seedless raisins
½ cup water

Serving size: ¼ cup
Calories per serving: 42
Approximate nutrient
    values per serving:
        Protein 0 g
        Fat 0 g
        Carbohydrate 11 g
        Sodium 7 mg
        Potassium 104 mg
        Cholesterol 0 mg
Exchanges:
    Fruit 1

*The Cranberry Mixture*
2 cups fresh cranberries
½ cup chopped unpeeled apples
⅓ cup chopped celery
1½ teaspoons grated orange rind

*To prepare the purée:* In a small covered saucepan, bring the raisins and water to a boil. Remove from heat and let stand 10 minutes. Purée in an electric blender.

*To prepare the cranberry mixture:* Rinse cranberries and remove any stems. Using a medium blade, put cranberries through a food grinder or chop coarsely by hand.

Mix ground cranberries with the raisin purée and refrigerate overnight.

Before serving, stir in the apples, celery, and orange rind.

*Yield:* 2 cups

# VEGETABLES

*Once overcooked and forced on children, vegetables have at last come into their own. Americans are learning that cooked al dente (crisp-tender) vegetables can be the highlight of any meal. The ranks of vegetarians grow greater daily. We believe firmly in the nutritional importance of vegetables and urge you to eat your share of them every day. Remember, they are one of the five essential food groups discussed in the chapter on nutrition. If you are a dedicated vegan or vegetarian, stay with your beliefs, but be certain to balance your diet by choosing other foods that deliver certain nutrients vegetables alone cannot supply. A review of our vegetable recipes reveals imaginative combinations that can help you do this.*

# Asparagus Mozzarella

BASIC RECIPE

Serving size: 4 asparagus
  spears, ¼ cup sauce, 1⅓
  ounces cheese
Calories per serving: 163
Approximate nutrient
  values per serving:
    Protein 10 g
    Fat 9 g
    Carbohydrate 11 g
    Sodium 333 mg
    Potassium 526 mg
    Cholesterol 30 mg
Exchanges:
  Vegetable 2
  Meat 1
  Fat 1½

1½ cups Italian Tomato Sauce (page 392)
24 medium-size fresh asparagus spears, trimmed
½ teaspoon salt
8 ounces mozzarella cheese, thinly sliced

Prepare tomato sauce in advance and keep warm.

Fill a large skillet with about 1 inch of water. Add salt and bring water to boil.

Add asparagus and boil, uncovered, 5 minutes. Cover and boil gently about 5 minutes longer, or until asparagus is tender.

Drain thoroughly and arrange spears, tips pointing in the same direction, in a shallow baking dish.

Spoon heated tomato sauce over the center of the spears. Cover all except tips with cheese and broil until cheese melts and is golden brown.

*Yield:* 6 servings

*Change Asparagus Mozzarella as follows or use Basic Recipe, if indicated, for:*

LOW-CALORIE, DIABETIC, LOW-FAT, AND LOW-CHOLESTEROL DIETS

Calories per serving: 153
Approximate nutrient
  values per serving:
    Protein 12 g
    Fat 7 g
    Carbohydrate 11 g
    Sodium 369 mg
    Potassium 533 mg
    Cholesterol 22 mg
Exchanges:
  Vegetable 2
  Meat 1
  Fat 1

Substitute part-skim mozzarella cheese for mozzarella. Proceed as in Basic Recipe.

Calories per serving: 230
Approximate nutrient
   values per serving:
      Protein 12 g
      Fat 14 g
      Carbohydrate 11 g
      Sodium 89 mg
      Potassium 554 mg
      Cholesterol 13 mg

## LOW-SODIUM DIETS

Omit salt.
Substitute low-sodium Swiss cheese, thinly sliced, for
   mozzarella.
Proceed as in Basic Recipe.

## BLAND AND HIGH-FIBER DIETS

Use Basic Recipe.

Serving size: ½ cup
Calories per serving: 102
Approximate nutrient
   values per serving:
      Protein 2 g
      Fat 6 g
      Carbohydrate 10 g
      Sodium 307 mg
      Potassium 175 mg
      Cholesterol 0 mg
Exchanges:
   Vegetable 1
   Bread ½
   Fat 1

# Green Beans with Dill

### BASIC RECIPE

1½ cups fresh bread crumbs (page 38)
3 tablespoons polyunsaturated margarine
½ teaspoon dillweed
½ teaspoon salt
3 cups fresh green beans cut in 2-inch pieces
⅓ cup chopped fresh parsley

Sauté bread crumbs in margarine until lightly browned. Add dill and stir gently to blend. Set aside.

In a medium saucepan bring 1 inch salted water to a boil. Add beans and cook, uncovered, for 5 minutes. Cover, reduce heat, and continue cooking about 5 minutes longer or until crisp but tender. Drain thoroughly. Serve topped with reserved crumbs and chopped parsley.

*Yield:* 6 servings

*Change Green Beans with Dill as follows or use Basic Recipe, if indicated, for:*

LOW-CALORIE, DIABETIC, LOW-FAT, AND LOW-CHOLESTEROL DIETS

Reduce margarine to 2 tablespoons.
Proceed as in Basic Recipe.

Calories per serving: 86
Approximate nutrient
   values per serving:
      Protein 2 g
      Fat 4 g
      Carbohydrate 10 g
      Sodium 288 mg
      Potassium 174 mg
      Cholesterol 0 mg
Exchanges:
   Vegetable 1
   Bread ½
   Fat ½

LOW-SODIUM AND RENAL DIETS

Omit salt.
Substitute unsalted polyunsaturated margarine for margarine.
Proceed as in Basic Recipe.

Calories per serving: 102
Approximate nutrient
   values same as Basic
   Recipe except for:
      Calcium 51 mg
      Phosphorus 40 mg
      Sodium 67 mg

BLAND DIETS

Use Basic Recipe.

HIGH-FIBER DIETS

Substitute stone-ground whole wheat fresh bread crumbs (page 38) for bread crumbs.
Proceed as in Basic Recipe.

Calories per serving: 102

# Green Beans Vinaigrette

BASIC RECIPE

Serving size: ½ cup
Calories per serving: 80
Approximate nutrient
  values per serving:
    Protein 1 g
    Fat 7 g
    Carbohydrate 4 g
    Sodium 210 mg
    Potassium 143 mg
    Cholesterol 0 mg
Exchanges:
  Vegetable 1
  Fat 1½

2 cups water
½ teaspoon salt for boiling beans
4 cups fresh green beans cut in thin strips
4 tablespoons polyunsaturated oil
2 tablespoons lemon juice
1 tablespoon chopped chives
½ teaspoon dillweed
½ teaspoon dry mustard
¼ teaspoon salt for the dressing
⅛ teaspoon freshly ground pepper

Place 2 cups water in quart-size saucepan. Add ½ teaspoon salt and bring to a boil. Add beans and boil, uncovered, 5 minutes. Cover tightly, reduce heat, and simmer 5 minutes longer or until just tender. Drain thoroughly and cool to room temperature.

In a medium bowl prepare a vinaigrette dressing by mixing oil, lemon juice, chives, dill, mustard, the remaining ¼ teaspoon salt, and pepper until thoroughly blended.

Add the cooled beans to the dressing and toss gently.

*Yield:* 8 servings

*Change Green Beans Vinaigrette as follows for:*

## LOW-CALORIE, DIABETIC, LOW-FAT, AND LOW-CHOLESTEROL DIETS

Calories per serving: 50
Approximate nutrient
  values per serving:
    Protein 1 g
    Fat 4 g
    Carbohydrate 4 g
    Sodium 210 mg
    Potassium 143 mg
    Cholesterol 0 mg
Exchanges:
  Vegetable 1
  Fat 1

Reduce oil to 2 tablespoons.
Proceed as in Basic Recipe.

## LOW-SODIUM AND RENAL DIETS

Calories per serving: 80
Approximate nutrient
  values same as Basic
  Recipe except for:
    Calcium 33 mg
    Phosphorus 26 mg
    Sodium 4 mg

Omit salt.
Proceed as in Basic Recipe.

## BLAND DIETS

Calories per serving: 79

Omit pepper and mustard.
Proceed as in Basic Recipe.

## HIGH-FIBER DIETS

Calories per serving: 80

Add ½ teaspoon celery seed to the vinaigrette dressing.
Proceed as in Basic Recipe.

419

# Stir-Fried Broccoli Crisp

BASIC RECIPE

6 cups broccoli (stems and flowerets)
2 tablespoons polyunsaturated oil
½ teaspoon salt
⅓ cup water

Wash broccoli thoroughly. Cut flowerets into bite-size pieces. Peel the stems and cut into julienne strips approximately 2 inches long and ¼ inch wide.

Heat the oil in a large, heavy skillet. Add broccoli and salt; stir and cook over high heat 30 seconds or until broccoli turns a bright green. Lower heat immediately.

Add water; cook, covered, 5 minutes. Serve immediately.

*Yield:* 8 servings

*Change Stir-Fried Broccoli Crisp as follows or use Basic Recipe, if indicated, for:*

LOW-CALORIE, DIABETIC, LOW-FAT, LOW-CHOLESTEROL, BLAND, AND HIGH-FIBER DIETS

Use Basic Recipe.

LOW-SODIUM DIETS

Omit salt.
Proceed as in Basic Recipe.

# Broccoli and Bean Sprout Sauté

BASIC RECIPE

Serving size: ½ cup
Calories per serving: 80
Approximate nutrient
  values per serving:
    Protein 5 g
    Fat 5 g
    Carbohydrate 8 g
    Sodium 453 mg
    Potassium 391 mg
    Cholesterol 0 mg
Exchanges:
  Vegetable 2
  Fat 1

1 bunch fresh broccoli (1 pound)
1½ tablespoons polyunsaturated oil
½ tablespoon sliced peeled fresh ginger root
2 cloves garlic, halved
10 ounces fresh bean sprouts
2 tablespoons soy sauce
1 teaspoon sesame oil

Cut the stalk from the broccoli and separate top into small flowerets. Use only the flowerets for this recipe.

Combine oil, ginger root, and garlic in a large skillet; heat gently for about 3 minutes or until oil has ginger and garlic flavor. Remove and discard the ginger root and garlic.

Add the broccoli to the oil; toss over high heat for 3 minutes, being careful not to brown the flowerets.

Add the bean sprouts and soy sauce. Continue to toss until the bean sprouts begin to wilt, about 2 minutes. Sprinkle on the sesame oil, toss, and serve immediately.

*Yield:* 6 servings

*Change Broccoli and Bean Sprout Sauté as follows or use Basic Recipe, if indicated, for:*

## LOW-CALORIE, DIABETIC, LOW-FAT, AND LOW-CHOLESTEROL DIETS

Reduce polyunsaturated oil to 1 teaspoon.
Spray skillet with vegetable cooking spray.
Proceed as in Basic Recipe.

Calories per serving: 56
Approximate nutrient
 values per serving:
  Protein 5 g
  Fat 2 g
  Carbohydrate 8 g
  Sodium 453 mg
  Potassium 391 mg
  Cholesterol 0 mg
Exchanges:
 Vegetable 2
 Fat ½

## LOW-SODIUM DIETS

Omit polyunsaturated oil and sesame oil.
Substitute 2 tablespoons olive oil.
Omit soy sauce. Add 2 tablespoons lemon juice before serving.
Proceed as in Basic Recipe.

Calories per serving: 79
Approximate nutrient
 values same as Basic
 Recipe except for:
  Sodium 13 mg
  Potassium 369 mg

## BLAND AND HIGH-FIBER DIETS

Use Basic Recipe.

# Spinach Genoa

BASIC RECIPE

Serving size: ½ cup
Calories per serving: 192
Approximate nutrient
   values per serving:
      Protein 6 g
      Fat 13 g
      Carbohydrate 17 g
      Sodium 377 mg
      Potassium 825 mg
      Cholesterol 9 mg
Exchanges:
   Vegetable 1
   Fruit 1
   Fat 2½

⅓ cup golden raisins
1 cup boiling water
1¼ pounds fresh spinach, washed and trimmed
3 tablespoons olive oil
¼ cup pine nuts
½ teaspoon salt
⅛ teaspoon freshly ground pepper

Put raisins in a small bowl. Cover with boiling water and let stand about 15 minutes. Drain and set aside.

Put spinach in a large saucepan with only the water that clings to the leaves. Cook, covered, 5 to 10 minutes, or until tender. Drain thoroughly and chop coarsely.

In a large skillet, heat the oil. Add pine nuts and sauté until golden brown. Add plumped raisins, spinach, salt, and pepper. Cook, stirring gently, until ingredients are hot and well blended.

*Yield:* 4 servings

*Change Spinach Genoa as follows for:*

LOW-CALORIE, DIABETIC, LOW-FAT, AND LOW-CHOLESTEROL DIETS

Calories per serving: 82
Approximate nutrient
   values per serving:
      Protein 5 g
      Fat 6 g
      Carbohydrate 6 g
      Sodium 375 mg
      Potassium 667 mg
      Cholesterol 9 mg
Exchanges:
   Vegetable 1
   Fat 1

Omit raisins and pine nuts.
Spray skillet well with vegetable cooking spray. Reduce olive oil to 1½ tablespoons.
Add 1 clove garlic, halved, to oil and sauté for 2 minutes; then remove it.
Proceed as in Basic Recipe.

## LOW-SODIUM DIETS

Heat oil as in Basic Recipe. Add 1 clove garlic, halved, and
  sauté in oil for 2 minutes. Then remove.
Omit salt.
Substitute ⅛ teaspoon each sage, thyme, and marjoram, and
  add with the raisins, spinach, and pepper.
Proceed as in Basic Recipe.

## BLAND DIETS

Omit pepper.
Proceed as in Basic Recipe.

## HIGH-FIBER DIETS

Omit pine nuts. Add ¼ cup coarsely chopped walnuts.
Proceed as in Basic Recipe.

# Creamed Spinach

BASIC RECIPE

two 10-ounce packages frozen chopped spinach
2 tablespoons polyunsaturated margarine
2 tablespoons flour
1 cup heavy cream
½ teaspoon salt
⅛ teaspoon freshly ground pepper
⅛ teaspoon nutmeg
1 tablespoon lemon juice

Cook spinach according to package directions and drain thoroughly. Set aside.
   Melt the margarine in a medium-size saucepan. Blend in
flour. Add cream and cook over low heat, stirring constantly,

---

Calories per serving: 192
Approximate nutrient
  values same as Basic
  Recipe except for:
    Sodium 103 mg

Calories per serving: 192

Calories per serving: 208

Serving size: ½ cup
Calories per serving: 243
Approximate nutrient
  values per serving:
    Protein 5 g
    Fat 23 g
    Carbohydrate 8 g
    Sodium 342 mg
    Potassium 423 mg
    Cholesterol 65 mg
Exchanges:
    Vegetable 1½
    Fat 4½

until sauce is thickened and smooth. Cook and stir for 1 minute.

Remove from heat and stir in the salt, pepper, nutmeg, and lemon juice. Stir in cooked spinach.

*Yield:* 5 servings

*Change Creamed Spinach as follows or use Basic Recipe, if indicated, for:*

LOW-CALORIE, DIABETIC, LOW-FAT, AND LOW-CHOLESTEROL DIETS

Substitute skim milk for cream.
Proceed as in Basic Recipe.

Calories per serving: 96
Approximate nutrient
  values per serving:
    Protein 6 g
    Fat 5 g
    Carbohydrate 9 g
    Sodium 350 mg
    Potassium 468 mg
    Cholesterol 1 mg
Exchanges:
  Milk ¼
  Vegetable 1
  Fat 1

LOW-SODIUM DIETS

Omit salt.
Substitute unsalted polyunsaturated margarine for margarine.
Proceed as in Basic Recipe.

Calories per serving: 243
Approximate nutrient
  values same as Basic
  Recipe except for:
    Sodium 77 mg

BLAND DIETS

Omit pepper and nutmeg.
Proceed as in Basic Recipe.

Calories per serving: 243

HIGH-FIBER DIETS

Use Basic Recipe.

# Tomatoes Torinese

BASIC RECIPE

8 firm, ripe tomatoes (approximately 2½ pounds)

*The Creamed Spinach*
two 10-ounce packages frozen chopped spinach
2 tablespoons polyunsaturated margarine
2 tablespoons flour
1 cup heavy cream
½ teaspoon salt
⅛ teaspoon freshly ground pepper
⅛ teaspoon nutmeg
1 tablespoon lemon juice

*The Topping*
3 tablespoons polyunsaturated margarine
1 cup fresh bread crumbs (page 38)
3 tablespoons grated Parmesan cheese

Preheat oven to 375°F.
   Core and seed the tomatoes, but leave shells intact.

*To prepare the spinach:* Cook spinach according to package directions and drain well.
   Melt 2 tablespoons margarine in a large saucepan. Blend in flour. Add cream gradually and cook over low heat, stirring constantly, until thickened and smooth.
   When sauce bubbles slightly, cook and stir for 1 minute.
   Remove from heat and mix in salt, pepper, nutmeg, and lemon juice. Stir in cooked spinach.

*To prepare the topping:* Melt 3 tablespoons margarine in a small skillet; add bread crumbs and cheese, and toss gently to blend.

*To assemble the dish:* Fill tomatoes with spinach and top with crumb mixture.
   Arrange stuffed tomatoes in a shallow baking dish and bake 15 to 20 minutes or until crumbs are golden brown.

*Yield:* 8 servings

*Change Tomatoes Torinese as follows or use Basic Recipe, if indicated, for:*

LOW-CALORIE, DIABETIC, LOW-FAT, AND LOW-CHOLESTEROL DIETS

*The spinach:* Substitute skim milk for cream. Proceed as in Basic Recipe.

*The topping:* Omit margarine and cheese. Top tomatoes with fresh bread crumbs.
   Proceed as in Basic Recipe.

Calories per serving: 103
Approximate nutrient
   values per serving:
      Protein 5 g
      Fat 4 g
      Carbohydrate 15 g
      Sodium 253 mg
      Potassium 599 mg
      Cholesterol 1 mg
Exchanges:
   Vegetable 2
   Bread ½
   Fat ½

LOW-SODIUM DIETS

*The spinach:* Omit salt.
   Substitute unsalted polyunsaturated margarine for margarine. Proceed as in Basic Recipe.

*The topping:* Substitute unsalted polyunsaturated margarine for margarine.
   Substitute grated low-sodium Cheddar cheese for Parmesan. Proceed as in Basic Recipe.

Calories per serving: 243
Approximate nutrient
   values per serving:
      Protein 6 g
      Fat 20 g
      Carbohydrate 14 g
      Sodium 83 mg
      Potassium 576 mg
      Cholesterol 42 mg

BLAND DIETS

*The spinach:* Omit pepper and nutmeg. Proceed as in Basic Recipe.

*The topping:* Use Basic Recipe.

Calories per serving: 248

Calories per serving: 248

*The spinach:* Use Basic Recipe.

*The topping:* Substitute fresh whole wheat bread crumbs (page 38) for fresh plain bread crumbs.
  Proceed as in Basic Recipe.

# Carrots Vichy

BASIC RECIPE

Serving size: ½ cup
Calories per serving: 114
Approximate nutrient
  values per serving:
    Protein 1 g
    Fat 8 g
    Carbohydrate 11g
    Sodium 295 mg
    Potassium 231 mg
    Cholesterol 0 mg
Exchanges:
  Vegetable 1
  Bread ½
  Fat 1½

4 tablespoons polyunsaturated margarine
4 cups carrots cut into ¼-inch slices
2 tablespoons sugar
½ teaspoon salt
⅛ teaspoon freshly ground pepper
1 cup carbonated water
3 tablespoons chopped fresh parsley

Heat the margarine in a medium skillet. Add carrots and sprinkle with sugar, salt, and pepper. Toss gently. Add carbonated water. Cover and simmer slowly about 15 to 20 minutes or until carrots are tender.
  Uncover. Increase heat and cook, stirring gently, until liquid has evaporated and carrots are glazed.
  Sprinkle with parsley before serving.

*Yield:* 6 servings

*Change Carrots Vichy as follows or use Basic Recipe, if indicated, for:*

### LOW-CALORIE, DIABETIC, LOW-FAT, AND LOW-CHOLESTEROL DIETS

Reduce margarine to 1 tablespoon.
Reduce sugar to 1 tablespoon.
Proceed as in Basic Recipe.

Calories per serving: 55
Approximate nutrient
  values per serving:
    Protein 1 g
    Fat 2 g
    Carbohydrate 9 g
    Sodium 238 mg
    Potassium 229 mg
    Cholesterol 0 mg
Exchanges:
  Vegetable 1½
  Fat ½

### LOW-SODIUM AND RENAL DIETS

Omit salt.
Substitute unsalted polyunsaturated margarine for margarine.
Add ¼ teaspoon nutmeg.
Proceed as in Basic Recipe.

Calories per serving: 114
Approximate nutrient
  values same as Basic
  Recipe except for:
    Calcium 36 mg
    Phosphorus 31 mg
    Sodium 36 mg

### BLAND DIETS

Omit pepper.
Proceed as in Basic Recipe.

Calories per serving: 114

### HIGH-FIBER DIETS

Use Basic Recipe.

# Gingered Carrots

BASIC RECIPE

Serving size: ½ cup
Calories per serving: 131
Approximate nutrient
  values per serving:
  Protein 1 g
  Fat 8 g
  Carbohydrate 16 g
  Sodium 293 mg
  Potassium 235 mg
  Cholesterol 0 mg
Exchanges:
  Vegetable 1½
  Bread ½
  Fat 1½

4 cups carrots, cut into ¼-inch slices
½ teaspoon salt
4 tablespoons polyunsaturated margarine
4 tablespoons sugar
½ teaspoon ground ginger
2 teaspoons grated orange rind

Place carrots in a medium saucepan. Add water to cover. Season with salt. Bring to a boil. Reduce heat and simmer, covered, 15 to 20 minutes or until carrots are barely tender. Drain.

In a medium skillet, melt the margarine. Blend in sugar, ginger, and orange rind. Add carrots. Cook over low heat, stirring gently, until carrots are glazed.

*Yield:* 6 servings

*Change Gingered Carrots as follows or use Basic Recipe, if indicated, for:*

LOW-CALORIE, DIABETIC, LOW-FAT, AND LOW-CHOLESTEROL DIETS

Calories per serving: 71
Approximate nutrient
  values per serving:
  Protein 1 g
  Fat 4 g
  Carbohydrate 9 g
  Sodium 255 mg
  Potassium 254 mg
  Cholesterol 0 mg
Exchanges:
  Vegetable 2
  Fat 1

Omit sugar.
Reduce margarine to 2 tablespoons.
Reduce orange rind to 1 teaspoon. Add ¼ cup orange juice.
Proceed as in Basic Recipe.

Calories per serving: 131
Approximate nutrient
   values same as Basic
   Recipe except for:
      Calcium 35 mg
      Phosphorus 32 mg
      Sodium 34 mg

Omit salt.
Substitute unsalted polyunsaturated margarine for margarine.
Proceed as in Basic Recipe.

BLAND AND HIGH-FIBER DIETS

Use Basic Recipe.

# Belmont Butternut Squash

BASIC RECIPE

Serving size: ½ cup
Calories per serving: 199
Approximate nutrient
   values per serving:
      Protein 2 g
      Fat 12 g
      Carbohydrate 23 g
      Sodium 282 mg
      Potassium 359 mg
      Cholesterol 0 mg
Exchanges:
   Bread 1½
   Fat 2½

4 cups mashed cooked butternut squash (about 2 pounds)
⅓ cup polyunsaturated margarine for blending with spices
1 teaspoon ground cinnamon
½ teaspoon ground ginger
½ teaspoon salt
⅛ teaspoon freshly ground pepper
⅓ cup firmly packed dark-brown sugar
3 tablespoons polyunsaturated margarine for the bread
   crumbs
¾ cup fresh bread crumbs (page 38)

Peel and seed the squash and cut it into large chunks. Put in boiling water and boil about 20 minutes, until soft. Drain, and mash until lumps disappear.

Preheat oven to 375°F.

In a small saucepan, melt ⅓ cup margarine and blend in the spices, salt, and pepper. Set aside.

In a large bowl beat together the squash, brown sugar, and margarine-spice mixture.

Pour into a greased 1½-quart casserole or baking dish.

Melt the remaining 3 tablespoons margarine and mix gently with the bread crumbs. Spoon the crumb mixture over the squash and bake, uncovered, 15 minutes or until nicely browned.

*Yield:* 8 servings

*Change Belmont Butternut Squash as follows for:*

## LOW-SODIUM DIETS

Calories per serving: 199
Approximate nutrient
    values same as Basic
    Recipe except for:
    Sodium 27 mg

Omit salt.
Substitute unsalted polyunsaturated margarine for margarine wherever used.
Proceed as in Basic Recipe.

## BLAND DIETS

Calories per serving: 199

Omit pepper.
Proceed as in Basic Recipe.

## HIGH-FIBER DIETS

Calories per serving: 199

Add 2 teaspoons finely grated orange rind to the squash mixture.
Proceed as in Basic Recipe.

## BELMONT BUTTERNUT SQUASH FOR LOW-CALORIE, DIABETIC, LOW-FAT, AND LOW-CHOLESTEROL DIETS

Serving size: ½ cup
Calories per serving: 77
Approximate nutrient
    values per serving:
    Protein 2 g
    Fat 3 g

4 cups mashed cooked butternut squash (about 2 pounds)
2 tablespoons polyunsaturated margarine
½ cup chopped onions
½ teaspoon salt
1 teaspoon ground cinnamon

432

Carbohydrate 13 g
Sodium 168 mg
Potassium 337 mg
Cholesterol 0 mg
Exchanges:
Bread 1
Fat ½

½ teaspoon ground ginger
⅛ teaspoon freshly ground black pepper

Peel and seed the squash and cut it into large chunks. Put in boiling water and boil about 20 minutes, until soft. Drain and mash until lumps disappear. Set aside.

In a large skillet, melt the margarine and sauté the onions until soft. Add cooked squash and seasonings and heat thoroughly before serving.

*Yield:* 8 servings

# Zucchini with Apples

BASIC RECIPE

Serving size: ½ cup
Calories per serving: 62
Approximate nutrient
values per serving:
Protein 2 g
Fat 3 g
Carbohydrate 8 g
Sodium 216 mg
Potassium 264 mg
Cholesterol 0 mg
Exchanges:
Vegetable 1½
Fat ½

1½ tablespoons polyunsaturated margarine
½ cup chopped onions
1 pound zucchini, cut into ½-inch slices
1 cup coarsely chopped peeled tomatoes
½ teaspoon salt
¼ teaspoon freshly ground pepper
1 cup diced peeled apples
½ teaspoon basil
2 tablespoons chopped fresh parsley

Heat the margarine in a large casserole. Add onions and sauté until soft. Add zucchini, tomatoes, salt, and pepper. Mix gently.

Cover and simmer slowly for 10 minutes. Add apples and basil. Simmer, covered, for 5 minutes more. Uncover and cook approximately 5 minutes longer or until zucchini is tender and some of the liquid has evaporated.

Garnish with parsley before serving.

*Yield:* 6 servings

*Change Zucchini with Apples as follows or use Basic Recipe, if indicated, for:*

LOW-CALORIE, DIABETIC, LOW-FAT, AND LOW-CHOLESTEROL DIETS

Omit margarine.
Instead of sautéing the onions, place them in casserole with all other vegetables and spices.
Proceed as in Basic Recipe.

Calories per serving: 37
Approximate nutrient
  values per serving:
    Protein 2 g
    Fat 0 g
    Carbohydrate 8 g
    Sodium 187 mg
    Potassium 264 mg
    Cholesterol 0 mg
Exchanges:
  Vegetable 1½

LOW-SODIUM DIETS

Omit salt.
Substitute unsalted polyunsaturated margarine for margarine.
  Add ½ teaspoon thyme with basil.
Proceed as in Basic Recipe.

Calories per serving: 62
Approximate nutrient
  values same as Basic
  Recipe except for:
    Sodium 4 mg
    Potassium 265 mg

RENAL DIETS

Omit salt.
Substitute unsalted polyunsaturated margarine for margarine.
Reduce tomatoes to ¾ cup.
Add ½ teaspoon thyme with basil.
Proceed as in Basic Recipe.

Calories per serving: 60
Approximate nutrient
  values per serving:
    Protein 1 g
    Fat 3 g
    Carbohydrate 8 g
    Calcium 35 mg
    Phosphorus 35 mg
    Sodium 4 mg
    Potassium 240 mg
    Cholesterol 0 mg

BLAND DIETS

Omit pepper. Proceed as in Basic Recipe.

Calories per serving: 62

Use Basic Recipe.

# Ratatouille with Sprouts

BASIC RECIPE

Serving size: ½ cup
Calories per serving: 79
Approximate nutrient
 values per serving:
  Protein 2 g
  Fat 5 g
  Carbohydrate 8 g
  Sodium 292 mg
  Potassium 360 mg
  Cholesterol 0 mg
Exchanges:
 Vegetable 1½
 Fat 1

¼ cup polyunsaturated oil
1 cup sliced onions
1 cup thinly sliced celery
½ cup diced seeded green pepper
1 clove garlic, put through garlic press
1 pound eggplant, peeled and cubed
1 pound zucchini, cut into ¼-inch slices
3 cups coarsely chopped peeled and seeded tomatoes
1½ teaspoons salt
¼ teaspoon freshly ground pepper
1 teaspoon basil
1 teaspoon thyme
2 cups fresh bean sprouts

Heat the oil in a large, heavy skillet. Add the onions, celery, green pepper, and garlic. Sauté until onions are soft. Add the eggplant, zucchini, tomatoes, salt, pepper, basil, and thyme. Stir gently to blend.

Simmer the ratatouille, covered, over low heat for 45 minutes, stirring occasionally. Uncover and simmer until most of the liquid has evaporated. Stir in the bean sprouts. Serve hot or cold.

*Yield:* 12 servings

*Change Ratatouille with Sprouts as follows or use Basic Recipe, if indicated, for:*

## LOW-SODIUM DIETS

Omit salt.
Proceed as in Basic Recipe.

Calories per serving: 79
Approximate nutrient
  values same as Basic
  Recipe except for:
    Sodium 18 mg

## BLAND DIETS

Omit ground pepper.
Proceed as in Basic Recipe.

Calories per serving: 79

## HIGH-FIBER DIETS

Use Basic Recipe.

## RATATOUILLE WITH SPROUTS FOR LOW-CALORIE, DIABETIC, LOW-FAT, AND LOW-CHOLESTEROL DIETS

1 cup sliced onions
1 cup thinly sliced celery
½ cup diced seeded green pepper
1 clove garlic, put through garlic press
½ cup Chicken Stock (page 114)
1 pound eggplant, peeled and cubed
1 pound zucchini, cut into ¼-inch slices
3 cups coarsely chopped peeled and seeded tomatoes
1½ teaspoons salt
¼ teaspoon freshly ground pepper
1 teaspoon basil
1 teaspoon thyme
2 cups fresh bean sprouts

Serving size: ½ cup
Calories per serving: 39
Approximate nutrient
  values per serving:
    Protein 2 g
    Fat 0 g
    Carbohydrate 8 g
    Sodium 296 mg
    Potassium 367 mg
    Cholesterol 0 mg
Exchanges:
  Vegetable 1½

Simmer the onions, celery, green pepper, and garlic in chicken stock for 10 minutes in a medium saucepan, covered. Add

436

remaining ingredients except the bean sprouts and simmer, covered, over low heat for 45 minutes, stirring occasionally. Uncover and simmer until most of the liquid has evaporated. Stir in bean sprouts. Serve hot or cold.

*Yield:* 12 servings

# Eggplant Soufflé

BASIC RECIPE

*The Sauce*
3 tablespoons olive oil
½ cup chopped celery
½ cup chopped onions
2 cloves garlic, put through garlic press
28-ounce can Italian plum tomatoes, undrained
½ teaspoon salt
⅛ teaspoon freshly ground pepper
½ teaspoon basil
¼ teaspoon oregano
½ cup heavy cream

*The Soufflé*
2 teaspoons polyunsaturated margarine for soufflé dish
2 eggplants (1 pound each), peeled and cubed
½ cup chopped onions
2 tablespoons polyunsaturated margarine for sautéing
½ teaspoon salt
½ teaspoon thyme
⅛ teaspoon freshly ground pepper
7½-ounce can minced clams, drained
½ cup fresh bread crumbs (page 38)
3 large eggs, separated, at room temperature

Prepare the sauce first, to the point where you start the simmering process. While it simmers prepare the soufflé and place in oven to bake.

Serving size: ⅔ cup soufflé, ¼ cup sauce
Calories per serving: 231
Approximate nutrient values per serving:
    Protein 9 g
    Fat 16 g
    Carbohydrate 14 g
    Sodium 508 mg
    Potassium 525 mg
    Cholesterol 162 mg
Exchanges:
    Vegetable 2
    Bread ½
    Meat 1
    Fat 2½

*To prepare the sauce:* In a large saucepan, heat the oil, then add celery, onions, and garlic. Sauté until onions are soft. Add tomatoes, salt, and pepper. Simmer, uncovered, approximately 40 minutes or until sauce is thickened and reduced by half. Stir occasionally. Add basil and oregano. Simmer 10 minutes longer.

Remove sauce from heat and allow to cool. Put into an electric blender and purée until smooth. If the soufflé is not quite ready, cover sauce and refrigerate it.

*To prepare the soufflé:* Grease a 1½-quart soufflé dish with 2 teaspoons margarine.

Put cubed eggplant in a large saucepan. Add just enough water to cover and bring to a boil. Reduce heat, cover, and boil gently 10 to 15 minutes or until tender. Drain thoroughly, spoon into a large bowl, and mash. Set aside.

In a small skillet, sauté onions in 2 tablespoons margarine until soft. Add to eggplant and then add salt, thyme, pepper, clams, bread crumbs, and egg yolks. Mix thoroughly.

Preheat oven to 375°F.

In a separate bowl, beat egg whites until soft peaks form. Fold into eggplant mixture and turn into prepared soufflé dish.

Set dish in a shallow pan of hot water and bake approximately 45 minutes or until lightly browned on top or when knife inserted in center comes out clean.

About 5 minutes before soufflé is ready, remove sauce from refrigerator, return to saucepan, and bring to a simmer. Add cream and cook for 1 minute longer. Place sauce in serving bowl and serve with the soufflé. You will need about half the sauce for the soufflé. The remainder may be frozen.

*Yield:* 6 servings soufflé, 3 cups sauce

*Change Eggplant Soufflé as follows or use Basic Recipe, if indicated, for:*

LOW-CALORIE, DIABETIC, LOW-FAT, AND LOW-CHOLESTEROL DIETS

*The sauce:* Reduce oil to 2 tablespoons. Substitute ½ cup buttermilk for cream.
    Proceed as in Basic Recipe.

*The soufflé:* Spray soufflé dish with vegetable cooking spray.
    Reduce margarine for sautéing to 1½ tablespoons.
    Increase bread crumbs to ¾ cup.
    Omit egg yolks.
    Proceed as in Basic Recipe.

Calories per serving: 146
Approximate nutrient
  values per serving:
    Protein 8 g
    Fat 6 g
    Carbohydrate 16 g
    Sodium 493 mg
    Potassium 524 mg
    Cholesterol 11 mg
Exchanges:
  Vegetable 2
  Bread ½
  Meat 1
  Fat 1

LOW-SODIUM DIETS

*The sauce:* Omit salt.
    Substitute 28-ounce can tomatoes packed with no salt added for Italian plum tomatoes.
    Proceed as in Basic Recipe.

*The soufflé:* Omit salt. Omit clams and substitute 6½-ounce can water-packed chunk white tuna with no salt added.
    Substitute unsalted polyunsaturated margarine for margarine wherever used.
    Proceed as in Basic Recipe.

Calories per serving: 247
Approximate nutrient
  values per serving:
    Protein 15 g
    Fat 16 g
    Carbohydrate 12 g
    Sodium 106 mg
    Potassium 447 mg
    Cholesterol 177 mg

BLAND DIETS

*The sauce and the soufflé:* Omit pepper.
    Proceed as in Basic Recipe.

Calories per serving: 231

Calories per serving: 232

*The sauce:* Add ½ teaspoon fennel seed with basil and oregano. Proceed as in Basic Recipe.

*The soufflé:* Use Basic Recipe.

## EGGPLANT SOUFFLÉ FOR RENAL DIETS

Serving size: ⅔ cup soufflé, ¼ cup sauce
Calories per serving: 381
Approximate nutrient values per serving:
    Protein 17 g
    Fat 29 g
    Carbohydrate 16 g
    Calcium 191 mg
    Phosphorus 239 mg
    Sodium 119 mg
    Potassium 440 mg
    Cholesterol 206 mg
Exchanges:
    Vegetable 2
    Bread ½
    Meat 2
    Fat 4

*The Soufflé*
2 teaspoons unsalted polyunsaturated margarine for the soufflé dish
2 eggplants (1 pound each), peeled and cubed
½ cup chopped onions
2 tablespoons unsalted polyunsaturated margarine for sautéing
½ teaspoon thyme
⅛ teaspoon freshly ground pepper
6½-ounce can chunk white tuna, without added salt
½ cup fresh bread crumbs (page 38)
3 large eggs, separated, at room temperature

*The Sauce*
3 tablespoons unsalted polyunsaturated margarine
3 tablespoons flour
¾ cup milk
¾ cup heavy cream
½ cup grated Swiss cheese
⅛ teaspoon cayenne pepper

*To prepare the soufflé:* Grease a 1½-quart soufflé dish with 2 teaspoons margarine. Peel eggplants, cut into cubes, and place in a large saucepan. Add just enough water to cover; bring to a boil, reduce heat, and boil gently, covered, 10 to 15 minutes or until tender. Drain thoroughly, spoon into a large bowl, and mash until there are no large pieces.

Preheat oven to 375°F.

In a small skillet, sauté onions in margarine until soft. Combine with eggplant. Add thyme, pepper, tuna, bread crumbs, and egg yolks; mix thoroughly.

In a separate bowl, beat egg whites until soft peaks form and fold into eggplant mixture. Turn into soufflé dish, set dish in a shallow pan of hot water, and bake 45 minutes or until a knife inserted in the center comes out clean.

*To prepare the sauce:* About 10 minutes before end of soufflé cooking time, make the sauce. In a medium saucepan, melt the margarine over low heat. Blend in flour. Gradually add milk and cream, stirring. Cook, stirring constantly, until sauce comes to a boil and thickens. Boil, stirring constantly, 1 minute. Remove from heat and blend in the Swiss cheese and pepper. If need be, keep sauce warm in the top of a double boiler over hot water.

*Yield:* 6 servings

# Cauliflower Mousse

BASIC RECIPE

Serving size: 1 cup
Calories per serving: 364
Approximate nutrient
   values per serving:
    Protein 14 g
    Fat 22 g
    Carbohydrate 28 g
    Sodium 800 mg
    Potassium 523 mg
    Cholesterol 285 mg
Exchanges:
   Milk ⅛
   Vegetable 1
   Bread 1
   Meat 1
   Fat 4

*The Cauliflower*
4 cups cauliflower flowerets
¾ cup fresh bread crumbs (page 38)
2 tablespoons polyunsaturated margarine

*The Sauce*
2½ tablespoons polyunsaturated margarine
2½ tablespoons flour
1⅓ cups milk, heated
¾ teaspoon salt
⅛ teaspoon freshly ground pepper
½ teaspoon ground ginger
4 large eggs, at room temperature

*To prepare the cauliflower:* Bring approximately 1 inch water to boil in a medium saucepan. Add cauliflower. Cover, reduce heat, and steam for 15 minutes or until cauliflower is tender; drain. Purée in blender and set aside.

Preheat oven to 350°F.

In a small skillet, sauté bread crumbs in 2 tablespoons margarine until lightly browned. Set aside.

*To prepare the sauce:* In a large saucepan, melt 2½ tablespoons margarine. Blend in flour. Add milk all at once, stirring vigorously; then add salt, pepper, and ginger and cook over moderate heat, stirring constantly, until sauce is thickened and smooth. Stir and cook for 1 minute. Remove from heat and set aside.

In a medium bowl, beat eggs lightly. Add about 3 tablespoons of the hot sauce to eggs and stir well. Then add egg mixture to sauce and stir gently until thoroughly mixed.

*To assemble the mousse:* Combine puréed cauliflower with sauce. Turn into an ungreased 1½-quart soufflé or baking dish. Top with reserved crumbs.

Place dish in a shallow pan of hot water and bake 50 minutes or until sharp knife inserted in center comes out clean. Place baking dish on a rack and let stand about 5 minutes before serving.

*Yield:* 4 servings

*Change Cauliflower Mousse as follows or use Basic Recipe, if indicated, for:*

LOW-CALORIE, DIABETIC, LOW-FAT, AND LOW-CHOLESTEROL DIETS

*The cauliflower:* Omit bread crumbs and margarine for sautéing them.

Then prepare cauliflower as in Basic Recipe.

*The sauce:* Substitute skim milk for milk.

Omit eggs. Substitute Low-Cholesterol Egg Substitute (page 189) equivalent to 4 large eggs.

Proceed as in Basic Recipe.

Assemble, bake, and cool the soufflé as in Basic Recipe. Just before serving, garnish with 2 tablespoons chopped fresh parsley.

Calories per serving: 186
Approximate nutrient
  values per serving:
    Protein 14 g
    Fat 8 g
    Carbohydrate 16 g
    Sodium 663 mg
    Potassium 617 mg
    Cholesterol 2 mg
Exchanges:
  Milk ⅓
  Vegetable 1
  Bread ½
  Meat 1
  Fat 1

*The cauliflower:* Use Basic Recipe.

*The sauce:* Omit salt.
    Substitute unsalted polyunsaturated margarine for margarine.
    Proceed as in Basic Recipe.

Calories per serving: 364
Approximate nutrient
    values same as Basic
    Recipe except for:
        Sodium 260 mg

BLAND DIETS

Omit pepper.
Proceed as in Basic Recipe.

Calories per serving: 364

HIGH-FIBER DIETS

Use Basic Recipe and garnish each serving with 2 tablespoons grated raw carrot.

Calories per serving: 370

# Cabbage and Mushrooms

BASIC RECIPE

Serving size: ¾ cup
Calories per serving: 84
Approximate nutrient
    values per serving:
        Protein 3 g
        Fat 4 g
        Carbohydrate 11 g
        Sodium 262 mg
        Potassium 515 mg
        Cholesterol 0 mg
Exchanges:
    Vegetable 2
    Fat 1

2½ pounds green cabbage
2 tablespoons polyunsaturated margarine
1 cup sliced fresh mushrooms
⅓ cup finely chopped fresh parsley
½ teaspoon salt
¼ teaspoon freshly ground pepper

Wash and quarter the cabbage. Cut away the core on each quarter. Finely shred the cabbage.
    Place cabbage in a large pot. Add boiling water to cover. Boil for 3 minutes. Pour into a colander and run under cold water. Drain well and set aside.

Heat margarine in a large skillet. Add mushrooms and sauté until light golden brown. Then add cabbage, parsley, salt, and pepper; toss over high heat until the cabbage is hot, but be careful not to brown it. Serve immediately.

*Yield:* 6 servings

*Change Cabbage and Mushrooms as follows for:*

LOW-CALORIE, DIABETIC, LOW-FAT, AND LOW-CHOLESTEROL DIETS

Prepare cabbage as in Basic Recipe.
Spray skillet thoroughly with vegetable cooking spray. Reduce margarine for sautéing to 1 tablespoon and add to skillet. Place on heat, add mushrooms, and sauté until light golden brown. Add cabbage and seasonings and proceed as in Basic Recipe.

LOW-SODIUM DIETS

Omit salt.
Substitute unsalted polyunsaturated margarine for margarine.
Proceed as in Basic Recipe.
Just before serving, stir in 2 tablespoons red wine vinegar.

BLAND DIETS

Omit pepper.
Proceed as in Basic Recipe.

HIGH-FIBER DIETS

Boil cabbage for 1 minute only,
Proceed as in Basic Recipe.

Calories per serving: 67
Approximate nutrient
 values per serving:
  Protein 3 g
  Fat 2 g
  Carbohydrate 11 g
  Sodium 243 mg
  Potassium 514 mg
  Cholesterol 0 mg
Exchanges:
 Vegetable 2
 Fat ½

Calories per serving: 84
Approximate nutrient
 values same as Basic
 Recipe except for:
  Sodium 41 mg
  Potassium 516 mg

Calories per serving: 84

Calories per serving: 84

# Red Cabbage Austrian Style

BASIC RECIPE

Serving size: ½ cup
Calories per serving: 55
Approximate nutrient
    values per serving:
        Protein 2 g
        Fat 3 g
        Carbohydrate 8 g
        Sodium 114 mg
        Potassium 251 mg
        Cholesterol 0 mg
Exchanges:
    Vegetable 1½
    Fat ½

2 pounds red cabbage
2 tablespoons red wine vinegar
½ teaspoon salt
¼ teaspoon freshly ground pepper
2 tablespoons polyunsaturated oil
½ cup thinly sliced onions
1 cup thinly sliced green pepper, in lengthwise strips
1 cup diced peeled tart apples

Wash, core, and shred cabbage. Mix cabbage, vinegar, salt, and pepper in a bowl and toss. Let stand 1 hour, tossing occasionally.

Heat oil in a large skillet. Add onions and green pepper. Sauté over moderate heat for 3 minutes. Then add cabbage, apples, and any liquid in the bowl. Stir over medium heat for 10 minutes, until the cabbage is cooked through.

*Yield:* 12 servings

*Change Red Cabbage Austrian Style as follows for:*

LOW-CALORIE, DIABETIC, LOW-FAT, AND LOW-CHOLESTEROL DIETS

Calories per serving: 45
Approximate nutrient
    values per serving:
        Protein 2 g
        Fat 1 g
        Carbohydrate 8 g
        Sodium 114 mg
        Potassium 251 mg
        Cholesterol 0 mg
Exchanges:
    Vegetable 1½

Reduce oil to 1 tablespoon.
Proceed as in Basic Recipe.

445

Calories per serving: 55
Approximate nutrient
  values same as Basic
  Recipe except for:
    Sodium 22 mg

Omit salt.
Proceed as in Basic Recipe.

BLAND DIETS

Calories per serving: 55

Omit ground pepper.
Proceed as in Basic Recipe.

HIGH-FIBER DIETS

Calories per serving: 55

Do not peel apples.
Proceed as in Basic Recipe.

# Sweet-and-Sour Cabbage

BASIC RECIPE

Serving size: ½ cup
Calories per serving: 115
Approximate nutrient
  values per serving:
    Protein 1 g
    Fat 6 g
    Carbohydrate 16 g
    Sodium 279 mg
    Potassium 215 mg
    Cholesterol 0 mg
Exchanges:
  Vegetable 1
  Fruit ½
  Bread ½
  Fat 1

1 cup chopped onions
4 tablespoons polyunsaturated margarine
5 cups finely shredded red cabbage
2 cups diced peeled apples
½ cup water
¼ cup dark-brown sugar
¾ teaspoon salt
¼ teaspoon freshly ground pepper
¼ cup cider vinegar

In a large skillet, sauté onions in margarine until soft. Add cabbage, apples, and water. Mix gently, cover tightly, and cook over low heat 5 to 10 minutes or until apples and cabbage are tender.

Add remaining ingredients; mix gently to blend.

*Yield:* 8 servings

*Change Sweet-and-Sour Cabbage as follows for:*

### LOW-CALORIE, DIABETIC, LOW-FAT, AND LOW-CHOLESTEROL DIETS

Reduce margarine to 2 tablespoons.
Omit water. Substitute ½ cup unsweetened apple juice.
Omit sugar.
Proceed as in Basic Recipe.

Calories per serving: 71
Approximate nutrient
  values per serving:
    Protein 1 g
    Fat 3 g
    Carbohydrate 11 g
    Sodium 248 mg
    Potassium 206 mg
    Cholesterol 0 mg
Exchanges:
  Vegetable 1
  Fruit ½
  Fat ½

### LOW-SODIUM DIETS

Omit salt.
Substitute unsalted polyunsaturated margarine for margarine.
Proceed as in Basic Recipe.

Calories per serving: 115
Approximate nutrient
  values same as Basic
  Recipe except for:
    Sodium 16 mg

### BLAND DIETS

Omit pepper.
Proceed as in Basic Recipe.

Calories per serving: 115

### HIGH-FIBER DIETS

Use unpeeled apples and proceed as in Basic Recipe.

Calories per serving: 115

# Harvard Beets

BASIC RECIPE

Serving size: ½ cup
Calories per serving: 96
Approximate nutrient
   values per serving:
     Protein 1 g
     Fat 4 g
     Carbohydrate 16 g
     Sodium 119 mg
     Potassium 189 mg
     Cholesterol 0 mg
Exchanges:
   Vegetable 1
   Bread ½
   Fat 1

3 cups fresh beets (1½ pounds)
¼ cup sugar
2 teaspoons cornstarch
⅛ teaspoon salt
¼ cup cider vinegar
¼ cup water for the roux
⅛ teaspoon ground cloves
2 tablespoons polyunsaturated margarine

To cook beets, wash them first; then place them in a medium saucepan, barely cover with water, and simmer them 30 to 45 minutes, until tender. Drain, cool slightly, then slip off the skins. Set aside to cool. Slice. (If you do this in advance, bring beets to room temperature before slicing them.)

Prepare a roux: in a medium saucepan, combine sugar, cornstarch, and salt. Stir in vinegar and water. Cook over low heat, stirring constantly, until thickened and smooth. Blend in cloves and margarine.

Add sliced beets and simmer, covered, 5 minutes. Baste occasionally with sauce.

*Yield:* 6 servings

*Change Harvard Beets as follows for:*

## LOW-CALORIE, DIABETIC, LOW-FAT, AND LOW-CHOLESTEROL DIETS

Calories per serving: 54
Approximate nutrient
  values per serving:
    Protein 1 g
    Fat 2 g
    Carbohydrate 9 g
    Sodium 100 mg
    Potassium 198 mg
    Cholesterol 0 mg
Exchanges:
  Vegetable 2
  Fat ½

Omit sugar.
Omit water for the roux. Substitute ¼ cup unsweetened apple cider.
Reduce margarine to 1 tablespoon.
Proceed as in Basic Recipe.

## LOW-SODIUM DIETS

Calories per serving: 96
Approximate nutrient
  values same as Basic
  Recipe except for:
    Sodium 37 mg

Omit salt.
Substitute unsalted polyunsaturated margarine for margarine.
Proceed as in Basic Recipe.

## RENAL DIETS

Calories per serving: 100
Approximate nutrient
  values per serving:
    Protein 1 g
    Fat 4 g
    Carbohydrate 17 g
    Calcium 17 mg
    Phosphorus 16 mg
    Sodium 39 mg
    Potassium 154 mg
    Cholesterol 0 mg

Substitute 3 cups low-sodium canned small whole beets for beets.
Omit salt. Substitute unsalted polyunsaturated margarine for margarine.
Proceed as in Basic Recipe.

## BLAND DIETS

Calories per serving: 96

Omit ground cloves.
Proceed as in Basic Recipe.

Calories per serving: 97

Add ½ teaspoon caraway seeds with cloves and margarine. Proceed as in Basic Recipe.

# Fresh Fried Corn

BASIC RECIPE

Serving size: ½ cup
Calories per serving: 101
Approximate nutrient
  values per serving:
    Protein 3 g
    Fat 5 g
    Carbohydrate 15 g
    Sodium 134 mg
    Potassium 341 mg
    Cholesterol 0 mg
Exchanges:
  Bread 1
  Fat 1

4 ears fresh corn
2 tablespoons polyunsaturated margarine
2 cups chopped peeled tomatoes
½ tablespoon basil
⅓ cup chopped fresh parsley
¼ teaspoon salt
½ teaspoon freshly ground pepper

Cut the kernels from the corn.
  Melt margarine in a large skillet. Sauté corn on medium heat for 3 minutes. Add tomatoes, basil, and parsley. Cook for 3 minutes, stirring often. Season with salt and pepper. Cook an additional minute. Serve immediately.

*Yield:* 6 servings

*Change Fresh Fried Corn as follows or use Basic Recipe, if indicated, for:*

LOW-CALORIE, DIABETIC, LOW-FAT, LOW-CHOLESTEROL, AND HIGH-FIBER DIETS

Use Basic Recipe.

## LOW-SODIUM DIETS

Omit salt. Substitute unsalted polyunsaturated margarine for
    margarine.
Proceed as in Basic Recipe.
Add ¼ teaspoon Tabasco with the pepper before the final min-
    ute of cooking.

Calories per serving: 101
Approximate nutrient
    values same as Basic
    Recipe except for:
    Sodium 5 mg

## BLAND DIETS

Omit pepper.
Proceed as in Basic Recipe.

Calories per serving: 101

# Baked Kidney Beans

## BASIC RECIPE

This recipe requires overnight preparation.

1 pound dried red kidney beans
2 quarts water
¼ pound sliced bacon
1 cup coarsely chopped red onions
2 cloves garlic, put through garlic press
2 cups coarsely chopped peeled tomatoes
1½ teaspoons salt
1 teaspoon sugar
½ teaspoon thyme
½ teaspoon sage
¼ teaspoon freshly ground pepper
1 bay leaf
2 tablespoons wine vinegar

Serving size: ¾ cup
Calories per serving: 137
Approximate nutrient
    values per serving:
    Protein 6 g
    Fat 7 g
    Carbohydrate 15 g
    Sodium 372 mg
    Potassium 315 mg
    Cholesterol 10 mg
Exchanges:
    Bread 1
    Fat 1½

Rinse beans thoroughly under cool running water. Put into
large saucepan, cover with 2 quarts cold water, and soak
overnight.

The next day, bring beans to boil in the soaking water.

Reduce heat and simmer, covered, 1½ hours or until tender. Skim foam as it rises. Drain beans and reserve 1 cup cooking liquid.

Preheat oven to 350°F.

In a large skillet, cook bacon until crisp. Drain on a paper towel.

Add onions and garlic to skillet and sauté in bacon drippings until onions start to brown.

In a large bowl, combine tomatoes, salt, sugar, thyme, sage, pepper, bay leaf, and vinegar. Add reserved cooking liquid, onions, and garlic. Mix thoroughly.

Pour tomato mixture over beans and mix well.

Spoon into 2½-quart baking dish. Crumble bacon on top. Bake, covered, for 40 minutes.

*Yield:* 10 servings

*Change Baked Kidney Beans as follows or use Basic Recipe, if indicated, for:*

LOW-CALORIE, DIABETIC, LOW-FAT, AND LOW-CHOLESTEROL DIETS

Calories per serving: 95
Approximate nutrient
values per serving:
   Protein 6 g
   Fat 2 g
   Carbohydrate 14 g
   Sodium 372 mg
   Potassium 315 mg
   Cholesterol 10 mg
Exchanges:
   Bread 1
   Fat ½

Omit sugar.
Drain bacon thoroughly. Discard pan drippings.
Add uncooked onions and garlic directly to tomato mixture.
Proceed as in Basic Recipe.

Calories per serving: 110
Approximate nutrient
   values per serving:
      Protein 4 g
      Fat 4 g
      Carbohydrate 14 g
      Sodium 5 mg
      Potassium 306 mg
      Cholesterol 0 mg

Omit bacon.
Omit salt.
Substitute 3 tablespoons polyunsaturated oil for bacon
   drippings.
Proceed as in Basic Recipe.

## BLAND DIETS

Calories per serving: 137

Omit pepper.
Proceed as in Basic Recipe.

## HIGH-FIBER DIETS

Use Basic Recipe.

# Parsnips Parma

## BASIC RECIPE

Serving size: ½ cup
Calories per serving: 94
Approximate nutrient
   values per serving:
      Protein 2 g
      Fat 4 g
      Carbohydrate 13 g
      Sodium 65 mg
      Potassium 288 mg
      Cholesterol 0 mg
Exchanges:
   Vegetable 2
   Fat 1

1 pound parsnips, washed and scraped
2½ cups Chicken Stock (page 114)
2 tablespoons polyunsaturated margarine
½ cup fresh bread crumbs (page 38)
⅛ teaspoon oregano
⅛ teaspoon basil
⅛ teaspoon rosemary

Trim ends of parsnips and slice into rounds approximately ¼
inch thick. Place parsnips in a medium saucepan. Add chicken
stock just to cover. Bring to a boil, reduce heat, and simmer,
covered, 20 minutes or until parsnips are tender. Drain.

Preheat broiler.

Arrange parsnips in a shallow baking dish and dot with margarine. Combine bread crumbs with seasonings and sprinkle mixture over parsnips. Place under broiler until crumbs are golden brown.

*Yield:* 6 servings

*Change Parnsips Parma as follows or use Basic Recipe, if indicated, for:*

LOW-CALORIE, DIABETIC, LOW-FAT, LOW-CHOLESTEROL, AND BLAND DIETS

Use Basic Recipe.

LOW-SODIUM DIETS

Calories per serving: 94
Approximate nutrient
values same as Basic
Recipe except for:
Sodium 27 mg

Substitute unsalted polyunsaturated margarine for margarine. Proceed as in Basic Recipe.

HIGH-FIBER DIETS

Calories per serving: 130

Add ⅛ cup coarsely chopped walnuts to bread crumb and herb topping.
Proceed as in Basic Recipe.

# Parslied Potatoes with Sesame Seeds

BASIC RECIPE

Serving size: ½ cup
Calories per serving: 164
Approximate nutrient
 values per serving:
   Protein 3 g
   Fat 12 g
   Carbohydrate 14 g
   Sodium 381 mg
   Potassium 289 mg
   Cholesterol 0 mg
Exchanges:
 Bread 1
 Fat 2

3 cups diced peeled potatoes
½ teaspoon salt for boiling potatoes
3 cups water
⅓ cup polyunsaturated margarine
⅔ cup chopped onions
⅓ cup chopped fresh parsley
¼ teaspoon salt
⅛ teaspoon freshly ground pepper
2 tablespoons toasted sesame seeds (page 38)

In a medium saucepan cook potatoes in 3 cups boiling salted water for about 8 minutes or until potatoes are just tender. Drain.

In a large skillet, heat the margarine. Add onions and cooked potatoes and sauté until vegetables start to brown. Add parsley, ¼ teaspoon salt, pepper, and sesame seeds. Mix gently and thoroughly to blend.

*Yield:* 6 servings

*Change Parslied Potatoes with Sesame Seeds as follows or use Basic Recipe, if indicated, for:*

LOW-CALORIE, DIABETIC, LOW-FAT, AND LOW-CHOLESTEROL DIETS

Spray large skillet with vegetable cooking spray.
Reduce margarine to 2 tablespoons.
Proceed as in Basic Recipe.

Calories per serving: 108
Approximate nutrient
values per serving:
Protein 3 g
Fat 5 g
Carbohydrate 14 g
Sodium 319 mg
Potassium 287 mg
Cholesterol 0 mg
Exchanges:
Bread 1
Fat 1

LOW-SODIUM AND RENAL DIETS

Omit salt.
Substitute unsalted polyunsaturated margarine for margarine.
Add ½ teaspoon dried dillweed with seasonings.
Proceed as in Basic Recipe.

Calories per serving: 164
Approximate nutrient
values per serving:
Protein 3 g
Fat 12 g
Carbohydrate 14 g
Calcium 22 mg
Phosphorus 63 mg
Sodium 6 mg
Potassium 292 mg
Cholesterol 0 mg

BLAND DIETS

Omit pepper.
Proceed as in Basic Recipe.

Calories per serving: 164

HIGH-FIBER DIETS

Use Basic Recipe.

# Delmonico Potatoes

BASIC RECIPE

Serving size: ½ cup
Calories per serving: 218
Approximate nutrient
  values per serving:
    Protein 8 g
    Fat 13 g
    Carbohydrate 19 g
    Sodium 591 mg
    Potassium 371 mg
    Cholesterol 23 mg
Exchanges:
  Milk ¼
  Bread 1
  Meat ½
  Fat 2

4 cups diced peeled potatoes
1½ teaspoons salt
⅔ cup chopped onions
¼ cup polyunsaturated margarine
¼ cup flour
2 cups milk
¼ cup chopped fresh parsley
½ teaspoon dillweed
⅛ teaspoon freshly ground pepper
1 cup grated sharp Cheddar cheese

Place potatoes in a large saucepan. Add water to cover and 1 teaspoon of the salt. Cover and bring to a boil; reduce heat and boil gently 10 minutes or until tender. Drain and set aside.

Preheat oven to 400°F.

In a medium saucepan, sauté onions in margarine until soft. Blend in flour. Gradually add milk; cook over moderate heat, stirring constantly, until sauce comes to a boil.

Remove from heat and stir in the remaining ½ teaspoon salt, parsley, dillweed, and pepper. Gently mix in the cheese and finally the potatoes.

Turn into a 2-quart baking dish. Bake, uncovered, 25 minutes or until top is golden.

*Yield:* 8 servings

*Change Delmonico Potatoes as follows or use Basic Recipe, if indicated, for:*

## LOW-CALORIE, DIABETIC, LOW-FAT, AND LOW-CHOLESTEROL DIETS

Calories per serving: 154
Approximate nutrient
  values per serving:
    Protein 8 g
    Fat 5 g
    Carbohydrate 19 g
    Sodium 542 mg
    Potassium 378 mg
    Cholesterol 9 mg
Exchanges:
  Milk ¼
  Bread 1
  Meat ½
  Fat 1

Reduce margarine to 2 tablespoons.
Substitute skim milk for milk.
Substitute grated part-skim mozzarella cheese for Cheddar.
Proceed as in Basic Recipe.

## LOW-SODIUM DIETS

Calories per serving: 215
Approximate nutrient
  values per serving:
    Protein 8 g
    Fat 13 g
    Carbohydrate 19 g
    Sodium 37 mg
    Potassium 377 mg
    Cholesterol 14 mg

Omit salt.
Substitute unsalted polyunsaturated margarine for margarine.
Substitute grated low-sodium Cheddar cheese for Cheddar.
Proceed as in Basic Recipe.

## BLAND DIETS

Calories per serving: 218

Omit pepper.
Proceed as in Basic Recipe.

## HIGH-FIBER DIETS

Use Basic Recipe.

# Sweet Potatoes with Orange

BASIC RECIPE

6 medium sweet potatoes (2 pounds)
⅓ cup polyunsaturated margarine
½ cup firmly packed dark-brown sugar
⅓ cup orange juice
1 teaspoon grated orange rind

Boil potatoes in water to cover and cook 25 to 30 minutes or until tender. Drain thoroughly. When cool enough to handle, peel potatoes and cut lengthwise into quarters.

In a large skillet, melt the margarine. Stir in sugar, orange juice, and orange rind and bring to a boil. Reduce heat so liquid bubbles gently.

Add potatoes and simmer, turning carefully and basting with syrup, until well glazed.

*Yield:* 6 servings

*Change Sweet Potatoes with Orange as follows or use Basic Recipe, if indicated, for:*

LOW-SODIUM DIETS

Substitute unsalted polyunsaturated margarine for margarine. Proceed as in Basic Recipe.

BLAND DIETS

Use Basic Recipe.

HIGH-FIBER DIETS

Use Basic Recipe. Add ⅓ cup chopped pecans and sprinkle on top of potatoes just before serving.

## SWEET POTATOES WITH ORANGE FOR LOW-CALORIE, DIABETIC, LOW-FAT, AND LOW-CHOLESTEROL DIETS

Serving size: ½ cup
Calories per serving: 169
Approximate nutrient
  values per serving:
    Protein 2 g
    Fat 5 g
    Carbohydrate 30 g
    Sodium 191 mg
    Potassium 285 mg
    Cholesterol 0 mg
Exchanges:
  Bread 2
  Fat 1

6 medium sweet potatoes (2 pounds)
3 tablespoons polyunsaturated margarine
½ teaspoon salt
1 teaspoon grated orange rind
2 tablespoons orange juice

Place potatoes in a large saucepan and cover with water. Cover and bring to a boil. Cook potatoes 25 to 30 minutes or until tender. Drain thoroughly.

When cool enough to handle, peel potatoes and mash with remaining ingredients until well blended.

*Yield:* 8 servings

# Sweet Potato Tzimmes

BASIC RECIPE

Serving size: ¾ cup
Calories per serving: 211
Approximate nutrient
  values per serving:
    Protein 2 g
    Fat 6 g
    Carbohydrate 39 g
    Sodium 291 mg
    Potassium 384 mg
    Cholesterol 0 mg
Exchanges:
  Fruit 1
  Bread 2
  Fat 1

1½ pounds sweet potatoes
2½ cups carrots, cut into ¼-inch slices
¾ teaspoon salt
⅛ teaspoon freshly ground pepper
4 tablespoons firmly packed dark-brown sugar
1½ cups sliced peeled apples
1½ teaspoons grated lemon rind
4 tablespoons polyunsaturated margarine, melted
⅔ cup unsweetened apple cider

In a medium saucepan boil sweet potatoes, covered, approximately 25 minutes or until tender. Drain. Allow potatoes to cool; then peel and cut into ¼-inch slices. Set aside.

Cook carrots, covered, in boiling water to cover 10 minutes or until tender. Drain.

Preheat oven to 350°F.

Combine salt, pepper, and brown sugar. Set mixture aside.

Alternate layers of sweet potatoes, carrots, and apples in a shallow 2-quart baking dish. Sprinkle each layer with the salt, pepper, and brown sugar mixture.

Combine lemon rind and melted margarine and sprinkle over top of mixture. Pour cider over all.

Cover and bake 10 minutes. Uncover and bake 10 minutes longer or until apples are tender and top is lightly browned.

*Yield:* 8 servings

*Change Sweet Potato Tzimmes as follows for:*

LOW-CALORIE, DIABETIC, LOW-FAT, AND LOW-CHOLESTEROL DIETS

Omit sugar.
Reduce margarine to 2 tablespoons.
Proceed as in Basic Recipe.

Calories per serving: 160
Approximate nutrient
  values per serving:
    Protein 2 g
    Fat 3 g
    Carbohydrate 32 g
    Sodium 260 mg
    Potassium 359 mg
    Cholesterol 0 mg
Exchanges:
  Fruit 1
  Bread 1½
  Fat ½

LOW-SODIUM DIETS

Omit salt.
Substitute unsalted polyunsaturated margarine for margarine.
Proceed as in Basic Recipe.

Calories per serving: 211
Approximate nutrient
  values same as Basic
  Recipe except for:
    Sodium 28 mg

Calories per serving: 211

Omit pepper.
Proceed as in Basic Recipe.

HIGH-FIBER DIETS

Calories per serving: 211

Use unpeeled sliced apples and proceed as in Basic Recipe.

# SALADS AND SALAD DRESSINGS

Salads may be appetizers or appetite discouragers, if large portions are served as a first course. They may fill an intermission between the entrée and the dessert, or star at a buffet table in a shimmering mold. If the dressing served with them boasts both piquancy in flavor and restraint in caloric content, a salad can be decidedly satisfactory as a luncheon dish or even as the main course, especially if it incorporates meat, fish, shellfish, or poultry. We offer all varieties, and you'll find the selection both delectable and carefully calculated to fit diet and diet combination requirements.

# Swedish Seafood Salad

BASIC RECIPE

Serving size: ¾ cup
Calories per serving: 243
Approximate nutrient
  values per serving:
    Protein 34 g
    Fat 9 g
    Carbohydrate 5 g
    Sodium 576 mg
    Potassium 582 mg
    Cholesterol 103 mg
Exchanges:
  Vegetable 1
  Meat 4
  Fat 1½

4½ cups Fish Stock (page 115)
1½ pounds cod fillets
½ pound raw medium shrimp, shelled and deveined
1 cup finely diced celery
⅓ cup finely sliced scallions, both white and green parts
⅓ cup fresh dillweed
⅓ cup finely chopped fresh parsley
1 teaspoon grated lemon rind
2 tablespoons lemon juice
1 teaspoon salt
½ teaspoon freshly ground pepper
1 cup sour cream

Bring the fish stock to a boil, add the cod, and gently poach for 10 minutes. Remove fish to a bowl and with a fork break into bite-size pieces. Add just enough stock to cover. Allow to cool.

Simmer the shrimp in remaining stock about 3 minutes; scoop out and add to cod fillets.

Mix the remaining ingredients in a large bowl, blending thoroughly to make a sour cream dressing.

Remove cod and shrimp from the cool stock and add to the sour cream dressing. Toss just until mixed, being careful not to crumble the fish. Put salad in a serving dish, cover, and chill for at least 2 hours.

*Yield:* 6 servings

*Change Swedish Seafood Salad as follows or use Basic Recipe, if indicated, for:*

## LOW-CALORIE, DIABETIC, LOW-FAT, AND LOW-CHOLESTEROL DIETS

Calories per serving: 158
Approximate nutrient
  values per serving:
    Protein 29 g
    Fat 2 g
    Carbohydrate 6 g
    Sodium 680 mg
    Potassium 588 mg
    Cholesterol 60 mg
Exchanges:
  Vegetable 1
  Meat 3½

Omit shrimp.
Substitute 6½-ounce can water-packed crabmeat, drained.
Make a yogurt dressing to substitute for sour cream dressing: omit sour cream. Substitute 1 cup plain low-fat yogurt. Mix with remaining ingredients and proceed as in Basic Recipe.

## LOW-SODIUM DIETS

Calories per serving: 244
Approximate nutrient
  values same as Basic
  Recipe except for:
    Sodium 210 mg
    Potassium 585 mg

Omit salt.
Increase lemon juice to 3 tablespoons.
Proceed as in Basic Recipe.

## BLAND DIETS

Calories per serving: 243

Omit pepper.
Proceed as in Basic Recipe.

## HIGH-FIBER DIETS

Use Basic Recipe.

# Lobster Salad

BASIC RECIPE

Serving size: ¾ cup
Calories per serving: 257
Approximate nutrient
  values per serving:
    Protein 18 g
    Fat 19 g
    Carbohydrate 4 g
    Sodium 367 mg
    Potassium 327 mg
    Cholesterol 96 mg
Exchanges:
  Vegetable 1
  Meat 2
  Fat 3½

3 cups cooked lobster in bite-size pieces
⅔ cup thinly sliced celery
2 tablespoons minced green pepper
2 tablespoons chopped fresh parsley
½ cup Homemade Mayonnaise (page 499)
¼ teaspoon salt
⅛ teaspoon freshly ground pepper
2 tablespoons lemon juice
16 leaves escarole or other loose-leaf variety of lettuce
¼ cup thinly sliced scallions, both white and green parts

In a large bowl, combine the lobster, celery, green pepper, and parsley.

In a separate bowl, stir together the mayonnaise, salt, pepper, and lemon juice. Pour dressing over lobster salad and mix gently.

Spoon salad on lettuce leaves; garnish with sliced scallions.

*Yield:* 5 servings

*Change Lobster Salad as follows or use Basic Recipe, if indicated, for:*

### LOW-CALORIE, DIABETIC, LOW-FAT, AND LOW-CHOLESTEROL DIETS

Substitute low-calorie Homemade Mayonnaise (page 500) for Basic Homemade Mayonnaise.
Proceed as in Basic Recipe.

Calories per serving: 128
Approximate nutrient
  values per serving:
    Protein 18 g
    Fat 3 g
    Carbohydrate 6 g
    Sodium 387 mg
    Potassium 358 mg
    Cholesterol 102 mg
Exchanges:
  Vegetable 1
  Meat 2
  Fat ½

### LOW-SODIUM AND RENAL DIETS

Substitute low-sodium Homemade Mayonnaise (page 499) for basic Homemade Mayonnaise. Omit salt in mayonnaise mixture. Add ½ teaspoon curry powder to mayonnaise with pepper and lemon juice.
Proceed as in Basic Recipe.

Calories per serving: 257
Approximate nutrient
  values per serving:
    Protein 18 g
    Fat 19 g
    Carbohydrate 4 g
    Calcium 91 mg
    Phosphorus 197 mg
    Sodium 213 mg
    Potassium 331 mg
    Cholesterol 96 mg

### BLAND DIETS

Substitute bland Homemade Mayonnaise (page 499) for basic Homemade Mayonnaise. Omit ground pepper.
Proceed as in Basic Recipe.

Calories per serving: 257

### HIGH-FIBER DIETS

Use Basic Recipe.

# Mussels Marinière

BASIC RECIPE

Serving size: 6 mussels
Calories per serving: 173
Approximate nutrient
   values per serving:
      Protein 13 g
      Fat 9 g
      Carbohydrate 11 g
      Sodium 263 mg
      Potassium 258 mg
      Cholesterol 51 mg
Exchanges:
   Vegetable 1
   Bread ½
   Meat 2
   Fat 1½

*The Mussels*
24 mussels
2 cups dry white wine
1 onion, sliced
½ bay leaf

*The Marinade*
2 tablespoons polyunsaturated oil
¼ cup lemon juice
1 teaspoon thyme
2 cloves garlic, put through garlic press
¼ teaspoon salt
¼ teaspoon freshly ground pepper

*To prepare the mussels:* Soak the mussels for 30 minutes; scrub them well and discard any in open shells.

Place the wine, onion, and bay leaf in a large saucepan. Bring to a boil and simmer 10 minutes.

Add the mussels, 12 at a time, to the wine mixture and simmer, covered, about 5 minutes or until all the shells open. Scoop from pan with slotted spoon and repeat process for the remaining mussels.

Remove the mussels from shells and set aside.

*To prepare the marinade:* Beat the marinade ingredients until well blended. Place the mussels in the marinade while still warm. Refrigerate for at least 1 hour before serving. To serve, remove mussels from marinade.

*Yield:* 4 servings

*Change Mussels Marinière as follows or use Basic Recipe, if indicated, for:*

## LOW-CALORIE, DIABETIC, LOW-FAT, AND LOW-CHOLESTEROL DIETS

*The mussels:* Use Basic Recipe.

*The marinade:* Reduce the oil to 1 tablespoon.
Proceed as in Basic Recipe.

Calories per serving: 143
Approximate nutrient
    values per serving:
        Protein 13 g
        Fat 5 g
        Carbohydrate 11 g
        Sodium 263 mg
        Potassium 258 mg
        Cholesterol 51 mg
Exchanges:
    Vegetable 1
    Bread ½
    Meat 2
    Fat 1

## LOW-SODIUM AND RENAL DIETS

*The mussels:* Use Basic Recipe.

*The marinade:* Omit salt. Increase pepper to ½ teaspoon.
Proceed as in Basic Recipe.

Calories per serving: 173
Approximate nutrient
    values per serving:
        Protein 14 g
        Fat 9 g
        Carbohydrate 11 g
        Calcium 87 mg
        Phosphorus 180 mg
        Sodium 126 mg
        Potassium 260 mg
        Cholesterol 51 mg

## BLAND DIETS

*The mussels:* Use Basic Recipe.

*The marinade:* Omit pepper.
Proceed as in Basic Recipe.

Calories per serving: 173

Calories per serving: 173

*The mussels:* Use Basic Recipe.

*The marinade:* Add 1 tablespoon chopped fresh parsley to marinade.
    Proceed as in Basic Recipe.
    For extra fiber, serve with pumpernickel bread or whole wheat crackers.

# Mediterranean Fish Salad

BASIC RECIPE

Serving size: ⅔ cup
Calories per serving: 182
Approximate nutrient
  values per serving:
    Protein 19 g
    Fat 10 g
    Carbohydrate 5 g
    Sodium 349 mg
    Potassium 540 mg
    Cholesterol 54 mg
Exchanges:
  Vegetable 1
  Meat 3
  Fat 2

4 cups Fish Stock (page 115)
1½ pounds fresh haddock fillets
¼ cup olive oil
1 tablespoon tomato paste
2 tablespoons fresh lemon juice
½ cup finely chopped fresh parsley
½ teaspoon salt
¼ teaspoon freshly ground pepper
3 medium tomatoes, peeled, thinly sliced
¼ onion, thinly sliced

Heat the fish stock in a large skillet. Add the haddock and gently simmer 10 minutes or until fish flakes. Carefully remove fish from stock to a platter. Allow to cool.
    Mix the olive oil, tomato paste, lemon juice, parsley, salt, and pepper in a bowl until well blended. Add tomatoes and onion.
    Flake the fish into large pieces and add to the tomato mixture. Toss gently and chill at least 2 hours before serving.

*Yield:* 6 servings

*Change Mediterranean Fish Salad as follows or use Basic Recipe, if indicated, for:*

LOW-CALORIE, DIABETIC, LOW-FAT, AND LOW-CHOLESTEROL DIETS

Calories per serving: 125
Approximate nutrient
  values per serving:
    Protein 19 g
    Fat 3 g
    Carbohydrate 5 g
    Sodium 350 mg
    Potassium 565 mg
    Cholesterol 54 mg
Exchanges:
  Vegetable 1
  Meat 3
  Fat ½

Reduce oil to 1 tablespoon.
Increase tomato paste to 2 tablespoons.
Proceed as in Basic Recipe.

LOW-SODIUM DIETS

Calories per serving: 182
Approximate nutrient
  values same as Basic
  Recipe except for:
    Sodium 168 mg
    Potassium 541 mg

Omit salt.
Add ½ teaspoon Tabasco sauce.
Proceed as in Basic Recipe.

BLAND DIETS

Calories per serving: 182

Omit pepper.
Add ⅛ teaspoon allspice.
Proceed as in Basic Recipe.

HIGH-FIBER DIETS

Use Basic Recipe.

# Rice Salad with Tuna

BASIC RECIPE

Serving size: 1 cup
Calories per serving: 318
Approximate nutrient
  values per serving:
    Protein 13 g
    Fat 20 g
    Carbohydrate 22 g
    Sodium 552 mg
    Potassium 266 mg
    Cholesterol 22 mg
Exchanges:
    Bread 1½
    Meat 1½
    Fat 4

2½ cups cold water
1 cup raw long-grain rice
¾ cup Vinaigrette Dressing (page 500)
two 6½-ounce cans chunk tuna packed in water
1 cup thinly sliced celery
1 cup cooked diced carrots
⅓ cup toasted slivered almonds (page 38)
½ cup sliced stuffed olives

In a medium saucepan bring water to a boil. Stir in rice. Reduce heat and simmer, tightly covered, 20 minutes. Remove from heat and allow to stand, covered, 5 minutes. Drain rice and transfer to a large bowl. Add dressing and stir gently to blend. Refrigerate until thoroughly chilled.

Just before serving, drain tuna. Combine celery, carrots, almonds, and tuna, and toss carefully until well mixed. Add to rice and toss again. Garnish with sliced olives.

*Yield:* 8 servings

*Change Rice Salad with Tuna as follows or use Basic Recipe, if indicated, for:*

## LOW-CALORIE, DIABETIC, LOW-FAT, AND LOW-CHOLESTEROL DIETS

Calories per serving: 197
Approximate nutrient
  values per serving:
    Protein 12 g
    Fat 7 g
    Carbohydrate 22 g
    Sodium 385 mg
    Potassium 248 mg
    Cholesterol 22 mg
Exchanges:
  Bread 1½
  Meat 1½
  Fat 1

Substitute low-calorie Vinaigrette Dressing (page 502) for basic Vinaigrette Dressing.
Omit olives and almonds.
Increase celery to 1⅛ cups.
Add ½ cup chopped seeded green pepper.
Proceed as in Basic Recipe.

## LOW-SODIUM DIETS

Calories per serving: 315
Approximate nutrient
  values per serving:
    Protein 13 g
    Fat 19 g
    Carbohydrate 23 g
    Sodium 39 mg
    Potassium 271 mg
    Cholesterol 22 mg

Substitute low-sodium Vinaigrette Dressing (page 501) for basic Vinaigrette Dressing.
Substitute tuna with no salt added for tuna.
Omit olives.
Add ½ cup diced unpeeled apples.
Proceed as in Basic Recipe.

## BLAND DIETS

Calories per serving: 318

Substitute bland Vinaigrette Dressing (page 501) for basic Vinaigrette Dressing.
Proceed as in Basic Recipe.

## HIGH-FIBER DIETS

Use Basic Recipe.

Serving size: 1 cup salad,
  1½ tablespoons dressing
Calories per serving: 286
Approximate nutrient
  values per serving:
    Protein 12 g
    Fat 16 g
    Carbohydrate 23 g
    Calcium 24 mg
    Phosphorus 97 mg
    Sodium 27 mg
    Potassium 199 mg
    Cholesterol 22 mg
Exchanges:
  Bread 1½
  Meat 1
  Fat 3

*The Dressing*
1 cup polyunsaturated oil
⅓ cup wine vinegar
2 tablespoons minced fresh parsley
½ teaspoon basil
½ teaspoon dry mustard
1 clove garlic, put through garlic press
½ teaspoon thyme
⅛ teaspoon freshly ground pepper
¼ teaspoon paprika

*The Salad*
2½ cups water
1 cup raw long-grain rice
two 6½-ounce cans chunk light tuna in water without added
    salt, drained
½ cup thinly sliced celery
½ cup cooked diced carrots
1½ cups diced unpeeled apples

*To prepare the dressing:* Measure all dressing ingredients into a
jar. Cover tightly and shake well to blend. Refrigerate until
thoroughly chilled and shake vigorously before serving.
Reserve ¾ cup for this recipe and store the remaining dressing
in the refrigerator.

*To prepare the salad:* In a medium saucepan, bring water to a
boil. Stir in rice. Reduce heat and simmer, tightly covered, 20
minutes. Remove from heat and let stand, covered, 5 minutes.
Drain any excess liquid and spoon rice into a large bowl. Add
the ¾ cup reserved dressing and toss gently to blend. Refrigerate until thoroughly chilled.

Just before serving, add tuna, celery, carrots, and apple. Mix
well.

*Yield:* 8 servings salad, 1⅓ cups dressing

# Beef Salad Vinaigrette

BASIC RECIPE

Serving size: 1 cup
Calories per serving: 253
Approximate nutrient
  values per serving:
    Protein 16 g
    Fat 20 g
    Carbohydrate 5 g
    Sodium 263 mg
    Potassium 451 mg
    Cholesterol 53 mg
Exchanges:
  Vegetable 1
  Meat 2
  Fat 3

4 cups cauliflower flowerets
½ teaspoon salt
¾ teaspoon dry mustard
½ cup Vinaigrette Dressing (page 500)
¾ pound lean cooked roast beef
¼ cup chopped fresh parsley
¼ cup thinly sliced scallions, both white and green parts

Place cauliflower in a large saucepan. Add just enough water to cover; season with salt. Cover and bring to boil. Reduce heat; boil gently 5 to 8 minutes or until cauliflower is tender. Drain thoroughly and chill.

Blend mustard with dressing. Let stand while preparing salad.

Slice beef thinly and cut into bite-size strips.

Place beef and cauliflower into large bowl. Add dressing; toss gently to blend. Spoon onto serving plates; garnish with parsley and scallions.

*Yield:* 6 servings

*Change Beef Salad Vinaigrette as follows or use Basic Recipe, if indicated, for:*

## LOW-CALORIE, DIABETIC, LOW-FAT, AND LOW-CHOLESTEROL DIETS

Calories per serving: 179
Approximate nutrient
  values per serving:
    Protein 16 g
    Fat 11 g
    Carbohydrate 5 g
    Sodium 270 mg
    Potassium 458 mg
    Cholesterol 53 mg
Exchanges:
  Vegetable 1
  Meat 2
  Fat 1

Substitute low-calorie Vinaigrette Dressing (page 502) for basic Vinaigrette Dressing.
Proceed as in Basic Recipe.

## LOW-SODIUM DIETS

Calories per serving: 253
Approximate nutrient
  values same as Basic
  Recipe except for:
    Sodium 228 mg

Substitute low-sodium Vinaigrette Dressing (page 501) for basic Vinaigrette Dressing.
Proceed as in Basic Recipe.

## BLAND DIETS

Calories per serving: 253

Omit mustard; add ⅛ teaspoon ground cumin.
Substitute bland Vinaigrette Dressing (page 501) for basic Vinaigrette Dressing.
Proceed as in Basic Recipe.

## HIGH-FIBER DIETS

Use Basic Recipe.

# Lamb Salad with Mint

BASIC RECIPE

Serving size: 1 cup
Calories per serving: 480
Approximate nutrient
  values per serving:
    Protein 22 g
    Fat 35 g
    Carbohydrate 22 g
    Sodium 152 mg
    Potassium 1024 mg
    Cholesterol 69 mg
Exchanges:
  Vegetable 1
  Bread 1
  Meat 2
  Fat 6

2 cups diced cooked lamb
2 cups peeled and diced cooked potatoes
1 cup thinly sliced celery
½ cup sliced scallions, both white and green parts
½ cup Vinaigrette Dressing (page 500)
12 lettuce leaves
4 medium tomatoes, quartered
4 tablespoons finely chopped fresh mint

In a large bowl, combine lamb, potatoes, celery, and scallions. Pour dressing over salad and mix gently. Refrigerate, covered, until serving time. Serve on lettuce leaves and garnish with tomato quarters and mint.

*Yield:* 4 servings

*Change Lamb Salad with Mint as follows or use Basic Recipe, as indicated, for:*

LOW-CALORIE, DIABETIC, LOW-FAT, AND LOW-CHOLESTEROL DIETS

Calories per serving: 370
Approximate nutrient
  values per serving:
    Protein 22 g
    Fat 22 g
    Carbohydrate 22 g
    Sodium 162 mg
    Potassium 1035 mg
    Cholesterol 69 mg
Exchanges:
  Vegetable 1
  Bread 1
  Meat 2
  Fat 3

Substitute low-calorie Vinaigrette Dressing (page 502) for basic Vinaigrette Dressing.
Proceed as in Basic Recipe.

Substitute low-sodium Vinaigrette Dressing (page 501) for basic Vinaigrette Dressing.
Proceed as in Basic Recipe.

Calories per serving: 480
Approximate nutrient
  values same as Basic
  Recipe except for:
    Sodium 99 mg
    Potassium 1025 mg

BLAND DIETS

Substitute bland Vinaigrette Dressing (page 501) for basic Vinaigrette Dressing.

Calories per serving: 480

HIGH-FIBER DIETS

Use Basic Recipe.

# Chicken Salad Somerset

BASIC RECIPE

Serving size: 1 cup
Calories per serving: 480
Approximate nutrient
  values per serving:
    Protein 26 g
    Fat 38 g
    Carbohydrate 10 g
    Sodium 358 mg
    Potassium 528 mg
    Cholesterol 180 mg
Exchanges:
  Fruit 1
  Meat 3
  Fat 7

1 cup Homemade Mayonnaise (page 499)
2 tablespoons lemon juice
½ teaspoon salt
¼ teaspoon freshly ground pepper
3 cups diced cooked chicken
1 cup thinly sliced celery
⅓ cup toasted slivered almonds (page 38)
¼ cup chopped fresh parsley
1½ cups seedless grapes
2 hard-cooked large eggs, coarsely chopped

In a small bowl, combine mayonnaise, lemon juice, salt, and pepper.

In a separate bowl combine chicken, celery, almonds, and parsley. Add mayonnaise mixture to the chicken and toss gently. Refrigerate until well chilled.

Just before serving add grapes, mixing well. Garnish with hard-cooked eggs.

*Yield:* 6 servings

*Change Chicken Salad Somerset as follows or use Basic Recipe, if indicated, for:*

### LOW-CALORIE, DIABETIC, LOW-FAT, AND LOW-CHOLESTEROL DIETS

Calories per serving: 199
Approximate nutrient
  values per serving:
    Protein 24 g
    Fat 6 g
    Carbohydrate 13 g
    Sodium 371 mg
    Potassium 529 mg
    Cholesterol 98 mg
Exchanges:
  Fruit 1
  Meat 3
  Fat ½

Omit almonds and eggs.
Substitute low-calorie Homemade Mayonnaise (page 500) for basic Homemade Mayonnaise.
Proceed as in Basic Recipe.
Garnish with ½ cup chopped green pepper.

### LOW-SODIUM DIETS

Calories per serving: 480
Approximate nutrient
  values same as Basic
  Recipe except for:
    Sodium 102 mg

Omit salt.
Substitute low-sodium Homemade Mayonnaise (page 499) for basic Homemade Mayonnaise.
Proceed as in Basic Recipe.

### BLAND DIETS

Calories per serving: 480

Omit pepper.
Substitute bland Homemade Mayonnaise (page 499) for basic Homemade Mayonnaise.
Proceed as in Basic Recipe.

Use Basic Recipe.

## CHICKEN SALAD SOMERSET FOR RENAL DIETS

This requires at least ½ hour refrigeration before serving.

Serving size: ½ green
pepper, ⅓ cup salad
Calories per serving: 624
Approximate nutrient
values per serving:
Protein 18 g
Fat 59 g
Carbohydrate 7 g
Calcium 40 mg
Phosphorus 210 mg
Sodium 48 mg
Potassium 416 mg
Cholesterol 175 mg
Exchanges:
Vegetable 1
Meat 2
Fat 11

*The Lemon Mayonnaise*
2 large egg yolks
¾ teaspoon dry mustard
⅛ teaspoon cayenne pepper
1 teaspoon celery seed
1 teaspoon lime juice
1 cup polyunsaturated oil
3 tablespoons plus 1 teaspoon lemon juice

*The Salad*
2 tablespoons lemon juice
¼ teaspoon ground cumin
¼ teaspoon ground ginger
¼ teaspoon turmeric
⅛ teaspoon cayenne pepper
1½ cups finely minced cooked chicken
2 medium-size green peppers
⅛ teaspoon paprika

*To prepare the lemon mayonnaise:* Place egg yolks in container of electric blender. Cover and blend at high speed until they turn lemon color. Uncover, keep motor running, and add mustard, cayenne pepper, celery seed, and lime juice. Then, with motor still running, add ½ cup of the oil, a little at a time; continue to blend until mixture is thick. Next, with motor still running, add the lemon juice and the remaining ½ cup oil, alternately and slowly—about 1 teaspoon at a time. Cover and blend another few seconds. Transfer to a bowl, cover, and refrigerate until ready to use.

*To prepare the salad:* In a medium bowl, combine ½ cup of the lemon mayonnaise, lemon juice, cumin, ginger, turmeric, and cayenne pepper. Add chicken and blend thoroughly. Cover and refrigerate.

Cut the green peppers in half lengthwise and remove seeds. Place in cold water to cover, bring to boil, and simmer for 5 minutes or until tender. Rinse immediately in cold water and drain thoroughly. Cover and refrigerate until well chilled.

Just before serving spoon ⅓ cup stuffing into each pepper half, top with 2 tablespoons lemon mayonnaise, and sprinkle with paprika.

*Yield:* 4 servings salad, 1 cup lemon mayonnaise

# American Potato Salad

BASIC RECIPE

*The Salad*
3 cups water
½ teaspoon salt
4 cups diced peeled potatoes
1½ cups thinly sliced celery
⅓ cup chopped fresh parsley
2 hard-cooked eggs, coarsely chopped
3 tablespoons chopped fresh chives for garnish

*The Dressing*
½ cup cottage cheese
½ cup Homemade Mayonnaise (page 499)
1 teaspoon dry mustard
1 teaspoon salt
⅛ teaspoon freshly ground pepper
3 tablespoons cider vinegar

*To prepare the salad:* Bring water and salt to boil. Add potatoes and cook 10 minutes or until just tender. Drain thoroughly. Allow to cool. Combine celery and parsley with potatoes.

Serving size: ½ cup
Calories per serving: 191
Approximate nutrient
  values per serving:
    Protein 5 g
    Fat 13 g
    Carbohydrate 13 g
    Sodium 544 mg
    Potassium 359 mg
    Cholesterol 84 mg
Exchanges:
  Bread 1
  Meat ½
  Fat 2

*To prepare the dressing:* In a small bowl, combine cottage cheese, mayonnaise, mustard, salt, pepper, and vinegar. Beat until well blended.

*To assemble the salad:* Add dressing to potato mixture; toss gently and refrigerate until thoroughly chilled.
  Before serving, carefully mix in chopped eggs. Garnish with chives.

*Yield:* 8 servings

*Change American Potato Salad as follows or use Basic Recipe, if indicated, for:*

LOW-CALORIE, DIABETIC, LOW-FAT, AND LOW-CHOLESTEROL DIETS

*The salad:* Omit eggs.

*The dressing:* Substitute 1 percent low-fat cottage cheese for cottage cheese.
  Substitute low-calorie Homemade Mayonnaise (page 500) for basic Homemade Mayonnaise.
  Proceed as in Basic Recipe.

Calories per serving: 88
Approximate nutrient
  values per serving:
    Protein 5 g
    Fat 2 g
    Carbohydrate 15 g
    Sodium 544 mg
    Potassium 363 mg
    Cholesterol 18 mg
Exchanges:
  Bread 1
  Fat ½

LOW-SODIUM DIETS

*The salad:* Omit salt.

*The dressing:* Omit salt.
  Substitute low-sodium Homemade Mayonnaise (page 499) for basic Homemade Mayonnaise.
  Proceed as in Basic Recipe.

Calories per serving: 191
Approximate nutrient
  values same as Basic
  Recipe except for:
    Sodium 105 mg

Calories per serving: 188
Approximate nutrient
  values per serving:
    Protein 5 g
    Fat 13 g
    Carbohydrate 13 g
    Calcium 27 mg
    Phosphorus 82 mg
    Sodium 85 mg
    Potassium 294 mg
    Cholesterol 84 mg

*The salad:* Omit salt.
   Reduce celery to ½ cup.
   Omit chives and garnish with 2 tablespoons chopped fresh parsley.

*The dressing:* Omit salt.
   Substitute low-sodium Homemade Mayonnaise (page 499) for basic Homemade Mayonnaise.
   Proceed as in Basic Recipe.

### BLAND DIETS

Calories per serving: 191

*The salad:* Use Basic Recipe.

*The dressing:* Omit mustard and pepper. Substitute bland Homemade Mayonnaise (page 499) for basic Homemade Mayonnaise.
   Proceed as in Basic Recipe.

### HIGH-FIBER DIETS

Use Basic Recipe.

# Beet and Potato Salad

### BASIC RECIPE

Serving size: 1 cup
Calories per serving: 147
Approximate nutrient
  values per serving:
    Protein 2 g
    Fat 10 g
    Carbohydrate 13 g

5 medium-size fresh beets
8 small red potatoes
2 tablespoons red wine vinegar
¼ teaspoon salt
¼ teaspoon freshly ground pepper
½ teaspoon dry mustard

Sodium 85 mg
Potassium 295 mg
Cholesterol 0 mg
Exchanges:
  Vegetable 1
  Bread ½
  Fat 2

6 tablespoons polyunsaturated oil
¼ cup chopped fresh parsley
2 scallions, chopped, both white and green parts
1 cucumber, peeled, seeded, and diced

Wash beets and cut off stems. In large saucepan, cover beets with cold water and boil 40 to 45 minutes or until tender. Slip off skins under cold running water. Cut beets into ¼-inch cubes, place in a large bowl, and set aside.

Boil potatoes 15 minutes or until just tender. Drain, peel, and cut into quarters. Add to beets.

Mix the vinegar, salt, pepper, mustard, oil, and parsley. Pour this dressing over beets and potatoes. Add scallions and gently mix. Stir cucumber into salad.

Cover salad tightly and refrigerate until serving time.

*Yield:* 8 servings

*Change Beet and Potato Salad as follows or use Basic Recipe, if indicated, for:*

LOW-CALORIE, DIABETIC, LOW-FAT, AND LOW-CHOLESTEROL DIETS

Increase vinegar to ⅓ cup.
Reduce oil to 4 teaspoons.
Proceed as in Basic Recipe.

Calories per serving: 76
Approximate nutrient
  values per serving:
  Protein 2 g
  Fat 2 g
  Carbohydrate 13 g
  Sodium 85 mg
  Potassium 295 mg
  Cholesterol 0 mg
Exchanges:
  Vegetable 1
  Bread ½
  Fat ½

Omit salt.
Add 1 teaspoon lemon juice with vinegar. Add 1 teaspoon rosemary.
Proceed as in Basic Recipe.

Calories per serving: 147
Approximate nutrient
 values same as Basic
 Recipe except for:
  Sodium 17 mg
  Potassium 297 mg

BLAND DIETS

Omit pepper and mustard.
Proceed as in Basic Recipe.

Calories per serving: 147

HIGH-FIBER DIETS

Use Basic Recipe.

# Neapolitan Salad

BASIC RECIPE

Serving size: ½ cup
Calories per serving: 331
Approximate nutrient
 values per serving:
  Protein 9 g
  Fat 27 g
  Carbohydrate 19 g
  Sodium 151 mg
  Potassium 898 mg
  Cholesterol 31 mg
Exchanges:
 Vegetable 4
 Fat 5½

1 large head cauliflower
3 green peppers, cored and halved
1 bunch scallions, both white and green parts
¾ cup Homemade Mayonnaise (page 499)
¾ cup plain yogurt
¼ cup blanched slivered almonds (page 38)
⅛ teaspoon salt
¼ teaspoon freshly ground pepper
1 teaspoon lemon juice
2 tablespoons shredded pimiento
3 tomatoes, peeled, seeded, and cut into wedges

Separate cauliflower into flowerets. Place in large saucepan of boiling water and cook for 4 minutes or until they are just tender but still slightly crunchy. Drain, rinse with cold water, and allow to cool.

Cut the peppers into very thin 1-inch-long strips. Cut scallions into thin strips 1 inch long. Mix mayonnaise with yogurt, almonds, salt, pepper, and lemon juice.

Place cauliflower in the center of a large serving platter. Spoon the mayonnaise over it. Top with green peppers, scallions, and pimiento. Arrange tomato wedges around salad. Cover loosely and refrigerate until ready to serve.

*Yield:* 6 servings

*Change Neapolitan Salad as follows for:*

LOW-CALORIE, DIABETIC, LOW-FAT, AND LOW-CHOLESTEROL DIETS

Substitute low-calorie Homemade Mayonnaise (page 500) for basic Homemade Mayonnaise.
Substitute plain low-fat yogurt for yogurt.
Proceed as in Basic Recipe.

Calories per serving: 171
Approximate nutrient
  values per serving:
    Protein 10 g
    Fat 7 g
    Carbohydrate 23 g
    Sodium 184 mg
    Potassium 959 mg
    Cholesterol 36 mg
Exchanges:
  Vegetable 3
  Bread ½
  Fat 1½

LOW-SODIUM DIETS

Omit salt.
Substitute low-sodium Homemade Mayonnaise (page 499) for basic Homemade Mayonnaise.
Omit pimiento; substitute 2 tablespoons shredded sweet red pepper.
Proceed as in Basic Recipe.

Calories per serving: 331
Approximate nutrient
  values same as Basic
  Recipe except for:
    Sodium 53 mg
    Potassium 904 mg

Calories per serving: 331

Substitute ¾ cup bland Homemade Mayonnaise (page 499) for
  basic Homemade Mayonnaise.
Omit ground pepper.
Proceed as in Basic Recipe.

HIGH-FIBER DIETS

Calories per serving: 363

Increase almonds to ½ cup.
Proceed as in Basic Recipe.

# Cauliflower and Mushroom Salad

BASIC RECIPE

Serving size: ¾ cup
Calories per serving: 252
Approximate nutrient
  values per serving:
    Protein 4 g
    Fat 24 g
    Carbohydrate 9 g
    Sodium 132 mg
    Potassium 481 mg
    Cholesterol 0 mg
Exchanges:
  Vegetable 2
  Fat 5

2 cups raw cauliflower flowerets
2 cups thinly sliced mushrooms
½ cup thinly sliced carrots
½ cup thinly sliced scallions, both white and green parts
⅓ cup chopped fresh parsley
¾ cup Lemon Salad Dressing with Dill (page 502)
15 Boston lettuce leaves
2 tablespoons toasted sesame seeds (page 38)

In a large bowl combine cauliflower, mushrooms, carrots, scallions, and parsley. Pour dressing over salad and toss gently.
Arrange each serving on 3 lettuce leaves and garnish with
toasted sesame seeds.

*Yield:* 5 servings

*Change Cauliflower and Mushroom Salad as follows or use Basic Recipe, if indicated, for:*

LOW-CALORIE, DIABETIC, LOW-FAT, AND LOW-CHOLESTEROL DIETS

Calories per serving: 125
Approximate nutrient
  values per serving:
    Protein 4 g
    Fat 9 g
    Carbohydrate 9 g
    Sodium 132 mg
    Potassium 481 mg
    Cholesterol 0 mg
Exchanges:
  Vegetable 2
  Fat 2

Substitute low-calorie Lemon Salad Dressing with Dill (page 503) for basic Lemon Salad Dressing.
Proceed as in Basic Recipe.

LOW-SODIUM DIETS

Calories per serving: 252
Approximate nutrient
  values same as Basic
  Recipe except for:
    Sodium 23 mg

Substitute low-sodium Lemon Salad Dressing with Dill (page 503) for basic Lemon Salad Dressing.
Proceed as in Basic Recipe.

BLAND DIETS

Calories per serving: 252

Substitute bland Lemon Salad Dressing with Dill (page 503) for basic Lemon Salad Dressing.
Proceed as in Basic Recipe.

HIGH-FIBER DIETS

Use Basic Recipe.

# Cole Slaw with Celery

BASIC RECIPE

½ cup Homemade Mayonnaise (page 499)
1 teaspoon dill seed
½ teaspoon salt
⅛ teaspoon freshly ground pepper
3½ cups shredded cabbage
1½ cups thinly sliced celery
⅓ cup grated raw carrot

In a large bowl, mix together mayonnaise, dill seed, salt, and pepper.

Add remaining ingredients; mix gently to blend. Cover and refrigerate at least 1 hour before serving.

*Yield:* 6 servings

*Change Cole Slaw with Celery as follows or use Basic Recipe, if indicated, for:*

LOW-CALORIE, DIABETIC, LOW-FAT, AND LOW-CHOLESTEROL DIETS

Substitute low-calorie Homemade Mayonnaise (page 500) for basic Homemade Mayonnaise.
Proceed as in Basic Recipe.

Calories per serving: 153
Approximate nutrient
values same as Basic
Recipe except for:
Sodium 54 mg

Omit salt.
Substitute low-sodium Homemade Mayonnaise (page 499) for basic Homemade Mayonnaise.
Proceed as in Basic Recipe.

BLAND DIETS

Calories per serving: 153

Omit pepper.
Substitute bland Homemade Mayonnaise (page 499) for basic Homemade Mayonnaise.
Proceed as in Basic Recipe.

HIGH-FIBER DIETS

Use Basic Recipe.

# Oriental Radish Salad

BASIC RECIPE

Serving size: ½ cup
Calories per serving: 16
Approximate nutrient
values per serving:
  Protein 1 g
  Fat 0 g
  Carbohydrate 4 g
  Sodium 189 mg
  Potassium 139 mg
  Cholesterol 0 mg
Exchanges:
  Vegetable 1

2 cups thinly sliced peeled cucumbers
1 cup thinly sliced red radishes
2 teaspoons sugar
½ teaspoon salt
¼ teaspoon freshly ground pepper
¼ cup white vinegar

Put cucumbers and radishes in a bowl. Mix together remaining ingredients and pour over vegetables. Mix gently to blend.

*Yield:* 6 servings

*Change Oriental Radish Salad as follows or use Basic Recipe, if indicated, for:*

## LOW-CALORIE, DIABETIC, LOW-FAT, AND LOW-CHOLESTEROL DIETS

Use Basic Recipe.

## LOW-SODIUM DIETS

Calories per serving: 16
Approximate nutrient
  values same as Basic
  Recipe except for:
    Sodium 6 mg

Omit salt.
Proceed as in Basic Recipe.

## RENAL DIETS

Calories per serving: 20
Approximate nutrient
  values per serving:
    Protein 1 g
    Fat 0 g
    Carbohydrate 5 g
    Calcium 15 mg
    Phosphorus 17 mg
    Sodium 6 mg
    Potassium 130 mg
    Cholesterol 0 mg

Omit salt.
Reduce radishes to ½ cup. Add ½ cup thinly sliced red onions.
Proceed as in Basic Recipe.

## BLAND DIETS

Calories per serving: 16

Omit pepper.
Proceed as in Basic Recipe.

## HIGH-FIBER DIETS

Calories per serving: 18

Use Basic Recipe. Add 3 tablespoons thinly sliced scallions, both white and green parts, and mix with other vegetables.

# Artichoke and Avocado Salad

BASIC RECIPE

Serving size: 1 cup salad, 4
 lettuce leaves, ½ tomato
Calories per serving: 318
Approximate nutrient
 values per serving:
  Protein 11 g
  Fat 27 g
  Carbohydrate 11 g
  Sodium 336 mg
  Potassium 821 mg
  Cholesterol 22 mg
Exchanges:
 Vegetable 2
 Meat 1
 Fat 5

9-ounce package frozen artichoke hearts
2½ cups avocado cubes
1 cup diced cooked ham
1 cup diced cooked chicken
1½ cups sliced small fresh mushrooms
1 cup thinly sliced celery
⅓ cup thinly sliced radishes
¾ cup Vinaigrette Dressing (page 500)
1 head Boston lettuce, separated into leaves
4 medium tomatoes, quartered

Cook artichoke hearts as directed on the package. Drain thoroughly, cool, and cut into bite-size pieces.

In a large mixing bowl combine artichokes, avocado, ham, chicken, mushrooms, celery, and radishes. Add Vinaigrette Dressing and toss gently until well mixed.

Arrange lettuce leaves on serving plates. Spoon salad on lettuce and garnish with tomato wedges.

*Yield:* 8 servings

*Change Artichoke and Avocado Salad as follows or use Basic Recipe, if indicated, for:*

### LOW-CALORIE, DIABETIC, LOW-FAT, AND LOW-CHOLESTEROL DIETS

Calories per serving: 235
Approximate nutrient
  values per serving:
    Protein 11 g
    Fat 17 g
    Carbohydrate 11 g
    Sodium 344 mg
    Potassium 821 mg
    Cholesterol 22 mg
Exchanges:
  Vegetable 2
  Meat 1
  Fat 3

Substitute low-calorie Vinaigrette Dressing (page 502) for basic Vinaigrette Dressing.
Proceed as in Basic Recipe.

### LOW-SODIUM DIETS

Calories per serving: 305
Approximate nutrient
  values per serving:
    Protein 14 g
    Fat 25 g
    Carbohydrate 10 g
    Sodium 64 mg
    Potassium 832 mg
    Cholesterol 26 mg

Omit ham. Increase chicken to 2 cups.
Substitute low-sodium Vinaigrette Dressing (page 501) for basic Vinaigrette Dressing.
Proceed as in Basic Recipe.

### BLAND DIETS

Calories per serving: 318

Substitute bland Vinaigrette Dressing (page 501) for basic Vinaigrette Dressing.
Proceed as in Basic Recipe.

### HIGH-FIBER DIETS

Use Basic Recipe.

# Pear and Watercress Salad

BASIC RECIPE

Serving size: ½ pear, 2½
  tablespoons dressing
Calories per serving: 83
Approximate nutrient
  values per serving:
    Protein 2 g
    Fat 2 g
    Carbohydrate 17 g
    Sodium 112 mg
    Potassium 267 mg
    Cholesterol 5 mg
Exchanges:
  Fruit 1
  Bread ½
  Fat ½

3 ripe pears, peeled
2 tablespoons lemon juice
1 cup plain yogurt
2 teaspoons grated orange rind
1 tablespoon undiluted orange juice concentrate
¼ teaspoon salt
¼ teaspoon freshly ground pepper
1 bunch watercress, large stems removed

Cut pears in half lengthwise and remove core. Sprinkle them with the lemon juice.

Make a dressing by combining yogurt, orange rind, orange juice concentrate, salt, and pepper. Mix thoroughly until well blended.

Arrange the watercress on a serving plate. Place the pears on top and spoon dressing on each pear half.

*Yield:* 6 servings

*Change Pear and Watercress Salad as follows or use Basic Recipe, if indicated, for:*

LOW-CALORIE, DIABETIC, LOW-FAT, AND LOW-CHOLESTEROL DIETS

Substitute plain low-fat yogurt for yogurt.
Proceed as in Basic Recipe.

Calories per serving: 84
Approximate nutrient
  values per serving:
    Protein 3 g
    Fat 1 g
    Carbohydrate 18 g
    Sodium 121 mg
    Potassium 296 mg
    Cholesterol 2 mg
Exchanges:
  Fruit 1
  Bread ½

## LOW-SODIUM DIETS

Omit salt.
Increase orange juice concentrate to 2 tablespoons and add 1
    teaspoon tarragon to the dressing.
Proceed as in Basic Recipe.

Calories per serving: 89
Approximate nutrient
    values per serving:
        Protein 2 g
        Fat 2 g
        Carbohydrate 18 g
        Sodium 21 mg
        Potassium 295 mg
        Cholesterol 5 mg

## BLAND DIETS

Omit pepper.
Proceed as in Basic Recipe.

Calories per serving: 83

## HIGH-FIBER DIETS

Use Basic Recipe.

# Herbed Cucumber Mold

## BASIC RECIPE

⅓ cup water
1½ tablespoons unflavored gelatin
3 cucumbers, peeled, seeded, and grated
¼ cup chopped fresh mint
¼ cup chopped fresh parsley
¼ cup chopped fresh dillweed
2 cups Chicken Stock (page 114)
¼ cup lemon juice
½ teaspoon salt
¼ teaspoon freshly ground pepper

Serving size: ½ cup
Calories per serving: 16
Approximate nutrient
    values per serving:
        Protein 2 g
        Fat 0 g
        Carbohydrate 3 g
        Sodium 166 mg
        Potassium 166 mg
        Cholesterol 0 mg
Exchanges:
    Vegetable 1

Place water in a small saucepan and sprinkle with gelatin. Let stand 10 minutes, then dissolve over low heat, stirring. Turn off heat.

Combine the cucumbers, mint, parsley, dill, chicken stock, lemon juice, salt, and pepper in a large bowl. Add the gelatin and mix well. Pour into a 5-cup mold and chill in the refrigerator at least 1½ hours before serving.

To unmold, dip mold in hot water for a few seconds. Place a plate against top of mold and flip mold upside down onto it.

*Yield:* 8 servings

*Change Herbed Cucumber Mold as follows or use Basic Recipe, if indicated, for:*

LOW-CALORIE, DIABETIC, LOW-FAT, AND LOW-CHOLESTEROL DIETS

Use Basic Recipe.

LOW-SODIUM DIETS

Calories per serving: 17
Approximate nutrient values same as Basic Recipe except for:
Sodium 29 mg
Potassium 169 mg

Omit salt.
Increase lemon juice to ⅓ cup.
Proceed as in Basic Recipe.

BLAND DIETS

Calories per serving: 17

Omit pepper.
Increase lemon juice to ⅓ cup.
Proceed as in Basic Recipe.

HIGH-FIBER DIETS

Calories per serving: 17

Increase parsley to ½ cup.
Proceed as in Basic Recipe.

# Molded Cranberry Salad

BASIC RECIPE

Serving size: ½ cup
Calories per serving: 190
Approximate nutrient
 values per serving:
   Protein 3 g
   Fat 7 g
   Carbohydrate 32 g
   Sodium 114 mg
   Potassium 140 mg
   Cholesterol 0 mg
Exchanges:
   Fruit 1½
   Bread 1
   Fat 1½

1 tablespoon unflavored gelatin
1¼ cups unsweetened apple juice
½ cup fresh cranberries, rinsed
¼ teaspoon salt
½ cup sugar
1 cup diced unpeeled apples
½ cup chopped walnuts

Sprinkle gelatin over ¼ cup of the apple juice and let stand 10 minutes.

Cook cranberries in remaining 1 cup apple juice in a medium saucepan, covered, over moderate heat until juice comes to a boil and cranberries open.

Add salt and sugar and simmer gently, uncovered, for 5 minutes, stirring frequently.

Remove from heat and stir in softened gelatin. Cool until mixture thickens slightly. Stir in apples and walnuts. Rinse out 5 half-cup individual molds with cold water and fill with cranberry salad. Refrigerate until set, at least 2 hours.

To unmold, dip each mold into hot water for a few seconds. Place cold plate against top of mold and flip mold upside down onto it.

*Yield:* 5 servings

*Change Molded Cranberry Salad as follows or use Basic Recipe, if indicated, for:*

LOW-SODIUM DIETS

Omit salt.
Proceed as in Basic Recipe.

Calories per serving: 190
Approximate nutrient
 values same as Basic
 Recipe except for:
   Sodium 4 mg

Use Basic Recipe.


MOLDED CRANBERRY SALAD FOR LOW-CALORIE, DIABETIC, LOW-FAT, AND LOW-CHOLESTEROL DIETS

Serving size: ½ cup
Calories per serving: 73
Approximate nutrient
  values per serving:
    Protein 2 g
    Fat 0 g
    Carbohydrate 17 g
    Sodium 114 mg
    Potassium 154 mg
    Cholesterol 0 mg
Exchanges:
  Fruit 2

1 tablespoon unflavored gelatin
1¼ cups unsweetened apple juice
½ cup fresh cranberries, rinsed
¼ teaspoon salt
⅔ cup diced unpeeled apples
8-ounce can undrained crushed pineapple, packed in
  unsweetened juice

Sprinkle gelatin over ¼ cup apple juice and let stand 10 minutes.

In a medium saucepan, cook cranberries with remaining 1 cup apple juice, covered, over moderate heat until juice comes to a boil and cranberries open. Add salt and simmer gently, uncovered, for 5 minutes, stirring frequently. Remove from heat and stir in softened gelatin. Cool until mixture thickens slightly. Stir in apples and pineapple. Rinse out 5 half-cup individual molds with cold water and fill with cranberry salad. Refrigerate for about 2 hours or until set.

To unmold, dip mold into hot water for a few seconds. Place cold plate against top of mold and flip mold upside down onto it.

*Yield:* 5 servings

# Homemade Mayonnaise

BASIC RECIPE

1 large egg, at room temperature
½ teaspoon dry mustard
¼ teaspoon salt
⅛ teaspoon cayenne pepper
2 tablespoons fresh lemon juice
1 cup polyunsaturated oil

Place egg, mustard, salt, and cayenne in container of electric blender. Cover and blend at high speed for about 5 seconds or until foamy.

With motor still running at high speed, uncover blender and add lemon juice all at once. Then slowly add oil in a very thin and steady stream until mayonnaise is thick. It should be finished in about 30 seconds.

*Yield:* 1¼ cups

*Change Homemade Mayonnaise as follows or use Basic Recipe, if indicated, for:*

LOW-SODIUM AND RENAL DIETS

Omit salt.
Proceed as in Basic Recipe.

BLAND DIETS

Omit cayenne pepper and mustard.
Proceed as in Basic Recipe.

HIGH-FIBER DIETS

Use Basic Recipe.


HOMEMADE MAYONNAISE FOR LOW-CALORIE, DIABETIC, LOW-FAT, AND LOW-CHOLESTEROL DIETS

Serving size: 1 tablespoon
Calories per serving: 20
Approximate nutrient
    values per serving:
        Protein 1 g
        Fat 1 g
        Carbohydrate 2 g
        Sodium 44 mg
        Potassium 25 mg
        Cholesterol 17 mg
Exchanges:
    Fat ½

2 tablespoons flour
⅔ cup skim milk, heated
1 large egg, at room temperature
½ teaspoon dry mustard
¼ teaspoon salt
⅛ teaspoon cayenne pepper
2 tablespoons fresh lemon juice
1 tablespoon polyunsaturated oil

Over low heat, in the top of a double boiler, whisk together flour and milk.

Stir in egg, mustard, salt, and cayenne. Cook over barely simmering water, stirring constantly, until sauce is thickened and smooth.

Remove from heat and stir in lemon juice and oil.

Cool and refrigerate, tightly covered.

*Yield:* 1 cup


# Vinaigrette Dressing

BASIC RECIPE

Serving size: 2 tablespoons
Calories per serving: 195
Approximate nutrient
    values per serving:
        Protein 0 g
        Fat 22 g
        Carbohydrate 1 g

1 cup polyunsaturated oil
⅓ cup wine vinegar
2 tablespoons chopped fresh parsley
½ teaspoon basil
½ teaspoon dry mustard
1 clove garlic, put through garlic press

Sodium 55 mg
Potassium 13 mg
Cholesterol 0 mg
Exchanges:
  Fat 4½

¼ teaspoon salt
⅛ teaspoon freshly ground pepper
¼ teaspoon paprika

Measure all ingredients into a jar. Cover tightly and shake well to blend. Refrigerate, tightly covered, until thoroughly chilled. Shake vigorously before serving.

*Yield:* 1⅓ cups

*Change Vinaigrette Dressing as follows or use Basic Recipe, if indicated, for:*

LOW-SODIUM AND RENAL DIETS

Calories per serving: 195
Approximate nutrient
  values per serving:
  Protein 0 g
  Fat 22 g
  Carbohydrate 1 g
  Calcium 5 mg
  Phosphorus 2 mg
  Sodium 1 mg
  Potassium 14 mg
  Cholesterol 0 mg

Omit salt.
Add ½ teaspoon thyme.
Proceed as in Basic Recipe.

BLAND DIETS

Calories per serving: 195

Omit pepper and mustard.
Proceed as in Basic Recipe.

HIGH-FIBER DIETS

Use Basic Recipe.

## VINAIGRETTE DRESSING FOR LOW-CALORIE, DIABETIC, LOW-FAT, AND LOW-CHOLESTEROL DIETS

Serving size: 1 tablespoon
Calories per serving: 38
Approximate nutrient
  values per serving:
    Protein 0 g
    Fat 4 g
    Carbohydrate 1 g
    Sodium 31 mg
    Potassium 7 mg
    Cholesterol 0 mg
Exchanges:
  Fat 1

2 teaspoons arrowroot
⅔ cup cold water
½ cup polyunsaturated oil
⅛ cup wine vinegar
2 tablespoons chopped fresh parsley
½ teaspoon basil
½ teaspoon dry mustard
1 clove garlic, put through garlic press
¼ teaspoon salt
⅛ teaspoon freshly ground pepper
¼ teaspoon paprika

In a small saucepan, blend arrowroot and water. Cook and stir over low heat until mixture comes to a boil and thickens. Remove from heat and allow to cool to room temperature.

Measure remaining ingredients into a jar and add arrowroot mixture. Shake well to blend. Refrigerate, tightly covered, until thoroughly chilled. Shake vigorously before serving.

*Yield:* 1⅛ cups

# Lemon Salad Dressing with Dill

## BASIC RECIPE

Serving size: 2 tablespoons
Calories per serving: 163
Approximate nutrient
  values per serving:
    Protein 0 g
    Fat 18 g
    Carbohydrate 1 g
    Sodium 92 mg

1 cup polyunsaturated oil
½ cup lemon juice
1 teaspoon dillweed
½ teaspoon salt
¼ teaspoon cayenne pepper
½ teaspoon grated lemon rind
2 teaspoons chopped fresh chives

Potassium 18 mg
Cholesterol 0 mg
Exchanges:
  Fat 4

Combine all ingredients in a jar with a tight-fitting lid. Shake vigorously to blend. Refrigerate until thoroughly chilled. Shake well before serving.

Store in refrigerator.

*Yield:* 1½ cups

*Change Lemon Salad Dressing with Dill as follows or use Basic Recipe, if indicated, for:*

LOW-SODIUM AND RENAL DIETS

Calories per serving: 163
Approximate nutrient
  values same as Basic
  Recipe except for:
    Calcium 3 mg
    Phosphorus 2 mg
    Sodium 0 mg

Omit salt.
Proceed as in Basic Recipe.

BLAND DIETS

Calories per serving: 163

Omit cayenne pepper.
Proceed as in Basic Recipe.

HIGH-FIBER DIETS

Use Basic Recipe.

LEMON SALAD DRESSING WITH DILL FOR LOW-CALORIE, DIABETIC, LOW-FAT, AND LOW-CHOLESTEROL DIETS

Serving size: 2 tablespoons
Calories per serving: 57
Approximate nutrient
  values per serving:
    Protein 0 g
    Fat 6 g

2 teaspoons arrowroot
⅔ cup cold water
⅓ cup polyunsatured oil
½ cup lemon juice
1 teaspoon dillweed

Carbohydrate 1 g
Sodium 92 mg
Potassium 18 mg
Cholesterol 0 mg
Exchanges:
Fat 1

½ teaspoon salt
¼ teaspoon cayenne pepper
½ teaspoon grated lemon rind
2 teaspoons chopped fresh chives

In a small saucepan, blend arrowroot in water. Cook and stir over low heat until mixture comes to a boil and thickens. Remove from heat and allow to cool to room temperature.

Combine arrowroot and remaining ingredients in a jar with a tight-fitting lid. Shake vigorously. Refrigerate until thoroughly chilled.

*Yield:* 1½ cups

# Herbed Cottage Cheese Dressing

BASIC RECIPE

This is excellent with raw vegetables or on top of avocado halves.

Serving size: 2 tablespoons
Calories per serving: 53
Approximate nutrient
  values per serving:
    Protein 2 g
    Fat 5 g
    Carbohydrate 1 g
    Sodium 89 mg
    Potassium 33 mg
    Cholesterol 15 mg
Exchanges:
Fat 1

⅓ cup heavy cream
½ cup sour cream
½ cup cottage cheese
2 tablespoons chopped fresh parsley
¼ teaspoon salt
⅛ teaspoon freshly ground pepper
¼ teaspoon dillweed
¼ teaspoon thyme
¼ teaspoon chervil
1 small clove garlic, put through garlic press

Place ingredients, in the order listed, in the container of an electric blender and blend until smooth.

It is best to make this fresh, but it will keep refrigerated for 2 to 3 days.

*Yield:* 1½ cups

*Change Herbed Cottage Cheese Dressing as follows or use Basic Recipe, if indicated, for:*

### LOW-CALORIE, DIABETIC, LOW-FAT, AND LOW-CHOLESTEROL DIETS

Omit heavy cream.
Substitute plain low-fat yogurt for sour cream.
Substitute low-fat 1 percent cottage cheese for cottage cheese.
Proceed as in Basic Recipe.

*Yield:* 1 cup

Calories per serving: 20
Approximate nutrient
  values per serving:
    Protein 3 g
    Fat 0 g
    Carbohydrate 2 g
    Sodium 136 mg
    Potassium 56 mg
    Cholesterol 1 mg
Exchanges:
  Meat ½

### LOW-SODIUM AND RENAL DIETS

Omit salt.
Proceed as in Basic Recipe.

Calories per serving: 53
Approximate nutrient
  values same as Basic
  Recipe except for:
    Calcium 23 mg
    Phosphorus 25 mg
    Sodium 43 mg

### BLAND DIETS

Omit pepper.
Proceed as in Basic Recipe.

Calories per serving: 53

### HIGH-FIBER DIETS

Use Basic Recipe.

# Roquefort Cheese Dressing

BASIC RECIPE

Serving size: 2 tablespoons
Calories per serving: 131
Approximate nutrient
values per serving:
Protein 2 g
Fat 14 g
Carbohydrate 1 g
Sodium 159 mg
Potassium 28 mg
Cholesterol 22 mg
Exchanges:
Fat 3

½ cup sour cream
½ cup Homemade Mayonnaise (page 499)
½ cup crumbled Roquefort cheese
⅛ teaspoon cayenne pepper

Mix together all ingredients. Refrigerate, covered, at least 1 hour. Stir before serving.

*Yield:* 1¼ cups

*Change Roquefort Cheese Dressing as follows or use Basic Recipe, if indicated, for:*

LOW-SODIUM AND RENAL DIETS

Note that this variation contains no Roquefort cheese, but it serves well as a substitute for that old favorite.

Calories per serving: 116
Approximate nutrient
values per serving:
Protein 2 g
Fat 12 g
Carbohydrate 1 g
Calcium 23 mg
Phosphorus 28 mg
Sodium 51 mg
Potassium 33 mg
Cholesterol 18 mg

Substitute low-sodium Homemade Mayonnaise (page 499) for basic Homemade Mayonnaise.
Substitute cottage cheese for Roquefort. Season with ¼ teaspoon marjoram, ¼ teaspoon tarragon, and ¼ teaspoon basil. Proceed as in Basic Recipe.

BLAND DIETS

Calories per serving: 131

Omit cayenne pepper.
Substitute bland Homemade Mayonnaise (page 499) for basic Homemade Mayonnaise. Proceed as in Basic Recipe.

Use Basic Recipe. For extra fiber, serve as a dip with raw vegetables or as a dressing for green salads.

## ROQUEFORT CHEESE DRESSING FOR LOW-CALORIE, DIABETIC, LOW-FAT, AND LOW-CHOLESTEROL DIETS

This version contains no Roquefort cheese, but it serves well as a substitute for that old favorite.

Serving size: 2 tablespoons
Calories per serving: 27
Approximate nutrient
 values per serving:
  Protein 2 g
  Fat 1 g
  Carbohydrate 2 g
  Sodium 74 mg
  Potassium 49 mg
  Cholesterol 12 mg
Exchanges:
 Fat ½

½ cup plain low-fat yogurt
½ cup low-calorie Homemade Mayonnaise (page 500)
½ cup 1 percent low-fat cottage cheese
¼ teaspoon marjoram
¼ teaspoon tarragon
¼ teaspoon basil

Mix together all ingredients. Refrigerate, covered, at least 1 hour. Stir before serving.

*Yield:* 1½ cups

# Spicy Tomato Dressing

## BASIC RECIPE

This makes a piquant accompaniment for spinach salad or a mixed green salad.

Serving size: 2 tablespoons
Calories per serving: 100
Approximate nutrient
 values per serving:
  Protein 0 g
  Fat 11 g
  Carbohydrate 1 g

½ cup tomato juice
½ cup polyunsaturated oil
¼ cup wine vinegar
½ teaspoon basil
¼ teaspoon dry mustard
¼ teaspoon salt

Sodium 79 mg
Potassium 33 mg
Cholesterol 0 mg
Exchanges:
  Fat 2

⅛ teaspoon freshly ground pepper
1 clove garlic, put through garlic press

Measure all ingredients into a jar with a tight-fitting cover and shake well. Refrigerate until thoroughly chilled.
  Shake vigorously before serving.

*Yield:* 1¼ cups

*Change Spicy Tomato Dressing as follows or use Basic Recipe, if indicated, for:*

LOW-CALORIE, DIABETIC, LOW-FAT, AND LOW-CHOLESTEROL DIETS

Serving size: 1 tablespoon
Calories per serving: 20
Approximate nutrient
  values per serving:
    Protein 0 g
    Fat 2 g
    Carbohydrate 1 g
    Sodium 57 mg
    Potassium 24 mg
    Cholesterol 0 mg
Exchanges:
  Fat ½

Reduce oil to 2 tablespoons.
Proceed as in Basic Recipe.

*Yield:* 14 tablespoons

LOW-SODIUM DIETS

Calories per serving: 100
Approximate nutrient
  values same as Basic
  Recipe except for:
    Sodium 1 mg

Omit salt.
Substitute low-sodium tomato juice for tomato juice.
Proceed as in Basic Recipe.

BLAND DIETS

Calories per serving: 100

Omit pepper and mustard.
Proceed as in Basic Recipe.

HIGH-FIBER DIETS

Use Basic Recipe.

# Carlisle Dressing

BASIC RECIPE

This is delicious with asparagus or artichoke hearts in salads.

1 cup polyunsaturated oil
⅓ cup red wine vinegar
2 tablespoons chopped fresh parsley
½ teaspoon basil
½ teaspoon dry mustard
1 clove garlic, put through garlic press
¼ teaspoon salt
⅛ teaspoon freshly ground pepper
¼ teaspoon paprika
½ cup peeled and diced cooked fresh beets
1 hard-cooked large egg, coarsely chopped

Measure all ingredients into a jar. Cover tightly and shake well to blend. Refrigerate, tightly covered, until thoroughly chilled. Shake vigorously before serving.

*Yield:* 1½ cups

*Change Carlisle Dressing as follows or use Basic Recipe, if indicated, for:*

LOW-SODIUM DIETS

Omit salt.
Proceed as in Basic Recipe.

BLAND DIETS

Omit pepper and mustard.
Proceed as in Basic Recipe.

Use Basic Recipe.


CARLISLE DRESSING FOR LOW-CALORIE, DIABETIC, LOW-FAT, AND LOW-CHOLESTEROL DIETS

Serving size: 2 tablespoons
Calories per serving: 60
Approximate nutrient
  values per serving:
    Protein 0 g
    Fat 6 g
    Carbohydrate 2 g
    Sodium 50 mg
    Potassium 35 mg
    Cholesterol 0 mg
Exchanges:
    Fat 1½

2 teaspoons arrowroot
⅔ cup cold water
⅓ cup polyunsaturated oil
⅓ cup red wine vinegar
2 tablespoons chopped fresh parsley
½ teaspoon basil
½ teaspoon dry mustard
1 clove garlic, put through garlic press
¼ teaspoon salt
⅛ teaspoon freshly ground pepper
¼ teaspoon paprika
½ cup peeled and diced cooked fresh beets
½ cup finely diced peeled cucumber

In a small saucepan, blend arrowroot and water. Cook and stir over low heat until mixture comes to a boil and thickens. Remove from heat and allow to cool to room temperature.

Measure remaining ingredients into a jar. Cover tightly and shake well to blend. Add arrowroot mixture and mix well. Refrigerate, tightly covered, until thoroughly chilled. Shake vigorously before serving.

*Yield:* 1½ cups

# Salsa Verde

BASIC RECIPE

This goes well with chilled seafood, stewed chicken, or boiled beef.

Serving size: 2 tablespoons
Calories per serving: 147
Approximate nutrient
  values per serving:
    Protein 0 g
    Fat 16 g
    Carbohydrate 0 g
    Sodium 51 mg
    Potassium 63 mg
    Cholesterol 20 mg
Exchanges:
    Fat 3

1 cup water
2 cups chopped fresh spinach
⅓ cup watercress leaves
⅓ cup chopped fresh parsley
2 tablespoons minced unpeeled cucumber
1 tablespoon chopped fresh chives
1 large egg, at room temperature
½ teaspoon dry mustard
¼ teaspoon salt
2 tablespoons lemon juice
1 cup polyunsaturated oil

Bring water to a boil in a medium saucepan. Add spinach, watercress, parsley, cucumber, and chives. Cover tightly; boil 3 minutes or until leaves are wilted. Remove to colander and rinse under cool running water. Press out all moisture. Purée in an electric blender, put in a medium bowl, and set aside.

Place egg, mustard, and salt in electric blender and blend at high speed until foamy. Turn off motor and add lemon juice. Then, with blender turned on at high speed, add oil in a thin, steady stream until sauce is thickened.

Add reserved spinach mixture and blend briefly.

Cover and refrigerate.

*Yield:* 1¾ cups

*Change Salsa Verde as follows or use Basic Recipe, if indicated, for:*

LOW-SODIUM DIETS

Calories per serving: 147
Approximate nutrient
values same as Basic
Recipe except for:
Sodium 11 mg

Omit salt.
Proceed as in Basic Recipe.

BLAND DIETS

Calories per serving: 147

Omit mustard.
Proceed as in Basic Recipe.

HIGH-FIBER DIETS

Use Basic Recipe.

SALSA VERDE FOR LOW-CALORIE, DIABETIC, LOW-FAT, AND LOW-CHOLESTEROL DIETS

Serving size: 2 tablespoons
Calories per serving: 31
Approximate nutrient
values per serving:
  Protein 2 g
  Fat 2 g
  Carbohydrate 3 g
  Sodium 66 mg
  Potassium 97 mg
  Cholesterol 24 mg
Exchanges:
  Vegetable ½
  Fat ½

1 cup water
2 cups chopped fresh spinach
⅓ cup watercress leaves
⅓ cup chopped fresh parsley
2 tablespoons minced unpeeled cucumber
1 tablespoon chopped fresh chives
2 tablespoons flour
⅔ cup skim milk, heated
1 large egg, at room temperature
½ teaspoon dry mustard
¼ teaspoon salt
2 tablespoons lemon juice
1 tablespoon polyunsaturated oil

Bring water to a boil in a medium saucepan. Add spinach, watercress, parsley, cucumber, and chives. Cover tightly; boil 3 minutes or until leaves are wilted. Remove to a colander and rinse under cool running water. Press out all moisture. Purée in an electric blender, put in a medium bowl, and set aside.

Over low heat, in the top of a double boiler, whisk together flour and milk. Blend in egg, mustard, and salt and cook over hot, not boiling, water, stirring constantly, until sauce is thickened and smooth.

Remove from heat and stir in lemon juice and oil. Stir in reserved spinach mixture and mix well. Cover and refrigerate.

*Yield:* 1½ cups

# Country Dressing

BASIC RECIPE

This is delicious with cooked vegetable salads.

Serving size: 2 tablespoons
Calories per serving: 46
Approximate nutrient
  values per serving:
    Protein 1 g
    Fat 4 g
    Carbohydrate 2 g
    Sodium 94 mg
    Potassium 46 mg
    Cholesterol 30 mg
Exchanges:
    Fat 1

1½ tablespoons flour
½ teaspoon dry mustard
¼ teaspoon salt
⅛ teaspoon cayenne pepper
¾ cup cold milk
1 large egg, lightly beaten
2 tablespoons polyunsaturated margarine
¼ cup lemon juice

Over low heat, in the top of a double boiler, mix flour, mustard, salt, cayenne, milk, and egg until blended.

Cook over hot, not boiling, water, stirring constantly, until thickened.

Remove from heat. Stir in margarine and lemon juice until margarine melts. Cool and refrigerate, tightly covered.

*Yield:* 1¼ cups

*Change Country Dressing as follows or use Basic Recipe, if indicated, for:*

## LOW-CALORIE, DIABETIC, LOW-FAT, AND LOW-CHOLESTEROL DIETS

Increase flour to 2 tablespoons.
Substitute skim milk for milk.
Omit egg and use Low-Cholesterol Egg Substitute (page 189) equivalent to 1 large egg.
Reduce margarine to 1 tablespoon. Proceed as in Basic Recipe.

*Yield:* 1¼ cups

Calories per serving: 29
Approximate nutrient
  values per serving:
    Protein 2 g
    Fat 1 g
    Carbohydrate 3 g
    Sodium 88 mg
    Potassium 58 mg
    Cholesterol 0 mg
Exchanges:
  Bread ½

## LOW-SODIUM DIETS

Omit salt.
Substitute unsalted polyunsaturated margarine for margarine.
Proceed as in Basic Recipe.

Calories per serving: 46
Approximate nutrient
  values same as Basic
  Recipe except for:
    Sodium 16 mg

## RENAL DIETS

Omit salt.
Substitute unsalted polyunsaturated margarine for margarine.
Substitute light cream for milk.
Proceed as in Basic Recipe.

Calories per serving: 86
Approximate nutrient
  values per serving:
    Protein 1 g
    Fat 8 g
    Carbohydrate 2 g
    Calcium 16 mg
    Phosphorus 22 mg
    Sodium 13 mg
    Potassium 35 mg
    Cholesterol 47 mg

Calories per serving: 46

Omit mustard and cayenne pepper.
Add ¼ teaspoon tarragon.
Proceed as in Basic Recipe.

HIGH-FIBER DIETS

Use Basic Recipe.

# Whipped Cream Dressing with Chutney

BASIC RECIPE

Delicious with Herbed Cucumber Mold (page 495) or with green vegetable salads.

Serving size: 2 tablespoons
Calories per serving: 70
Approximate nutrient
  values per serving:
    Protein 1 g
    Fat 6 g
    Carbohydrate 4 g
    Sodium 41 mg
    Potassium 39 mg
    Cholesterol 16 mg
Exchanges:
    Fruit ½
    Fat 1

½ cup heavy cream
2 tablespoons minced chives
¼ teaspoon dillweed
⅛ teaspoon salt
⅛ teaspoon freshly ground pepper
4 teaspoons lemon juice
3 tablespoons chutney
¼ cup chopped walnuts

Whip cream until it holds its shape. Fold in remaining ingredients. Refrigerate, covered, for 1 hour.

Fold together once again before serving. Serve immediately.

*Yield:* 1¼ cups

*Change Whipped Cream Dressing with Chutney as follows or use Basic Recipe, if indicated, for:*

LOW-CALORIE, DIABETIC, LOW-FAT, AND LOW-CHOLESTEROL DIETS

Substitute 1 cup plain low-fat yogurt for cream.
Omit nuts. Substitute ¼ cup finely chopped unpeeled apples.
Reduce lemon juice to 2 teaspoons.
Proceed as in Basic Recipe.

Calories per serving: 28
Approximate nutrient
  values per serving:
    Protein 1 g
    Fat 0 g
    Carbohydrate 5 g
    Sodium 52 mg
    Potassium 73 mg
    Cholesterol 1 mg
Exchanges:
  Fruit ½

LOW-SODIUM DIETS

Omit salt and chutney.
Add 1 teaspoon grated peeled fresh ginger root.
Proceed as in Basic Recipe.

Calories per serving: 58
Approximate nutrient
  values per serving:
    Protein 1 g
    Fat 6 g
    Carbohydrate 1 g
    Sodium 5 mg
    Potassium 26 mg
    Cholesterol 16 mg

BLAND DIETS

Omit pepper.
Proceed as in Basic Recipe.

Calories per serving: 70

HIGH-FIBER DIETS

Use Basic Recipe.

# Pineapple Cream Dressing

BASIC RECIPE

This is very good as a marinade for fresh pineapple or as a dressing for fresh fruit salad.

Serving size: 2 tablespoons
Calories per serving: 57
Approximate nutrient
  values per serving:
    Protein 1 g
    Fat 5 g
    Carbohydrate 3 g
    Sodium 67 mg
    Potassium 49 mg
    Cholesterol 10 mg
Exchanges:
  Fruit ½
  Fat 1

1 cup sour cream
⅓ cup unsweetened pineapple juice
2 teaspoons dark-brown sugar
1 teaspoon grated lemon rind
¼ teaspoon salt
¼ teaspoon ground cinnamon

In a medium bowl stir all ingredients together until smooth. Refrigerate, covered, at least 1 hour.
  Stir before serving.

*Yield:* 1⅓ cups

*Change Pineapple Cream Dressing as follows or use Basic Recipe, if indicated, for:*

LOW-CALORIE, DIABETIC, LOW-FAT, AND LOW-CHOLESTEROL DIETS

Calories per serving: 19
Approximate nutrient
  values per serving:
    Protein 1 g
    Fat 0 g
    Carbohydrate 3 g
    Sodium 71 mg
    Potassium 66 mg
    Cholesterol 1 mg
Exchanges:
  Fruit ½

Omit brown sugar.
Substitute plain low-fat yogurt for sour cream.
Proceed as in Basic Recipe.

Calories per serving: 57
Approximate nutrient
    values same as Basic
    Recipe except for:
        Sodium 13 mg

Omit salt.
Proceed as in Basic Recipe.

## BLAND AND HIGH-FIBER DIETS

Use Basic Recipe.

## PINEAPPLE CREAM DRESSING FOR RENAL DIETS

Serving size: 2 tablespoons
Calories per serving: 46
Approximate nutrient
    values per serving:
        Protein 0 g
        Fat 4 g
        Carbohydrate 2 g
        Calcium 9 mg
        Phosphorus 8 mg
        Sodium 5 mg
        Potassium 19 mg
        Cholesterol 16 mg
Exchanges:
    Fat 1

½ cup heavy cream
¼ teaspoon dillweed
¼ cup crushed pineapple
1 teaspoon grated peeled fresh ginger root
4 teaspoons lemon juice

Whip cream until it holds its shape. Fold in remaining ingredients. Refrigerate, covered, for 1 hour.
    Mix gently before serving and serve immediately.

*Yield:* 1¼ cups

# Tomato Catsup

BASIC RECIPE

Serving size: 1 tablespoon
Calories per serving: 20
Approximate nutrient
    values per serving:
        Protein 1 g
        Fat 0 g

3 pounds tomatoes, chopped
¾ cup chopped onions
⅓ cup brown sugar
2 teaspoons salt
⅛ teaspoon dry mustard

Carbohydrate 5 g
Sodium 140 mg
Potassium 122 mg
Cholesterol 0 mg
Exchanges:
  Vegetable 1

⅛ teaspoon celery seed
6 whole cloves
6 black peppercorns
1 cinnamon stick
½ cup cider vinegar

Cook tomatoes and onions in a medium saucepan for 20 minutes, stirring occasionally. Purée mixture in a blender, then strain through a food mill or sieve to remove seeds and skin.

Return sauce to pan and add the brown sugar, salt, mustard, and celery seed. Tie cloves, peppercorns, and cinnamon stick in cheesecloth or spice bag and add to sauce. Bring to a boil, lower heat, and simmer, uncovered, until thick and reduced by half (about 50 minutes).

Remove spice bag, add vinegar, and cook at least 10 minutes. Keep in covered container in the refrigerator.

*Yield:* 2 cups

*Change Tomato Catsup as follows or use Basic Recipe, if indicated, for:*

LOW-CALORIE, DIABETIC, LOW-FAT, LOW-CHOLESTEROL, AND HIGH-FIBER DIETS

Use Basic Recipe.

LOW-SODIUM DIETS

Calories per serving: 20
Approximate nutrient
  values same as Basic
  Recipe except for:
  Sodium 2 mg

Omit salt.
Proceed as in Basic Recipe.

BLAND DIETS

Calories per serving: 20

Omit mustard, cloves, and peppercorns.
Proceed as in Basic Recipe.

# Tarragon Mustard

BASIC RECIPE

This is delicious with roast meats, particularly veal, and it makes an excellent coating for grilled meats.

½ cup tarragon vinegar
2 ounces dry mustard
3 eggs
6 tablespoons sugar
4 tablespoons polyunsaturated margarine, melted
½ teaspoon salt

Pour vinegar over mustard and mix well. Let stand at least 3 hours or overnight, but do not stir.

Pour vinegar-mustard mixture into the top of a double boiler. Over low heat, add eggs one at a time, mixing well after each addition.

Add sugar, margarine, and salt and cook over hot, not boiling, water for 5 minutes. Stir occasionally.

Store in 2 screw-top jars in the refrigerator.

*Yield:* 2 cups

*Change Tarragon Mustard as follows or use Basic Recipe, if indicated, for:*

LOW-SODIUM AND RENAL DIETS

Omit salt.
Substitute unsalted polyunsaturated margarine for margarine.
Proceed as in Basic Recipe.

Serving size: 2 teaspoons
Calories per serving: 26
Approximate nutrient
  values per serving:
    Protein 1 g
    Fat 2 g
    Carbohydrate 2 g
    Sodium 37 mg
    Potassium 15 mg
    Cholesterol 17 mg
Exchanges:
    Fat ½

Calories per serving: 26
Approximate nutrient
  values same as Basic
  Recipe except for:
    Calcium 5 mg
    Phosphorus 15 mg
    Sodium 4 mg

# HIGH-FIBER DIETS

Use Basic Recipe.

## TARRAGON MUSTARD FOR LOW-CALORIE, DIABETIC, LOW-FAT, AND LOW-CHOLESTEROL DIETS

½ cup tarragon vinegar
2 ounces dry mustard
4 tablespoons polyunsaturated margarine
½ tablespoon cornstarch
¼ cup dry white wine
¼ cup Chicken Stock (page 114)
1 egg
2 tablespoons sugar
½ teaspoon salt

Pour vinegar over mustard and mix well. Let stand at least 3 hours or overnight, but do not stir.

In a small saucepan, melt margarine. Add cornstarch and mix until a smooth paste is formed. Add wine and stock and cook about 5 minutes or until thick and smooth.

Pour vinegar-mustard mixture into the top of a double boiler. Over low heat, add egg, mixing in well. Then add wine mixture, sugar, and salt; stir in well and cook over hot water another 5 minutes, stirring often. The mustard should be thick.

Store in 2 screw-top jars in the refrigerator.

*Yield:* 2 cups

Serving size: 2 teaspoons
Calories per serving: 20
Approximate nutrient
values per serving:
Protein 1 g
Fat 2 g
Carbohydrate 1 g
Sodium 34 mg
Potassium 13 mg
Cholesterol 6 mg
Exchanges:
Fat ½

# DESSERTS AND DESSERT SAUCES

You may think that the words "diet" and "dessert" are mutually exclusive. Not at all—if you choose the dessert that matches your diet requirements. We offer so many possibilities that your main problem will be one of selection, not search; how to choose one, not how to find one, be it cake, pie, tart, fruit, whip, pudding, soufflé, or even ice cream cake. There are a wealth of possibilities—but fortunately none so rich that you cannot afford to eat it. Our modifications of mouth-watering basic dessert recipes make each of them appropriate for almost any diet.

We include our recipes for pie crusts, choux puffs, and pâte brisée in this section, and have developed them and their modifications with an eye to their versatility. In addition to their roles in dessert preparation, they can serve as the bases of appetizers or luncheon dishes, depending on their fillings.

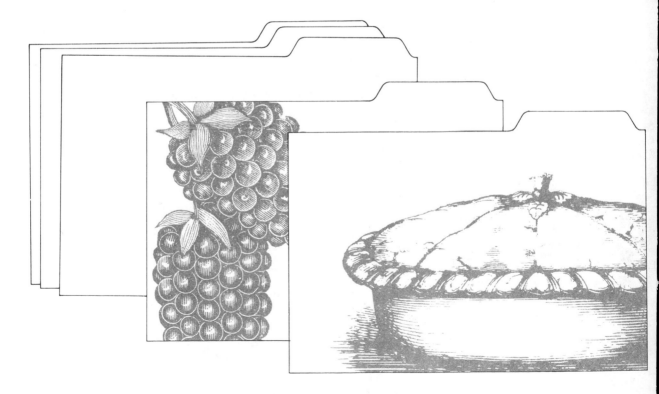

# Angel Food Cake

BASIC RECIPE

12 egg whites (1¼ cups), at room temperature
¾ cup superfine sugar
1 teaspoon almond extract
1 cup cake flour, sifted twice

Preheat oven to 350°F.

Beat egg whites until foamy. Then beat in sugar, a little at a time, until stiff peaks form. Add the almond extract; beat a little more, until glossy.

Fold in flour, ¼ cup at a time, until just blended. Pour into an ungreased 9-inch tube pan and bake for 50 to 60 minutes, or until cake tester inserted in center comes out clean. Invert pan on wire rack to cool. Remove cake from pan.

*Yield:* **10 servings**

*Change Angel Food Cake as follows or use Basic Recipe, if indicated, for:*

LOW-CALORIE, DIABETIC, LOW-FAT, AND LOW-CHOLESTEROL DIETS

Reduce sugar to ½ cup.
Proceed as in Basic Recipe.

*Yield:* **12 servings**

Use Basic Recipe.

### HIGH-FIBER DIETS

Use Basic Recipe. For extra fiber, serve with poached peaches or stewed berries.

# Chocolate Angel Food Cake

BASIC RECIPE

Serving size: 1/16 cake
Calories per serving: 102
Approximate nutrient
  values per serving:
    Protein 3 g
    Fat 1 g
    Carbohydrate 22 g
    Sodium 72 mg
    Potassium 67 mg
    Cholesterol 0 mg
Exchanges:
    Bread 1½

1 cup sifted cake flour
¼ cup cocoa
⅓ cup sugar for the batter
¼ teaspoon salt
12 egg whites (1¼ cups), at room temperature
1 teaspoon cream of tartar
1 cup sugar for the egg whites
1 teaspoon vanilla extract

Preheat oven to 375°F.
   Sift together the flour, cocoa, ⅓ cup sugar, and salt.
   In a large mixing bowl beat the egg whites until foamy. Beat in the cream of tartar and gradually beat in the 1 cup sugar. Continue to beat until stiff peaks form. Add vanilla.
   Sift flour mixture, one quarter at a time, over beaten egg whites and fold in carefully until just blended. When all the flour has been added turn batter into ungreased 9-inch tube pan and bake 35 to 45 minutes or until cake tester inserted in the center comes out clean. Invert pan on wire rack to cool. Remove from pan when completely cooled.

*Yield:* 16 servings

*Change Chocolate Angel Food Cake as follows or use Basic Recipe, if indicated, for:*

## LOW-CALORIE, DIABETIC, LOW-FAT, AND LOW-CHOLESTEROL DIETS

Omit sugar in flour mixture.
Reduce sugar to ¾ cup for egg whites.
Proceed as in Basic Recipe.

Calories per serving: 75
Approximate nutrient
  values per serving:
    Protein 3 g
    Fat 1 g
    Carbohydrate 15 g
    Sodium 72 mg
    Potassium 67 mg
    Cholesterol 0 mg
Exchanges:
  Bread 1

## LOW-SODIUM AND RENAL DIETS

Omit salt.
Proceed as in Basic Recipe.

Calories per serving: 102
Approximate nutrient
  values same as Basic
  Recipe except for:
    Calcium 6 mg
    Phosphorus 19 mg
    Sodium 38 mg

## BLAND DIETS

Use Basic Recipe.

## HIGH-FIBER DIETS

Add ¼ cup shredded coconut to dry ingredients and fold into
  batter.
Proceed as in Basic Recipe.

Calories per serving: 107

# Chocolate Cupcakes

BASIC RECIPE

1 tablespoon polyunsaturated margarine for greasing muffin cups
1 cup sifted cake flour
½ teaspoon baking soda
¼ teaspoon salt
1 square (1 ounce) unsweetened chocolate
¼ cup polyunsaturated margarine, at room temperature
½ cup sugar
½ teaspoon vanilla extract
1 large egg
½ cup ice water
1 tablespoon confectioners' sugar for dusting cupcakes

Preheat oven to 350°F.

Grease 12-cup muffin tin (2-inch cups) with 1 tablespoon margarine.

Sift cake flour, baking soda, and salt together onto waxed paper and set aside.

Melt chocolate slowly in top of double boiler over hot water and allow to cool slightly.

Meanwhile, cream margarine in the bowl of an electric mixer at moderate speed until soft and light. Gradually beat in sugar until thoroughly blended. Beat in vanilla and egg. (The mixture at this point probably will look curdled.) Beat in cooled melted chocolate.

Set the mixer at the lowest speed and proceed to beat in ice water alternately with the flour mixture, scraping down the sides of the bowl from time to time.

Divide the batter among the muffin cups and bake for 30 minutes or until the tops spring back when touched. Leave cupcakes in the cups to cool for 10 minutes. Then remove them to a wire rack to finish cooling. Dust with confectioners' sugar when cool.

*Yield:* 12 cupcakes

*Change Chocolate Cupcakes as follows or use Basic Recipe, if indicated, for:*

## LOW-SODIUM DIETS

Calories per serving: 124
Approximate nutrient
   values same as Basic
   Recipe except for:
      Sodium 42 mg

Omit salt.
Substitute unsalted polyunsaturated margarine for margarine
   wherever used.
Proceed as in Basic Recipe.

## BLAND DIETS

Use Basic Recipe.

## HIGH-FIBER DIETS

Calories per serving: 151

Add ½ cup chopped walnuts. Stir into batter after the ice water
   and flour have been added and just before placing in muffin
   cups.
Proceed as in Basic Recipe.

## CHOCOLATE CUPCAKES FOR LOW-CALORIE, DIABETIC, LOW-FAT, AND LOW-CHOLESTEROL DIETS

Serving size: 1 cupcake
Calories per serving: 81
Approximate nutrient
   values per serving:
      Protein 5 g
      Fat 2 g
      Carbohydrate 15 g
      Sodium 51 mg
      Potassium 188 mg
      Cholesterol 0 mg
Exchanges:
   Bread 1
   Meat ½
   Fat ½

vegetable cooking spray
6 egg whites, at room temperature
2 tablespoons confectioners' sugar for the egg whites
⅓ cup confectioners' sugar
½ cup unsweetened cocoa

Preheat oven to 300°F.
   Spray 6 ramekins or custard cups with vegetable cooking
spray.
   Beat egg whites until they hold their shape. Beat in 2 tablespoons confectioners' sugar and continue beating until whites
are stiff.
   Sift remaining sugar with cocoa and fold into egg whites.

Divide batter among ramekins and set them in a roasting pan in approximately 1 inch of boiling water.

Bake for 50 minutes or until firm to the touch.

Remove individual cups and allow to cool to room temperature. Run a knife around inside of cups and remove cakes.

*Yield:* 6 servings

# Cheesecake

BASIC RECIPE

This recipe requires overnight refrigeration.

*The Crust*
1 tablespoon polyunsaturated margarine, at room temperature
⅓ cup graham cracker crumbs

*The Filling*
four 8-ounce packages cream cheese, at room temperature
1¾ cups sugar
4 large eggs, lightly beaten
1 teaspoon grated lemon rind
2 tablespoons lemon juice
1 teaspoon vanilla extract

*To prepare the crust:* Grease an 8-inch springform pan with the margarine. Sprinkle bottom and sides of the pan with the graham cracker crumbs and set aside.

Preheat oven to 350°F.

*To prepare the filling:* Beat cream cheese in the bowl of an electric mixer until soft and light. Gradually add the sugar and continue beating until smooth and fluffy.

Beat in the eggs one at a time; then add lemon rind, lemon juice, and vanilla and mix well. Pour batter into the springform.

Serving size: ½ cheesecake
Calories per serving: 424
Approximate nutrient
  values per serving:
    Protein 8 g
    Fat 30 g
    Carbohydrate 33 g
    Calcium 70 mg
    Phosphorus 114 mg
    Sodium 276 mg
    Potassium 124 mg
    Cholesterol 175 mg
Exchanges:
  Bread 2
  Meat 1
  Fat 5

*To bake the cheesecake:* Wrap the bottom and sides of spring-form pan in aluminum foil to make it waterproof. Set spring-form in a large deep pan (a roasting pan will do nicely). Prepare a water bath as follows: Pour boiling water into the pan so the water comes halfway up the sides of the springform, and place in the center of the oven.

Bake for 1½ hours or until top is set and slightly puffed. Turn oven off and leave the cheesecake inside for another hour to prevent top from sinking.

Remove pan from the water bath and leave it at room temperature until completely cooled. Remove foil and refrigerate in springform pan overnight.

*Yield:* 12 servings

*Change Cheesecake as follows or use Basic Recipe, if indicated, for:*

LOW-SODIUM AND RENAL DIETS

*The crust:* Substitute unsalted polyunsaturated margarine for margarine.
Proceed as in Basic Recipe.

*The filling:* Use Basic Recipe.

Calories per serving: 424
Approximate nutrient
   values same as Basic
Recipe except for:
   Calcium 70 mg
   Phosphorus 114 mg
   Sodium 266 mg

BLAND DIETS

Use Basic Recipe.

HIGH-FIBER DIETS

*The crust:* Add ½ cup ground almonds to graham cracker crumbs before sprinkling in pan.
Proceed as in Basic Recipe.

*The filling:* Use Basic Recipe.

Calories per serving: 456

## CHEESECAKE FOR LOW-CALORIE, DIABETIC, LOW-FAT, AND LOW-CHOLESTEROL DIETS

Serving size: ½ cheesecake
Calories per serving: 114
Approximate nutrient
 values per serving:
  Protein 8 g
  Fat 3 g
  Carbohydrate 13 g
  Sodium 208 mg
  Potassium 70 mg
  Cholesterol 8 mg
Exchanges:
  Bread 1
  Meat 1

*The Crust*
1 tablespoon polyunsaturated margarine, at room temperature
⅓ cup graham cracker crumbs

*The Filling*
2 cups 1 percent low-fat cottage cheese
1 cup part-skim ricotta cheese
½ cup sugar
1 teaspoon grated lemon rind
1 teaspoon vanilla extract
2 tablespoons lemon juice
2 tablespoons cold water
1 tablespoon plus 1 teaspoon unflavored gelatin

*To prepare the crust:* Grease an 8-inch springform pan with the margarine. Sprinkle the bottom and sides of the pan with the graham cracker crumbs and set aside.

*To prepare the filling:* Purée the cottage cheese and ricotta cheese in an electric blender until smooth. Add sugar and beat until smooth. Stir in lemon rind and vanilla.

 Mix lemon juice with water. Sprinkle gelatin over liquid and let stand 5 minutes. Dissolve the gelatin over low heat, then allow to cool but not set. Stir gelatin into cheese mixture and pour into prepared pan. Refrigerate for 3 hours or until set.

*Yield:* 12 servings

# Orange Cheesecake

BASIC RECIPE

Serving size: ½ cake
Calories per serving: 309
Approximate nutrient
   values per serving:
      Protein 6 g
      Fat 20 g
      Carbohydrate 27 g
      Sodium 197 mg
      Potassium 92 mg
      Cholesterol 101 mg
Exchanges:
   Bread 2
   Fat 4

*The Sponge Cake*
½ teaspoon polyunsaturated oil for the cake pan
⅓ cup sugar for the batter
½ cup all-purpose flour
1½ teaspoons baking powder
2 egg yolks
2 tablespoons polyunsaturated oil
1½ tablespoons water
1½ teaspoons grated orange rind
3 egg whites, at room temperature
2 tablespoons sugar for the egg whites

*The Filling*
two 8-ounce packages cream cheese, at room temperature
1 tablespoon grated orange rind
⅓ cup orange marmalade
½ cup heavy cream
4 egg whites, at room temperature
½ cup superfine sugar

Preheat oven to 350°F.
   Line the bottom of a 9-inch round cake pan with waxed paper and lightly brush with ½ teaspoon oil.

*To prepare the sponge cake:* In a bowl, mix ⅓ cup sugar, the flour, and the baking powder. Make a well in the center.
   Place the egg yolks, 2 tablespoons oil, water, and orange rind in the center of the flour and mix thoroughly. Beat with electric or hand beater until smooth.
   In a separate bowl, beat the egg whites until frothy; then gradually beat in the 2 tablespoons sugar until stiff peaks form.
   Fold one-fourth of the egg white mixture into the batter. Gradually fold in the remaining whites, until just blended.
   Pour the batter into the cake pan and bake for 20 to 30 minutes or until cake tester inserted in center comes out clean. Allow the cake to cool in the pan for 10 minutes before removing.

After the cake has cooled, remove from pan and cut, horizontally, to make two thin round layers. Cover each layer with waxed paper and set aside.

*To prepare the filling:* While the sponge cake is baking, cut the cream cheese into small pieces and leave at room temperature.

When the cake has cooled and been cut, mix the orange rind into the marmalade and spread this mixture over the top of each layer of the cake.

In a large bowl beat the cream cheese with the heavy cream until light and fluffy.

In a separate bowl, beat the egg whites until frothy; then gradually beat in the sugar, just until egg whites hold their shape. Fold a third of the egg-white mixture into the cream cheese. Gently fold in the remaining whites.

*To finish the cake:* Place one sponge cake layer, orange marmalade side up, in a 9-inch springform pan and spread half the cheese mixture on top. Place the other cake half on top and spread over it remaining cheese mixture.

Place in the freezer for 1 hour and then in the refrigerator for at least 2 hours before serving or prepare in advance and refrigerate overnight.

*Yield:* 12 servings


*Change Orange Cheesecake as follows or use Basic Recipe, if indicated, for:*

LOW-SODIUM AND BLAND DIETS

Use Basic Recipe.


HIGH-FIBER DIETS

Use Basic Recipe. For extra fiber, garnish with strawberries.

## ORANGE CHEESECAKE FOR LOW-CALORIE, DIABETIC, LOW-FAT, AND LOW-CHOLESTEROL DIETS

Serving size: ½ cake
Calories per serving: 133
Approximate nutrient
 values per serving:
  Protein 8 g
  Fat 3 g
  Carbohydrate 18 g
  Sodium 233 mg
  Potassium 123 mg
  Cholesterol 24 mg
Exchanges:
 Bread 1
 Meat 1

*The Sponge Cake*
vegetable cooking spray
2 tablespoons sugar for the batter
½ cup flour
1½ teaspoons baking powder
1 egg yolk
2 tablespoons polyunsaturated oil
1½ tablespoons water
1½ teaspoons grated orange rind
3 egg whites, at room temperature
2 tablespoons sugar for the egg whites

*The Filling*
2 cups 1 percent low-fat cottage cheese
1 tablespoon unflavored gelatin
⅓ cup undiluted orange juice concentrate
1 tablespoon grated orange rind
4 egg whites
⅓ cup superfine sugar

Preheat oven to 350°F.

Line the bottom of a 9-inch round cake pan with waxed paper and spray with vegetable cooking spray.

*To prepare the sponge cake:* In a bowl, mix sugar, flour, and baking powder together and make a well in the center. Place the egg yolk, oil, water, and orange rind in the center of the flour and mix thoroughly. Beat until smooth.

In a separate bowl, beat the egg whites until frothy; then gradually beat in the sugar until stiff peaks form. Fold one-fourth of the egg-white mixture into the batter. Gradually fold in the remaining whites, until just blended.

Pour the batter into the prepared cake pan and bake for 20 to 30 minutes or until cake tester inserted in center comes out clean. Allow the cake to cool in the pan for 10 minutes before removing.

After the cake has cooled, cut in half horizontally, to make two thin layers. Cover each layer with waxed paper and set aside.

*To prepare the filling:* Purée cottage cheese in an electric blender.

In a small saucepan, sprinkle gelatin over orange juice concentrate and let stand 10 minutes, then dissolve over low heat. Cool slightly.

Mix the gelatin into cottage cheese, add the orange rind, and refrigerate until it just begins to set.

Beat the egg whites until frothy; then gradually beat in the sugar until stiff peaks form. Fold one-fourth of the whites into cottage cheese mixture; gradually fold in the rest until just blended.

*To finish the cake:* Place one sponge cake layer, cut side up, in a 9-inch springform pan and cover with half the cottage cheese mixture. Place the other cake half on top and cover it with remaining cottage cheese mixture. Refrigerate for at least 2 hours before serving, or prepare in advance and refrigerate overnight.

*Yield:* 12 servings

# Orange Sponge Cake

BASIC RECIPE

This is marvelous served with Custard Sauce (page 632). Also, it makes an excellent layer cake, split horizontally and spread with Orange Cream Filling (page 635).

Serving size: ½ cake
Calories per serving: 143
Approximate nutrient
  values per serving:
    Protein 3 g
    Fat 6 g
    Carbohydrate 19 g

1 teaspoon polyunsaturated oil for greasing pan
½ cup sugar for the cake mix
¾ cup all-purpose flour
1 tablespoon baking powder
3 egg yolks
4 tablespoons polyunsaturated oil

Calcium 28 mg
Phosphorus 57 mg
Sodium 126 mg
Potassium 37 mg
Cholesterol 68 mg
Exchanges:
 Bread 1½
 Fat 1

4 tablespoons water
1 tablespoon grated orange rind
6 egg whites, at room temperature
¼ cup sugar for the egg whites

Preheat oven to 325°F.

Line the bottom of a 10-inch tube pan with waxed paper and lightly brush the paper and sides of pan with 1 teaspoon oil.

In a large bowl, mix ½ cup sugar, flour, and baking powder together and make a well in the center. Place the egg yolks, 4 tablespoons oil, water, and orange rind in the well and mix thoroughly. Beat until smooth.

In a separate bowl, beat the egg whites until frothy; then gradually beat in the ¼ cup sugar until stiff peaks form. Fold one-fourth of the egg white mixture into the batter. Gradually fold in the remaining whites, until just blended.

Pour batter into the prepared tube pan and bake for about 45 minutes or until cake tester inserted in cake comes out clean. Invert tube pan on a rack and allow cake to cool completely before removing.

*Yield:* 12 servings

*Change Orange Sponge Cake as follows or use Basic Recipe, if indicated, for:*

LOW-CALORIE, DIABETIC, LOW-FAT, AND LOW-CHOLESTEROL DIETS

Reduce sugar for the cake mix to ¼ cup.
Reduce egg yolks to 1.
Omit oil for greasing tube pan and spray well with vegetable cooking spray.
Proceed as in Basic Recipe.

Calories per serving: 114
Approximate nutrient
 values per serving:
 Protein 3 g
 Fat 5 g
 Carbohydrate 15 g
 Sodium 125 mg
 Potassium 34 mg
 Cholesterol 23 mg
Exchanges:
 Bread 1
 Fat 1

Use Basic Recipe.

HIGH-FIBER DIETS

Use Basic Recipe. For extra fiber, garnish with Bing cherries.

# Fresh Cherry Cream Torte

BASIC RECIPE

Serving size: ⅛ cake
Calories per serving: 226
Approximate nutrient
  values per serving:
    Protein 4 g
    Fat 11 g
    Carbohydrate 29 g
    Sodium 129 mg
    Potassium 85 mg
    Cholesterol 123 mg
Exchanges:
  Fruit ½
  Bread 1½
  Meat ½
  Fat 2

*The Cake*
2 tablespoons polyunsaturated margarine for greasing pan
1 tablespoon flour for dusting pan
1 tablespoon sugar for dusting pan
¾ cup all-purpose flour, sifted 3 times
¼ teaspoon salt
3 large eggs
½ cup sugar

*The Filling*
½ cup heavy cream
1 cup pitted, halved fresh cherries
3 tablespoons confectioners' sugar

Preheat oven to 350°F.
  Grease an 8-inch springform pan with margarine and dust with 1 tablespoon each of flour and sugar.

*To prepare the cake:* Sift the flour a fourth time with the salt. Set aside.
  Beat the eggs in the bowl of an electric mixer, gradually adding the sugar, and continue beating about 20 minutes or until thick. Gently fold the flour into the egg mixture and pour the batter into the prepared pan. Bake for 30 to 35 minutes or until a cake tester inserted in the center comes out clean.

Remove pan to a rack and allow cake to cool completely. Remove cake and split it horizontally into two thin layers.

*To prepare the filling:* Whip the heavy cream until stiff. Stir the cherries into the whipped cream and add 1 tablespoon of the confectioners' sugar.

*To assemble cake:* Spread filling between layers and sprinkle top with the remaining 2 tablespoons confectioners' sugar.
The torte can be refrigerated for up to 3 hours before serving.

*Yield:* 8 servings

*Change Fresh Cherry Cream Torte as follows or use Basic Recipe, if indicated, for:*

LOW-SODIUM DIETS

*The cake:* Omit salt.
Substitute unsalted polyunsaturated margarine for margarine.
Proceed as in Basic Recipe.

*The filling:* Use Basic Recipe.

Calories per serving: 226
Approximate nutrient values same as Basic Recipe except for:
Sodium 32 mg

BLAND DIETS

Use Basic Recipe.

HIGH-FIBER DIETS

Calories per serving: 228

*The cake:* Use unsifted all-purpose flour and reduce to ½ cup; sift only once with the salt. Add ¼ cup stone-ground whole wheat flour.
Proceed as in Basic Recipe.

*The filling:* Use Basic Recipe.

## FRESH CHERRY CREAM TORTE FOR LOW-CALORIE, DIABETIC, LOW-FAT, AND LOW-CHOLESTEROL DIETS

Serving size: ⅛ cake
Calories per serving: 163
Approximate nutrient
   values per serving:
      Protein 8 g
      Fat 3 g
      Carbohydrate 26 g
      Sodium 147 mg
      Potassium 135 mg
      Cholesterol 44 mg
Exchanges:
   Fruit ½
   Bread 1½
   Meat 1

*The Cake*
vegetable cooking spray
¾ cup all-purpose flour, sifted 3 times
¼ teaspoon salt
1 large egg
Low-Cholesterol Egg Substitute (page 189) equivalent to
   2 large eggs
½ cup sugar

*The Filling*
1 cup part-skim ricotta cheese
1 cup pitted, halved fresh cherries

Preheat oven to 350°F. Spray an 8-inch springform pan with vegetable cooking spray.

*To prepare the cake:* Sift the flour a fourth time with the salt. Set aside.

   Beat the egg and egg substitute in the bowl of an electric mixer, gradually adding the sugar, and continue beating about 20 minutes or until thick. Gently fold the flour into the egg mixture and pour the batter into prepared pan. Bake for 30 to 35 minutes or until a cake tester inserted in center comes out clean. Remove pan to a rack and allow cake to cool completely. Remove cake and split horizontally into two thin layers.

*To prepare the filling:* Purée the ricotta cheese in an electric blender until smooth. Stir in the cherries.

*To assemble cake:* Spread filling between layers. Refrigerate until ready to serve.

*Yield:* 8 servings

# Old-Fashioned Carrot Cake

BASIC RECIPE

*The Cake*
2 large eggs
⅔ cup polyunsaturated oil
1⅓ cups sugar
2 teaspoons baking powder
1 teaspoon allspice
¼ teaspoon salt
¼ cup undiluted orange juice concentrate
1½ cups unsifted whole wheat flour
1⅓ cups grated raw carrots

*The Cream Cheese Frosting*
4 ounces cream cheese, at room temperature
1 tablespoon polyunsaturated margarine
1¾ cups sifted confectioners' sugar
1 teaspoon vanilla extract

Preheat oven to 350°F.

*To prepare the cake:* In a large mixing bowl, beat eggs until light. Add oil, sugar, baking powder, allspice, salt, and orange juice concentrate and beat until smooth and thoroughly blended.

Add flour alternately with carrots, stirring after each addition until blended.

Turn batter into an ungreased 8-by-8-by-2-inch baking pan and bake for 45 minutes or until a cake tester inserted in the middle comes out clean. Remove to rack and allow to cool.

*To prepare the frosting:* Combine all ingredients in a large mixing bowl and beat until smooth and thoroughly blended. Remove cake from pan and cover with cream cheese frosting.

*Yield:* 12 servings

Serving size: ½₂ cake
Calories per serving: 371
Approximate nutrient
  values per serving:
    Protein 4 g
    Fat 18 g
    Carbohydrate 52 g
    Sodium 167 mg
    Potassium 165 mg
    Cholesterol 56 mg
Exchanges:
  Bread 3½
  Fat 3½

*Change Old-Fashioned Carrot Cake as follows or use Basic Recipe, if indicated, for:*

LOW-SODIUM DIETS

Calories per serving: 371
Approximate nutrient
  values same as Basic
  Recipe except for:
    Sodium 112 mg

*The cake:* Omit salt.
  Proceed as in Basic Recipe.

*The frosting:* Substitute unsalted polyunsaturated margarine for margarine.
  Proceed as in Basic Recipe.

BLAND DIETS

Use Basic Recipe.

HIGH-FIBER DIETS

Calories per serving: 398
Serving size: ½ cake

*The cake:* Use Basic Recipe.

*The frosting:* Use Basic Recipe.
  Add ½ cup coarsely chopped walnuts and sprinkle on top of frosting.

OLD-FASHIONED CARROT CAKE FOR LOW-CALORIE, DIABETIC, LOW-FAT, AND LOW-CHOLESTEROL DIETS

Calories per serving: 189
Approximate nutrient
  values per serving:
    Protein 3 g
    Fat 9 g
    Carbohydrate 25 g
    Sodium 137 mg
    Potassium 126 mg
    Cholesterol 0 mg
Exchanges:
  Bread 2
  Fat 2

1 cup sifted all-purpose flour
2 teaspoons baking powder
¼ teaspoon salt
Low-Cholesterol Egg Substitute (page 189) equivalent to
    2 large eggs
½ cup polyunsaturated oil
⅓ cup undiluted orange juice concentrate
¾ cup sugar
1 teaspoon allspice
1 cup grated raw carrots
1½ teaspoons confectioners' sugar for topping

Preheat oven to 350°F.

Sift together the flour, baking powder, and salt in a large bowl.

In a separate bowl, beat egg substitute, oil, orange juice concentrate, sugar, and allspice until well blended. Stir egg mixture into flour mixture alternately with carrots.

Pour batter into an ungreased 8-by-8-by-2-inch baking pan and bake for 35 minutes. Allow to cool. Remove from pan and sift confectioners' sugar over top of cake.

*Yield:* 12 servings

# Spice Coffee Cake

BASIC RECIPE

Serving size: ½ cake
Calories per serving: 323
Approximate nutrient
  values per serving:
    Protein 4 g
    Fat 15 g
    Carbohydrate 43 g
    Sodium 214 mg
    Potassium 130 mg
    Cholesterol 54 mg
Exchanges:
  Bread 3
  Fat 3

*The Cake*
½ cup polyunsaturated margarine
1 teaspoon ground cinnamon
½ teaspoon nutmeg
¾ teaspoon ground ginger
¼ teaspoon vanilla extract
¾ cup sugar
¾ cup firmly packed dark-brown sugar
2 large eggs
2 cups sifted all-purpose flour
2 teaspoons baking powder
¼ teaspoon salt
1 cup sour cream

*The Topping*
1 tablespoon sugar
½ cup chopped walnuts

Preheat oven to 350°F.

*To prepare the cake:* In a large mixing bowl, cream margarine until light. Blend in cinnamon, nutmeg, ginger, and vanilla.

Add white and brown sugars; mix until thoroughly blended. Beat in eggs, one at a time.

Sift together flour, baking powder, and salt; add to batter alternately with sour cream. Stir after each addition until mixture is blended—batter will be fairly stiff.

Turn into an ungreased 9-by-9-by-2-inch baking pan; sprinkle with sugar and walnut topping.

Bake 45 minutes or until cake tester inserted in the center comes out clean. Place pan on rack to cool. Serve cake either warm or at room temperature.

*Yield:* 12 servings

*Change Spice Coffee Cake as follows or use Basic Recipe, if indicated, for:*

LOW-SODIUM DIETS

*The cake:* Omit salt.
Substitute unsalted polyunsaturated margarine for margarine. Proceed as in Basic Recipe.

*The topping:* Use Basic Recipe.

RENAL DIETS

*The cake:* Omit salt.
Substitute unsalted polyunsaturated margarine for margarine. Proceed as in Basic Recipe.

*The topping:* Omit walnuts.

Calories per serving: 323
Approximate nutrient
  values same as Basic
  Recipe except for:
    Sodium 92 mg

Calories per serving: 295
Approximate nutrient
  values per serving:
    Protein 4 g
    Fat 13 g
    Carbohydrate 42 g
    Calcium 56 mg
    Phosphorus 69 mg
    Sodium 92 mg
    Potassium 111 mg
    Cholesterol 54 mg

BLAND DIETS

*The cake:* Omit nutmeg. Proceed as in Basic Recipe.

*The topping:* Use Basic Recipe.

HIGH-FIBER DIETS

Use Basic Recipe.

SPICE COFFEE CAKE FOR LOW-CALORIE, DIABETIC, LOW-FAT, AND LOW-CHOLESTEROL DIETS

½ cup polyunsaturated margarine
1 teaspoon ground cinnamon
½ teaspoon nutmeg
¾ teaspoon ground ginger
¼ teaspoon vanilla extract
½ cup sugar
¼ cup firmly packed dark-brown sugar
Low-Cholesterol Egg Substitute (page 189) equivalent to
    2 large eggs
2 cups sifted flour
2 teaspoons baking powder
¼ teaspoon salt
1 cup plain low-fat yogurt

Preheat oven to 350°F.

In a large mixing bowl, cream margarine until light. Blend in cinnamon, nutmeg, ginger, and vanilla. Add white and brown sugars; mix until thoroughly blended. Beat in egg substitute.

Sift together flour, baking powder, and salt; add to batter alternately with low-fat yogurt. Stir after each addition until mixture is blended—batter will be fairly stiff.

Turn into an ungreased 9-by-9-by-2-inch baking pan. Bake 45 minutes or until cake tester inserted in the center comes out clean. Place pan on rack to cool. Serve cake either warm or at room temperature.

*Yield:* 12 servings

Serving size: ⅟₁₂ cake
Calories per serving: 207
Approximate nutrient
  values per serving:
    Protein 4 g
    Fat 8 g
    Carbohydrate 30 g
    Sodium 223 mg
    Potassium 112 mg
    Cholesterol 1 mg
Exchanges:
  Bread 2
  Fat 1½

# Streusel-Topped Plum Cake

BASIC RECIPE

Serving size: ⅓ cake
Calories per serving: 215
Approximate nutrient
    values per serving:
        Protein 3 g
        Fat 11 g
        Carbohydrate 27 g
        Sodium 158 mg
        Potassium 86 mg
        Cholesterol 32 mg
Exchanges:
    Fruit ½
    Bread 1½
    Fat 2

*The Cake*
1 tablespoon polyunsaturated margarine for greasing cake pan
1 cup sifted all-purpose flour
1 teaspoon baking powder
5 tablespoons polyunsaturated margarine
5 tablespoons sugar
1 egg, slightly beaten
⅓ cup milk
9 fresh prune plums, pitted and halved

*Streusel Topping*
2 tablespoons polyunsaturated margarine
2 tablespoons sugar
2 tablespoons all-purpose flour

Preheat oven to 350°F.

Grease an 8-inch square cake pan with 1 tablespoon margarine.

*To prepare the cake:* Sift together the flour and baking powder.

In a medium bowl, cream margarine until soft and light. Add sugar gradually and beat, using an electric or hand beater. Continue beating until well blended. Add egg and beat well. Stir in the flour and the milk, alternately, beginning and ending with the flour.

Spread batter in the pan, and arrange the plums, cut side down, in rows on the batter.

*To prepare the topping:* Blend ingredients in a small bowl until mixture is crumbly. Sprinkle the mixture over plums and bake for 55 minutes or until cake tester inserted in center comes out clean.

Remove cake from oven, place on rack, and allow to cool. Serve warm. Cut into 9 squares for serving.

*Yield:* 9 servings

*Change Streusel-Topped Plum Cake as follows or use Basic Recipe, if indicated, for:*

LOW-CALORIE, DIABETIC, LOW-FAT, AND LOW-CHOLESTEROL DIETS

*The cake:* Omit margarine for greasing. Spray pan well with vegetable cooking spray.
   Reduce sugar to 3 tablespoons.
   Omit egg and use Low-Cholesterol Egg Substitute (page 189) equivalent to 1 large egg.
   Substitute skim milk for milk.
   Reduce plums to 9 halves arranged cut side down on the batter.

*The topping:* Omit streusel topping, and reduce cooking time to 50 minutes.

LOW-SODIUM DIETS

*The cake and the topping:* Substitute unsalted polyunsaturated margarine for margarine wherever used.
   Proceed as in Basic Recipe.

BLAND DIETS

Use Basic Recipe.

HIGH-FIBER DIETS

*The cake:* Reduce all-purpose flour to ½ cup. Add to it ½ cup unsifted stone-ground whole wheat flour.
Proceed as in Basic Recipe.

*The topping:* Use Basic Recipe.

Calories per serving: 139
Approximate nutrient
   values per serving:
      Protein 3 g
      Fat 7 g
      Carbohydrate 18 g
      Sodium 126 mg
      Potassium 74 mg
      Cholesterol 0 mg
Exchanges:
   Fruit ½
   Bread 1
   Fat 1

Calories per serving: 215
Approximate nutrient
   values same as Basic
   Recipe except for:
      Sodium 57 mg

Calories per serving: 214

# Blueberry Teacake

BASIC RECIPE

Serving size: ½ cake
Calories per serving: 331
Approximate nutrient
  values per serving:
    Protein 5 g
    Fat 19 g
    Carbohydrate 38 g
    Sodium 326 mg
    Potassium 91 mg
    Cholesterol 54 mg
Exchanges:
    Fruit 1
    Bread 2
    Fat 4

*The Crumb Topping*
⅓ cup sugar
½ cup sifted all-purpose flour
¾ teaspoon ground cinnamon
¼ cup polyunsaturated margarine
⅓ cup chopped walnuts

*The Cake*
½ teaspoon polyunsaturated margarine for greasing baking pan
2 cups sifted cake flour
1½ teaspoons baking powder
½ teaspoon baking soda
½ teaspoon salt
1½ cups fresh blueberries
½ cup polyunsaturated margarine
1 teaspoon vanilla extract
¾ cup sugar
2 large eggs
1 cup sour cream

Preheat oven to 375°F.

*To prepare the crumb topping:* In a medium bowl, mix sugar, flour, and cinnamon. Cut in the margarine until mixture is crumbly. Add nuts and mix gently. Set aside.

*To prepare the cake:* Grease a 9-by-9-by-2-inch baking pan with ½ teaspoon margarine.

Sift together flour, baking powder, baking soda, and salt into a medium-size bowl. Add blueberries and mix gently to coat berries with flour.

In a large bowl beat the margarine, vanilla, sugar, and eggs together until well blended.

Add flour-blueberry mixture alternately with the sour cream, stirring after each addition until mixture is thoroughly blended.

Pour batter into baking pan and sprinkle with reserved topping.

Bake 50 minutes or until cake tester inserted in the center comes out clean.

Place on a rack to cool. Serve warm or cold.

*Yield:* 12 servings

*Change Blueberry Teacake as follows or use Basic Recipe, if indicated, for:*

LOW-SODIUM DIETS

*The topping:* Substitute unsalted polyunsaturated margarine for margarine. Proceed as in Basic Recipe.

*The cake:* Omit salt. Substitute unsalted polyunsaturated margarine for margarine wherever used.

Add ½ teaspoon almond extract to batter.

Proceed as in Basic Recipe.

RENAL DIETS

*The topping:* Substitute unsalted polyunsaturated magarine for margarine. Omit walnuts. Proceed as in Basic Recipe.

*The cake:* Omit salt. Substitute unsalted polyunsaturated margarine for margarine wherever used.

Add ½ teaspoon almond extract to the batter.

Proceed as in Basic Recipe.

BLAND AND HIGH-FIBER DIETS

Use Basic Recipe.

Calories per serving: 331
Approximate nutrient
  values same as Basic
  Recipe except for:
    Sodium 119 mg

Calories per serving: 314
Approximate nutrient
  values per serving:
    Protein 4 g
    Fat 17 g
    Carbohydrate 38 g
    Calcium 44 mg
    Phosphorus 66 mg
    Sodium 119 mg
    Potassium 79 mg
    Cholesterol 54 mg

## BLUEBERRY TEACAKES FOR LOW-CALORIE, DIABETIC, LOW-FAT, AND LOW-CHOLESTEROL DIETS

For these diets, you will be making small cupcakes, not a cake.

Serving size: 2 cupcakes
Calories per serving: 102
Approximate nutrient
  values per serving:
    Protein 2 g
    Fat 4 g
    Carbohydrate 14 g
    Sodium 117 mg
    Potassium 44 mg
    Cholesterol 0 mg
Exchanges:
  Bread 1
  Fat 1

1¾ cups sifted all-purpose flour
2 teaspoons baking powder
½ teaspoon ground cinnamon
½ teaspoon salt
1 cup fresh blueberries
⅓ cup sugar
⅓ cup polyunsaturated oil
¾ cup skim milk
Low-Cholesterol Egg Substitute (page 189) equivalent to
    1 large egg
1 teaspoon grated orange rind
1 teaspoon vanilla extract

Preheat oven to 400°F.

Put 36 little cupcake paper liners in cupcake tins 1¾ inches in diameter.

Sift flour, baking powder, cinnamon, and salt. Add blueberries and mix gently to coat berries with flour.

In a separate bowl combine sugar, oil, milk, egg substitute, orange rind, and vanilla. Add to flour mixture and stir until just blended.

Spoon batter into lined tins, allowing 1 tablespoon batter per cake.

Bake 20 minutes or until a cake tester inserted in center comes out clean. Place on a rack to cool. Serve warm or cold.

*Yield:* 36 cupcakes

# Strawberry Pavlova

BASIC RECIPE

*The Meringue Pie Shell*
1 tablespoon polyunsaturated margarine, melted
1 tablespoon all-purpose flour
3 egg whites
⅛ teaspoon salt
⅓ cup superfine sugar
1 teaspoon distilled white vinegar
½ teaspoon vanilla extract

*The Filling*
1 cup heavy cream
1 teaspoon vanilla extract
1 teaspoon confectioners' sugar
1 pint fresh ripe strawberries, hulled and quartered
3 whole strawberries reserved for garnish

Preheat oven to 275°F.

Grease a 9-inch pie plate with margarine and dust with flour. Set aside.

*To prepare the meringue pie shell:* Beat egg whites with salt until very stiff. Fold in sugar, then the vinegar and vanilla.

Spoon meringue into pie plate, scooping a hollow in the center to hold filling.

Bake for 1 hour or until firm at the edges and elsewhere slightly sticky. Remove to rack and allow to cool completely.

*To prepare the filling:* Beat cream until it holds soft shape. Beat in vanilla and confectioners' sugar. Gently fold in quartered strawberries. Pile filling on cooled shell. Cut reserved whole berries into halves, through stem ends. Arrange in center of pie, pointed ends out. Refrigerate no longer than 1 hour. To serve, cut into 6 slices with strawberry garnish for each slice.

*Yield:* 6 servings

Serving size: ⅙ pie
Calories per serving: 234
Approximate nutrient
   values per serving:
      Protein 3 g
      Fat 17 g
      Carbohydrate 19 g
      Sodium 104 mg
      Potassium 151 mg
      Cholesterol 54 mg
Exchanges:
   Fruit ½
   Bread 1
   Fat 3½

*Change Strawberry Pavlova as follows or use Basic Recipe, if indicated, for:*

LOW-CALORIE, DIABETIC, LOW-FAT, AND LOW-CHOLESTEROL DIETS

*The meringue pie shell:* Omit margarine and flour for preparing pie plate. Instead, spray pie plate with vegetable cooking spray.
   Proceed as in Basic Recipe.

*The filling:* Omit heavy cream, vanilla, and sugar. Substitute 1 cup part-skim ricotta cheese beaten until soft and light. Fold in strawberries.
   Proceed as in Basic Recipe.

Calories per serving: 129
Approximate nutrient
  values per serving:
    Protein 7 g
    Fat 4 g
    Carbohydrate 18 g
    Sodium 121 mg
    Potassium 171 mg
    Cholesterol 13 mg
Exchanges:
    Fruit ½
    Bread 1
    Meat 1

LOW-SODIUM AND RENAL DIETS

*The meringue pie shell:* Omit salt. Substitute unsalted polyunsaturated margarine for margarine.
   Proceed as in Basic Recipe.

*The filling:* Use Basic Recipe.

Calories per serving: 234
Approximate nutrient
  values same as Basic
  Recipe except for:
    Calcium 40 mg
    Phosphorus 40 mg
    Sodium 41 mg

BLAND AND HIGH-FIBER DIETS

Use Basic Recipe.

# Fresh Fruit Tart

BASIC RECIPE

This tart would be equally delicious filled with raspberries or blackberries.

*The Glaze*
1 cup apricot preserves
2 tablespoons sugar

*The Tart*
9-inch Easy-Mix Flaky Pie Crust, baked (page 555)
1 quart strawberries, washed and hulled

*To prepare the glaze:* Rub apricot preserves through a sieve into a small saucepan. Stir in sugar. Simmer 1 minute. Remove from heat and cool slightly.

*To prepare the tart:* Brush 3 tablespoons warm glaze on inside of pie crust.
Arrange berries in crust stem side down. Brush with remaining glaze. Refrigerate for 1 hour before serving.

*Yield:* 8 servings

*Change Fresh Fruit Tart as follows or use Basic Recipe, if indicated, for:*

LOW-SODIUM AND RENAL DIETS

Substitute low-sodium Easy-Mix Flaky Pie Crust (page 555) for
   basic Easy-Mix Flaky Pie Crust.
Proceed as in Basic Recipe.

---

Serving size: ⅛ tart
Calories per serving: 300
Approximate nutrient
   values per serving:
      Protein 3 g
      Fat 10 g
      Carbohydrate 53 g
      Sodium 143 mg
      Potassium 177 mg
      Cholesterol 0 mg
Exchanges:
   Fruit 3
   Bread 1½
   Fat 2

Calories per serving: 300
Approximate nutrient
   values same as Basic
   Recipe except for:
      Calcium 27 mg
      Phosphorus 37 mg
      Sodium 6 mg

## BLAND DIETS

Use Basic Recipe.

## HIGH-FIBER DIETS

Calories per serving: 321

Substitute high-fiber Easy-Mix Flaky Pie Crust (page 556) for basic Easy-Mix Flaky Pie Crust.
Proceed as in Basic Recipe.
Sprinkle top of pie with ½ cup grated coconut.

## FRESH FRUIT TART FOR LOW-CALORIE, DIABETIC, LOW-FAT, AND LOW-CHOLESTEROL DIETS

Serving size: ⅛ tart
Calories per serving: 210
Approximate nutrient
  values per serving:
    Protein 3 g
    Fat 10 g
    Carbohydrate 28 g
    Sodium 139 mg
    Potassium 218 mg
    Cholesterol 0 mg
Exchanges:
    Fruit 1
    Bread 1½
    Fat 2

*The Glaze*
2 cups strawberries, washed and hulled
¼ cup unsweetened orange juice
4 teaspoons cornstarch
1 tablespoon sugar
1 teaspoon vanilla extract

*The Tart*
9-inch Easy-Mix Flaky Pie Crust, baked (page 555)
1 quart whole strawberries, washed and hulled

*To prepare the glaze:* Crush strawberries in a saucepan.
    In a small bowl, combine orange juice with cornstarch until smooth. Add to berries.
    Cook, stirring constantly, over moderate heat until mixture comes to a boil and starts to thicken. Remove from heat.
    In an electric blender, purée mixture until smooth. Strain, then stir in sugar and vanilla. Allow to cool to room temperature.

*To prepare the tart:* Brush 3 tablespoons warm glaze on inside of pie crust. Arrange whole berries stem side down in crust and brush with remaining glaze.
    Refrigerate for 1 hour before serving.

*Yield:* 8 servings

# Key Lime Pie

BASIC RECIPE

Serving size: ⅒ pie
Calories per serving: 315
Approximate nutrient
  values per serving:
    Protein 7 g
    Fat 13 g
    Carbohydrate 45 g
    Sodium 208 mg
    Potassium 196 mg
    Cholesterol 96 mg
Exchanges:
  Milk ½
  Bread 2½
  Fat 2½

3 large eggs, separated
14-ounce can sweetened condensed milk
½ cup fresh lime juice
2 teaspoons grated lime rind
⅛ teaspoon salt
⅛ teaspoon nutmeg
1 teaspoon vanilla extract
9-inch Easy-Mix Flaky Pie Crust, baked (page 555)
¼ teaspoon cream of tartar
½ cup sugar for meringue

Preheat oven to 350°F.

In a large bowl beat egg yolks until thick and lemon-colored. Blend in condensed milk, lime juice, rind, salt, nutmeg, and vanilla. Pour mixture into baked pie crust.

In a separate bowl, beat egg whites until foamy. Beat in cream of tartar. Gradually add sugar, beating until soft peaks form. Spread meringue over top of pie, sealing to edge of the crust. Bake 8 to 10 minutes or until meringue is golden. Cool pie on rack. Refrigerate until thoroughly chilled, about 3 hours.

*Yield:* 10 servings

*Change Key Lime Pie as follows for:*

LOW-SODIUM AND RENAL DIETS

Calories per serving: 315
Approximate nutrient
  values same as Basic
  Recipe except for:
    Calcium 125 mg
    Phosphorus 143 mg
    Sodium 72 mg

Substitute low-sodium Easy-Mix Flaky Pie Crust (page 555) for basic Easy-Mix Flaky Pie Crust.
Omit salt in filling.
Proceed as in Basic Recipe.

## BLAND DIETS

Calories per serving: 315

Omit nutmeg.
Proceed as in Basic Recipe.

## HIGH-FIBER DIETS

Calories per serving: 323

Substitute high-fiber Easy-Mix Flaky Pie Crust (page 556) for basic Easy-Mix Flaky Pie Crust.
Add ¼ cup grated coconut; fold into meringue.
Proceed as in Basic Recipe.

## KEY LIME PIE FOR LOW-CALORIE, DIABETIC, LOW-FAT, AND LOW-CHOLESTEROL DIETS

Serving size: ⅒ pie
Calories per serving: 191
Approximate nutrient
 values per serving:
  Protein 4 g
  Fat 7 g
  Carbohydrate 28 g
  Sodium 139 mg
  Potassium 83 mg
  Cholesterol 0 mg
Exchanges:
  Bread 2
  Fat 1½

1 tablespoon unflavored gelatin
½ cup fresh lime juice
¾ cup boiling water
⅓ cup sugar for filling
1 cup skim milk
1 teaspoon vanilla extract
1½ teaspoons grated lime rind
⅛ teaspoon nutmeg
3 large egg whites
¼ teaspoon cream of tartar
⅓ cup sugar for meringue
9-inch Easy-Mix Flaky Pie Crust, baked (page 555)

Soften gelatin in the lime juice, about 5 minutes. Pour softened gelatin, boiling water, ⅓ cup sugar, and skim milk into container of electric blender. Blend until mixed thoroughly. Pour into a large bowl and stir in vanilla, lime rind, and nutmeg. Chill until mixture begins to thicken.

In a separate bowl, beat egg whites until foamy. Beat in cream of tartar. Gradually beat in remaining ⅓ cup sugar until soft peaks form. Fold whites into lime mixture, until just blended, and turn into baked crust. Refrigerate until set.

*Yield:* 10 servings

# Easy-Mix Flaky Pie Crust

BASIC RECIPE

1⅓ cups sifted all-purpose flour
½ teaspoon salt
⅓ cup polyunsaturated oil
3 tablespoons ice water
1 tablespoon flour

Preheat oven to 450°F.

In a large bowl, mix flour and salt. Add oil and water; stir with a fork until dough is well blended. Shape into a ball; then flatten it slightly.

Roll out dough between two pieces of lightly floured waxed paper forming a circle 12 inches in diameter. Peel away paper.

Fit dough into a 9-inch pie plate. Trim excess and pinch dough evenly around the rim. Prick pastry with a fork.

Bake 12 to 15 minutes or until golden brown. Remove from oven and place on rack. Cool before filling.

*Yield:* 9-inch pie crust

*Change Easy-Mix Flaky Pie Crust as follows or use Basic Recipe, if indicated, for:*

LOW-CALORIE, DIABETIC, LOW-FAT, LOW-CHOLESTEROL, AND BLAND DIETS

Use Basic Recipe.

LOW-SODIUM AND RENAL DIETS

Omit salt.
Proceed as in Basic Recipe.

Serving size: ⅛ pie crust
Calories per serving: 153
Approximate nutrient
  values per serving:
    Protein 2 g
    Fat 9 g
    Carbohydrate 15 g
    Sodium 138 mg
    Potassium 19 mg
    Cholesterol 0 mg
Exchanges:
  Bread 1
  Fat 2

Calories per serving: 153
Approximate nutrient
  values same as Basic
  Recipe except for:
    Calcium 3 mg
    Phosphorus 17 mg
    Sodium 0 mg

Calories per serving: 152

Reduce all-purpose flour to 1 cup. Add to it ⅛ cup stone-ground whole wheat flour.
Proceed as in Basic Recipe.

# Choux Puffs

BASIC RECIPE

Delicious filled with Orange Cream Filling (page 635) or Vanilla Ice Cream (page 615) served with Apricot Sauce (page 622). They may also be used as appetizers filled with cheese, fish, meat, or chicken mixtures.

Serving size: 2 puffs
Calories per serving: 62
Approximate nutrient
 values per serving:
  Protein 1 g
  Fat 5 g
  Carbohydrate 3 g
  Sodium 90 mg
  Potassium 14 mg
  Cholesterol 39 mg
Exchanges:
  Bread ¼
  Fat 1

¼ cup polyunsaturated margarine for the puff dough
½ cup water
½ cup sifted flour
¼ teaspoon salt
2 large eggs
1 tablespoon polyunsaturated margarine for greasing cookie sheets

In a medium saucepan, bring margarine and water to a boil. Reduce heat and add flour and salt, all at once, and stir vigorously until mixture leaves the sides of the saucepan and forms a ball.

Remove from heat. Add eggs, one at a time, beating after each addition until mixture is well blended. Allow to cool to room temperature.

Drop by rounded teaspoonsful onto cookie sheet greased with the 1 tablespoon margarine.

Refrigerate for at least 1 hour.

Preheat oven to 425°F.

Bake puffs approximately 18 to 20 minutes or until golden brown and crusty.

Place on a rack and allow to cool.

*Yield:* 28 puffs

*Change Choux Puffs as follows or use Basic Recipe, if indicated, for:*

LOW-CALORIE, DIABETIC, LOW-FAT, LOW-CHOLESTEROL, BLAND, AND HIGH-FIBER DIETS

Use Basic Recipe.

LOW-SODIUM AND RENAL DIETS

Calories per serving: 62
Approximate nutrient
  values same as Basic
  Recipe except for:
    Calcium 5 mg
    Phosphorus 16 mg
    Sodium 10 mg

Omit salt.
Substitute unsalted polyunsaturated margarine for margarine wherever used.
Proceed as in Basic Recipe.

# Pâte Brisée

BASIC RECIPE

This is a crunchy pastry shell for dessert tarts, fruit pies, or luncheon quiches.

Serving size: ⅛ pastry shell
Calories per serving: 136
Approximate nutrient
  values per serving:
    Protein 2 g
    Fat 8 g
    Carbohydrate 15 g
    Sodium 144 mg
    Potassium 20 mg
    Cholesterol 0 mg
Exchanges:
  Bread 1
  Fat 1½

1¼ cups sifted all-purpose flour
¼ teaspoon salt
⅓ cup polyunsaturated margarine, at room temperature
¼ cup ice water
1 tablespoon flour for dusting the board

Mix 1¼ cups flour and salt in a large bowl. Cut in margarine until mixture is crumbly. Add ice water to form a soft dough. Wrap dough in plastic and refrigerate at least 2 hours or overnight.
  Preheat oven to 425°F.
  Dust board with 1 tablespoon flour. Roll out dough into a 12-inch circle and fit into a 9-inch pie plate. Trim excess pastry and flute the edge.

If crust is to be baked with its filling, do not prick pastry. If it is to be filled after baking, prick inside of pastry with a fork and bake 12 to 15 minutes or until lightly browned. Check after 5 minutes and prick any areas that have puffed up.

Cool on rack before filling.

*Yield:* 9-inch pastry shell

*Change Pâte Brisée as follows or use Basic Recipe, if indicated, for:*

LOW-CALORIE, DIABETIC, LOW-FAT, LOW-CHOLESTEROL, BLAND, AND HIGH-FIBER DIETS

Use Basic Recipe.

LOW-SODIUM AND RENAL DIETS

Omit salt.
Substitute unsalted polyunsaturated margarine for margarine.
Proceed as in Basic Recipe.

# Peach Tarts

SUITABLE FOR LOW-CALORIE, DIABETIC, LOW-FAT, LOW-CHOLESTEROL, LOW-SODIUM, BLAND, AND HIGH-FIBER DIETS

*The Tarts*
2 large egg whites, at room temperature
¼ cup superfine sugar
¼ cup unsifted all-purpose flour
¼ teaspoon ground cinnamon
¼ teaspoon ground coriander
¼ cup polyunsaturated margarine, softened
vegetable cooking spray

Sodium 71 mg
Potassium 181 mg
Cholesterol 0 mg
Exchanges:
 Fruit 1
 Bread ½
 Fat 1

*The Filling*
1 pint fresh strawberries
1 tablespoon honey
4 medium-size ripe peaches

Preheat oven to 375°F.

*To prepare the tarts:* Beat the egg whites until frothy. Gradually beat in the sugar, then the flour, cinnamon, and coriander, and continue beating. Add margarine and beat until smooth.

On a baking sheet sprayed lightly with vegetable cooking spray, spread two thin 4-inch rounds of batter about 2 inches apart. Bake for 10 to 12 minutes or until golden brown—watch them carefully. It is important to bake only two at a time to complete the next step.

While tarts are baking, spray four custard cups inside and out with vegetable cooking spray—the cups should be large enough to hold a peach half. Turn cups upside down. Remove the two baked tarts and, while they are still soft, quickly mold them over the bottoms of two of the cups. Slip the remaining cups over the top of each tart to shape it while it cools. (If they become too brittle while molding place them in the oven for a minute to soften.) Repeat the process until all dough is used.

*To prepare the filling:* Wash and slice the strawberries. Place in a blender with the honey and purée until smooth. Set aside.

Place the whole peaches in boiling water for 1 minute. Remove and cool. Peel, cut in half, and remove the pits.

*To assemble the tarts:* Place a peach half, cut side down, in each tart shell and spoon strawberry sauce over each peach.

*Yield:* 8 servings

# Kichlach

BASIC RECIPE

1 tablespoon polyunsaturated margarine
2 cups sifted all-purpose flour
2 tablespoons sugar
4 large eggs
1 tablespoon polyunsaturated oil

*The Topping*
½ teaspoon ground cinnamon
½ teaspoon sugar

Preheat oven to 425°F.
　Grease two baking sheets with margarine and set aside.
　Mix the flour, sugar, eggs, and oil in a bowl with your hands to form a smooth, sticky dough.
　Combine the cinnamon and sugar in a small bowl.
　Drop dough by teaspoons about 2 inches apart onto prepared baking sheets. Sprinkle with the cinnamon-sugar mixture and bake for 12 minutes or until puffed and brown. Lift from baking sheets with spatula and allow to cool on wire racks.

*Yield:* 4 dozen cookies

*Change Kichlach as follows or use Basic Recipe, if indicated, for:*

LOW-SODIUM AND RENAL DIETS

Substitute unsalted polyunsaturated margarine for margarine wherever used.
Proceed as in Basic Recipe.

Serving size: 2 cookies
Calories per serving: 62
Approximate nutrient
　values per serving:
　　Protein 2 g
　　Fat 2 g
　　Carbohydrate 9 g
　　Sodium 16 mg
　　Potassium 20 mg
　　Cholesterol 46 mg
Exchanges:
　Bread ½
　Fat ½

Calories per serving: 62
Approximate nutrient
　values same as Basic
　Recipe except for:
　　Calcium 7 mg
　　Phosphorus 23 mg
　　Sodium 12 mg

## BLAND DIETS

Use Basic Recipe.

## HIGH-FIBER DIETS

Calories per serving: 75

Add ½ cup chopped walnuts to dough before mixing. Proceed as in Basic Recipe.

## KICHLACH FOR LOW-CALORIE, DIABETIC, LOW-FAT, AND LOW-CHOLESTEROL DIETS

Serving size: 2 cookies
Calories per serving: 52
Approximate nutrient
    values per serving:
        Protein 1 g
        Fat 4 g
        Carbohydrate 4 g
        Sodium 12 mg
        Potassium 20 mg
        Cholesterol 0 mg
Exchanges:
    Bread ½
    Fat ½

vegetable cooking spray
1 cup sifted all-purpose flour
1 tablespoon sugar
Low-Cholesterol Egg Substitute (page 189) equivalent to 3
    large eggs
½ cup polyunsaturated oil
½ teaspoon ground cinnamon

Preheat oven to 300°F.
    Spray baking sheets well with vegetable cooking spray.
    Beat flour, sugar, egg substitute, and oil with electric mixer for 20 minutes. (Dough will be very soft and will drop off the beaters.) Drop dough by teaspoons onto sprayed baking sheets—about 2 inches apart. Sprinkle with cinnamon and bake 20 to 25 minutes or until puffed brown. Lift from baking sheets with spatula and allow to cool on wire racks.

*Yield:* 5 dozen cookies

# Ladyfingers

SUITABLE FOR LOW-CALORIE, DIABETIC, LOW-FAT, LOW-CHOLESTEROL, LOW-SODIUM, RENAL, BLAND, AND HIGH-FIBER DIETS

These are good alone as a cookie, or as a lining for charlotte molds.

Serving size: 1 ladyfinger
Calories per serving: 84
Approximate nutrient
  values per serving:
    Protein 1 g
    Fat 5 g
    Carbohydrate 9 g
    Calcium 3 mg
    Phosphorus 10 mg
    Sodium 11 mg
    Potassium 14 mg
    Cholesterol 19 mg
Exchanges:
  Bread ½
  Fat 1

1 teaspoon polyunsaturated oil for greasing cookie sheet
1 teaspoon flour for dusting cookie sheet
½ cup sugar
⅓ cup all-purpose flour
1 egg yolk
4 tablespoons polyunsaturated oil
½ teaspoon vanilla extract
3 egg whites

Preheat oven to 375°F.

Oil cookie sheet with 1 teaspoon oil. Dust with 1 teaspoon flour.

Mix ¼ cup of the sugar and ⅓ cup flour in a bowl. Make a well in the center. Pour the egg yolk, oil, and vanilla into the well. Gradually mix the egg mixture with the flour until well blended.

Beat the egg whites until frothy. Then gradually beat in the remaining ¼ cup sugar until stiff peaks form. Fold one-third of the beaten whites into the flour mixture until thoroughly blended. Fold in the remaining egg whites until just blended.

Press dough through a pastry tube or shape into oblongs 1 inch wide, 3 inches long. Place on cookie sheet.

Bake 7 to 12 minutes or until lightly browned. Remove from cookie sheet while still hot and place on wire racks.

*Yield:* 14 ladyfingers

# Chocolate Fork Cookies

BASIC RECIPE

Serving size: 2 cookies
Calories per serving: 101
Approximate nutrient
 values per serving:
  Protein 1 g
  Fat 6 g
  Carbohydrate 14 g
  Sodium 48 mg
  Potassium 53 mg
  Cholesterol 0 mg
Exchanges:
  Bread 1
  Fat 1

1 tablespoon polyunsaturated margarine for greasing cookie
 sheet
½ cup flour
⅓ cup unsweetened cocoa
¼ cup polyunsaturated margarine
½ cup superfine sugar

Preheat oven to 350°F.
 Grease cookie sheet with 1 tablespoon margarine.
 Sift together the flour and cocoa and set aside.
 Cream margarine and sugar until light and fluffy. Gradually blend in the flour mixture and mix until a dough is formed.
 Divide dough equally into 24 small balls. Place balls on the greased cookie sheet. Dip a fork into hot water and flatten each cookie with the tines.
 Bake 8 to 10 minutes. Remove from the cookie sheet while still hot, and place on racks to cool.

*Yield:* 24 cookies

*Change Chocolate Fork Cookies as follows or use Basic Recipe, if indicated, for:*

LOW-CALORIE, DIABETIC, LOW-FAT, AND LOW-CHOLESTEROL DIETS

Calories per serving: 77
Approximate nutrient
 values per serving:
  Protein 1 g
  Fat 5 g
  Carbohydrate 10 g
  Sodium 38 mg
  Potassium 53 mg
  Cholesterol 0 mg
Exchanges:
  Bread ½
  Fat 1

Reduce superfine sugar to ¼ cup.
Omit margarine for greasing cookie sheet. Spray cookie sheet
 with vegetable cooking spray instead.
Proceed as in Basic Recipe.

Calories per serving: 101
Approximate nutrient
values same as Basic
Recipe except for:
Sodium 0 mg

## LOW-SODIUM DIETS

Substitute unsalted polyunsaturated margarine for margarine
wherever used.
Proceed as in Basic Recipe.

## BLAND DIETS

Use Basic Recipe.

## HIGH-FIBER DIETS

Calories per serving: 119

Add ⅛ cup chopped walnuts and blend in with the flour.
Proceed as in Basic Recipe.

# Old-Fashioned Oatmeal Cookies

## BASIC RECIPE

Serving size: 2 cookies
Calories per serving: 196
Approximate nutrient
values per serving:
Protein 3 g
Fat 9 g
Carbohydrate 29 g
Sodium 158 mg
Potassium 98 mg
Cholesterol 18 mg
Exchanges:
Bread 2
Fat 1½

2 cups all-purpose flour
1 teaspoon baking powder
1 teaspoon salt
1 cup polyunsaturated margarine
1 teaspoon vanilla extract
1 cup sugar
1 cup firmly packed dark-brown sugar
2 large eggs
2 cups quick-cooking oats
⅔ cup chocolate chips
⅔ cup raisins
2 teaspoons polyunsaturated margarine for greasing cookie
sheets

Preheat oven to 375°F.

Sift together flour, baking powder, and salt. Set aside.

In a large bowl beat together margarine, vanilla, sugar, brown sugar, and eggs. Blend in flour mixture, oats, chocolate chips, and raisins.

Drop by tablespoons onto lightly greased cookie sheets about 1½ inches apart. Bake 10 to 12 minutes or until nicely browned. Remove to racks and allow to cool.

*Yield:* 5 dozen cookies

*Change Old-Fashioned Oatmeal Cookies as follows or use Basic Recipe, if indicated, for:*

### LOW-SODIUM DIETS

Calories per serving: 196
Approximate nutrient values same as Basic Recipe except for: Sodium 21 mg

Omit salt.

Substitute unsalted polyunsaturated margarine for margarine wherever used.

Proceed as in Basic Recipe.

### BLAND DIETS

Use Basic Recipe.

### HIGH-FIBER DIETS

Calories per serving: 199

Omit raisins; substitute ⅔ cup chopped walnuts.

Proceed as in Basic Recipe.

### OLD-FASHIONED OATMEAL COOKIES FOR LOW-CALORIE, DIABETIC, LOW-FAT, AND LOW-CHOLESTEROL DIETS

Serving size: 3 cookies
Calories per serving: 95

vegetable cooking spray
1 cup all-purpose flour

½ teaspoon baking powder
½ teaspoon salt
⅓ cup polyunsaturated margarine
⅓ cup honey
1 teaspoon ground cinnamon
½ teaspoon ground ginger
¼ teaspoon nutmeg
1 teaspoon vanilla extract
Low-Cholesterol Egg Substitute (page 189) equivalent to
    1 large egg
1 cup quick-cooking oats
⅓ cup raisins

Preheat oven to 375°F.
  Spray cookie sheet with vegetable cooking spray.
  Sift together flour, baking powder, and salt. Set aside.
  Beat together margarine, honey, cinnamon, ginger, nutmeg,
and vanilla. Blend in egg substitute. Add flour mixture, oats,
and raisins, and mix well.
  Drop by teaspoons onto cookie sheets about 1½ inches apart.
Bake 8 to 10 minutes or until golden brown. Remove to racks
and allow to cool.

*Yield:* 5 dozen cookies

# Mandel Brot

BASIC RECIPE

3 cups sifted all-purpose flour
2 teaspoons baking powder
¼ teaspoon salt
2 large eggs
½ cup polyunsaturated oil
⅓ cup sugar
2 teaspoons grated orange rind
1 teaspoon almond extract

Potassium 27 mg
Cholesterol 12 mg
Exchanges:
  Bread ½
  Fat 1

1 teaspoon vanilla extract
¾ cup chopped almonds

Preheat oven to 350°F.

Sift together flour, baking powder, and salt. Set aside.

In a large bowl, beat eggs, oil, sugar, orange rind, almond extract, and vanilla extract until well blended. Gradually beat in flour mixture—batter must be stiff. Add almonds and work them in until they are evenly distributed.

Divide dough into three pieces and shape each piece into a roll 9 inches long, 2 inches wide.

Place rolls about 2 inches apart on an ungreased cookie sheet. Bake 25 minutes or until rolls are dry on top.

Remove from oven and cut hot rolls at an angle, in ½-inch slices. Arrange slices on ungreased cookie sheet and bake 15 minutes longer or until golden brown. Remove to racks, allow to cool, and store in airtight container.

*Yield:* 45 mandel brot

*Change Mandel Brot as follows or use Basic Recipe, if indicated, for:*

LOW-CALORIE, DIABETIC, LOW-FAT, AND LOW-CHOLESTEROL DIETS

Omit eggs; use Low-Cholesterol Egg Substitute (page 189) equivalent to 1 large egg.
Reduce oil to ⅓ cup.
Omit almonds.
Proceed as in Basic Recipe.

Calories per serving: 49
Approximate nutrient
  values per serving:
    Protein 1 g
    Fat 2 g
    Carbohydrate 7 g
    Sodium 33 mg
    Potassium 11 mg
    Cholesterol 0 mg
Exchanges:
  Bread ½
  Fat ½

Calories per serving: 72
Approximate nutrient
  values same as Basic
  Recipe except for:
    Sodium 21 mg

LOW-SODIUM DIETS

Omit salt.
Proceed as in Basic Recipe.

BLAND AND HIGH-FIBER DIETS

Use Basic Recipe.

# Apple Cobbler

BASIC RECIPE

*The Apple Filling*
1 teaspoon polyunsaturated margarine for greasing pie plate
4½ cups sliced peeled apples
⅓ cup sugar
⅓ cup all-purpose flour
½ teaspoon nutmeg
2 tablespoons lemon juice
1 teaspoon grated lemon rind
2 tablespoons polyunsaturated margarine for dotting the
  apples

*The Biscuit Topping*
2 cups all-purpose flour
2½ teaspoons baking powder
¼ cup sugar
1 teaspoon salt
¼ cup vegetable shortening
¾ cup milk
2 tablespoons all-purpose flour for pastry board

Preheat oven to 400°F.

Serving size: ½ cup apple
  filling, 1 biscuit
Calories per serving: 266
Approximate nutrient
  values per serving:
    Protein 4 g
    Fat 9 g
    Carbohydrate 43 g
    Sodium 355 mg
    Potassium 119 mg
    Cholesterol 3 mg
Exchanges:
  Fruit 1
  Bread 2
  Fat 2

*To prepare the filling:* Grease a deep 9½-inch pie plate with 1 teaspoon margarine.

Combine apples, sugar, flour, and nutmeg. Transfer to greased pie plate and bake for 15 minutes or until apples are just tender.

Remove the pie plate from the oven and sprinkle the apples with lemon juice and rind; dot with 2 tablespoons margarine. Set aside.

*To prepare the biscuit topping:* Sift flour, baking powder, sugar, and salt into a large bowl. Cut in the shortening until mixture is crumbly.

Stir in two-thirds of the milk. Add remaining milk, 1 tablespoon at a time, until a soft, sticky dough is formed.

Dust pastry board with 2 tablespoons of flour and turn dough onto it.

Knead until smooth.

Roll the dough out until it is approximately ¾ inch thick. Cut out ten 2-inch circles.

Place the biscuit circles on the apple mixture, return to the oven, and continue baking for 35 minutes or until biscuits are lightly browned. Allow to cool 10 minutes before serving.

*Yield:* 10 servings

*Change Apple Cobbler as follows or use Basic Recipe, if indicated, for:*

LOW-SODIUM AND RENAL DIETS

*The apple filling:* Substitute unsalted polyunsaturated margarine for margarine wherever used. Proceed as in Basic Recipe.

*The biscuit topping:* Omit salt.
Proceed as in Basic Recipe.

Calories per serving: 266
Approximate nutrient
values same as Basic
Recipe except for:
Calcium 46 mg
Phosphorus 74 mg
Sodium 109 mg

Calories per serving: 266

*The apple filling:* Omit nutmeg. Substitute cinnamon.
    Proceed as in Basic Recipe.

*The biscuit topping:* Use Basic Recipe.

HIGH-FIBER DIETS

Calories per serving: 260

*The apple filling:* Use Basic Recipe.

*The biscuit topping:* Reduce all-purpose flour to 1 cup. Add to it
1 cup stone-ground whole wheat flour.
    Proceed as in Basic Recipe.

APPLE COBBLER FOR LOW-CALORIE, DIABETIC,
LOW-FAT, AND LOW-CHOLESTEROL DIETS

Serving size: ½ cup apple
    filling, 1 biscuit
Calories per serving: 161
Approximate nutrient
    values per serving:
        Protein 2 g
        Fat 5 g
        Carbohydrate 28 g
        Sodium 154 mg
        Potassium 91 mg
        Cholesterol 0 mg
Exchanges:
    Fruit 1
    Bread 1
    Fat 1

*The Apple Filling*
vegetable cooking spray
4½ cups sliced peeled apples
⅓ cup sugar
⅓ cup all-purpose flour
½ teaspoon nutmeg
2 tablespoons lemon juice
1 teaspoon grated lemon rind

*The Biscuit Topping*
1 cup all-purpose flour
1 teaspoon baking powder
½ teaspoon salt
3 tablespoons polyunsaturated oil
⅓ cup skim milk
2 tablespoons all-purpose flour for pastry board

Preheat oven to 400°F.

*To prepare the filling:* Spray a deep 9½-inch pie plate with vegetable cooking spray.

Combine apples, sugar, flour, and nutmeg. Transfer into sprayed pie plate and bake for 15 minutes or until apples are barely tender.

Remove the pie plate from the oven and sprinkle the apples with lemon juice and rind.

*To prepare the biscuit topping:* Sift flour, baking powder, and salt into a medium bowl.

Add enough oil and milk to moisten flour. Add remaining oil and milk and stir until a soft, sticky dough is formed.

Dust pastry board with 2 tablespoons of flour and turn the dough onto the board. Knead until smooth.

Roll the dough out until it is approximately ½ inch thick. Cut out ten 2-inch circles.

Place biscuit circles on the apple mixture, return to the oven, and continue baking for 25 to 30 minutes or until biscuits are lightly browned.

Allow to cool for 10 minutes before serving.

*Yield:* 10 servings

# Fruit Clafoutis

BASIC RECIPE

*The Pie Plate*
1 teaspoon polyunsaturated margarine
1 tablespoon sugar

*The Fruit*
½ cup sliced peeled peaches
½ cup sliced bananas
½ cup halved pitted cherries
½ cup sliced pitted plums
3 tablespoons sugar
1 tablespoon grated lemon rind

Serving size: ⅛ tart
Calories per serving: 182
Approximate nutrient
  values per serving:
    Protein 5 g
    Fat 4 g
    Carbohydrate 34 g
    Sodium 79 mg
    Potassium 161 mg
    Cholesterol 107 mg
Exchanges:
  Fruit 1
  Bread 1½
  Meat ½
  Fat ½

*The Batter*
½ cup all-purpose flour
⅛ teaspoon salt
½ cup sugar
3 eggs, lightly beaten
1 cup milk
2 tablespoons confectioners' sugar

Preheat oven to 350°F.

*To prepare the pie plate:* Grease a deep 9½-inch pie plate with the margarine and sprinkle with the tablespoon sugar.

*To prepare the fruit:* Arrange fruit in the pie plate and sprinkle with the 3 tablespoons sugar and lemon rind.

*To prepare the batter:* Combine flour, salt, sugar, eggs, and milk in the container of an electric blender and blend until smooth.
    Pour batter over fruit and bake for 1 hour or until puffed and browned. Sprinkle with confectioners' sugar and serve at once.

*Yield:* 8 servings

*Change Fruit Clafoutis as follows or use Basic Recipe, if indicated, for:*

LOW-SODIUM DIETS

*The pie plate:* Substitute unsalted polyunsaturated margarine for margarine.
    Proceed as in Basic Recipe.

*The fruit:* Use Basic Recipe.

*The batter:* Omit salt.
    Proceed as in Basic Recipe.

Calories per serving: 182
Approximate nutrient
    values same as Basic
    Recipe except for:
    Sodium 42 mg

Use Basic Recipe.

## FRUIT CLAFOUTIS FOR LOW-CALORIE, DIABETIC, LOW-FAT, AND LOW-CHOLESTEROL DIETS

vegetable cooking spray

Serving size: ⅛ tart
Calories per serving: 92
Approximate nutrient
  values per serving:
    Protein 5 g
    Fat 0 g
    Carbohydrate 18 g
    Sodium 96 mg
    Potassium 202 mg
    Cholesterol 1 mg
Exchanges:
  Fruit 1
  Bread ½
  Meat ½

*The Fruit*
½ cup sliced peeled peaches
½ cup sliced bananas
½ cup halved pitted cherries
½ cup sliced pitted plums
1 tablespoon grated lemon rind

*The Batter*
½ cup flour
⅛ teaspoon salt
2 tablespoons sugar
Low-Cholesterol Egg Substitute (page 189) equivalent to 3
  large eggs
1 cup skim milk

Preheat oven to 350°F.
  Spray a deep 9½-inch pie plate with vegetable cooking spray.

*To prepare the fruit:* Arrange fruit in the pie plate and sprinkle with lemon rind.

*To prepare batter:* Combine flour, salt, sugar, egg substitute, and milk in the container of an electric blender and blend until smooth.
  Pour batter over fruit and bake for 1 hour or until puffed and browned. Serve at once.

*Yield:* 8 servings

# Peach Shortcake

BASIC RECIPE

*The Shortcake*
1 tablespoon polyunsaturated margarine, melted
2 cups all-purpose flour
2½ teaspoons baking powder
¼ cup sugar
1 teaspoon salt
¼ cup solid vegetable shortening
¾ cup milk
1 tablespoon flour for dusting board

*The Filling*
8 ripe medium-size peaches
1½ cups water
½ cup sugar
1 cup heavy cream

Preheat oven to 425°F.

Grease a baking sheet with 1 tablespoon melted margarine.

*To prepare the shortcake:* Sift together flour, baking powder, sugar, and salt into a medium bowl. Cut in shortening until mixture is crumbly.

Stir in ⅔ cup milk. Add remaining milk, 1 tablespoon at a time, until a soft dough is formed.

Turn the dough onto a lightly floured board and knead lightly until smooth. Roll the dough out until about ½ inch thick. Cut into ten 3-inch rounds and place on baking sheet.

Bake in upper third of oven for 20 minutes or until tops of shortcakes are lightly golden and sides firm. Remove to a rack and allow to cool.

*To prepare the filling:* Blanch the peaches in boiling water for 1 minute, then peel. Combine 1½ cups water and sugar in a saucepan and cook over low heat until sugar dissolves.

Slice peaches into water and sugar syrup and poach gently for 5 minutes or until soft.

*To serve:* Split the shortcakes horizontally and arrange bottom halves on dessert plates. Spoon peaches onto the shortcakes with slotted spoon. Add 1 teaspoon syrup to each serving to moisten the peaches. Whip the heavy cream until soft peaks form. Do not overbeat. Spoon whipped cream on top of peaches, add top halves of shortcakes, and serve at once.

*Yield:* 10 servings

*Change Peach Shortcake as follows or use Basic Recipe, if indicated, for:*

### LOW-SODIUM DIETS

Calories per serving: 330
Approximate nutrient values same as Basic Recipe except for:
Sodium 118 mg

*The shortcake:* Omit salt.
Substitute unsalted polyunsaturated margarine for margarine.
Proceed as in Basic Recipe.

*The filling:* Use Basic Recipe.

### BLAND DIETS

Use Basic Recipe.

### HIGH-FIBER DIETS

Calories per serving: 327

*The shortcake:* Reduce all-purpose flour to 1½ cups; add to it ½ cup unsifted stone-ground whole wheat flour.
Proceed as in Basic Recipe.

*The filling:* Use Basic Recipe.

## PEACH SHORTCAKE FOR LOW-CALORIE, DIABETIC, LOW-FAT, AND LOW-CHOLESTEROL DIETS

Serving size: 1 shortcake, ⅓ cup peaches, 1½ tablespoons ricotta cheese
Calories per serving: 155
Approximate nutrient values per serving:
    Protein 5 g
    Fat 6 g
    Carbohydrate 21 g
    Sodium 186 mg
    Potassium 218 mg
    Cholesterol 8 mg
Exchanges:
    Fruit 1
    Bread 1
    Meat ½
    Fat 1

*The Shortcake*
vegetable cooking spray
1 cup all-purpose flour
1 teaspoon baking powder
½ teaspoon salt
3 tablespoons polyunsaturated oil
⅓ cup skim milk
1 tablespoon flour for dusting board

*The Filling*
8 ripe medium-size peaches
1½ cups water
2 tablespoons sugar
1 cup part-skim ricotta cheese, puréed in blender

Preheat oven to 400°F.
    Spray baking sheet with vegetable cooking spray.

*To prepare the shortcake:* Sift together the flour, baking powder, and salt into a large bowl. Add the oil and milk and stir until a soft dough is formed. Turn the dough onto a lightly floured board and knead lightly until smooth. Roll the dough out until about ⅜ inch thick. Cut into ten 2-inch rounds and place on baking sheet. Bake on top rack of oven for 20 minutes or until shortcakes are lightly golden on top and the sides are firm. Remove to a rack and allow to cool.

*To prepare the filling:* Immerse whole peaches in boiling water for 1 minute. Remove peaches with slotted spoon and peel. Combine the 1½ cups water and sugar in a saucepan and cook over low heat until sugar dissolves. Slice the peaches into the syrup and poach gently for 5 minutes or until soft.

*To serve:* Split the shortcakes and arrange on ten dessert plates. Spoon the peaches onto the shortcakes with slotted spoon. Add 1 teaspoon syrup to each serving to moisten the peaches and top with puréed ricotta cheese. Serve at once.

*Yield:* 10 servings

# Peaches Marsala

BASIC RECIPE

Serving size: 2 peach
halves, ¼ cup sauce
Calories per serving: 190
Approximate nutrient
values per serving:
    Protein 2 g
    Fat 9 g
    Carbohydrate 27 g
    Sodium 127 mg
    Potassium 221 mg
    Cholesterol 68 mg
Exchanges:
    Fruit 1
    Bread 1
    Fat 2

*The Peaches*
6 medium-size ripe peaches
3 quarts boiling water

*The Marsala Sauce*
¼ cup Marsala wine
⅓ cup polyunsaturated margarine, at room temperature
1¼ cups sifted confectioners' sugar
2 large eggs, separated
½ teaspoon grated lemon rind
⅛ teaspoon salt

*To prepare the peaches:* Immerse whole peaches in boiling water and poach for 5 minutes. Immediately drain and cover with cold water. When cool enough to handle, peel, cut in half, and remove pits. Set peaches aside.

*To prepare the Marsala sauce:* Place Marsala in a small saucepan. Bring to a boil for 1 minute and remove from heat immediately. Set aside.

In a large bowl, beat margarine, sugar, and egg yolks until blended smoothly. Transfer mixture to the top of a double boiler and cook over hot water, stirring constantly, until smooth and thickened.

Remove from heat and stir in Marsala, lemon rind, and salt.

In a separate bowl, beat egg whites until soft peaks form. Fold one-fourth of the whites into the sauce and then fold in remaining whites.

Place two peach halves, cut side down, in each serving dish and spoon sauce over peaches. Serve at once.

*Yield:* 6 servings, 2 cups sauce

Change Peaches Marsala as follows or use Basic Recipe, if indicated, for:

LOW-SODIUM AND RENAL DIETS

*The peaches:* Use Basic Recipe.

*The sauce:* Omit salt.
   Substitute unsalted polyunsaturated margarine for margarine.
   Proceed as in Basic Recipe.

Calories per serving: 190
Approximate nutrient
   values same as Basic
   Recipe except for:
      Calcium 16 mg
      Phosphorus 42 mg
      Sodium 19 mg

BLAND AND HIGH-FIBER DIETS

Use Basic Recipe.

PEACHES MARSALA FOR LOW-CALORIE, DIABETIC, LOW-FAT, AND LOW-CHOLESTEROL DIETS

*The Peaches*
6 medium-size ripe peaches
3 quarts boiling water

*The Sauce*
¼ cup Marsala wine
1 tablespoon polyunsaturated margarine
2 teaspoons cornstarch
⅔ cup skim milk
½ teaspoon grated lemon rind
⅛ teaspoon salt
2 egg whites
2 tablespoons sugar

Serving size: 2 peach
   halves, ¼ cup sauce
Calories per serving: 78
Approximate nutrient
   values per serving:
      Protein 2 g
      Fat 2 g
      Carbohydrate 15 g
      Sodium 71 mg
      Potassium 248 mg
      Cholesterol 0 mg
Exchanges:
   Fruit 1
   Bread ½

*To prepare the peaches:* Immerse whole peaches in boiling water and poach for 5 minutes. Immediately drain and cover with cold water. When cool enough to handle, peel, cut in half, and remove pits. Set peaches aside.

*To prepare the sauce:* Place Marsala wine in a small saucepan. Bring to a boil for 1 minute and remove from heat immediately. Set aside.

Melt margarine in a small saucepan. Blend in cornstarch, then gradually add milk, and cook over moderate heat, stirring constantly, until sauce comes to a boil. Boil and stir for 1 minute. Remove from heat and stir in Marsala, lemon rind, and salt.

In a separate bowl, beat egg whites until foamy. Add sugar and continue beating until soft peaks form. Fold one-fourth of the whites into the sauce, then fold in remaining whites.

Place two peach halves, cut side down, into each serving dish and spoon sauce over peaches. Serve at once.

*Yield:* 6 servings, 2 cups sauce

# Poached Spiced Peaches

BASIC RECIPE

6 ripe medium-size peaches
1½ cups water
½ cup honey
2 whole cloves
1 cinnamon stick
2 whole allspice
⅛ cup brandy

Immerse whole peaches in boiling water for 1 minute. Peel the peaches and set aside.

In a large saucepan, make a syrup by combining water, honey, cloves, cinnamon, and allspice. Boil for 5 minutes.

Pour brandy into metal measuring cup or small saucepan. Heat container briefly, ignite brandy, then let flames subside. Add to the syrup.

Add whole peaches and simmer slowly for 5 minutes. Remove from heat and allow to cool in syrup. Remove cloves, cinnamon stick, and allspice. Serve peaches either hot or cold.

*Yield:* 6 servings

Serving size: 1 whole peach
Calories per serving: 123
Approximate nutrient values per serving:
   Protein 0 g
   Fat 0 g
   Carbohydrate 33 g
   Calcium 10 mg
   Phosphorus 21 mg
   Sodium 2 mg
   Potassium 216 mg
   Cholesterol 0 mg
Exchanges:
   Fruit 3

*Change Poached Spiced Peaches as follows or use Basic Recipe, if indicated, for:*

## LOW-CALORIE, DIABETIC, LOW-FAT, AND LOW-CHOLESTEROL DIETS

Calories per serving: 48
Approximate nutrient
  values per serving:
  Protein 0 g
  Fat 0 g
  Carbohydrate 12 g
  Sodium 2 mg
  Potassium 226 mg
  Cholesterol 0 mg
Exchanges:
  Fruit 1

Omit honey. Substitute 2 tablespoons Raisin Purée (page 591)
Proceed as in Basic Recipe.

## LOW-SODIUM AND RENAL DIETS

Use Basic Recipe.

## BLAND DIETS

Calories per serving: 123

Omit cloves.
Proceed as in Basic Recipe.

## HIGH-FIBER DIETS

Calories per serving: 131

Use Basic Recipe.
While peaches are cooling, cut the rind of half an orange into thin julienne strips about 2 inches long. Gently simmer the orange rind in ⅓ cup water and 2 tablespoons sugar for 3 minutes. Drain and garnish the peaches with the orange rind.

# Pears in Fruit Sauce

BASIC RECIPE

Serving size: 2 pear halves,
2 tablespoons sauce
Calories per serving: 125
Approximate nutrient
values per serving:
Protein 2 g
Fat 1 g
Carbohydrate 31 g
Sodium 4 mg
Potassium 317 mg
Cholesterol 0 mg
Exchanges:
Fruit 3

6 medium-size pears, peeled, cored, and halved
1¼ cups fresh orange juice
¼ cup water
⅛ teaspoon ground ginger
2 tablespoons Grand Marnier

Preheat oven to 325°F.

Arrange pears, cut side up, in baking dish.

Mix together orange juice, water, and ginger. Pour over pears. Bake, covered, for 1 hour or until pears are tender but still firm. Baste occasionally.

Remove pears with a slotted spoon to a serving bowl; pour juice into a small saucepan. Simmer until liquid is reduced to 1 cup.

Stir in Grand Marnier; simmer 2 minutes longer. Pour sauce over pears. Serve at room temperature or refrigerate and serve chilled.

*Yield:* 6 servings

*Change Pears in Fruit Sauce as follows or use Basic Recipe, if indicated, for:*

LOW-CALORIE, DIABETIC, LOW-FAT, LOW-CHOLESTEROL, LOW-SODIUM, AND BLAND DIETS

Use Basic Recipe.

HIGH-FIBER DIETS

Calories per serving: 149

Use Basic Recipe.
Add 3 tablespoons toasted slivered almonds (page 38) as a garnish.

Serving size: 2 pear halves,
2 tablespoons sauce
Calories per serving: 139
Approximate nutrient
values per serving:
Protein 1 g
Fat 1 g
Carbohydrate 35 g
Calcium 15 mg
Phosphorus 20 mg
Sodium 4 mg
Potassium 243 mg
Cholesterol 0 mg
Exchanges:
Fruit 3½

1 teaspoon grated lemon rind
¼ cup dry white wine
2 tablespoons honey
6 fresh medium-size pears, peeled, cored, and halved
1 tart apple, peeled, cored, and quartered
1½ tablespoons rum
½ tablespoon cornstarch
2 tablespoons water

Combine the lemon rind, wine, and honey in a medium saucepan. Simmer for 3 minutes. Add the pear halves and simmer gently, covered, 5 to 8 minutes or until tender. Remove pears with slotted spoon and set aside to cool.

Add the apple to wine and honey mixture and simmer, covered, for 15 minutes. Add rum and simmer, uncovered, 2 to 3 minutes. Transfer to an electric blender and purée until smooth. Return purée to the saucepan.

Blend the cornstarch and water. Add to the purée and bring to boil, stirring constantly. Cover and allow to cool.

To serve, arrange the pear halves on dessert plates and spoon the apple purée over the pears. Serve at room temperature or refrigerate and serve chilled.

*Yield:* 6 servings

# Pear and Berry Compote

SUITABLE FOR LOW-CALORIE, DIABETIC, LOW-FAT, LOW-CHOLESTEROL, LOW-SODIUM, RENAL, BLAND, AND HIGH-FIBER DIETS

Serving size: ½ pear, 3
tablespoons sauce
Calories per serving: 80

4 ripe pears, peeled, cored, and quartered
½ cup water
½ teaspoon allspice

2 tablespoons honey
2 teaspoons cornstarch
¼ cup cold water
1 cup fresh blueberries

Slice the pears into quarters. Bring the ½ cup water, allspice, and honey to a boil. Add the pears, reduce heat until water simmers, then poach gently for 3 minutes. Remove the pears to a plate. Reserve liquid.

Mix the cornstarch with remaining ¼ cup cold water. Add to poaching liquid and gently stir until the cornstarch is translucent.

Bring to a boil; cool.

Return pears to the cool syrup and add the blueberries. Stir to combine. Pour into a serving bowl and serve either warm or chilled.

*Yield:* 8 servings

# Oranges Porto

BASIC RECIPE

3 medium-size oranges
¼ cup water
2 tablespoons sugar
½ cup port wine
½ cup red currant jelly

Peel the rind from the oranges as thinly as possible, and cut it into very fine julienne strips about 2 inches long. Reserve the oranges.

Boil water and sugar together for 1 minute to make a thin syrup. Add the rind strips and simmer gently for 3 minutes.

Drain and reserve the syrup and the rind separately.

Bring the port wine to a boil, remove from heat, and ignite

it; let it flame for 1 minute. Blend in the red currant jelly, return to heat, and simmer for 3 minutes.

Add 2 tablespoons of the reserved syrup and two-thirds of the orange rind strips. Continue to simmer gently for 3 minutes. Cool.

Slice the peeled oranges into thin circles and arrange in a serving dish. Pour the port wine mixture over the oranges and marinate for at least 1 hour at room temperature. Then chill for at least 30 minutes. Decorate with remaining orange rind strips.

*Yield:* 6 servings

*Change Oranges Porto as follows or use Basic Recipe, if indicated, for:*

LOW-CALORIE, DIABETIC, LOW-FAT, AND LOW-CHOLESTEROL DIETS

Omit sugar.
Boil the julienned orange rind in water instead of in syrup.
Reduce red currant jelly to ¼ cup.
Proceed as in Basic Recipe.

Calories per serving: 79
Approximate nutrient
  values per serving:
    Protein 1 g
    Fat 0 g
    Carbohydrate 20 g
    Sodium 3 mg
    Potassium 157 mg
    Cholesterol 0 mg
Exchanges:
  Fruit 2

LOW-SODIUM, BLAND, AND HIGH-FIBER DIETS

Use Basic Recipe.

# Oranges Vigneronne

BASIC RECIPE

Serving size: ½ orange, 2
   tablespoons sauce
Calories per serving: 113
Approximate nutrient
   values per serving:
      Protein 2 g
      Fat 4 g
      Carbohydrate 20 g
      Sodium 2 mg
      Potassium 216 mg
      Cholesterol 0 mg
Exchanges:
   Fruit 2
   Fat 1

3 medium-size oranges
1 teaspoon grated lemon rind
¼ cup dry white wine
2 tablespoons honey
1 tart apple, peeled, cored, and quartered
1½ tablespoons rum
½ tablespoon cornstarch
2 tablespoons water
⅓ cup toasted slivered almonds (page 38)

Peel and slice oranges into thin rounds; set aside.

Place the lemon rind, wine, and honey in a medium saucepan and simmer for 3 minutes. Add the apple and simmer, covered, for 10 minutes. Add the rum, transfer the mixture to an electric blender, and purée until smooth. Return to the saucepan.

Mix the cornstarch and water together in a cup, add to the purée, and bring to a boil, stirring constantly. Cover and allow to cool.

Arrange oranges on dessert plates, spoon the cooled apple purée over them, and garnish with the almonds.

*Yield:* 6 servings

*Change Oranges Vigneronne as follows or use Basic Recipe, if indicated, for:*

LOW-CALORIE, DIABETIC, LOW-FAT, AND LOW-CHOLESTEROL DIETS

Omit almonds.
Proceed as in Basic Recipe.

Calories per serving: 71
Approximate nutrient
  values per serving:
    Protein 1 g
    Fat 0 g
    Carbohydrate 18 g
    Sodium 1 mg
    Potassium 160 mg
    Cholesterol 0 mg
Exchanges:
    Fruit 2

LOW-SODIUM, BLAND, AND HIGH-FIBER DIETS

Use Basic Recipe.

# Fresh Fruit Georgianna

BASIC RECIPE

Serving size: ½ cup
Calories per serving: 54
Approximate nutrient
  values per serving:
    Protein 1 g
    Fat 0 g
    Carbohydrate 14 g
    Sodium 3 mg
    Potassium 217 mg
    Cholesterol 0 mg
Exchanges:
    Fruit 1½

1 cup water
3 tablespoons sugar
1 cinnamon stick
6 ripe medium-size peaches, peeled and halved
1 cup cantaloupe balls
1 cup sliced bananas

Combine the water, sugar, and cinnamon stick and bring to a boil. Lower heat, add peach halves, and poach gently for 10 minutes or until tender. Allow to cool and refrigerate in the syrup until well chilled.

Remove cinnamon stick. Slice peaches and put them back in the syrup; add cantaloupe and bananas.

*Yield:* 10 servings

*Change Fresh Fruit Georgianna as follows or use Basic Recipe, if indicated, for:*

**LOW-CALORIE, DIABETIC, LOW-FAT, AND LOW-CHOLESTEROL DIETS**

Omit sugar.
Proceed as in Basic Recipe.

Calories per serving: 40
Approximate nutrient
  values per serving:
    Protein 1 g
    Fat 0 g
    Carbohydrate 10 g
    Sodium 3 mg
    Potassium 217 mg
    Cholesterol 0 mg
Exchanges:
  Fruit 1

**LOW-SODIUM, BLAND, AND HIGH-FIBER DIETS**

Use Basic Recipe.

# Compote of Dried Fruit

BASIC RECIPE

Serving size: ¼ cup
Calories per serving: 120
Approximate nutrient
  values per serving:
    Protein 1 g
    Fat 0 g
    Carbohydrate 31 g
    Sodium 8 mg
    Potassium 310 mg
    Cholesterol 0 mg
Exchanges:
  Fruit 3

¼ pound dried figs
¼ pound dried pitted prunes
¼ pound dried apricots
¼ pound dried peaches
3 cups water
⅓ cup sugar
2 lemon slices, ⅛ inch thick
1 cinnamon stick
2 tablespoons Cognac

Snip stems off figs. Combine fruit and water in medium saucepan. Add sugar, lemon slices, and cinnamon stick.

Bring to simmer and cook, covered, about 30 minutes or until fruit is puffed and tender. Add Cognac and simmer, uncovered, 2 minutes longer. Serve warm or cold with a little of the liquid spooned over the fruit.

*Yield:* 12 servings

*Change Compote of Dried Fruit as follows or use Basic Recipe, if indicated, for:*

LOW-CALORIE, DIABETIC, LOW-FAT, AND LOW-CHOLESTEROL DIETS

Omit sugar.
Proceed as in Basic Recipe.

Calories per serving: 100
Approximate nutrient
 values per serving:
  Protein 1 g
  Fat 0 g
  Carbohydrate 26 g
  Sodium 8 mg
  Potassium 310 mg
  Cholesterol 0 mg
Exchanges:
 Fruit 2½

LOW-SODIUM, BLAND, AND HIGH-FIBER DIETS

Use Basic Recipe.

# Cherries Jubilee

BASIC RECIPE

Serving size: ½ cup ice
 cream, ¼ cup cherries
Calories per serving: 333
Approximate nutrient
 values per serving:
  Protein 4 g

1½ quarts Vanilla Ice Cream (page 615)
two 1-pound packages frozen cherries without sugar, thawed
2 teaspoons grated orange rind
3 tablespoons confectioners' sugar
¼ cup brandy

Fat 25 g
Carbohydrate 26 g
Sodium 39 mg
Potassium 222 mg
Cholesterol 173 mg
Exchanges:
  Fruit 1
  Bread 1
  Fat 5

Allow the ice cream to soften in the container for 10 minutes. Invert it onto a large platter. Place the platter in the freezer until the ice cream is firm.

Spoon the cherries on top and around the sides of the ice cream. Sprinkle with orange rind and confectioners' sugar.

Heat the brandy in a small saucepan. Turn off heat, ignite the brandy, and pour it, still flaming, over the cherries and ice cream. Serve at once.

*Yield:* 12 servings

*Change Cherries Jubilee as follows or use Basic Recipe, if indicated, for:*

LOW-CALORIE, DIABETIC, LOW-FAT, AND LOW-CHOLESTEROL DIETS

Substitute 1½ quarts low-calorie Vanilla Ice Cream (page 615) for basic Vanilla Ice Cream.
Reduce confectioners' sugar to 1 tablespoon.
Proceed as in Basic Recipe.

Calories per serving: 134
Approximate nutrient
  values per serving:
    Protein 6 g
    Fat 2 g
    Carbohydrate 25 g
    Sodium 81 mg
    Potassium 300 mg
    Cholesterol 7 mg
Exchanges:
  Fruit 1
  Bread 1
  Fat ½

LOW-SODIUM, BLAND, AND HIGH-FIBER DIETS

Use Basic Recipe.

# Melon Bowls

BASIC RECIPE

1 large ripe melon (Cranshaw or honeydew)
1 pint fresh strawberries
1 cup seedless green grapes
1 cup fresh blueberries
3 tablespoons Kirsch
10 fresh mint leaves, for garnish

Cut the melon in half and use the halves for bowls. Cut a thin slice from the bottom so they will stand well.

Using a small scoop, cut out melon balls and place in a colander to drain off juice.

Mix melon balls with remaining fruits and sprinkle with Kirsch. Fill bowls with fruit mixture, wrap in aluminum foil and refrigerate until ready to serve. Garnish with mint leaves before serving.

*Yield:* 8 servings

*Change Melon Bowls as follows or use Basic Recipe, if indicated, for:*

LOW-CALORIE, DIABETIC, LOW-FAT, LOW-CHOLESTEROL, AND BLAND DIETS

Omit Kirsch; substitute ½ teaspoon mint extract.
Proceed as in Basic Recipe.

Serving size: ¾ cup
Calories per serving: 177
Approximate nutrient
   values per serving:
      Protein 4 g
      Fat 2 g
      Carbohydrate 39 g
      Sodium 46 mg
      Potassium 1051 mg
      Cholesterol 0 mg
Exchanges:
   Fruit 4

Calories per serving: 162
Approximate nutrient
   values per serving:
      Protein 4 g
      Fat 2 g
      Carbohydrate 38 g
      Sodium 46 mg
      Potassium 1051 mg
      Cholesterol 0 mg
Exchanges:
   Fruit 4

Use Basic Recipe.

# Raisin Purée

SUITABLE FOR LOW-CALORIE, DIABETIC, LOW-FAT,
LOW-CHOLESTEROL, LOW-SODIUM, BLAND, AND
HIGH-FIBER DIETS

Raisin purée is used in some recipes as a sugar substitute for
low-calorie diets.

2 cups seedless raisins
2 cups water

Bring raisins and water to a boil in a medium-size saucepan,
covered. Remove pan from heat and allow to stand for 10 minutes. Pour into a blender and purée mixture. Store in covered
jar in refrigerator.

*Yield:* 2 cups

Serving size: 2 teaspoons
Calories per serving: 20
Approximate nutrient
  values per serving:
    Protein 0 g
    Fat 0 g
    Carbohydrate 5 g
    Sodium 2 mg
    Potassium 48 mg
    Cholesterol 0 mg
Exchanges:
  Fruit ½

# Bavarian Custard

BASIC RECIPE

*The Custard*
4 egg yolks
¼ cup sugar
1 cup light cream
1 teaspoon vanilla extract
2 teaspoons instant coffee granules
1 tablespoon plus 1 teaspoon unflavored gelatin
¼ cup cold water

Serving size: ½ cup
Calories per serving: 439
Approximate nutrient
  values per serving:
    Protein 6 g
    Fat 39 g
    Carbohydrate 18 g
    Sodium 46 mg
    Potassium 122 mg
    Cholesterol 307 mg

1 cup heavy cream
¼ teaspoon polyunsaturated oil

*The Decorations*
½ cup heavy cream
¼ cup crushed peanut brittle

*To prepare the custard:* Beat the egg yolks, sugar, and ¼ cup of the light cream in medium bowl.

In medium saucepan, scald remaining ¾ cup light cream and when it is very hot stir it gradually into the yolks. Return mixture to saucepan and stir over low heat until the mixture coats the back of a spoon. Do not let the mixture boil.

Remove from heat; stir in vanilla and instant coffee granules until granules dissolve.

Sprinkle gelatin over cold water and let stand for 5 minutes. Then stir gelatin into the coffee mixture until it dissolves.

Whip 1 cup heavy cream until it holds a soft shape. Set aside.

Cool the coffee custard over bowl of ice, stirring constantly, until it thickens slightly. Fold in whipped cream and continue stirring until the custard is at the point of setting.

Grease a 4-cup ring mold with the oil. Pour the custard into the mold. Refrigerate for 4 hours or until set.

To unmold, dip the bottom of the mold into hot water for a second or two. Put a chilled serving plate (bottom side up) on the open top of the mold, then reverse mold so plate is at the bottom and custard will slip out on it.

*The decorations:* Whip ½ cup heavy cream, spread it on the custard, and sprinkle with crushed peanut brittle. Keep refrigerated until ready to serve.

*Yield:* 6 servings

*Change Bavarian Custard as follows or use Basic Recipe, if indicated, for:*

LOW-SODIUM AND HIGH-FIBER DIETS

Use Basic Recipe.

Calories per serving: 291

*The custard:* Reduce light cream to ½ cup. Beat in ¼ cup with egg yolks and sugar. Scald remaining ¼ cup and add gradually to the egg yolks.

Omit coffee granules. Substitute 1 cup strawberries puréed in an electric blender and add with vanilla.

Reduce heavy cream for whipping to ½ cup and fold into the custard as in the Basic Recipe.

Proceed as in Basic Recipe.

*The decorations:* Omit peanut brittle. Garnish with whipped cream only.

## BAVARIAN CUSTARD FOR LOW-CALORIE, DIABETIC, LOW-FAT, AND LOW-CHOLESTEROL DIETS

Serving size: ½ cup
Calories per serving: 129
Approximate nutrient
  values per serving:
    Protein 10 g
    Fat 5 g
    Carbohydrate 10 g
    Sodium 112 mg
    Potassium 153 mg
    Cholesterol 20 mg
Exchanges:
  Bread ½
  Meat 1
  Fat ½

½ cup buttermilk
1¼ cups part-skim ricotta cheese
1 teaspoon vanilla extract
2 tablespoons sugar
2 teaspoons instant coffee granules
1 tablespoon plus 1 teaspoon unflavored gelatin
¼ cup skim milk
¼ teaspoon polyunsaturated oil

Purée buttermilk, ricotta, vanilla, sugar, and coffee granules in an electric blender until smooth.

Sprinkle the gelatin over the milk and let stand 5 minutes. Set the gelatin over a bowl of hot water and stir until it dissolves. Stir into coffee mixture.

Grease a 4-cup ring mold with oil. Fill with coffee mixture and refrigerate 3 hours or until set. To unmold, see Basic Recipe.

*Yield:* 5 servings

# Maple Coconut Custard

BASIC RECIPE

4 large eggs
2½ cups milk
½ cup maple syrup
¼ teaspoon salt
⅛ teaspoon nutmeg
1½ teaspoons vanilla extract
½ cup heavy cream
½ cup toasted shredded coconut (page 38)

Preheat oven to 325°F.

In a large bowl, beat eggs, milk, maple syrup, salt, nutmeg, and vanilla. Pour into eight 6-ounce custard cups. Set cups in a shallow baking dish and fill dish with hot water to ¾ inch from top of cups.

Bake approximately 40 minutes or until a knife inserted near the center of custard comes out clean. Remove cups from pan and cool. Refrigerate if you wish.

Before serving, whip the cream until almost stiff. Top each custard with a dollop of cream and 1 tablespoon coconut.

*Yield:* 8 servings

*Change Maple Coconut Custard as follows or use Basic Recipe, if indicated, for:*

LOW-SODIUM DIETS

Omit salt.
Proceed as in Basic Recipe.

## BLAND DIETS

Omit nutmeg. Add ⅛ teaspoon ground cinnamon.
Proceed as in Basic Recipe.


## HIGH-FIBER DIETS

Use Basic Recipe.


## MAPLE COCONUT CUSTARD FOR LOW-CALORIE, DIABETIC, LOW-FAT, AND LOW-CHOLESTEROL DIETS

Serving size: 1 custard
cup, 2 tablespoons
whipped topping
Calories per serving: 74
Approximate nutrient
values per serving:
Protein 6 g
Fat 0 g
Carbohydrate 12 g
Sodium 166 mg
Potassium 185 mg
Cholesterol 2 mg
Exchanges:
Milk ½
Bread ½

Low-Cholesterol Egg Substitute (page 189) equivalent to
3 large eggs
2 cups skim milk
¼ cup maple syrup
¼ teaspoon salt
1½ teaspoons vanilla extract
½ teaspoon coconut extract
1 cup Whipped Topping (page 636)
1 teaspoon nutmeg

Preheat oven to 325°F.

In a large bowl, beat egg substitute, milk, maple syrup, salt, vanilla, and coconut extract. Pour mixture into eight 6-ounce custard cups. Set cups in a shallow baking dish and fill dish with hot water to ¾ inch from top of cups.

Bake approximately 40 minutes or until a knife inserted near the center of custard comes out clean. Remove cups from pan and cool. Refrigerate if you wish.

Garnish with whipped topping and sprinkle with nutmeg before serving.

*Yield:* 8 servings

# Lemon Bread Pudding

BASIC RECIPE

Serving size: ¾ cup
Calories per serving: 264
Approximate nutrient
  values per serving:
    Protein 9 g
    Fat 13 g
    Carbohydrate 28 g
    Sodium 305 mg
    Potassium 214 mg
    Cholesterol 151 mg
Exchanges:
  Milk ½
  Bread 1½
  Meat 1½
  Fat 2

1 tablespoon polyunsaturated margarine for greasing dish
12 slices French bread, ¼ inch thick, 2½ inches wide
2 tablespoons polyunsaturated margarine for bread
1 teaspoon grated lemon rind
2 tablespoons lemon juice
2½ cups milk
2 large eggs
1 egg yolk
3 tablespoons sugar

Preheat oven to 350°F.

Grease a 1½-quart baking dish with 1 tablespoon margarine.

Spread French bread slices on both sides with 2 tablespoons margarine. Arrange bread slices in layers in the dish, sprinkling each layer with some of the lemon rind and lemon juice.

Bring milk to the boiling point. Remove from heat. Beat eggs and egg yolk in a bowl with 1 tablespoon sugar. Gradually add scalded milk, beating constantly. Strain mixture directly over bread in the baking dish. Sprinkle the top with the remaining 2 tablespoons sugar.

Set baking dish in a large roasting pan. Pour hot water around dish so it comes halfway up the sides of the baking dish.

Bake for 1 hour, 10 minutes or until pudding is set and knife inserted in center comes out clean. Serve at once.

*Yield:* 6 servings

*Change Lemon Bread Pudding as follows or use Basic Recipe, if indicated, for:*

LOW-SODIUM AND RENAL DIETS

Calories per serving: 264
Approximate nutrient
  values same as Basic
  Recipe except for:
    Calcium 148 mg
    Phosphorus 165 mg
    Sodium 248 mg

Substitute unsalted polyunsaturated margarine for margarine
  wherever used.
Proceed as in Basic Recipe.

BLAND DIETS

Use Basic Recipe.

HIGH-FIBER DIETS

Calories per serving: 365

Add ¾ cup chopped pecans, scattering some on each bread
  layer with lemon rind and lemon juice.
Proceed as in Basic Recipe.

LEMON BREAD PUDDING FOR LOW-CALORIE,
DIABETIC, LOW-FAT, AND LOW-CHOLESTEROL
DIETS

Serving size: ⅙ pudding
Calories per serving: 135
Approximate nutrient
  values per serving:
    Protein 8 g
    Fat 1 g
    Carbohydrate 24 g
    Sodium 214 mg
    Potassium 173 mg
    Cholesterol 1 mg
Exchanges:
  Milk ½
  Bread 1½

6 slices French bread, ¼ inch thick, 2½ inches wide
½ cup flour
⅛ teaspoon salt
1 teaspoon grated lemon rind
1 cup skim milk
2 tablespoons sugar
Low-Cholesterol Egg Substitute (page 189) equivalent to
  3 large eggs
vegetable cooking spray

Preheat broiler.
  Place French bread slices on cookie sheet and broil until
lightly browned on both sides. Set aside.

597

Preheat oven to 350°F.

In the container of an electric blender, combine flour, salt, lemon rind, milk, sugar, and egg substitute. Blend until smooth.

Spray a deep 9-inch pie plate with vegetable cooking spray. Pour in flour, milk, and egg substitute mixture. Arrange bread slices in the dish so they form a circle. Bake for 55 to 60 minutes or until puffed and browned.

Cut into six wedges and serve at once.

*Yield:* 6 servings

# Snow Pudding with Golden Sauce

BASIC RECIPE

*The Pudding*
½ cup sugar
1 cup boiling water
1 tablespoon grated lemon rind
⅓ cup lemon juice
1 tablespoon unflavored gelatin
¼ cup cold water
3 egg whites

*The Golden Sauce*
2 large egg yolks
¼ cup sugar
⅛ teaspoon salt
½ cup milk
½ cup light cream
½ teaspoon vanilla extract

*To prepare the pudding:* Pour the sugar into the boiling water and stir until dissolved. Remove from heat and pour into a medium bowl. Stir in lemon rind and lemon juice and allow to cool.

Sprinkle the gelatin over the cold water in a small pan and

Serving size: ½ cup pudding, 2 tablespoons sauce
Calories per serving: 170
Approximate nutrient values per serving:
Protein 4 g
Fat 7 g
Carbohydrate 25 g
Sodium 58 mg
Potassium 85 mg
Cholesterol 87 mg
Exchanges:
Bread 2
Fat 1

let stand for 10 minutes. Then dissolve the gelatin over low heat. Add the gelatin to the lemon mixture, stir, and refrigerate for 10 to 15 minutes or until mixture begins to set, stirring occasionally. When it starts to set, beat until frothy.

Beat the egg whites until stiff; then fold one-third of them into the gelatin until well blended. Gently fold in the remaining whites. Pour into a serving bowl and chill at least 1 hour before serving.

*To prepare the golden sauce:* In the top of a double boiler, over moderate heat, beat egg yolks lightly with a fork or whisk. Blend in sugar and salt, and gradually stir in milk and cream. Cook over simmering water, stirring constantly, until sauce thickens. Remove from heat and strain into a bowl. Stir in vanilla. Serve immediately with pudding.

*Yield:* 6 servings, 1¼ cups sauce

*Change Snow Pudding with Golden Sauce as follows or use Basic Recipe, if indicated, for:*

LOW-CALORIE, DIABETIC, LOW-FAT, AND LOW-CHOLESTEROL DIETS

Calories per serving: 91
Approximate nutrient
  values per serving:
    Protein 6 g
    Fat 0 g
    Carbohydrate 17 g
    Sodium 90 mg
    Potassium 135 mg
    Cholesterol 1 mg
Exchanges:
  Meat ½
  Bread 1

*The pudding:* Reduce the sugar to ⅓ cup.
    Proceed as in Basic Recipe.

*The sauce:* Omit egg yolks. Use Low-Cholesterol Egg Substitute (page 189) equivalent to 2 large eggs.
    Reduce the sugar to 2 tablespoons.
    Omit milk and light cream. Substitute 1 cup skim milk.
    Proceed as in Basic Recipe.

Calories per serving: 170
Approximate nutrient
  values same as Basic
  Recipe except for:
    Calcium 39 mg
    Phosphorus 48 mg
    Sodium 41 mg

*The pudding:* Use Basic Recipe.

*The sauce:* Omit salt and substitute ⅛ teaspoon nutmeg. Proceed as in Basic Recipe.

## BLAND DIETS

Use Basic Recipe.

## HIGH-FIBER DIETS

Calories per serving: 175

*The pudding:* Use Basic Recipe.

*The sauce:* Add ¼ cup toasted shredded coconut (page 38) to cooked golden sauce.

# Snow Eggs with Fresh Strawberries

## BASIC RECIPE

Serving size: 1 meringue, ¼
  cup strawberries, ¼ cup
  custard
Calories per serving: 188
Approximate nutrient
  values per serving:
    Protein 5 g
    Fat 5 g
    Carbohydrate 30 g
    Sodium 93 mg
    Potassium 180 mg
    Cholesterol 144 mg
Exchanges:
  Milk ¼
  Fruit 3
  Meat ½

2 cups fresh strawberries

*The Meringues*
4 large egg whites, at room temperature
¼ teaspoon cream of tartar
½ cup sugar
2 cups milk

*The Custard*
4 large egg yolks, lightly beaten
½ cup sugar
⅛ teaspoon salt
1 teaspoon vanilla extract

Wash strawberries in cold water. Slice and place in a medium bowl. Cover and refrigerate.

*To prepare the meringues:* Beat egg whites until foamy. Beat in cream of tartar and gradually add sugar. Continue beating until stiff peaks form.

Scald milk in a medium saucepan. Lower heat until milk is barely simmering. Scoop up a large spoonful of beaten egg whites and drop onto the milk. Poach the meringue 4 minutes, turning once with a slotted spoon. The meringue should be firm to the touch. After poaching, carefully remove meringue to paper towels to drain. Repeat poaching, one large spoonful at a time until you have made eight meringues. Refrigerate the meringues.

Reserve warm poaching milk for the custard.

*To prepare the custard:* Place lightly beaten egg yolks, sugar, and salt in the top of a double boiler. Cook mixture over barely simmering water, gradually adding reserved poaching milk and stirring constantly until custard thickens.

Strain custard into a bowl. Stir in vanilla. Cool and refrigerate until thoroughly chilled.

When ready to serve, spoon custard into eight individual serving dishes; top with meringues and strawberries.

*Yield:* 8 servings

*Change Snow Eggs with Fresh Strawberries as follows or use Basic Recipe, if indicated, for:*

LOW-SODIUM AND RENAL DIETS

*The meringues:* Use Basic Recipe.

*The custard:* Omit salt.
Proceed as in Basic Recipe.

Calories per serving: 188
Approximate nutrient
values same as Basic
Recipe except for:
Calcium 96 mg
Phosphorus 110 mg
Sodium 60 mg

Use Basic Recipe.

## SNOW EGGS WITH FRESH STRAWBERRIES FOR LOW-CALORIE, DIABETIC, LOW-FAT, AND LOW-CHOLESTEROL DIETS

2 cups fresh strawberries

*The Meringues*
4 large egg whites
¼ teaspoon cream of tartar
1 tablespoon honey
2 cups skim milk

*The Custard*
Low-Cholesterol Egg Substitute (page 189) equivalent to
   4 large eggs
2 tablespoons honey
⅛ teaspoon salt
1 teaspoon vanilla extract

Serving size: 1 meringue, ¼ cup strawberries, ¼ cup custard
Calories per serving: 94
Approximate nutrient values per serving:
   Protein 8 g
   Fat 0 g
   Carbohydrate 15 g
   Sodium 153 mg
   Potassium 259 mg
   Cholesterol 2 mg
Exchanges:
   Fruit 2
   Meat ½

Wash strawberries in cold water. Slice and place in a bowl; cover and refrigerate.

*To prepare the meringues:* Beat egg whites until foamy. Beat in cream of tartar; gradually beat in honey. Continue beating until stiff peaks form.

Scald the milk in a medium saucepan. Lower the heat so the milk barely simmers. Scoop up a large spoonful of beaten egg whites and drop onto the milk. Poach the meringue 4 minutes, turning once with slotted spoon. The meringue should be firm to the touch. After poaching, remove meringue to paper towels to drain. Repeat poaching, one large spoonful at a time, until you have made eight meringues. Refrigerate. Reserve warm poaching milk for custard sauce.

*To prepare the custard:* In the top of a double boiler, mix together egg substitute, honey, and salt. Over low heat, gradually add reserved milk, stirring constantly. Cook, stirring constantly, until custard thickens. Strain sauce and stir in vanilla. Cool and refrigerate until thoroughly chilled.

When ready to serve, spoon custard into individual serving dishes; top with meringues and strawberries.

*Yield:* 8 servings

# Apple Rice Pudding

BASIC RECIPE

½ cup thinly sliced dried apricots
1 cup boiling water for the apricots
½ cup raw short-grain white rice
4 cups boiling water for the rice
1½ cups milk
2 cups diced unpeeled apples
½ teaspoon ground cinnamon
¼ teaspoon nutmeg
¼ teaspoon allspice
1 tablespoon polyunsaturated oil

Preheat oven to 325°F.

Soak apricots in boiling water for 30 minutes. Drain.

Cook rice in 4 cups boiling water for about 12 minutes, or until soft. Drain well.

Mix milk, apples, apricots, and spices into cooked rice.

Grease a 1½-quart baking dish with the oil. Pour pudding into dish. Bake for 1 hour or until nicely browned.

*Yield:* 6 servings

Serving size: ½ cup
Calories per serving: 164
Approximate nutrient
  values per serving:
    Protein 4 g
    Fat 5 g
    Carbohydrate 28 g
    Sodium 33 mg
    Potassium 255 mg
    Cholesterol 8 mg
Exchanges:
  Fruit 1½
  Bread 1
  Fat 1

*Change Apple Rice Pudding as follows or use Basic Recipe, if indicated, for:*

## LOW-CALORIE, DIABETIC, LOW-FAT, AND LOW-CHOLESTEROL DIETS

Calories per serving: 119
Approximate nutrient
  values per serving:
    Protein 3 g
    Fat 3 g
    Carbohydrate 21 g
    Sodium 31 mg
    Potassium 149 mg
    Cholesterol 0 mg
Exchanges:
  Fruit ½
  Bread 1
  Fat 1

Omit dried apricots.
Substitute skim milk for milk.
Proceed as in Basic Recipe.

## LOW-SODIUM DIETS

Use Basic Recipe.

## RENAL DIETS

Calories per serving: 205
Approximate nutrient
  values per serving:
    Protein 4 g
    Fat 5 g
    Carbohydrate 37 g
    Calcium 95 mg
    Phosphorus 85 mg
    Sodium 36 mg
    Potassium 179 mg
    Cholesterol 9 mg

Omit dried apricots.
Add 4 tablespoons honey to milk, apples, and spice mixture.
  Mix into cooked rice.
Proceed as in Basic Recipe.

## BLAND DIETS

Calories per serving: 164

Omit nutmeg.
Proceed as in Basic Recipe.

Calories per serving: 168

Substitute brown rice for short-grain white rice.
Proceed as in Basic Recipe.

# Rice Cream Mold with Apricot Sauce

BASIC RECIPE

Serving size: ⅙ mold, 2
  tablespoons sauce
Calories per serving: 211
Approximate nutrient
  values per serving:
    Protein 6 g
    Fat 8 g
    Carbohydrate 31 g
    Sodium 57 mg
    Potassium 332 mg
    Cholesterol 28 mg
Exchanges:
  Milk ½
  Fruit 1
  Bread 1
  Fat 1½

*Rice Cream Mold*
¼ teaspoon polyunsaturated oil
¼ cup raw short-grain white rice
2½ cups milk
¼ cup sugar
1 tablespoon unflavored gelatin
¼ cup undiluted orange juice concentrate
¼ cup heavy cream

*Apricot Sauce*
½ cup dried apricots
¾ cup water for stewing apricots
rind of ½ lemon, cut into julienne strips
1 tablespoon Grand Marnier
¼ cup water
1 tablespoon sugar

*To prepare rice cream mold:* Grease a 3-cup ring mold with oil.

Combine rice and milk in a medium saucepan and bring to boil; lower heat, cover, and simmer steadily for 35 minutes or until rice is tender. Remove from heat and stir in sugar.

Sprinkle gelatin over orange juice concentrate and let stand for 10 minutes. Stir this mixture into the rice until dissolved. Allow to cool completely.

Whip the cream until it holds soft peaks. Fold cream into rice mixture and pour into the mold. Cover with plastic wrap and refrigerate for 2 hours or until set.

*To prepare apricot sauce:* Combine the apricots, water, lemon rind, and Grand Marnier in a saucepan and bring to boil. Simmer gently for 15 minutes or until the apricots are very tender. Transfer mixture to an electric blender and purée.

Stir in remaining water and sugar and chill in the refrigerator.

Just before serving, unmold by dipping mold into hot water for a few seconds. Hold plate against top of mold and flip over sharply. Serve rice cream mold with apricot sauce.

*Yield:* 6 servings rice cream mold, 1 cup sauce

*Change Rice Cream Mold with Apricot Sauce as follows or use Basic Recipe, if indicated, for:*

LOW-CALORIE, DIABETIC, LOW-FAT, AND LOW-CHOLESTEROL DIETS

*The rice cream mold:* Substitute skim milk for milk.
   Reduce sugar to 2 tablespoons.
   Substitute ¼ cup diluted orange juice concentrate for undiluted concentrate.
   Substitute ½ cup plain low-fat yogurt for heavy cream.
   Proceed as in Basic Recipe.

*The apricot sauce:* Omit sugar.
   Proceed as in Basic Recipe.

Calories per serving: 123
Approximate nutrient
   values per serving:
      Protein 7 g
      Fat 1 g
      Carbohydrate 23 g
      Sodium 70 mg
      Potassium 322 mg
      Cholesterol 3 mg
Exchanges:
   Milk ½
   Fruit ½
   Bread 1

LOW-SODIUM, BLAND, AND HIGH-FIBER DIETS

Use Basic Recipe.

# Banana Mold

BASIC RECIPE

1½ tablespoons honey
1 piece peeled fresh ginger root, the size of a walnut
⅓ cup water
1 tablespoon unflavored gelatin
1½ cups mashed bananas
1½ cups sour cream
½ cup chopped walnuts

Combine honey, ginger root, and water in a small pan. Cover and simmer gently for 10 minutes. Scoop out ginger root and discard it. Let liquid cool.

Sprinkle the gelatin over the cooled liquid and set aside for 10 minutes. Then, over low heat, stir until gelatin is completely dissolved.

In a medium bowl, mix bananas, sour cream, and walnuts. Then stir in the liquid gelatin mixture.

Pour into 3-cup mold and refrigerate at least 2 hours before serving.

To unmold, dip mold briefly in very hot water, turn upside down onto an iced serving plate.

*Yield:* 6 servings

*Change Banana Mold as follows or use Basic Recipe, if indicated, for:*

## LOW-CALORIE, DIABETIC, LOW-FAT, AND LOW-CHOLESTEROL DIETS

Substitute plain low-fat yogurt for sour cream.
Omit walnuts.
Proceed as in Basic Recipe.

Calories per serving: 107
Approximate nutrient
  values per serving:
    Protein 5 g
    Fat 1 g
    Carbohydrate 22 g
    Sodium 42 mg
    Potassium 376 mg
    Cholesterol 3 mg
Exchanges:
  Fruit 1
  Bread 1

## LOW-SODIUM, BLAND, AND HIGH-FIBER DIETS

Use Basic Recipe.

# Prune Whip

BASIC RECIPE

Serving size: ¾ cup
Calories per serving: 95
Approximate nutrient
  values per serving:
    Protein 4 g
    Fat 0 g
    Carbohydrate 22 g
    Sodium 40 mg
    Potassium 211 mg
    Cholesterol 0 mg
Exchanges:
  Fruit 2½

1 cup brewed tea
1 cup pitted dried prunes
2 teaspoons grated lemon rind
2 tablespoons honey
1 tablespoon unflavored gelatin
⅓ cup cold water for the gelatin
5 egg whites, at room temperature

Heat the tea in a small saucepan, add the prunes, remove from heat, and allow to soak for 1 hour. Then, over low heat, cook the prunes in the tea about 20 minutes until soft. Cool, drain, and purée the prunes in a blender. Pour into a bowl and add the lemon rind and honey.

Sprinkle gelatin over cold water in a small pan and allow to stand 10 minutes. Dissolve over low heat. Add gelatin mixture to the prune purée.

In a separate bowl beat egg whites until stiff. Fold one-third of the whites into the purée and blend well. Gently fold in the remaining whites.

Spoon into a serving dish and chill for at least 1 hour before serving.

*Yield:* 7 servings

*Change Prune Whip as follows or use Basic Recipe, if indicated, for:*

LOW-SODIUM AND HIGH-FIBER DIETS

Use Basic Recipe.

BLAND DIETS

Omit tea. Substitute 1 cup water.
Proceed as in Basic Recipe.

PRUNE WHIP FOR LOW-CALORIE, DIABETIC, LOW-FAT, AND LOW-CHOLESTEROL DIETS

1 cup water for cooking prunes
1 cup pitted dried prunes
2 teaspoons grated lemon rind
¼ teaspoon almond extract
⅓ cup cold water for the gelatin
1 tablespoon unflavored gelatin
5 egg whites

Heat 1 cup water in a small saucepan, add prunes, remove from heat, and allow to soak for 1 hour. Then, over low heat,

Calories per serving: 95

Serving size: ¾ cup
Calories per serving: 77
Approximate nutrient
  values per serving:
    Protein 4 g
    Fat 0 g
    Carbohydrate 17 g
    Sodium 39 mg
    Potassium 200 mg
    Cholesterol 0 mg
Exchanges:
    Fruit 2

cook prunes in the water for about 20 minutes until soft. Cool, drain, and purée prunes in a blender. Pour into a bowl; add lemon rind and almond extract.

Place remaining ⅛ cup water in a small pan, add gelatin, and allow to stand 10 minutes. Dissolve over low heat. Add gelatin mixture to the prune purée.

In a separate bowl beat egg whites until stiff. Fold one-third of the whites into the purée and blend well. Gently fold in remaining whites.

Spoon into a serving dish and chill for at least 1 hour before serving.

*Yield:* 7 servings

# Strawberry Frappé

BASIC RECIPE

Serving size: ½ cup
Calories per serving: 161
Approximate nutrient
  values per serving:
    Protein 1 g
    Fat 1 g
    Carbohydrate 41 g
    Calcium 21 mg
    Phosphorus 21 mg
    Sodium 1 mg
    Potassium 171 mg
    Cholesterol 0 mg
Exchanges:
    Fruit 4

1 quart ripe hulled strawberries
¼ cup water
1 cup sugar
2 tablespoons lemon juice

In a medium saucepan combine strawberries and water and cook over medium high heat for 5 minutes or until berries are soft. Put mixture through a food mill or press through a sieve into a bowl. Stir in sugar and lemon juice.

Chill until completely cold. Then pour into medium-size shallow pan and set in freezer. When the mixture has a rough texture, stir well and return to freezer. Repeat three times until the frappé has the consistency of a coarse sherbet.

Spoon the frappé into a bowl, cover tightly, and freeze for several hours or overnight. Transfer to the refrigerator 15 minutes before serving.

*Yield:* 6 servings

*Change Strawberry Frappé as follows or use Basic Recipe, if indicated, for:*

LOW-CALORIE, DIABETIC, LOW-FAT, AND LOW-CHOLESTEROL DIETS

Reduce sugar to ⅓ cup.
Proceed as in Basic Recipe.

LOW-SODIUM, RENAL, BLAND, AND HIGH-FIBER DIETS

Use Basic Recipe.

Calories per serving: 79
Approximate nutrient
  values per serving:
    Protein 1 g
    Fat 1 g
    Carbohydrate 19 g
    Sodium 1 mg
    Potassium 170 mg
    Cholesterol 0 mg
Exchanges:
  Fruit 2

# Blueberry Mousse

BASIC RECIPE

1 cup port wine
1 tablespoon grated orange rind
½ teaspoon ground cinnamon
1 pint fresh blueberries
¼ cup cold water
1 tablespoon unflavored gelatin
3 egg whites, at room temperature
⅓ cup sugar

Serving size: ½ cup
Calories per serving: 82
Approximate nutrient
  values per serving:
    Protein 3 g
    Fat 0 g
    Carbohydrate 19 g
    Calcium 11 mg
    Phosphorus 7 mg
    Sodium 23 mg
    Potassium 56 mg
    Cholesterol 0 mg
Exchanges:
  Fruit 2

Place port wine in a medium saucepan over moderate heat. Bring to a boil, turn off heat, then blaze by igniting. Let flames die, then return to heat.

Add the orange rind and cinnamon. Cover and simmer gently for 10 minutes. Add the blueberries and cook for 1 minute. Pour into a bowl and cool to room temperature.

Place the water in a small saucepan and sprinkle with gelatin. Allow to stand 10 minutes, then dissolve over low heat.

Stir gelatin into the blueberry mixture, place over a bowl of ice, and stir until mixture starts to thicken.

Beat the egg whites until glossy, gradually adding sugar until stiff peaks form. Stir one-third of the beaten whites into the blueberry mixture. Fold in remaining whites and pour carefully into a serving dish.

Place in the freezer until firm. Remove from freezer and place in refrigerator 20 to 30 minutes before serving.

*Yield:* 7 servings

*Change Blueberry Mousse as follows or use Basic Recipe, if indicated, for:*

LOW-CALORIE, DIABETIC, LOW-FAT, AND LOW-CHOLESTEROL DIETS

Reduce sugar to 3½ tablespoons.
Proceed as in Basic Recipe.

Calories per serving: 70
Approximate nutrient
  values per serving:
    Protein 3 g
    Fat 0 g
    Carbohydrate 16 g
    Sodium 23 mg
    Potassium 56 mg
    Cholesterol 0 mg
Exchanges:
  Fruit 1½

LOW-SODIUM, RENAL, BLAND, AND HIGH-FIBER DIETS

Use Basic Recipe.

# Frozen Orange Yogurt

BASIC RECIPE

Serving size: ½ cup
Calories per serving: 92
Approximate nutrient
  values per serving:
    Protein 5 g
    Fat 2 g
    Carbohydrate 16 g
    Sodium 53 mg
    Potassium 167 mg
    Cholesterol 6 mg
Exchanges:
  Bread 1
  Meat ½

½ cup orange juice
¼ cup lemon juice
2 teaspoons unflavored gelatin
1 tablespoon grated orange rind
1 cup plain yogurt
3 egg whites, at room temperature
4 tablespoons sugar

Combine the fruit juices. Pour ¼ cup into a saucepan. Sprinkle gelatin over the juice, let stand for 10 minutes, then dissolve by stirring over low heat.

Whisk the remaining juice, orange rind, and yogurt together until smooth. Stir the gelatin into the yogurt mixture.

In a separate bowl beat the egg whites, gradually adding the sugar, until the mixture is glossy and forms peaks.

Stir one-third of the egg whites into yogurt mixture until well blended. Fold in remaining whites.

Pour into a freezer tray and freeze until firm. Remove from freezer and place in refrigerator 20 to 30 minutes before serving. Serve in individual dessert bowls.

*Yield:* 5 servings

*Change Frozen Orange Yogurt as follows or use Basic Recipe, if indicated, for:*

## LOW-CALORIE, DIABETIC, LOW-FAT, AND LOW-CHOLESTEROL DIETS

Substitute 1 cup plain low-fat yogurt for yogurt.
Proceed as in Basic Recipe.

Calories per serving: 93
Approximate nutrient
  values per serving:
    Protein 5 g
    Fat 1 g
    Carbohydrate 17 g
    Sodium 63 mg
    Potassium 203 mg
    Cholesterol 3 mg
Exchanges:
  Bread 1
  Meat ½

## LOW-SODIUM AND BLAND DIETS

Use Basic Recipe.

## HIGH-FIBER DIETS

Calories per serving: 114

Use Basic Recipe.
Prepare 5 tablespoons grated toasted coconut (page 38). Set aside. Just before serving, garnish each portion with 1 tablespoon coconut.

# Vanilla Ice Cream

BASIC RECIPE

Serving size: ½ cup
Calories per serving: 272
Approximate nutrient
  values per serving:
    Protein 3 g
    Fat 25 g
    Carbohydrate 11 g
    Calcium 56 mg
    Phosphorus 72 mg
    Sodium 37 mg
    Potassium 77 mg
    Cholesterol 173 mg
Exchanges:
  Bread 1
  Fat 5

2 large eggs
2 egg yolks
½ cup sugar
2½ cups light cream
1 vanilla bean, split in half
1 cup heavy cream
1 tablespoon sugar

In a medium bowl, whisk eggs, egg yolks, and sugar. Gradually add ½ cup light cream, beating constantly. Set aside.

Pour remaining 2 cups light cream into a saucepan, add vanilla bean, and bring the mixture to the scalding point. Remove from heat and let stand for 10 minutes. Remove vanilla bean.

Return the light cream mixture to the scalding point, then stir it into the egg mixture. Return to saucepan and stir over low heat until mixture coats the back of a spoon; do not let it boil.

Transfer to a bowl; stir in the heavy cream and sugar. Allow to cool completely.

Pour the mixture into an ice cream freezer and follow directions for freezing.

*Yield:* 1½ quarts

*Change Vanilla Ice Cream as follows or use Basic Recipe, if indicated, for:*

LOW-SODIUM, RENAL, AND BLAND DIETS

Use Basic Recipe.

Use Basic Recipe. For extra fiber, serve with glacéed fruits, chopped nuts, or stewed berries.

## VANILLA ICE CREAM FOR LOW-CALORIE, DIABETIC, LOW-FAT, AND LOW-CHOLESTEROL DIETS

¼ cup sugar
2 cups skim milk
½ cup buttermilk
½ cup part-skim ricotta cheese
1½ teaspoons vanilla extract
2 egg whites, at room temperature

In the container of an electric blender, mix the sugar, skim milk, buttermilk, ricotta cheese, and vanilla. Blend until smooth. Pour into an ice cream freezer and freeze until it is just slushy.

In a separate bowl, beat the egg whites until stiff. Add whites to the mixture in ice cream freezer and continue freezing until mixture is firm.

*Yield:* 1 quart

Serving size: ½ cup
Calories per serving: 78
Approximate nutrient
  values per serving:
    Protein 4 g
    Fat 1 g
    Carbohydrate 11 g
    Sodium 80 mg
    Potassium 155 mg
    Cholesterol 7 mg
Exchanges:
  Bread 1

# Chocolate Ice Cream Roll

BASIC RECIPE

*The Cake*
¼ teaspoon polyunsaturated oil
4 large eggs
¾ cup sugar
3 tablespoons cold water
1 teaspoon vanilla extract
1 teaspoon baking powder
¼ teaspoon salt

Serving size: ½2 cake
Calories per serving: 209
Approximate nutrient
  values per serving:
    Protein 4 g
    Fat 11 g
    Carbohydrate 25 g
    Sodium 115 mg
    Potassium 90 mg
    Cholesterol 149 mg

¾ cup all-purpose sifted flour
¼ cup unsweetened cocoa powder
2 tablespoons confectioners' sugar

*The Filling and Topping*
2 cups Vanilla Ice Cream (page 615)
2 tablespoons confectioners' sugar

Preheat oven to 350°F.

Grease an 11-by-16-inch jelly-roll pan with oil. Line with wax paper that comes right up sides of pan.

*To prepare the cake:* In the bowl of an electric mixer, beat the eggs and sugar until thick. Beat in water and vanilla.

Sift the baking powder, salt, flour, and cocoa together and add to the egg mixture just until blended.

Pour batter into the prepared pan. Smooth the top with a rubber spatula and bake for 15 to 18 minutes or until top springs back when pressed with a fingertip.

Place a clean kitchen towel on the counter and sprinkle it with 2 tablespoons confectioners' sugar.

Quickly turn jelly-roll pan upside down onto towel so waxed paper lining is on top side of cake. Lift off pan and carefully peel away the wax paper. Roll the cake up with the towel, starting at one long side. Allow to cool, wrapped up, on a rack.

*To prepare the filling:* Let ice cream soften until spreadable. Unroll the cake from the towel and spread it with ice cream. Reroll without towel and set on a long platter. Cut off both ends at a diagonal and sift the remaining confectioners' sugar on top. Serve at once.

*Yield:* 12 servings

*Change Chocolate Ice Cream Roll as follows or use Basic Recipe, if indicated, for:*

LOW-CALORIE, DIABETIC, LOW-FAT, AND LOW-CHOLESTEROL DIETS

*The cake:* Reduce eggs to 2. Add to them Low-Cholesterol Egg Substitute (page 189) equivalent to 1 large egg, and beat with other ingredients in bowl of electric mixer, as in the Basic Recipe.

Omit confectioners' sugar for sprinkling on towel.

Proceed as in Basic Recipe.

*The filling and topping:* Substitute low-calorie Vanilla Ice Cream (page 616) for basic Vanilla Ice Cream.

Proceed as in Basic Recipe.

LOW-SODIUM DIETS

*The cake:* Omit salt.

Proceed as in Basic Recipe.

*The filling and topping:* Use Basic Recipe.

BLAND DIETS

Use Basic Recipe.

HIGH-FIBER DIETS

*The cake:* Use Basic Recipe.

*The filling and topping:* Add ¼ cup finely chopped toasted almonds (page 38) and sprinkle on ice cream before rolling up cake.

Calories per serving: 137
Approximate nutrient
  values per serving:
    Protein 5 g
    Fat 3 g
    Carbohydrate 24 g
    Sodium 134 mg
    Potassium 126 mg
    Cholesterol 49 mg
Exchanges:
  Bread 1½
  Meat ½

Calories per serving: 209
Approximate nutrient
  values same as Basic
  Recipe except for:
    Sodium 69 mg

Calories per serving: 225

# Hot Apple Soufflé with Fruit Sauce

BASIC RECIPE

The fruit sauce would also be delicious with angel food cake, baked custards, or steamed fruit puddings.

For this recipe, prepare the sauce while the soufflé is cooking if you want it warm. Prepare it earlier and refrigerate if you prefer it chilled.

Serving size: 1 cup soufflé,
    2 tablespoons sauce
Calories per serving: 134
Approximate nutrient
    values per serving:
    Protein 3 g
    Fat 3 g
    Carbohydrate 25 g
    Sodium 235 mg
    Potassium 153 mg
    Cholesterol 0 mg
Exchanges:
    Fruit 1
    Bread 1
    Meat ½

*The Soufflé*
1½ cups diced peeled apples
¼ cup unsweetened apple juice
¼ teaspoon ground cinnamon
⅛ teaspoon salt for apple mixture
½ teaspoon grated peeled fresh ginger root
1½ teaspoons polyunsaturated margarine for greasing
    soufflé dish
1½ tablespoons sugar for preparing soufflé dish
5 large egg whites, at room temperature
¼ teaspoon cream of tartar
¼ teaspoon salt for egg whites
¼ cup sugar

*The Sauce*
1⅛ cups orange juice
2 teaspoons cornstarch
⅛ teaspoon salt
1 tablespoon polyunsaturated margarine
⅛ teaspoon nutmeg
1 teaspoon grated orange rind
1 teaspoon vanilla extract
2 tablespoons honey

*To prepare the soufflé:* Bring apples and apple juice to a boil in a medium saucepan. Reduce heat and simmer gently, covered, 8 to 10 minutes or until apples are tender. Remove from heat.

Stir in cinnamon, salt, and ginger. Cool to room temperature. Preheat oven to 425°F.

Grease a 6-cup soufflé dish with margarine. Sprinkle bottom and sides of dish with sugar.

In a large bowl, beat egg whites until foamy. Beat in cream of tartar and salt. Gradually add sugar and continue beating until stiff peaks form. Stir about one-fourth of the egg whites into the apple mixture. Gently fold in the remaining whites.

Pour into greased soufflé dish. Bake 15 minutes or until top is browned and soufflé is firm to the touch. Serve at once with fruit sauce.

*To prepare the sauce:* In a small saucepan combine orange juice, cornstarch, and salt. Cook and stir over low heat until mixture comes to a boil and is thickened and smooth.

Boil gently, stirring, for 1 minute. Remove from heat; blend in remaining ingredients. Serve warm or chilled.

*Yield:* 6 servings soufflé, 1 cup sauce

*Change Hot Apple Soufflé with Fruit Sauce as follows or use Basic Recipe, if indicated, for:*

LOW-CALORIE, DIABETIC, LOW-FAT, AND LOW-CHOLESTEROL DIETS

*The soufflé:* Omit margarine. Omit sugar for preparing soufflé dish.

Proceed as in Basic Recipe.

*The sauce:* Reduce margarine to 1½ teaspoons. Reduce honey to 1 tablespoon.

Proceed as in Basic Recipe.

Calories per serving: 100
Approximate nutrient
  values per serving:
    Protein 3 g
    Fat 1 g
    Carbohydrate 20 g
    Sodium 218 mg
    Potassium 151 mg
    Cholesterol 0 mg
Exchanges:
  Fruit ½
  Bread 1

LOW-SODIUM DIETS

*The soufflé:* Omit salt.

Substitute unsalted polyunsaturated margarine for margarine.

Proceed as in Basic Recipe.

Calories per serving: 134
Approximate nutrient
  values same as Basic
  Recipe except for:
    Sodium 43 mg

620

*The sauce:* Omit salt.

Substitute unsalted polyunsaturated margarine for margarine.

Proceed as in Basic Recipe.

### RENAL DIETS

*The soufflé:* Omit salt.

Substitute 1 tablespoon unsalted polyunsaturated margarine for margarine.

Proceed as in Basic Recipe.

*The sauce:* Omit fruit sauce. Substitute ¾ cup heavy cream, whipped until stiff.

### BLAND DIETS

*The soufflé:* Use Basic Recipe.

*The sauce:* Omit nutmeg. Substitute ⅛ teaspoon ground cinnamon.

Proceed as in Basic Recipe.

### HIGH-FIBER DIETS

Use Basic Recipe. For extra fiber, serve with canned lingonberries or canned mandarin oranges.

Serving size: 1 cup soufflé, ¼ cup whipped cream
Calories per serving: 188
Approximate nutrient
  values per serving:
    Protein 4 g
    Fat 12 g
    Carbohydrate 17 g
    Calcium 25 mg
    Phosphorus 24 mg
    Sodium 54 mg
    Potassium 102 mg
    Cholesterol 41 mg

Calories per serving: 134

# Cinnamon Vanilla Soufflé with Apricot Sauce

BASIC RECIPE

The apricot sauce here would also go beautifully with Soufflé Grand Marnier (page 625), Lemon Bread Pudding (page 596), or Vanilla Ice Cream (page 615).

(page 625), (page 596), (page 615)

*The Apricot Sauce*
½ cup dried apricots
¾ cup water for stewing apricots
rind of 1 lemon, cut into julienne strips
1 tablespoon Grand Marnier
¼ cup water
1 tablespoon sugar

*The Soufflé*
1 tablespoon polyunsaturated margarine for greasing
  soufflé dish
2 tablespoons sugar for sprinkling soufflé dish
3 tablespoons polyunsaturated margarine
¾ teaspoon ground cinnamon
3 tablespoons flour
¾ cup light cream
¼ cup sugar
⅛ teaspoon salt
4 large eggs, separated, at room temperature
2 teaspoons vanilla extract
¼ teaspoon cream of tartar
1 tablespoon sifted confectioners' sugar

*To prepare the sauce:* You can make the sauce ahead of time or while the soufflé is baking. Combine the apricots, water, lemon rind, and Grand Marnier in a saucepan and bring to a boil. Simmer gently for 15 minutes or until the apricots are very tender. Transfer the mixture to an electric blender and purée. Stir in remaining water and sugar and set aside to cool.
  Preheat oven to 400°F.

Serving size: ¼ soufflé, 2
  tablespoons sauce
Calories per serving: 444
Approximate nutrient
  values per serving:
    Protein 8 g
    Fat 31 g
    Carbohydrate 34 g
    Sodium 267 mg
    Potassium 200 mg
    Cholesterol 324 mg
Exchanges:
  Fruit 1
  Bread 1½
  Meat 1
  Fat 5½

*To prepare the soufflé:* Grease a 1½-quart soufflé dish with 1 tablespoon margarine. Sprinkle 2 tablespoons sugar into the dish and rotate it to coat the bottom and sides.

In a small saucepan melt the remaining 3 tablespoons margarine. Blend in the cinnamon and flour. Gradually stir in the cream, sugar, and salt. Cook over moderate heat, stirring constantly, until thickened and smooth.

Remove from heat and add egg yolks, one at a time, beating well after each addition. Blend in vanilla.

In a large bowl beat egg whites until foamy. Add cream of tartar and continue to beat until stiff but not dry. Stir about one-fourth of the whites into cinnamon mixture. Fold in remaining whites.

Turn into prepared soufflé dish and place in preheated oven. Immediately reduce temperature to 375°F. and bake about 35 minutes or until nicely browned and firm on top. Sprinkle with confectioners' sugar after removing from oven. Serve at once with warm apricot sauce.

*Yield:* 4 servings soufflé, 1 cup sauce

*Change Cinnamon Vanilla Soufflé with Apricot Sauce as follows or use Basic Recipe, if indicated, for:*

LOW-SODIUM DIETS

*The sauce:* Use Basic Recipe.

*The soufflé:* Omit salt.
Substitute unsalted polyunsaturated margarine for margarine wherever used.
Proceed as in Basic Recipe.

BLAND DIETS

Use Basic Recipe.

Calories per serving: 444
Approximate nutrient
values same as Basic
Recipe except for:
Sodium 87 mg

Calories per serving: 492

*The sauce:* Use Basic Recipe.

*The soufflé:* Add ¼ cup chopped toasted almonds (page 38); fold in with the egg whites.
Proceed as in Basic Recipe.

## CINNAMON VANILLA SOUFFLÉ WITH APRICOT SAUCE FOR LOW-CALORIE, DIABETIC, LOW-FAT, AND LOW-CHOLESTEROL DIETS

Serving size: ¼ soufflé, 2 tablespoons sauce
Calories per serving: 237
Approximate nutrient values per serving:
    Protein 7 g
    Fat 12 g
    Carbohydrate 26 g
    Sodium 232 mg
    Potassium 220 mg
    Cholesterol 137 mg
Exchanges:
    Fruit 1
    Bread 1
    Meat ½
    Fat 2

*The Apricot Sauce*
½ cup dried apricots
¾ cup water for stewing apricots
rind of 1 lemon, cut into julienne strips
1 tablespoon Grand Marnier
¼ cup water

*The Soufflé*
vegetable cooking spray
3 tablespoons polyunsaturated margarine
¾ teaspoon ground cinnamon
3 tablespoons flour
¾ cup skim milk
¼ cup sugar
⅛ teaspoon salt
2 large egg yolks
2 teaspoons vanilla extract
4 large egg whites
¼ teaspoon cream of tartar

*To prepare the sauce:* The sauce may be prepared ahead of time or started as soon as soufflé is placed in the oven.
Combine the apricots, water, lemon rind, and Grand Marnier in a saucepan and bring to a boil. Simmer gently for 15 minutes or until the apricots are very tender. Transfer the mixture to an electric blender and purée. Stir in remaining water and set aside to cool.
Preheat oven to 400°F.

*To prepare the soufflé:* Spray a 1½-quart soufflé dish with vegetable cooking spray.

In a small saucepan melt the margarine. Using a wire whisk, blend in the cinnamon and flour. Gradually stir in milk, sugar, and salt. Cook over moderate heat, stirring constantly, until thickened and smooth. Remove from heat and add egg yolks, one at a time, beating well after each addition. Blend in vanilla.

In a large bowl beat the egg whites until foamy. Add the cream of tartar and continue to beat until whites are stiff but not dry. Stir about one-fourth of the whites into the cinnamon mixture, then fold in the remaining whites.

Turn into a prepared soufflé dish and place in preheated oven. Immediately reduce the temperature to 375°F. and bake about 35 minutes or until nicely browned and firm on top. Serve at once with warm apricot sauce.

*Yield:* 4 servings soufflé, 1 cup sauce

# Soufflé Grand Marnier

BASIC RECIPE

Serving size: ⅛ soufflé
Calories per serving: 158
Approximate nutrient
  values per serving:
    Protein 7 g
    Fat 7 g
    Carbohydrate 17 g
    Sodium 122 mg
    Potassium 139 mg
    Cholesterol 212 mg
Exchanges:
  Bread 1
  Meat 1
  Fat 1

1 tablespoon polyunsaturated margarine for greasing
   soufflé dish
1 tablespoon sugar for sprinkling soufflé dish
1½ cups milk
¼ cup sugar
⅛ teaspoon salt
6 eggs, separated, at room temperature
¼ cup flour
¼ cup Grand Marnier
1 tablespoon grated orange rind
¼ cup orange juice
2 tablespoons confectioners' sugar for dusting the finished
   soufflé

Grease a 2-quart soufflé dish with margarine and sprinkle the inside, bottom, and sides with sugar. Set aside.

Preheat oven to 375°F.

Scald 1 cup of the milk in medium saucepan and set aside.

Pour remaining milk into bowl. Add sugar, salt, egg yolks, and flour; beat until smooth. Stir scalded milk into mixture.

Return mixture to saucepan. Whisk over medium heat until it comes to a boil. Lower heat and simmer 2 minutes, stirring constantly. Remove from heat. Stir in Grand Marnier, orange rind, and juice. Set aside.

Beat egg whites until they hold stiff peaks. Fold one-fourth of whites into Grand Marnier mixture until they disappear. Lightly fold in remaining whites and pour into soufflé dish.

Bake soufflé 40 minutes or until puffed and golden brown. Dust top with confectioners' sugar and serve at once.

*Yield:* 8 servings

*Change Soufflé Grand Marnier as follows or use Basic Recipe, if indicated, for:*

### LOW-SODIUM DIETS

Calories per serving: 158
Approximate nutrient values same as Basic Recipe except for: Sodium 74 mg

Omit salt.

Substitute unsalted polyunsaturated margarine for margarine used to grease soufflé dish.

Proceed as in Basic Recipe.

### BLAND DIETS

Calories per serving: 158

Boil Grand Marnier in a separate saucepan for 1 minute. Then stir in with orange rind and juice.

Proceed as in Basic Recipe.

### HIGH-FIBER DIETS

Use Basic Recipe. For extra fiber, garnish with orange sections.

## SOUFFLÉ GRAND MARNIER FOR LOW-CALORIE, DIABETIC, LOW-FAT, AND LOW-CHOLESTEROL DIETS

Serving size: ⅛ soufflé
Calories per serving: 77
Approximate nutrient
  values per serving:
    Protein 5 g
    Fat 0 g
    Carbohydrate 14 g
    Sodium 103 mg
    Potassium 158 mg
    Cholesterol 1 mg
Exchanges:
    Bread 1

vegetable cooking spray
1½ cups skim milk
¼ cup sugar
⅛ teaspoon salt
Low-Cholesterol Egg Substitute (page 189) equivalent to
    3 large eggs
¼ cup flour
¼ cup Grand Marnier
1 tablespoon grated orange rind
¼ cup orange juice

Spray 2-quart soufflé dish with vegetable cooking spray. Set aside.

Preheat oven to 375°F.

Scald milk in medium saucepan. Beat in sugar, salt, egg substitute, and flour. Whisk over medium heat until it comes to boil. Lower heat and simmer 2 minutes, whisking constantly. Remove from heat.

Boil Grand Marnier in a separate saucepan for 1 minute. Combine with orange rind and orange juice, then stir into milk and egg mixture. Whisk until smooth.

Pour into soufflé dish. Bake 40 minutes or until puffed and golden brown. Serve at once.

*Yield:* 8 servings

# Columbia Dessert Soufflé

BASIC RECIPE

Serving size: ¾ cup
Calories per serving: 106
Approximate nutrient
  values per serving:
    Protein 3 g

1⅔ cups strong coffee
1 cinnamon stick
5 tablespoons honey
⅓ cup strong cold coffee

Fat 6 g
Carbohydrate 12 g
Sodium 39 mg
Potassium 99 mg
Cholesterol 20 mg
Exchanges:
Bread 1
Fat 1

1 tablespoon unflavored gelatin
5 egg whites, at room temperature
½ cup heavy cream, whipped

Place 1⅔ cups coffee and cinnamon stick in a small pan and simmer until reduced to 1 cup. Remove cinnamon, add honey, and allow to cool.

Place the other ⅓ cup cold coffee in a small pan. Sprinkle gelatin over coffee and let stand 10 minutes. Dissolve over low heat.

In a medium bowl combine gelatin mixture with cinnamon-coffee mixture. Let stand 5 to 10 minutes or until the mixture begins to set.

In a separate bowl, beat the egg whites until stiff. Whip the cream. Fold one-third of the egg whites and one-third of the whipped cream alternately into the coffee mixture. Fold in the remaining whites and whipped cream lightly, until just blended.

Pour into a 2-quart soufflé dish and place in freezer for at least 30 minutes.

At least 1 hour before serving, transfer soufflé from freezer to refrigerator.

*Yield:* 8 servings

*Change Columbia Dessert Soufflé as follows or use Basic Recipe, if indicated, for:*

LOW-CALORIE, DIABETIC, LOW-FAT, AND LOW-CHOLESTEROL DIETS

Reduce honey to ¼ cup.
Omit heavy cream and increase egg whites to 6.
Proceed as in Basic Recipe.

Calories per serving: 49
Approximate nutrient
  values per serving:
    Protein 3 g
    Fat 0 g
    Carbohydrate 9 g
    Sodium 40 mg
    Potassium 92 mg
    Cholesterol 0 mg
Exchanges:
  Bread ½

## LOW-SODIUM DIETS

Use Basic Recipe.

## BLAND DIETS

Omit coffee. Substitute apple juice for coffee wherever used.
Proceed as in Basic Recipe.

Calories per serving: 133

## HIGH-FIBER DIETS

Use Basic Recipe.
Sprinkle soufflé with ⅓ cup toasted slivered almonds (page 38)
  before serving.

Calories per serving: 138

# Crêpes Suzette

BASIC RECIPE

*The Crêpes*
2 large eggs
1⅛ cups milk
2 tablespoons polyunsaturated oil
¼ teaspoon salt
1 cup sifted all-purpose flour
1 teaspoon polyunsaturated oil for greasing crêpe pan

*The Sauce*
⅓ cup polyunsaturated margarine
1 teaspoon grated orange rind
⅓ cup sugar
½ cup orange juice
2 tablespoons orange liqueur
2 tablespoons Kirsch

Serving size: 2 crêpes
Calories per serving: 246
Approximate nutrient
  values per serving:
    Protein 5 g
    Fat 15 g
    Carbohydrate 25 g
    Sodium 182 mg
    Potassium 125 mg
    Cholesterol 74 mg
Exchanges:
  Bread 1½
  Fat 3

*To prepare the crêpes:* Place eggs, milk, 2 tablespoons oil, salt, and flour in the container of an electric blender. Blend until smooth. Cover blender and refrigerate at least 2 hours.

Heat a 6-inch crêpe pan over moderate heat and brush with 1 teaspoon oil. Pour 2 tablespoons batter into pan and tip to distribute evenly. Cook until lightly browned on bottom. Turn crêpe and cook another 30 seconds.

As each crêpe is cooked, put it on a plate and fold in half, then in half again to form wedge. Set aside. You should have sixteen crêpes. If you do them ahead of time, reheat, covered, in a low oven, or over simmering water.

*To prepare the sauce:* Melt margarine in a large skillet. Add orange rind, sugar, and orange juice.

Heat, stirring, until sauce comes to a simmer and is slightly reduced.

*To assemble Crêpes Suzette:* Add folded crêpes to sauce in skillet and baste with sauce.

In a small pan warm orange liqueur and Kirsch. Pour over crêpes and ignite, basting crêpes with flaming sauce.

When flames subside, transfer crêpes to warm serving dishes and spoon sauce over crêpes. Serve immediately.

*Yield:* 8 servings

Change *Crêpes Suzette* as follows or use *Basic Recipe, if indicated, for:*

## LOW-CALORIE, DIABETIC, LOW-FAT, AND LOW-CHOLESTEROL DIETS

*The crêpes:* Substitute 1⅛ cups skim milk for milk.
  Proceed as in Basic Recipe.

*The sauce:* Reduce margarine to 3 tablespoons.
  Reduce sugar to 2 tablespoons.
  Increase orange juice to ¾ cup.
  Proceed as in Basic Recipe.

Calories per serving: 190
Approximate nutrient
  values per serving:
    Protein 5 g
    Fat 10 g
    Carbohydrate 21 g
    Sodium 150 mg
    Potassium 146 mg
    Cholesterol 69 mg
Exchanges:
  Bread 1½
  Fat 2

## LOW-SODIUM DIETS

*The crêpes:* Omit salt.
  Proceed as in Basic Recipe.

*The sauce:* Substitute unsalted polyunsaturated margarine for margarine.
  Proceed as in Basic Recipe.

Calories per serving: 246
Approximate nutrient
  values same as Basic
  Recipe except for:
    Sodium 38 mg

## BLAND DIETS

Use Basic Recipe.

## HIGH-FIBER DIETS

Use Basic Recipe. For extra fiber, top with fresh strawberries
  or garnish with grated orange peel.

# Custom Sauce

BASIC RECIPE

This is good with gingerbread or rice pudding or spooned over berries.

4 large egg yolks
½ cup sugar
⅛ teaspoon salt
1 cup milk
1 cup light cream
1 teaspoon vanilla extract

In a bowl, beat egg yolks lightly with a whisk. Beat in sugar and salt until mixture makes light ribbons. Gradually beat in milk and cream.

Put in top of double boiler and stir constantly, until custard thickens and coats a metal spoon.

Remove from heat and strain into a bowl. Stir in vanilla. Cool and refrigerate.

*Yield:* 2 cups

*Change Custard Sauce as follows or use Basic Recipe, if indicated, for:*

LOW-CALORIE, DIABETIC, LOW-FAT, AND LOW-CHOLESTEROL DIETS

Omit egg yolks and substitute Low-Cholesterol Egg Substitute (page 189) equivalent to 4 large eggs.
Reduce sugar to ¼ cup.
Substitute 2 cups skim milk for milk and cream.
Proceed as in Basic Recipe.

Serving size: 2 tablespoons
Calories per serving: 93
Approximate nutrient
  values per serving:
    Protein 2 g
    Fat 7 g
    Carbohydrate 7 g
    Sodium 31 mg
    Potassium 42 mg
    Cholesterol 87 mg
Exchanges:
  Bread ½
  Fat 1

Calories per serving: 35
Approximate nutrient
  values per serving:
    Protein 3 g
    Fat 0 g
    Carbohydrate 5 g
    Sodium 63 mg
    Potassium 92 mg
    Cholesterol 1 mg
Exchanges:
  Bread ½

Omit salt.
Add ⅛ teaspoon nutmeg.
Proceed as in Basic Recipe.

Calories per serving: 93
Approximate nutrient
  values same as Basic
  Recipe except for:
    Calcium 35 mg
    Phosphorus 45 mg
    Sodium 15 mg

## BLAND DIETS

Use Basic Recipe.

## HIGH-FIBER DIETS

Calories per serving: 98

Use Basic Recipe. When sauce is cool, add ¼ cup toasted coconut (page 38) to it.

# Apple Purée with Rum

## BASIC RECIPE

This is delicious with fruit, puddings, and vanilla ice cream.

Serving size: ⅓ cup
Calories per serving: 34
Approximate nutrient
  values per serving:
    Protein 0 g
    Fat 0 g
    Carbohydrate 9 g
    Sodium 46 mg
    Potassium 65 mg
    Cholesterol 0 mg
Exchanges:
  Fruit 1

2 cups unsweetened applesauce
¼ teaspoon ground cinnamon
⅛ teaspoon salt
¾ teaspoon grated peeled fresh ginger root
2 tablespoons light rum

Combine all ingredients in a small saucepan. Cook over low heat, stirring constantly, until sauce starts to simmer.
    Remove from heat. Serve warm.

*Yield:* 2 cups

*Change Apple Purée with Rum as follows or use Basic Recipe, if indicated, for:*

LOW-CALORIE, DIABETIC, LOW-FAT, LOW-CHOLESTEROL, AND BLAND DIETS

Use Basic Recipe.

LOW-SODIUM AND RENAL DIETS

Calories per serving: 34
Approximate nutrient
   values same as Basic
   Recipe except for:
   Calcium 4 mg
   Phosphorus 4 mg
   Sodium 2 mg

Omit salt.
Proceed as in Basic Recipe.

HIGH-FIBER DIETS

Use Basic Recipe.
For extra fiber, serve with fruit or puddings garnished with nuts or grated coconut.

# Orange Cream Filling

BASIC RECIPE

This is good as a filling for jelly rolls or sponge cakes—for instance, as a substitute for the ice cream in the Chocolate Ice Cream Roll (page 616) or as a filling for Orange Sponge Cake (page 534).

⅔ cup sugar
2½ tablespoons cornstarch
⅛ teaspoon salt
2 tablespoons lemon juice
1 cup orange juice
1 tablespoon orange liqueur
¾ teaspoon grated orange rind
1 tablespoon polyunsaturated margarine

In the top of a double boiler, mix sugar, cornstarch, and salt. Gradually add in lemon juice, orange juice, and orange liqueur and blend until smooth. Place over boiling water and cook, stirring constantly, until thickened. Remove from heat. Blend in orange rind and margarine.

*Yield:* 1⅓ cups

*Change Orange Cream Filling as follows or use Basic Recipe, if indicated, for:*

LOW-CALORIE, DIABETIC, LOW-FAT, AND LOW-CHOLESTEROL DIETS

Omit lemon juice.
Reduce sugar to ⅛ cup.
Proceed as in Basic Recipe.

*Yield:* 1 cup

Calories per serving: 66
Approximate nutrient
    values per serving:
        Protein 0 g
        Fat 2 g
        Carbohydrate 13 g
        Sodium 48 mg
        Potassium 63 mg
        Cholesterol 0 mg
Exchanges:
    Bread 1

LOW-SODIUM DIETS

Omit salt.
Substitute unsalted polyunsaturated margarine for margarine.
Proceed as in Basic Recipe.

Calories per serving: 72
Approximate nutrient
    values same as Basic
    Recipe except for:
        Sodium 0 mg

BLAND AND HIGH-FIBER DIETS

Use Basic Recipe.

# Whipped Topping

BASIC RECIPE

This is a tasty topping for puddings and fruit molds.

Serving size: ¼ cup
Calories per serving: 14

½ teaspoon unflavored gelatin
4 tablespoons cold water
2 large egg whites

636

⅛ teaspoon salt
⅛ teaspoon cream of tartar
2 tablespoons sugar
½ teaspoon vanilla extract

Sprinkle gelatin over cold water in a small saucepan. Let stand for 10 minutes. Cook over low heat, stirring constantly, until gelatin dissolves. Remove from heat.

In a bowl, beat egg whites until foamy. Beat in salt, cream of tartar, and sugar. Add dissolved gelatin in a slow, steady stream, beating constantly until stiff peaks form. Beat in vanilla.

Pour into top of double boiler, insert top in double boiler base half-filled with hot water and continue beating mixture for 1 minute.

Serve immediately.

*Yield:* 2½ cups

*Change Whipped Topping as follows or use Basic Recipe, if indicated, for:*

LOW-CALORIE, DIABETIC, LOW-FAT, LOW-CHOLESTEROL, BLAND, AND HIGH-FIBER DIETS

Use Basic Recipe.

LOW-SODIUM AND RENAL DIETS

Omit salt.
Proceed as in Basic Recipe.

# Crème Fraîche

BASIC RECIPE

This is superb with berries, poached pears, and baked apples.

1 cup heavy cream
2 tablespoons buttermilk

In a small saucepan, heat ingredients together until lukewarm.

Pour into a jar, cover loosely, and let stand at room temperature 8 to 10 hours or overnight. If the temperature is below 75°F., the cream will take longer to thicken.

Stir, cover tightly, and refrigerate. Serve very cold. It will keep for 2 to 3 weeks.

*Yield:* 1 cup

*Change Crème Fraîche as follows or use Basic Recipe, if indicated, for:*

LOW-CALORIE, DIABETIC, LOW-FAT, AND LOW-CHOLESTEROL DIETS

Substitute 1 cup 1 percent low-fat cottage cheese for heavy cream.
Increase buttermilk to ¼ cup.
Combine ingredients in an electric blender. Blend until smooth.
Proceed as in Basic Recipe.

LOW-SODIUM, RENAL, BLAND, AND HIGH-FIBER DIETS

Use Basic Recipe.

---

Serving size: 2 tablespoons
Calories per serving: 104
Approximate nutrient
values per serving:
Protein 1 g
Fat 11 g
Carbohydrate 1 g
Calcium 24 mg
Phosphorus 22 mg
Sodium 15 mg
Potassium 28 mg
Cholesterol 41 mg
Exchanges:
Fat 2

Calories per serving: 23
Approximate nutrient
values per serving:
Protein 4 g
Fat 0 g
Carbohydrate 1 g
Sodium 123 mg
Potassium 36 mg
Cholesterol 1 mg
Exchanges:
Meat ½

# Strawberry Pineapple Conserve

BASIC RECIPE SUITABLE FOR LOW-SODIUM,
RENAL, BLAND, AND HIGH-FIBER DIETS

This would be lovely on Homemade English Muffins (page 135), Apple Muffins (page 131), or Popovers (page 137). It would also be good spread over Crêpes (page 184) as a dessert.

Serving size: 2 tablespoons
Calories per serving: 128
Approximate nutrient
  values per serving:
    Protein 0 g
    Fat 0 g
    Carbohydrate 32 g
    Calcium 8 mg
    Phosphorus 8 mg
    Sodium 0 mg
    Potassium 66 mg
    Cholesterol 0 mg
Exchanges:
  Fruit 3

3 cups peeled, cored, and finely chopped fresh pineapple
6 cups sugar
2 quarts hulled strawberries (if large, cut into quarters)

Place pineapple in a large enameled or stainless-steel casserole or kettle. Sprinkle with sugar; mix to distribute fruit with sugar. Cook over low heat, stirring frequently to prevent scorching, until sugar dissolves.

Add strawberries; increase heat. Boil rapidly, stirring frequently, for 40 minutes or until syrup is thickened and the temperature on a candy thermometer registers 220°F.

Skim off foam. Pour conserve, boiling hot, into hot, sterile jars. Adjust caps; process in a water bath at simmering temperature for 10 minutes. Cool. Check seals; store in a dark, dry, cool place.

*Yield:* 5 cups

*Change Strawberry Pineapple Conserve as follows for:*

LOW-CALORIE, DIABETIC, LOW-FAT, AND
LOW-CHOLESTEROL DIETS

Serving size: 2 tablespoons
Calories per serving: 18
Approximate nutrient
  values per serving:
    Protein 0 g
    Fat 0 g
    Carbohydrate 5 g
    Sodium 0 mg
    Potassium 52 mg
    Cholesterol 0 mg
Exchanges:
  Fruit ½

2 cups sliced ripe strawberries
8-ounce can unsweetened crushed pineapple
2 tablespoons cornstarch

Crush strawberries in a medium saucepan with a potato masher.

Drain juice from pineapple can into a small cup. Reserve pineapple.

Combine pineapple juice with the cornstarch and stir until smooth. Stir into strawberries; cook and stir over moderate heat until mixture comes to a boil and thickens.

Purée in an electric blender. Pour purée mixture into a jar; stir in reserved crushed pineapple. Cover and refrigerate. This will keep for several days.

*Yield:* 2 cups

# Strawberry Sunshine Sauce

BASIC RECIPE

This is delicious with puddings and dessert soufflés.

Serving size: ⅓ cup
Calories per serving: 198
Approximate nutrient
  values per serving:
    Protein 3 g
    Fat 12 g
    Carbohydrate 21 g

2 cups sliced fresh strawberries
¾ cup sugar
4 large egg yolks
⅛ teaspoon salt
1 cup milk
1 cup light cream
1 teaspoon vanilla extract

Sodium 56 mg
Potassium 128 mg
Cholesterol 154 mg
Exchanges:
 Fruit 2
 Fat 2½

Place strawberries in bowl or glass pie plate and sprinkle with ¼ cup of the sugar. Let stand at room temperature about 1 hour. Mix with rubber spatula occasionally.

Meanwhile, in the top of a double boiler, beat egg yolks lightly with a whisk. Blend in remaining ½ cup sugar and salt. Gradually stir in milk and cream.

Insert top in double boiler base half-filled with hot water and cook, stirring constantly, until sauce thickens and coats a metal spoon.

Remove from heat and strain into a bowl. Stir in vanilla. Chill and refrigerate, if you wish, or serve warm.

Just before serving gently stir in strawberries and juice.

*Yield:* 3 cups

*Change Strawberry Sunshine Sauce as follows or use Basic Recipe, if indicated, for:*

LOW-SODIUM DIETS

Calories per serving: 198
Approximate nutrient values same as Basic Recipe except for:
 Sodium 27 mg

Omit salt and add ⅛ teaspoon nutmeg.
Proceed as in Basic Recipe.

BLAND AND HIGH-FIBER DIETS

Use Basic Recipe.

STRAWBERRY SUNSHINE SAUCE FOR LOW-CALORIE, DIABETIC, LOW-FAT, AND LOW-CHOLESTEROL DIETS

Serving size: ⅓ cup
Calories per serving: 75
Approximate nutrient values per serving:
 Protein 6 g
 Fat 0 g
 Carbohydrate 12 g
 Sodium 113 mg

Low-Cholesterol Egg Substitute (page 189) equivalent to
 4 large eggs
¼ cup sugar
⅛ teaspoon salt
2 cups skim milk
1 teaspoon vanilla extract
2 cups sliced fresh strawberries

641

Potassium 217 mg
Cholesterol 1 mg
Exchanges:
Milk ½
Fruit 1

In the top of a double boiler, beat egg substitute lightly with a fork. Blend in sugar and salt. Gradually stir in milk. Insert top in double boiler base half-filled with hot water and cook, stirring constantly, until custard thickens and coats a metal spoon. Remove from heat and strain into a bowl. Stir in vanilla. Gently fold in sliced strawberries.

*Yield:* 3 cups

# Herbs and Spices to Enjoy

Enjoy these herbs and spices *unless* your special diet is marked *NO*.

| | LOW-CALORIE | DIABETIC | LOW-FAT | LOW-CHOLESTEROL | LOW-SODIUM | RENAL | BLAND | HIGH-FIBER |
|---|---|---|---|---|---|---|---|---|
| Allspice, cracked | | | | | | | | |
| Allspice, ground | | | | | | | | |
| Allspice, whole | | | | | | | | |
| Anise, ground | | | | | | | | |
| Anise seed | | | | | | | | |
| Basil, dried | | | | | | | | |
| Basil, fresh | | | | | | | | |
| Bay leaf | | | | | | | | |
| Capers | | | | | NO | NO | | |
| Caraway seed | | | | | | | | |
| Cardamom, ground | | | | | | | | |
| Cardamom seed | | | | | | | | |
| Cayenne | | | | | | | NO | |

| | LOW-CALORIE | DIABETIC | LOW-FAT | LOW-CHOLESTEROL | LOW-SODIUM | RENAL | BLAND | HIGH-FIBER |
|---|---|---|---|---|---|---|---|---|
| Celery flakes | | | | | | | | |
| Celery salt | | | | | NO | NO | | |
| Celery seed | | | | | | | | |
| Celery seed, ground | | | | | | | | |
| Chervil | | | | | | | | |
| Chili powder | | | | | | | NO | |
| Chives, dried | | | | | | | | |
| Chives, fresh | | | | | | | | |
| Cinnamon, ground | | | | | | | | |
| Clove, ground | | | | | | | NO | |
| Clove, whole | | | | | | | NO | |
| Coriander, cracked | | | | | | | | |
| Coriander, ground | | | | | | | | |
| Coriander seed | | | | | | | | |
| Cumin, ground | | | | | | | | |
| Cumin seed | | | | | | | | |
| Curry powder | | | | | | | | |
| Dill, fresh | | | | | | | | |
| Dill seed | | | | | | | | |
| Dillweed, dried | | | | | | | | |
| Fennel, fresh | | | | | | | | |
| Fennel seed | | | | | | | | |

| | LOW-CALORIE | DIABETIC | LOW-FAT | LOW-CHOLESTEROL | LOW-SODIUM | RENAL | BLAND | HIGH-FIBER |
|---|---|---|---|---|---|---|---|---|
| Garlic flakes | | | | | | | | |
| Garlic, fresh (bud) | | | | | | | | |
| Garlic juice | | | | | | | | |
| Garlic, minced | | | | | | | | |
| Garlic, powder | | | | | | | | |
| Garlic, pressed | | | | | | | | |
| Garlic salt | | | | | NO | NO | | |
| Ginger, ground | | | | | | | | |
| Ginger root, fresh | | | | | | | | |
| Horseradish, fresh | | | | | | | NO | |
| Horseradish, prepared | | | | | NO | NO | NO | |
| Mace | | | | | | | NO | |
| Marjoram | | | | | | | | |
| Mint, dried | | | | | | | | |
| Mint, fresh | | | | | | | | |
| MSG | | | | | NO | NO | | |
| Mustard, dry | | | | | | | NO | |
| Nutmeg | | | | | | | NO | |
| Onion, dehydrated | | | | | | | | |
| Onion flakes | | | | | | | | |
| Onion juice | | | | | | | | |
| Onion powder | | | | | | | | |

| | LOW-CALORIE | DIABETIC | LOW-FAT | LOW-CHOLESTEROL | LOW-SODIUM | RENAL | BLAND | HIGH-FIBER |
|---|---|---|---|---|---|---|---|---|
| Onion salt | | | | | NO | NO | | |
| Oregano | | | | | | | | |
| Paprika | | | | | | | | |
| Parsley, dried | | | | | | | | |
| Parsley, fresh | | | | | | | | |
| Peppercorns | | | | | | | NO | |
| Pepper, ground | | | | | | | NO | |
| Pepper, red, crushed | | | | | | | NO | |
| Poppy seed | | | | | | | | |
| Poultry seasoning | | | | | | | NO | |
| Rosemary | | | | | | | | |
| Saffron | | | | | | | | |
| Sage | | | | | | | | |
| Salt | | | | | NO | NO | | |
| Savory | | | | | | | | |
| Sesame seed | | | | | | | | |
| Tarragon | | | | | | | | |
| Thyme | | | | | | | | |
| Turmeric | | | | | | | | |
| Vanilla bean | | | | | | | | |

# Equivalent Amounts of Food Before and After Processing

| | |
|---|---|
| Apples, 1 pound | = 3 medium or 3 cups sliced |
| Bananas, 1 pound | = 3 medium or 2½ cups sliced |
| Beans, dried, 1 pound uncooked or 2½ cups uncooked | = 6 cups cooked |
| Beans, green, fresh, 1 pound | = 3 cups chopped and cooked |
| Beets, fresh, 1 pound medium-size | = 2 cups cooked and sliced |
| Bell pepper, 1 large, ½ pound | = 1 cup seeded and finely chopped |
| Bread | |
|   1 slice dry | = ⅛ cup grated bread crumbs |
|   1 slice fresh | = ¾ cup broken up |
| Broccoli, fresh, 1 bunch, 1 pound | = 6 cups chopped and cooked |
| Butter and shortening | |
|   butter or margarine, 1 ounce | = 2 tablespoons |
|   butter or margarine, ½ stick | = ¼ cup |
|   butter or margarine, 1 stick | = ½ cup |
|   butter or margarine, 1 pound | = 2 cups |
|   vegetable shortening, 1 pound | = 2½ cups |
| Cabbage, 1 pound | = 4 cups shredded or 2½ cups cooked |
| Carrots, 1 pound | = 8 small or 4 cups chopped |
| Cauliflower, 1 average head | = 1½ pounds or 6 cups chopped and cooked |
| Celery, stalk | = ½ cup finely chopped |
| Cheese | |
|   Cheddar, 1 pound | = 4 cups shredded |
|   cottage cheese, 8 ounces | = 1 cup |
|   cream cheese, 3-ounce package | = ⅜ cup or 6 tablespoons |
|   cream cheese, 8-ounce package | = 1 cup |
| Cherries, fresh, 1 pint | = 1 cup pitted |
| Chocolate, 1 square | = 1 ounce |
| Coffee, ¼ pound ground | = 10–12 cups brewed coffee |
| Cornmeal, 1 pound | = 3 cups |

| | |
|---|---|
| Cornstarch, 1 pound | = 3 cups |
| Cracker crumbs | |
|     soda type, 23 | = 1 cup |
|     graham, 15 | = 1 cup |
| Cranberries, fresh, 1 pound | = 4½ cups |
| Cream | |
|     heavy cream, 1 cup | = 2 cups whipped |
|     sour cream, 8 ounces | = 1 cup |
| Eggs | |
|     8 to 10 whites (large eggs) | = 1 cup |
|     12 to 14 yolks (large eggs) | = 1 cup |
|     5 to 6 whole eggs | = 1 cup |
|     1 large whole egg | = 4 tablespoons |
| Flour | |
|     all-purpose, 1 pound; | = 4 cups sifted |
|         1 cup minus 2 tablespoons unsifted | = 1 cup sifted |
|     cake flour, 1 pound | = 4¾ to 5 cups sifted |
|     whole wheat flour, 1 pound | = 3½ to 3¾ cups unsifted |
|     rye flour, 1 pound | = 4½ to 5 cups |
| Gelatin | |
|     unflavored envelope, ¼ ounce | = 1 tablespoon |
|     flavored package, 3¼ ounces | = ½ cup |
| Grapes | |
|     Concord, ¼ pound | = 1 cup or 30 grapes |
|     Thompson seedless, ¼ pound | = 1 cup or 40 grapes |
| Lemon | |
|     1 medium | = 3 tablespoons juice |
| |    1 tablespoon grated rind |
| Lettuce, 1 average head | = 6 cups bite-size pieces |
| Lime, 1 medium | = 2 tablespoons juice |
| |    2 teaspoons grated rind |
| Macaroni, 1 pound uncooked, 5 cups | = 12 cups cooked |
| Marshmallows, 16 large | = ¼ pound |
| Milk | |
|     evaporated, 1 cup | = 3 cups whipped |
|     evaporated, 5⅓-ounce can | = ⅔ cup |
|     evaporated, 13-ounce can | = 1¼ cups |
|     1 quart | = 4 cups |
| Mushrooms, fresh, ½ pound | |
|     (20 medium) | = 2 cups sliced |
| Noodles, 1 pound uncooked, 5½ cups | = 10 cups cooked |
| Nuts | |
|     almonds, 1 pound unshelled | = 1¼ cups shelled |
|     almonds, 1 pound shelled | = 3 cups |

| | |
|---|---|
| peanuts, 1 pound unshelled | = 2 cups shelled |
| peanuts, 1 pound shelled | = 4 cups |
| pecans, 1 pound unshelled | = 2¼ cups shelled |
| pecans, 1 pound shelled | = 4 cups |
| walnuts, 1 pound unshelled | = 2 cups shelled |
| walnuts, 1 pound shelled | = 4 cups |
| Oatmeal, quick-cooking, 1 cup | = 2 cups cooked |
| Onion | |
| 1 medium, chopped | = 1 cup |
| Orange, 1 medium | = ⅓ cup juice<br>2 tablespoons grated rind |
| Peaches, 1 pound | = 3 medium or<br>2 cups chopped |
| Pears, 1 pound | = 3 medium or<br>2 cups chopped |
| Peas in pods, 1 pound | = 1 cup shelled and cooked |
| Pineapple, 1 medium, 3 pounds | = 2½ cups chopped |
| Plums, 1 pound | = 4 medium or<br>2 cups chopped |
| Potatoes, 1 pound | = 3 medium |
| Raisins, 1 pound | = 3 cups |
| Rice, 1 cup uncooked | = 3 cups cooked |
| Spaghetti, 1 pound | = 9 cups cooked |
| Spinach, fresh, 8 cups | = 2 cups cooked |
| Squash, summer, 1 pound | = 4 medium<br>1 cup cooked |
| Squash, zucchini, 1 pound | = 2 average,<br>1¼ cups cooked or<br>3 cups raw diced |
| Sugar | |
| granulated, 1 pound | = 2 cups |
| brown, 1 pound | = 2¼ cups packed |
| confectioners', 1 pound | = 3 to 3½ cups sifted |
| Syrup | |
| corn syrup, 16 ounces | = 2 cups |
| maple syrup, 12 ounces | = 1½ cups |
| Tea, ¼ pound loose | = 75 cups brewed tea |
| Tomatoes, 1 pound | = 3 medium |
| Turnips, 1 pound | = 3 small,<br>1¼ cups cooked and mashed |
| Yeast, 1 package (¼ ounce) active dry | = 1 tablespoon |

# Ingredient Substitutions

If you run out of an ingredient, use one of these substitutions, but remember that best results will come from using the ingredients specified in our recipes.

*If You Don't Have:*

*Use Instead:*

Baking powder, 1 teaspoon

¼ teaspoon baking soda plus ½ teaspoon cream of tartar

Bread crumbs, 1 cup

¾ cup cracker crumbs

Broth, 1 cup

1 bouillon cube; or
1 teaspoon powdered broth dissolved in 1 cup boiling water

Butter, 1 cup

1 cup margarine; or
1 cup hydrogenated fat plus ½ teaspoon salt; or
⅞ cup oil plus ½ teaspoon salt

Catsup or chili sauce, 1 cup

1 cup tomato sauce plus ½ cup sugar and 2 tablespoons vinegar (for cooking)

Chocolate, unsweetened 1 ounce (1 square)

3 tablespoons cocoa plus 1 tablespoon margarine or butter

Coconut, 1 tablespoon grated dry

1½ tablespoons fresh grated

Coconut milk, 1 cup

1 cup milk

Cornstarch, 1 tablespoon

2 tablespoons all-purpose flour

Corn syrup, 1 cup

¾ cup sugar plus ¼ cup water

Cream, heavy, 1 cup

¾ cup milk plus ⅓ cup margarine or butter

Cream, light, 1 cup

⅞ cup milk plus 3 tablespoons margarine or butter

Cream, whipped, 2 cups

2 cups whipped dessert topping

Cream, sour, 1 cup

3 tablespoons margarine or butter plus ⅞ cup sour milk or buttermilk

Egg, 1 large whole

4 tablespoons beaten egg; or
2 yolks plus 1 tablespoon water

Flour, 1 tablespoon as a thickener

½ tablespoon cornstarch, potato starch, arrowroot, or rice starch; or
1 tablespoon granulated tapioca; or
2 teaspoons quick-cooking tapioca

| If You Don't Have: | Use Instead: |
|---|---|
| Flour, all-purpose, 1 cup sifted | 1 cup sifted cake flour plus 2 tablespoons; or |
| | ⅞ cup cornmeal; or |
| | 1 cup rolled oats; or |
| | ½ cup bran or whole wheat flour plus ½ cup all-purpose flour |
| Flour, cake, 1 cup | ⅞ cup sifted all-purpose flour |
| Flour, self-rising, 1 cup | 1 cup all-purpose flour plus 1 teaspoon baking powder and ½ teaspoon salt |
| Garlic, 1 small clove | ⅛ teaspoon garlic powder; or ⅛ teaspoon dried minced garlic; or |
| | 1 teaspoon garlic salt |
| Ginger, ⅛ teaspoon powdered | 1 tablespoon candied ginger rinsed and finely chopped |
| Herbs, 1 tablespoon fresh minced | 1 teaspoon dried, ground, or crushed herbs |
| Honey, 1 cup | 1 cup granulated sugar plus ¼ cup liquid |
| Lemon peel, 1 teaspoon grated | ½ teaspoon lemon extract |
| Milk, 1 quart whole | 1 quart skim milk plus 3 tablespoons margarine or butter |
| 1 cup whole | ¼ cup whole dry milk plus 1 cup water; or |
| | ½ cup evaporated milk plus ½ cup water; or |
| | 1 cup skim milk plus 2 teaspoons margarine or butter; or |
| | 1 cup reconstituted nonfat dry milk plus 2 teaspoons margarine or butter |
| 1 cup skim | ¼ cup nonfat dry milk plus 1 cup water |
| 1 cup buttermilk or sour milk | 1 tablespoon vinegar or lemon juice plus enough whole or skim milk to make 1 cup (let stand 5 minutes); or |
| | 1¾ teaspoons cream of tartar plus 1 cup whole or skim milk; or |
| | 1 cup plain yogurt |
| Mushrooms, 1 pound fresh | 3 ounces dried; or 8-ounce can |
| Mustard, 1 tablespoon prepared | 1 teaspoon dry mustard |

| If You Don't Have: | Use Instead: |
|---|---|
| Onion, 1 small | 1 teaspoon onion powder; or<br>1 tablespoon minced dried onion |
| Rice, white, 1 cup uncooked | 1 cup brown or wild rice uncooked; or<br>3 cups cooked |
| Shrimp, 1 cup cleaned, shelled, and cooked | ¾ pound raw, in shell; or<br>7-ounce package frozen peeled and cooked shrimp; or<br>4½ to 5-ounce can shrimp |
| Sour cream, 1 cup | 1 tablespoon lemon juice plus enough evaporated milk to make 1 cup |
| Sugar, 1 cup granulated | 1 cup packed brown sugar; or<br>2 cups sifted powdered sugar; or<br>2 cups corn syrup (reduce liquid in recipe); or<br>¾ cup honey (reduce liquid in recipe) |
| Tapioca, 1 tablespoon instant granulated | 1 tablespoon flour; or<br>2 tablespoons pearl tapioca |
| Tomatoes, 1 cup canned | 1⅛ cups cut-up fresh tomatoes, simmered 10 minutes |
| Tomato juice, 1 cup | ½ cup tomato sauce plus ½ cup water |
| Yeast, 1 tablespoon, active dry | 1 cake compressed; or<br>1 package (¼ ounce) active dry yeast |
| Yogurt, 1 cup plain | 1 cup buttermilk or sour milk |

# Nutrients: What They Do for You and Where to Find Them*

We list below the key nutrients you need to stay in the best of health: fats, proteins, carbohydrates, vitamins, and minerals. We have marked the ten most important ones, the leader nutrients, with this symbol ◊.

In addition, we explain what each nutrient does for the body and list the foods in which they are primarily found.

| Nutrient | What They Do for You | Where to Find Them |
|---|---|---|
| ◊ **Proteins**<br>4 calories per gram, or 112 calories per ounce | Make important contributions to growth of muscles, ligaments, bones, organs, skin, hair, and nails. Build and maintain body tissues. They are part of hemoglobin, which carries oxygen in the blood; of insulin, which regulates blood sugar; and of enzymes, which regulate the body's metabolism and are necessary for digesting food. | Meats, poultry, fish, eggs, milk, cheese, dried beans, peas |
| ◊ **Carbohydrates**<br>4 calories per gram, or 112 calories per ounce | Supply energy, so body does not draw on protein for it, leaving the latter free for body-building and repairs. | Cereals, potatoes, rice, spaghetti, macaroni, noodles and other pastas, dried beans and peas, corn, lima beans, sugars |
| ◊ **Fats**<br>9 calories per gram, or 152 calories per ounce | The most concentrated source of energy, essential for growth, for repairing and replacing body cells. Fats carry vitamins A, D, E, and K into the body and help in their absorption. They add flavor to foods. | Shortening and oils, butter, margarine, salad dressings |

*See Note 20.

| Nutrient | What They Do for You | Where to Find Them |
| --- | --- | --- |
| ◇ **Thiamine** (B₁) | Helps body cells obtain energy from food. Helps keep nerves in healthy condition. Promotes good appetite and digestion. | Lean pork, nuts, fortified cereal, dry beans, peas |
| ◇ **Niacin** (one of the B-complex vitamins) | Helps cells use oxygen to promote energy. Essential to the action of carbohydrates, which in turn help the body use fat. Maintains healthy skin, tongue, digestive tract, and nervous system. | Liver, meat, fish, poultry, peanuts, fortified cereal |
| ◇ **Vitamin C** (Ascorbic acid) | A water-soluble vitamin that helps the body resist infection and heal wounds. It forms a cementing material that holds body cells together. | Oranges, cantaloupe, orange juice, grapefruit, fresh strawberries, broccoli, spinach and other greens, sweet and white potatoes cooked in jackets, raw cabbage, tomatoes, tomato juice, papayas, mangoes |
| ◇ **Vitamin A** (Retinol) | Necessary for vision. Helps keep skin, lining of mouth, nose, throat, and digestive tract healthy and resistant to infection. Promotes growth. | Liver, dark green and deep yellow vegetables, butter, margarine, yellow fruits, eggs, milk |
| ◇ **Riboflavin** (B₂) | Helps the body release energy from carbohydrates and proteins. Necessary for the healing of tissues and the optimum condition of tissues and skin. Helps maintain good vision. | Milk, liver, yogurt, cottage cheese |
| **Vitamin D** (Calciferol) | Helps body absorb and use calcium and phosphorus to build strong bones and teeth. | Vitamin D–enriched milk, butter, egg yolk, saltwater fish, liver |

| Nutrient | What They Do for You | Where to Find Them |
|---|---|---|
| **Vitamin E** (Tocopherol) | Acts as an antioxidant to help prevent oxygen from destroying other substances in the body. In this sense it is a preservative helping to protect the activities of other components like vitamin A. | Wheat germ, oatmeal, other whole grain cereals, vegetable oil, margarine, milk, peanuts |
| **Vitamin B$_6$** (Pyridoxine) | Maintains health of skin. Prevents certain types of anemia. | Most fish and shellfish, chicken, egg yolks, dark green leafy vegetables, meat, liver, potatoes, wheat germ, oatmeal and other whole grain cereals, dry legumes, bananas, prunes, raisins |
| **Folacin** (one of the B-complex vitamins) | Aids metabolism by helping the body utilize proteins. Helps manufacture red blood cells. | Dark green leafy vegetables, dry beans, wheat germ, liver, peanuts |
| **Vitamin B$_{12}$** (Cyanocobalamin) | Essential for normal development of red blood cells, particularly in the bone marrow, nervous system, and intestines. | Liver, kidneys, heart, lean meats, fish, milk, eggs, most cheeses, shellfish |
| **Biotin** (one of the B-complex vitamins) | Plays an important role in the metabolism of carbohydrates, proteins, and fats. | Liver, meat, eggs, and milk |
| **Pantothenic Acid** (one of the B-complex vitamins) | Necessary for healthy skin and sound functioning of the nervous system. Helps the body absorb carbohydrates, which in turn supply energy. | Liver, meat, eggs, milk, sweet and white potatoes, whole grain cereals, peas |
| ◊ **Calcium** | Helps give structure and strength to bones and teeth. Helps blood clotting. Helps nerves, muscles, and heart to function properly. | Milk, yogurt, cheese, sardines, citrus fruits, dried peas and beans, leafy vegetables such as collards, dandelions, kale, mustard, and turnip greens |

| Nutrient | What They Do for You | Where to Find Them |
|---|---|---|
| ◇ Iron | An important part of compounds needed to transport oxygen to the cells and use it when it arrives. Helps form hemoglobin in the blood and prevents iron-deficiency anemia. | Enriched breads and cereals, liver, red meat, egg yolk, fish, prune juice, dried beans and peas, green leafy vegetables, dried fruits, whole grain cereals |
| Phosphorus | Needed for metabolism of fat and carbohydrate. Helps to build bones and teeth. | Milk, egg yolk, meat, poultry, fish, nuts, whole grains, legumes |
| Iodine | Vital to the normal functioning of the thyroid gland and prevention of iodine-deficiency goiter. Important to normal body metabolism. | Seafood, iodized salt |
| Magnesium | Constituent of bones, teeth, muscles, red blood cells. Essential to activate certain enzyme systems that initiate the metabolism of food and the release of energy in the body. | Wheat germ, other whole grain cereals, most dark green vegetables, meat, milk, peanuts, peanut butter, bananas |
| Zinc | Helps the body utilize proteins and carbohydrates. Helps heal wounds and regulate the appetite, contributes to body growth, good vision, healthy skin, and sexual functioning. | Shellfish, meat, cheese, oatmeal, wheat germ and other whole grain cereals, dry beans, cocoa, nuts |
| Copper | Necessary for the formation of hemoglobin and for the body's use of ascorbic acid. | Liver, oysters, meat, legumes, nuts, whole grain foods |
| Water | Prevents friction between moving parts of the body; helps food pass into the intestinal tract and into the bloodstream; regulates the body temperature. Fifty-five to seventy percent of the body is water, depending on one's age and sex. | Liquids, fruits, vegetables, limited amounts in all solid foods |

# Glossary of Nutrition

**Absorption**  The process of transferring nutrients from the digestive tract to the body.

**Acetic acid**  The acid in vinegar, used as an additive to prevent food spoilage by slowing up the growth of bacteria.

**Additive**  A substance or mixture, other than a basic foodstuff, which is added in the production, processing, storage, or packaging of foods.

**Albumin**  A protein that, with hemoglobin, comprises the two principal proteins in the blood. Albumin is found in egg white and in milk.

**Alginate**  An additive used to prevent the separation of fat from other ingredients in some liquid and semisolid foods. It is made of seaweed.

**Amino acids**  Component parts of proteins. There are twenty-two amino acids necessary for life. Twelve of these, known as nonessential amino acids, are liberated during digestion. The other ten, known as essential amino acids, are not produced in adequate amounts by the body and therefore must be derived from food.

**Ammonium carbonate**  An additive used as a leavening agent and to prevent the breakdown of ingredients in cookies, candies, and soda crackers.

**Ammonium phosphate**  An additive used to prevent the breakdown of ingredients in certain foods.

**Amylopectin**  A component of starch, which, in water, forms a gel. It is used in making jellies and jams.

**Antioxidant**  A widely used synthetic or natural substance added to a product to prevent or delay its deterioration by the action of the oxygen in the air. Vegetable oils and prepared foods contain antioxidants.

**Ascorbic acid**  *See* vitamin C.

**Basal metabolism**  The minimum amount of energy produced by the body at rest. This amount is measured in calories.

| | |
|---|---|
| **B-complex vitamins** | A group of water-soluble vitamins necessary for normal growth and function of the human body. These include biotin, choline, folacin, niacin, pantothenic acid, riboflavin ($B_2$), thiamine ($B_1$), pyridoxine ($B_6$), and cyanocobalamin ($B_{12}$). (*See* specific vitamins.) |
| **Beta carotene** | A plant form of vitamin A. Food sources include carrots and sweet potatoes. It has a characteristic yellow color and as an additive may be used to color food. |
| **Bile** | A substance produced in the gall bladder. It helps break down fat. |
| **Biotin** | One of the B-complex vitamins. |
| **BHA** | (BUTYLATED HYDROXYANISOLE) An additive used as an antioxidant to slow down or prevent spoilage in fresh pork, dry yeast, beverages, desserts, dry breakfast cereals; also used as a stabilizer in shortening, margarine, and potato flakes. |
| **BHT** | (BUTYLATED HYDROXYTOLUENE) An additive with the same uses as BHA. |
| **Bulk** | A nonnutrient substance necessary for intestinal functioning. It is found in plant tissues and fibers. |
| **Calciferol** | *See* vitamin D. |
| **Calcium** | An essential mineral necessary for building and maintaining bones and teeth, for blood clotting, and for nerve function. It is found in milk and milk products and in green vegetables. Its absorption into the body depends upon an adequate supply of vitamin D. |
| **Calcium chloride** | An additive used as a stabilizer. It prevents canned fruits and vegetables from softening. |
| **Calcium disodium EDTA** | An additive used as a preservative in mayonnaise. (*See* EDTA.) |
| **Calcium lactate** | An additive used as a stabilizer. It prevents canned fruits and vegetables from softening and helps to reduce changes in acidity and alkalinity. |
| **Calcium propionate** | An additive used to slow down or prevent mold growth in cheese and baked goods. |
| **Calcium stearoyl-2-lactate** | An additive used for a stable foam in whipping agents. |
| **Calcium sulfate** | An additive used in the bleaching of flour. |

**Calorie**　A unit of energy measurement, used to measure heat-producing or energy-producing value in food.

**Carbohydrate**　A sugar or starch providing the major source of energy in the body. Each gram of carbohydrate yields four calories.

**Carotene**　A yellow substance found in green and yellow vegetables, egg yolk, and milk fat. It is changed in the body to vitamin A.

**Carrageenin**　An additive derived from seaweed. It is used as a thickening agent, an emulsifier, and a stabilizer.

**Casein**　The principal protein of milk, the basis of curd and cheese.

**Catabolism**　The breakdown of tissues within the body.

**Cellulose**　A carbohydrate substance forming the skeleton of most plant structures. It adds bulk to food but has no nutritional value.

**Chlorine dioxide**　An additive used as a bleaching and maturing agent for flour.

**Cholesterol**　A substance that is present in foods of animal origin but that is also made within the body. It is essential for the production of hormones and for the repair of membranes.

**Choline**　A component of lecithin, sometimes classified as a B-complex vitamin.

**Citric acid**　An acid obtained from citrus fruits. It is used for a sour flavor in beverages and confectionery and as an antioxidant in shortening, margarine, and dry sausage.

**Cobalt**　A trace mineral (a component of vitamin $B_{12}$) found in liver.

**Complete proteins**　Those proteins that supply all the essential amino acids to maintain body tissues and promote growth. They are found in meat, poultry, fish, eggs, milk, and cheese.

**Copper**　A mineral necessary for the formation of hemoglobin and connective tissue, and for the body's use of ascorbic acid. It is found in liver, oysters, meat, legumes, nuts, and whole grain foods.

**Cyanocobalamin**　*See* vitamin $B_{12}$.

**Dextrin**　A carbohydrate used as an emulsifying and thickening agent in foods.

**Dextrose**　A sugar used in candy, baked goods, and cereals. It is also known as glucose.

| | |
|---|---|
| **Dicalcium phosphate** | An additive used in the bleaching of flour. |
| **Digestion** | The process by which food is converted in the intestinal tract into chemical substances that can be absorbed by the body. |
| **Diglyceride** | A substance that is part fatty acid and part glycerol. As a food additive, it is used as an emulsifier. |
| **Disaccharide** | A carbohydrate composed of two simple sugars. Lactose, maltose, and sucrose are disaccharides. |
| **Disodium EDTA** | An additive used as a preservative in mayonnaise. |
| **Edema** | An excess accumulation of fluid in the body tissues. |
| **EDTA** | (ETHYLENE DIAMINE TEXTRAACETIC ACID) An additive used as an antioxidant. |
| **Emulsifier** | The substance or agent that holds tiny drops of one liquid in suspension in another liquid. Its main function is to prevent the separation of ingredients in some liquid and semisolid foods. Lecithin, glycerol, and glycerides may be used as emulsifiers to form such emulsions as mayonnaise, margarine, and ice cream. |
| **Endocrine gland** | A gland whose function is to secrete a hormone into the blood that has a specific effect on another gland or organ. |
| **Enrichment** | Replacement of nutrients originally present in the food but removed by processing. |
| **Enzyme** | A substance that catalyzes specific chemical reactions in plants and animals, as in the digestion of foods. |
| **Essential fatty acid** | A fatty acid that is necessary for growth and for the well-being of vital organs and skin but cannot be produced by the body and must therefore be provided by food. Linoleic acid is currently considered to be the only essential fatty acid in humans. |
| **Exchanges, food** | A way of organizing foods of similar types and nutritional values in basic food groups or exchanges. |
| **Fats** | Compounds composed of fatty acids and glycerol. Fats are derived from plants and animals, occurring usually in combination with proteins and carbohydrates. Fat is the most concentrated source of energy; each gram of fat yields nine calories. Fat is necessary for repairing and replacing body cells |

and for the absorption and protection of the fat-soluble vitamins A, D, E, and K. Fats are either saturated or unsaturated. Some sources of unsaturated fats are vegetable oils, wheat germ, and nuts. Animal fats such as lard, fatty meats, butter, cream, and egg yolk are sources of saturated fats.

**Fat-soluble vitamins**   These are vitamins A, D, E, and K. They can be stored in the body.

**Fatty acids**   Organic acids that combine with glycerol to form fat. There are saturated, monounsaturated, and polyunsaturated fatty acids. *See* essential fatty acid.

**FDA**   Food and Drug Administration.

**Fiber**   In nutritional context, a term referring to dietary fiber, the indigestible parts of food, necessary for intestinal functioning.

**Fluoride**   An element found in bones and teeth. It increases resistance to dental cavities.

**Folacin**   Official name of folic acid, a vitamin of the B complex, important in regulating metabolism.

**Folic acid**   Lay term for folacin.

**Fortification**   Addition of one or more nutrients to a food so that it contains more of the nutrients than were present originally.

**Fructose**   A simple sugar, found mainly in fruits and also in sugarcane and honey.

**Fruitarian**   One who eats only fruits.

**Fumaric acid**   An additive used for tartness.

**Galactose**   A simple sugar derived from lactose.

**Gelatin**   An incomplete protein, used as an additive to make liquids thicken and gel.

**Glucose**   A simple sugar found in sweet fruits and vegetables. Also known as dextrose. A form of carbohydrate that circulates in the blood and is used by the tissues for energy.

**Gluten**   One of the proteins of wheat and other grains. It gives dough its elastic and adhesive character.

**Glyceride**   A substance that is part fatty acid and part glycerol. Monoglycerides and diglycerides are used as food additives. They act as emulsifiers in baked goods, margarine, peanut butter, and candy.

| | |
|---|---|
| **Glycerine** | An additive used to retain moisture. |
| **Glycerol** | A substance found in animal fats and vegetable oils and in the body itself as one of the products of digestion of fats. |
| **Gram (g)** | A measure of weight used in the metric system. One ounce equals 28 grams. |
| **GRAS** | Abbreviation for "Generally Recognized as Safe," used by the FDA in connection with additives. |
| **Guar** | An additive used as a thickening and stabilizing agent. |
| **Hemicellulose** | A carbohydrate found in plants more soluble in water than cellulose. It is a fiber that gives bulk to food but has no nutritive value. |
| **Hemoglobin** | A protein in the blood that contains iron and that carries oxygen from the lungs to the tissues. |
| **Homogenize** | To break into small particles of uniform size; in homogenized milk, for instance, the fat has been broken into such small globules that it remains in suspension uniformly. |
| **Hormone** | A specific chemical product of a gland, organ, or certain cells of an organ (transported by the blood or other body fluids) that has a specific regulatory effect upon some other cells. |
| **Hydrogenation** | The addition of hydrogen to any unsaturated fat. By this process, vegetable oils are changed to solid fats. Hydrogenated vegetable oils are cooking shortenings and most margarines. |
| **Hydrolized vegetable protein (HVP)** | An additive used as a thickener and stabilizer. It is sometimes used as a protein supplement. |
| **Hypertension** | High blood pressure. |
| **Incomplete proteins** | Those proteins that do not supply enough of all of the essential amino acids. They are not capable of replacing or building new tissues. They must be supplemented with other foods to supply the essential complete proteins. Examples of foods that contain incomplete proteins are gelatin, legumes, and grains. |
| **Insulin** | A hormone formed by the pancreas and secreted into the blood. It is essential for the maintenance of the proper blood sugar level. It is also used therapeutically in the treatment of diabetes mellitus. |

| | |
|---|---|
| **Iodine** | A mineral, essential for formation of hormones secreted by the thyroid gland, which controls the basal metabolism of the body. |
| **Iron** | A mineral, an essential constituent of hemoglobin. Its absorption is promoted by vitamin C. |
| **I.U. (International Unit)** | A unit of measurement, internationally accepted, to express amounts of vitamins A, D, E, and other biological substances. |
| **Joule** | A measurement of heat or energy used in the metric system. One calorie equals 4.184 joules. |
| **Ketone** | A substance that increases simultaneously in the blood and in the urine during starvation, diabetic acidosis, pregnancy, after ether anesthesia, and after protein-sparing diets. A ketone is one of the end products of fat metabolism. |
| **Kilogram (kg)** | A measure of weight used in the metric system. One kilogram equals 1000 grams or 2.2 pounds. |
| **Lactic acid** | A syrupy liquid present in sour milk, molasses, wines, and various fruits. It is used as a flavoring and preservative in confectionery and soft drinks. |
| **Lacto-ovo-vegetarian** | A person who eats foods derived only from milk, eggs, and plants. |
| **Lactose** | The sugar occurring naturally in milk. It is used as an additive in infant foods, bakery products, confections, and pharmaceuticals, and in some frozen vegetables to add sweetness. |
| **Lacto-vegetarian** | One who eats only milk and plant products. |
| **Lecithin** | A fatty substance found in plant and animal tissues. It is an emulsifier, produced by the liver, and is the source of the nutrient choline. Lecithin, working with bile, helps the body absorb cholesterol. |
| **Linoleic acid** | An essential fatty acid, necessary for the growth and the well-being of vital organs and skin. It is a polyunsaturated fatty acid. |
| **Linolenic acid** | A polyunsaturated fatty acid that can be synthesized by the body. |
| **Lipid** | A term for fat. |
| **Lysine** | One of the essential amino acids. |
| **Magnesium** | A mineral. It is a constituent of bones, teeth, muscles, and red blood cells and is important in energy metabolism. |

| | |
|---|---|
| **Malic acid** | An acid obtained from a number of fruits, such as apples. |
| **Mannitol** | An additive used as a sweetener in chewing gum and low-calorie foods. |
| **Metabolism** | The process of transforming and utilizing substances within the body. Through this process energy is produced and body tissues are broken down and rebuilt continuously. |
| **Metric system** | A decimal system of weights and measures. The FDA prescribes the metric system for nutrition labeling because its measuring units (grams, milligrams, etc.) are small enough to express the amounts of individual nutrients in foods. |
| **Microgram (mcg)** | A measure of weight in the metric system and equal to one-millionth of a gram. |
| **Milligram (mg)** | A measure of weight in the metric system, and equal to one-thousandth of a gram. |
| **Mineral** | A substance found in the skeletal structure and tissues of the body. |
| **Modified starch** | An additive used as a thickener and stabilizer. |
| **Monoglyceride** | A food additive that acts as an emulsifier. |
| **Monosaccharide** | A simple sugar. Glucose, fructose, and galactose are simple sugars. |
| **Monosodium glutamate** | An additive used to enhance flavor. |
| **Monounsaturated fats** | Fat in which monounsaturated fatty acids predominate. They include olive oil, peanut oil, avocado, and most nuts. |
| **Niacin** | A member of the vitamin-B complex. It is needed for a healthy nervous system, healthy tissues, proper brain function, and healthy skin. |
| **Nicotinic acid** | Niacin. |
| **Nitrate** | An additive primarily used to attain and retain attractive color in meat and fish. It is particularly useful in preventing botulism in semiperishable products like smoked meats and fish. |
| **Nitrite** | An additive, used for the same purposes as nitrates. |
| **Nitrosamine** | A compound generated in the body, under some circumstances, by the combination of nitrites and amines. (Amines are the natural breakdown products of proteins during metabolism.) |

| | |
|---|---|
| **Nutrient** | A substance that provides nourishment for the body—i.e., proteins, carbohydrates, fats, vitamins, minerals, and water. |
| **Oleic acid** | An unsaturated fatty acid present as a glyceride in most fats. |
| **Ovo-vegetarian** | One who eats only egg and plant products. |
| **Oxystearin** | An additive used to inhibit crystallization in foods. |
| **Pantothenic acid** | One of the vitamin B-complex group necessary to convert carbohydrates, fats, and proteins into energy. |
| **Pectin** | A substance contained in the cell walls of various fruits and vegetables—e.g., apples, oranges, lemons. It is used to thicken jams and as an emulsifier and stabilizer in many food products. |
| **PER (protein efficiency ratio)** | The protein quality of a food compared to that of casein, the principal protein of milk. |
| **Phospholipid** | A type of lipid or fat contained in all biological cells. It is an emulsifying agent with an affinity for water and is therefore esential to the digestion and absorption of fats. |
| **Phosphorus** | A mineral present in the tissues of all animals and plants. It is important for the metabolism of fat and carbohydrates and helps to build bones and teeth. |
| **Phytosterol** | Sterols occurring in the oil or fat of plants, not of animals. Peanut oil, sesame oil, and olive oil are sources of phytosterol. |
| **Polysaccharides** | Carbohydrates formed from simple sugars. Starch, dextrin, pectin, cellulose, and glycogen are polysaccharides. |
| **Polysorbates** | Additives used as flavorings and emulsifiers in shortenings, dressings, chocolates, cakes, and prepared mixes. |
| **Polyunsaturated fats** | Fats in which polyunsaturated fatty acids predominate are referred to as polyunsaturated fats. They are usually liquid at room temperature and of vegetable origin. They include corn oil, safflower oil, and sesame seed oil. |
| **Potassium** | A mineral that regulates nervous and muscular sensitivity and the heart rhythm. |
| **Potassium sorbate** | An additive used as a preservative. |
| **Preservative** | An additive used to slow down or stop spoilage of foods. |

| | |
|---|---|
| **Propylene glycol monostearate** | An additive used to prevent the separation of fat from other ingredients in liquid and semisolid foods. |
| **Protein** | A nutrient necessary for life. It contributes to the growth and well-being of muscle, bones, organs, skin, hair, and nails. *See* complete proteins and incomplete proteins. |
| **P/S value** | The ratio of polyunsaturated fat to saturated fat. |
| **Pyridoxine** | *See* vitamin $B_6$. |
| **RDA (recommended daily allowances)** | The levels of essential nutrients needed to meet the known nutritional needs of practically all healthy persons in the U.S.A. This, on the basis of available scientific knowledge, is the judgment of the Food and Nutrition Board, National Academy of Sciences–National Research Council. |
| **Renal** | Pertaining to the kidneys. |
| **Retinol** | *See* vitamin A. |
| **Riboflavin** | *See* vitamin $B_2$. |
| **Saccharin** | An artificial sweetener over five hundred times as sweet as sugar. It has no nutritive value. |
| **Salt** | Sodium chloride. An additive used as a flavoring and a preservative. |
| **Saturated fats** | Fats in which saturated fatty acids predominate. They are usually solid at room temperature and of animal origin. They include the fats of whole milk, cream cheese, butter, eggs, meat, some hydrogenated or solid vegetable shortenings, and coconut oil. |
| **Sitosterol** | A sterol found in plant tissues. |
| **Sodium** | An element in the form of table salt (sodium chloride) that maintains the necessary balance of water in the body and regulates muscle and nerve sensitivity. |
| **Sodium benzoate** | An additive used in fruit drinks and juices, purées, margarine, pie filling, and dressings to retard or prevent mold growth. |
| **Sodium bicarbonate** | Baking soda. An additive used to help make dough rise. |
| **Sodium chloride** | Table salt. *See* sodium. |

| | |
|---|---|
| **Sodium citrate** | An additive used in dairy products as an emulsifying agent and for greater acidity in beverages and candy. |
| **Sodium diacetale** | An additive used to retard growth of mold. |
| **Sodium phosphate** | An additive used in dairy products as an emulsifying agent. |
| **Sorbic acid** | An additive used as a preservative. |
| **Sorbitol** | A sweet substance found in berries and fruit. It is often used as a sweetening agent in diet candy and gum. It is also a softening and moistening agent and inhibits crystal formation. |
| **Stabilizer** | An additive that improves texture and keeps component parts of food from separating. |
| **Stearic acid** | A saturated fatty acid used in formulas of many skin creams and some pill coatings. Found in butter, meat, eggs, and, in smaller amounts, in vegetables. |
| **Stearoyl-2-lactylate acid** | An additive used as an emulsifier in shortening. |
| **Sterol** | A substance occurring in the fatty tissues of plants and animals. |
| **Sucrose** | A sweet carbohydrate found chiefly in sugarcane and beet sugar. We know it as table sugar. |
| **Sugar** | A sweetening agent. *See* monosaccharide, disaccharide, polysaccharide, dextrose, fructose, glucose, lactose, galactose, and sucrose. |
| **Tartaric acid** | An additive used for tartness in fruit drinks. |
| **Thiamine** | *See* vitamin $B_1$. |
| **Tocopherol** | *See* vitamin E. |
| **Tragacanth gum** | An additive used as a thickening and stabilizing agent. |
| **Triglyceride** | The chief form in which fats occur in humans, animals, and vegetables. |
| **Unsaturated fats** | Fats in which polyunsaturated fatty acids predominate are referred to as either polyunsaturated or unsaturated fats. |
| **USDA** | United States Department of Agriculture. |

**U.S. RDA**   United States Recommended Daily Allowances used in nutrition labeling. *See* RDA.

**Vegan**   One who eats only plant products.

**Vitamin**   An organic compound that is essential for normal growth and maintenance of the human body. The body cannot manufacture vitamins so they must be included in the diet. Fat-soluble vitamins (A, D, E, and K) can be stored in the body. Water-soluble vitamins (all of the B-complex group and vitamin C) must be replaced daily.

**Vitamin A**   Retinol, a fat-soluble vitamin that is stored in the liver. It is essential for vision, helps keep tissue healthy, and promotes cell growth.

**Vitamin B$_1$**   Thiamine, one of the B-complex vitamins. It is essential for the metabolism of carbohydrates, for the regulation of nerve sensitivity, and for carrying air from the lungs to the tissues.

**Vitamin B$_2$**   Riboflavin, one of the B-complex vitamins. It is necessary for the metabolism of protein, the healing of tissues, and the optimum condition of tissues and skin.

**Vitamin B$_6$**   Pyridoxine, one of the B-complex vitamins. It is important in maintaining healthy skin and in preventing certain types of anemia.

**Vitamin B$_{12}$**   Cyanocobalamin, one of the B-complex vitamins. It is essential for normal development of red blood cells and functioning of all cells, particularly in the bone marrow, nervous system, and intestines.

**Vitamin C**   Ascorbic acid, a water-soluble vitamin that helps the body to resist infection and heal wounds. As an additive it is used as an antioxidant and stabilizer.

**Vitamin D**   Calciferol, a fat-soluble vitamin that helps the body use calcium and phosphorus to build strong bones and teeth.

**Vitamin E**   Tocopherol, the principal form of vitamin E, acts as an antioxidant to help prevent oxygen from destroying vitamins A and C and carotene in the digestive tract and the body cells.

**Vitamin K**   A fat-soluble vitamin that acts as a coagulant and promotes normal blood clotting.

**Water-soluble vitamins**   *See* B-complex vitamins; vitamin.

**Xanthum gum**  An additive used as a thickening and stabilizing agent.

**Zinc**  A trace mineral that plays an important role in growth and in appetite regulation. A diet that supplies sufficient animal protein will also furnish enough zinc.

For precise, fully detailed definitions, consult nutrition textbooks and medical dictionaries (Note 21).

# Metric Equivalents and Common Measures*

The recipes will work whether you measure as usual or switch to metric. The proportions of ingredients called for will be approximately the same, but the recipe will yield about 5 percent more in quantity when measuring in metric units. For example: the U.S. standard cup is 237 milliliters; the metric cup is 250 milliliters or ½ liter. The metric teaspoon measures 5 milliliters versus the usual teaspoon, which holds 4.9 milliliters. The recipes will translate into metric measures equally well for special diets, since the differences in ingredient amounts are so slight that their effect on nutrient values will be negligible. These lists of approximate metric equivalents and the metric conversion table below will start you on the way to feeling at home with them.

COMMON METRIC UNITS

| *Weight* | *Equals* |
|---|---|
| kilogram | 1000 grams (a little more than 2 pounds—about 2.2 pounds) |
| gram | 0.001 ($\frac{1}{1000}$ kilogram) |
| milligram | 0.001 ($\frac{1}{1000}$ gram) |

*Liquid Measure*

| | |
|---|---|
| 1 liter | a little more than 1 quart |
| 1 deciliter | 0.1 liter ($\frac{1}{10}$ liter) |
| 1 milliliter | 0.001 liter ($\frac{1}{1000}$ liter) |

*Length*

| | |
|---|---|
| kilometer | 1000 meters (a little more than ½ mile) |
| meter | a little more than a yard (about $1\frac{1}{10}$ yards) |
| centimeter | 0.01 meter (25 centimeters = 1 inch) |
| millimeter | 0.001 meter |

*See Note 22.

*Approximate Weight Equivalents*
Ounces and pounds equal the following weights in grams and kilograms:

| Ounces and Pounds | Grams and Kilograms |
|---|---|
| ½ ounce | 14 grams |
| 1 ounce | 28 grams |
| ½ pound (8 ounces) | 227 grams |
| 1 pound (16 ounces) | 454 grams |
| 2.2 pounds | 1 kilogram (1000 grams) |

*Approximate Liquid Equivalents*
Spoons, cups, pints, and quarts equal the following liquid measure in milliliters, deciliters, and liters:

| Spoons, Cups | Ounces, Pints, Quarts | Milliliters, Deciliters, Liters |
|---|---|---|
| 1 teaspoon | ⅙ fluid ounce | 5 milliliters |
| 1 tablespoon | ½ fluid ounce | 15 milliliters |
| ¼ cup | 2 fluid ounces | ½ deciliter plus 10 milliliters (2 teaspoons) |
| ⅓ cup | 2⅔ fluid ounces | 1 deciliter minus 20 milliliters (4 teaspoons) |
| 1 cup | 8 fluid ounces | ¼ liter |
| 2 cups | 1 pint (16 fluid ounces) | ½ liter minus 20 milliliters (1½ tablespoons) |
| 4 cups | 1 quart (32 fluid ounces) | 1 liter minus 1 deciliter |

Identical amounts of some liquids vary in weight, but the differences are so small they are negligible.

*Approximate Temperature Equivalents*

| Degrees in Fahrenheit | Degrees in Celsius |
|---|---|
| 100 | 38 |
| 140 | 60 |
| 200 | 93 |
| 250 | 121 |
| 300 | 149 |
| 350 | 177 |
| 400 | 204 |
| 450 | 232 |
| 500 | 260 |

## Equivalent Familiar Measures (Note 23)

| | |
|---|---|
| 1 teaspoon | ⅛ ounce |
| 3 teaspoons | 1 tablespoon or ½ ounce |
| 2 tablespoons | 1 ounce |
| 4 tablespoons | ¼ cup or 2 ounces |
| 5⅓ tablespoons | ⅓ cup |
| 8 tablespoons | ½ cup or 4 ounces |
| 16 tablespoons | 1 cup or 8 ounces |
| 1 cup | 8 ounces |
| 2 cups | 1 pint or 16 ounces |
| 2 pints | 1 quart or 32 ounces |
| 4 quarts | 1 gallon or 128 ounces |
| 16 ounces | 1 pound |
| 1 jigger | 1½ ounces or 3 tablespoons |

## Metric Conversion
(Note 24)

*How to Convert Familiar Measures into Approximate Metric Measures*

| SYMBOL | WHEN YOU KNOW | MULTIPLY BY | TO FIND | SYMBOL |
|---|---|---|---|---|
| oz | ounces | 28.35 | grams | g |
| lb | pounds | 0.45 | kilograms | kg |
| tsp | teaspoons | 5 | milliliters | ml |
| tbsp | tablespoons | 15 | milliliters | ml |
| fl oz | fluid ounces | 30 | milliliters | ml |
| c | cups | 2.4 | deciliters | dl |
| pt | pints | 0.47 | liters | l |
| qt | quarts | 0.95 | liters | l |
| gal | gallons | 3.8 | liters | l |
| in | inches | 2.5 | centimeters | cm |
| °F | degrees Fahrenheit | subtract 32, multiply by 5, and divide by 9 | degrees Celsius | °C |
| cal | calories | 4.184 | joules | j |

*How to Convert Metric Measures into Familiar Ones*

| SYMBOL | WHEN YOU KNOW | MULTIPLY BY | TO FIND | SYMBOL |
|---|---|---|---|---|
| g | grams | 0.035 | ounces | oz |
| kg | kilograms | 2.2 | pounds | lb |
| ml | milliliters | 0.03 | fluid ounces | fl oz |
| dl | deciliters | .21 | pints | pt |
| l | liters | 1.06 | quarts | qt |
| l | liters | 0.26 | gallons | gal |
| mm | millimeters | 0.04 | inches | in |
| cm | centimeters | 0.4 | inches | in |
| °C | degrees Celsius | multiply by 9, divide by 5, and add 32 | degrees Fahrenheit | °F |

# Equivalent Amounts of Selected Ingredients in Cups, Ounces, and Grams

An ounce is an ounce and a pound is a pound, but a cupful of one food may weigh far more or far less than a cupful of another. This is of little concern as long as you use ingredient amounts as we give them—in nonmetric spoons, cups, pints, and so forth. But if, at some future time, you need to convert familiar nonmetric measures into grams, kilograms, and liters, you can accomplish this with your calculator or with some not-so-simple arithmetic. The preceding metric conversion tables tell you how. Or you can simplify the solutions with measuring utensils and a good kitchen scale, marked in both metric and nonmetric units. Here are equivalent amounts of a few ingredients you are apt to use often:

| Amount (1 cup) | Ounces | Grams |
|---|---|---|
| Apples, peeled, diced, or sliced | 4 | 110 |
| Apricots, dried, uncooked | 4½ | 130 |
| Asparagus, chopped, raw, or cooked | 5 | 140 |
| Barley, uncooked | 7 | 200 |
| Beans, dry | 6½ | 180 |
| Beef, ground | 8 | 226 |
| Blueberries, raw | 5 | 145 |
| Bread, crumbs, dry | 1½ | 45 |
| Butter, margarine, cooking oil | 8 | 227 |
| Carrots, diced or sliced, raw or cooked | 5½ | 150 |
| Celery, sliced or diced | 4 | 120 |
| Cheese, grated, Cheddar or Swiss, lightly packed | 4 | 120 |
| Chicken, cooked, diced | 5 | 140 |
| Cocoa | 3 | 86 |
| Flour, cake, sifted | 3½ | 96 |
| Flour, wheat, all-purpose, sifted | 4 | 115 |
| Flour, wheat, all-purpose, unsifted | 4½ | 125 |
| Mayonnaise | 8 | 220 |
| Milk, dry, nonfat | 4 | 120 |
| Milk, dry, regular | 4½ | 128 |

| Amount (1 cup) | Ounces | Grams |
|---|---|---|
| Mushrooms, raw, chopped or sliced | 2½ | 70 |
| Nuts, pieces | 4 | 120 |
| Onions, chopped | 6 | 170 |
| Onions, sliced | 4 | 115 |
| Parsley, fresh, chopped | 2 | 60 |
| Peas, fresh | 5 | 145 |
| Potatoes, peeled, diced, or sliced, raw or cooked | 5½ | 150 |
| Raisins | 5 | 145 |
| Rice, long-grain, cooked | 7 | 205 |
| Rice, long-grain, raw | 6½ | 185 |
| Squash, summer | 4½ | 130 |
| Sugar, brown, firmly packed | 8 | 220 |
| Sugar, confectioners', sifted | 3½ | 100 |
| Sugar, granulated, superfine | 7 | 200 |
| Tomatoes, fresh, cooked, or canned | 8½ | 241 |

Note: Weights are approximate. The above gram weights per cup are based on information available in the U.S. Department of Agriculture Handbook No. 456 (Note 25). In converting grams to ounces we rounded off the figures to the nearest digit or digit and a half. Handbook No. 456 offers similar information for hundreds of food items.

# Notes

*Note*

1 *Dietary Goals for the United States*, 2nd edition. Select Committee on Nutrition and Human Needs, United States Senate, Washington, D.C., 1977.

2 *Guide to Good Eating*, 4th Edition, National Dairy Council, Rosemont, Illinois 60018, 1978.

3 Adapted from *Food*, U.S. Department of Agriculture, Home and Garden Bulletin No. 228.

4 F. J. Stare, P. J. Cifrino, and J. Witschi. Adapted from *What Everyone Should Know About Nutrition*, Food and Fitness, Blue Cross Association, Chicago, Illinois, 1973.

5 Adapted from the *1983 Metropolitan Height & Weight Tables*, Metropolitan Life Insurance Company, Society of Actuaries.

6 L. Page, and N. Raper, *Food and Your Weight*, U.S. Department of Agriculture, Home and Garden Bulletin No. 74, 1977.

7 See Note 3 and Note 6.

8 See Note 3.

9 M. Morrison, *A Consumer's Guide to Food Labels*, reprinted from FDA Consumer, 1977, U.S. Department of Health, Education and Welfare, No. 77-2083.

10 Recommended Dietary Allowances, 1980, reprinted with permission of The National Academy of Sciences, Washington, D.C.

11 *Nutrition Labeling—Terms You Should Know*, FDA Consumer Memo, 1974, No. 76-2012.

12 See Note 9.

13 *Code of Federal Regulations*, Title 21, Parts 100 to 169. Revised 1980.

14 P. Lehmann, *More Than You Ever Thought You Would Know About Food Additives*, reprinted from FDA Consumer, April, May and June, 1979, U.S. Department of Health, Education and Welfare, Nos. 79-2115, 79-2118, 79-2119.

15 H. Hopkins, *The GRAS List Revisited*, reprinted from FDA Consumer, May 1978, U.S. Department of Health, Education and Welfare, No. 78-2103.

16 Calculations based on current data supplied by the Case Western Reserve University Data Base with cooperation of the Harvard School of Public Health. For their major source of nutrient values see Note 19.

*Note*

17 Adapted from the following: M. Robinson, and L. Fulton, *Freezing Combination Main Dishes*, U.S. Department of Agriculture, Home and Garden Bulletin No. 40, 1976; R. Vittel, and D. Davis, *Storing Perishable Foods in the Home*, U.S. Department of Agriculture, Home and Garden Bulletin No. 78, 1973.

18 The exchange lists are based on material in *Exchange Lists for Meal Planning* prepared by the Committee of the American Diabetes Association, Inc., and the American Dietetic Association, in cooperation with the National Institute of Arthritis, Metabolism and Digestive Diseases and the National Heart and Lung Institute, National Institutes of Health, Public Health Service, Department of Health, Education and Welfare (now called U.S. Department of Health and Human Services), 1976. Exchange calculations based on lean meat figures.

19 C. F. Adams, *Nutritive Values of American Foods in Common Units*, Agriculture Handbook No. 456, Agricultural Research Service, U.S. Department of Agriculture, Washington, D.C., 1975.

20 Adapted from the following: *Guide to Good Eating*, 4th Edition, National Dairy Council, Rosemont, Illinois, 1978; *Key Nutrients*, Federal Extension Service, U.S. Department of Agriculture, 1977.

21 *Dorland's Illustrated Medical Dictionary*, 25th Edition, W. B. Saunders, Philadelphia, London, Toronto, 1974; R. S. Goodhart and M. E. Shils, *Modern Nutrition in Health and Disease*, 5th Edition, Lea and Febiger, Philadelphia, 1973; *Stedman's Medical Dictionary*, 22nd Edition, the Williams and Wilkins Company, Baltimore, Maryland 21202, 1973.

22 Adapted from the following: *Household Weights and Measures*, U.S. Department of Commerce, National Bureau of Standards, Washington, D.C. 20234, January Special Publication 430, reprint March, 1979; *Metric Conversion Factors*, U.S. Department of Commerce, National Bureau of Standards, Washington, D.C. 20234, NBS Letter Circular 1051, Rev. September, 1976; *Units and Systems of Weights and Measures, Their Origin, Development and Present Status*, U.S. Department of Commerce, National Bureau of Standards, Washington, D.C. 20234, Letter Circular LC 1035, January, 1980.

23 *Favorite American Recipes*—A Collection of Classics from Around The Country, Food and Nutrition Service, U.S. Department of Agriculture, 1974, FNS-109.

24 See Note 22.

25 See Note 19.

# Resources for Further Information

If you are interested in reading more about nutrition, diet, and health, you will find that various special health associations, research associations, and government agencies all publish a variety of pamphlets, brochures, and books on these subjects. Most of these sources offer lists and brief descriptions of their publications from which you may order by mail or telephone.

Many of these are national organizations with local chapters in major cities. In all the following listings, we give addresses of national headquarters, but where there are local offices, you are requested to address your inquiries to them. If none is listed in your telephone book, write the national headquarters for further information.

**HEALTH AND RESEARCH ASSOCIATIONS**

American Diabetes Association, Inc.
1 West 48th Street (600 Fifth
    Avenue)
New York, NY 10020

The American Heart Association
7320 Greenville Avenue
Dallas, TX 75231

National Academy of Sciences–
    National Research Council and
    Nutrition Board
Office of Publications
2101 Constitution Avenue
Washington, D.C. 20418

National Dairy Council
6300 North River Road
Rosemont, IL 60018

Nutrition Foundation, Inc., Office of
    Education
888 17th Street, N.W.
Washington, D.C. 20006

Society for Nutrition Education
2140 Shattuck Avenue, Suite 1110
Berkeley, CA 94704

**GOVERNMENT AGENCIES**

Consumer Information Center (CIC)
Pueblo, CO 81009
    The starting point for acquiring
    lists of government publications
    and instructions on how to order
    them.

Federal Information Centers (FIC)
    See General Services
    Administration

Food and Drug Administration
    (FDA)
Consumer Communications
5600 Fishers Lane
Rockville, MD 20857

677

General Services Administration (GSA)
Washington, D.C. 20405
A government agency with Federal Information Centers in most states and in many major cities. The Federal Information Centers specialize in telling you which government office has the answer to your question.

U.S. Department of Agriculture (USDA)
Office of Governmental and Public Affairs
Washington, D.C. 20250

U.S. Government Printing Office
Superintendent of Documents
Washington, D.C. 20402
Though government publications may be ordered at this address, many are available at Government Printing Office Bookstores in major cities. See your telephone book for GPO addresses.

Government Publication Printing Office Bookstore (GPO)
See U.S. Government Printing Office.

# Index

*NOTE: Specific instructions for Low-Calorie, Diabetic, Low-Fat, and Low-Cholesterol Diets are grouped together under each recipe. This cluster is designated "Four-in-One Diet" in the Index. Under any citation for Four-in-One Diet, you will find all four of these diets. For a further explanation of Four-in-One, *see* pp. 2–3.

683

# About the Authors

*H*ARRIET WILINSKY GOODMAN is a Trustee of Beth Israel Hospital. For twenty-five years she was marketing director of Filene's department store in Boston. She was the first woman to head Boston's Chamber of Commerce.

*B*ARBARA MORSE supervised the dietitians who created the recipes for this book and is herself an accomplished cook.